The Egyptian Sudan (in two volumes), Vol.II

Its History and Monuments

SIR ERNEST A. WALLIS BUDGE

COSIMO CLASSICS

NEW YORK

The Egyptian Sudan (in two volumes), Vol.II
First published in 1907
Current edition published by Cosimo Classics in 2010.

Cover design by www.popshopstudio.com
Cover image, "An Arab Caravan outside a Fortified Town, Egypt"
by Jean -Léon Gérôme.

ISBN: 978-1-61640-455-0

Cosimo, Inc.
P.O. Box 416, Old Chelsea Station
New York, NY 10011

info@cosimobooks.com

or visit us at:
www.cosimobooks.com

"The country is full of mines; the higher it is ascended the richer it is found to be in gold. There are mines of silver, copper, iron, lead, loadstone, marcasite, hamest, emeralds, and a very brittle stone, of which if a piece is rubbed with oil, it burns like a wick; other similar productions are found in their researches after gold; but the Beja work none of these mines except those of gold."

—from Appendix to Chapter XI, The Blemmyes of Beja

TABLE OF CONTENTS

VOL. II.

PART II.—(*Continued*).

CHAPTER IV.

PAGE

The Rise of the Nubian or Sûdânî Kingdom of Piānkhi 1

CHAPTER V.

The Successors of Piānkhi 27

CHAPTER VI.

The Successors of Tanuath-Àmen 56

CHAPTER VII.

The Successors of Piānkhi 83

CHAPTER VIII.

The Sûdân in the Ptolemaïc Period 104

CHAPTER IX.

The Nubian Kingdom on the Island of Meroë . 114

CHAPTER X.

The Sûdân in the First Century before, and the First Century after, Christ 153

TABLE OF CONTENTS

CHAPTER XI.

PAGE

THE SÛDÂN IN THE ROMAN PERIOD 166

CHAPTER XII.

THE MUḤAMMADAN INVASION AND OCCUPATION OF THE SÛDÂN 184

CHAPTER XIII.

THE RULE OF MUḤAMMAD 'ALÎ AND HIS DESCENDANTS IN THE SÛDÂN 209

CHAPTER XIV.

THE MAHDÎ IN THE SÛDÂN 240

CHAPTER XV.

CHRISTIANITY IN THE NORTHERN SÛDÂN 288

APPENDIX TO CHAPTER XV.—THE INSCRIPTION OF SILKO, KING OF THE NOBADAE 308

CHAPTER XVI.

CHRISTIANITY IN THE SÛDÂN. MODERN MISSIONARY ENTERPRISE 312

CHAPTER XVII.

THE GOLD MINES OF THE SÛDÂN 324

CHAPTER XVIII.

THE MODERN SÛDÂN 343

CHAPTER XIX.

THE BRITISH IN THE SÛDÂN 448

BIBLIOGRAPHY OF THE SÛDÂN 515

INDEX 573

LIST OF PLATES

VOLUME II.

PAGE

Harua, an official of Queen Åmenårṭâs, holding statues of Hathor and Tefnut 30
Ornamentation of the Egypto-Roman Temple at Nagaa . . . 138
Scene from north wall of Temple A at Nagaa 142
Scene from west wall of Temple A at Nagaa 144
Doorway of a Temple at Nagaa 146
Cailliaud's plan of Temples, &c., at Maṣawwarât Aṣ-Ṣufra . . . 148
Lepsius' plan of Temples, &c., at Maṣawwarât Aṣ-Ṣufra 150
"Anak" in Eastern Desert drawing water 174
"Anak" dwellings at Gebel Maman 176
"Anak" house at Gebel Maman 178
Scenery in Kordofan 231
Major Marchand in Steam-launch *Faidherbe* at Fâshôda . . . 279
Fâshôda—Major Marchand's house and guns 280
Agar Dinka woman at Shambî 284
Shilluks at the American Mission on the Sobat River 320
Conquest of Nubia by Rameses II. 325
Payment of tribute by Nubians to the King of Egypt's representative . 326
Plan of gold mines in the Eastern Sûdân worked in the reign of Seti I. 335
View of Gondokoro in 1905 349
Kagera River 352
Native hut on the White Nile 375
Tawfîḳîya 378
Floating sudd on the White Nile 379
Woman grinding *dhurra* at Kîrô 381
Women washing clothes at Lâdô 382
Gondokoro 384
Natives in an ambatch canoe 386
Woman drawing water at Omdurmân 394
Cotton spinners at Omdurmân 396
Shilluks on the White Nile resting 398
Khor Arab in flood 400
Modern Sûdânî silver work 406, 408
Woman of Omdurmân 428
Shilluks at Fâshôda 434
Altar with Meroïtic inscription 444
Sirdar inspecting the construction of the Nile-Red Sea Railway . . 476
Nile-Red Sea Railway 478
Nile-Red Sea Railway near Gebêt 480

ILLUSTRATIONS IN THE TEXT

VOLUME II.

PAGE

Portrait of Shabaka 29
Portrait of Shabataka 31
Shrine with seated figure of Åmen-Rā 32
Relief on altar of Tirhâḳâh 36
Row of captives roped together 37
Tirhâḳâh offering to Åmen-Rā 43
Stele with account of the Dream of Tanuath-Åmen 47
Stele with account of the coronation of King Åspelta 59
Stele with account of dedication of gifts to Åmen-Rā at Napata by King Åspelta and his Queen 67
Stele with Edict against Eaters of Raw Meat at Gebel Barkal . . 71
Reliefs and text from Stele of Ḥeru-Sa-Åtef 77
Reliefs and opening lines of stele of Nåstasenen, or Nåstasen . . 85
Native boats on Nile near Ad-Dâmar 103
Sûdân Elephant 107
Portrait of Rā-Mer-Ka Åmen-Tarit 121
Remains of Temple on east bank of Nile near 'Amâra 122
Plan of Temple of 'Amâra 123
Bes columns of Temple at Wâd Bâ Nagaa 124
Portrait of Netek-Åmen 125
King Netek-Åmen : from altar at Wâd Bâ Nagaa 126
Queen Åmen-Tarit : from altar at Wâd Bâ Nagaa 127
Plan of Temple at Nagaa 128
Outline of remains of Temples at Nagaa 129
The Queen who built Temple A at Nagaa and her Consort slaughtering their foes 132, 133
Lions' heads above lotus pillar in shrine of Åmen-ḥetep II.'s time . 135
God worshipped at Nagaa 136
Lion-headed serpent rising from a lotus (?) 137
Lion banner of Queen Åmen-Tarit 137
Plan of Temples C, D at Nagaa 139
King adoring hawk-headed crocodile 140

ILLUSTRATIONS IN THE TEXT

	PAGE
Åmen-Tarit	140
Netek-Åmen	140
God worshipped at Nagaa (Jupiter Sarapis?)	141
Ark-Teten	143
Egypto-Roman Temple at Nagaa	143
Plans of Temple E, F, and G at Nagaa	144, 145, 146
Sculptures on columns of Great Temple at Nagaa	149, 151
River Atbara	161
Khor Arab	162
Papyrus on Baḥr Al-Gebel	171
View of village of Kassâm, near Fâzôglî, in 1837	215
View of the Blue Nile, near Fâzôglî, in 1837	215
Gebel Kasala, as seen from the New Government Buildings	216
View of Al-Obêd in 1837	217
Ripon Falls, Victoria Nyanza	219
Victoria Nyanza at the Ripon Falls	219
Five-piastre note of Gordon	251
Twenty-piastre pieces of the Khalîfa	267
Transport of gunboats by railway	269
Mahdî's Tomb, Omdurmân, before the bombardment	277
Baḥr Al-Gebel at Kîrô and Mongalla	283
Pyramids of Meroë	287
Plan of church in the Christian monastery in the Wâdî Al-Ghazâl	300
Christian monastery in the Wâdî Al-Ghazâl	301
Ruined church at Siedever	305
Plan of gold mines of the reign of Rameses II.	337
Southern Sûdân and district of the Great Lakes	344
Ankoli district mountains	352
Lake Albert Edward	353
View on the Semliki River	354
Upper Fall on Wakki River	355
Junction of the Asua River with the Baḥr Al-Gebel	357
Sobat River	358
River Abâî, from bridge of Agam Deldi	359
Abâî near Lake Ṣânâ	360
Lake Ṣânâ	361
Abâî Rapids	362
Portuguese bridge at Agam Deldi	363
Fola Rapids on Baḥr Al-Gebel	367
Cataract at Semna and Kumma	369
Fâshôda	377
River Bank at Bôr	381
Lâdô	382
"Earthquake Hill"	383

ILLUSTRATIONS IN THE TEXT

	PAGE
Murchison Falls on Victoria Nile	385
Kharṭûm and Omdurman	392
Palace at Kharṭûm	393
Mosque at Kharṭûm	395
Sûdânî silver-work cigarette case	405
Sawâkin	408
Gordon Gate, Sawâkin	409
Sawâkin Bazaar	410
Main street, Sawâkin	411
Dongolâwî merchant	418
Sûdânî woman	419
Sûdânî young man	421
Sûdânî man	423
Sûdânî woman	425
Sûdânî maiden	426
Sûdânî youth of Negro origin	427
Sûdânî woman wearing the râhat	429
Meroïtic inscriptions	444
Altar with Meroïtic inscription	445
Ḥalfa-Abû-Hamed Railway	464
Sûdân Railways	465
The Driver of the "Gedaref"	467
American engine on the Ḥalfa-Abu-Hamed Railway	468
A shady resting-place	469
Atbara-Sawâkin Railway	474
Railway shops, Sawâkin	475
Material train leaving Sawâkin	476
Laying the Atbara-Red Sea Railway	477
Sir W. Garstin's proposed Canal in the Sûdân	485

PART II.

[CONTINUED]

A HISTORY

OF THE

EGYPTIAN SUDAN, ANCIENT AND MODERN.

CHAPTER IV.

THE RISE OF THE NUBIAN OR SÛDÂNÎ KINGDOM OF PIĀNKHI.

AFTER the departure of the priests of Ȧmen from Thebes to seek a refuge for their god and themselves at Napata, the condition of affairs in Egypt passed from bad to worse, and no man was able to make himself truly the king of Egypt. In Upper Egypt disturbances broke out everywhere, and such influence as the priests who remained at Thebes possessed was used by them to thwart every attempt of the kings of the North to increase their power in the South. In the Delta itself the authority of the Bubastite kings was lightly regarded, and little by little each governor of a large city arrogated to himself the authority of a king. Taking advantage of these circumstances, the native princes of Napata soon made themselves independent rulers of Nubia, and by degrees their authority was recognized over a tract of country which extended from the First Cataract in the north to the Blue Nile in the south. Under the influence of the priests of Ȧmen who had settled in their capital and had established on a firm base the worship of the Nubian Ȧmen, they began to regard Thebes in Egypt and the country between that city and the First Cataract as parts of their kingdom, and they spared no pains in trying to turn the fertile Dongola province into a copy of Upper Egypt, which, indeed, in many particulars it closely resembled.

The time was ripe for the making of this attempt, and the population of this portion of the Nile Valley, containing as it did a large Egyptian element, was ready and willing to be ruled according to the laws of Egypt, with the civilization and religion and manners and customs of which they had been familiar for about fifteen centuries. Since the time of Amen-ḥetep II. Napata had been regarded as a second Thebes by the Nubians, and we may be sure that when Ḥer-Ḥeru usurped the title of "Prince of Kash," the act had a profound political as well as religious signification. Whilst the petty kings in the Delta were fighting among themselves, and the chiefs in Upper Egypt were striving for sovereignty, the princes of Nubia were consolidating their power, and apparently waiting for a favourable opportunity of making a descent upon Egypt. The kings of the North were far too much occupied with their own affairs to have either time or attention to give to the Sûdân, and, as they had not sufficient power to take over the gold mines and work them as a government monopoly, that country interested them but little, and it was free from the interference of Egypt for several generations.

About the year B.C 750 there reigned at Napata a Nubian king called Piānkhi.[1] Of his origin and of the circumstances which brought him to the throne we know nothing, though his name suggests that there was a strain of Egyptian blood in him, and he may well have been a descendant of the great Theban royal line of which Åmen was the ancestor. We may note in passing that on a pillar in the temple which he built at Gebel Barkal he styles himself the "son of Bast,"[2] i.e., the great goddess of the city of Bubastis in the Delta, but it is difficult to see how he could be connected with that city. Be this as it may, he enclosed his name in a cartouche, he adopted the prenomen USR-MAĀT RĀ,[3] which he also enclosed in a cartouche, and placed in front of it the title  *Suten Båt*, which Menå, the first king of Egypt, used to express

[1] Probably the Ψαμμοῦς of Manetho.

[2] There is preserved in the Louvre a figure of Bast which appears to have been dedicated to the goddess by Piānkhi and his wife Kenensat; see Pierret, *Recueil*, p. 44.

[3] .

his sovereignty over the South and the North, and he styled himself "Meri Åmen " (beloved of Åmen), son of Bast." These facts are interesting, for they prove that a Nubian prince of Napata in the eighth century before Christ endeavoured to connect himself with the ancient monarchy of the Pharaohs, and used their titles, apparently not realizing their exact signification, and, it may be added, his absurdity in doing so, and described himself as the son of an alien goddess, and the " beloved " of a foreign god. He also called himself " son of Rā." In Northern Nubia we see on the reliefs in the temples built by the kings of Egypt figures of Ṭeṭun, certainly one of the oldest gods of Nubia, if not the oldest, but nowhere in Piānkhi's inscription, or on his buildings, is there any mention of this god, and it is clear from this fact that Åmen had been made to absorb the attributes of the indigenous gods of the country, and had become the " king of the gods " in Nubia as in Egypt. In the Sûdân, as in Egypt, Åmen appears in the form of a man, wearing a pair of high feathers on his head, or as a man with a ram's head, or as a ram, and the Nubians never confounded him with the ram-headed god Khnemu, who was especially worshipped in the Cataracts. The horns of the species of ram sacred to Khnemu project horizontally from the sides of his head, whilst those of the ram sacred to Åmen curl down on each side of the animal's face. As Piānkhi assumed the titles of the ancient kings of Egypt, so his Queen Kenensat also adopted the titles of the ancient queens, and her name was enclosed within a cartouche;[1] of her origin likewise nothing is known, but her name does not appear to be Egyptian.[2]

The greatest event in the life of Piānkhi was his expedition to Egypt, of which he caused a lengthy account to be cut upon a massive block of black basalt and set up in temple built by him at Gebel Barkal; this object was found by an Egyptian officer in the Sûdân in 1862, and was subsequently brought with great difficulty to Cairo, where it is now preserved in the Museum of

[1] Thus, .

[2] The title of the goddess Bast worshipped by herself and her husband is *uatch taui* 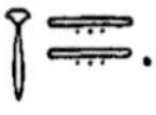.

Egyptian Antiquities.[1] The text is the longest and fullest of any Nubian king known to us, and is of the greatest interest and value for the history of the period. It should, of course, be remembered that it is only a one-sided statement of facts, but, on the other hand, it is the *sole* authority on Piānkhi's conquest of Egypt, and as such must be highly prized. The Stele of Piānkhi is about 5 feet 10 inches high, 6 feet wide, and 1 foot 4 inches thick, and the text fills one hundred and fifty-nine lines. On the face of the rounded part of the stele we see Amen seated, and behind him the goddess Mut; before him stands the king receiving the address which is made to him by Nemareth, who is bringing a horse as a gift. At the feet of Piānkhi kneel three kings, and behind the goddess are five more; the name of each is above him.

The narrative sets forth that Piānkhi, the son of Rā, the counterpart of Tem, and the offspring of a god, was a *suten*, i.e., king from his mother's womb, and that a certain man came to him and reported that the whole of the North of Egypt was in revolt, that Tafnekhth, a local chief of the town of Neter in the Delta, had first seized the whole country as far as Memphis, and had then sailed up the Nile with a large number of soldiers, and that the governors of the great cities of Mêdûm, Oxyrhynchus, Crocodilopolis, and other cities on the west bank of the Nile, had thrown open their gates and received him. This done, Tafnekhth crossed the river, and several cities on the east bank submitted to him in a similar manner. The only one that stood out against Tafnekhth was Herakleopolis, the governor of which was Peftchāā-Bast: this he besieged vigorously, and in a very short time no one could either come out of it or go into it. When Piānkhi received this intelligence it must have been clear to him that Tafnekhth was the kind of man to succeed, and to force his way southwards until he had Thebes at his mercy, but Piānkhi appears to have taken no steps to arrest his progress. Later moreover, we find from the narrative that the heads of the civil and military powers in all the cities of Egypt sent frequent messengers to Piānkhi, begging him not "to keep silent," for otherwise

[1] For the text, see Mariette, *Mon. Divers.*, plates i.-vi. It was first translated by E. de Rougé, in 1868 (see *Chrestomathie Égyptienne*, Fasc. iv., Paris, 1876). See also Brugsch, *Geschichte*, 1877, pp. 676-707, and its English translation, vol. ii., pp. 225-248; Wiedemann, *Aeg. Geschichte*, p. 564 ff.

all the nomes of Middle Egypt and the Land of the South would fall into the hands of Tafnekhth. They reported also that king Nemareth, after resisting for some time, had at length thrown in his lot with Tafnekhth.

Matters now appeared to be serious, so Piānkhi sent a message to his generals Puarma and Lāmersekni, who were stationed in Egypt, and commanded his forces there, to go and seize all the men and cattle, and all the boats on the river, to stop all work in the fields and to draw up a force before the nome of Hermopolis in order to check the advance of Tafnekhth. From this statement it is clear that there must have been a force of Nubian troops stationed somewhere on the southern border of Egypt, which was always ready to defend Piānkhi's interest in Upper Egypt. Piānkhi sent his soldiers some excellent advice, and bade them fight in the way in which they were accustomed to fight, and with boldness, because they were fighting for Åmen. He also bade them perform religious ceremonies when they arrived at Thebes, so that Åmen, who was able to make one man to capture a thousand, may give them his potent help. His advice is so paternal that he even provides them with a formula of prayer to Åmen, which runs :—

"O open thou the way before us, and
"Let us fight under the shadow of thy sword : for
"A child, if he be sent forth by thee,
"Shall overcome him that hath overcome multitudes."

Piānkhi's soldiers returned him a suitable answer, and vowed that in his name they would do great things. When they arrived at Thebes they worshipped Åmen according to their instructions, and then they embarked in their boats and sailed down the river. On their way they met a force of Tafnekhth's sailing up, and a fight took place in which the Nubians were victorious, capturing many boats and prisoners, and so destroying Tafnekhth's chance of reducing Herakleopolis. Piānkhi's troops then marched on to the relief of Herakleopolis, and when they arrived there they found that the siege was being directed by Tafnekhth himself, assisted by Nemareth, Åuapeth, Shashanq, and several other chiefs, including the governors of Busiris, Mendes, Hermopolis Parva, and Bubastis. The Nubians attacked the confederates without delay, and defeated them and captured several of their boats, but a remnant managed to escape, and succeeded in finding refuge at Pa-peḳ, which, as Prof. Maspero has pointed out, may well be near the modern Al-Fûḳa'i. At dawn the next morning the Nubians left their boats and marched against the foe, and, according to Piānkhi, his soldiers slew such a large number of men and horses that it was impossible to count them. The remainder fled, having suffered the "worst and most disastrous "defeat which they had ever known."

Meanwhile Nemareth escaped and went to Hermopolis, and having gathered together the people and the cattle, he went with them into the city and entrenched himself behind its earthworks, and here Piānkhi's soldiers found him when they arrived. They surrounded Hermopolis, and then sent to report to their master what they had done. When Piānkhi received the news he became like a panther in a rage, and swore by Amen that as soon as he had performed the festival ceremonies of that god at Thebes, he would come in person, and make "the Land of "the North to taste the taste of his claws." Leaving a force to besiege Hermopolis, the remainder of the Nubians set out to attack Oxyrhynchus, and having captured the city with all the fury of a water-flood, they sent a report to this effect to Piānkhi, but the king's wrath was not appeased. They next attacked Tatehen and captured it, beating down its walls with a battering ram; they killed many of its inhabitants, including a son of Tafnekhth, but when they sent the report of their success to the king his wrath was not appeased. They next attacked Hipponon, and captured it, but still the king was not satisfied.

On the ninth day of the month Thoth (August-September) Piānkhi set out from Napata, and came down quickly on the waters of the inundation to Thebes. Having performed all the ceremonies, and made all the offerings proper for the New Year festivals, he re-embarked and went on to Hermopolis. He left his boat, and mounted his chariot, and attacked the city at the head of his troops, and the enemy trembled. He had his tent pitched to the south-west of the city, and made his soldiers build earthworks, stiffened with poles, up to the level of the tops of the walls, and, having caused wooden shelters to be erected on these, he filled them with archers and slingers, who poured their missiles among the people and slew many of them. After three days

Hermopolis capitulated, and Nemareth sent messengers, laden with rich gifts, to offer his submission to Piānkhi; he also sent his queen and her women to entreat for mercy from the Nubian queen and princesses and ladies, who had accompanied the Nubian king to Egypt. In due course Nemareth himself appeared, leading a horse with one hand and holding a sistrum in the other, and, having made a suitable speech, he offered to Piānkhi rich tribute. Having made an offering to Thoth, the great god of the city, Piānkhi went through the palace and the storehouses of Nemareth, and had all their contents brought out before him, including the ladies of the royal *harîm*, but on these last he did not look at all. Then he passed on to the royal stud farm, and when he found that the brood mares and foals had been allowed to go hungry, he swore by the Sun-god that he considered this neglect of the horses to be the very worst of all the offences which Nemareth had committed. Piānkhi divided the spoil of Hermopolis into two lots one he gave to Åmen, and the other he kept for himself. At this time Pef-tchāā-Bast, governor of Herakleopolis, also brought tribute, including a number of very fine horses. He tendered his submission in picturesque words, saying that he had fallen deep down into hell, and was buried in the blackness of night, when the light of Piānkhi fell upon him, and his darkness was rolled away, &c.

Piānkhi then passed on to Al-Lâhûn, which submitted to him, and he thus became master of the Fayyûm; the son of Tafnekhth was allowed to march out with his followers unmolested. Mêdûm and Thet-taui also opened their gates to Piānkhi, and then he was able to go straight on to Memphis. Here, however, the gates were shut against him. He found some means of addressing the people of the city, and told them that if they let him in he would offer sacrifice to Ptah and Seker, and then sail down the river, and that not even a child should cry out in alarm. These words the people did not believe, and they kept their gates fast shut, and, when they found a few Nubian artificers who were examining the quay, or the harbour, separated from the main body of the Nubian army, they fell upon them and killed them. One night Tafnekhth appeared and addressed the garrison of Memphis, which numbered 8,000 men, and pointed out to them how well the place was provisioned, and how strongly it was fortified, and he advised them to offer resistance to Piānkhi, at all events until he (Tafnekhth) returned. He then mounted his horse and rode away. The next morning Piānkhi went to the west side of the city and examined the fortifications, and he found them very strong. When his soldiers saw them they made up their minds that the city could only be taken by casting up mounds against it, and attacking it under cover of wooden towers; but Piānkhi thought otherwise, and ordering his boats to advance, they dashed in among the vessels which lined the quay sides, and as the water was up to the walls, their bows projected over them into the city. From the bows of the boats the soldiers leaped into the city, and captured it with all the force of a water-flood. At dawn next day the king sent men to protect the temples, and then he went and made an offering to the gods, and he purified the city, and made sacrifices to Ptaḥ and Seker. At this time Āuapeth, and Merkanshu, and Peṭā-Āst tendered their submission and brought him gifts. The following day Piānkhi crossed the river to Kher-Āḥa and sacrificed to Temu, and then he went on to Heliopolis to perform ceremonies in honour of the gods there. He first purified himself by bathing his face in the Sun Well, and then he offered up white oxen, &c., to Rā. He entered the temple of Rā, and prayed many prayers there, and the high-priest also prayed on his behalf. This done, he asperged and censed himself, and then, taking with him flowers and perfume, he mounted the steps of the shrine, and opened the doors of the ark, and saw Rā face to face. He then adored the Boats of Rā and Tem, and, having shut the doors of the ark and sealed them, he ordered the priests to let no other king enter the sanctuary. Piānkhi was thus acknowledged king of Egypt by the god Āmen-Rā, and all the people knew that they must tender to him their submission as the god's vice-gerent upon earth. The following day the *Erpā* Peṭā-Āst submitted and paid him large tribute, and fifteen other kings, and dukes, and governors followed his example.

Meanwhile Tafnekhth, the leader of the rebellion, dismantled his fortifications, set fire to his treasure-houses, and, taking his soldiers with him, fled to the city of Mest. Thither Piānkhi sent soldiers under the *Erpā* Peṭā-Āst, and they slew every man they found there. Tafnekhth seems to have escaped to some place among the salt lagoons near the sea-coast, and from this place he sent an envoy bearing his submission. He acknowledged his faults in picturesque language, and begged Piānkhi not to punish him according to his deserts; in weighing his offences he begs the king to hold the scales of his judgment in such a way that such merit as he possesses by reason of his submission, and his sufferings and misery, may tell in his favour as much as possible. Finally, he said he was ready to pay tribute to Piānkhi and to swear an oath of allegiance, and he asked the king to send an envoy to receive the tribute, and to hear him swear the oath. This Piānkhi did, and Tafnekhth went into the house of his god, and in the presence of the Nubian commander-in-chief and a high-priest, he swore never to offend again; this satisfied Piānkhi, who accepted the tribute, and granted peace to Tafnekhth. Soon after this the cities of Cynopolis and Aphroditopolis submitted to Piānkhi, and thus the whole of Egypt was in his power. Finally, two Governors of the North and two of the South, and all the other chiefs of the country, came and tendered their submission in person, but as all save one, Nemareth, were uncircumcised, and were fish-eaters, they were not admitted to the royal tent, and they stood outside in awe, "their legs (trembling) like those of women."

There was nothing further for Piānkhi to do, so his boats were loaded with the masses of tribute which had been given to him, and he sailed up the river with a glad heart, the people everywhere receiving him with joy. He had added the kingdom of the North, which at its conquest by him extended from the Mediterranean to Asyût, to his own kingdom of the South, and the Nile Valley so far south as Napata was once more subject to one king, just as it had been under the XVIIIth Dynasty, only that king was a Sûdânî instead of an Egyptian. Piānkhi did not rule from Thebes as might have been expected, but he returned to Napata with his spoil, a large portion of which fell, no doubt, to the share of the priests of Åmen and their god. Probably with the view of commemorating his conquest of Egypt, Piānkhi built a large temple on the plain at the foot of Gebel Barkal, which was dedicated to Åmen-Rā and the other deities of his triad. It was at least 500 feet long and 135 feet wide, and contained two courts, a hypostyle hall, a vestibule, and a sanctuary, which held probably three shrines. The pylon which divided the first court from the second was decorated with battle-scenes, processions, &c., copied, no doubt, from the temples of Egypt. The temple is now a mass of ruins, but thanks to the plans and descriptions made by Cailliaud, Hoskins, and Lepsius, when they were in a less confused state than now, its general arrangement can be satisfactorily made out. As this has been discussed elsewhere in the present work, nothing need be said about it here. It is a moot point whether Piānkhi repaired and enlarged a temple erected by one of the great kings of the XVIIIth or XIXth Dynasty, or built an entirely new edifice; it seems, however, most probable that he adopted the former course. It is impossible to think that the Thothmes and Ȧmen-ḥetep kings did not build temples in the capital of their Sûdân kingdom, especially as under their reigns Napata must have been the great trading centre to which the slaves of the countries on the White and Blue Niles, and the gold, red stones, ivory, ebony, ostrich feathers, skins, &c., were brought. Hoskins tells[1] us that he found in the burial ground at Merawi a stone bearing one half of the name of Rameses II.; and Lepsius, probably referring to the same stone,[2] says that the oldest remains which existed at Gebel Barkal were confined to "one temple which Rameses the Great erected to Ȧmen-Rā." The occurrence of the name of this king on an isolated block of stone proves nothing beyond the fact that some admirer of this king cut his name on it. As a matter of fact, Rameses II. had little interest in Napata, for in the Wâdî 'Ulâki, near Dakka, he found a rich gold-producing country which was far nearer Egypt than the mines of the region further south. And we know that his name appears prominently in places where he built nothing.

Piānkhi seems to have neither restored nor built any temples in Egypt; if he did, no traces of them remain. The black basalt stele on which he caused to be cut the history of his campaign in Egypt tells us nothing concerning his subsequent acts, and therefore nothing is known about his dealings with the chiefs further to the south in the Sûdân, or the system on which he ruled

[1] *Travels*, p. 288.

[2] *Letters*, p. 222.

his kingdom. The one document which he has left us is, however, most valuable, and its contents are of more than ordinary interest; moreover, the information which it gives us is not to be obtained elsewhere. No other Nubian king has supplied us with such a full account of the chief events of his reign, and that the reader may be able to judge of his narrative in a consecutive form, an English rendering of it is here appended. A few passages are obscure to modern investigators of it, and the meanings of some of the words in it are not yet known accurately, but the general sense of the document is quite clear, and it proves that the Nubian Piānkhi was no mere savage conqueror, but a man endowed with a full belief in his divine origin, a capable and energetic soldier, and a ruler who, in the hour of his triumph, exhibited moderation in his dealings with the vanquished, and who knew how to respect the temples and gods of Egypt, and the civil and religious institutions of the country whence his own civilization, and religion, and laws were drawn.

TRANSLATION OF THE INSCRIPTION OF PIĀNKHI MERI ÅMEN, KING OF THE EGYPTIAN SÛDÂN, ABOUT B.C. 730.

On the first day of the month Thoth, in the twenty-first year of the reign of the king of the South and North (Piānkhi-meri-Åmen), the ever-living, His Majesty pronounced the [following] words: Hearken ye to the things which I have done more than [my] ancestors. I am a *suten* (king), the emanation of God, and the living counterpart of Tem; [when I] came forth from the womb I was decreed (literally, written down) to be a ruler (*ḥeq*) who should strike fear into his chiefs. I was recognized as a ruler by my mother when I was in the egg (i.e., in embryonic state), and as a well-doing god, and the beloved of the gods, the son of Rā, the work of his hands (Piānkhi-meri-Åmen).

One came and said unto His Majesty: "The governor of the "country of the West (Åmentet), the great duke (*ḥā*) in the city of "Neter (Saïs), Tafnekhth, [hath made himself master] in the nome "of . . . . , in the nome Ka-ḥeseb, in Ḥāp, in Ān, in Pa-nub, and "in White Wall (Memphis); he hath taken possession of the whole "of the West Country, from the region of the swamps (on the "north) to Thet-taui [a district of Memphis]; he hath sailed up "the river with a large number of soldiers, and all the lands on "both sides of the Nile have joined themselves unto him, and the "dukes and the governors of the towns and cities which have "temples in them guard his feet like so many dogs. None of the "cities which are fortified hath shut its gates against him . . . . . in "the nomes of the south. The city of Mer-Tem, the city of Pa-Rā-"sekhem-kheper, the city of Neter-ḥet-Sebek (Crocodilopolis), the "city of Pa-Matchet (Oxyrhynchus), the city of Thekansh, and "every town in the West Country, have unbolted their gates, by "reason of their fear of him. Then he betook himself to the "nomes of the East Country, and they also opened their gates before "him, namely, Ḥet-Bennu (Hipponon), Taiutchait, Suten-ḥet and "Pa-neb-ṭep-aḥet (Aphroditopolis); verily [thus have they "done]. He hath also beleaguered Suten-ḥenen (Herakleopolis), "and he hath completely surrounded it.[1] Of those who want to "come out none cometh out, and of those who would go into it "none goeth in by reason of the fighting which goeth on each day "(or, all day long) He hath invested the city closely at every "point, and every duke (*ḥā*) knoweth the portion of the wall "[which he is to attack]. He hath allowed every man among "the dukes and the governors of cities, which have temples in "them, to dwell in his own district. [These things hath he done] "by reason of the arrogance of his rebellious heart, and his heart is "swollen with pride and joy."

And moreover, the chiefs, and the dukes, and the generals of the army which were in every town were sending messages to His Majesty every day, saying: "If thou keepest silence "in this matter then all the Land of the South, and the "nomes of Middle Egypt, will be lost; Tafnekhth carrieth all "before him, and findeth none to resist him. Nemareth . . . . "the duke of Ḥet-urt hath thrown down the fortifications of "the city of Neferus, and hath himself laid waste his own town, "being afraid that Tafnekhth will capture it; but when he was "besieged by him in another city, verily he departed and "became a watcher of his feet. Nemareth hath now forsaken His "Majesty and hath become an adherent of Tafnekhth, whom he "serveth, and Tafnekhth hath handed over to him the nome of "Oxyrhynchus, and hath given to him everything that his heart "desireth."

Then His Majesty sent messages to the dukes and to the Commanders-in-chief who were in Egypt, namely to the general Puarma, and the general Lāmersekni, and to every general of His Majesty in Egypt, telling them to go quickly with boldness, and set in array the battle . . . . and to seize the men, and the cattle, and the barges which were on the river, and to prevent the labourers from going out to the fields, and to stop every ploughman from ploughing the land, and to beleaguer closely the country in front of the nome of Un (Hermopolis), and to fight against it each day. And thus did they.

[1] Literally, "he hath made himself [like a serpent] with [its] tail in [its] mouth."

INSCRIPTION OF PIANKHI

Then His Majesty made soldiers march into Egypt, and gave them strict commands, saying: "Ye shall not [pass] the night in "pleasure,[1] but as soon as ye see that he hath set his troops in "marching order, do battle with him. If any man shall say, He "hath marched his infantry and cavalry to another city, then abide "ye where ye are until his soldiers arrive. Attack ye when one "shall tell you that he is with his forces in another town, and let "the dukes whom he hath brought to help him be gathered together, "[and] let the Thehennu (Libyans), [and] as many soldiers as he "pleaseth muster [where they will], and let the battle be set in "array according to ancient custom. And say, We do not know "how to command him, and to give orders to his soldiers, and to "harness the finest horses of the stable. Then fight in battle "boldly, for we know that it is the god Amen who hath sent us "forth. And when ye arrive at the sanctuary of Uast (Thebes), "opposite the Apts (i.e., Karnak and Luxor), go ye into the water, "and cleanse ye yourselves in the waters of the stream. Undress "yourselves at the head of the lake, unstring your bows, lay aside "your arrows, and let not any chief imagine himself to be the "equal of the lord of two-fold strength, for the strength of no "mighty man shall prevail without his help. Him who is feeble "of arm he maketh strong of arm; if the enemy be many, he "maketh them to flee before the hand of the impotent man, and "he maketh one man to lead captive a thousand. Wet ye "yourselves in the water of his altars, and smell ye the earth "before him, and say ye unto him; 'O make thou a way for us, "and let us fight under the shadow of thy sword, for a child, if he "be sent by thee, shall overcome him that hath overcome "multitudes.'"

Then the soldiers cast themselves on their bellies before His Majesty, saying: "Through thy name Amen will work mighty "deeds by us. Thy counsel leadeth thy soldiers, thy bread is in "our bodies on every road, and thy beer quencheth our thirst, "thy might giveth to us the sword of battle, and victory shall "come to us by the mention of thy name. The soldiers who are "led by a captain having unnatural passions shall not stand firm. "Who is like unto thee? Verily thou art a strong king, thou "workest with thy hands, and thou art the overseer of the opera- "tions of war."

Then the soldiers made their passage down the river, and they arrived at the city of Thebes, and they did everything which His Majesty had commanded them to do. And they continued their journey down the river, and they met several large boats sailing up the river containing soldiers, and sailors, and mighty captains of every kind of the Land of the North, and every man of them was equipped with the weapons of war and ready to do battle with the troops of His Majesty. Then the soldiers of His Majesty

[1] De Rougé translates: N' (attaquez pas) pendant la nuit, comme pour un jeu.

inflicted a mighty defeat on them, and slew a countless number, and made prisoners of their soldiers, and captured their boats, and they brought the captives alive to the place where His Majesty was. Then they marched on to the territory before the city of Suten-ḥenen (Herakleopolis) in order to set in array the battle against the dukes and the kings of the Land of the North, that is to say, to attack king Nemareth, and king Āuapeth, and Shashanq, the chief of the Māshuasha, of the city of Pa-Asȧr-neb-Ṭeṭ, i.e., Busiris); and Tchet-Ȧmen-ȧf-ānkh, the great chief of the Māshuasha, of the city of Pa-ba-neb-Ṭeṭ (i.e., Mendes); and his eldest son who was commander of the troops of the city of Pa-Teḥuti-ȧp-reḥeḥui (i.e., Hermopolis Parva); and the soldiers of the *Erpā* Bakennifi; and his eldest son Nesnaqeti, the chief of the Māshuasha in the nome of Ka-ḥeseb; and every prince who carrieth a fan in the Land of the North; and king Uasarken, who is in Pa-Bast (Bubastis) and the city of Uu-en-Rā-nefert; and every duke, and every governor of a city wherein there is a temple on the west of the river, and on the east of the river, and in the lands which are between them. All these had joined themselves together, and had become guardians of the feet of Tafnekhth, the great chief of the Land of the West, the governor of all the temple-cities of the Land of the North, the prophet of Neith, the lady of Saïs, and the *sem* priest of the god Ptaḥ.

The soldiers of His Majesty marched against them, and they inflicted defeat upon them, the greatest defeat there ever was, and they captured their boats on the river. A remnant of them made their escape and succeeded in reaching a place in the country on the western bank called Pa-peḳ. As soon as the dawn came on the following morning the soldiers of His Majesty set out to attack them, and they rushed in among them and slew such a large number of men and horses that it was impossible to say how many had died. Then panic seized the rest of them, and they fled to the Land of the North, having suffered a defeat which was greater and more disastrous than they had ever known.[1]

And king Nemareth sailed up the river, having been told that the city of Khemennu (Hermopolis) was [open] before the enemy, that is, the soldiers of His Majesty [Piānkhi]. He captured its people and its cattle, and he himself went into the city of Un. Now the soldiers of His Majesty [Piānkhi] were [in boats] on the river, and [encamped] on the territory of the nome of Un, and when they heard this, they surrounded the nome of Un on all its four sides, and they allowed no man either to come in or to go out; and they sent messengers to announce to His Majesty, the King of the South and North (Piānkhi-meri-Ȧmen), the life-giver, each defeat which had been inflicted on the enemy by the forces

[1] When complete, the text at this point gave the number of the people who were slain in the two engagements, but the figures have either been erased wittingly, or broken away accidentally.

of His Majesty. And His Majesty raged like a panther, and said: "If it should happen that they leave alive a remnant of the soldiers "of the Land of the North, and if any one of them escape to "relate the story thereof, and if they do not slay utterly every one "of them, I swear by my own life, and by the love which I bear to "Rā, and by the grace which Father Åmen hath shown to me, "that I myself will go down the river and will overthrow every-"thing which he (i.e., Tafnekhth) hath made, and will make him "to retreat from the fight for evermore. When I have performed "the ceremonies which belong to the Festival of the New Year, "and I have made my offering to Father Amen during his beauti-"ful festival, wherein he maketh his beautiful appearance at "the Festival of the New Year, he shall send me away in peace "to see Åmen during the beautiful festival of the Festival of Åpt, "and I shall make him to appear in his divine form in the Åpt of the "South [1] in his beautiful festival of the Festival of the Åpt, on the "night of the Festival which is stablished in Thebes, the Festival "which Rā ordained [2] when time began, and I shall make him to "appear in his temple, and he shall take his position on his throne "on the day whereon the god entereth, which is the second day of "the third month of the summer, on that day, I say, will I make "the Land of the North to taste the taste of my fingers."

Now when the soldiers [of His Majesty Piānkhi] who were in Egypt heard of the wrath which His Majesty nursed against them they waged war against the nome of Uaseb at Pa-Matchet (Oxyrhynchus), and they captured it like a water-flood. They sent messengers to His Majesty [to announce this], but his heart was not satisfied thereat. Then they attacked Tatehen,[3] which was very strongly fortified, and they found it to be full of mighty men of war of all kinds of the Land of the North. And they constructed a tower [4] to send against it to beat down its walls, and they made so great a slaughter among its people that the dead could not be counted; among these was the son of Tafnekhth, the prince of the Māshuasha. They sent messengers to His Majesty [to announce this], but his heart was not satisfied thereat. Then they attacked Ḥet Bennu, and it opened its fortress, and the soldiers of His Majesty entered therein. They sent messengers to His Majesty [to announce this], but his heart was not satisfied thereat.

On the ninth day of the first month of the summer, His Majesty set out on his journey and went down the river to Ṭhebes, and he took part in the celebration of the Festival of Åmen, the Festival of Åpt. Then His Majesty continued his journey down the river to the city of Un. And His Majesty came forth from the cabin of his barge, and he harnessed his horses, and mounted his chariot, and the terror of His Majesty

[1] I.e., the temple of Luxor.
[2] Literally, made.
[3] A fortress near Memphis.
[4] I.e., a battering ram.

penetrated even to the remotest parts of the country of the Sati (Asia ?), and every heart quaked with the fear of him. And His Majesty rushed forth and threw himself upon those whom his soldiers hated, and he raged at them like a panther, and said : "If ye still continue to fight, and if ye still gainsay my com-"mands, and if ye, moreover, persist in your rebellion I must in "truth put the fear of me in the Land of the North." And he inflicted upon them a terrible defeat, disastrous and crushing.

Then a tent was pitched for him to the south-west of the city of Hermopolis, and he besieged the city every day. He made heaps of earth to cover the walls, and he set up wooden stagings to scale them. And the archers [who were in them] shot forth arrows, and the leathern slings hurled forth stones to kill people [in the city] every day. And it came to pass on the third day that the city of Un was in a stinking state, and the people thereof could not breathe by reason of the stench [of the corpses]. Then the city of Un cast itself upon its belly, and it offered up supplications for mercy before the king (*bät*, i.e., His Majesty Piānkhi). And envoys came forth with things of every kind which were beautiful to look upon, that is to say, gold, precious stones of every kind, and apparel made of the finest linen, [and they said]; "He hath risen! The uraeus is on his brow, he hath "placed his terror [in our hearts], and it is unnecessary for us to "allow many days to pass before making supplication to his "crown." Then he [i.e., Nemareth] made his wife to come, the wife of a king and the daughter of a king, Nesthentmeḥ, to make supplication before the queen and royal concubines, and princesses, and sisters of the king (i.e., of Piānkhi), and she cast herself upon her belly in the house of the women, before the queens, saying, "O come with me, queens, and princesses, and "royal sisters, and make ye to be at peace Horus, the lord of the "palace, whose souls are mighty, and whose word cometh to pass "with great effect indeed, O come ye . . . . ."

[Fifteen lines of the text are here broken away]

". . . . . the way of life.[1] If I were to ascend into the sky like an "arrow, I should be [caught by thee. Have submitted to thee] "the countries of the South, and the land of the North bows in "homage before thee. We beseech thee to let us live under "thy shadow . . . . Not a grown man is seen with his father, "and thy nomes are filled with children." And he cast himself upon his belly before His Majesty . . . . saying: "O Horus, "lord of the palace, behold, it is thy souls who have done this "thing unto me. I am one of thy royal vassals, who are bound "to pay tribute into thy treasury, whose tribute thou dost "compute, but I will pay unto thee more than they all." Then he brought the tribute which had been laid upon him, silver, gold, lapis-lazuli, turquoises, copper (?), and [precious] stones of

[1] This is a part of the speech of the conquered rebel to Piānkhi.

every kind in large quantities, and he filled the treasure-house with these offerings. He led a horse in his right hand, and in his left he held a sistrum, a sistrum of gold and lapis-lazuli.

Then [Piānkhi] rose in his palace, and he came forth and went to the Temple of Thoth, the Lord of the Eight Gods, and he slaughtered oxen, and calves, and geese, to Father Thoth, the Lord of the Eight Gods in the House of the Eight Gods, and the fighting men of the nome of Un [Hermopolis] shouted for joy, and the priests said: "Right well hath Horus, the son of "Rā, (Piānkhi), taken up his place in his town. Thou hast "made for us a festival inasmuch as thou hast protected the nome "of Un."

Then His Majesty set out to go to the palace of king Nemareth, and he went through every chamber of the royal house, and his treasury, and his store-houses. Then he made them bring to him the queens and the princesses, and they were loud in their praises of His Majesty after the manner of women, but His Majesty did not permit his face to turn towards them. And His Majesty went on to the place where the horses were kept, and into the stalls of the foals, and he perceived that they had been suffering from hunger, and he said: "I swear by my "own life, and by the love which I have for Rā, who reneweth "the [breath of] life which is in my nostrils, that, to my mind, "to have allowed my horses to suffer hunger, is the worst of all "the evil things which thou hast done in the violence of thy "heart. I can testify to the terror of a lord in thy people.[1] "Knowest thou not that the shadow of God is upon me, and that "my luck never faileth me? I swear that if any man whom I "had not known had done this thing to me I would never have "remitted to him his offence. I was brought forth from [my "mother's] womb having been brought into being from a divine "egg, and the god begot me and set his person [in me]. I have "never done anything without him, and he himself hath decreed "that which I have done."

Then His Majesty took count of the spoil for the treasury, and of his storehouses [which he dedicated] as an offering for Āmen in the Āpts. And the governor of Suten-ḥenen (Herakleopolis), Pef-tch-āā-Bast, came with his gifts to Pharaoh, gold, silver, [precious] stones of all kinds, and the finest horses from his stables, and he cast himself upon his belly in the presence of His Majesty, and he said: "Homage to thee, O Horus, thou mighty "king, thou bull who subduest bulls! I dug out a place for "myself in the Ṭuat,[2] I was sunk deep down in the darkness,

[1] A difficult passage. De Rougé reads: "Ne rebelle pas ton cœur! j'attesterai la terreur du maître à tes gens:" and Brugsch renders: "That thou hast laid thy heart bare through this, evidence is furnished me of thy habitual views" (?).

[2] I.e., the Other World. He means to say, "I was in the blackest hell."

"when light was cast in on me. I found no friend in the day of "evil, or any one who supported me in the day of battle except "thyself, O king. Thou hast rolled away the darkness which "was over me. Henceforward I will be thy servant, and all my "possessions are thine. Suten-ḥenen shall pay tribute into thy "palace, for behold, thou art the image of Rā-Harmachis and "thou art above the stars which never fail (*akhemu seku*). His "existence is thine in thy capacity of king; he never diminisheth "and thou shalt never diminish, O king of the South and North, "(Piānkhi), who livest for ever!"

Then His Majesty sailed down the river to Ȧp-she (i.e., the Fayyûm), near to Reḥent (Al-Lâhûn), and he found the city of Pa (Rā-sekhem-kheper), with its fortifications manned, and its fortress shut against him, and it was filled with mighty men of war of all kinds from the Land of the North. And His Majesty sent a message unto them, saying: "O ye who live in the death "of the Ṭuat, deprived of . . . . . ye wretched ones! O ye who "live in death, if another moment pass without your having "opened your gates to me, verily ye shall suffer the doom of "vanquished folk, and it shall be disastrous to the king. Do not "ye close the doors of your lives at the block of slaughter this "day; do not love death and hate life. . . . . ." Then they sent messengers unto His Majesty, saying: "Indeed the shadow of "god is on thy head, O son of Nut,[1] and he hath given unto thee "his two hands. The thing which is imagined in thy heart "cometh to pass straightway, even as that which cometh forth "from the mouth of God, for verily, thou art born of God; [this]. "we see by the work[2] of thy two hands. Verily [this is] thy city, "and its enclosed fortifications [are thine] . . . . . let every man "enter and let every man go forth, and let His Majesty's will be done." Then they came forth with the son of the Prince of Māshuasha, Tafnekhth. And the soldiers of His Majesty entered into the city, and he did not slay any man whom he found therein. [Then His Majesty sent men] with those who had the seals to seal up his documents (?), and he had a list made of the things in his treasury for the treasury, and the contents of the store-houses were counted as offerings for his father Ȧmen-Rā, the lord of the thrones of the Two Lands.

And His Majesty continued his journey down the river, and he found the city of Mer-Tem, the Temple of Seker-neb-sehetch, with [its gates] shut, but before he came thereto, a conflict broke out within it . . . . . and fear [seized] them, and terror closed their mouths. Then His Majesty sent messengers unto them, saying: "Verily there are two ways before you; choose ye according "to your desire. Open your gates and ye shall live; keep

[1] I.e., the goddess of the sky.
[2] Literally, "from the mouth of thy two hands."

"them closed and ye shall die; for My Majesty passeth by no "city that keepeth its gates shut." Thereupon His Majesty entered straightway into the innermost part of this city, and he dedicated . . . . . [and offered sacrifices] to the goddess Menḥi-khent-Seḥetch. And he made a list of the contents of his treasury and store-houses which he set apart as offerings to Ȧmen of the Ȧpts.

Then His Majesty continued his journey down the river to Thet-taui,[1] and he found its fortifications closed and manned by mighty men of war of all kinds of the Land of the South. And they opened the gates of their strong places, and they cast themselves upon their bellies, [and they sent messengers to] His Majesty, [saying]: "Thy father hath decreed that thou shalt "possess his heritage of the lordship of the Two Lands: thou "hast taken possession of them, and thou art the lord over [all] "the earth." Then His Majesty went forth [from the cabin of his boat], and he offered up a great sacrifice to the gods who dwelt in this city, oxen, calves, geese, and good and pure things of every kind. And he had a list of the contents of the treasury made for his treasury, and of the contents of the store-houses he made offerings [to Ȧmen of the Ȧpts].

[Then His Majesty advanced to] White Wall (i.e., Memphis), and he sent messengers unto the inhabitants thereof, saying: "Shut ye not your gates, and there shall be no fighting inside "your city. My entry therein shall be like unto the entry of the "god Shu, who is from primeval time, and my going forth shall "be as his going forth, and my passage shall not be obstructed. "I will make an offering unto Ptaḥ and the gods who are within "White Wall, I will perform all the ceremonies appertaining to "Seker in the secret sanctuary, I will look upon the god who is "on his southern wall (i.e., Ptaḥ), and then I will sail on down "the river in peace . . . . . White Wall shall remain unharmed "and safe, and not a child shall raise a cry of distress. Consider "ye now the nomes to the south. Not a man in them, except "such as hath uttered blasphemies against god and hath revolted, "hath been slain, for the block of slaughter hath only been "prepared for those who have rebelled."

[Nevertheless the inhabitants of White Wall] shut fast their gates, and they caused a company of soldiers to go forth against a few of the soldiers of His Majesty who were artificers, and master-masons, and boatmen [and they slew them on] the river bank of White Wall. And behold that Prince of Saïs (Tafnekhth) came to White Wall by night, and he gave orders to his soldiers, and to his transport-men, and to every officer of his soldiers [who were in all] eight thousand men, and he admonished them very strictly indeed [saying]:—" Verily

[1] This strong fortress was built by Ȧmenemhāt I., and marked the division between Lower and Upper Egypt. It lay a little to the south of Memphis.

"Men-Nefer is filled with the bravest, mightiest men of war of "all kinds of the Land of the North, and its granaries are over-"flowing with wheat, and barley, and grain of all kinds, and "weapons of all kinds are [stored therein], and [the city is "surrounded by] a wall, and the great bastions are built as "strongly as the craft of the mason can build them, and [as] the "river floweth round its eastern side no place for attacking it can "be found there. The byres remain full of cattle, and the treasury is stored with silver, gold, bronze, clothing, incense, "honey, and unguents. I am going away, and I commit "[this] property to the chiefs of the North, I will open their "nomes for them, and I will become . . . [defend ye these "for a few] days until I come." Then he mounted his horse, for he could not depend upon his chariot, and he went down the river through fear of His Majesty.

And as soon as it was dawn on the following day, His Majesty set out for White Wall; he landed on the northern side of the city, finding that the waters reached up to the walls, and the boats came up close to the [quay] of Men-Nefer (Memphis). And His Majesty saw that it was strongly fortified, and that the walls thereof had been made higher by means of new buildings, and that the bastions thereof were provided with fortifications, and that there was no place available whereat it might be attacked. Now every man among the soldiers of His Majesty spake his opinion as to the method which ought to be followed in attacking [the city], and every one said:—"Come, let us surround it on all "sides . . . . verily its soldiers are very many. And the master "of affairs [or, works] said:—Make a passage to it. We will "throw up earth against the walls thereof, and on this we will lay "planks of olive wood firmly fastened together, and we will erect "wooden towers, and will make wooden . . . . round about "its whole circuit, and with these we will make breaches every-"where in it from the mounds of earth and the . . . . to raise "the ground by its walls, and we shall [thus] find a path for our "feet."

Then was His Majesty filled with rage like a panther, and he said;—"I swear by my own life, and by the love of Rā, and by "the grace of my father Åmen, that I believe[1] this hath "happened in respect of it by the decree of Åmen. This (i.e., the "speech given above) is the speech of a man . . . . and the "nomes of the south; they opened their gates to him [whilst he "was] on the road. They have not set Åmen in their hearts, "and they know not his decree; this hath he done so that he "might make his souls cause his terror to be seen. I shall "capture the city like a water-flood, and this hath [my father "Åmen] ordered me to do." Then he made his boats to advance, and his soldiers to attack the quay of Men-Nefer; and

[1] Literally, "I find" (?).

they passed in among the barges, and transports, and all boats with decks, and all the boats without, and these, in very large numbers, they tied up their own boats to the quay of Men-Nefer, with their bows close in to the houses of the city . . . . and none of the soldiers of His Majesty caused one child to cry out in distress. Then His Majesty himself had the vessels, and they were very many, drawn close to [the quay]. And His Majesty said unto his soldiers:—"It resteth now upon you "to act; surround the walls, and enter the houses on the "waters of the river. If any man among you entereth by the "wall, let him not stay upon the place where he is . . . . Offer "no resistance to the captains [who wish to submit], for that "would be an abominable thing [to do]. We have closed the "country of the South, and we have arrived at the country of the "North, and we sit upon Makhi-taui."[1]

And His Majesty captured the town of Men-Nefer like a water-flood, and he slew a large number of the people who were therein, and the prisoners were brought alive to the place where His Majesty was. And when it was dawn on the following day, His Majesty caused men to go there to protect the temples of God, and he performed acts of worship in the sanctuary of the gods, and he poured out libations to the divine chiefs of Ḥet-ka-Ptaḥ, and he purified Men-Nefer with natron and incense, and he set the priests in their appointed places. Then His Majesty went to the temple [of Ptaḥ] and he poured out a libation at the entrance thereof, and he performed all the ceremonies which are prescribed for performance by the king, he entered into the divine house, and he offered up a great sacrifice to Ptaḥ upon his Southern Wall, consisting of oxen, calves, geese, and every kind of good thing.

Then His Majesty went into his house, and he heard that all the towns which were in the district of Men-Nefer, that is to say, the town of Ḥeripeṭmȧi, and Peni- . . . . naunāā, and Pebekhen-nebiu, and Tauḥibit, had opened their gates, and that all the inhabitants thereof had betaken themselves to flight, and that no man knew where they had gone. And Ȧuapeth and Merkanshu, the chief of the Māshuasha, and the *erpā* Peṭā-Ȧsteta, and all the dukes of the Land of the North came bearing their offerings to look upon the beauties[2] of His Majesty. And he adjudged the contents of the treasuries and store-houses of Memphis as offerings for Ȧmen, and Ptaḥ, and the company of the gods who were in Ḥet-ka-Ptaḥ (Memphis).

And at dawn on the following day His Majesty made a journey to the east side of the river, and he made an offering to Tem in

[1] A name meaning, "The Balance of the Two Lands." This place was near Memphis.

[2] I.e., to experience the noble qualities of forgiveness and magnanimity of Piānkhi.

Kher-Āḥa,[1] and to the company of the gods in the temple, and to the company of the gods of the Ȧmḥet, and to the gods who are therein, consisting of oxen, calves, and geese, so that they might give life, strength, and health to the king of the South and North, Piānkhi, living for ever.

Then His Majesty set out for Ȧnnu (Heliopolis), over the mountain of Kher-Āḥa, by the road of the god Sep to Kher-Āḥa, and His Majesty went on to the camp to the west of the town of the two wells (or lakes) Merti (i.e., the modern Maṭarîya), and he made an offering there, and he purified himself in the pool of water, and he bathed his face in the milk (i.e., water) of Nut, wherein Rā bathed his face. And he passed on to Shāi-qa-em Ȧnnu, and he offered up a great offering there before Rā as he rose, consisting of white oxen, milk, *ānti*, incense, and sweet-smelling wood of all kinds. And as he was going along he went into the House of Rā, and he entered the temple, and prayed many prayers therein. And the chief ***kher ḥeb*** priest offered up prayers that the attacks of fiends on the king might be repulsed. And he performed the ceremonies of the ***per sba*** (?) chamber, and he girded about him the ***seṭeb*** garment, and he purified himself with incense, and he sprinkled himself with water, and he brought the ***ānkhiu*** flowers of the shrine (***ḥet-benbent***, i.e., the house of the obelisk), and he took perfume, and he ascended the steps to the great ark in order that he might look upon Rā himself in the shrine (***ḥet-benbent***). And His Majesty stood up there by himself, he drew back the bolts, and opened the doors of the ark, and he gazed upon Rā in the shrine, and he made adorations before the Māṭet Boat of Rā, and the Sektet Boat of Tem. Then he drew together the doors [of the sanctuary] and set clay [upon them], whereon he impressed the seal of the king himself. And he admonished the priests, saying: "I have set [my] seal; let no "other king whatsoever who may stand [here] enter." And the priests cast themselves upon their bellies before His Majesty, saying: "Horus, who loveth Ȧnnu (Heliopolis) shall endure, "and flourish, and shall never diminish!"

And His Majesty went on and entered into the house of Tem, and he performed the ceremonies connected with the offering of figures made of *ānti* of Tem-Kheperȧ, the prince of Ȧnnu.

Then the king Uasarken came to see the beauties of His Majesty.

And His Majesty set out on the following morning at dawn, at the head of his boats from the river bank, and journeyed to Ka qem. And his Majesty's tent was pitched to the south of Kaheni, and to the east of Ka-qem, and the kings and the dukes of the Land of the North, and all the chiefs, and all the fan-bearers and all the umbrella-bearers, and all the nobles, and all the royal kinsfolk from the East and from the West Countries,

[1] A city which occupied the site of Old Cairo.

and from the regions of Middle Egypt, came to look upon the beauties of His Majesty. And the *Erpā* Paṭā-Astet threw himself upon his belly before His Majesty, saying: "Come thou "to Ka-qem, and may the god Khent-Khatthi look upon thee, "and the goddess Khuit protect thee. Offer thou sacrifices to "Horus in his temple, oxen, calves, and geese. Enter thou into "my house, open the doors of my treasury, and make thyself "lord of the property of my father. I will give unto thee as "much gold as thine heart can desire, and a mass of copper (or "turquoise) as large as thyself, and the finest horses which are "in my stud-farm, and the best and strongest which are in "my stables." Then His Majesty went to the temple of Ḥeru-khent-Khatthi and made an offering of oxen, and calves, and geese to his father Ḥeru-khent-Khatthi, the lord of Qem-ur. And His Majesty went into the palace of the *Erpā* Peṭā-Àst, who presented to him gold, silver, lapis-lazuli, copper (or turquoise), and a great mass of property of all kinds, that is to say, suits of apparel made of byssus of every quality, and couches, and coverlets of fine linen, and *ānti* perfume, and vases full of unguents, and all the best horses and mares in his stables. Then Peṭā-Ast purified himself and swore an oath by [his] god before the kings and governors of the Land of the North, saying: "Whosoever shall conceal his horses, or hide any property "which he hath [from His Majesty] shall most assuredly die the "death of his father. These things I declare so that ye may "cease to offer opposition to him. And if ye know of anything "that belongeth to me which I have hidden from His Majesty of "the things of my father's house ye shall certainly declare it, "whether it be gold, or silver (?), or [precious] stones, or metal "vessels, or bracelets, or gold ornaments for the neck, or metal "collars inlaid with [precious] stones, or amulets for any "member of the body, or crowns for the head, or rings for the "ears, or ornaments worn by the king, or gold vases wherein "the king performeth the ceremonies of purification, or [precious] "stones of any sort or kind whatsoever. I have given to the "king thousands of suits of apparel made of the finest linen, "every kind being of the best which I have in my house, and I "know [O king] that thou wilt be satisfied therewith. Pass "thou now into my stud-farm and choose thereout as many of the "horses which please thee as thou desirest." And His Majesty did so.

Then the kings and dukes spake unto His Majesty, saying: "Permit us to depart unto our towns, and we will open our "treasure-houses, and we will choose thereout the things which "thy heart loveth, and we will bring unto thee the best horses "from our stud-farms, and the finest of our chargers." And His Majesty did so. [Here followeth] the list of the names of the kings:—

King Osorkon in Bubastis and Rā-nefer.

King Ȧnapeth in Thenteremu and Ta-an.
Duke Tchet-Ȧmen-ȧuf-ānkh in Mendes and Ta- . . . -Rā.
His eldest son, Āmkh-Ḥeru, commander-in-chief in Pa-Teḥuti-ȧp-reḥeḥ.
Duke Merkanesh in Sebennytus, and Pa-Ḥebi, and Sma-Beḥuṭet.
Duke and Prince of the Māshuasha, Pathenf in Pa Sept, and . . . pen-ȧneb ḥetchet
Duke and Prince of the Māshuasha, Pemau in Busiris.
Duke and Prince of the Māshuasha, Nesnaḳeti in Pharbaeṭites (?).
Duke and Prince of the Māshuasha, Nekht-Ḥeru-na-shennu, in Paḳerer.
Prince of the Māshuasha [in] Pentaurt.
Prince of the Māshuasha [in] Penth-bekhent.
The Prophet of Ḥorus, lord of Sekhem, Petā-Ḥeru-sma-taui.
Duke Ḥurbasa in Pa-Sekhet-nebt-Saut and in Pa-Sekhet-neb-Reḥesaui
Duke Tcheṭ-khiȧu in Khent-Nefer.
Duke Pa-Bas in Kher-āḥa and in Pa-Ḥāp.

[These came] with their offerings of fine objects of all kinds, that is to say, gold, silver, [lapis-lazuli,] copper (or turquoise), [and a great mass of property of all kinds, that is to say, suits of apparel made of byssus of every quality], and couches, and coverlets of fine linen, and *ānti* perfume in vases, ... and all the best horses and mares [in his stables] . . . .

[And it came to pass after] these things that one came and told His Majesty, saying: "[Tafnekhth] hath [gathered together] "his soldiers, and he hath [torn down] his walls through fear of "thee, he hath set fire to his treasure-houses, [he hath fled in a "boat on the river, and he hath entrenched himself strongly in "the city of Mesṭ [with his] soldiers." And His Majesty caused fighting men to go and see what had happened, and they did so under the command of the *Erpā* Peṭā-Ȧst. And they came back and reported to His Majesty, saying: "We have killed every man whom we found there;" and His Majesty gave a reward to the *Erpā* Peṭā-Ȧst. Then Tafnekhth, the Prince of Māshuasha, heard of this, and he sent an envoy to the place where His Majesty was to make supplication, saying: "Be thou at peace "[with me]. I have not seen thy face during the days of shame. "I cannot stand against thy fire, and the terror of thine onset "hath vanquished me. Behold, thou art the god Nubt, the "governor of the South, and the god Menthu, the mighty bull! "In every matter whereto thou hast set thy face thou hast "found none who could resist thee. I have reached the utter-"most swamps on the coast of the Great Green Water (i.e., the "Mediterranean), but I am afraid of thy souls because thy word "of fire hath become an enemy to me. Is not the heart of Thy "Majesty refreshed by reason of the things which thou hast "done unto me? Behold, I am in very truth a most miserable "man; punish thou me not in proportion to [my] abominable "deeds. The measure of the scales taketh count of *qeṭet* weights, "and do thou double them on my behalf in forgetting [my "misdeeds]. If thou sowest seed thou wilt meet it [again] in "[its] season, and dig thou not up the trees when they are in "blossom. Thou hast sown the terror of thee in my body, and "the fear of thee is in my bones. I do not any longer sit in the "beer-hall, and no man bringeth to me the harp. Behold, I only "eat the bread [required] by hunger, and I only drink the water "[demanded] by thirst. Since the day when thou didst hear my "name wretchedness hath been in my bones. My head hath "lost its hair, and my apparel is rags. I have fled and taken "refuge with the goddess Nit (Neith), O come to me and turn thou "thy face to me! Seeing that I have separated myself from my "sin, hold then thy servant guiltless, and lift his [sin] from him. "I beseech thee to receive my goods into [thy] treasury, the gold, "and the [precious] stones, together with the best of my horses, "and an abundant supply of every thing. I beseech thee to send "to me an envoy to take them, and to remove the fear which "is in my heart. Verily I will go in his presence into the "temple, and I will purge myself of my sin by swearing an oath "[of allegiance to thee] by God."

Then His Majesty sent the *kher heb* priest Peṭā-Ȧmen-[neb]-nest-taui and the commander-in-chief Puarma, and Tafnekhth loaded them with silver, and gold, and raiment, and [precious] stones, and he went into the house of [his] god, and prayed unto him, and purged himself of his sin, and swore an oath of allegiance by God, saying: "I will never again transgress the "decree of the king, and I will never oppose the words of His "Majesty. I will never again injure (?) any duke without thy "knowledge, and I will perform the king's behests, and I will "never transgress any decree which he hath uttered." And with these words the heart of His Majesty was satisfied.

Then one came and reported to His Majesty, saying: "The "city of Cynopolis hath opened its gates, and the city of "Aphroditopolis hath cast itself on its belly. There is now no "nome shut against His Majesty of the nomes of the South, or of "the North, or of the West, or of the East. The districts of "the Interior are on their bellies through fear of thee, and they "have brought their property, as they were bound to do, to the "place where His Majesty is, even like servants of the palace."

And at dawn on the following day the two governors of the South, and the two governors of the North, with their uraei on their foreheads, came to smell the ground of (i.e., do homage to) the souls of His Majesty, and behold the kings and dukes of the Land of the North came also to look upon the beauties of His Majesty. Now their legs were like the legs of women. And they did not enter into the house of the king, because they were uncircumcised, and they were eaters of fish, [a habit] which is held in abomination in the royal house. And behold, king Nemareth did enter the royal house, because he was ceremonially pure, and was not an eater of fish; [but the other chiefs] stood on their feet, and not one of them entered the royal house. Then [His Majesty] loaded the barges with silver, and gold, and copper, and raiment, and every kind of product of the Land of the North, and with products of all kinds from Syria, and with spices of Ta-neter, and he sailed up the river, and his heart was glad, and both sides of the river, the West and the East, rejoiced. And the people welcomed him with rejoicings, and they shouted and cried out with gladness, saying: " Hail, divine Governor and Conqueror! " Hail, divine Governor and Conqueror! (Piānkhi), the " Governor and Conqueror! Thou hast come and hast made thy-" self governor of the Land of the North. Thou hast made men " to be as women. Let the heart of the mother rejoice who " hath given birth to a man. He who dwelleth in Ȧnt (i.e., Ȧmen) " hath poured out the seed which produced thee. Let praise " be ascribed to the Cow which gave birth to the Bull. Mayest " thou live for ever, and may thy strength endure eternally, O " Governor, who lovest Thebes!"

CHAPTER V.

THE SUCCESSORS OF PIĀNKHI.

THE great inscription of Piānkhi, of which a translation has been given in the preceding pages, gives us, unfortunately, no particulars of his ancestry, and tells us nothing of his descendants. The list of kings compiled by Lepsius, and adopted by Brugsch and Bouriant in their work,[1] gives as the immediate ancestor of Piānkhi another king of Napata of the same name, whose Horus name was "ḤERU SEḤETEP TAUI-F,"[2] whose prenomen was "SENEFER-RĀ,"[3] and who called himself "son of Rā," and "King of the South and North." Why this king was made to head the list of the kings of Napata is not clear, but from the form of his prenomen, which resembles those of Senka-Ȧmen-seken[4] and Atlanersa,[5] it is probable that he reigned *after* Piānkhi Meri-Ȧmen. Be that as it may, on the death of Piānkhi Meri-Ȧmen the sovereignty appears to have passed into the hands of a Nubian called Kashta,[6] who was then ruling in some capacity at Thebes. His claim to the throne is not clear, but he may have been a son of Piānkhi Meri-Ȧmen, or his mother may have been a descendant of one of the priest-kings at Thebes. It is a remarkable fact that his name is not found on any monument at Gebel Barkal, and we may therefore conclude that he usurped the kingdom whilst Napata was still in the hands of one of Piānkhi's offspring. By some Kashta has been identified with the Zêt, *Ζήτ*, or Xêt, *Ξήτ*, whom Manetho makes to be one of the two last kings of the

1 *Le Livre des Rois*: Cairo, 1887.

2 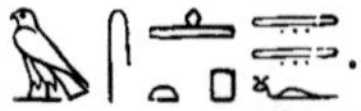.

3 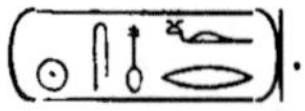.

4 Ḥeru-seh-taui 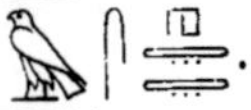.

5 Ḥeru-ḳer-taui .

6 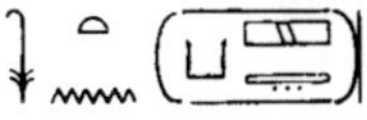. His prenomen is unknown.

XXIIIrd Dynasty. Kashta married Shep-en-Ȧpt,[1] a daughter of Osorkon III., the great high-priestess of Ȧmen, whose official title was "Neter-Ṭuat," i.e., "divine adorer," or "morning star." By her he had issue Shabaka, who became king of Egypt and Nubia, and Ȧmenȧrṭās, who attained to the rank of high-priestess of Ȧmen. Kashta's influence in Egypt and the Sûdân was not great, and he made no attempt to slay Bakenrenf, who had succeeded his father Tafnekhth at Saïs, and who was regarded as the king of Lower Egypt. Bakenrenf, who is called Bocchoris by the Greek writers, was one of the six great law-givers of Egypt, and he is described as a wise and prudent man.

Kashta's son and successor, SHABAKA,[2] who was the first of the Nubian or Sûdânî Dynasty, ascended the throne between B.C. 716 and 710, and reigned at least twelve years. His home appears to have been at Napata, and it is probable that he began to reign there, but he found that the kingdom of the North was becoming stronger and stronger, and he set out to reduce to submission the country which Piānkhi had made a province of his dominions. He left Napata and passed triumphantly into and through Egypt, and he defeated all who took up arms against him. Bakenrenf, the son of Tafnekhth, king of Saïs and Memphis, and a vassal of Piānkhi, was either burned or flayed alive by Shabaka, who took up his abode at Thebes and ruled Egypt and the Sûdân from that city. The rule of Shabaka was beneficial to Egypt, especially in matters connected with the agriculture of the country. He made a law that criminals, who would in the ordinary way be put to death,[3] should be made to labour at raising the foundations of the cities and towns above the level of the waters of the inundation, and he had the canals cleared out by the same means. We must not assume that Shabaka was the first king to have such works undertaken, but, with the peace which came on the country under his reign, it became possible to carry

1 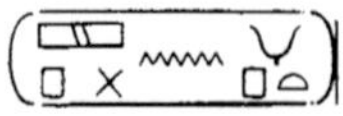.

2 His full titles are 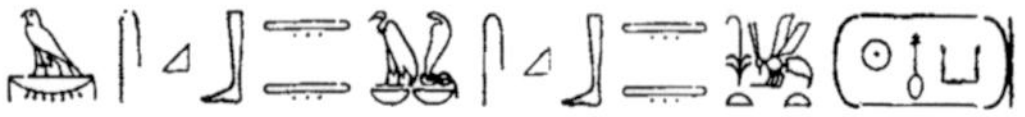
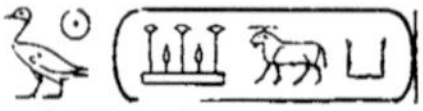.

3 Herodotus, ii. 137 ; Diodorus, i. 65.

out works of public utility. The city in the Delta which most benefited by the system of forced labour inaugurated by Shabaka

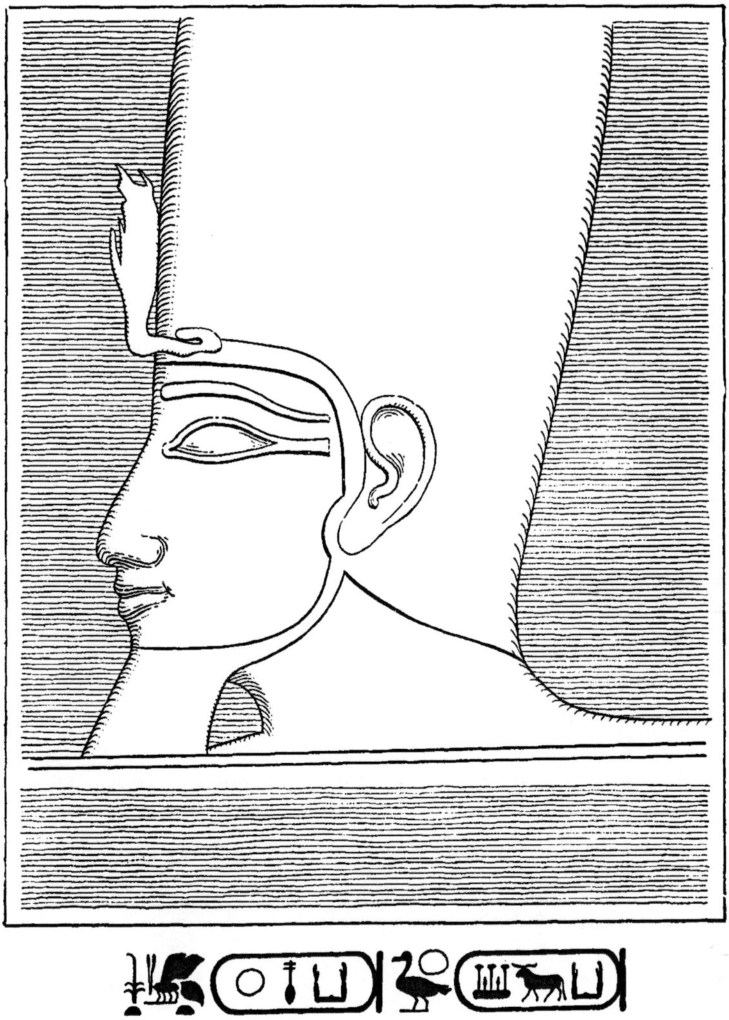

PORTRAIT OF SHABAKA.

[Drawn from Lepsius, *Denkmäler*, Abth. III. Bl. 301.

was Bubastis, the temple of which evoked such great admiration in Herodotus. In Shabaka some writers have identified " So, the king of Egypt," who is mentioned in 2 Kings xvii. 4, but there can be no doubt now [1] that So is no other than the Sib', or Sib'e, of the cuneiform inscriptions, who was the *turdannu* or commander-in-chief of Egypt. That Shabaka was in communication with Sargon, king of Assyria, is clear from the fact that clay seals inscribed with his name and titles were found among the tablets of the Royal Library of Nineveh at Kuyunjik,[2] and the two kings certainly exchanged gifts.

Shabaka repaired and added to several of the older temples in Egypt, but he appears to have done little or nothing of the kind in Nubia. He carried out building operations at Bubastis, in which city he took special interest, at Memphis, and at Thebes, where his name is found at Karnak, Luxor, and Madînat Habû. His sister Åmenårṭås,[3] the high-priestess of Åmen, lived with her husband Piānkhi [4] at Thebes, and the monuments there prove that he carried out on them a series of important repairs. In conjunction with her brother she built a sanctuary near the great north door of the temple of Karnak, and it is probable that from this place came her fine alabaster statue, which is now in the Museum in Cairo. Her position in Thebes must have been of considerable importance, for her name occurs side by side with that of her brother Shabaka, and even in remote places like the Wâdî Ḥammâmât her cartouche appears [5] between those of her father and brother. On a scarab in the British Museum [6] her cartouche is cut by the side of that of her father, and her name is accorded a prominent position between the figures of two goddesses which are held on the knees of the figure of the high official Ḥarua in the British Museum.[7]

Of Shabaka Diodorus, after speaking of his piety and his kind-

[1] See my *History of Egypt*, vol. vi., pp. 124 ff.

[2] The British Museum registration numbers are 51-9-2, 43, and 81-2-4, 352; for descriptions, see my *Mummy*, p. 249, and Bezold, *Catalogue*, p. 1784. One of the objects is exhibited in Table-case I., No. 32, in the Nineveh Gallery.

[3] Her prenomen was Mut-khā-neferu .

[4] His titles are 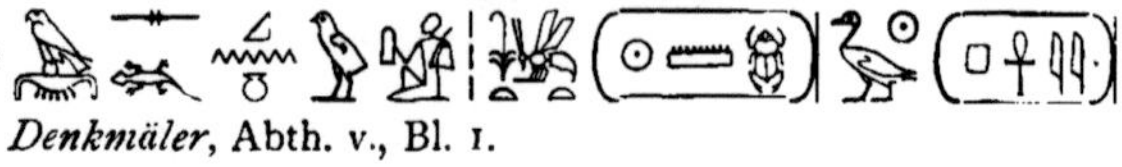.

[5] See Lepsius, *Denkmäler*, Abth. v., Bl. 1.

[6] Fourth Egyptian Room, Table-case D., No. 1308.

[7] Third Egyptian Room, No. 32,555.

HARUA, A HIGH OFFICIAL OF QUEEN AMENARTAS, SISTER OF KING SHABAKA, HOLDING SEATED STATUES OF HATHOR AND TEFNUT.

[British Museum, No. 32555.

ness to men, says: "A man may likewise judge of his extraordinary "piety, from his dream, and his abdication of the government; "for the tutelar god of Thebes seemed to speak to him in his sleep,

PORTRAIT OF SHABATAKA, BELOVED OF ÀMEN.

[Drawn from Lepsius, *Denkmäler*, Abth. III. Bl. 301.

"and told him, that he could not long reign happily and "prosperously in Egypt unless he cut all the priests to pieces "when he passed through the midst of them with his guards and "servants; which advice being often repeated, he at length sent "for the priests from all parts, and told them that if he stayed in "Egypt any longer he found that he should displease God, who "never at any time before, by dreams or visions, commanded any

BRONZE SHRINE CONTAINING A SEATED FIGURE OF ÀMEN-RĀ. IT WAS DEDICATED TO THE GOD BY SHABATAKA, KING OF EGYPT, ABOUT B.C. 650.

[British Museum, No. 11,013.

"such thing. And that he would rather be gone and lose his "life, being pure and innocent, than displease God, or enjoy "the crown of Egypt, by staining his life with the horrid "murder of the innocent. And so at length, giving up the "kingdom into the hands of the people, he returned into "Ethiopia."

SHABATAKA

Shabaka was succeeded by his son Shabataka[1] in the first or second year of the reign of Sennacherib, who ascended the Assyrian throne B.C. 705. It seems that Shabataka was associated with his father and aunt Åmenårṭās in the rule of the kingdom a few years before Shabaka's death, for on a painted stele at Turin, which is described by the late Dr. Pleyte,[2] we find the cartouches of Shabataka, Shabaka, Shep-en-Åpt, the high-priestess of Åmen, Piānkhi, and Shep-en-Åpt's mother, Åmenårṭās, the high-priestess of Åmen. On this stele is a figure of the double god Horus-Set, with outstretched arms, which seems to indicate that one arm specially protects the two royal personages who were connected with the South, and the other the two who were connected with the North. It may be noted in connection with this, that the text, which was copied in the reign of Shabaka from a worm-eaten [wooden][3] tablet on to the black slab preserved in the British Museum (No. 32,555), deals with the combat which went on perpetually between Horus and Set through the disappearance of Osiris into the sea. Of the reign of Shabataka, we learn very little from the hieroglyphic inscriptions, but he built a chamber at Karnak,[4] and seems to have repaired some portion of the temple of Ptaḥ at Memphis. His name is found nowhere in the Sûdân, but one of the small temples now in ruins at Gebel Barkal may have been built by him. That he was a devotee of Åmen Rā goes without saying, and if proof of this be needed we have it from the small bronze shrine in the British Museum,[5] which contains a figure of this god, and is inscribed with the king's name.

The greatest event in his reign was the agreement which he made with Hezekiah, king of Judah, wherein he promised to help

[1] His Horus name was 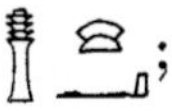; his  name was  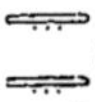; his Horus-of-gold name was ; and his cartouches are .

[2] *Aeg. Zeit.*, 1876, p. 51.

[3] .

[4] See Lepsius, *Denkmäler*, Abth. v., Bl. 3 and 4.

[5] Third Egyptian Room, No. 11,013.

him to resist the threatened attack of Jerusalem by Sennacherib, king of Assyria. In his second campaign Sennacherib set out to reduce Hezekiah of Jerusalem and Ṣidkai of Ascalon to submission, and before the troops which Shabataka had sent from Egypt could reach them, Ṣidkai had been taken prisoner and deported to Assyria, and Sharruludari had been made king of Ascalon in his stead. The Egyptians, with their bowmen, and chariots, and horses, and large numbers of men from the Eastern Desert, came to Altakû (the Eltekeh of Joshua xix. 44), and there they determined to do battle against the Assyrians. In the fight which took place immediately afterwards, Sennacherib captured alive the sons of the king of Egypt, and the generals of the chariots of the Egyptians and of the king of Milukhkhi, and defeated the allies with great slaughter. He then marched against Ekron, which he captured, and slew the chiefs of the city and hung their dead bodies upon poles round about the city. He next attacked Jerusalem, which fell into his hands after a siege, and Hezekiah had to pay 30 talents of gold, 800 talents of silver, &c., and to deliver up his wives, and concubines, and daughters, and 200,150 people were made prisoners. Sennacherib, exasperated with the Egyptians because of the help which they had sent to the kings of Jerusalem and Ascalon, set out from Jerusalem to invade Egypt, but when he reached the region near Pelusium, a great calamity overtook him whereby he lost probably more than one half of his army. The cuneiform inscriptions tell us nothing about the disaster, but we may be sure that something fraught with dire consequences happened to his army, otherwise he would have marched into Egypt and punished her people.

The Bible narrative states,[1] "that the angel of the LORD went "out, and smote in the camp of the Assyrians an hundred four-"score and five thousand; and when they arose early in the "morning, behold, they were all dead corpses;" according to Herodotus[2] a legion of field mice came by night, no one knowing whence, and quietly gnawed the quivers, bowstrings, buckler straps, &c., and when the soldiers woke up in the morning, they found themselves practically disarmed, and, after making a feeble resistance, they fled.

[1] 2 Kings xix. 6-35; Isaiah xxxvii. 6-36. [2] ii., cxli.

TIRHAKAH

After the battle of Altaḳû the Egyptians did not during the reign of Shabataka attempt to assist the kings of Palestine against the Assyrians. From the statement made in Sennacherib's Annals it is clear that Shabataka did not lead his troops at the battle of Altaḳû, but it is not unreasonable to suppose that he was awaiting in the Delta the result of their efforts. It is thought by some that when planning to help Hezekiah he appealed for help to the king of Napata, who was called Taharq, but is more commonly known from the Bible narrative as Tirhâḳâh, and that the Nubian king set out with an army to join him in the re-conquest for the Egyptians of a portion of Syria. Others, admitting that Taharq set out with an army from Napata, think that he did so because he wished to overthrow Shabataka, and thought that a time favourable for his purpose had arrived. Be this as it may, he marched into Egypt, and sailed down to the Delta, where he found Shabataka, and, finding that his army had been routed by the Assyrians, made him prisoner, and after a time put him to death. Such is the tradition preserved by Greek writers.

Taherqa, Taharq,[1] or Tirhâḳâh, appears to have seized the supreme power in Egypt about B.C. 693. From a short inscription found at Tanis about thirty years ago[2] it seems that he was only twenty years of age when he ascended the throne of Egypt, and that he came to the North not expecting to be made king. A little before his coronation at Tanis he sent to Napata for his mother Āqreq or Āqleq, and when she arrived she found that her son, who had spent the earlier years of his life in working with his father on their farm, had become the "king of the South and North." Taharqa's father was not a man of high rank, but he must have been a landed proprietor of some importance at Napata; he superintended the management of the live stock, and

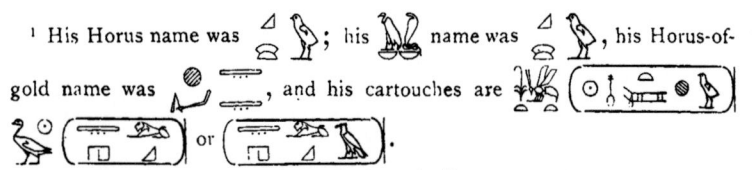

[1] His Horus name was 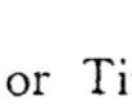; his 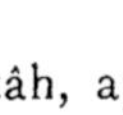 name was 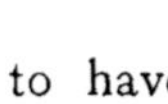, his Horus-of-gold name was 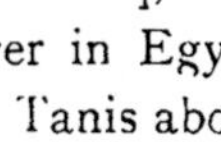, and his cartouches are 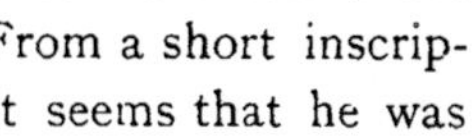 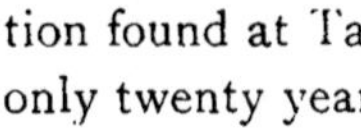 or 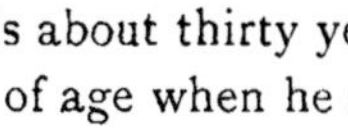.

[2] See Birch, *Trans. Soc. Bibl. Arch.*, vol. vii., p. 193; E. de Rougé, *Mélanges*, tom. i., p. 21 f.; and Griffith, *Tanis*, vol. ii., p. 29, plate 9, No. 163.

his son looked after the crops. The first coronation of Taharqa took place at Tanis, and was performed with great pomp and ceremony, and with all the details which were so much appreciated in Egypt. On this occasion a number of exalted titles were bestowed by Taharqa upon his mother, and upon his wife Ṭākehet-Åmen,[1] who was the widow of Shabaka.

During the first few years of his reign Taharqa was fully

RELIEF ON AN ALTAR OF TAHARQ.

[From Lepsius, *Denkmäler*, Abth. V. Bl. 13.

occupied in restoring the administration of Egypt on the lines followed by the great kings of the XVIIIth Dynasty, and he succeeded admirably. The people felt that peace was assured as long as he lived, and under his protection the trade of the country increased, and means were forthcoming for the repair of ancient temples and the building of new ones. That he should one day win back some of the former possessions of Egypt in Syria must have been an idea always present in his mind, and

1 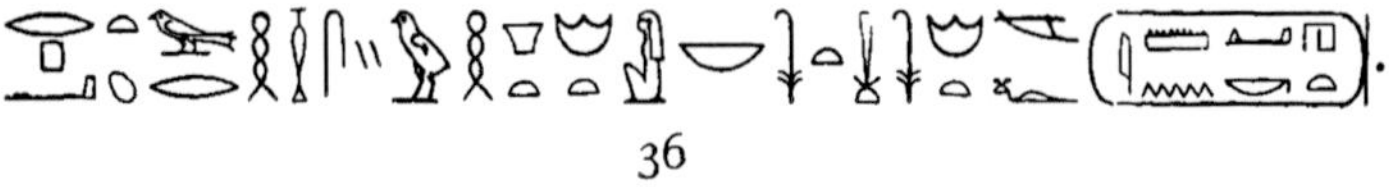

that the manner of his dealings with the kings and governors of Syria was dictated with it always in view is evident from many considerations. His friendship with the kings of that country was disapproved of by Sennacherib, who appears to have made a second expedition into Palestine with the view of invading Egypt, but nothing came of it so far as Egypt was concerned, and Taharqa continued his friendly relations with the kings on the Palestinian sea-coast until the middle of the reign of Esarhaddon, who succeeded to the throne of Assyria after the murder of his father Sennacherib, B.C. 681.

About B.C. 676 Esarhaddon sent an expedition against Milukhkha, i.e., against the tribes of the desert on the east and north-east of the Delta, for he felt that the combination of these tribes, if backed by help from Egypt, might result in the loss to Assyria of Jerusalem, and all the neighbouring towns. The success of this expedition was not decisive, for Esarhaddon was not able to reduce the tribes at once to submission. Some three years later he made a second attempt to break up the combination of people which he now knew to be in league against him, but this also failed, at any rate, the Assyrian king did not advance against Egypt, and invade her territories. On this Taharqa rejoiced greatly, for he foolishly assumed that it was the fear of his arms which kept Esarhaddon out of Egypt. And in commemoration of a campaign, which he did

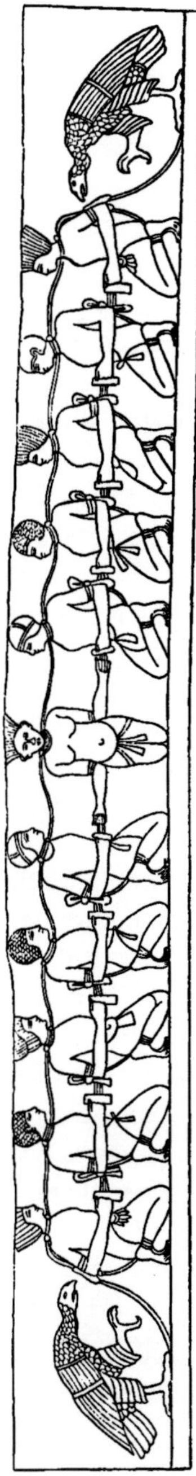

A ROW OF CAPTIVES ROPED TOGETHER.

From the pedestal of an altar found in the ruins of a temple (Lepsius, I.) at Gebel Barkal.

not fight, in a country which he never entered, he caused a list of the great peoples of Syria and Palestine to be cut on the base of his statue as nations which he had conquered! In this list we find the names of Kadesh, Assur, Kheta, Nehernu, and of many other Western Asiatic places,[2] together with the names of several districts of the Sûdân.

Among those who hastened to profit by the retreat of Esarhaddon was Baal, king of Tyre, who made a treaty quickly with Taharqa, and, following his example, the neighbouring princes did the same. For nearly three years Taharqa was permitted to indulge without hindrance his wish to intrigue in Syria and in Palestine, for it was not until the spring of the year B.C. 670 that Esarhaddon was ready to strike. In the month of Nisan he left Nineveh and set out for Syria, and having visited the mainland opposite Tyre, and cut off the water supply of Baal, its king, he went on to Aphek. He did not go straight on to Egypt from this place, but turned off to the south-east, and marched for a considerable distance in the desert. This journey was a terrible one for his troops, on account of the heat, and the serpents and scorpions which infested the country, but, thanks to the arrangements which he had made for the supply of water with the local shêkhs, his army marched triumphantly through the desert. At length he reached Raphia, and, after another march into the desert, made in order to avoid the ordinary caravan route into Egypt from Syria, arrived at some point on the eastern frontier of the Delta about three months after he set out from Nineveh. On the third day of the month Tammuz, Esarhaddon appears to have engaged the Egyptian frontier troops, and on the sixteenth and eighteenth days of the same month two battles were fought by him, no doubt against Taharqa's regular army which he had sent to the Eastern Delta.

On each of these occasions the Assyrians were the conquerors, and Taharqa's soldiers were driven back from town to town towards Memphis. Four days after the second battle, Esarhaddon appeared before Memphis with his army, and captured the

[1] This object was found in the temple of Mut at Karnak.

[2] Mariette, *Karnak*, plate 45, *a* 2.

city by assault, and the Assyrian soldiers pillaged it so thoroughly that even the Nubian warriors must have been surprised. Taharqa himself managed to escape, but he was obliged to leave behind him the queen and the other women of the royal *harîm* and all their children, and they became the conqueror's property. Esarhaddon did not attempt to pursue Taharqa, who had probably fled to Napata, but he appointed some twenty governors or more, over twenty large cities, which they were to rule in his interest, and having fixed the amount of tribute which they were to pay to him annually, and gathered together a vast amount of spoil, he set out to return to Nineveh. On his way northwards he stopped at the mouth of the Nahr al-Kalb River near Bêrût, and set up a monument to commemorate his victory over Egypt and Tyre. Henceforward he styled himself in his Annals, " King of Lower Egypt, of Upper Egypt, and of Kash " (Nubia, or the Sûdân). At many places he set up stelae to record his triumph, and on the large monumental tablet found at Sinjirli [1] is sculptured a figure of Esarhaddon, who holds in his hand cords to which are tied figures of Taharqa and Baal of Tyre. The former is kneeling and the latter is standing before the king, and each has his hands raised in an attitude of supplication. As Taharqa pretended in his inscriptions that he had conquered all Syria and Assur, so we find Esarhaddon pretending that he had captured Taharqa and Baal, and had them fettered at his feet. Both text and sculptures are to be understood symbolically, but such examples show that the evidence of the monuments of some of these old warriors cannot be relied on implicitly.

Soon after Esarhaddon returned to Nineveh the chiefs of the Delta principalities split up into two parties, one being led by Paḳrer,[2] or Paqrer, the governor of the nome of Pa-Sept in the Eastern Delta, and the other by Nekau, prince of Saïs. Taharqa, hearing of this, and knowing that Esarhaddon was in Nineveh, gathered together an army and marched to Memphis. It is probable that the native chiefs of the Delta would have flocked

[1] See Luschan, *Ausgrabungen in Sendschirli*, vol. i., p. 30.

[2] 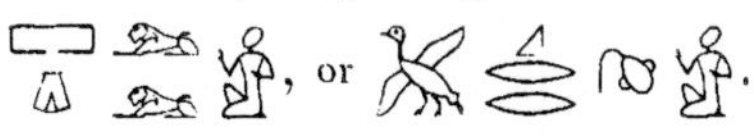

to his standard gladly, for they had no love for the rule of the king of Assyria, but they were afraid to do so, because the Assyrians in the Delta had sent news of what had happened to Nineveh, and it was pretty certain that an Assyrian army would be sent to restore order. When Esarhaddon received the report he made haste to make one of his sons, Shamash-shum-ukin, king of Babylon, and another, Ashur-bani-pal, king of Nineveh, and then, even though his health was failing, he set out on his third campaign against Egypt. This was in the year B C. 668. On the way his illness increased, and he died in the month of May, having reigned about twelve years. The death of Esarhaddon did not, however, retard the advance of the Assyrian army, which pursued its way to Egypt under the leadership of the "Turdannu" (Tartan), or commander-in-chief When it arrived in Syria the twenty-two kings who had been appointed tendered their fealty to the Tartan, and the Assyrians approached Egypt by the old caravan route from Syria. At a place called Karbanit they found Taharqa's troops, but in the battle which took place they were utterly defeated, and such large numbers of them were slain that any attempt to rally at Memphis and defend that city was hopeless. Meanwhile Taharqa had once more escaped, and had found his way to Thebes, which he fortified to the best of his ability.

Unlike Esarhaddon, the new Assyrian king, Ashur-bani-pal, was not content with suppressing the rebellion in the Delta and occupying Memphis, but he ordered the commander-in-chief of the army which he sent to the aid of the Tartan to ascend the Nile and sack Thebes. On his arrival near Egypt, this commander-in-chief, whose official title was Rab-saki (Rabshakeh), collected a fleet of boats and sailed up the Nile to Memphis, where he joined his forces to those of the Tartan, and as soon as possible they set out for Thebes. During the six weeks which were occupied by the Assyrians in sailing up to Thebes, Taharqa began to intrigue with the chief rulers in the Delta, i.e., Nekau of Saïs, Paḳrer of Pa-Sept, and Sharru-ludari of Tanis, against the Assyrians, but his messengers bearing their despatches were caught by the Assyrians, who proceeded to punish the conspirators according to their usual methods. Their troops in the

Delta destroyed the cities of Saïs, Tanis, and Pa-Sept, the ringleaders of the revolt among the people were either flayed alive or impaled, and Nekau and Sharru-ludari were sent in fetters to Nineveh. Pakrer managed to escape. Taharqa, divining from these events what his fate was likely to be if caught, fled from Thebes to the south, leaving that city to the mercy of Ashur-bani-pal's soldiers. Menthu-em-ḥāt,[1] its governor, promptly surrendered, and thus Upper and Lower Egypt, and the Sûdân, became a province of the Assyrian Empire. The fate of Taharqa is unknown, but the Assyrian annalist says that Taharqa fled to Kush and that the terror of the soldiers of Ashur overwhelmed him in the place whither he had gone, and he went to his destiny of night.[2]

Taharqa was a capable and energetic king, and under his able rule the country, notwithstanding his wars with the Assyrians, enjoyed a period of prosperity for about twenty-five years. That he should have been able to offer such steadfast resistance to Esarhaddon and Ashur-bani-pal says much for his capacity as a soldier and leader of men. There must have been something attractive in his personality, and his deeds appealed so strongly to the popular imagination, at all events in Greek times, that they were regarded as the exploits of a hero, and he had the reputation of being a great traveller as well as a great conqueror.[3] As a builder he displayed great activity, and remains of several of his edifices have come down to us. Near the temple of Karnak he built a small temple in commemoration of his coronation at Thebes. On the walls here we see Taharqa's mother, Āqleq,[4] and a priest performing ceremonies connected with the enthronement of her son, who appears under the forms of Ṭeṭun, Sepṭ, Āmen, and Ḥeru, thereby signifying that he is lord of the four quarters of the world. Next, a high priestly official called Ḥeru-em-ḥeb,

[1] .

[2] *Cuneiform Inscriptions*, vol. v. pl. 2, l. 20 f. 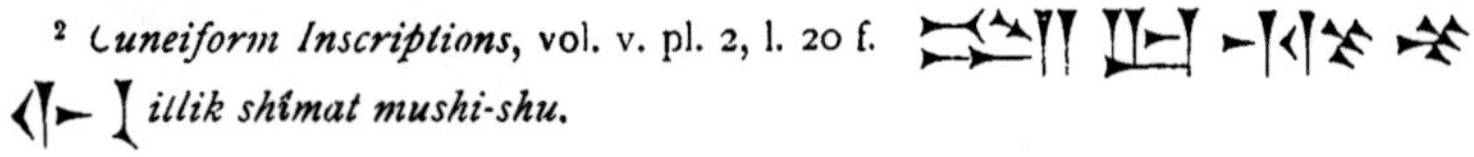 *illik shîmat mushi-shu.*

[3] See Strabo, i. 3, 21, and xv. 1, 6, where he quotes Megasthenes.

[4] 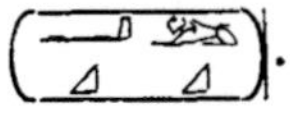.

makes an address to the people in words which express their acceptance of Taharqa as king before Ȧmen-Rā. Elsewhere, standing on one side of a sacred tree which grows out of the funeral coffer of Osiris, is Queen Ȧqleq, holding a bow in her hands, and shooting arrows into symbols of the four quarters of the world; on the other side of the tree is Taharqa dancing, and hurling stones with his left hand into the four quarters of the world. In his right hand he holds the Sûdânî club . It will be remembered that Piānkhi tells us in his great stele that his slingers hurled stones into a city which he besieged, and from the scene described above it seems as if Taharqa was proud to be regarded as a "slinger of stones." The text which refers to the shooting of arrows by the queen reads: "the divine wife hath "grasped the bow, she hath shot arrows into the South, the "North, the West, and the East, against the enemies whom "[Ȧmen] hath given unto him."

The greater number of Taharqa's building operations were carried out after his conquest of Lower Egypt, when he was, comparatively, a young man, and in these works he was ably assisted by Menthu-em-ḥāt, the governor of Thebes. At Karnak he began to build a large temple, but abandoned the work after he had set up a few pillars; he built a little sanctuary in honour of Ptaḥ, and to the south of the great temple of Ȧmen is another, on the walls of which he is represented with his wife's son Tanut-Ȧmen. On the other side of the river, at Madînat Habû, he restored portions of the temple of Thothmes III., and his name appears at a few places in the Delta. At Semna, just above the "great gate" of the Cataract, and immediately to the south of the temple of Thothmes III., he built a temple of mud brick, with stone doorways and pillars, in honour of Usertsen III., the conqueror of the Sûdân. This temple was, when in a complete state, about 23 metres long, and 12 metres 50 centimetres wide. It consisted of a fore-court containing six columns, and a chamber, within which is a rectangular sanctuary, 5 metres 48 centimetres long, and 3 metres 80 centimetres wide, inside measures. The outer walls are 1 metre 45 centimetres thick, and the space

[1] See Prisse d'Avennes, *Monuments*, plates 31-33.

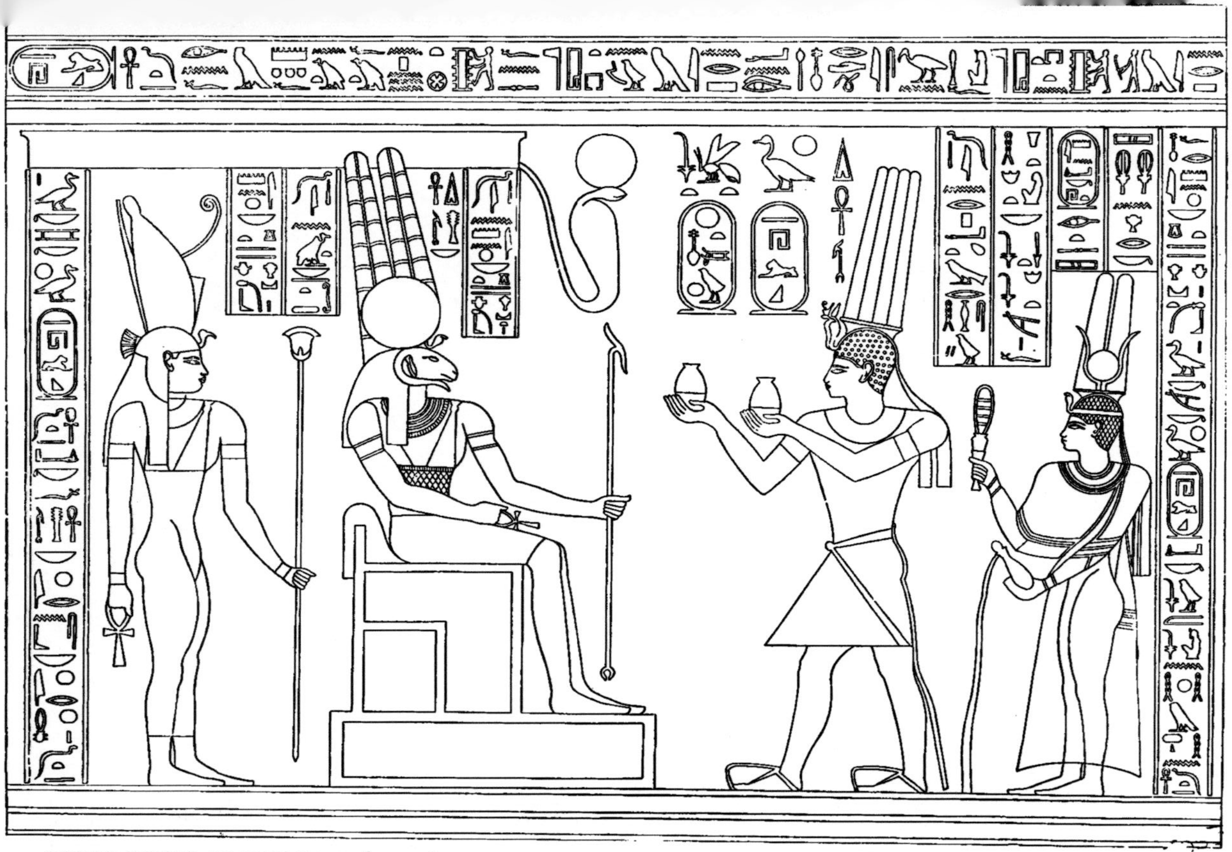

TAHARQ MAKING AN OFFERING TO ÅMEN-RĀ, GOD OF THE HOLY MOUNTAIN, OR GEBEL BARKAL. BEHIND ÅMEN-RĀ STANDS THE GODDESS MUT, AND BEHIND THE KING HIS QUEEN, CALLED ṬĀKHET-ÅMEN.

[From Lepsius, *Denkmäler*, Abth. V. Bl. 5.

between them and the sanctuary is 1 metre 95 centimetres. The sanctuary walls are 1 metre 19 centimetres thick. In the sanctuary stands an altar with the cartouches of Taharqa and Usertsen III. arranged side by side, within four lines forming a square.[1] This temple is oriented due south

At Gebel Barkal he built a fine temple in honour of Amen-Rā, the "dweller in the Holy Mountain," Ṭut-āb , i.e., Mount Barkal, and of Mut, the lady of Kenset. On the walls the king is seen offering vases of wine, &c., to the ram-headed Amen, who wears a disk and plumes on his head. Behind Amen stands Mut, and behind the king is his wife Ṭākhet-Åmen, holding a sistrum in her hand. Among the gods worshipped by the king here we find Amen-Rā-khu-Aten, Ṭeṭun, Rā-Ḥeru-khuti, Thoth and his company, Tem, Nefer-Tem, An-Ḥer, Shu, Menu, Khensu-em-Uast-Nefer-ḥetep, Hathor, &c., in fact, all the great gods at Thebes, among whom is included the old Sûdânî god Ṭeṭun. This is now a mass of ruins. On the western side of the mountain he built a temple, with a sanctuary hewn in the living rock; here the pillars were ornamented with sculptured reliefs of Bes, whose worship flourished at Napata in Taharqa's time. Time, and apparently the hand of man, have wrought irreparable damage to Taharqa's buildings at Gebel Barkal, but enough of them remains to show that they were as well built, and as well decorated, as any in Egypt. The inscriptions are cut in bold hieroglyphics,[2] and those who made them were either expert masons and sculptors from Thebes, or men who had been trained to their work under their guidance. The work generally is far better than that found at Ṣulb, of the time of Åmen-ḥetep III., and it proves that the people of Napata had absorbed the arts and crafts, and civilization, and religion of Egypt most successfully, and that the city was rightly regarded by its inhabitants as a second Thebes. We unfortunately know nothing about the home affairs of Napata in the reign of Piānkhi, but it is quite certain that the trade between Nubia and Egypt was considerable, and intercourse frequent. Nubia and Egypt, in fact, formed one

[1] The discovery of this temple has been described in Vol. I., p. 487 ff.

[2] See the texts and drawings in Lepsius, *Denkmäler*, Abth. v., Bl. 5-12.

country, as they must ever do, but Taharqa was the first to prove that a Nubian king could reign both at Thebes and Napata with the greatest benefit to both countries.

During the last few years of his reign Taharqa appears to have associated his step-son, Tanuath-Ȧmen, with himself in the rule of the kingdom, and it seems that this man was in Thebes when his stepfather went to his "destiny of night," probably two or three years after the accession of Ashur-bani-pal, B.C. 668. When the news of Taharqa's death reached Tanuath-Ȧmen, he declared himself king, and made preparations to go to Napata to be crowned. Whilst these were in progress one night he had a dream, which had such far-reaching results that subsequently he caused an account of it to be inscribed on a stele of gray granite, which he had placed near the famous stele of Piānkhi, in the great temple at Gebel Barkal. This stele was discovered by an Egyptian officer in the Sûdân, and was brought to the Bûlâḳ Museum at Cairo in the time of Mariette's administration. On the upper, rounded portion of it are two scenes.[1] In that to the right Tanuath-Ȧmen is offering a necklace and a pectoral to Ȧmen, and behind him stands the princess, his sister Qelhetat,[2] holding a sistrum in her right hand, and pouring out a libation with her left. Here Ȧmen is ram-headed. In the scene to the left the king is making an offering of Maāt, , to Ȧmen, who appears in the form of a man, with the disk and plumes on his head. Behind him stands the queen Ḳuruȧr-*ḥi*[3] (?), holding a sistrum and pouring out a libation, like the princess. Each form of Ȧmen is said to reside in the "Holy Mountain," i.e., Gebel Barkal; the ram-headed form gives the king a seat on the throne of Horus, and the man-form makes him to rule over all

[1] For the text, see Mariette, *Monuments Divers*, plates 7 and 8. For translations, see Maspero, *Revue Arch.*, 1868, tom. xvii., p. 329 ff.; Maspero, *Records of the Past*, vol. iv., p. 81 ff.; Brugsch, *Geschichte Aegyptens*, pp. 707-715; English translation, vol. ii., p. 248 ff. See also Maspero, *Mélanges*, tom. iii., p. 5 ff., p. 217 ff.; Schaefer, *Zur Erklärung der Traumstele*, in *Aeg. Zeit.*, 1868, p. 80; Steindorff, *Beiträge zur Assyriologie*, vol. i., p. 356; Mariette, *Rev. Arch.*, N.S., tom. xii., p. 162; de Rougé, *Mélanges*, tom. i., p. 89 ff.

[2] . [3] 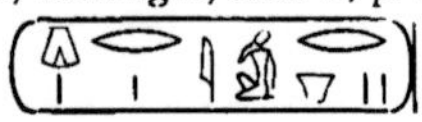.

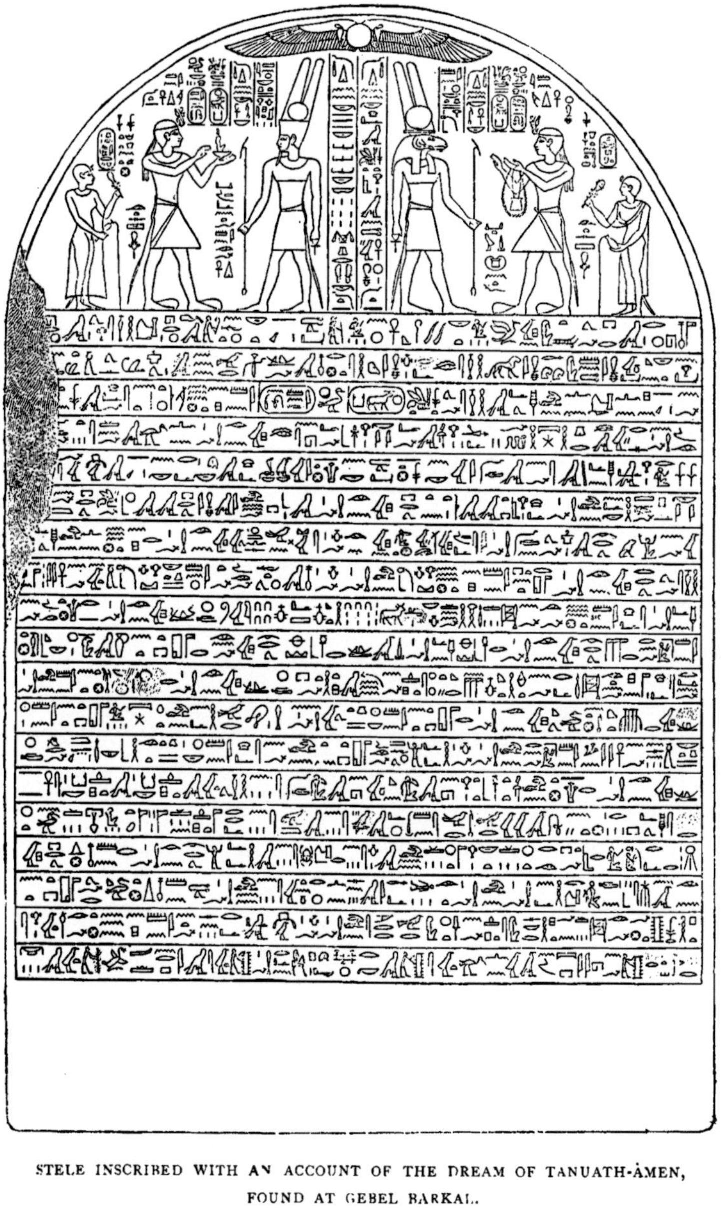

STELE INSCRIBED WITH AN ACCOUNT OF THE DREAM OF TANUATH-ÅMEN, FOUND AT GEBEL BARKAL.

countries, and all deserts and mountains, and places all the Nine Tribes of the Bow under his sandals.

The text opens with a string of titles, and the king is described as a "fierce lion," and like unto "the dweller in Ḥesert." The document is dated in the first year of the king's reign, and in that same year he dreamed a dream wherein he saw two serpents, one on his right hand and the other on his left, and when His Majesty awoke he saw them no longer. Such is the dream. When the king asked his wise men what it portended, they told him that he already held the South, and that he must seize the North, so that he might wear the crowns of both countries, for the whole world would be his, and that none should vie with him in power. Then the king went to Napata, and was acknowledged by Ȧmen, to whom he offered thirty-six oxen, forty large vessels of beer, and one hundred ostrich feathers; a gift of *ānkham* flowers of the god was given to the king, and he was crowned forthwith. The remainder of the text describes the next acts of the king. He set out for the North, and when he arrived at Elephantine he made offerings to Khnemu-Rā, the lord of the First Cataract, and to Ḥāpi, the Nile-god, the source of whose stream was supposed to be in the neighbourhood. He then went on to Thebes, where he offered gifts to Ȧmen-Rā, and amid the acclamations of the people on both sides of the river he sailed down to Memphis to "repair the temples, to set the statues and "emblems of the god on their pedestals, to provide offerings for "the gods and goddesses, and the dead, to re-establish the "priests in their grades, and to cause all proper ceremonies "connected with the worship of the gods to be performed."

At Memphis his progress was barred by the Assyrian garrison, but in the fight which took place Tanuath-Ȧmen was victorious, and he took possession of the city, and made offerings to Ptaḥ, its great god. He then sailed on to reduce the garrison towns to the north, but the troops in these would not come forth to do battle with him, and he therefore returned to Memphis. From this city he made some arrangement with the governors of the chief cities in the Delta, for after a time they came to Memphis, with Paḳrer, the governor of Pa-Sept, as their leader, and they begged for their lives, and promised to be his faithful vassals.

At this Tanuath-Åmen was very pleased, and made a feast, and he and the Delta chiefs partook of cakes, and ale, and "all good things." After some days they said to him, "Why tarry we here, O king our Lord?" And the king replied "Why?" Thereupon they departed, each to his city, and sent back gifts to the king. Here the text comes to an end, and the Egyptian inscriptions tell us nothing about subsequent events. The Assyrian Annals, however, help us, and from these we find that whilst Tanuath-Amen was at Memphis, the report of his arrival and proceedings was carried to Ashur-bani-pal at Nineveh. The king of Assyria, hearing that his troops in Memphis had been slain by the Nubian king, whom he regarded as a rebel, set forth without delay for Egypt. On his arrival, Tanuath-Åmen fled to Thebes, and the governors of the cities who had given gifts to him promptly tendered their submission to the king of Assyria. Ashur-bani-pal and his soldiers advanced to Memphis, and then followed the fugitive up the Nile. On hearing of their advance, Tanuath-Åmen fled to Kipkip,[1] without attempting to defend Thebes, and thus the city fell into the hands of the Assyrians, who plundered it in their usual fashion.

On their return to the North they carried off gold, silver, precious stones, rich apparel, costly furniture, fine horses, men, women and children, and two objects of which the Assyrian king seems to have been especially proud. These objects, which were called *dimmi* in the Assyrian texts, weighed two thousand five hundred talents, and they were made of wood, which was overlaid with some precious metal. Ashur-bani-pal was now master of the kingdoms of the South and the North; he took no steps to assert his authority over Nubia, and so far as we know he made no attempt to capture Tanuath-Åmen. On his return to Memphis he ordered the affairs of the Delta to his own satisfaction, and then, laden with spoil, returned to Nineveh, and Egypt saw him no more. Of the fate of Tanuath-Åmen the inscriptions of Egypt tell us nothing, but with his downfall the XXVth Dynasty came to an end, and the power of Nubia in Egypt was broken, and

[1] In Assyrian  Ki-ip-ki-pi, in Egyptian . Qepqepa.

none of her kings or queens again obtained dominion over that country. The Nubian rule in Egypt came to an end B.C. 663 or 662.

When the late Mr. G. Smith first translated the Annals of Ashur-bani-pal, and thus made the valuable information which they contain available to students of Oriental History, he read the name of the successor of Taharqa who defied the Assyrian king as "Urdamanie,"[1] and this king was supposed by many to be the Egyptian king Åmen-ruṭ Meri Amen, whose prenomen was "Usr-Maāt-Rā-setep-en-Åmen."[2] This was soon found to be impossible, and scholars were driven to the conclusion that the king who set up the Stele of the Dream at Gebel Barkal and Urdamanie were one and the same person. Now the cartouche containing the king's name Åmen was at first not clear; but subsequent examination showed[3] that the unclear sign was *ta* ═, and that the name must be read Tanuath-Åmen. Again, however, a difficulty arose, for it was impossible to get the Assyrian name Urdamanie from the Egyptian name, and then it was thought that Tanuath-Åmen was a successor of the Urdamanie of the Assyrian text, and not Urdamanie himself. Later, doubt was thrown upon the correctness of the reading *ur* for the first sign in Urdamanie's name, which is polyphonous and has several values,[4] and finally Dr. Steindorff substituted the very unusual value of *tan* for *ur*, and thus obtained the reading of "Tandamanie" instead of Urdamanie. There is now no doubt that the Tandamanie of the Assyrian texts is the Tanuath-Åmen, king of the Sûdân and of Egypt, who set up the Stele of the Dream at Gebel Barkal.[5]

The evidence available on the subject, unfortunately, does not

1 

2 

3 See Steindorff, in *Beitrage zur Assyriologie*, Bd. i., p. 356.

4 Lik, liḳ, tas, tash, das, dash, tish, tiz, tiṣ, and tan.

5 His full titles are 

enable us to decide how long Tanuath-Ȧmen reigned. From the fact that figures of him appear side by side with those of Taharqa in one of the little sanctuaries which this king built at Thebes, it has been assumed that he reigned conjointly with him during the last few years of his rule over Egypt. But then, as Professor Maspero has pointed out, it is equally possible to assume that he appears on the walls of the temple because he finished the building of it, which his predecessor began. Most probably he held some position of importance at Thebes during Taharqa's life, and there is no doubt that he was actually in Egypt and not at Napata when he had the dream which he recorded on his stele. At Thebes, at one time at least, he was regarded as the lawful king of the country, and this fact is proved by a monument at Berlin,[1] the text on which refers to the entrance of Peṭā-Khensu, a priest, into the brotherhood of the priests of Amen-Rā at Thebes. This man was a priest of Ȧmen, Mut, and Khensu, and belonged to a very old Theban family, and his ancestors had been priests at Thebes for seventeen generations. This monument is dated in the third year of Tanuath-Ȧmen, and the fact that Peṭā-Khensu acknowledges his sovereignty in this way makes it quite clear that for three years at least Tanuath-Ȧmen was king of Upper Egypt as well as of Nubia.

As for Lower Egypt, or the kingdom of the North, that had passed into the hands of Psammetichus, the son of Nekau, king of Saïs. It will be remembered that Nekau, king of Saïs and Memphis, was the leader of the revolt which broke out in Egypt in the reign of Ashur-bani-pal, and that he, with Sharru-ludari, was deported by the Assyrian king to Nineveh. Soon after he arrived there the Assyrian king forgave him, and gave him rich apparel to wear, and rings for his fingers, and a dagger inlaid with gold and inscribed with the king's name. After a time he reinstated Nekau in his sovereignty at Saïs, whither he sent him with horses and chariots, and an escort suitable to the position of the viceroy of Ashur-bani-pal in Egypt. He also appointed Psammetichus,[2] Nekau's son, king of Athribis, and gave him the

[1] No. 2,096. See the official *Verzeichnis*, p. 253.

[2] In Assyrian

Assyrian name of "Nabû-shezib-anni"; to Saïs also and Athribis he gave Assyrian names, that of the former being "Kar Bêl-matati," and that of the latter "Limir patesi Ashur." After the flight of Tanuath-Åmen the power of Psammetichus I. extended by degrees from the Delta to Thebes, and it is quite certain that he, the founder of the XXVIth Dynasty, was the next ruler of the kingdoms of the South and North. Thus the period of the rule of the Nubian kings over Egypt, which began with Piānkhi and ended with Tanuath-Åmen, was about ninety years, i.e., from about B.C. 750 to B.C. 660.

Soon after Psammetichus I. became king of all Egypt he adopted a policy different from that followed by his predecessors, and so far as Egypt is concerned it succeeded admirably. Having, by the help of the Mediterranean mercenaries, succeeded in expelling the Assyrian garrisons, he determined to make use of these allies in keeping his country intact; in other words, he dispensed with the services of the Nubians, of whom a strong force had usually been massed at Thebes and in the neighbouring district, and established a garrison of mercenaries at Elephantine, which he regarded as the southern boundary of Egypt. He placed another garrison at Pelusium Daphnae against the Arabians and Syrians, and another at Marea against the Libyans. During the reign of Psammetichus I., which lasted for fifty-four years, there was no war between Egypt and Nubia, and no record of any Egyptian expedition for trading purposes into the Sûdân has come down to us. Having established a garrison at Elephantine to prevent any energetic prince or king of Napata from troubling Egypt by raid or invasion, Psammetichus I. took no further thought about the Sûdân.

During the reign of Psammetichus I. an event happened which must have been fraught with important results in the Sûdân. Psammetichus, as we know from Herodotus (ii. 152), conferred many benefits on his Carian and Ionian mercenaries, and he formed them into a body-guard, and gave to them the place of honour on his right hand when reviewing his army, thus dispossessing a large number of native soldiers who had formerly enjoyed the privileges which were now given to foreigners. The Egyptians became discontented, and did not approve of the new scheme of defence of the country which had been adopted by Psammetichus, for it relegated them to the three great garrisons which had recently been formed at Daphne, Marea, and Elephantine. Service in these places was regarded practically as exile, and the discontent of the Egyptians increased. On one occasion these garrisons were not relieved for three years; "the soldiers, therefore, at the end of that time, consulted "together, and having determined by common consent to "revolt, marched away to Ethiopia (Nubia)."[1]

Psammetichus set out in pursuit of them, and overtook them, and begged them not to forsake the Gods of their country and their wives and children.[2] The deserters refused to listen to him, and, saying that they were certain to find wives and children wherever they went, pressed on into Nubia. When they arrived there they offered their services to the king [of Napata?], who gave them a tract of land which was at that time in the possession of his foes, telling the soldiers to turn out his enemies, and occupy it. This the new-comers promptly did, and they settled down in the Sûdân, and in a few generations became a powerful nation. The number of these deserters from the Egyptian garrisons is given by Herodotus (ii. 30) as two hundred and forty thousand, but there must be some mistake in the figures; the desertions probably went on for a space of several years, and the number given above may represent the total number of the men who emigrated from Egypt during the reign of Psammetichus.

Herodotus says that these Automoloi,[3] or "Deserters," called themselves "Asmakh," Ἀσμαχ, a word which he says means, "the men who stand on the left hand of the king," the allusion being to the fact that Psammetichus had given to his foreign mercenaries the place on his right hand which had been formerly held by the Egyptians. Diodorus (i. 67) says plainly that the Egyptian troops deserted because they had been placed in the left wing, whilst the right was given to strangers. The meaning

[1] Herodotus, ii. 30.

[2] Τῶν δέ τινα λέγεται δείξαντα τὸ αἰδοῖον εἶπαι, ἔνθα ἂν τοῦτο ᾖ, ἔσεσθαι αὐτοῖσι ἐνθαῦτα καὶ τέκνα καὶ γυναῖκας.

[3] These are the Sembritai of Strabo, and the Semberritae of Pliny (vi. 30).

of "Asmakh" has been debated by many scholars, but as there are variant readings of the name it is not easy to arrive at a final conclusion about it. M. de Horrack believed [1] that it represented the Egyptian word, suggested by Brugsch, "semeḥi," [2] i.e., "to be left," "the left," and, as Professor Maspero says, "it is certain "that the Egyptians, whatever may have been the real significa- "tion of the name, had in their minds the word indicated by "M. de Horrack, and the very expression used by Herodotus, *οἱ* "ἐξ ἀριστερῆς χειρός, proves it." [3]

Prof. Wiedemann rejects this derivation,[4] and prefers to think that *Asmakh,* or *Askam* represents some "Ethiopian word, the "meaning of which is not connected with the Egyptian word "*semeḥi.*" He further points out that "fan-bearer on the left hand of the king" was a position of the highest honour, and that when the god separated the good from the bad, the latter were placed on the right hand, and the former on the left. According to Professor Maspero, the deserters from the Egyptian garrisons belonged to the Mashuasha, or Libyan tribes, who henceforward disappear from Egyptian history. They were a warlike and turbulent people, as we know from the inscriptions of the XXIst and following dynasties, but they felt that they could not withstand successfully the Greek mercenaries, and so retreated to the South, where they must have modified profoundly the civilization of the inhabitants.

[1] *Revue Arch.*, tom. ii., 1862, p. 268.

[2] 

[3] *Passing of the Empires*, p. 500.

[4] *Herodots zweites Buch*, Leipzig, 1890, p. 128.

CHAPTER VI.

THE SUCCESSORS OF TANUATH-ÀMEN.

TURNING now to Napata, it is impossible to say what happened there after the flight, and presumably death, of Tanuath-Àmen. It is probable that one of the immediate descendants of Taharqa seized the throne, but the inscriptions are silent on the matter. To the second half of the seventh century before Christ the following kings may be attributed :—

1. PIĀNKHI, with prenomen of SENEFER-RĀ, and the Horus name of SEḤETEP-TAIU-F. His names occur on an altar which was found in the village of Merawi,[1] near Gebel Barkal, whence it had no doubt, been taken. It will be seen from the text here given that the altar was dedicated to "Mut, "the great lady, the dweller in Ta-kenset." From this it appears that there was a temple at Gebel Barkal specially dedicated to the goddess and consort of Àmen. The style of the hieroglyphics suggests that they were cut not very long after the inscriptions on Taharqa's temple.

2. NETCH-KA-MEN 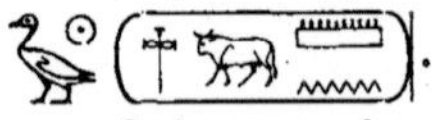. His name is found on a door-curve in a room of the temple at Gebel Barkal, where the name of a PIĀNKHI MERI-ÀMEN-SA-BAST occurs.[2]

3. . . . ḤERU-NEKHT 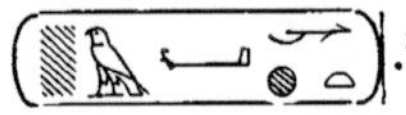.[3]

[1] Lepsius, *Denkmäler*, Abth. v., Bl. 14 *l*.

[2] *Ibid.*, *g*.

[3] *Ibid.*, *e*.

4. SENKA-ÅMEN-SEKEN, with the prenomen of SEKHEPER-EN-RĀ, and the Horus name of SEH [ER] TAUI. His name and titles occur on an altar which Lepsius took from the ruins of a temple at Gebel Barkal to Berlin[1] (No. 1481). In the inscription here given he calls himself "beloved of Åmen-Rā, lord of "the throne of the Two Lands, the "dweller in the Holy Mountain"; three copies of this inscription appear on the altar. The surface of the altar shows marks of long usage.

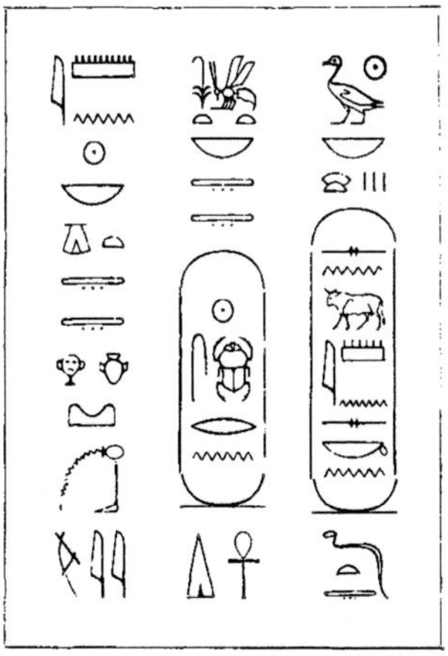

5. ÅTHLENERSA, with the prenomen KHU-KA-RĀ, and the Horus name of ḤETEP(?)-TAUI,[2] i.e., "the peace of the Two Lands," and the Nekhebet-Uatchet title of MERI MAĀT,[3] and the Golden Horus title of SMEN-EN-HEPU.[4] On an altar, which Lepsius found among the ruins of a temple at Gebel Barkal,[5] in addition to his other titles this king calls himself "beloved of Åmen-Rā, lord of the throne of the Two Lands, at the head of the Apts," and "stablished by his soldiers."[6]

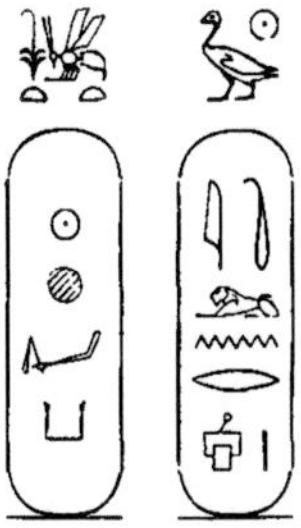

6. AMATHEL. with the prenomen UATCH-KA-RĀ; the other names are broken away from the headless granite statue of this king, on which his prenomen and nomen are given. The statue was found at Gebel Barkal by Lepsius, who took it to Berlin, where it is now preserved in the Royal Museum (No. 2240, *Verzeichnis*, p. 401). The inscription upon it reads:—"All life, all permanence, all joy, all health, all

[1] Lepsius, *Denkmäler*, Abth. v., Bl. 15 *a*; see the official *Verzeichnis*, p. 401.

[2] 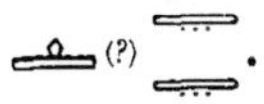 [3] 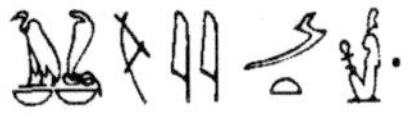 [4] 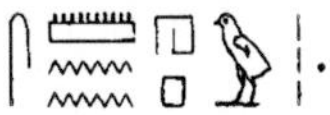

[5] See *Denkmäler*, Abth. v., Bl. 15 *b*. [6] 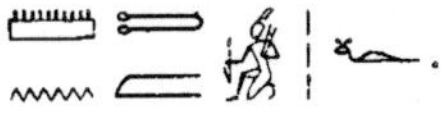

"happiness are at the feet of this good god, whom all men "adore."

7. ÅSPELTA, with the prenomen MER-KA-RĀ, and the Horus name of NEFER-KHĀ, and the Nekhebet-Uatchet name of Nefer-khā, and the Golden Horus name of USR-ÅB.[1] Of the reign of this king we know nothing. He seems to have flourished during the reign of Psammetichus I., and Dr. Schaefer has come to the conclusion[2] that his date may be fixed at B.C. 625. The principal monument of his reign is a large gray granite stele which was found at Gebel Barkal, and brought to Cairo during Mariette's Directorship of Antiquities. On its upper portion the ram-headed Åmen is seen seated on a throne, with a king kneeling in front of him; behind the god stands the goddess Mut, and in front of the king stands the royal sister, royal mother, "the mistress of Kash," holding a sistrum in each hand. The name of this "royal mother," as well as that of Åspelta, has been obliterated on the monument, but we may restore it from the stele in the Louvre, which was first published by Pierret.[3] From this we learn that Aspelta's mother was called Enenselsa, and his wife Māṭ . . ḥenen, and his daughter Khebit.[4] The god before whom the king kneels is Amen of Nept (Napata), and he tells Åspelta that he has established the uraei of sovereignty on his brow as the heavens upon their four pillars. Below this scene are inscribed thirty lines of hieroglyphics, in which Åspelta describes the ceremonies that were performed at his coronation or enthronement, and for this reason the monument is generally known as the "Stele of the Coronation," or the "Stele of the Enthronement." It will be remembered that Diodorus tells us that when a king was to be crowned in Nubia the priests first of all selected a number of suitable candidates, that these were led

1 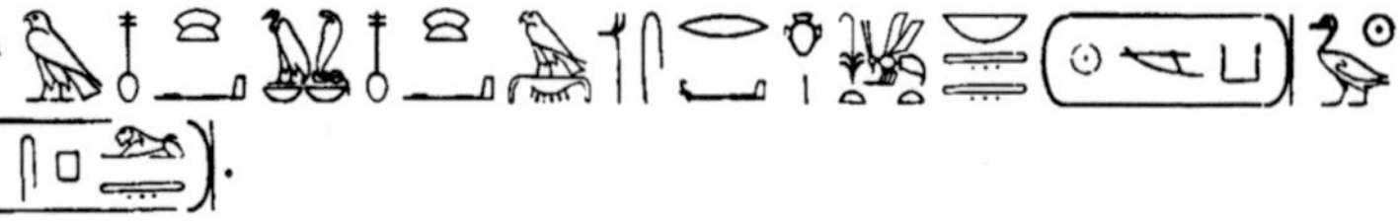

2 *Aeg. Zeit.*, xxxiii., 1895, p. 101 ff.

3 *Études Égyptologiques*, tom. i., pp. 96-100; *Records of the Past*, vol. iv., p. 87; see also Schaefer, *Aeg. Zeit.*, 1895, p. 101 ff

4 

STELE INSCRIBED WITH AN ACCOUNT OF THE CORONATION OF KING ȦSPELTA.
FOUND AT GEBEL BARKAL.

in by them before the statue of the god during the performance of certain festival rites, and that the candidate whom the statue of the god touched or embraced was regarded as chosen by him to be king. This done, all present fell on their faces and adored the king-elect as a god, believing that the divine power had been transferred to him by the touch or embrace of the image.[1] Now Diodorus was, as we shall see, well-informed on this matter, and the Stele of the Coronation supplies a number of details which supplement his statement in a striking manner.

The document is dated in the first year of the king's reign, and sets forth that all the soldiers of His Majesty were in the town of Ṭu-āb (the Holy Mountain, i.e., Gebel Barkal), the seat of Ṭeṭun Khenti-Nefert, i.e., the god of the country of the Second and Third Cataracts. With these were assembled twenty-four great officers of the kingdom, six being chosen captains of the army, and six of the seal-bearing caste of priests,[2] and six of the caste of learned scribes, and six of the chief chancellors of the palace, and they agreed to elect a king. And they said, "There is a lord among us, but we know him not," and they earnestly desired that he might be made manifest to them. And the twenty-four officials said one to the other, that none knew who he was save Rā, and prayed that he would be defended from all evil. Next, allusion was made to the death of the late king, and the vacant throne, and then they all decided to go to Amen-Rā, and to lay the matter before him, and to make offerings and pray for his guidance. When the twenty-four officials arrived at the temple of Åmen-Rā, they found the prophets and priests already assembled, and they told them the object of their coming. Then the priests proceeded to asperge and cense the temple, and to pour out libations of water and wine, and when they had done this, they prayed to Amen-Rā, and asked him to

[1] Οἱ μὲν γὰρ ἱερεῖς ἐξ αὐτῶν τοὺς ἀρίστους προκρίνουσιν, ἐκ δὲ τῶν καταλεχθέντων, ὃν ἂν ὁ θεὸς κωμάζων κατά τινα συνήθειαν περιφερόμενος λάβῃ, τοῦτον τὸ πλῆθος αἱρεῖται βασιλέα· εὐθὺς δὲ καὶ προσκυνεῖ καὶ τιμᾷ καθάπερ θεόν, ὡς ὑπὸ τῆς τοῦ δαιμονίου προνοίας ἐγκεχειρισμένης αὐτῷ τῆς ἀρχῆς. Book iii. 5. 1 (Didot's ed. p 129).

[2] .

give them a king who would carry out his good works among them.

After their prayer they placed the candidates for the throne, who were styled "royal brethren,"[1] before the god, but the god would have none of them; among these, presumably, was Ȧspelta. Then they brought Ȧspelta before the god a second time, whereupon Ȧmen-Rā declared that he was to be their lord. When complete the text stated that Ȧspelta was the son of Enenselsa, queen of Kash, and grandson of a high-priestess of Ȧmen-Rā, and gave the name of Enenselsa's mother, grandmother, great-grandmother, great-great-grandmother, and great-great-great-grandmother, but the cartouches of all these royal ladies have been obliterated. It is important to note that Aspelta's maternal ancestress in the sixth generation was a queen of Kash. When Amen-Rā had spoken, all present fell on their bellies and "smelt the earth," i.e., adored Aspelta as the son of Amen-Rā, and acknowledged him as their king. Then Ȧspelta went into the presence of the god, and prayed for strength and guidance to do his will, and Amen-Rā promised to give him these. The king then rose up, and put on the crown, and, taking the sceptre in his hand, prostrated himself before the god, and prayed for "life, stability, power, health, gladness, and long life." When Ȧmen-Rā had further promised to give him dominion over all lands, the king came forth and was greeted with cries of joy and shouts of acclamation by his assembled subjects. As a thank-offering to Ȧmen-Rā Aspelta founded several festivals which were to be celebrated yearly, and he made large gifts, including one hundred and forty barrels of beer, to the god and his priests.

The last lines of the text are, unfortunately, much mutilated, but the general sense of the remaining portions is clear. From the above summary it is evident that Aspelta was no adventurer or usurper, and that on his mother's side, at least, he was the legitimate occupant of the throne of Napata. His ancestress in the sixth generation was probably a contemporary of the great Piānkhi, and may have belonged to the same branch of the royal

1 .

house of Napata as he. The inscription which records Åspelta's coronation[1] is very important as illustrating Nubian customs in the seventh century before Christ, and a translation of all the portions of it now remaining is therefore given here.

THE CORONATION OF ASPELTA—TRANSLATION.

(1) On the fifteenth day of the second month of spring of the first year of the Majesty of Horus NEFER-KHÅ, the king of the shrines of Nekhebet and Uatchet, NEFER-KHÅ, the Horus of gold USR-ÅB, the king of the South and North, the lord of the Two Lands, (Mer-ka-Rā), the son of the Sun, the lord of crowns, (Åspelta), the beloved of Åmen-Rā, the lord of the throne of the Two Lands, who dwelleth in ṬU-ĀB—now behold (2) all the soldiers of His Majesty were in the temple-hall of the city of ṬU-ĀB —now the name of the god who dwelleth therein is Ṭeṭun Khenti-Nefert, the god of Kash,—after the god (i.e., the late king) had departed to his place of rest. (3) And there were there six captains who filled the heart [of the king] of the army of his Majesty, and six of the chiefs who filled the heart [of the king] who were overseers of the seal, and (4) six overseers of the archives who filled the heart [of the king], and six nobles who were overseers of the chancery of the palace. And they said unto all his soldiers, "Come, let us "(5) make a king for ourselves, who shall be like unto a bull whom "none can resist." And the soldiers pondered anxiously and said, "Our lord abideth among us, but we know him not. (6) We "wish indeed that we did know him so that we might enter into "his service, even as the Two Lands served Horus the son of "Isis after he had taken his seat upon the throne of his father "Osiris, and ascribed adoration to the two uraei [on his brow]." (7) And one spake unto his neighbour, saying, "No man knoweth "him, save only Rā himself: may the god drive away from him "evil in every place wheresoever he may be!" And [again] one (8) spake unto his neighbour, saying, "Rā (i.e., the late king) "hath taken up his place in the Land of Life (Ānkhtet), and his "crown is [empty] among us." And [again] one spake unto his neighbour, saying, "It hath been a fixed and unalterable decree of "Rā since the time when heaven came into being, and (9) since "the crown of royalty existed, that he should give [the crown] to "his beloved son, for the king is his image among the living, and "hath not Rā placed himself in this land because of his love for it,

[1] For the text, see Mariette, *Monuments*, plate 9; and for translations, see Maspero, *Rev. Arch.*, 1873, tom. xxv., p. 300 ff.; Maspero, *Records of the Past*, vol. vi., p. 71; Maspero, *Annales Éthiopiennes*, § ii; Müller, *Aethiopien*, p. 27.

"and that this land may have peace?" And [again] one said (10) unto his neighbour, "Hath not Rā[1] entered into heaven, and "is not his throne empty without a king? And do not his rank "and his beneficence remain in his hands to give unto his son who "loveth him? For Rā knoweth that by means of them he (i.e., "the king) will make good laws on his throne."

(11) Then all the soldiers pondered anxiously, saying, "Our "lord abideth among us, but we know him not." And each and all the soldiers of His Majesty said with one voice, "Now, moreover, "this god Ȧmen Rā, lord of the throne of the Two Lands, the "dweller in Ṭu-āb is the god of Kash. Come, (12) let us go to "him, and let us do nothing without him, for not good is the thing "which is done without him. And let us place the matter with "the god, for he hath been the god of the kingdom of Kash since "the time of Rā, and he will lead us. For (13) the kingdom of "Kash is in his hands, and he giveth it unto the son whom he "loveth. We will adore him, and we will smell the earth [as we "lie on] our bellies before him, and we will declare before him, "saying, 'We have come unto thee, O Ȧmen, do thou give unto "us our lord to vivify us, to build the temples of all the gods and "goddesses of the South and North, and to provide (14) offerings "for them. We will do nothing without thee, thou art our guide, "and nothing whatsoever shall be done without thee.'" Then each and every soldier said, "This is a saying which is good, and "we declare it to be so a hundred thousand times."[2]

Then the captains of His Majesty went (15) with the chief officers of the palace of Ȧmen, and they found the prophets and the chief libationers standing at the door of the temple, and they said unto them, "[We] come before this god Ȧmen-Rā, the "dweller in Ṭu-āb, so that he may give unto us our lord to vivify "us, to build the temples (16) of all the gods and all the goddesses, "of the South and North, and to provide offerings for them, and "we will do nothing whatsoever without this god, for he is our "guide." Then the prophets and the chief libationers went into the temple, and they performed all the ceremonies of purification by the pouring out of water therein. And the captains of His Majesty (17) and the nobles of the palace went into the temple, and they threw themselves on their bellies before this god, and they said, "We have come unto thee, O Ȧmen-Rā, the lord of the "throne of the Two Lands, the dweller in Ṭu-āb, give thou us a lord "to vivify us, to build the temples of the gods of the South and "of the North, and to provide offerings [for them], and [to receive] "the gracious (18) dignity from thy two hands which thou givest "unto thy beloved son."

And they set the royal brethren in the presence of this god, but

[1] I.e., the dead king.

[2] Em shes maāt ḥeḥ en sep: this is an old phrase borrowed from the rubrics of the Book of the Dead.

he did not draw to himself one of them. Then they set a second time [before the God] the Royal Brother, the son of ȦMEN, born of MUT, the lady of heaven, the son of Rā, (Ȧspelta), who liveth for ever, and the god Amen-Rā, (19) the lord of the throne of the Two Lands, said, "He it is who is the king your lord, and he shall "vivify you, and he shall build all the temples of the Lords of the "South and North, and provide offerings therefor. His father "was the divine son, the son of Rā (. . . . . .), *maā kheru*,[1] whose "mother was the royal sister, the royal mother, the mistress of "Kash, (20) the daughter of Rā (. . . . . .), who liveth for ever; "whose mother was the royal sister, the *Neter Ṭuat* (i.e., high-"priestess) of Ȧmen-Rā, the king of the gods of Thebes, (. . . . . .), "*maāt kheru*; whose mother was the royal sister (. . . . . .), "*maāt kheru*; whose mother was the royal sister (. . . . . .), *maāt* "*kheru*; whose mother was the royal sister (. . . . . .), *maāt kheru*; "whose mother was the royal sister (. . . . . .), (21) *maāt kheru*; "whose mother was the royal sister, the mistress of Kash, "(. . . . . .), *maāt kheru*. He shall be your lord."

Then the captains of His Majesty and the nobles of the palace cast themselves down on their bellies before this god, and smelt the earth in the deepest humility, and gave thanks unto this god for the mighty (22) deed which he had done for his beloved son, the king of the South and North, (Ȧspelta), who liveth for ever. And His Majesty entered in to let himself be crowned before Father Ȧmen-Rā, the Lord of the throne of the Two Lands, and he found every kind of crown, and the royal apparel of the kings of Kash, and their sceptres, laid before this god. Then His Majesty spake in the presence of this god, saying: (23) "Come thou to "me, O Ȧmen-Rā the lord of the throne of the Two Lands, who "dwellest in Ṭu-āb, grant thou unto me thy beneficent dignity "which is not in my heart, and let me love thee (?). Give thou "to me the crown, according to the desire of thy heart, and the "sceptre." Then the god said, "Thine is the crown of the royal "brother, the king of the South and North (. . . . . .), *maā* "*kheru* (24); and his diadem is stablished on thy head, even as "is stablished . . . . on thy head; and his sceptre is in thy

[1] "He whose word is maāt," i.e., he who has attained the power of making every order he gives to take effect. Thus we know that Ȧspelta's father was dead.

"hand, and it shall overthrow all thine enemies." Then His Majesty rose up before Åmen-Rā, [the lord of the throne of the Two Lands], ... and he took the sceptre in his hand, and His Majesty cast himself upon his belly before this god (25) to smell the earth in the deepest humility. And he said: "Come thou to "me, O Åmen-Rā, the lord of the throne of the Two Lands, who "dwellest in Ṭu-āb . . . ." From this point onwards the text is much mutilated, but enough of it remains to prove that when the king came out from the temple he was received by his soldiers with shouts of joy (line 28), and that he established festivals in honour of the gods, and gave gifts to the priests.

In connection with the reign of Åspelta mention must be made of the Stele set up by his Queen Māṭ . . . . ḥenen (?) at Gebel Barkal, to commemorate the gifts which she made to the temple of Åmen-Rā there. This Stele, after it was removed from the Sûdân, came into the possession of Linant Bey, and it passed into the hands of Prince Napoleon and E. de Rougé, and after the death of the latter was given to the Museum of the Louvre by J. de Rougé.[1] On the upper portion of it is sculptured a scene wherein Aspelta is making an offering of *Maāt*, , to Åmen-Rā, Mut, and Khensu, and behind him stand his mother Enselsa, his wife Māṭ . . . ḥenen (?), and his sister Khebit, each pouring out a libation with her right hand, and holding a sceptre in her left. Each of the three royal ladies is steatopygous, and their figures resemble those of the ladies who are seen represented on the chapel-walls of the pyramids of Meroë. Beneath the sculptured scene are twenty-three lines of text, which set forth that on the twenty-fourth day of the fourth month of the season Shat, in the third year of Åspelta's reign, the following officers of the kingdom of Napata came to the temple: six overseers of the seal called Rum-Åmen, Amen-tarhaknen . . . . a-Åmen-saknen, the *Ånauasasu* official Kuru-Åmen-tanen, ... samākhinen, Nastaåbusaknen,[2] and the chief scribe of Kash, Mārubiua-

[1] First published and translated by P. Pierret, in *Études Égypt.*, tom. i., pp. 96-106, plate 2, Paris, 1873; also published and translated by Schaefer, in *Aeg. Zeit.*, 1895, p. 101.

[2] 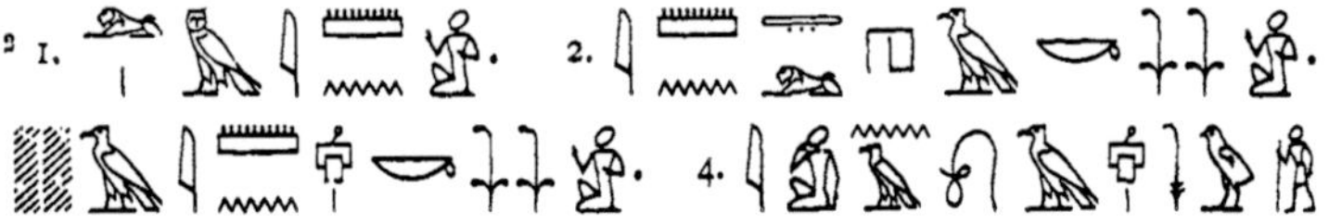

STELE INSCRIBED WITH AN ACCOUNT OF THE DEDICATION OF GIFTS TO THE TEMPLE OF ÅMEN-RĀ AT NAPATA BY KING ASPELTA. FOUND AT GEBEL BARKAL.

Amen,[1] and the scribe of the granary, Khensu-Årṭās,[2] the chief chancellor of the marches of Ta-Kenset, Arta,[3] the royal scribe Takarta,[4] the chancellor Paṭa-nub,[5] in all, eleven officials. In the presence of these stood the queen, with a silver bowl in her right hand, and a sistrum in her left, and she made an offering to Åmen and agreed to give to the god fifteen loaves of bread, ten of one sort and five of another, each day, and every month fifteen measures of beer, and every year three oxen, and on festival days she promised to give a measure of some kind of beer, and two measures of another, extra. These gifts were to be maintained by the queen during her life, and by her children and grandchildren after her death. Every descendant of hers who carried out her wishes would be favourably regarded by Åmen-Rā, and would have a son to succeed him, but whosoever diminished these offerings would be smitten by the sword of Åmen-Rā, and be burned by the fire of Sekhet, and have no son to succeed him. There were present also at the dedication of this endowment, the second, third, and fourth prophets of Åmen, who were called Uahmāni-Åmen, Ṭanen-Åmen, Tanenbuta, respectively; and the scribe of the divine words of Åmen, whose name is erased; the seven chief libationer-priests, Sapåkhi, Sab, Peṭā-Amen, Nemkhi, Kurumut, Khent(?)-ruhi, Kuru-tanen-Åmen; the three presidents, Nes-Ånḥer, Bes . . . ., and Un-nefer, and the temple scribe Nes-Mut.

Here for convenience' sake, and because the document probably belongs to the end of the seventh century before Christ, reference must be made to the edict against the eaters of raw meat, which was promulgated at Napata by a king whose name has been

obliterated.[1] The edict is inscribed upon a stone slab, with a rounded top, which was found by an Egyptian officer at Gebel Barkal, and which was subsequently brought to Cairo, under Mariette's Directorship of Antiquities; this monument is generally known as the "Stele of the Excommunication." On the rounded part is sculptured a scene wherein the king, whose name has been erased from the cartouche, is making an offering of Maāt , to Åmen-Rā, who is represented with a ram's head surmounted by a disk and plumes; behind the god stand Mut and Khensu. Åmen promises to give him "all life and power"; and Mut, "all health," and Khensu, "the veritable scribe of the company of the gods, and Horus, the lord of joy of heart, all joy of heart." Beneath the scene are ten lines of text, the first three of which contain the king's names and titles. The rest of the inscription sets forth that, in the second year after His Majesty had ascended the throne of Seb, he went into the temple of Father Åmen of Napata, the dweller in Ṭu-āb, to drive away these men (or tribes), who were haters of the god [Åmen], and were called "Tem pesiu per ṭet khaiu," saying; "They shall not enter into the temple of "Åmen of Napata, the dweller in Ṭu-āb, because of that thing, "whereof to speak is an abomination, which they did in the "temple of Åmen." Now they did a thing, which the god had not given the command to do, and they made a blasphemous design in their hearts, in respect of slaying the man in whom there existed no abomination, the which the god had given no command to perform. But the god made their words [empty whilst yet] in their mouths, and their words wherein they had pleasure turned into things which rose up against them in an evil manner. And the god smote them, and he made the fire of the king to pass through their midst. In order to put into all prophets, and into all libationers, who enter into the place where this holy god is, the fear of the greatness of his souls and of the might of his living power, His Majesty saith thus:—

"All prophets and all libationers who shall commit an evil act "in the temple shall [the god Amen] slay. And their feet shall

[1] For the text, see Mariette, *Mon. Divers*, plate 10; and for translations, see Maspero, *Revue Arch.*, 1871, tom. xxi., p. 329; *Records of the Past*, vol. iv., p. 95 ff.; *Études de Mythologie*, tom. iii., p. 229; and see Mariette, *Revue Arch.*, 1865, tom. ii., p. 161.

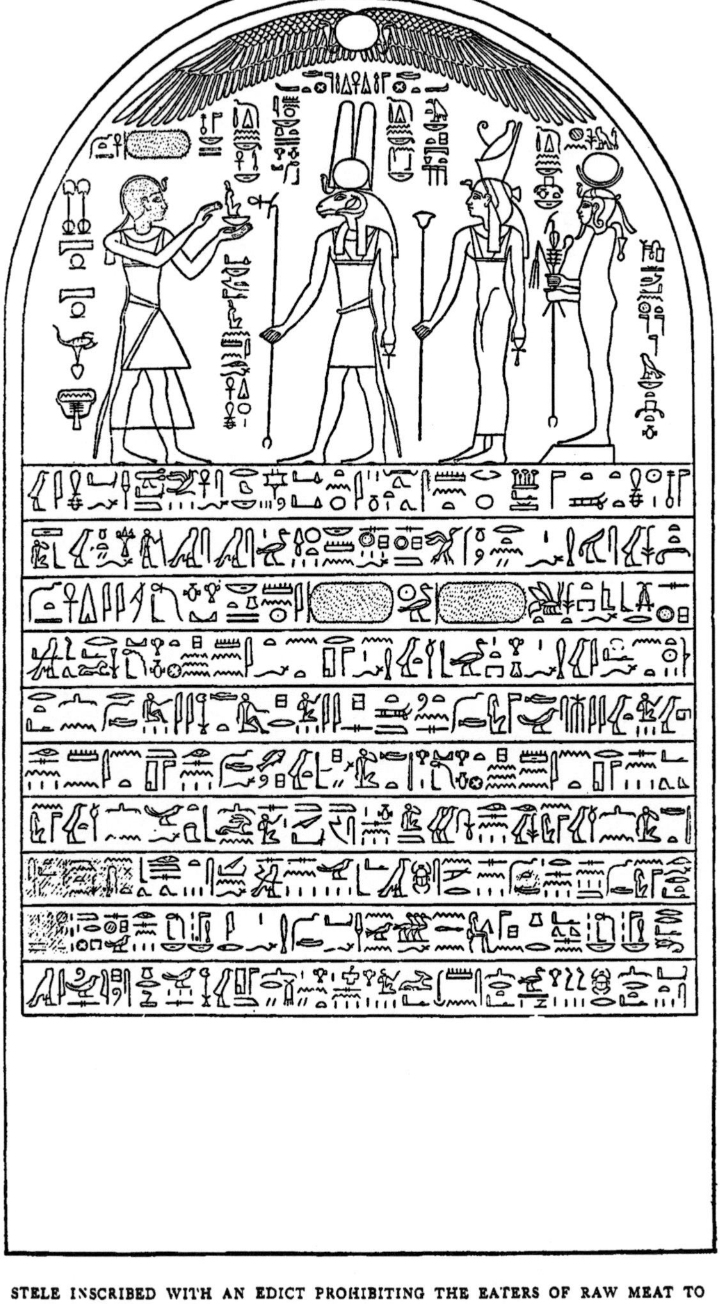

STELE INSCRIBED WITH AN EDICT PROHIBITING THE EATERS OF RAW MEAT TO ENTER THE TEMPLE OF ÅMEN-RĀ AT GEBEL BARKAL. FOUND AT GEBEL BARKAL.

"not be permitted to [stand] upon the earth, and their posterity "shall not be firmly stablished after them; therefore shall the "temple be free from their pollution, and their defilement shall "not be therein."

From this extract it is clear that the edict was directed against a class of people who tried to introduce into the town of Napata a custom which was abhorred by the priests and their nominee the king, and, though it is impossible to supply details of the custom, and to give the exact meaning of the formula which expressed the views of these people, it is not difficult to show what they were. The first two words of the phrase,[1] *tem pesi*, seem to mean "do not cook," and therefore Professor Maspero, the first to translate the edict, believes that the people who incurred the wrath of Ȧmen and the king endeavoured to introduce the custom of eating raw meat. That it found favour among certain of the priests and libationers is clear from the fact that the last paragraph of the edict is directed against them. Now, the eating of raw meat has been a practice among the Ethiopians from time immemorial, and the custom survives to this day among many of the tribes on the Abyssinian frontier and in Abyssinia itself. The Amharic language, in fact, contains a word for "meat which is eaten raw," i.e., *brûndô*, or *brendô*,[2] and the Abyssinians, as has already been said (see Vol. I., pp. 18, 19), love raw meat. The priests of Ȧmen and the men of Egyptian descent in Napata hated the innovation, or perhaps the continuation of an old custom, hence the edict; but, seeing that the name of the king who promulgated it was obliterated in later days, it may be assumed that he was unpopular because of his edict, and that the custom of eating raw meat became common in Napata.

During the reign of Nekau (Necho), the second king of the XXVIth Dynasty, Egypt was too much occupied with Syria to trouble about Nubia, or the Sûdân, and, so far as we know, the mercenaries who garrisoned Elephantine had no serious trouble with the people who lived to the south of the First Cataract. Nekau began to reign about B.C. 611 and died about 594. In a battle with him in the Valley of Megiddo Josiah, king of Judah,

[1] *Tum pesi. Per tot khaï*, "Do not cook. Let violence kill" (Maspero).

[2] ብሩንዶ ፡ or ብርንዶ ፡

was slain,[1] and Nekau made himself master of all Syria whilst the Babylonians and Medes were attacking Nineveh. After the fall of Nineveh Nebuchadnezzar II. marched against him, and in a pitched battle fought at Karkĕmîsh the Egyptians, Nubians, and Libyans were routed with great slaughter, and Nekau sought safety in flight; he reached Egypt safely, and died two years after his defeat. During his reign he cleared out the old Red Sea Canal, in the course of which work 120,000 men perished; he also established a fleet of triremes.

Psammetichus II., the son and successor of Nekau, ascended the throne when very young, and in the early years of his reign he went to Elephantine to superintend an expedition into Nubia; on his return he died, about B.C. 589. Whilst he was at Elephantine his officers caused his titles and cartouches to be cut on rocks on the Islands of Bigga, Abaton, Konosso, &c., and about this time the rock-hewn chapel at Philae, made in honour of Khnemu and other gods of the Cataract country, was probably dedicated. The object of the expedition into Nubia is not clear, and there is no evidence that it met with any opposition on the way. How far south the officers of Psammetichus II. went is not known, but they certainly reached Abû Simbel, for they left inscriptions there which make this certain. These inscriptions[2] are in Greek, Carian, and Phoenician, and are found on a leg of one of the colossal statues of Rameses II. The most important of those in Greek is that which states that it was cut by the comrades of Psammetichus, the son of Theokles, when king Psammetichus came to Elephantine. The expedition, it goes on to say, sailed by way of Kerkis to the source of the river, Deche-Potasimto commanding the foreigners, and Amasis the Egyptians. The men who wrote were Damerarchon, the son of Amoibichos, and Pelekos, the son of Udamos.[3] The name Kerkis[4] has been

[1] See 2 Kings xxiii. 29.

[2] See Lepsius, *Denkmäler*, Abth. vi., Bl. 98 ff.; *Corpus Inscrip. Semit.*, tom. i., pl. 19, 20, text, tom. i., pp. 128-137; Sayce, *Trans. Soc. Bibl. Arch.*, vol. ix., p. 144 ff.

[3] Βασιλέος ἐλθόντος ἐς Ἐλεφαντίναν Ψαμματίκο
ταῦτα ἔγραψαντ οἱ σὺν Ψαμματίχοι τοὶ Θέοκλος
ἔπλεον ἦλλον δὲ Κέρκιος κατυπερ θένισσο ποταμὸς
ἀνίη ἀλόγλοσος Δηχεποτάσιμτο Αἰγύπτιος δὲ Ἄμασις
ἔγραφε Δαμεραρχον Ἀμοίβιχου καὶ Πέλεκος Οὐδάμου.

[4] See Wiedemann, in *Rheinisches Museum*, Bd. xxxv., p. 372.

the subject of much discussion, but the reading is well-established, and it seems better to look for this place to the south of Abû Simbel, than to identify it either with Kirsh, opposite to Garf Ḥusên, or with Korti, a little above Dakka. Practically speaking, the expedition sailed nearly to Wâdî Ḥalfa, the Egyptians of the time considering that the Nile Valley from Elephantine to this point belonged to them. Wâdî Ḥalfa, or Behen as it was then called, had lost its importance, but this was certain to happen when it ceased to be a central market for the products of the Southern Sûdân. This ancient frontier town was situated in a most unproductive portion of the Nile Valley, and it was to the interest neither of the kings of Napata nor of the kings of Egypt to maintain or defend it against each other at this period.

During the rule of the early kings of the XXVIth Dynasty of Egypt there flourished at Napata, probably between B.C. 610 and B.C. 580, a king called P-ĀNKH-ÀLURU, whose name occurs in this form:—

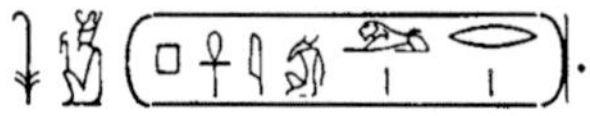.

Nothing whatever is known about his reign, but his name occurs twice in the Stele of Nàstasenen, once in connection with a vineyard, or garden, which he planted at Ta-ḥeḥet, and once in connection with Ḥeru-sa-àtef.

Following close on the period of his rule came the reign of ḤERU-SA-ÀTEF, whose prenomen was SA-MER-ÀMEN. His Horus name was KA-NEKHT-KHĀ-EM-NEPT,[1] his Nekhebet-Uatchet name was NETCH-NETERU,[2] and his Golden Horus name was UAF-TH-ṬĀT-SEMT-SEMT-NEBT.[3] The only known monument of this king is the famous gray granite stele from Gebel Barkal which is now in the Egyptian Museum at Cairo. On the upper portion of the obverse is sculptured a figure of the winged disk, with pendent uraei, between

1 .

2 .

3 .

which is a cartouche containing the name of Ḥeru-sa-àtef Beneath are two scenes: in that to the right the king is standing, and is making an offering of a string of beads, a necklace and a pectoral to the ram-headed Àmen of Napata, and behind him is the "royal mother, royal sister, mistress of Kash, Thesma nefer-ru";[1] in the scene to the left the king is making the same kind of offerings to the man-headed Àmen, and behind him stands the "royal sister and wife Behthàlis (?). On the four sides of the stele are 161 lines of hieroglyphics, wherein is recorded the history of the principal events of the reign of Ḥeru-sa-àtef.[3] The following rendering of them will illustrate their contents:—

(1 The thirteenth day of the second month of the season of Pert, in the thirty-fifth year under the majesty of the Horus, the Mighty Bull crowned in Nept (Napata), the lord of the shrines of Nekhebet and Uatchet, (2) the Advocate of the gods, the Golden Horus, the conqueror (?) of all foreign lands, the king of the South and North, (Sa-mer-Àmen), the son of Rā, the lord of the Two Lands, the lord of crowns, (3) the lord who hath made creation, the son of Rā [proceeding] from his body, beloved by him, (Ḥeru-sa-àtef), who liveth for ever, beloved of Àmen-Rā, the lord of the thrones of the Two Lands, who dwelleth in the Holy [Mountain]. We give him (4) life, stability, and all power, and all health, and all joy of heart, like Rā, for ever.

In the beginning they decided that Àmen of (5) Napata . . . . my beneficent Father, should give unto me Ta-Neḥeset (i.e., the Land of the Blacks, or Sûdân); in the beginning it was they who (6) bound on the royal tiara, in the beginning it was they who looked upon me with their kind eyes, and who spake unto me, saying. (7) "O get thee gone to the temple of Àmen of Napata, "who dwelleth in the Hall of the (8) North." Then was I afraid, and I made supplication unto a certain aged man, and did reverence [to him], and he (9) spake unto me, saying: "Seek on "behalf of thy two hands; he who buildeth up my (10) holy "places shall be protected." Then they caused me to come into the presence of Àmen of Napata, my (11) beneficent Father, saying: "I beseech thee to give unto me the diadem of the Land

1 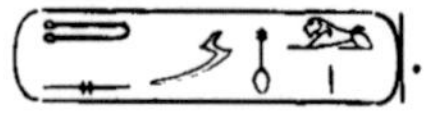.   2 .

3 For the text, see Mariette, *Mon. Divers*, plates 11-13; and for translations, see Maspero, *Records of the Past*, vol. vi., pp. 85-96; *Études de Mythologie*, tom. iii., p. 233.

RELIEFS AND TEXT FROM THE FRONT OF THE STELE OF HERU-SA-ÀTEF.
FOUND AT GEBEL BARKAL.

"of the Blacks"; and (12) Åmen of Napata said unto me, "I "have given unto thee the diadem of the Land of the Blacks; "and I have given (13) unto thee the Four Quarters of the whole "earth; and I have given unto thee the water which is good; "and I have given unto thee (14) the water which is foul; and I "have placed all thy foes so that they may be beneath thy "sandals." (15) If any country maketh a [hostile] advance on "thy two sides it shall not succeed; but if thou (16) makest an "expedition against any country which is on either side of thee, "(17) the thigh and the legs thereof shall come to nought." And having seen him I poured out a great libation in return for that which Åmen of Napata, (18) my beneficent Father, had given me, and I stood up in the hall of the Apts of Åmen of Napata, (19) within the sanctuary.

And it came to pass after these things that [I] made a journey to Åmen-Rā (20), the lord who dwelleth in the city of Qemten, and I spake, saying, "Åmen of Napata." And I made a journey to Åmen-Rā, the lord who dwelleth (21) within Pa-Nebes. and I spake, saying, "Åmen of Napata." And I made a journey to Bast of (22) Taret, and I spake, saying, "Åmen of Napata."

Then they spake to me, saying, "Get thee gone (23) to the temple "of Åmen of Tarukhet(?)-reset, for men say that the building "thereof is not complete." (24) Then I turned back a second time, and I builded it, and I provided materials, and I adorned it completely in five months. And when I looked at the (25) temple of the Apts of Åmen of Napata, and saw that it lacked gold, I gave (26) unto the temple of the Apts . . . . . forty *teben* of gold, and of worked gold (?) five thousand one hundred and twenty *pek*. (27) Then one spake unto me saying, "The *pa shennut* lacketh gold." And I (28) caused them to bring *shenṭ* (acacia) wood, and wood of Årkaret, in abundance, (29) and I made them bring it to Napata, and I made them to lay plates of gold on both sides of it [in weight] forty *teben*. (30) And I gave to the treasury (?) of the temple twenty *teben* of gold, and of worked gold one hundred pieces.

(31) O Åmen of Napata, I have given unto thee [a pectoral] and beads for thy neck . . . . and a statue of Åmen-Rā . . . . inlaid with . . . . and gold, and three . . . . of gold, which were inlaid with [precious stones], and a figure of Rā inlaid with gold, and three gold figures of the head of Åmen, and two censers (?) of gold, and one hundred and thirty-four bands (?) of gold, and one hundred *teben* of silver, and one *māhen* vessel of silver, and one *haru* vessel of silver, and five *sekaru* vessels of silver, and one *haru* vessel of silver, and one *māhen* vessel of silver, and one *ȧbrek* vessel of silver, and nine *mennu* vessels of silver, and four *karu* vessels of copper, and . . . . *meḳatmi* vessels of copper, and two *ḥāḥrȧmȧu* vessels of copper, and two fire-holders of copper, and one *ukhakh* vessel of copper, and fifteen *sekaru* bowls of copper, and five *paṭennu* vessels of copper, and two large lavers

of copper—total, thirty-two [vessels]. And two hundred *teben* of spices, and three jars of incense, and five jars of honey (56).

And on another occasion, when the House of a Thousand Years began to fall into ruin, I rebuilt it for thee. I made for it a roof with pillars; I built for thee a stable for oxen, two hundred and fifty-four cubits [long]. I restored for thee a temple, which though small had gone to ruin, and I made supplication, saying, "Adoration [to thee]." And I spake, saying, "Behold, as a king of Egypt have I built for thee, and I have "provided for its supply of offerings." And again, I gave unto thee five hundred oxen, and I gave unto thee two *māhen* vessels of milk, and very many geese (?) on many occasions. And I gave unto thee ten ministrants. And I gave unto thee captives, fifty men and fifty women, in all one hundred. O Åmen of Napata, I have not reckoned [what I gave] unto thee. I am the man who provided for thee that which I vowed. (72) And on the twenty-third day of the third month of the season Pert, in the second year, they made him set out on an expedition against the rebels, and I slaughtered the Rehrehsa, and Åmen hamstrung the thighs that were stretched out against me. I did acts of bravery among them, and defeated them utterly.

(77) And on the fourth day of the second month of the season Pert, in the third year, I did acts of bravery among the Meṭeṭ rebels, and I defeated them utterly . . . . and it was thou who workedst for me.

(79) And on the twelfth day of the second month of the season Shemu, in the fifth year of the son of Rā, the king of the South and North (Ḥeru-sa-åtef), life, strength, health [to him] for ever! I caused my bowmen and my horsemen to go against the rebels in the country of Meṭeṭ, and they performed mighty deeds in the towns of Ånerua . . . ru, and they defeated them, and slew large numbers of them, and they took many prisoners, and defeated the Prince Aruḳa . . . . th.

(84) And on the fourth day of the second month of the season Shemu, in the sixth year of the son of Rā, (Ḥeru-sa-åtef), who liveth for ever, I called together a multitude [of soldiers] against the country of Meṭeṭ, and I did great acts of bravery among them and their towns, and I defeated and routed them utterly in the town of Hebsi (?). I captured the bulls, and cows, and asses, and sheep, and goats, and men slaves, and women slaves thereof, and the . . . . thereof, and it was thy terror which worked graciously on my behalf. Then the chief of the land of Meṭeṭ sent unto me, saying, "Thou art my god, I am thy servant, I am a woman, O come (?) to me." And he caused the *åṭennut*[1] to be brought unto me in

[1] The emblems of his sovereignty, or the money which he paid to Ḥeru-sa-åtef as his overlord.

the hands of an envoy (?). And I came and [I] performed the ceremonies of Ȧmen of Napata, my beneficent Father. And I gave unto thee oxen in very large numbers.

(92) And on the fourth day of the first month of the season Pert, in the eleventh year [of my reign], I made my bowmen to set out on an expedition against the country of Taqnat, under the leadership of Ḳasȧu, for the troops of the chiefs Baruḳa and Sȧmensa had reached the city of Sunt. He did mighty deeds of valour there and defeated Baruḳa and Sȧmensa, and slew all the people of the city. It was through the terror of thee which was beneficent [towards me] that I did [this].

(96) And on the fifteenth day of the first month of the season Sha, in the sixteenth year [of my reign], I caused my bowmen and my horsemen to set out on an expedition against the rebels of the land of Mekhetsa (?) and they performed mighty deeds of valour among them, and my bowmen defeated them with slaughter, and captured the finest of their cattle.

(99) And on the thirteenth day of the first month of the season Pert, in the eighteenth year of [the reign of] the son of Rā, (Ḥeru-sa-ȧtef), who liveth for ever, the rebels of the country of Rehrehsa came under the leadership of . . . . . with his men into the city of Baruat (Meroë), and I repulsed him. Thy auspicious terror and thy two mighty thighs smote him bravely, and I defeated him and overthrew him with very great slaughter, and scattered his men. And thou thyself didst so work for me in the lands (?) that he rose up in the middle of the night and took to flight.

(105) And on the eighteenth day of the third month of Shemu, in the twenty-third year of [the reign of] the son of Rā, (Ḥeru-sa-ȧtef), who liveth for ever, Ȧrua, the chief of the countries of Rehrehsa, and all his men came against me in the city of Baruat (Meroë). And I did mighty deeds of valour among them, and I defeated him and overthrew him with very great slaughter, and I repulsed him and put him to flight. And I defeated Shaikaru who came to his assistance under an agreement with him. It was thy auspicious terror and thy two thighs [which smote] the chief . . . . . and my bowmen and my horsemen drove him off.

(111) And on the fifteenth day of the first month of the season Pert, in the thirty-fourth year of [the reign of] the son of Rā, (Ḥeru-sa-ȧtef), who liveth for ever, I sent a messenger to Ȧmen of Napata, my beneficent Father, saying, "Shall I send "my bowmen against the countries of Mekhetsai?" And Ȧmen sent a message unto me, saying: "Certainly send them." Then I caused to set out fifty scouts and horsemen, and the people of the four lands of Mekhetsai who were gathered together did they defeat with slaughter, and none remained, and none of them

was able to escape, and none of them was able to take the road, and none of them was able to put his feet [to ground], and none of them was able . . . . . and none of them was able to grasp a bow (?), and they gave themselves up as prisoners (?).

(119) And, moreover, so soon as they spake unto me, saying, "The temple fell into ruin in the third month of the season Pert "during the festival of Ptaḥ," I built the temple for thee. I built for thee a temple of gold . . . . of wood, six chambers of wood, and four pillars of stone. And moreover, so soon as they spake unto me, saying: "The house of the king (i.e., palace) hath "become in such a state of ruin that no man can enter therein," I built the house of the king, and four houses in Napata, and sixty houses which I caused to be enclosed within a wall. And, moreover, I built a place of . . . . . each side of which was fifty cubits [long], making in all two hundred cubits. And, moreover, I planted six gardens with a vine in each, making in all six vines in Napata. And I gave unto thee most beautiful gardens in Baruat (Meroë), making in all six. And I caused to be offered up unto thee offerings on the twelfth (or, twenty-second) night [of each month] one hundred and fifteen measures of grain, and thirty-eight measures of barley, making in all one hundred and fifty-three measures of wheat and barley. [The next four lines are mutilated, but the text seems to mean that the king carried out repairs of temples in every town which needed them]. I made Osiris to rise (i.e., celebrated a festival to the god) in . . . . thit; I made to rise Osiris, the dweller in Baruat (Meroë); I made to rise Osiris and Isis in Merthet; I made to rise Osiris and Isis four times in Ḳarert; I made to rise Osiris and Isis and Horus in Sehreset; I made to rise Osiris and Ȧmen-Ȧbṭi[1] in Sekaruḳat; I made to rise Horus in Karuthet (Korti ?); I made to rise Rā in Mehat (?); I made to rise An-ḥer in Ȧruthnait; I made to rise Osiris in Napata; I made to rise Osiris in Nehanat; I made to rise Osiris and Isis in Pa-Qemt; and I made to rise Osiris three times in Pa-Nebes, for ever.

[1] 

CHAPTER VII.

THE SUCCESSORS OF PIĀNKHI.

THE information to be gained from Ḥeru-sa-ȧtef's inscription is of a most interesting nature, and it proves that in the sixth century before Christ there lived at Napata a king, who, by means of the nine expeditions which he made during his reign of at least thirty-five years, made himself master of the Nile Valley from Pa-nebes, the *Πνουψ* of Ptolemy, near Wâdî Ḥalfa, to Sennaar on the Blue Nile, and Dâr Fûr on the White Nile. How far to the west his rule extended cannot be said, but he was certainly conqueror of all the country on both banks of the Atbara. He made no attempt to wage war against the Egyptians, and he seems to have laid claim to no country north of Pa-nebes, a city which lay to the south of Wâdî Ḥalfa. He devoted all his energies to the conquest of the various savage, or half savage tribes, whether with black, or red, or white skins, and whether of pure Sûdânî or Semitic origin, that lived south of the Island of Meroë, and his success was great. With the spoil which he took from the vanquished chiefs he endowed the great temple of Ȧmen at Napata, and he rebuilt the sanctuaries of the gods in many cities, and established one or more annual festivals in each of the twelve chief cities of his kingdom. It is clear that he was wholly in the hands of the priests of Ȧmen, and that he took their advice about going to war. We see also that the bulk of the spoil went to them and to their god, and that Ḥeru-sa-ȧtef bestowed upon Ȧmen of Napata a new endowment after each of his great expeditions.

The gods chosen by him for endowment besides Ȧmen of Napata were Osiris, Isis, Horus, Rā, Ȧn-Ḥer, and a local form of Ȧmen called "Ȧmen-Abṭi." Ḥeru-sa-ȧtef copied the great Egyptian kings of the XVIIIth Dynasty in causing a summary of his deeds in the form of Annals to be drawn up, and, like them, he attributed to Amen the successful results which he achieved. The exact length of his reign is unknown, and nothing is known of the events which followed his death. He may have been succeeded by a son, but the materials at present available do not permit any statement to be made on this point, and we do not reach a period concerning which historical facts exist until the reign of Nåstasenen.

NÅSTASENEN, with the prenomen of ĀNKH-KA-RĀ, and the

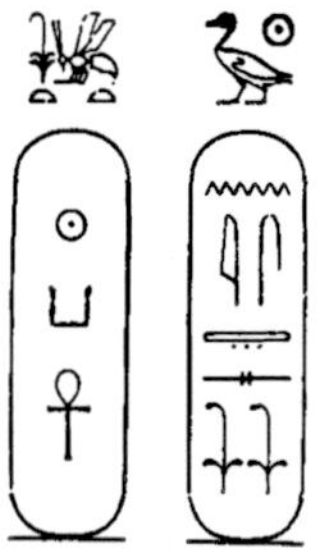

Horus name of KA NEKHT MER PAUT NETERU KHĀ EM NEPITA,[1] and the title of "son of Rā," ascended the throne about B.C. 525, and he appears to have been the king of the Sûdân against whom Cambyses directed his campaign. The only known monument of his reign is the massive gray granite slab about 5 feet, 6 inches high, inscribed on both sides in hieroglyphics, which is called by Lepsius the "Stele of Dongola." In a note printed at the end of Brugsch's translation of the text,[2] Lepsius says that the stele was obtained through the agency of Graf Wilhelm von Schlieffen, through whom it was given by Muḥammad Alî to the Berlin Museum in 1854, but there is some mistake here, for Muḥammad Alî died in 1849. The difficulty is partially cleared up by a communication which Graf Wilhelm von Schlieffen has made to Dr. Schäfer,[3] wherein he says that he first saw the stele in New Dongola lying flat on its side in 1853; he cleared away the dust from it, and took a paper impression of the text on one side. When he returned to Cairo the following winter he was instructed by the Prussian Consul-General to obtain the stele from 'Abbâs Pâshâ, who was then the Ruler of Egypt, and 'Abbâs Pâshâ presented it to His Majesty Frederick William IV. The stele, however, remained at New Dongola, and it was not until 1869, when the Crown Prince Frederick William took a personal

[1] "Mighty Bull, beloved of the company of the gods, crowned in Napata."

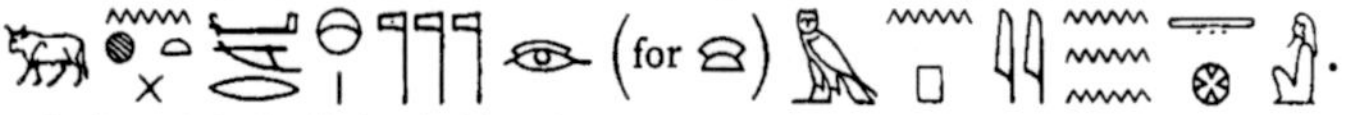

[2] *Aegyptische Zeitschrift*, 1877, pp. 23-27.

[3] *Die Aethiopische Königsinschrift des Berliner Museums*, p. 2. Leipzig, 1901.

THE RELIEFS AND OPENING LINES OF THE STELE OF NÅSTASENEN, OR NÅSTASEN.

[From Lepsius, *Denkmäler*, Abth. V. Bl. 16.

interest in the matter, that the monument was brought to Cairo; in 1871 it was taken to the Museum in Berlin (No. 2268).[1] By some means or other, Lepsius managed to obtain a paper impression of the text on the reverse soon after the discovery of the stele, for he published the complete text from both sides in 1856.[2] The stele, as has already been said, was found by Graf Wilhelm von Schlieffen at New Dongola, but it is pretty certain that it was not originally set up there by the king who had it made, and although it cannot be said when, or by whom, it was brought there, it is tolerably certain that its original home was Gebel Barkal, and that it stood there near the Stele of Piānkhi, the Stele of Tanuath-Åmen, the Stele of Åspelta, the Stele of Ḥeru-sa-åtef, and the Stele of the Excommunication. It is probable that it was brought away from there by the person who removed the Stele of Queen Māṭ . . . ḥenen (?), and who gave it or sold it to Linant Bey, and that on account of its weight, and the great difficulties which would be encountered in passing through the Third and Second Cataracts, it was dropped at New Dongola to await a more favourable opportunity for its removal.

On the upper part of the stele are sculptured two scenes: in that to the right Nåstasenen is standing before the ram-headed Åmen of Napata, to whom he offers a necklace of beads, and a necklace with a pectoral attached, and in that to the left he makes the same offering to the man-headed Åmen-Rā. In the former scene he is accompanied by the Queen Sekhmakh,[3] and in the latter by the Queen Mother Pelkha.[4] Above these scenes is the winged disk, with pendent uraei, between which is the king's name enclosed within a cartouche; the text referring to the winged disk reads, "the great god of Beḥuṭet (Edfû), the lord of heaven, giveth "life and power." Of the ram-headed Åmen it is said; "Åmen "of Napata, the dweller in the Holy Mountain, the great god, the "governor of Ta-Kenset, giveth life and all power for ever," and he says to the king, "I give thee all life and power, all stability, "all health, and joy of heart. I give thee the years of eternity,

[1] See the official *Verzeichnis*, p. 402.

[2] See *Denkmäler*, Abth. v., Bl. 16.

[3] 

[4] 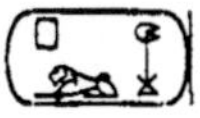.

"wherein to rise upon the throne of Horus for ever." The king is said to be "giving a pectoral to his father," and he must say four times, "I give thee . . . . *teben* of gold in the first month of "the season Shemut." The Queen Sekhmakh is pouring out a libation with one hand, and holding a sistrum in the other. Of the man-headed Åmen it is said; "Åmen-Rā, the lord of "the thrones of the two lands, the governor of the Apts, the "giver of all life, stability and power, like Rā, for ever," and he says to the king; "I give to thee all lands, and all mountains "and deserts, and the Nine Peoples who fight with the bow shall "be fettered together beneath thy sandals, like Rā, for ever."

The text[1] which runs beneath these scenes and is continued on the reverse of the stele gives a good account of the election to the throne, the coronation, and the wars, or rather raids of Nåstasenen. As a young man he lived in Beruat, where he received from Amen of Napata a call which said, "Come" This statement is interesting, for it shows that about B.C. 525 the priesthood of Napata, on the death of Ḥeru-sa-åtef, found no one in their city who was suitable for the throne. At Meroë Nåstasenen took counsel with the members of the royal house, and as they acknowledged that Åmen regarded him as his son, he set out early one morning for the city of Åsṭersat, which was perhaps his native town or village, and passed the night there. The situation of this place is unknown, but it was probably on the river, as it seems unlikely that Nåstasenen would go to Napata by a great desert route, one of which started opposite Meroë, and the other a little to the north of the junction of the Atbara with the Nile. From Åsṭersat he went to Ta-ḥeḥet (?), another place the site of which is unknown. This town was connected in some way with (P-ānkhi-Aluru), a former king of Napata, and Nåstasenen no doubt wished to gain the support of its inhabitants. Here he was met by a company of men from the temple of Åmen of Napata and a number of local magnates, and, as they informed

[1] See Lepsius, *Denkmäler*, Abth. v., Bl. 16; for translations, see Maspero, *Trans. Soc. Bibl. Arch.*, vol. iv., p. 2, 1876; *Records of the Past*, vol. x., p. 55 ff.; *Études de Mythologie*, vol. iii., p. 239 ff.; Brugsch, *Aeg. Zeit.*, 1877, p. 23; Erman, in *Ausführliches Verzeichnis* of the Royal Museum in Berlin, p. 402; Schaefer, *Die Aethiopische Königsinschrift des Berliner Museums*, Leipzig, 1901.

him that Àmen had laid the sovereignty of the country at his feet, he continued his journey, and arrived, by the west bank of the river, at Napata.

He crossed the river and rode on a "large horse" to the temple at Gebel Barkal, and when he had performed all the appointed ceremonies, Àmen gave him the kingdom of the Sûdân, which extended from the neighbourhood of the modern village of Kôsha, about one hundred and twenty miles south of Wâdî Ḥalfa, to the country of Àlut, the Alwah of Muḥammadan writers, the southern limits of which extended along the Blue and White Niles some two or three hundred miles south of the modern city of Kharṭûm. The capital of this country was probably on the site of the ruins on the right bank of the Blue Nile, a little above Kharṭûm, now known as Sôba. All the country between the Nile and the Red Sea formed a part of Nȧstasenen's dominions, and all the Bayûda desert, and the regions to the north and south of it. After returning thanks to Àmen, the new king danced before his god, and sacrificed two oxen or bulls, and then went up and took his seat on the Golden Throne, amid the acclamations of gentle and simple, who rejoiced in the appearance of a king who would renew the prosperity of their country.

It was now necessary for Nȧstasenen to show himself in the northern parts of his kingdom, and he therefore journeyed to the shrine of Àmen of Pa-Qem, which was probably situated between the Third and Second Cataracts. Here he was received by the god, in whose honour he celebrated a festival, and when Àmen had confirmed his rule the king went up and sat upon the Golden Throne. From Pa-Qem he went to Pa-Nebes, which was situated near Wâdî Ḥalfa, and the Àmen who was worshipped in this place having confirmed his rule, the king went up and sat upon the Golden Throne. At Pa-Qem he received a bow from the god, and at Pa-Nebes he received a leather-laced club, and thus, having been acknowledged as king in the two chief religious centres in the northern parts of his kingdom, he returned to Napata. Here he offered up further sacrifices, and then he spent four nights in the *tchaut* chamber in the temple, and during the four days he performed some kind of acts or ceremonies, of the nature and import of which nothing is known. When these days were accomplished he offered up as sacrifices two more oxen or bulls, and then he went and seated himself upon the throne which is in the house of the Golden Garden (?).

Up the river from Napata, at a place called Tert, was a famous sanctuary of the goddess Bast. Thither Nȧstasenen journeyed, and presented himself before the goddess, who embraced him, and gave him her left breast [to suck], and presented him with a strong club (?). The site of Tert is unknown. The king occupied five days in going there and coming back, and we may assume therefore that the sanctuary was situated some distance up the Fourth Cataract, perhaps near the modern Berti. When Nȧstasenen had visited Tert his religious pilgrimages, which were also somewhat of a political character, came to an end, and he was free to consider a course of action which would fill the treasury of Ȧmen with gold. From his private possessions he dedicated to Ȧmen of Napata four gardens and thirty-six men to work them, a gold statue of Ȧmen of Pa-Qem-Ȧten, and two gold statues of Horus, several sets of silver and copper vessels for use in the sanctuary, and large quantities of incense, honey, and myrrh. To Ȧmen in Apt he dedicated ten very fine bulls and cows, and several sets of copper vessels.

Now whilst Nȧstasenen was consolidating his rule, and carrying out the behests of the priests of Ȧmen, events of importance were happening in Egypt. Cambyses, king of Persia, had quarrelled with Amāsis II., king of Egypt, and was making preparations to invade Egypt. The causes of the quarrel do not concern us here, for once having made up his mind to invade Egypt, Cambyses would not have much difficulty in finding an excuse. Assisted by Phanes, who had been formerly an officer in the service of Amāsis II., he obtained guides and water from the Arabs who lived on the north-east frontier of Egypt, and in a very short time he appeared with his host at Pelusium, where, however, he learned that Amāsis II. had just died after a short illness, and that his son, Psammetichus III., had succeeded him. Psammetichus III. marched out with the Egyptians and his mercenaries to fight Cambyses, but in the fierce battle which took place at Pelusium his forces were beaten, and he retreated to Memphis. A few days later, having captured Pelusium, Cambyses advanced on Memphis, which in due course fell into his hands, and thus Egypt and Nubia so far south as Wâdî Ḥalfa became a sàtrapy of the Persian Empire. According to one account, Psammetichus III. was compelled by Cambyses to commit suicide by drinking bulls' blood,[1] according to another, he was exiled, with six thousand Egyptians, to Susa.

Cambyses next determined to conquer the country to the west of Egypt, and Carthage, and Nubia (the Sûdân). Before, however, he began to do this, he appears to have set to work to gain the affections of the Egyptians by adopting their manners and customs. He caused his name to be written within a cartouche, and he adopted a Horus name (SMA TAUI, i.e., the "uniter of the two lands,") and a prenomen, MESUTH-RĀ;[2] he also styled himself "son of Rā," as if he had been a true Egyptian Pharaoh. With the view of further conciliating the Egyptians, he went to Saïs, restored at his own expense the temple of Neith, which had suffered greatly during the war, and under the tuition of the "*ḥā* prince and real royal kinsman," Utcha-Ḥeru-Resenet, learned something of the mythology of the goddess who was the mother of Rā, the Sun-god. Cambyses purified the temple, reinstated the priests, restored their incomes, and performed an act of worship to Neith and poured out a libation to her. With the money which Cambyses restored to him, the priest of Saïs did good to all, and it is expressly said of him that he provided coffins for those whose relatives were too poor to buy them, and that "he took care of the children." According to Herodotus (iii. 16), Cambyses had the body of his old enemy, Amāsis II., brought out from its tomb, and then beaten and stabbed, and when he found that he could not destroy it, he ordered it to be burned. Herodotus says that he did not believe this story, and most people will share his scepticism in this respect.

When Cambyses thought that the fitting time had arrived, he determined to send his fleet to Carthage, and a portion of his army against the dwellers in the Oasis of Jupiter Ammon, and

[1] The ancients believed that bulls' blood was poisonous, and that Midas, king of Phrygia, Themistocles, and Smerdis, all died through drinking it.

[2] .

another portion against the Nubians.[1] The expedition to Carthage broke down because the Phoenicians in the fleet of Cambyses refused to fight against their kinsmen, the Carthaginians, and the king thereupon decided to send an army to Carthage by land. He sent to Elephantine[2] for a number of the Fish-eaters who were acquainted with the Nubian tongue, and when they had come he gave them their instructions, and sent them into the Sûdân with the following gifts: a purple robe, a gold neck-chain, amulets, an alabaster box of myrrh, and a cask of palm wine. He also wanted to know whether the "table of the Sun" really existed in Nubia. The "table of the Sun" was a meadow full of boiled flesh of all kinds of beasts, which the magistrates stored with meat each night, and whosoever liked came and ate during the day.

The Nubians to whom the Fish-eaters went were the "tallest and handsomest of men," and their king was the tallest citizen, whose strength equalled his height. When the Fish-eaters arrived, they told the king of Nubia that Cambyses wished to be his friend and ally, and that the gifts they bore to him from him were those wherein he most delighted. The Nubian king told the envoys that their words were untrue, that they were spies, and that their king was not a just man because he coveted his country. He then gave them a bow and told them that when the Persians could pull it easily they might come against the Nubians; thus saying he unstrung the bow. Of the gifts which Cambyses sent, the only one he approved was the wine, which he confessed was better than anything they had of the kind in Nubia. In answer to the questions of the Fish-eaters the Nubian king told them that most of his people lived one hundred and twenty years, some even more; that they ate boiled flesh and drank nothing but milk; he showed them a fountain, the waters of which made their flesh glossy and sleek, and smell of perfume like that of violets; he showed them the prisoners in the gaol whose fetters were of gold, and the "table of the Sun"; and the crystal coffins wherein the dead were placed for one year before burial.[3]

When the Fish-eaters returned to Cambyses and gave him their

[1] Herodotus, iii. 17. [2] *Ibid.*, 19. [3] *Ibid.*, 23, 24.

report, he was furious, and immediately set out against the Nubians, without making arrangements for feeding his troops. When he arrived at Thebes he detached fifty thousand men from his main army, and sent them off to the Oasis of Jupiter Ammon, with orders to take all the people captives, and to burn the temple of Jupiter Ammon. These men by the help of guides reached the Oasis of Khârga in seven days, and then set out for the Oasis of Jupiter Ammon, but when they were half-way across, they were overtaken whilst eating their mid-day meal by a "strong and deadly" south wind, which buried them all in the sand that it brought with it, and never a man returned to Egypt. Meanwhile Cambyses continued his journey up the Nile, but before he had advanced one-fifth of the distance to the Nubian capital his army had eaten all the provisions, and the soldiers began to eat the transport animals, and the grass and the herbs which grew on the skirts of the desert. When, however, the great sandy desert was reached, even these failed, and the troops began to kill and eat their comrades, every ten men selecting a victim.[1] Then Cambyses became frightened and retreated to Thebes with the few soldiers that remained to him.

Such is the story, as told by Herodotus, of the mad attempt made by Cambyses to conquer the Sûdân. Details of the route chosen by Cambyses are wanting, and we do not know whether he intended to go to Napata or Meroë. If to the former place, he would have to go to Wâdî Ḥalfa, then traverse the awful "Belly of Stones," and the howling wilderness of the Third Cataract, and then march from Kerma to Napata along the river bank, a distance of at least two hundred miles. If to Meroë, he would leave the Nile at Korosko, and cross the desert to Abû Ḥamed, a distance of two hundred and thirty miles, and then proceed along the river bank for two hundred and twenty miles more. In either case it seems impossible for Cambyses to have reached his destination. Several historians, both ancient and modern, have, however, thought that Cambyses conquered the Sûdân. Strabo says[2] that he conquered the capital of "Ethiopia," and gave it his sister's name "Meroë," and the

[1] Herodotus, iii. 25.

[2] Bk. xvii.

statement is repeated by Josephus[1] and Diodorus.[2] The modern authorities who accept this statement adduce the fact of the existence of a city somewhere near the Third Cataract, called by Pliny[3] "Cambusis," and by Ptolemy[4] *Καμβύσου ταμιεῖα*, or "the store places of Cambyses." The hieroglyphic texts also mention a city called "Qem-baiu-set,"[5] which Brugsch was prepared to identify with the "Cambusis" of Pliny. Whether this identification be true or not, matters comparatively little, for the real question is whether there exists in the hieroglyphic inscriptions any evidence that Cambyses conquered the Sûdân. On this point the Stele of Nȧstasenen, the contents of which have already been partially described, throws much light, and its evidence goes to show that Cambyses did invade the Sûdân, and that his troops were defeated by Nȧstasenen with such slaughter that Cambyses was compelled to retreat to Egypt.

In lines thirty-nine and forty it is said: "The Chief Kambasu-"ṭen came, and I made my bowmen to advance against him from "the city Tchart. There was a great slaughter. [I captured] "all his . . . . . I made myself master of all the boats of his "captains, I routed and overthrew him. I seized all his lands (or "territory), and all his oxen, bulls, cows, calves, and animals of "every kind, and everything whereon men live, from the city of "Karṭept unto the city of Taruṭi-peḥt . . . ." The name of the chief whom Nȧstasenen overthrew is written in the inscription

Ka-m- ba-sa-u-ṭ-n-?

Brugsch transcribed these signs by Kambi . . . . uṭen, the fourth character being to him illegible, but Dr. Schaefer, after an examination of the stele itself, identified it as  *sa*, and there is no doubt about the correctness of his reading. The last sign may be ⊗, the determinative of "city," and , the last character of all, proves that the preceding characters are intended to form the name of the chief against whom Nȧstasenen fought. When

[1] *Antiq. Jud.*, ii. 102. [2] i. 33. [3] vi. 35.

[4] iv. 7. [5] 

we compare the group of characters with the variant spellings of the hieroglyphic forms of the name of Cambyses which are known from other monuments, there is no reasonable room for doubt that the foe of Nȧstasenen was Cambyses.

The position of the city of Tchart, from which the bowmen sallied, is unknown, and it is futile at present to hazard guesses as to its situation. The boats which Nȧstasenen seized probably belonged to the natives on the river whom Cambyses pressed into his service. The camp, or camps, where the Persian had stored such supplies as he had were captured by the Nubians and all his cattle, but it is instructive to note the absence of any mention of gold or women among the articles of spoil. From his campaigns in the south Nȧstasenen obtained large numbers of women and gold, the quantities of which are carefully noted. Cambyses coming from the north had, naturally, no stores of gold, and the number of women who followed his army was probably small. The attack on Cambyses' soldiers by the Nubian bowmen resembled a modern Dervish raid upon a town on the Nile under the rule of the Mahdî or Khalîfa, and, as the Persians were unused to Sûdânî methods of warfare, they must have suffered severely under the attacks of the Nubian "bowmen." After the defeat of Cambyses Nȧstasenen gave twelve bulls to the city of Tarumen, and six bulls to the city of Saksakṭit, a lamp to the city of Taqtetet, and to Ȧmen of Napata he dedicated twelve pectorals, all the crops which were produced on the Nile between Karṭept and Tarreqet, six hundred cattle, and two hundred men. Thus it seems that the priests of Ȧmen were slave-owners on a considerable scale.

Nȧstasenen next undertook five expeditions against the various enemies of his country. The first was directed against Ȧikhentka (?), Chief of Mekhenteqnent, to the south of Meroë, in the Eastern Desert. The second was against Reb-khenṭent, Chief of Rebaru and Ȧkarkarḥent (?). The third was against Ȧbskhent (?), Chief of Ȧrersa. The fourth was against the land of Mekhsherkherthet (?). The fifth was against Tamakhith, Chief of Mai-khentka (?). The positions of all these places are unknown, but there is no doubt that they were situated in the Eastern Desert between the Nile and the Red Sea, in places where gold was plentiful, and where the local shêkhs possessed large numbers of cattle. The names of the chief shêkhs of all the countries save one are mentioned. The spoil taken in the third expedition was dedicated to Ȧmen of Napata, and that taken during the fourth expedition the king kept for himself. The amount of spoil taken on the five expeditions was enormous; it consisted of 673,471 oxen and bulls; 1,252,232 cows, calves, sheep and goats; 3,212 ṭen or ṭeben of gold, i.e., about 800 lbs. troy, besides a "large quantity of gold," and "a quantity of gold so large that it could not be told;" 2,236 women from Mekhenteqnent, besides "all the women" from the four other conquered countries; 322 figures in gold (?), and all stores of provisions from most of the districts which Nåstasenen invaded.

The large quantities of gold mentioned prove that some of these places lay along the countries on the Blue Nile, and the great numbers of cattle suggest that the king raided so far south as Dâr Fûr and perhaps Kordôfân also. It is quite clear that when Nåstasenen had raided a country he left it a wilderness, and in much the same state as the Sûdân was in on the death of the Khalîfa in November, 1899. Cattle, women, and gold were the three things desired by the Nubian king five hundred years before Christ, and it is interesting to note how closely his views on this matter resembled those of Muḥammad Alî, twenty-four centuries later! The gifts which Nåstasenen made to Ȧmen were on a large scale, a fact which proves that he was merely the instrument of the priesthood of Napata, and his frequent laudations of Ȧmen suggest that he was a narrow-minded and fanatical adherent of this god, and remind us of the frequent references to the mercy and power of Allah with which the Mahdî and Khalîfa interspersed their edicts and proclamations. He was prudent in his benefactions, and the restoration, at his own expense, of the temple property which had been stolen from Ȧmen Pa-Qem-Ȧten and from the goddess Bast of Thert, in the Fourth Cataract, was clearly due to motives which were less religious than political.

The inscription of Nåstasenen is a most interesting document, for it illustrates the system of conquest which was followed by a king who was probably an usurper, and of pure Sûdânî origin. Linguistically it is of the first importance, as may be seen from the excellent monograph which Dr. Schaefer has devoted to it. As a genuine Sûdânî historical composition its value is very high, and a rendering of it in full is therefore given here.

Inscription of Nastasenen.

The ninth day of the first month of the season Pert, in the eighth year under Horus, the Mighty Bull, beloved of the company of the gods, who hath risen in Nepita, lord of the shrine of Nekhebet, lord of the shrine of Uatchet,[1] the son of Rā, (Nåstasenen), Horus, the Bull who trampleth those who rebel against him beneath his sandals, the great and tearing Lion, who stablisheth all the two lands, the son of Åmen, whose thighs are great, who maketh broad every part of the two lands, the son of the gods, the most mighty one who is . . . . . adored by all the two lands and the gods, who comprehendeth all knowledge like Thoth, who marcheth with long steps, who buildeth the house (?) of all the two lands like unto the god Pet (Ptaḥ ?), who provideth the means of living for every one like unto Åmen, the son of Isis, the most mighty one, whose birth the gods decided to bring about, the protector of the two lands, the son of Rā (Nåstasenen), the son of Åmen, who hath been proclaimed blessed in heaven.

I would have you to know that the king of the South and North, (Ānkh-ka-Rā), the son of Rā, the lord of the two lands, (Nåstasenen), who liveth for ever, speaketh, saying: When I was a good boy in the city of Beruat (Meroë), Åmen of Napata, my good Father, called to me, saying, "Come." Then I cried unto the members of the royal family throughout all the city of Beruat, and I said unto them, "Arise ye, and come with "me and let us search out for us a judge for our . . . . ." And they said, "We will not go with thee. Thou art his good child, "and Åmen of Napata, thy good Father, loveth thee."

At dawn on the following day I set out on my journey, and I arrived at the city of Åsṭersat,[2] and I slept there, for there was my home (?). And I heard those who were journeying from Napata say: "He is in the city (?) of all lands." I set out on the morning of the second day, and I arrived at Ta-ḥeḥet (?), which is the great lion, the vineyard wherein king (P-ānkhi-Åluru), grew. And as my hand was stretched out (?) straightway to benefit (?) and to . . . . . the temple of Åmen, there came unto me all the men from the temple of Åmen of Napata and from the

[1] Or, "lord of the vulture crown, lord of the uraeus crown."

[2] 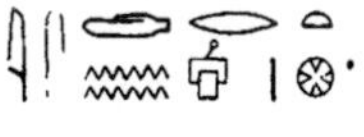

towns, and they were all great (i.e., rich) men, and they spake unto me, saying, "Åmen of Napata, thy good Father, hath set "before thee the sovereignty of the Land [of Kenset]." And all the men said: "When will he land?" Then I spake unto them, saying, "Get you down the river, and I entreat you to make an "agreement with my good Father, Åmen of Napata, on my behalf; "get you gone, and prostrate ye yourselves before Åmen of "Napata."

Then I set out and went down to the quay, and crossed over the river to the House of Rā, and I mounted a large horse and arrived at the Great House. And all the great men and the servants of the god Åmen prostrated themselves before me, and every mouth declared my praises. And I went up and opened the great doors, and I performed the ceremonies which it was my duty to perform, and the good nobles [brought me] to the Golden Apt (or, Golden Temple). I told Amen of Napata, my good Father, everything which was in my heart, and Åmen of Napata hearkened unto [the words of] my mouth. And Åmen of Napata, my good Father, gave unto me the sovereignty of Ta-Kenset, and the crown of king (Ḥeru-sa-âtef), and the strength of king (P-ânkhi-Åluru).

And on the last day of the third month of the season Shat, I made my good Father, Åmen of Napata, to rise, and he came forth from the Great House, and he made me to be king over Ta-Kenset, and Ålut,[1] and the Nine Tribes who fight with bows, and the country on both sides of the river, and the Four Quarters of the world. Then I spake my fair words unto Rā, and unto Amen of Napata I spake, saying: "It is thou thyself who hast wrought "this thing for me, and all lands and all people have heard "concerning it. Thou didst call me from the city of Beruat "(Meroë), and I have come doing thy bidding, and thou hast laid "before me the sovereignty of Ta-Kenset. It was not men who "made me king on that twenty-fourth day, whereon thou didst "give unto me the sovereignty [of Ta-Kenset]." And there were men of power and men who were destitute, of every kind on the road.[2] And I danced with joy before Rā, and I came to the places where sacrifices were made, and I took two oxen and slew them, and I went up and sat upon the Golden Throne, in the Golden Åpt, in the shade, on this day. And all men spake, saying: "He shall make all things to prosper, Åmen of Napata "hath given unto him the sovereignty, with life, strength, and

[1] , i.e., Alwah, the capital of which was Sôba. This city was situated on the right bank of the Blue Nile, about ten miles above Kharṭûm.

[2] I.e., the wealthy and the poor, or, gentle and simple, were there.

"health, over Ta-Kenset. The son of Rā (Nȧstasenen). "hath gone up and taken his seat on the Golden Throne in the "shade on this day. He shall reign as king, and shall sit and "abide in Beruat."

On the twelfth day of the first month of the season Sha, I set out and went down the river to Ȧmen of Pa-Qem,[1] my good Father, and I caused Ȧmen of Pa-Qem to rise and to come forth from the Great House, and I spake my fair words with him [and] with Rā. And he gave unto me the sovereignty of Ta-Kenset, and of the country on each side of the river, and of the Nine Peoples who fight with the bow, and his own mighty bow. And he said unto me the same words which Ȧmen of Napata, my gracious Father, had said unto me, and I went up and took my seat upon the Golden Throne.

Then I went to Ȧmen of Pa-Nebes,[2] my good Father, and he came from the Great House and gave unto me the sovereignty of Ta-Kenset, and his own leather-covered club (?), and I spake the fair words which I had to say to Rā, and I went up and sat upon the Golden Throne.

Then I came up [the river] to Ȧmen of Napata, my good Father. And on the nineteenth day of the second month of the season of Pert, I caused Ȧmen of Napata to rise, and he came forth from the Great House. And I spake fair words[3] to Rā, and I repeated to him all the favourable words which Ȧmen of Pa-Qem, and Ȧmen of Pa-Nebes, and all the gods had spoken unto me. And I danced with joy. Then I came to the places where sacrifices were made, and I took two oxen and slew them. And I went down into the *tchaut* chamber, and I lay down therein for four nights, and for four days I performed . . . . of every kind. Then I went up out of the chamber and came to the place where sacrifices were made, and I took two oxen and slew them, and then I went into the temple, and I seated myself upon the throne which is in the house of the Golden Garden (?).

On the twenty-fourth day of the month I went up to Bast, who dwelleth in Hert,[4] my good Mother, and she gave me life, and great age, and happiness, and her left breast, placing me in her bosom of beautiful life, and she gave unto me her strong club (?).

Then I came [back] to Napata, and on the twenty-ninth day I caused to rise Ȧmen of Napata, and he gave unto me all the

[1] A place which was probably situated near Suwârda.

[2] The Πνουψ of Ptolemy, to the south of Wâdî Ḥalfa.

[3] I.e., words of an auspicious character.

[4] A town two or three days' journey above Napata. It was probably situated near the modern town of Berti, about half-way between Merawî and Abû Ḥamed.

heavens, and all the lands, and all the rivers, and all peoples. And I went up and seated myself upon the Golden Throne.

And I dedicated unto thee four gardens, O Ȧmen of Napata, in the city of Napata, whereto were attached thirty-six men. And I gave unto thee three large copper *kalulu* vessels full of incense, and four large *kalulu* vessels full of honey, and three [packets] of *ānti* spice; one figure of Ȧmen of Pa-qem-Ȧten, of gold, and two figures of Horus [weighing in all] three *ṭeben*; three silver *mesṭi* vessels, three *katcha* vessels of silver, and seven *ȧpet* vessels of silver, making in all thirteen vessels, and [weighing] 134 *ṭeben*; two large copper bowls, thirteen copper skimming pans for milk, two copper vessels for beer, six copper buckets (?), twelve copper *kas* vessels, and six copper *mesṭi* vessels.

And on the last day of the first month of the season Shemu I dedicated unto thee, Ȧmen in Ȧpt, two young oxen and two full grown, in all four oxen, two heifers and two full grown, in all four cows; one young ox (?) and one full grown, in all two oxen; . . . . . sixteen *khirurteba* vessels in copper, two *tekht* vessels in copper, ten *reb* vessels in copper, two *bāṭcha* vessels in copper, two *ȧpet* vessels in copper.

The chief Kambasuṭen came, and I made my bowmen to advance against him from the city Tchart. There was a great defeat (*or* slaughter); [I captured] all his weapons (?), and I made myself master of all the boats of his captains, and I routed and overthrew him. I seized all his lands, and all his oxen, cows, calves, and animals of every kind, and everything whereon men live, from the city of Karṭept to the city of Taruṭi-peḥt . . . . . . I gave to the city of Tarumen twelve sacred bulls of those which were [given] to Ȧmen of Napata, and they were brought down from Napata.

On the twenty-sixth day of the fourth month of the season Shat, on the birthday of the son of Rā (Nȧstasenen), I gave to the city of Saksakṭit six bulls of the property of Ȧmen of Napata, my good Father, and they came down the river from Napata. On the last day of the fourth month of the season Sha, which is the day whereon the crown was given to the son of Rā (Nastasenen), I dedicated to thee, O Ȧmen of Napata, twelve breast-plates (or pectorals), and the crops (?) and green herbs (?) from the city of Karṭept to Tarreqet. I dedicated to thee, O Ȧmen of Napata, my good Father, a lamp in Taqtetet, and of the spoil which I captured I brought to thee three hundred oxen, and three hundred cows and calves, and two hundred men. O Ȧmen of Napata, thy

[1] Here follows a sentence of which it is difficult to make connected sense. The latest published rendering is by Dr. Schaefer (*op. cit.*, p. 121), who translates, "Ich überliess den Würmen (?) das, worin Wunden waren, das, wovon "die Menschen leben konnten, liess ich am Leben . . . . "

two thighs and thine excellent, overwhelming might brought these things to pass. I gave thee, O Ȧmen of Napata . . . . . . one hundred and ten women.

Moreover, I caused my bowmen to set out on an expedition against the rebels of the country of Mekhenṭeqnent,[1] and I fought against them, and I inflicted great slaughter upon them, and I took prisoner their Chief Ȧikhentkat (?).[2] And I captured all the women, all the cattle, a large quantity of gold, 209,659 oxen, 505,349 cows, calves, and sheep, 2,236 women, and 322 *ȧqit*[3] of the city of Katarṭit. I left for the . . . . [to eat] whatsoever the land on both sides of the river produced for food.

I dedicated unto thee, O Ȧmen of Napata, a lamp in Katarṭit, and twelve *ȧqit.* I dedicated unto thee two massive copper lamp standards, and I set them up in the city of Uast. O Ȧmen of Napata, my good Father, I dedicated unto thee six breast-plates (or, pectorals) in the city of Katarṭit, and I opened the Temple of the Gold Bull, whose form (?) is that of Ȧmen of Napata, my good Father.

Moreover I caused my bowmen to set out on an expedition against the rebels of the land of Rebarut[4] and the land of Ȧkarkarḥent (?),[5] and I defeated them with great slaughter. I took prisoner their Chief Rebkhenṭent,[6] and [I captured] all his gold, the quantity whereof was so great that it could not be told, and 203,216 bulls and oxen, and 603,107 cows, calves and sheep, and all the women, and everything which men could eat for food. I gave the Chief to Ȧmen of Napata, my good Father. [O Ȧmen of Napata], thy thigh is mighty, and thy wisdom is good.

Moreover I caused many threatenings to go against the rebel land of Ȧrersat,[7] and I defeated [the people thereof] with great slaughter. I took prisoner Ȧbskhent (?)[8] the Chief of the country of Mashat,[9] and I captured all the women, and all the cattle, and 1,212 *teben* of gold, and 22,120 oxen and bulls, and all the women, and 55,200 cows and calves, and I gave the Chief and all his property to Ȧmen of Napata, my good Father. [O Ȧmen of Napata], thy name is great and good, and thy overwhelming power is good.

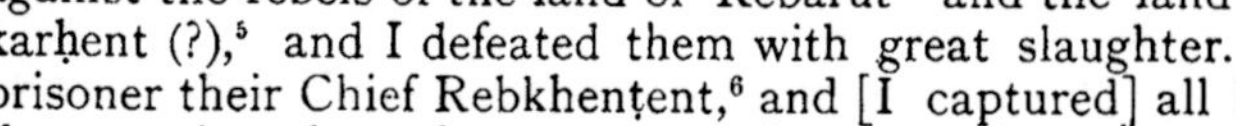

[3] Objects made of one of the precious metals, gold or silver? Perhaps figures of sacred animals or gods.

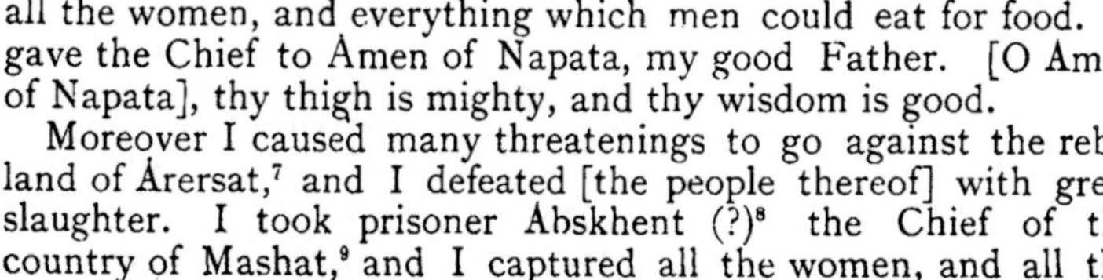

Moreover I made my bowmen set out on an expedition against the rebel land of Mekhsherkherthet,[1] and I defeated the people thereof with great slaughter. I took the Chief thereof prisoner, and captured all the food of man in the country, and all the women. And I seized for my own share 203,146 oxen and bulls, and 33,050 cows, calves and sheep. O Åmen of Napata, my good Father, thy thigh is strong, and thy name is great and beautiful.

Moreover I made very many threatenings to go forth against the rebel country of Maikhentkat (?),[2] and the rebels attacked me at the sycamore tree of Sarsart;[3] I did battle with them there, and I defeated them with great slaughter. I took prisoner their Chief Tamakhithet,[4] and I captured all his women, and all his cattle, and 2,000 *teben* of gold, and 35,330 oxen and bulls, and 55,526 cows, calves and sheep, and everything which men eat for food Åmen of Napata, my good Father, hath given unto me all lands, his thigh is mighty, his power is good, his name is great and beautiful, like the heavens. Åmen of Napata, my good Father, hath done [these things for me].

Moreover, certain things which had been dedicated as votive offerings to the temple of Pa-Qem Åten by the King, life, strength, health! (Aspelta), had been carried off (i.e., stolen). Thereupon many urgent appeals went forth to the finest of my soldiers [for the restoration of the property which had been dedicated by the King, life, strength, health! (Aspelta)], and for the punishment of the enemy who belonged to the Meṭi country, [but the property could not be recovered]. Then they took some of my own treasure to replace it. It was Åmen of Napata, my good Father, who gave it to me, and I gave it [back] to Amen of Pa-Qem-Åten, my good Father. Then Åmen of Pa-Qem-Aten, my good Father, said unto me: "I give thee my bow, wherein are strength "and might, and I will make all thine enemies to be prisoners "beneath thy sandals."

And moreover, the enemies in the Meṭit country[5] stole some of the treasure which belonged to the goddess Bast, of the city of Thert,[6] which had been dedicated by king (Aspelta). Then there came some of my own treasure which I dedicated to the goddess Bast, who dwelleth in the city of Thert, my good Mother. And she gave unto me a great and beautiful flower-shaped sceptre,

a good long life extending into an advanced old age, and her might, and she said unto me: "This shall be thy protection, and thy renewing of power (?)" Ȧmen of Napata, my good Father, made [the treasure] for me, he made my wealth abundant (*or* good), his thigh is strong.

Verily, O Ȧmen of Napata, my good Father, the things which thou utterest with thy mouth cannot come to nought; and verily, when thou closest thy mouth no man hath the wherewithal to feed himself beneath the heavens.

NATIVE BOATS ON THE NILE NEAR AD-DÂMAR.

CHAPTER VIII.

THE SÛDÂN IN THE PTOLEMAÏC PERIOD.

NÂSTASENEN died B.C. 517, i.e., about the time when Darius the Great came to Egypt, and nothing is known about his successor. We may assume that at his death the throne reverted to some descendant of the legitimate kings of Napata, who probably took up his abode there, and appointed a governor to rule over the Island of Meroë. From Egypt the kingdom of Napata had nothing to fear, for Darius was wholly occupied in developing her resources, and rendering the country prosperous. He honoured the Egyptian gods, and studied the religious works which treated of them, and finally he came to be regarded as the sixth of the great lawgivers which the country had produced. Egypt, with Libya, Cyrene, and Barce, formed the sixth of the twenty satrapies into which he divided his kingdom, and it paid to him seven hundred talents of gold as its annual tribute, besides a heavy tax on the fisheries of Lake Moeris, and sufficient corn for the maintenance of 120,000 men at Memphis. The gold which the Egyptians paid to Darius came no doubt from the mines in the Eastern Desert, i.e., from Wâdî 'Ulâḳî, where it was probably obtained by an arrangement made with the Nubians who lived south of Aswân. As a result of the peaceful policy pursued by Darius, trade caravans were enabled to travel in safety from the Sûdân to Egypt, and their owners did a thriving business in slaves, gold, ivory, ebony, &c. The Persians were fond of describing Darius as a "huckster," saying that "he looked to making a gain in everything," [2] and it was not long before he perceived the advantages which accrued to the Nubians from his rule.

[1] Herodotus, iii. 91.

[2] *Ibid.*, 89.

He then, according to Herodotus, made the "Ethiopians" bordering upon Egypt, who were reduced by Cambyses when he made war on the long-lived Ethiopians, and the Calantian Indians, bring every third year two schoenices of virgin gold, two hundred logs of ebony, five Ethiopian boys, and twenty elephant tusks. Herodotus adds that these gifts were paid to the Persians down to his own time. A little consideration shows us, however, that the "Ethiopians" who sent these gifts were probably those who lived between Philae and Korosko, or Derr; in other words, they belonged to that portion of Northern Nubia which the Egyptians had for centuries regarded as a portion of their Empire. If they were not, they must have been the chiefs of caravans who gave a fixed quantity of gold, &c., to the Government officials of the chief towns on their route for the privilege of bringing their wares into the markets. One hundred years ago the governor of Asyût who levied heavy tax upon the caravans from Dâr Fûr and Kordôfân might, in the same way as Darius, have claimed the overlordship of these countries, because he made the merchants who traded in products from them pay import duties. The Persians had never any authority over the Nile Valley south of Wâdî Ḥalfa, and it is doubtful if the Island of Meroë was to them any more than a name.

The information about the Sûdân collected by Herodotus is, on the whole, very good. He first says (ii. 29) that beyond Elephantine the land rises, and that it is necessary to tie a rope to the boat on each side; if the rope snaps, the vessel is borne down stream by the force of the current. After four days, the distance travelled is, he says, twelve schoenes, and then a plain is reached, and also the Island of Tachompsos, round which the Nile flows in two branches. Half this island is occupied by the "Ethiopians," who live south of Elephantine, and the other half by Egyptians. Beyond the Island is a lake, on the shores of which live nomad "Ethiopians," and when this is passed, the Nile is again reached. Here the traveller lands, and he must journey along the banks of the river for forty days, since it is impossible to proceed further in a boat on account of the sharp rocks which jut out from the water, and the sunken rocks which abound in that

[1] Herodotus, iii. 97.

part of the stream. At the end of this time he takes boat again, and after twelve days more arrives at a great city called Meroë, "which is said to be the capital of the other 'Ethiopians.'" The only gods worshipped by the inhabitants are Jupiter (i.e., Ȧmen-Rā), and Bacchus (i.e., Osiris), to whom great honours are paid. There is an oracle of Jupiter in the city, which directs the warlike expeditions of the "Ethiopians"; [1] when it commands they go to war, and in whichever direction it bids them march, thither straightway they carry their arms. Going onward, after the same number of days which it took the traveller to reach Meroë from Elephantine, the traveller reaches the "Automoli," or "Asmakh" (see above, p. 54), who are the descendants of the Egyptians of the warrior caste, who went over to the "Ethiopians" in the reign of Psammetichus (I.), to the number of two hundred and forty thousand men, because they had not been relieved of their garrison duty for three years. From this statement it is clear that Herodotus placed the "Automoli," or "Deserters" (the "Sembritae" of Strabo) in a country on the White Nile four months' journey south of Elephantine, i.e., some hundreds of miles south of Kharṭûm, and he, no doubt, refers to the tribes who were not negroes, and whose skins were not black, that lived in and about the modern kingdom of Sennaar. His statement about the river flowing from west to east is to me inexplicable, but when he goes on to say that beyond this point "no one has any "knowledge of its source, since the country is uninhabited by "reason of the excessive heat," it seems that he must be alluding to the swamps about the Bahr al Ghazâl.

The information which the Ichthyophagi brought back to Cambyses has already been described (see above, p. 90), and we may pass on therefore to the statement of Herodotus (ii. 104) about circumcision. He says that the Colchians, Egyptians, and "Ethiopians" are the only nations who have practised circumcision from the earliest times, but he could not make out whether the "Ethiopians" learned the practice from the Egyptians, or the Egyptians from the "Ethiopians." In any case, he says, it is undoubtedly of very ancient date in

[1] A proof of this statement is found in the Stele of Nȧstasenen, wherein it is said that this king asked Ȧmen if he should go on a certain war, or not.

"Ethiopia." As to the clothing of the "Ethiopians" he says (vii. 69) that they wore skins of leopards and lions, and that they were armed with palm-stem bows, four cubits long; the arrows were short and tipped, not with iron, but with a stone. Their spears were tipped with the horns of antelopes, and they had knotted clubs. When they went into battle they painted their bodies half with chalk and half with vermilion. The monuments prove the truth of all these statements except the last, and if we had reliefs with coloured battle scenes upon them, we should probably find it to be true also. Herodotus divided (vii. 70) the "Ethiopians" into two classes, "Eastern," and "Western," the

SÛDÂN ELEPHANT.

[From Lepsius, *Denkmäler*, Abth. V. Bl. 75.

languages and hair of each being different; the former had straight hair, and the latter woolly hair.

From this we see that Herodotus calls the negro tribes to the west of the White Nile "Western Ethiopians," and the light or red-skinned tribes of the Eastern Desert and Blue Nile "Eastern Ethiopians." He adds the interesting information that the "Eastern Ethiopians" wore upon their heads the scalps of horses, with the ears and mane attached; the ears were made to stand upright, and the mane served as a crest. For shields this people made use of the skins of cranes. Finally, he says (iii. 114), where the south declines towards the setting sun, lies the country called Ethiopia, the last inhabited land in that direction. There gold is obtained in great plenty, huge elephants abound, and wild trees of all sorts, and ebony; and the men are taller, handsomer, and longer-lived than anywhere else. Herodotus here undoubtedly refers to the countries on the Blue Nile, and his information as to their products is correct.

From B.C. 517 to the beginning of the Ptolemaïc Period nothing is known of the Sûdân either from native or Egyptian sources, and even the world-conqueror, Alexander the Great, left that country uninvaded. Greek writers of historical romances about Alexander and his exploits, e.g., Pseudo-Callisthenes, were obliged to make their hero master of every country in the known world, and thus we find in their works impossible narratives of his travels into China and the remotest regions of India. Pseudo-Callisthenes in his book (iii. 18) introduces an account of a fabulous visit of Alexander to Queen Candace, who is described as a descendant of Semiramis, and declared to have possessed wondrous beauty. To her Alexander is made to write a letter in which, after referring to the graves and houses in her land, and her worship of the god Åmen, he invited her to meet him at the boundary of her territory so that they might worship Åmen together. To this "Candace, Queen of Meroë," replied that Åmen, by means of an oracle, has forbidden his image to be moved, that no one is to enter her country, and if he does he will be treated as an enemy. Alexander is not to think scorn because her people are dark-coloured, for they are whiter in soul than the white folk who are with him. Her tribes are eighty in number, and they are ready to punish any who attack them. She approves of his worship of Åmen, and she sends him by her ambassadors 100 large bars of gold, 500 Ethiopian maidens, 200 parrots, 200 sphinxes, and for Åmen on the borders of Egypt, a crown set with emeralds and unpierced pearls, and 10 string pearls, and 80 ivory boxes. Besides these things she gave him 308 elephants, 300 leopards, 13 rhinoceroses, 4 panthers, 300 man-eating dogs, 300 fighting bulls, 6 elephants' tusks, 300 panther-skins, and 1500 ebony rods, and told him to send men to fetch them away. The adventures of Alexander in the country of Candace do not concern us here, and for further information about them Müller's excellent edition of the Greek text of Pseudo-Callisthenes may be consulted. The writer of the story given above was ignorant of the exact position of Candace's kingdom, but the alleged visit to the queen by Alexander was capable of treatment which he knew would appeal to his readers, and historical accuracy was therefore disregarded by him.

Under the Ptolemies an attempt seems to have been made to bring the Sûdân and Egypt into relations which should be closer than those existing as a result of the passage to and fro of trading caravans. Ptolemy I. made no expedition into Nubia, but it seems that the terror of his arms was carried into surrounding countries by Eumachus. This general inflicted a great defeat on the Numidians, and then, Diodorus says (xx 58 ff.) he made an expedition into "higher Africa." He passed over a high mountain two hundred stadia in length, which was full of cats. He next entered a country abounding in apes, and came to three cities called Pithecussae; here the apes lived in the houses and were worshipped as gods by the natives, and children were called after their names. Eumachus took one of the three cities by storm, and razed it to the ground, and the other two capitulated. He went no further, however, for, hearing that the barbarians were gathering preparatory to coming against him in a large body, he retreated to the sea. It is impossible to identify the region to which Eumachus marched, but it was situated, clearly, in some portion of the Sûdân where apes abounded.

Ptolemy II. (B.C. 283-247) was on friendly terms with Ergamenes the king of Nubia, who, according to Diodorus (iii. 6), had been bred up in the Grecian discipline and philosophy;[1] whether this Ergamenes is the same as the Arq-Ȧmen who was a contemporary of Ptolemy IV. and Ptolemy V. is somewhat uncertain. The friend of Ptolemy II. set a precedent in the history of his country which is noteworthy. Diodorus tells us that the priests at Meroë, i.e., the priests of Ȧmen, who held the greatest possible power, had been, up to that time, accustomed to send whensoever they pleased a messenger to the king commanding him to put himself to death. They supported such commands with the statement that they were the will of the gods, and that it was unlawful to disregard them. The kings of Napata, who always held their authority from the priests, usually obeyed the orders of the priests, and so killed themselves, believing that

[1] μετεσχηκὼς Ἑλληνικῆς ἀγωγῆς καὶ φιλοσοφήσας.

they were performing a religious act. When, however, the order to commit suicide reached Ergamenes, instead of obeying he plucked up the spirit and courage which befitted a king, and collecting a considerable number of soldiers, he marched to the golden temple of the Ethiopians, and cut the throats of all the priests, and so put an end to a barbarous, though very ancient custom. The "golden temple" referred to is no doubt the Pa-nub, , wherein was the Golden Throne on which the king took his seat "in the shade" after his coronation; in the time of Nåstasenen (B.C. 525-517) this golden temple was at Napata, but when the capital was removed to Meroë another may have been built there. Diodorus says that the place where it was situated was "very difficult to reach," but Ergamenes built a temple at Dakka, and must therefore have lived near Egypt. When we remember the great development of trade which took place under the encouragement of Ptolemy II., it seems most probable that this astute ruler found it cheaper to conquer Northern Nubia by means of merchants and their caravans than by military expeditions.

His aim was, of course, to obtain possession of the gold mines in the Wâdî 'Ulâkî, and to effect this it was only necessary for him to be master of the Nile Valley so far as Dakka. Between Dakka and 'Amâra, about one hundred and thirty miles south of Wâdî Ḥalfa, the country was at that time a sort of No-man's-land. The portion of the Nile Valley in Nubia specially claimed by the Ptolemies was called by the Greeks "Dodekaschoinos,"[1] because it contained Twelve Schoinoi,[2] or one hundred and twenty stadia; it probably represented some ancient division of the country made in very early times. Originally the Dodekaschoinos represented the tract of land which the kings of Egypt set apart for the maintenance of the temples on the Island of Philae. It is difficult to state exactly the extent of this tract of land, but its length was probably between ninety and one hundred miles.

[1] See Ptolemy iv. 5, § 74; Herodotus ii. 29; and Sethe, *Dodekaschoinos*, Leipzig, 1901.

[2] In Egyptian .

The principal towns in it were: PAREMBOLE, the modern Dâbûd; TAPHIS, with CONTRA TAPHIS, the modern Tâfa; TALMIS, with CONTRA-TALMIS, the modern Kalâbsha; TUTZIS, the modern Garf Ḥusên; PSELCIS, the modern Dakka; CONTRA-PSELCIS, the modern Ḳubbân; TACHOMPSO, the modern Ḳûrta; HIERA-SYKAMINOS, the modern Mîḥarraḳa. The last-named town marked the southern limit of the DODEKASCHOINOS.[1]

As already said, Ptolemy II. made one expedition into the Sûdân by the route which had been followed by the kings of Egypt for centuries, but he took steps to develop the trade between Egypt and the seaports nearest the South Sûdân. From the "Stele of Pithom," which was discovered by Prof. Naville[2] in 1884, we learn that Ptolemy sent a fleet of ships to the southern land of Khemthithet,[3] and to the "borders of the land of the Blacks,"[4] and that his general brought back the things which were "beloved of the king and royal wife Arsinoe." He also tapped the supplies of the Eastern Desert by founding the city of Ptolemaïs Epithêras, which cannot have been far from the modern Sawâkin. From the country to the south of this city his officers brought large numbers of elephants which were shipped to Egypt, and the writer of the text is no doubt correct in saying that "the like of this was never before done for any "king in all the earth" In the last line on the stele Ptolemy is said to have Egypt in his grasp, and all the southern lands bow

[1] The district between the southern end of the Island of Meroë and Philae was divided into thirteen portions, thus: 1. PEḤQENNES. 2. MÂRAUAT (MEROË). 3. NÂPT (NAPATA). 4. PETEN-ḤERT. 5. PA-NEBES. 6. TA-UATCHET. 7 BEHENT (Wâdî Halfa). 8. ÂTEFTHIT. 9. NEHÂU. 10. MEHIT. 11. MAÂT. 12. BAKET. 13. HET-KHENT.

[2] See *The Store-city of Pithom*, London, 1885; and Brugsch, *Aeg. Zeit.*, 1894, p. 74.

[3]

[4]

before his souls, and all the nine nations who fight with bows are beneath his sandals.

Ptolemy IV. ascended the throne of Egypt B.C. 222, and died B.C. 205. During the last few years of his reign he sent expeditions into the Sûdân to hunt elephants, which were used in the army; these expeditions marched inland from ports on the Red Sea. An inscription mentioning Charimortos, a strategos of the elephant hunts in the reign of Ptolemy IV., is in the British Museum.[1] Among the building operations which he carried out must be mentioned the addition he made to the temple built at Dakka by Ȧrq-Ȧmen, king of Nubia. We have already seen that Diodorus speaks of a Nubian king called Ergamenes, i.e., Ȧrq-Ȧmen, who lived in the reign of Philadelphus, and had received a Greek education, but it is doubtful if the builder of the temple of Dakka is the same king as the friend of Ptolemy II.

It is quite possible that he was, for the Ergamenes of Diodorus may well have lived through the last few years of the life of Ptolemy II., and the whole of the reigns of Ptolemy III. and Ptolemy IV., and still have been at the death of Ptolemy IV. under seventy years of age. Arq-Ȧmen, the contemporary of Ptolemy IV., adopted the prenomen of "Ṭet-ānkh-Ȧmen tȧa-[en]-Rā,"[2] and called himself "Son of Rā," and the "ever-living, "beloved of Isis."[3] The temple of Ȧrq-Ȧmen at Dakka consists of a small building about twenty feet square, with an opening in the east wall leading to the sanctuary, and another in the west wall leading to a flight of steps.

In the inscriptions on the walls he calls himself the son of Osiris and Isis, the son of Khnemu and Sati, beloved of Ȧmen, Osiris, Isis, Ȧr-ḥes-nefer, and Thoth.[4] Ptolemy IV. built a chapel in front of this, with doors in the east and west walls, and Ptolemy IX. built the pro-naos, and the other portions of the temple as it now stands were built by a Roman emperor, probably

[1] See H. R. Hall, in the *Classical Review*, vol. xii., 1898, p. 274.

[2] I.e., "Living hand of Ȧmen, emanation of Rā" 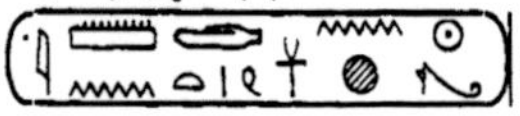.

[3] 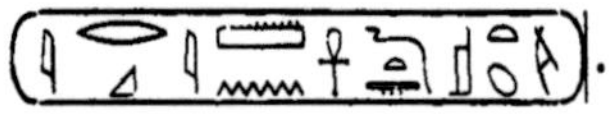.

[4] See Lepsius, *Denkmäler*, Abth. v., Bl. 17.

Augustus or Tiberius. The temple is dedicated to Thoth, and is oriented due south. Of the reign of Arq-Ȧmen nothing is known. His successor was, according to some, Ȧtchakhar-Ȧmen, "the ever-living, the beloved of Isis,"[1] who adopted the prenomen "Taa-en-Ȧmen-setep-en-neteru,"[2] and called himself "Son of Rā, lord of the two lands, lord of crowns." This king's name is found in a dedicatory inscription[3] on the temple of Dâbûd, which is close to the site of the ancient city of Parembole, a few miles south of Philae, but nowhere else in the country. Several of the Ptolemies who followed Ptolemy IV. restored and added to the temples built by their predecessors, but they limited their labours in Nubia to the district between Wâdî Ḥalfa and Abû Simbel; in fact, they carried on very little building work south of Dakka, the nearest point on the Nile to the gold mines of Wâdî 'Ulâkî. It is safe to assume that trade went on uninterruptedly between the Sûdân and Egypt, and that, speaking generally, trading caravans passing between the south and north had little to fear except the attacks of the ordinary highway robber, and the extortionate demands made by the local governors of the cities to which they brought their goods to market.

1 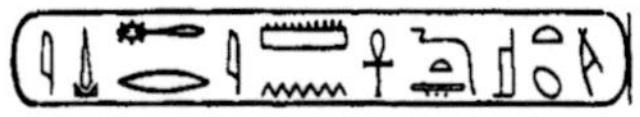. 2 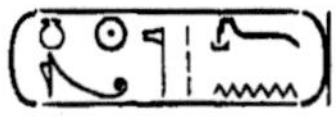.

3 See Lepsius, *Denkmäler*, Abth. v., Bl. 18.

CHAPTER IX.

THE NUBIAN KINGDOM ON THE ISLAND OF MEROË.

IN preceding chapters descriptions have been given of the reigns of the principal kings of the country of the Sûdân between B.C. 750 and B.C. 517, and the names of several kings who cannot be placed at present in strict chronological order have been mentioned. For a period of about three centuries after the death of Nastasenen, i.e., from B.C. 517 to about B.C. 200, nothing is known of Sûdân history, and whether the capital of the Meroïtic kingdom was still at Napata, or in the Island of Meroë during that period cannot be said. The descendants or kinsfolk of Nȧstasenen would probably continue to rule for some time after his death, but unless there were among them capable and warlike kings, it is unlikely that they were able to maintain their capital at Meroë, where they were at all times open to attack by combinations of desert tribes on the north, east, and south. The probabilities are that for some time between B.C. 500 and B.C. 200 the kings of the Meroïtic kingdom resided at Napata, or even further north. In any case they cannot have possessed much power, or we should have heard of their exploits and found some of their monuments. The first evidences we have of the recrudescence of the power of the Nubian kingdom is the temple which Ȧrq-Ȧmen (Ergamenes) and Ȧtchakhar-Ȧmen built in the Dodekaschoinos, the former at Dakka (Pselcis), and the latter at Dâbûd (Parembole). No other purely Sûdânî kings built temples so far to the north, and it is clear that they would not have done so unless the central seat of their power were sufficiently near to enable them to protect such buildings. It is, moreover, clear that they must have possessed material as well as spiritual interests in the region wherein they set up their temples, and that their power must have been sufficiently great to compel the Ptolemies who were their contemporaries to permit them to build temples so close to Egyptian frontier.

Whether we accept the statement of Diodorus that Årq-Amen was a contemporary of Ptolemy II., or that of recent writers, who say that he lived in the time of Ptolemy IV., it is certain that in the reign of the latter king he was the king of Nubia, and that he was master of the Dodekaschoinos. This was due, not to any special efforts made by the Nubians, but to the fact that towards the close of the reign of Ptolemy IV. (he died B.C. 205) the rebellion of the soldiers in Upper Egypt, which had been going on for many years, assumed such serious proportions that all Government administration in Upper Egypt ceased to exist. This rebellion continued in full force until the nineteenth year of the reign of Ptolemy V. (B.C. 186), and it was only suppressed then by great exertions on the part of the Government, and by an awful sacrifice of life. Whilst the rebellion was in progress, the Thebans appointed kings to reign over them, paying not the least regard to Ptolemy V., who passed the early years of his reign in the north; two of these kings bore the names of Ḥeru-khuti, and Ȧnkh-em-khu. Meanwhile Årq-Amen seized the opportunity which events in Egypt gave him, and declared himself to be the "King of the South and North," 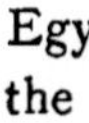, i.e., of all Egypt. His rule appears to have lasted about twenty-five years, and we may be sure that he gave all the assistance in his power to the rebels in Upper Egypt. His successor, Åtchakhar-Åmen, with even greater boldness, built his temple at Parembole, some ten or fifteen miles only from the Egyptian frontier. When Ptolemy V. succeeded in suppressing the rebellion, he took steps to reassert his authority in the Dodekaschoinos, and he appears to have succeeded. At all events, we hear no more of Nubian "kings of the South and North" in the Ptolemaïc Period.

We have now to consider briefly the extent of the Meroïtic Kingdom between B.C. 200 and the end of the second or third century after Christ, and to enumerate the names of the kings who probably reigned during this interval, and the towns, temples, and pyramid-tombs which they left behind them. The two great centres of such power as the Meroïtic kings and the queen-mothers possessed at this time were Meroë and Napata; their largest town to the south was Sôba, on the Blue Nile, and their frontier town on the north was probably near the modern village of 'Amâra, which stands on the Nile, a few miles above Kôsha. It is important to note that the kings of pure Sûdânî stock never employed the ancient forts of the great Egyptian kings of the XIIth, XVIIIth, and XIXth Dynasties as places of defence, though it is probable that they made use of them as quarries. No stronger natural situations for fortresses than Semna and Kumma could be found in the Sûdân, yet the only Nubian king who built at either place was Taharqa, who dedicated a temple to his great predecessor Usertsen III. at Semna.

The principal sites chosen by the pure Sûdânî kings of the Meroïtic Kingdom on which to build temples are:—1. 'AMÂRA, which lies on the east bank of the Nile, about 130 miles from Wâdî Ḥalfa. 2. NAPATA, on the west bank of the Nile, 648 miles from Wâdî Ḥalfa. Down-stream of this place are the pyramid fields of Tanḳâsî, Kurru, and Zûma; up-stream is the pyramid field of Nûri, or Belal, and opposite to it is the group of pyramids at Gebel Barkal. 3. MEROË, on the east bank, 877 from Wâdî Ḥalfa by river, and 554 miles by the route across the Ḥalfa-Abû Ḥamed Desert. To the south and east of the city ruins are four pyramid fields; they lie near the villages of Sur and Maraga. 4. WAD BÂ NAGAA, twenty-four miles south of Shendî. At the eastern end of the khôr, from seventeen to twenty miles to the east, are the ruins of several temples, and about fifteen miles to the north, at Masawwarât âṣ-Ṣûfra, are also the ruins of several temples. 5. SÔBA, on the right bank of the Blue Nile, a few miles from Kharṭûm. From the ruins of the temples and pyramids at these places Lepsius collected the cartouches of several kings and several queen-mothers of the Meroïtic Kingdom, but they, of course, only represent a small proportion of the number of kings and queens who reigned between B.C. 500 and the downfall of the kingdom. It will be convenient to give these cartouches here, but no correctness is claimed for the order in which they are placed.

KINGS OF THE SUDAN

1. The Queen-Mother KATIMAR, or KATIMAL 

.[1] Her name was found at Napata.

2. ÅMEN-TAUI-KALBATH .

Her name was found at Meroë.

3. 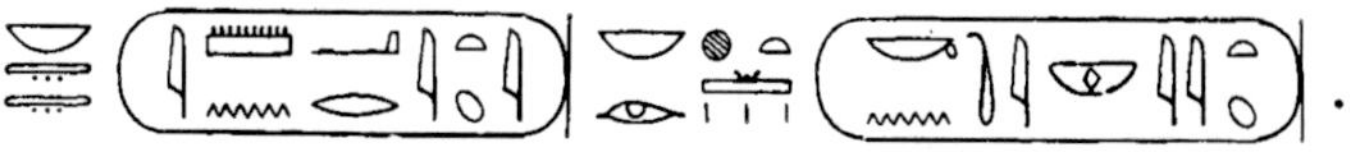.

The lady of the two lands, ÅMEN-ĀRIT, the lady, maker of things, KENTHA-ḤEBIT. Her pyramid-tomb[2] is near Meroë (Northern Group, No. 1). This name was first read "Kentakit," and was thought to be the original form of the name Candace, but it is clear that the fifth sign in the second cartouche is  *ḥeb*, not  *k*.

4. 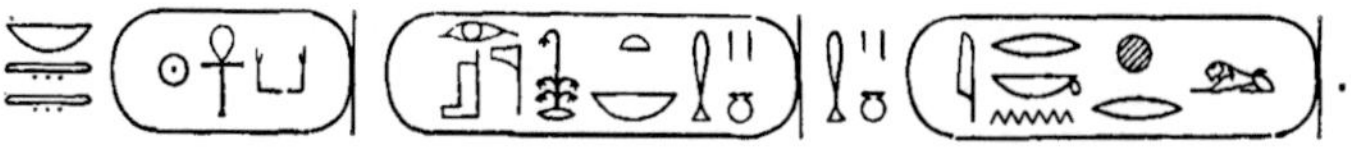.

"The lord of the two lands, ĀNKH-KA-RĀ,[3] priest of the second "order, ÅRKENKHEREL." In the second cartouche he styles himself "Priest of the second order of Osiris, the lord of the South." His pyramid-tomb is near Meroë (Northern Group, No. 5).

5. .

NEHÅRQ— . . . . NENTENI,[4] beloved of Mut. His pyramid-tomb is at Meroë.

6. 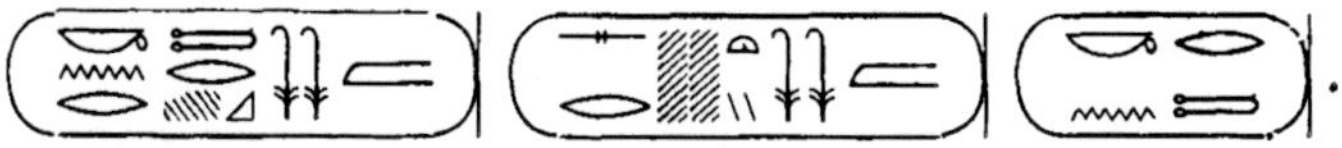.

Queen KENRETHREQNEN-M (?) SER . . . TINEN-M (?). Her pyramid-tomb[5] is near Meroë (Southern Group, No 4). The short form of the first name is KENRETH. In the inscriptions on the chapel walls two other cartouches are found, viz, PERUI, or PERU. 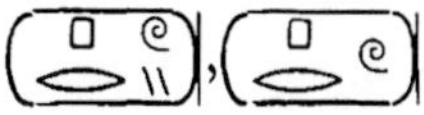, and KA-ĀAT 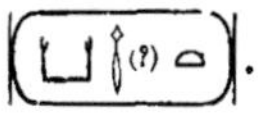.

[1] See Lepsius, *Königsbuch*, No. 939.

[2] Lepsius, *Denkmäler*, Abth. v., Bl. 47.

[3] *Ibid.*, Bl. 43.

[4] See Lepsius, *Königsbuch*, No. 945.

[5] See Lepsius, *Denkmäler*, Abth. v. Bl. 52.

7. 

KHNEM-ĀB-RĀ,[1] son of RĀ, AMEN-ÅRK-NEB (?). His pyramid-tomb is near Meroë (Southern Group, No. 6).

8. 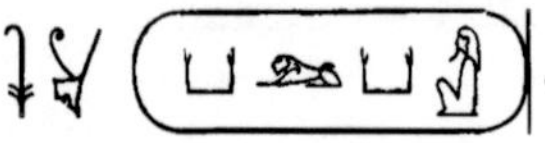

9. 

KARKA, or KALKA, and KARTERÅ, or KALTELÅ. Both these names[2] are found on a pyramid-tomb near Meroë (Southern Group, No. 10).

10. 

ÅNKH-NEFER-ÅB-RĀ, son of Rā, lord of crowns, ÅSRU,[3] Meri Åmen. His name is found on one of the two granite lions which Lord Prudhoe brought from Gebel Barkal, and presented to the British Museum (No. 34). The pyramid-tomb of this king is near Meroë (Southern Group, No. 5).

11. 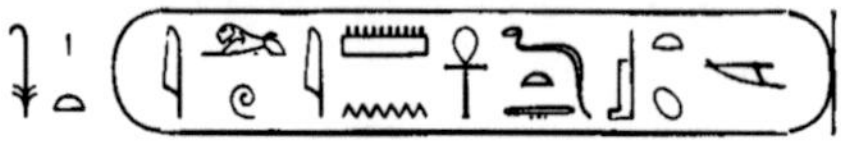

ÅRU-ÅMEN,[4] the ever-living, the beloved of Isis. He may be the Ārq-Åmen who was a contemporary of Ptolemy IV. (see above, Vol. II., p. 113), but it is unlikely. His pyramid-tomb is near Meroë (Northern Group, No. 7).

12. 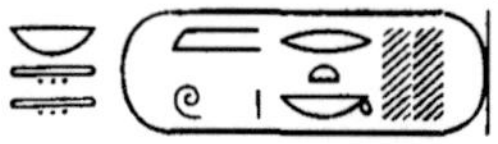

MURTEK . . . . His name is found on the walls of the chapel of No. 14.

13. 

KHEPER-KA-RĀ NETEK-ÅMEN.[5] The name of this king is found at Gebel Barkal, Wad Bâ Nagaa, and Meroë (Northern Group, No. 22).

[1] See Lepsius, *Denkmäler*, Abth. v., Bl. 55.
[2] *Ibid.*, 55.
[3] *Ibid.*, Bl. 54.
[4] *Ibid.*, Bl. 36.
[5] *Ibid.*, Bl. 25; *Königsbuch*, Nos. 963, 981.

14. 

ĀMEN. . . . . ĀKHA[1] . . . . . ab-en . . . . (Northern Group, No. 4).

15. 

ĀMEN-KHETASHEN[2] . . . . . (Northern Group, No. 18).

16. 

KHEPER-KA-RĀ[3] . . . . (Northern Group, Lepsius, No. 27).

17. 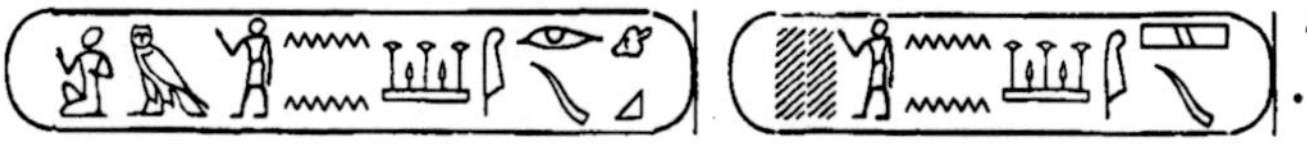 [4]

His pyramid-tomb is near Meroë (Northern Group, No. 6).

18. TIRIKANLAT (?)  [5]

His pyramid-tomb is near Meroë (Northern Group, No. 19).

19. 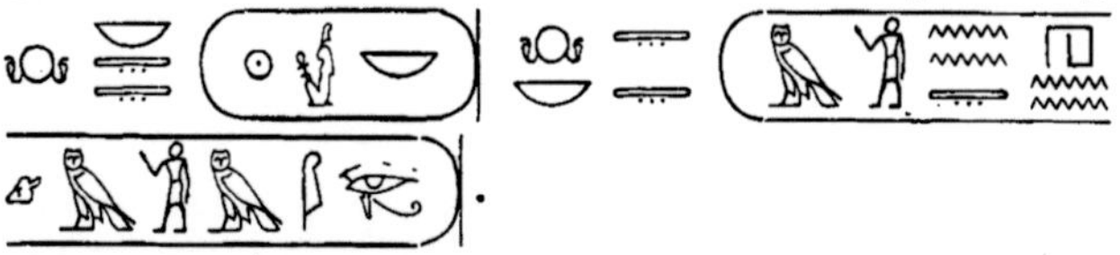

NEB-MAĀT-RĀ ĀMEN-TAHNAMAMIP (?) His pyramid-tomb is near Meroë (Northern Group, No. 17).

20. 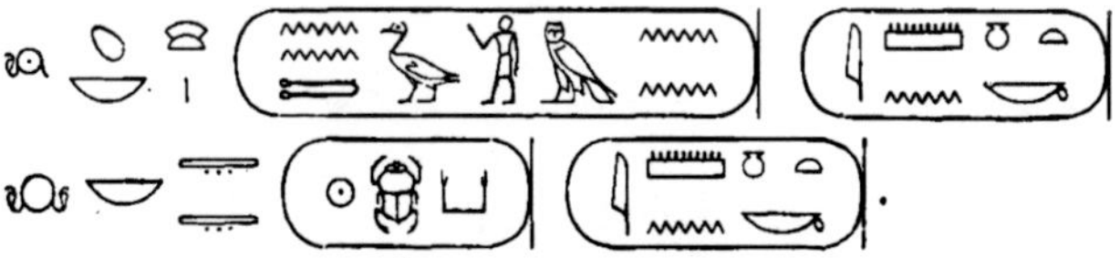

KHEPER-KA-RĀ NETEK-ĀMEN.[6] His name is found on monuments at Wad Bâ Nagaa, at Nagaa, and 'Amâra. His queen was called ĀMEN-TARI 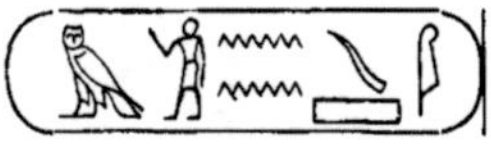 and her prenomen was 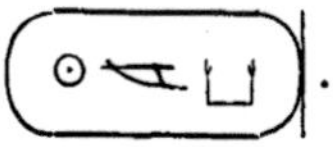. At Wad Bâ Nagaa he and his wife are associated with ARK-ATALAL (?), whose prenomen was ĀNKH-KA-RĀ, and at 'Amâra with a prince called SHARKRAR, or SHALKLAL.

[1] See Lepsius, *Denkmäler*, Abth. v. 45. [2] *Ibid.*, Bl. 51. [3] *Ibid.*, Bl. 48.
[4] *Ibid.*, Bl. 43. [5] *Ibid.*, Bl. 49. [6] *Ibid.*, Bll. 55, 57, 69.

21. 

ÅNKH-KA-RĀ ARK-ATALAL (?) His name appears at Nagaa.[1]

22. 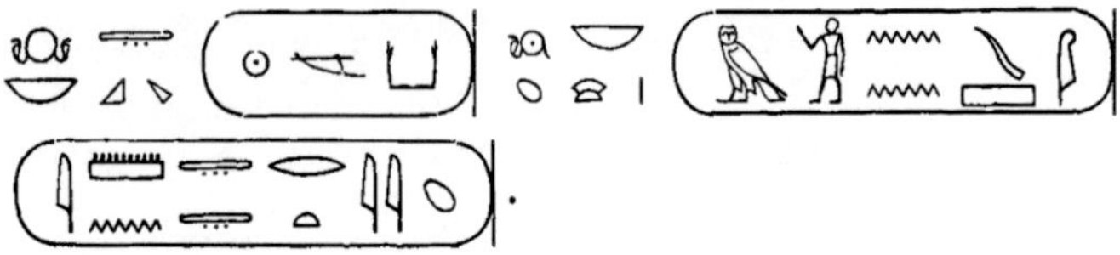

ÅMEN-TARIT[2] was the wife of Netek-Amen (No. 20), and her name is found at Wad Bâ Nagaa, Nagaa, and 'Amâra ; it is clear that during her reign building operations were carried on at all these places, and that the Meroïtic kingdom must have been in a state of great prosperity. The fact that she or her husband built a temple at 'Amâra proves that the Nubian power in the Northern Sûdân must have been great, and it is probable that this queen was the Candace who came in conflict with the Romans.

23. 

SHARKRAH, or SHALKLAL. This personage must have been a contemporary of Netek-Åmen and the queen mentioned above, for his name occurs with theirs on the pillars of the temple of 'Amâra.[3]

On temple A at Nagaa are also found the following names :—

24.  [4]

25. King  [5]

26. Queen 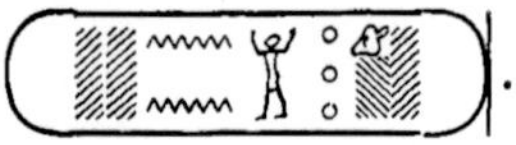

27. 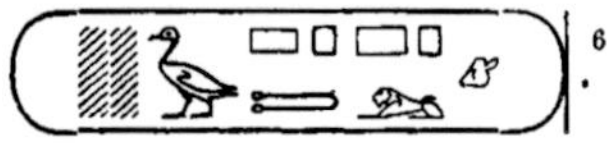 [6]

[1] Lepsius, *Denkmäler*, Bl. 66. [2] *Ibid.*, Bll. 55, 57, 69. [3] *Ibid.*, Bl. 69.
[4] *Ibid.*, Bll. 59, 60. [5] *Ibid.*, Bl. 56. [6] *Ibid.*, Bl. 62.

28. SHANKPITAH (?)  [1]

This name occurs at Nagaa, Temple F.

PORTRAIT OF THE MEROÏTIC SOVEREIGN, RĀ-MER-KA ȦMEN-TARIT.

[Drawn from Lepsius, *Denkmäler*, Abth. III. Bl. 304.

It now remains to enumerate the principal ruins in the Sûdân which belong to this period. The most northerly of these is a

[1] Lepsius, *Denkmäler*, Bl. 68.

temple at 'Amâra, on the right bank of the Nile, a few miles above Kôsha. When complete it probably consisted of two chambers, each wider than it was long, with a court containing from six to ten pillars. At the time when Lepsius had his plan made,[1] it was only possible to trace the walls of the sanctuary chamber, and only six of the columns were standing. The columns are decorated with scenes wherein a king, a queen, and a prince are represented in the act of making offerings to Khnemu, Àmen-Rā, Isis, Sekhet (?) Osiris, Thoth, Menu, and

REMAINS OF THE TEMPLE BUILT BY A MEROÏTIC QUEEN ON THE EAST BANK OF THE NILE NEAR 'AMÂRA.

[From Lepsius, *Denkmäler*, Abth. I. Bl. 114.

other deities of the Cataract country. The scenes on each column are divided by horizontal rows of stars, and by perpendicular rows of hieroglyphics, each containing three cartouches, consisting presumably of dedications to the gods. The cartouches are identical with those found at Wad Bâ Nagaa, and Nagaa, and they prove that this temple was built by Netek-Àmen and his queen Àmen-tarit, probably about B.C. 30.

Of the temples which existed at Meroë, on the island of the same name, very little can be said, for their remains are

[1] Lepsius, *Denkmäler*, Abth. i., Bl. 115.

extremely scanty. From the plan published by Lepsius[1] we see that this scholar was able to trace the walls which surrounded a space containing the remains of three or four temples (*c*, *d*, *e*), and that to the north and east of the enclosure he found ruins of six or seven other small temples. To the south of these may be

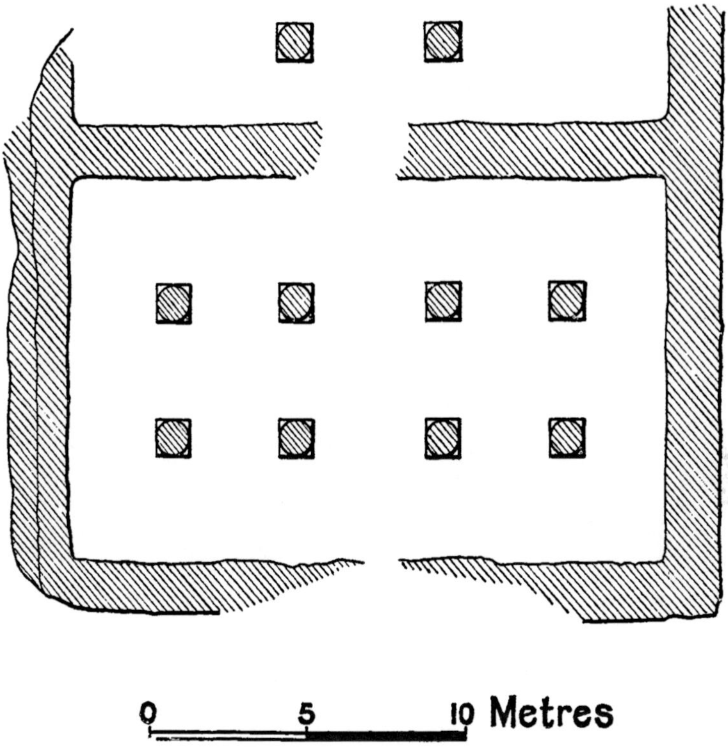

PLAN OF THE TEMPLE OF 'AMÂRA.

[From Lepsius, *Denkmäler*, Abth. I. Bl 115.

traced another rectangular enclosure,[2] which had a doorway in the centre of its east and west sides. The temple itself was rectangular, and was entered through a doorway with pylons; inside was a rectangular chamber, entered on the east side, which probably was used as a sanctuary, and contained the shrine of the god. A passage ran round all four sides of this chamber. The temple

[1] *Denkmäler*, i., Bl. 132.

[2] *Ibid.*, i., Bl. 133.

was approached by a flight of steps. Immediately in a line with the doorway of the temple are the remains of two small buildings, also oriented to the east, and to the south-east may be traced the outline of the edge of a large reservoir. This reservoir was probably an appanage of the temple, and the revenues which the priests derived from the sale of the water in it from passing caravans were, no doubt, devoted to the support of their god and themselves.

Passing southwards to Wad Bâ Nagaa, there may still be seen in the so-called Wâdî Al-Kirbikân a number of mounds of bricks,

BES COLUMNS OF A TEMPLE AT WAD BÂ NAGAA.

[From Lepsius, *Denkmäler*, Abth. I. Bl. 139.

ruins of columns, &c., which mark the site of a once flourishing town. When, or by whom this town was founded is unknown, but a settlement of considerable size existed here in the XVIIIth Dynasty, for a kneeling statue of king Àmen-ḥetep II. was discovered among the ruins,[1] a fact that seems to prove conclusively that he made offerings in a temple which, even at that period, had stood for some time on the site. The most important remains of buildings which were seen there by Cailliaud[2] consisted of the ruins of two temples; the larger temple contained a number of rectangular pillars, ornamented with sculptured

[1] See above, p. 602. [2] See *Voyage à Méroé*, pll. 9, 10.

figures of the god Bes, surmounted by heads of the goddess Hathor in relief. Two of these pillars were in a tolerably good

PORTRAIT OF THE MEROÏTIC KING NETEK-ÀMEN, BUILDER OF A TEMPLE AT WAD BÂ NAGAA.

[Drawn from Lepsius, *Denkmäler*, Abth. III. Bl. 304.

state of preservation, even when the drawing of them published by Lepsius[1] was made. Cailliaud, mistaking the god Bes for Typhon, called this temple the "Typhonium." The building is

[1] *Denkmäler*, i. 139.

oriented, like the two other temples on this site, to the south. The town represented by the ruins at Wad Bâ Nagaa lay close to the river, and was clearly an important halting-place for caravans

KING NETEK-ÀMEN. FROM AN ALTAR FOUND BY LEPSIUS AT WAD BÂ NAGAA.

on the road between towns on the Nile above the Third Cataract, and Abû Harâz on the Blue Nile.

After leaving the Nile, the first halting-place was Nagaa, the site of which lies up the *khôr* at a distance of between seventeen and twenty miles; here the route joined the main road which ran from

Shendî to Abû Harâz. As the traveller journeys through the *khôr* the ground rises, and when Gebel Nagaa is reached he sees all round him a fine open space dotted all over with the ruins of ancient

QUEEN ÂMEN-TARIT. FROM AN ALTAR FOUND BY LEPSIUS AT WAD BÂ NAGAA.

temples, large and small. To the east, on the gentle slope of a hill, are the remains of a large number of tombs, and it is probable that royal personages and notables were buried here. Beyond this, to the south, was an enormous reservoir, the greater part of the sides of which was formed of the living rock of two conveniently placed hills; the gaps on the east and west sides were filled up by artifical embankments, traces of which are still to be seen. At the south-east corner of the reservoir was a temple,[1] which was oriented nearly south-east, and which stood

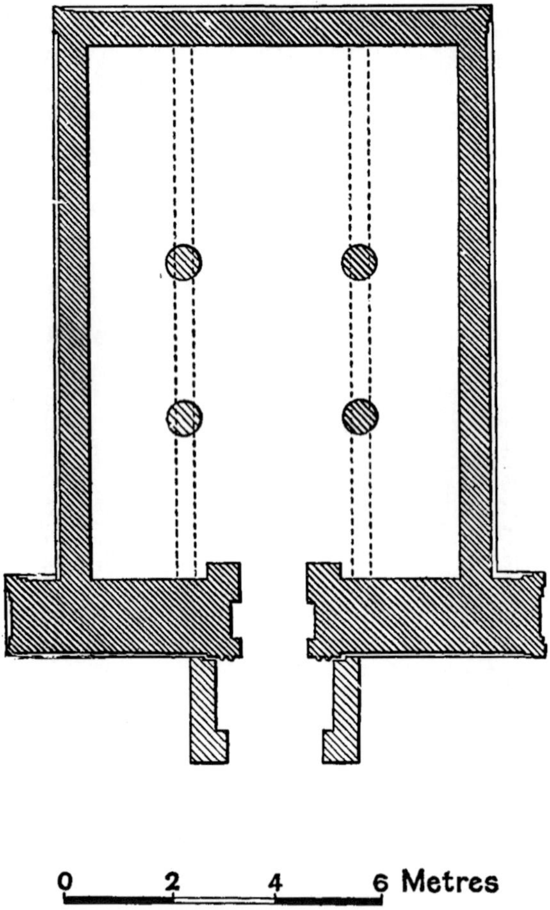

PLAN OF A TEMPLE AT NAGAA (LEPSIUS, A).

[From Lepsius, *Denkmäler*, Abth. I. Bl. 145.

within an enclosure surrounded by a wall. A colonnade ran round the whole of the outside of the temple; on the south-east side it had two rows of pillars. To the north-west of this temple are

[1] Lepsius, plan G. See *Denkmäler*, i., Bl. 143.

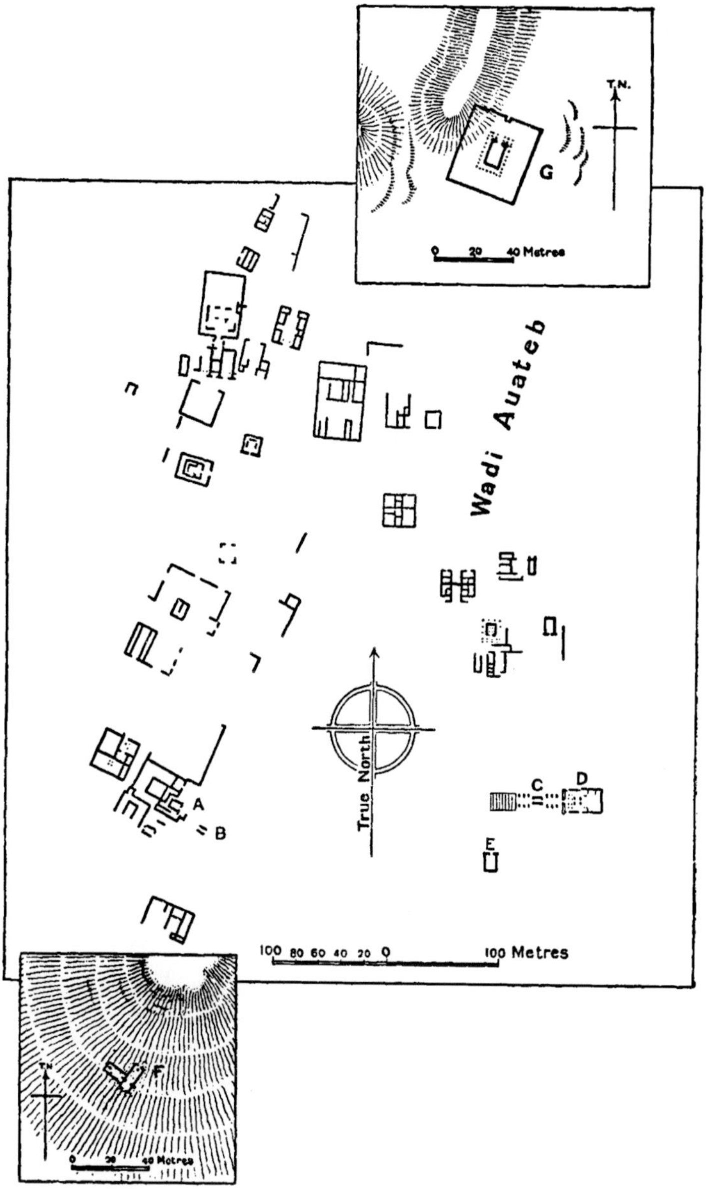

OUTLINE OF THE REMAINS OF THE TEMPLES AT NAGAA.

[From Lepsius, *Denkmäler*, Abth. I. Bl. 143.

the remains of another reservoir, and I was told by the natives that after the summer rains a considerable quantity of water remains in it for two months or more. An examination of the site shows that the ruins of some sixteen distinct buildings may be traced at Nagaa, but of most of them the remains are so scanty that is impossible to attempt to describe the plans of more than half a dozen.

The best preserved of all of them is the important little temple[1] which was built by one of the Candace queens called Amen-tarit (?) who flourished probably in the second or third century A.D. Her own name[2] and that of her consort[3] are mutilated, and there exists, unfortunately, no means of supplying the missing signs. This temple consists of a single chamber, about 45 feet long, and contained four columns, which supported the roof; it has, however, fallen in, and the greater part of each pillar is destroyed. The pylon is about 22 feet high; the cornice is practically destroyed; in front of the entrance through the pylon was a small rectangular portico. The doorway is ornamented with a cornice sculptured with uraei having disks on their heads, and with three winged disks, with pendent uraei, and closely resembles the sculptured shrines in the chapels of the Pyramids of Meroë. On the right façade is sculptured a colossal figure of a queen, wearing the characteristic Nubian head-dress, with uraei over the forehead. She wears a necklace of circular beads, to which is attached a pendant in the form of Amen; her bracelets and armlets are deep and richly ornamented. Her neck and arms are bare, but she wears a belt with a sheath for a scabbard attached, and skirts elaborately decorated with feather work. With her right hand she grasps the hair of thirty prisoners, representatives of conquered nations, who kneel at her feet with their hands raised beseechingly. Her left hand holds a short sword, or dagger, and is raised aloft as if about to smite the prisoners. By her side is a raging lion engaged in clawing the vanquished men before him. Above her head is the vulture-

[1] Called B by Cailliaud, and A by Lepsius (i., Bll. 144, 145).

[2] 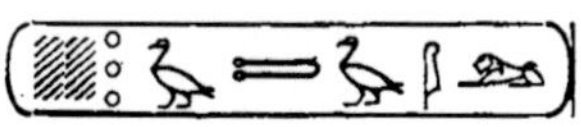.

[3] 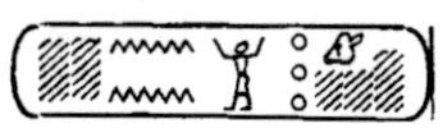.

THE CONSORT OF THE QUEEN WHO BUILT TEMPLE A AT NAGAA SLAUGHTERING HIS FOES.

[From Lepsius, *Denkmäler*, Abth. V. Bl. 56.

goddess Mut, and beneath her feet are seven captives with their arms tied at the elbows behind them; their bodies are in the form of jars

THE QUEEN WHO BUILT TEMPLE A AT NAGAA SLAUGHTERING HER FOES.
ABOVE HER IS THE VULTURE-GODDESS MUT.
[From Lepsius, *Denkmäler*, Abth. V. Bl. 56.

On the left façade is sculptured the figure of a king who is about to smite with his battle-axe a group of thirty rebels kneeling before him. Above his head is a hawk with outstretched wings, and beneath his feet is a lion gnawing the dead body of an enemy; in a lower register are seven captives as before.

On the north wall, outside, are sculptured eight colossal figures. The first is that of a king-consort, whose name is wanting; he wears on each hand a ring which covers the second joints of all four fingers, and his robe is ornamented with lions' winged heads. The second figure is that of queen , who wears the crown of Isis. The Egyptian name of this queen is Åmen-tarit, and she was the wife of Netek-Åmen; her native name is found at 'Amâra, and Wad Bâ Nagaa. The sceptre which she holds in her right hand is noteworthy. The third figure is that of her husband, who wears the crown of Osiris. Before him stands Isis (?), who is presenting to him a group of captives. Behind her stand two gods and two goddesses, three of whom hold papyrus sceptres surmounted by symbols of "life." The first pair are probably Mut and Khensu, and the second Isis and Osiris.

On the west wall are five large figures, the central one being that of a god, with three lions' heads and two pairs of outstretched hands and arms, and wearing the triple crown, with horns, uraei, disks, &c. In one of his right and one of his left hands he grasps a bunch of flowers. Three lions' heads are seen to form a very effective ornament above a lotus-pillar in a shrine of the time of Åmen-ḥetep II., but what they symbolize is unknown. On his right stands king , Netek-Amen, who is clearly of negro origin, wearing an elaborate crown and ornaments, and behind him is another royal personage whose robe is decorated with symbols , which are intended to represent , "life." On the left of the god is Netek-Åmen's queen, Åmen-tarit (?), and behind her is another royal attendant, whose name appears to be identical with that of the royal servant behind Netek-Åmen. Each figure wears two rings, with large bezels, on each hand.

On the south, as on the north wall, are sculptured eight figures, three being those of royal personages, i.e., Netek-Amen, his queen, and a prince, and five deities. The king, queen and prince wear very large rings, and the queen's finger-nails are several inches long. The first deity has the head of a lioness, and is probably Bast; she holds in one hand a lotus flower, and in the other the symbol of "life." Between her and the king is a

THREE LIONS' HEADS ABOVE A LOTUS PILLAR IN A SHRINE OF THE TIME OF AMEN-HETEP II.

[From Lepsius, *Denkmäler*, Abth. III. Bl. 63.

sort of banner, with tassels, on the top of which is a lion, wearing the triple crown; he may be intended to represent the queen's *ka*, or "double," or may be her fetish. The second deity is Rā, or one of the Horus gods, the third is Ȧmen, the fourth is Khensu, and the fifth is Khnemu. On the north, west, and south walls, on a level with the heads of the gods and royal personages, is a row of characters intended to represent the symbol of "life." The apparel of the gods is richly decorated with scale and feather work, and the forms of the crowns which they wear suggest that they were copied from models of the Ptolemaïc Period. The wings of the pylon are ornamented with:—1. A lion-headed serpent, with human hands and arms, rising out of a lotus flower; 2. A banner, surmounted by a lion wearing the triple crown, the pole of which is driven through the body of a captive enemy.

On the north wall, inside, figures of the same royal personages are seen adoring the gods; above these, in a sort of frieze, is a

A GOD WORSHIPPED AT NAGAA.

[From Lepsius, *Denkmäler*, Abth. V. Bl. 63.

series of figures adoring Åmen, Isis, and other gods. Among these most noteworthy is the god who is represented full-face, with rays emerging from his head; he is seated on a throne, and grasps a standard in his right hand. He is clearly a form of the Sun-god. Among the larger figures of the gods is one wearing the plumes of Åmen. He is arrayed in long, flowing robes, and his attitude somewhat suggests that of Jupiter Sarapis. He holds in each hand a number of cords, each of which is tied round the neck of a captive enemy, and the ends of these he is giving to the king who stands before him. Figures of this god also appear on the insides of the west and south walls. On the upper portion of the

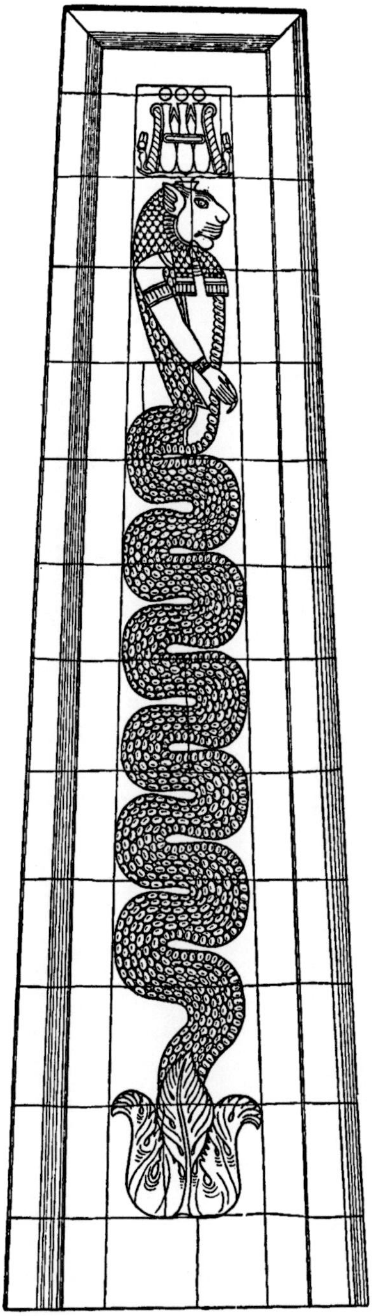

THE LION-HEADED SERPENT, ONE OF THE PROTECTORS OF THE TEMPLE OF QUEEN ÅMEN-TARIT AT NAGAA, RISING FROM A LOTUS (?).

[From Lepsius, *Denkmäler*, Abth. V. Bl. 60.

THE LION-BANNER OF QUEEN ÅMEN-TARIT.

[From Lepsius, *Denkmäler*, Abth. V. Bl. 60.

THE ORNAMENTATION OF THE EGYPTO-ROMANO TEMPLE AT NAGAA.

[From a photograph by Lieutenant S. F. Newcombe, R.E.

east wall, inside, three members of a royal family are seen adoring a hawk-headed crocodile, which has a disk and plumes, enclosed within a circle, upon his head. This temple is a very interesting and striking object at Nagaa, and it is to be hoped that steps will be taken by the Sûdân Government to prevent the cracked stones over the doorway from falling down.

The next most important ruins are those of the buildings called by Cailliaud[1] "Grand Temple de l'Est," and by Lepsius C and D;[2] they stand on the slope of a hill, at no great distance from the quarries whence the stone employed in building the town and its temples was taken. The total length of the ruins is about three hundred feet. The temples were approached by a flight of steps (A), at the top of which was a short avenue, consisting of three pairs of stone rams (B); next to these was a rectangular portico[3] with fourteen columns (C), and beyond this was another avenue, containing three more pairs of stone rams (D). The head of each ram when on its pedestal was about 8 feet from the ground.

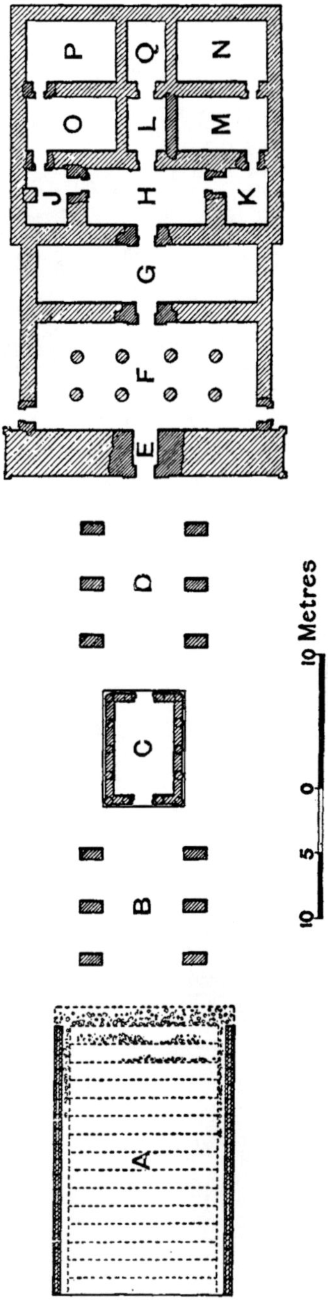

PLAN OF THE TEMPLES C, D AT NAGAA.
[From Lepsius, *Denkmäler* Abth. V. Bl. 145.

The hall of the temple (F) immediately behind the pylon (E)

[1] Planche xv.

[2] *Denkmäler*, i., Bl. 145; and see v., Bl. 66 f.

[3] *Ibid.*, v., Bl. 66*a*.

KING ADORING A HAWK-HEADED CROCODILE WITH THE HANDS AND ARMS OF A MAN.

[From Lepsius, *Denkmäler*, Abth. V. Bl. 65.

contained eight columns. Passing through the pro-naos (G) a group of rooms (H-P) are seen; these were used by the priests for the storage of temple property. In the sanctuary (Q) was the

AMEN-TARIT.

NETEK-AMEN.

A GOD WORSHIPPED AT NAGAA (JUPITER SARAPIS?).

[From Lepsius, *Denkmäler*, Abth. V. Bl. 64

SCENE FROM THE NORTH WALL OF TEMPLE A AT NAGAA. ISIS HOLDING THE ENDS OF THE CORD BY WHICH THE NECKS OF A GROUP OF FOES OF THE KING ARE TIED TOGETHER.

[From Lepsius, *Denkmäler*, Abth. v., Bl. 57.

figure of the god. The reliefs on the portions of the entrances and walls which now remain show that this temple was built by Netek-Ȧmen and his queen Ȧmen-Tarit, and their cartouches occur here, together with a cartouche of a prince whose prenomen was Ānkh-ka-Rā and whose native name was Ark-teten (?). Numerous figures of the Nile-god occur, and Ȧmen of Napata and Ȧmen of Thebes are represented in several places. Both the king and queen wear the disk and plumes of Ȧmen. On one of the pillars in the first hall [1] the three cartouches of the royal worshippers are arranged side by side, and in the panels each is seen adoring

[1] See Lepsius, *Denkmäler*, Abth. v., Bl. 67 *a*.

ARK-TETEN.

THE EGYPTO-ROMAN TEMPLE AT NAGAA.
[From a photograph by C. C. F. Mackenzie, Esq.

Amen, Menu, Horus, Bast, &c. Elsewhere the prince is seen standing between Isis and Thoth, and Isis and Horus.[1]

Close to the top of the mountain is a group of ruins of three small temples, one of which is oriented to the north-west, one to the north-east, and one to the south. The largest temple was built, apparently, by king Shankpitah (?) .[2]

About 40 feet to the south-east of the temple (*a*) is a small Egypto-Roman rectangular edifice, which appears to have no connection with any other building at Nagaa; it is about 28 feet long, and 13 feet 6 inches high. The ornamentation of the capitals of the pillars, and of the arches between them, proves that this portico belongs to the period of the most recent of the Pyramids of Meroë, and it is unlikely that it is older than the third century of our era. It is well preserved, and, if we except the buildings of a similar class at Khârga, is perhaps the best example extant of the architecture of the period to which it belongs.

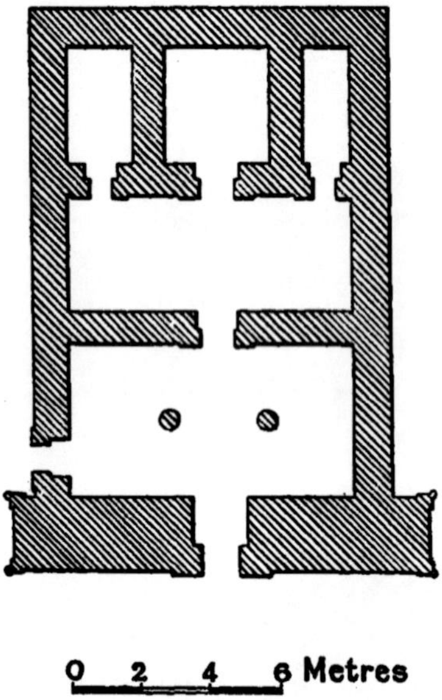

PLAN OF TEMPLE E AT NAGAA.
[From Lepsius, *Denkmäler*, Abth. I. Bl. 145.

Other ruins at Nagaa are:—

A small temple, marked E on the plan of Lepsius, about 50 feet long, and 30 feet wide, which consisted of two chambers. The first chamber contained two circular pillars, and had a door on the south side; in the second was the sanctuary, which held the shrine of the god, and two long narrow chambers wherein the dresses of the statue of the god were stored. The builder of this temple is unknown.

Two temples, the larger of which was connected by a wall with a small rectangular edifice, and consisted of a single chamber and

[1] See Lepsius, *Denkmäler*, Bl. 67 *c, d*. [2] *Ibid.*, Bl. 68 *d*.

a portico with six columns. In the hall of this temple were four columns, and an altar, and the statue of the god was placed in a niche in the end wall. The total length of the temple and portico was about 65 feet. The second temple was built at right angles to the first, and consisted of three chambers, in the first of which

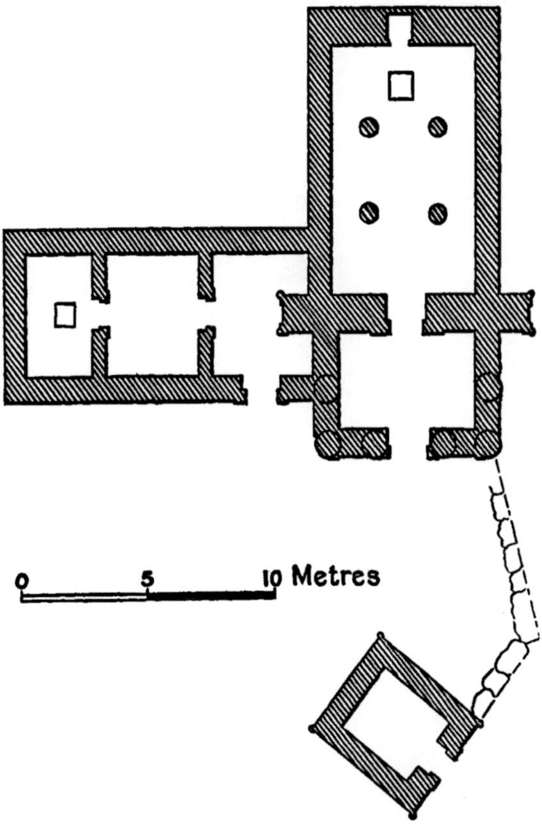

PLAN OF TEMPLE F AT NAGAA.

[From Lepsius, *Denkmäler*, Abth. I. Bl. 145.

were two doorways, and in the third an altar. This group stands on the slope of a hill and is marked F in the plan of Lepsius. The orientation is unusual.

A temple consisting of a single chamber, marked G′ in the plan of Lepsius. It was surrounded by a colonnade, which on the east side had two rows of pillars, and was enclosed within a mud-brick wall, with a gateway in front of the door of the temple. The temple enclosure was nearly a square, about 130 feet long and 118 feet wide. The orientation of the building is unusual.

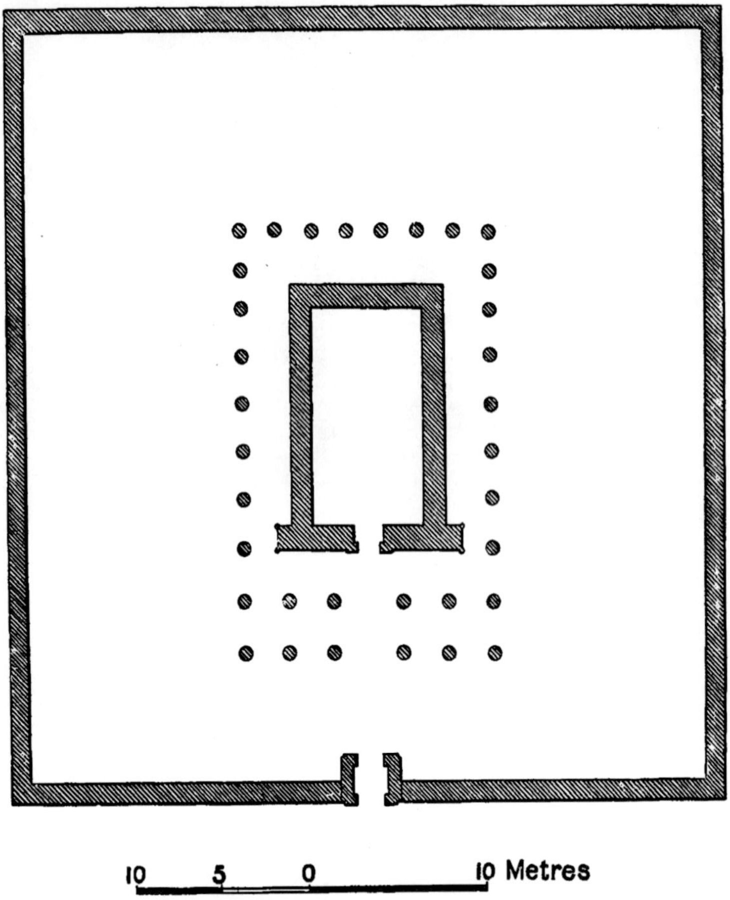

PLAN OF TEMPLE G AT NAGAA.

[From Lepsius, *Denkmäler*, Abth. I. Bl. 145.

The largest and probably the most perplexing of all the groups of ruins in the Sûdân is that which is found in the Wâdî Aṣ-Ṣufra, and which is commonly known as "Maṣawwarât aṣ-Ṣufra," or the "sculptures of Aṣ-Ṣufra." The ruins here, like those at Nagaa,

DOORWAY OF A TEMPLE AT NAGAA.

[From a photograph by Lieutenant S. F. Newcombe, R.E.

stand on raised ground at the head of a valley, and they lie on the older of the two routes between Shendî and Nagaa, about thirty miles from the former place.

On this same route, about half way between Shendî and Maṣ-awwarât, are the remains of some sculptures which Cailliaud thought belonged to a small temple, and on the same road, a few miles south of Shendî, is an ancient well. The temple,[1] when in a perfect state, was about 20 feet long. Its walls are formed of comparatively large stones, and were covered with sculptures, which are now in a ruined state. Cailliaud, however, was able to identify on them figures of women who were dressed in apparel similar to that worn by the queens of Nagaa and Meroë. Along this road Mr. J. W. Crowfoot discovered some interesting sculptures which had escaped the attention of Lepsius and other travellers.

The chief group of ruins in the Wâdî Aṣ-Ṣufra is found within an enclosure of the general shape of which a good idea will be gained from the accompanying plans, reproduced from the works of Cailliaud and Lepsius.[2] It is impossible to obtain an accurate plan of the ruins until many parts of the site have been carefully excavated The ruins consist of the remains of "chambers, "courts, corridors and temples, in an enclosure or parallelogram, "760 by 660 feet; but in more accurate numbers the entire cir-"cumference is 2,854 feet. The north-east side is 660 feet long; "the north-west, the only side on which there are entrances, "769½ feet; the south-west side 665 feet; and the south-east "760 feet."[3]

Opposite to the central entrance is a corridor 8 feet wide and 205 feet long; this leads to a temple which stands in an enclosure 94 feet long and 85 feet wide. The temple itself is 47 feet long, and 40½ feet wide, and stands very nearly in the centre of the enclosure. It contained four pillars, and was surrounded by a colonnade which had on its south-east side a double row of pillars. On each side of the door leading into the small temple on the east side are the remains of a colossal statue

[1] Cailliaud, *Voyage*, plate xxx., No. 9; and see tom. iii., p. 158.

[2] *Ibid.*, plate xxii.; *Denkmäler*, i., Bl. 139.

[3] Hoskins, *Travels*, p. 100.

sculptured in very high relief. This temple consisted of a single chamber, which contained four pillars, and had a portico in front of it; it was approached by a flight of steps, and was 53 feet long and 45 feet wide. The door is ornamented by two serpents, which in form and treatment remind us of Alexandrian Roman work of the third century of our era.

Another temple to the north-east of the largest temple is 52 feet long by 29 feet wide. It contained four columns, and had a colonnade with two rows of pillars in front of it. The use to which this group of buildings was put when complete has puzzled every traveller, and it seems impossible to understand its object. The most easily understood divisions of it are the temples, about the purpose of which there can be no doubt. Cailliaud thought the buildings formed a college. Hoskins believed them to have been a hospital, and Heeren declared them to be the Ammonium. One thing seems clear, namely, that the largest temple was the first building set up here. It is permissible to assume, until proof to the contrary is forthcoming, that chambers were built in the temple precincts for the use of the priests and of their royal masters, that these were in due course enclosed by walls, and that building after building was added and enclosed, and two other temples were built. Possibly the courts may have been used for driving cattle into when fighting was going on between the tribes, and the whole group of buildings made to serve the purposes of a *khân*, or desert rest-house.

To the south of the main group of buildings are the ruins of a large rectangular edifice which contained many chambers, and to the south of this are the remains of a small house (?) of irregular shape. To the north and east are the ruins of reservoirs, and to the south of the larger reservoir are the remains of three temples.[1] The largest of these consisted of a single chamber, containing six columns, and was entered through a pylon. There are no other ruins on this site, and it seems clear that no town stood here. The confusion which reigns here is chaotic, but every here and there among the ruins are mutilated reliefs and

[1] See Lepsius, *Denkmäler*, i., Bl. 140.

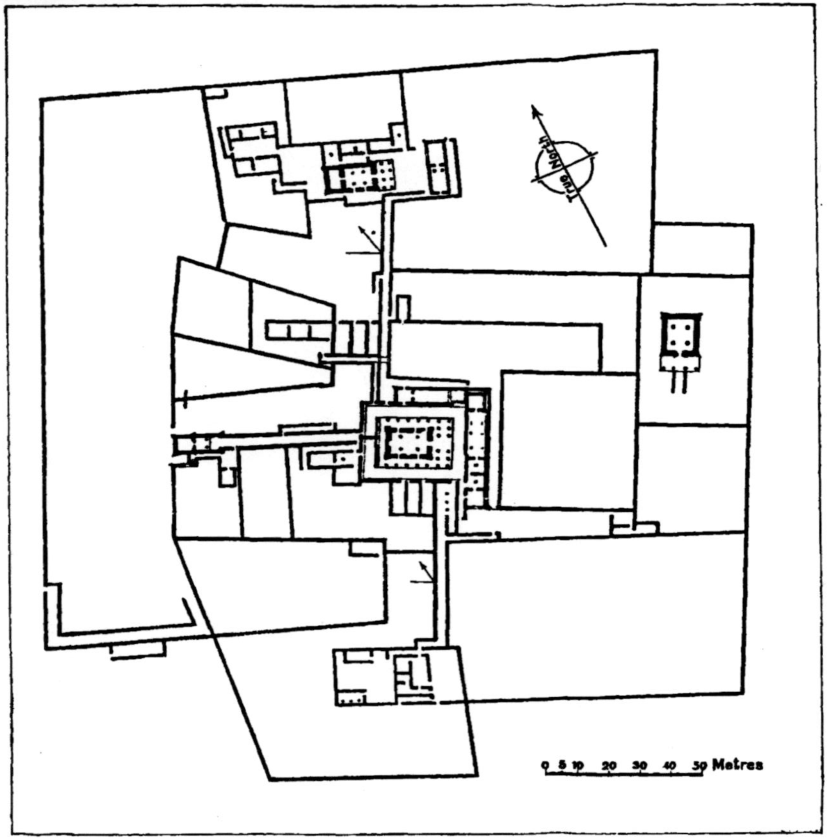

PLAN OF THE TEMPLES, ETC., AT MASAWWARAT AS-SUFRA.

[According to Cailliaud, *Voyage*, Plate xxii.

NO. 1.

columns which are of considerable interest.[1] The columns of the first row of the colonnade of the great temple are unlike any found elsewhere in the Sûdân, and display the high pitch of perfection attained in the sculptor's art by the artisans who set them up. Their capitals are ornamented with lotus flowers, and the flutings and ropework patterns which adorn the shafts give them a graceful appearance; round the drums and bases are sculptured figures of gods, warriors, athletes, &c., in high relief.[2] The reliefs in the panels into which the shafts of many of the pillars are divided are no less interesting. With many of the designs we are familiar from other temples in the Sûdân, e.g., 'Amâra and Nagaa.

NO. 2.

NO. 3.

Worthy, however, of special note are the large numbers of mythical and fantastic animals which are sculptured on the

[1] For general views of the site, see Cailliaud, *Voyage*, plates xxiii. ff.; Hoskins, *Travels*, plates 14 and 15; and Lepsius, *Denkmäler*, i., Bl. 141.

[2] See *Denkmäler*, v., Bl. 71.

NO. 4.

lower parts of the columns:—1. The ram-headed god Khnemu leading a child with his right hand, and a winged lioness, with a curly tail, by a string with his left. Under the right fore-paw of the lioness, which is stretched out, are two stricken gazelle (No. 1). 2. A winged, hawk-headed lion, wearing the *atef*-crown, crushing a prostrate man with his right fore-paw (No. 2). 3. A lion-headed god riding a lion which is gnawing the body of a man held between its fore-paws (No. 3). In these three scenes the lion probably typifies the king. 4. A hawk-headed god, with the solar disk on his head, riding a

NO. 5.

winged lioness with a woman's head, surmounted by a disk. With its right fore-paw the lioness is crushing a couple of gazelle (No. 4). The lioness probably symbolizes a queen. 5. The vulture-goddess Mut supporting her weight on the body of one prostrate foe, and holding a second

NO. 6.

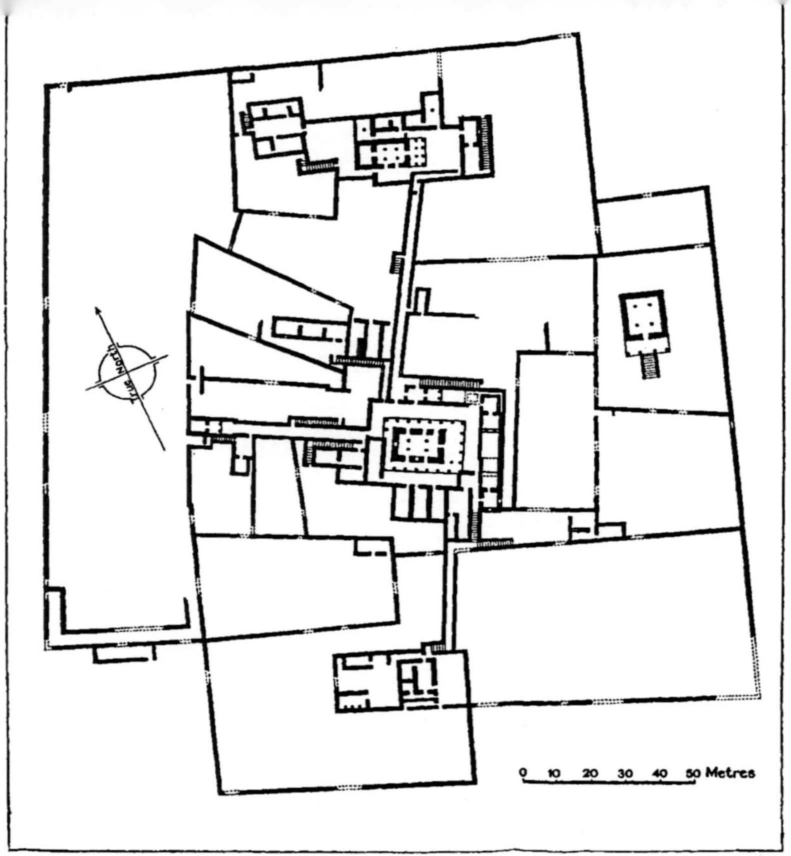

PLAN OF THE TEMPLES, ETC., AT MASAWWAHAT AS-SUFRA.

[According to Lepsius, Abth. i., Bl. 140.

in her claw and beak (No. 5). 6. A god wearing the double-crown, riding an elephant, the trunk of which is being held by a kneeling man (No. 6). 7. The god Bes, with plumes and a tail, playing the harp to a seated lion, which wears the triple crown and smells a flower (No. 7).[1]

These sculptures are full of spirit, and the expressions on the faces of some of the animals and their attitudes are strikingly comical, and can hardly have failed to appeal to the humorous side of all the Sûdânî folk who saw them. The style and character of the sculptures and reliefs on this site suggest that the ruins are the latest of all the Meroïtic buildings. The work is

NO. 7.

too good to have been done by natives guided by purely native overseers, and I believe that Egyptians who had been trained in the service of Roman architects were imported to carry it out, probably in the second or third century of our era. Several of the walls must belong to a far later period, and some are evidently built of stones which have been carried off from the older buildings.

The next great centre of trade that flourished when the Meroïtic kingdom existed was Sôba, a town of considerable extent, which stood on the bank of the Blue Nile a few miles above Kharṭûm. Of the history of the town during the first few centuries after the establishing of the Nubian kingdom on the Island of Meroë nothing is known, but it is tolerably certain that

[1] See *Denkmäler*, v., Bl. 74, 75.

it contained a number of temples, built of sandstone, similar to those of Napata, Aṣ-Ṣufra, Nagaa, Wad Bâ Nagaa, &c. One of these, as we may see from the ruins of it which still exist, was turned into a church by the Jacobite Nubians. A few facts concerning the town when it formed the capital of a Christian kingdom have been obtained, and these will be given in the chapter on Christianity in the Sûdân.

CHAPTER X.

THE SÛDÂN IN THE FIRST CENTURY BEFORE, AND THE FIRST CENTURY AFTER, CHRIST.

THE information which is to be derived from native sources about the Sûdân between B.C. 100 and A.D. 100 is scanty, but we may with advantage summarize here the statements about that country made by Diodorus, Strabo, and Pliny. The narratives of Diodorus and Pliny are in some respects not so valuable as those of Strabo, but the first was very well informed on many points connected with the history and civilization of Nubia, and many of his statements are supported by archaeological evidence.

According to Diodorus (i. 33), the Nile rises far away in Ethiopia, and in its course forms many islands, the largest of which is Meroë, whereon Cambyses built a city, and called it after his mother's name "Meroë." This island is shield-shaped, is 3,000 stadia long, and 1,000 stadia wide. It contains mines of gold, silver, iron, and brass, ebony trees and precious stones (i. 33). The Inundation begins at the summer solstice, and increases until the equinox; its waters bring down new soil for the land (i. 36). The inhabitants of the Island of Meroë call the Nile "Astapus"[1]; Diodorus rejects the opinion of Herodotus that the Nile rises from a lake (i. 37). The Ethiopians (i e., the Sûdânî folk) were the first men who ever lived (iii. 2), and are generally held to be autochthones; they were the first to institute the worship of the gods and sacrifices. The Egyptians were a colony from Ethiopia, and Egypt was formed of slime and mud brought down from Ethiopia. The laws of Ethiopia and Egypt are identical, and the writing in use in both countries is the same (iii. 3). Kings are chosen from the priesthood. The candidates are brought into the god's presence, and he whom the god

[1] They, of course, referred to the Blue Nile.

touches becomes king, and is worshipped as a god. (When the priests were tired of their king they ordered him to commit suicide; this custom lasted for centuries, but was broken by Ergamenes (Ȧrq-Amen), who refused to obey the priests, and, taking soldiers, went to the Golden House [at Napata ?] and slew the priests.) This happened in the reign of Ptolemy II. (iii. 6). No man is put to death, but he is compelled to commit suicide; when the king kills himself, his servants do the same. These are the laws of the people on the Island of Meroë.

There are, however, several other Ethiopian nations that dwell on each side of the river Nile; some border upon Arabia (i.e., the Eastern Desert), and others are seated in the heart of Africa. The greater part of these, especially those near the river (iii. 8), are blacks, flat-faced, have curled hair, are exceeding fierce and cruel, and are in their manners like unto the animals, not so much, however, in their natural temper, as in their studied and contrived acts of wickedness. Their whole bodies are filthy and nasty, their nails are long like the claws of beasts, and they are very cruel to each other. Some carry raw ox-hide shields and short lances; others darts with forked points; others have bows four cubits long, and when they have used up their arrows they fight with clubs. The women fight with men's weapons, many wearing a brass ring in their lips. Some of them go naked, some wear skins, and others wear sheep's tails hanging in front of them from their waists. Some wear breeches made of human hair. Their food consists of marsh fruit, young branches of trees, sesamus, lotus, roots of cane, &c. Those who are archers live on the game they kill, but most of them live upon flesh, milk, and cheese. Of the gods, some are mortal (iii. 9), and others immortal; among the former are Isis, Pan,[1] Hercules, and Jupiter,[2] and among the latter, the sun, moon, and the universe. Some believe in no gods at all, and when the sun rises they hide in the marshes as from an implacable enemy. The dead are disposed of: 1. By throwing the bodies into the river. 2. By pouring melted glass on them, and keeping them in their houses. 3. By burial in earthen coffins near their temples. An oath sworn by the

[1] Probably the Egyptian god Menu.

[2] Compare the illustration above, page 141.

names of the dead is the most sacred. Kings are chosen from among the handsomest men, or from the most industrious shepherds, or from the richest men, or from the bravest in war. The Ethiopians and Africans quarrel (iii. 10) for the possession of the lands near the river. Herds of elephants from higher Libya come down to the morasses for food. In the deserts are numerous large serpents, which are able to kill the elephants. We must not trust writers about Ethiopia too implicitly, for most of them were either too credulous, or invented lies as a diversion; Agatharcides of Cnidus and Artemidorus the Ephesian "have in their writings nearly pursued the truth." Diodorus then, quoting from Agatharcides, describes how gold is obtained; as his narrative will be given in the Chapter on Gold-mining in the Sûdân, we pass on to summarize his remarks on the nations in the Eastern Desert or Troglodyta, and Southern Ethiopia, i.e., Dâr Fûr, Kordôfân, Sennaar, &c.

The Ichthyophagi (iii. 15) live along the Red Sea coast. They go naked, and have their wives in common. The women and children catch the little fish in the shallows, and the men catch the lobsters, lampreys, dog-fish, sea-calves, &c. They kill them with goats' horns and stones. The fish are partly cooked in the sun and then boiled with the seed of a plant; each person eats as much as he can. They also eat shell-fish, breaking the shells with stones; when these fail they gnaw the fish bones, which they take care to keep. Every fifth day they go to the wells of the shepherds to drink, and they drink so much that they can hardly move for a whole day. They resemble herds of cattle, and make a horrid noise as they go about. Other fish-eating people do not drink at all. They speak to no stranger, they are interested in nothing; if assaulted with drawn swords, they stir not, and even if hurt they feel no anger. They are unconcerned if their wives and children be slain before their eyes. Some of them live in caves, and others in tents made of grass and whalebone. Another class lives under the branches of living trees plaited together, and a fourth lives in holes which they dig in sea-moss. The dead are laid on the shore at low tide, and when the sea flows back it carries the bodies away. A fifth class lives in holes in the high rocks.

The Chelonophagi (iii. 21) live on sea turtles. The Rhizophagi live on the roots of canes (iii. 23); many of these people are destroyed by lions, which are, however, kept in check by the gnats, which sting them and drive them out of the country. The Hylophagi are tree-climbers, and feed on the buds and branches of trees; they leap from tree to tree like birds (iii. 24). They go naked, have their wives in common, and fight with clubs. The Spermatophagi live on fruits and herbs. The Konegoi (iii. 25) sleep in trees, and eat the flesh of wild bulls, leopards, &c., and when this fails they eat the skins of animals which they have killed. They are good marksmen with the dart. The Elephantomachi (iii. 26) live in forests, and kill elephants by hamstringing them. To the west of these live the Simoes, and to the south the Struthophagi (iii. 27). Near these are the Acridophagi (iii. 29), who are smaller than other men, of lean and meagre bodies, and exceeding black. They are small, swift of foot, and short-lived; they rarely live more than forty years, and they die through winged lice breeding in their bodies. They live on locusts, which they kill by suffocation, and which they salt. Beyond these is a large country filled with spiders and scorpions (iii. 30), by which the inhabitants were driven out of the country.

To the south of these are the Canimulgos (iii. 31), who wear long beards, and keep large numbers of fierce dogs; they live on the flesh of oxen. "The nations that lie farthest south live the lives of beasts under the shapes of men." The Troglodytes, or Nomades (iii. 32), live pastoral lives; they are divided into tribes, and have a monarchical government. They have their wives in common, except only the wife of the king. They drink for a part of the year milk and blood boiled together. Cattle that are old or sick are killed and eaten. They call no man father, and no woman mother, but only a bull, an ox, a goat, or a sheep, of which they call the males fathers, and the females mothers, because they have their daily food from them and not from their parents (iii. 32). The common drink is made from the *paliurus* plant, but men of position drink a wine which is made from the juice of a flower. They go naked except for beasts' skins round their loins. All the Troglodytes are circumcised, and the cripples among them are mutilated.

The Megabarei fight with raw ox-hide shields, iron-bound clubs, and bows and spears. The dead are tied neck and heels, and carried to the top of a hill, where they are pelted with stones until they are covered over; upon each heap a goat's horn is stuck. They fight among themselves for the pastures. The old folk tie themselves by their necks to tails of oxen, and so end their days. The heat is so great at midday that two standing together cannot see each other (iii. 34). The animals in Ethiopia are rhinoceroses, sphinxes, and the cynocephali (iii. 35). The cepus has the face of a lion, is like a panther, and is as big as a deer. The wild bull lives on flesh. He is as swift as a horse, he is red in colour, and he can move his horns like his ears. His hair stands on end, and his skin is impenetrable. The crocotta is of a mixed nature, part wolf and part dog, and fiercer than both. The serpents are huge, some say a hundred cubits long, which no one believes; a serpent thirty cubits long was brought to Alexandria in the reign of Ptolemy II., and it became quite tame.

According to Strabo (i. 2, § 25), "Ethiopia" runs in the same direction as Egypt and is long, narrow, and subject to inundation. Beyond the reach of the waters the land is parched and desolate, and unfitted for human habitation. Near Meroë (xvi. 4, § 9) is the confluence of the rivers Astaboras, Astapus, and Astasobas with the Nile. On the banks live the Rhizophagi, or Root-eaters, and the Heleii, or marsh-men. Here live lions, which are driven from the country by large gnats at the rising of Sirius. Close by live the Spermophagi, who live on seeds of plants and trees. Far in the interior is Endera, where naked men live, who use bows and arrows. They generally shoot the animals from the trees. They live on the flesh of their cattle, and of other animals, and when this fails they roast the skins of animals and eat them.

Two rivers empty themselves into the Nile, which issue out of some lakes towards the east, and encircle Meroë, a considerable island. One of these rivers is called Astaboras [Tacazze], flowing along the eastern side of the island. The other is the Astapus, or, as some call it, Astasobas. But the Astapus is said to be another river which issues out of some lakes in the south, and this river forms nearly the body of the Nile, which flows in a straight line, and is filled by the summer rains; above the confluence of the Astaboras and the Nile, at the distance of 700 stadia, is Meroë, a city having the same name as the Island; and there is another Island above Meroë, occupied by the fugitive Egyptians, who revolted in the time of Psammetichus, and are called Sembritae, or foreigners. Their sovereign is a queen, but they obey the king of Meroë. The lower parts of the country on each side of Meroë, along the Nile towards the Red Sea, are occupied by Megabari and Blemmyes, who are subject to the Ethiopians, and border upon the Egyptians; about the sea are Troglodytae. The Troglodytae, in the latitude of Meroë, are distant ten or twelve days' journey from the Nile. On the left of the course of the Nile live Nubae in Libya, a populous nation. They begin from Meroë and extend as far as the bends [of the river]. They are not subject to the Ethiopians, but live independently, being distributed into several sovereignties. (Book xvii., chap. i., § 2.)

Strabo's remarks on the Elephant-eaters, the Struthophagi, and other nations in this country are derived for the most part from the writings of Artemidorus, and as they have been already quoted need no further reference. He continues:—

The Ethiopians at present lead for the most part a wandering life, and are destitute of the means of subsistence, on account of the barrenness of the soil, the disadvantages of climate, and their great distance from us. For the mode of life [of the Ethiopians] is wretched; they are for the most part naked, and wander from place to place with their flocks. Their flocks and herds are small in size, whether sheep, goats, or oxen; the dogs also, though fierce and quarrelsome, are small. It was perhaps from the diminutive size of these people, that the story of the Pygmies originated, whom no person, worthy of credit, has asserted that he himself has seen. They live on millet and barley, from which also a drink [marissa] is prepared. They have no oil, but use butter and fat instead. There are no fruits, except the produce of trees in the royal gardens. Some feed even upon grass, the tender twigs of trees, the lotus, or the roots of reeds. They live also upon the flesh and blood of animals, milk, and cheese. They reverence their kings as gods, who are for the most part shut up in their palaces. Their largest royal seat is the city of Meroë, of the same name as the Island. The shape of the Island is said to be that of a shield. Its size is perhaps exaggerated. Its length is about 3,000, and its breadth 1,000 stadia. It is very mountainous, and contains great forests. The inhabitants are nomades, who are partly hunters and partly husbandmen. There are also mines of copper, iron, gold, and various kinds of precious stones. It is surrounded on the side of Libya by great hills of sand, and on that of Arabia by continuous precipices. In the higher parts on the south, it is bounded by the confluent streams of the rivers Astaboras, Astapus, and Astasobas. On the north is the continuous course of the Nile to Egypt, with its windings, of which we have spoken before. The houses in the cities are formed by interweaving split pieces of palm wood or of bricks. They have rock salt, as in Arabia. Palm, the persea (peach), ebony, and carob trees are found in abundance. They hunt elephants, lions, and panthers. There are also serpents, which encounter elephants, and there are many other kinds of wild animals, which take refuge, from the hotter and parched districts. in watery and marshy districts. Above Meroë is Psebo, a large lake, containing a well-inhabited island. As the Libyans occupy the western bank of the Nile, and the Ethiopians the country on the other side of the river, they thus dispute by turns the possession of the islands and the banks of the river, one party repulsing the other, or yielding to the superiority of its opponents. The Ethiopians use bows of wood four cubits long, and hardened in the fire. The women also are armed, most of them wear in the upper lip a copper ring. They wear sheepskins, without wool; for the sheep have hair like goats. Some go naked, or wear small skins or girdles of well-woven hair round the loins. They regard as God one being who is immortal, the cause of all things; another who is mortal, a being without a name, whose nature is not clearly understood. In general they regard as gods benefactors and royal persons, some of whom are their kings, the common saviours and guardians of all; others are private persons, esteemed as gods by those who have individually received benefits from them. Of those who inhabit the torrid region, some are even supposed not to acknowledge any god, and are said to abhor even the sun, and to apply opprobrious names to him, when they behold him rising, because he scorches and tortures them with his heat; these people take refuge in the marshes. The inhabitants of Meroë worship Hercules, Pan, and Isis, besides some other barbaric deity. Some tribes throw the dead into the river; others keep them in the house, enclosed in hyalus (oriental alabaster?). Some bury them around the temples in coffins of baked clay. They swear an oath by them, which is reverenced as more sacred than all others. Kings are appointed from among persons distinguished for their personal beauty, or by their breeding of cattle, or for their courage, or for their riches. In Meroë the priests anciently held the highest rank, and sometimes sent orders even to the king, by a messenger, to put an end to himself, when they appointed another king in his place. At last one of their kings abolished this custom by going with an armed body to the temple, where the golden shrine is, and slaughtering all the priests. The following custom exists among the Ethiopians. If a king is mutilated in any part of the body, those who are most attached to his person, as attendants, mutilate themselves in the same manner, and even die with him. Hence the king is guarded with the utmost care. This will suffice on the subject of Ethiopia.

Pliny's account of "Ethiopia" will be found in his Sixth Book, section 35, and a perusal of it will show that classical writers had in his day a very good general idea of the extent of Nubia, or the Sûdân, and of its principal characteristics and products. It will be seen, however, that his geographical knowledge is not very accurate, and that he transmits a number of fanciful statements, compiled from the works of many writers, without question. His narrative is, nevertheless, of considerable interest, and is worth reproducing here:—[1]

On leaving Syene, and taking first the Arabian side, we find the nation of the Catadupi, then the Syenitae, and the town of Tacompsos, by some called Thatice, as also Aramasos, Sesamos, Sanduma, Masindomacam, Arabeta and Boggia, Leupitorga, Tantarene, Mecindita, Noa, Gloploa, Gystate, Megada, Lea, Renni, Nups, Direa, Patiga, Bacata, Dumana, Rhadata, at which place a golden cat was worshipped as a god, Boron, in the interior, and Mallos, near Meroë; this is the account given by Bion. Juba, however, gives another account; he says that there is a city on Mount Megatichos, which lies between Egypt and Æthiopia, by the Arabians known as Myrson, after which come Tacompsos, Aramus, Sesamos, Pide, Mamuda, Orambis, situate near a stream of bitumen, Amodita, Prosda, Parenta, Mama, Tessatta, Gallas, Zoton, Graucome, Emeus, the Pidibotae, the Hebdomecontacometae, Nomades, who dwell in tents, Cyste, Macadagale, Proaprimis, Nups, Detrelis, Patis, the Ganbreves, the Megasnei, Segasmala, Crandala, Denna, Cadeuma, Thena, Batta, Alana, Mascoa, the Scammi, Hora, situate on an island, and then Abala, Androgalis, Sesecre, the Malli, and Agole. On the African side we find mentioned, either what is another place with the same name of Tacompsos, or else a part of the one before-mentioned, and after it Moggore, Sæa, Edos, Plenariæ, Pinnis, Magassa, Buma, Linthuma, Spintum, Sydop, the Censi, Pindicitora, Acug, Orsum, Sansa, Maumarum, Urbim, the town of Molum, by the Greeks called Hypaton, Pagoarca, Zmanes, at which point elephants begin to be found, the Mambli, Berressa, and Acetuma; there was formerly a town also called Epis, over against Meroë, which had, however, been destroyed before Bion wrote.

These are the names of places given as far as Meroë; but at the present day hardly any of them on either side of the river are in existence; at all events, the praetorian troops that were sent

[1] The rendering is that of Messrs. Bostock and Riley, London, 1890.

by the Emperor Nero under the command of a tribune, for the purposes of inquiry, when, among his other wars, he was contemplating an expedition against Æthiopia, brought back word that they had met with nothing but deserts on their route. The Roman arms also penetrated into these regions in the time of the late Emperor Augustus, under the command of P. Petronius, a man of Equestrian rank, and prefect of Egypt. That general took the following cities, the only ones we now find mentioned there, in the following order:—Pselcis, Primis, Abuncis, Phthuris, Cambusis, Atteva, and Stadasis, where the river Nile, as it thunders down the precipices, has quite deprived the

RIVER ATBARA, NEAR ḲALLÂBÂT.

[From Sir W. Garstin's *Report*, by permission of the Comptroller of H.M. Stationery Office.

inhabitants of the power of hearing: he also sacked the town of Napata. The extreme distance to which he penetrated beyond Syene was 970 miles; but still, it was not the Roman arms that rendered these regions a desert. Æthiopia, in its turn gaining the mastery, and then again reduced to servitude, was at last worn out by its continual wars with Egypt, having been a famous and powerful country even at the time of the Trojan War, when Memnon was its king; it is also very evident from the fabulous stories about Andromeda, that it ruled over Syria in the time of king Cepheus, and that its sway extended as far as the shores of our sea.

In a similar manner, also, there have been conflicting accounts as to the extent of this country: first by Dalion, who travelled a considerable distance beyond Meroë, and after him by Aristocreon and Basilis, as well as the younger Simonides, who made a stay of five years at Meroë, when he wrote his account of Æthiopia. Timosthenes, however, the commander of the fleets of Philadelphus, without giving any other estimate as to the distance, says that Meroë is sixty days' journey from Syene; while Eratosthenes states that the distance is 625 miles, and Artemidorus 600. Sebosus says that from the extreme point of Egypt, the distance to Meroë is 1,675 miles, while the other writers last mentioned

KHOR ARUB, NEAR ḲALLÂBÂT.

[From Sir W. Garstin's *Report*, by permission of the Comptroller of H.M. Stationery Office.

make it 1,250. All these differences, however, have since been settled; for the persons sent by Nero for the purposes of discovery have reported that the distance from Syene to Meroë is 871 miles, the following being the items:—From Syene to Hiera-Sycaminos they make to be 54 miles, from thence to Tama 72, to the country of the Evonymitae, the first region of Æthiopia, 120, to Acina 54, to Pittara 25, and to Tergedus 106. They state also that the Island of Gagaudes lies at an equal distance from Syene and Meroë, and that it is at this place that the bird called the parrot was first seen; while at another island called Articula, the animal known as the sphingium was first discovered by them, and after passing Tergedus, the cynocephalus. The distance from thence to Napata is 80 miles, that little town being the only one of all of them that now survives. From thence to the Island of Meroë the distance is 360 miles. They also state that the grass in the vicinity of Meroë becomes of a greener and fresher colour, and that there is some slight appearance of forests, as also traces of the rhinoceros and elephant. They reported also that the city of Meroë stands at a distance of 70 miles from the first entrance of the Island of Meroë, and that close to it is another island, Tadu by name, which forms a harbour facing those who enter the right-hand channel of the river. The buildings in the city, they said, were but few in number, and they stated that a female, whose name was Candace, ruled over the district, that name having passed from queen to queen for many years. They related also that there was a temple of Jupiter Hammon there, held in great veneration, besides smaller shrines erected in honour of him throughout all the country. In addition to these particulars, they were informed that in the days of the Æthiopian dominion, the Island of Meroë enjoyed great renown, and that, according to tradition, it was in the habit of maintaining 200,000 armed men, and 4,000 artisans. The kings of Æthiopia are said even at the present day to be forty-five in number.

The whole of this country has successively had the names of Ætheria, Atlantia, and last of all, Æthiopia, from Aithiops, the son of Vulcan. It is not at all surprising that towards the extremity of this region the men and animals assume a monstrous form, when we consider the changeableness and volubility of fire, the heat of which is the great agent in imparting various forms and shapes to bodies. Indeed, it is reported that in the interior, on the eastern side, there is a people that have no noses, the whole face representing a plane surface; that others again are destitute of the upper lip, and others are without tongues. Others again, have the mouth grown together, and being destitute of nostrils, breathe through one passage only, inbibing their drink through it by means of the hollow stalk of the oat, which there grows spontaneously and supplies them with its grain for food. Some of these nations have to employ gestures by nodding the head and moving the limbs, instead of speech. Others again were unacquainted with the use of fire before the time of Ptolemy Lathyrus, king of Egypt. Some writers have also stated that there is a nation of Pygmies, which dwells among the marshes in which the river Nile takes its rise; while on the coast of Æthiopia, where we paused, there is a range of mountains, of a red colour, which have the appearance of being always burning.

All the country, after we pass Meroë, is bounded by the Troglodytae and the Red Sea, it being three days' journey from Napata to the shores of that sea; throughout the whole of this district the rain-water is carefully preserved at several places, while the country that lies between is extremely productive of gold. The parts beyond this are inhabited by the Adabuli, a nation of Æthiopia; and here, over against Meroë, are the Megabarri, by some writers called the Adiabari; they occupy the city of Apollo; some of them, however, are Nomades, living on the flesh of elephants. Opposite to them, on the African side, dwell the Macrobii, and then again, beyond the Megabarri, there are the Memnones and the Dabeli, and, at the distance of 20 days' journey, the Critensi. Beyond these are the Dochi, and then the Gymnetes, who always go naked; and after them the Andetae, the Mothitae, the Mesaches, and the Ipsodorae, who are of a black tint, but stain the body all over with a kind of red earth. On the African side again there are the Medimni, and then a nation of Nomades, who live on the milk of the cynocephalus, and then the Aladi and the Syrbotae, which last are said to be eight cubits in height. Aristocreon informs us that on the Libyan side, at a distance of five days' journey from Meroë, is the town of Tolles, and then at a further distance of twelve days' journey, Esar, a town founded by the Egyptians who fled from Psammetichus; he states also that they dwelt there for a period of 300 years, and that opposite, on the Arabian side, there is a town of theirs called Daron. The town, however, which he calls Esar, is by Bion called Sape, who says that the name means "the strangers"; their capital being Sembobitis, situate on an island, and a third place of theirs, Sinat in Arabia. Between the mountains and the river Nile are the Simbarri, the Palugges, and, on the mountains themselves, the Asachae, who are divided into numerous peoples; they are said to be distant five days' journey from the sea, and to procure their subsistence by the chase of the elephant. An island in the Nile, which belongs to the Semberritae, is governed by a queen; beyond it are the Æthiopian Nubei, at a distance of eight days' journey; their town is Tenupsis, situate on the Nile. There are the Sesambri also, a people among whom all the quadrupeds are without ears, the very elephants even. On the African side are the Tonobari, the Ptoenphae, a people who have a dog for their king, and divine from his movements what are his commands; the Auruspi, who have a town at a considerable distance from the Nile, and the Archisarmi, the Phaliges, the Marigerri, and the Casmari.

Bion makes mention also of some other towns situate on islands, the whole distance being twenty days' journey from Sembobitis to Meroë; a town in an adjoining island, under the queen of the Semberritae, with another called Asara, and another, in a second island, called Darde. The name of a third island is Medoë, upon which is the town of Asel, and a fourth is called Garodes, with a town upon it of the same name. Passing thence along the banks of the Nile, are the towns of Navi, Modunda, Andatis, Secundum, Colligat, Secande, Navectabe, Cumi, Agrospi, Ægipa, Candrogari, Araba, and Summara. Beyond is the region of

Sirbitum, at which the mountains terminate, and which by some writers is said to contain the maritime Æthiopians, the Nisacaethae, and the Nisyti, a word which signifies "men with three or four eyes,"—not that the people really have that conformation, but because they are remarkable for the unerring aim of their arrows. On that side of the Nile which extends along the borders of the Southern Ocean, beyond the Greater Syrtes, Dalion says that the people, who use rain-water only, are called the Cisori, and that the other nations are the Longompori, distant five days' journey from the Œcalices, the Usibalci, the Isveli, the Perusii, the Balii, and the Cispii, the rest being deserts, and inhabited by tribes of fable only. In a more westerly direction are the Nigroae, whose king has only one eye, and that in the forehead, the Agriophagi, who live principally on the flesh of panthers and lions, the Pamphagi, who will eat anything, the Anthropophagi, who live on human flesh, the Cynamolgi, a people with the heads of dogs, the Artabatitae, who have four feet, and wander about after the manner of wild beasts; and, after them, the Hesperiae and the Perorsi, whom we have already spoken of as dwelling on the confines of Mauritania. Some tribes, too, of the Æthiopians subsist on nothing but locusts, which are smoke-dried and salted as their provision for the year; these people do not live beyond their fortieth year.

M. Agrippa was of opinion that the length of the whole country of the Æthiopians, including the Red Sea, was 2,170 miles, and its breadth, including Upper Egypt, 1,297. Some authors again have made the following divisions of its length:—From Meroë to Sirbitum eleven days' sail, from Sirbitum to the Dabelli fifteen days', and from them to the Æthiopian Ocean six days' journey. It is agreed by most authors, that the distance altogether, from the Ocean to Meroë, is 625 miles, and from Meroë to Syene, that which we have already mentioned. Æthiopia lies from south-east to south-west. Situate as it is, in a southern hemisphere, forests of ebony are to be seen of the brightest verdure; and in the midst of these regions there is a mountain of immense height, which overhangs the sea, and emits a perpetual flame. By the Greeks this mountain is called Theon Ochema, and at a distance of four days' sail from it is a promontory, known as Hesperu Ceras, upon the confines of Africa, and close to the Hesperiae, an Æthiopian nation. There are some writers who affirm that in these regions there are hills of a moderate height, which afford a pleasant shade from the groves with which they are clad, and are the haunts of Ægipans and Satyrs.

[Book II., cap. 75]. At Meroë, an island in the Nile and the metropolis of the Æthiopians, which is 5,000 stadia from Syene, there are no shadows at two periods of the year, viz., when the sun is in the 18th degree of Taurus and in the 14th of Leo [May 8th and August 4th respectively].

CHAPTER XI.

THE SÛDÂN IN THE ROMAN PERIOD.

THE first prefect of Egypt was Cornelius Gallus, who was born about B.C. 69 and died B.C. 26; he was appointed by the Emperor Augustus, to whom he had rendered important services, B.C. 30, and he governed Egypt four years.[1] Cornelius, having attacked and taken the city of Heroopolis with a small body of men, advanced into Upper Egypt, and in a very short time reduced the Egyptians to subjection. The centres of the revolt were Coptos and Thebes, and it is pretty certain that the rebels were supported by the Nubians from beyond the First Cataract. Cornelius next proceeded to Syene, and interviewed the Nubian chiefs of the tract of territory which extended from Philae to a place a little to the south of Wâdî Ḥalfa, and which was called at that time Triakontaschoinoi, and, though asserting the rights of Rome to that portion of the Nile Valley, he allowed the chiefs to retain their independence. During the rule of the later Ptolemies the Nubians had remained unmolested, and it is probable that they were quite prepared to fight the Romans, unless Cornelius was willing to allow them to retain the privileges which they regarded as their rights. A trilingual inscription in Egyptian (hieroglyphics), Greek, and Latin, found by Captain H. G. Lyons[2] at Philae, records the suppression of a revolt B.C. 29, and we may therefore assume that the first agreement between the Nubians and Romans was made in that, or in the following year. According to Dion Cassius (liii., 23), Cornelius became so much puffed up through his success in Egypt that he set up statues of himself everywhere in the country, and had inscriptions describing his exploits cut on pyramids![3] He was denounced by

[1] Strabo, xvii. 1, 53; Dion Cassius, li. 9, 17.

[2] See Lyons, *Report on the Island and Temples of Philae*, p. 29; Lyons and Borchardt, *Sitzungsberichte d. kön. preuss. Akad. Wissen.*, April, 1896.

[3] καὶ τὰ ἔργα ὅσα ἐπεποιήκει, ἐστὰς πυραμίδας ἐσέγραψε.

Valerius Largus to the Emperor, and was deposed by Augustus, and later the Senate decreed his exile, and the confiscation of his estates ; at length he killed himself with his own sword.

Cornelius Gallus was succeeded by Gaius Petronius, who, according to Strabo,[1] was successful in quelling a revolt which broke out in Alexandria. He was in turn succeeded by Ælius Gallus, about B.C. 25, and was deputed by Augustus to go to Arabia Felix, and make friends with the tribes there, so that the Romans might get possession of the treasures with which the country was supposed to be filled. If the inhabitants refused to come to terms, Ælius Gallus was instructed to fight them. Ælius Gallus chose for his guide Syllaeus, the chamberlain of Obodas, king of the Nabataeans, and he led both the sea and land forces into serious difficulties. Gallus built eighty biremes, and triremes, and galleys, at Cleopatris (Arsinoë), but as these were useless, he built 130 vessels of burden, wherein he embarked 10,000 infantry, including 500 Jews and 1,000 Nabataeans. After much hardship he reached Leuce-Come in fifteen days, having lost many of his vessels, and some with all their crews. Large numbers of his soldiers fell ill of what would now be called enteric fever, and dysentery, and Gallus had to stay at Leuce-Come a whole year. Another six months were wasted through the perfidy of Syllaeus, but eventually Gallus returned to Alexandria with the remnants of his army. The whole expedition was a terrible failure in one respect, but Strabo admits that it was of "some small service."[2]

The Nubians, learning that the prefect Gallus had got into difficulties in the Eastern Desert, and seeing that a large number of Egyptian troops were engaged in fighting the Arabs, took the opportunity of invading the Thebaïd, and attacked the garrison, which consisted of three cohorts, near Syene. They captured Syene, Elephantine, and Philae, by a sudden inroad, and enslaved the inhabitants, and overthrew the statues of Caesar. When the news of this serious revolt reached the Romans, Petronius, who had already been prefect of Egypt, was despatched

[1] Strabo, xvii. 1, 53.

[2] *Ibid.*, xvi. 4, §§ 22-24; Dion Cassius, liii. 29.

with some 10,000 infantry and 800 cavalry to fight the enemy, whose army contained 30,000 men. The Nubians were either driven or withdrew to Pselcis, i.e., the modern Dakka, where Petronius opened a parley with them. He sent deputies who demanded the restitution of the things which the Nubians had carried off, and asked them to give their reasons for revolt. The Nubians replied that they had been ill-treated by the nomarchs, whereupon Petronius replied that they were not the sovereigns of the country, the lord of which was Caesar. The Nubians then asked for three days for consideration, but, as they made no overtures during this period, Petronius attacked them, and made them fight. Badly officered and poorly armed, the result for the Nubians was a foregone conclusion, and their skin shields, hatchets, spears, and swords, availed nothing. They soon fled, some to the city, others to the desert, and others swam away to an island in the river. Among the fugitives were the generals of Candace, queen of the Nubians, a masculine woman, who had lost an eye. Petronius pursued them in rafts and boats, and, having captured them all, sent them to Alexandria; he then attacked Pselcis and took it. Nearly all the Nubians were killed or taken prisoners.[1] From Pselcis Petronius went on to Premnis, the modern Ibrîm, "travelling over the hills of sand, beneath which "the army of Cambyses was overwhelmed by the setting in of a "whirlwind."[2] He took Premnis without difficulty, and then proceeded 500 miles up the river to Napata, the ancient Meroïtic capital, capturing on his way the cities of Abuncis, Phthuris, Cambusis, Atteva, and Stadasis.[3]

Queen Candace was not at Napata when Petronius arrived, but she sent to him ambassadors to treat for peace, and an offer to release the prisoners whom she had taken at Syene, and to give back the statues [of Caesar?]; on this Petronius attacked, captured, and destroyed Napata. He made many prisoners, and took much spoil, and then returned to the north, for the heat and the sand made it impossible to advance further. On his return

[1] Strabo, xvii. 1, 54.

[2] Cambyses' troops were overwhelmed in the Western Desert, between Khârga and Sîwa.

[3] Pliny, vi. 35.

to Premnis he fortified the place, and, placing a garrison of 400 men there, with provisions for two years, he returned to Alexandria. Some of the Nubians were sold as slaves, one thousand were sent to Caesar, and many died of disease. On the departure of Petronius, Candace attacked the garrison he had left at Premnis with an army of several thousand men, but he returned before the Nubians reduced it, and the queen was obliged to send messengers to treat for peace. In reply, Petronius referred them to Caesar, and when they said they knew neither who he was, nor where to find him, Petronius sent men to take them to Caesar at Samos. The ambassadors obtained all they asked for, and Caesar even remitted the tribute which he had imposed.[1]

It is clear from Strabo's narrative that in the year B.C. 24 the Nubians possessed a very large army, and that they were ruled by one of the Meroïtic queen-mothers, who bore the title of "Candace." According to Pliny,[2] this name "had passed from "queen to queen for many years," and in support of this statement it may be noted that a "Candace, queen of the Ethiopians," is referred to in Acts viii. 27, and that Pseudo-Callisthenes makes Alexander the Great visit "Candace," queen of Meroë. Neither of these Candaces can be the opponent of Petronius. Lepsius thought that he had recovered the hieroglyphic form of the name Candace from Pyramid No. 1 of the Northern Group of the Pyramids of Meroë.[3] Now the name of the queen for whom this pyramid was built is not "K(e)ntkit," but "Kenthehebit,"[4] and unless  is a mistake for , the name of "Candace" can hardly come from the name in the cartouche. Moreover, if "Kenthehebit" is a royal title we ought to find it on the pyramids of the other queens of Meroë; but it has not yet been found on them.[5]

To identify with certainty the Candace who defied the Romans is also at present impossible. So far as the monumental evidence is concerned, we may identify her with Amen-tarit, the wife of

[1] Dion Cassius, liv. 6. [2] vi. 35. [3] See Vol. I., p. 363.

[4] Not , but 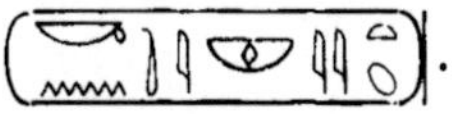.

[5] There still remain two chapels to clear out, and until this has been done it is impossible to say that Kenthehebit occurs but once.

Netek-Amen, whose prenomen and nomen occur on the temples of Wad Bâ Nagaa, Nagaa, and 'Amâra. This fact proves that she, or her consort, was an able and successful ruler of the Island of Meroë, and that her power was effective from Wad Bâ Nagaa, at least, in the south, to 'Amâra in the north, i.e., over a portion of the Nile Valley about 800 miles long. It is evident that if the country in her time had not been in a prosperous state these temples would not have been built. Trade also must have been in a flourishing condition, for we may note that all the temples bearing her name are close to important towns on the great trade routes from south to north, and at Nagaa they are near the great reservoirs which supplied the towns close by. If more remains of the temples in the city of Meroë existed, we should probably find that Queen Åmen-tarit was the builder of the largest of them; the same also may be said of Napata.

The invasion of Petronius proved to the Nubians that the Romans were a people against whom it was unsafe to rebel, and they learned well the lesson which he intended his severe chastisement to teach them. He took with him an ample force of infantry and cavalry, struck quickly and hard, and then marched to their royal city, and razed it to the ground; he deported numbers of them to Alexandria, where they were sold as slaves, and then carried off all the booty which he could collect. Pliny speaks of the country being "famous and powerful" under its king Memnon (Åmen-ḥetep III.), but it was only as a province of Egypt, and when administered by Egyptian officials, that it merits such a description. In saying that "Ethiopia" ruled over Syria in the time of king Cepheus,[1] he probably refers to the reign of Taharqa, who, as we have already seen (Vol. II., pp. 37, 38) was always intriguing in Syria.

During the reign of Augustus the building of the large temple at Talmis (Kalâbsha) was begun, and additions, at least, were made to the temples of Dendûr and Dakka.

In the reign of Claudius (A.D. 41-54) the Romans undertook various enterprises connected with the development of the trade between Arabia, India, and Egypt, and Nero (A.D. 54-68) meditated an invasion of Ethiopia (i.e., the Sûdân, not Abyssinia), with the

[1] Pliny, vi. 35.

view of making himself master of the products of the country. It is curious how little, even at this time, the Romans really knew about Sûdân geography, otherwise they would have known that the richest sources of wealth in the country were in Dâr Fûr, Kordôfân, and the lands on and between the Blue and

PAPYRUS ON THE BAḤR AL-GEBEL.

[From Sir W. Garstin's *Report*, by permission of the Comptroller of H.M. Stationery Office.

White Niles. Before, however, Nero attempted to invade Nubia he sent a tribune, with some praetorian troops, to report on the country in general, and when they returned they stated that they had found nothing on the banks of the Nile but wastes.[1] The

[1] "Certe solitudines nuper renuntiavere principi Neroni missi ab ea milites "praetoriani cum tribunum ad explorandum, inter reliqua bella et Aethiopicum "cogitandi." Pliny, vi. 35 (181).

information which they acquired about the Sûdân was considerable. They went from Syene to Meroë by the following cities:—Hiera-Sykaminos, 54 miles; Tama, 72 miles from Hiera-Sykaminos; the region of the Evonymitae, 120 miles from Tama; Acina, 64 miles from the Evonymitae; Pittara, 22 miles from the Acina; Tergedus, 103 miles from Pittara; Napata, 80 miles from Tergedus; Meroë, 360 miles from Napata; in all 875 miles. They said that the city of Meroë was 70 miles from the entrance to the island, which would make its site to be near Shendî, and that it formerly maintained 240,000 soldiers, and 3,000 artizans.[1] Nero's soldiers and the two centurions must have penetrated for a considerable distance into the Sûdân, and it is clear from a statement of Seneca that they reached the great marshes out of which the Nile was supposed to spring. The "Nili Paludes," or *αἱ τοῦ Νείλου λιμναι*,[2] were held to be situated at the foot of the mountains of the Moon, but it is incredible that the soldiers travelled so far south. They told Seneca that, after travelling an immense distance, they arrived at some marshes of enormous extent, that these were without outlet, and that the muddy water was covered over with an entangled mass of weeds, which it was impossible to wade through or to sail over. There, too, they saw two rocks, from which the river poured forth with tremendous force.[3] Now the first portion of this description suggests that Nero's centurions reached some portion of the region of the "Sadd," or "Sudd," the southern limit of which we know, on the authority of Sir William Garstin,[4] begins north of Bôr. Here the marshes are filled with papyrus and ambatch, and those reeds which require to have their roots under water for a great portion of the year. North of Shâmbî, "many islands

[1] Pliny, vi. 29 (34, 35), 184-186.

[2] Ptolemy, *Geography*, iv. 9. 3.

[3] "Ego quidem centuriones duos, quos Nero Caesar, aut aliarum virtutum, ita veritatis in primis amantissimus, ad investigandum caput Nili miserat, audivi narrantes, longum illos iter peregisse, quum a rege Aethiopiae instructi auxilio, commendatique proximis regibus, penetrassent. Ad ulteriora equidem, aiebant, pervenimus, ad immensas paludes, quarum exitum nec incolae, noverant, nec sperare quisquam potest. Ita implicitae aquis herbae sunt, et aquae nec pediti eluctabiles nec navigio, quod nisi parvum et unius capax limosa et obsit a palus non ferat. Ibi, inquit, vidimus duas petras, ex quibus ingens vis fluminis excidebat" (*Naturalium Quaestionum*, vi. 8, ed. Koeler, p. 163).

[4] *Report on the Basin of the Upper Nile*, p. 94.

"covered with ambatch and papyrus separate the stream "into numerous branches, and the whole country is a waste "of swamp."[1]

When we compare the description of the swamps of the Bahr al-Gebel by Sir William Garstin with that of the marshes, or swamps, of the two centurions it seems certain that they must have reached some portion of the Nile Valley through which that river flows.

"The scenery of the Bahr-el-Gebel throughout its course "through the 'Sudd' region is monotonous to a degree. There "are no banks at all, and, except at a few isolated spots, no "semblance of any ridge on the water's edge. The reedy swamps "stretch for many kilometres upon either side. Their expanse is "only broken at intervals by lagoons of open water. Their surface "is only a few centimetres above that of the water-level in the "river when at its lowest, and a rise of half a metre floods them "to an immense distance. These marshes are covered with a "dense growth of water-weeds extending in every direction to "the horizon. Of these reeds the principal is the papyrus, which "grows in extreme luxuriance. The stems are so close together "that it is difficult to force a way through them, and the plants "reach a height of from three to five metres above the marsh. In "addition to the papyrus large areas are covered with the reed "called *Um-soof*, or 'mother of wool,' by the Arabs, another "called *Bus*, and the tall feathery-headed grass so well known to "Indian sportsmen by the name of 'Tiger' grass. The extent of "these swamps is unknown, but more especially to the west of "the river, it must be enormous. In all probability the greater "portion of the region lying between the Bahr-el-Gebel and the "Bahr-el-Ghazal is in the rainy season a vast marsh . . . . . The "whole region has an aspect of desolation beyond the power of "words to describe. It must be seen to be understood."[2]

"North of Rejaf the 'marsh' formation commences. A low "ridge follows the water's edge on either bank. Beyond this "again on both sides is a wide depression full of tall elephant "grass and very swampy."[3]

[1] *Report on the Basin of the Upper Nile*, p. 95.
[2] *Ibid.*, p. 98.
[3] *Ibid.*, p. 90.

The two rocks through which, according to the centurions, the river rushed with tremendous force are hard to identify; some rapids appear to be referred to, and it is difficult not to think of the Fola Rapids in connection with their statement. These Rapids begin "in two or more falls with a drop of five or six "metres. . . . Below the falls the stream rushes down an extremely "narrow gorge with a very heavy slope, enclosed between vertical "walls of rocks. . . . The water tears through this channel in a "glassy green sheet with an incredible velocity. . . . At the foot of "this race the river leaps into a deep cauldron or pot, which it "fills with an apparently boiling mass of white water lashed into "foam." This cauldron is fifty metres long, and is not more than twelve metres across! Below this the channel widens out to thirty metres, "while the river thunders down in a series of rapids "for a considerable distance."[1] It is to be regretted that more details of the report of the centurions have not come down to us, but it seems quite clear that their description of the Nile swamps is based upon personal observation.

From about A.D. 54 to 260 the Nubians gave the Romans little trouble, and seem to have acquiesced in the arrangement which left them masters of the Nile Valley from Premnis (Ibrîm) southwards. Emperor after emperor added to the temples of Egypt, and a few of them, e.g., Trajan, Hadrian, and Verus, built at Philae, Talmis, and other places in the district between Syene and Dakka. The Emperors Vespasian and Titus carried on building operations in the Oasis of Dakhla[2] (Oasis Minor), which lies a journey of four days west of Al-Khârga, thereby, no doubt, attempting to establish friendly relations with the tribes of the Western Desert for the purposes of trade.

The tribes of the Eastern Desert, however, whom the ancient Egyptians knew as ÅNTI, or "Hill-men," towards the beginning of the third century A.D. began to encroach on the southern frontier of Egypt, and to occupy the lands immediately to the south of it, and to the east and west of the Thebaïd itself. It is said that these tribes had settlements even in the Oasis of Khârga. To

[1] *Report on the Basin of the Upper Nile*, p. 82.

[2] In Egyptian 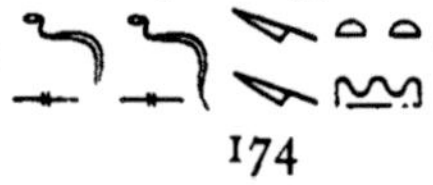 TCHESTCHESTET.

AN "ANAK" IN THE EASTERN DESERT DRAWING WATER.

[From a photograph by Sir Reginald Wingate, K.C.B.

these tribes the Greeks and Romans gave the name of "Blemyes"[1] or "Blemmyes." The Blemmyes, who at this period allied themselves to the Egyptians of the Thebaïd, were a Hamitic people who lived chiefly in the Eastern Desert, and moved from south to north and from north to south, according to the time of the year, seeking pasture for their flocks and herds; they are represented by the Bega of the Arabic writers, and by the Anaks and other modern tribes of the Bishârîn. To these joined themselves a number of negroid, or perhaps pure negro tribes, who lived near the Island of Meroë and along the White and Blue Niles, and a number of their kinsmen who dwelt in the Western Desert, and south of it so far as Kordôfân. The Blemmyes possessed an evil reputation for savagery and ferocity, and they made life a burden to the owners of trading caravans, which they pillaged at every opportunity. Their wild and fierce appearance caused them to be regarded as a class of men who were partly negroes and partly apes, and we find them grouped with the Satyrs, Aegipans, and Himantopodes. Pliny[2] goes so far as to repeat a tradition about them to the effect that they had no heads, and that their mouths and eyes were in their breasts.

About 250 A.D. the Blemmyes[3] were in Upper Egypt in considerable force, and they were plundering the villages, apparently unchecked. In 261 they were attacked by Marcus Julius Æmilianus, who had been made king of Egypt by the Alexandrians, and he succeeded in driving them back to the south of the First Cataract. Soon after Æmilianus was captured by the Roman general Theodotus, and sent to Rome, and the Blemmyes returned to the plunder of the Thebaïd. In the reign of Claudius II. they continued their acts of aggression, and with the help of Odaenathus, the son of Queen Zenobia, and the discontented Egyptians, they became masters of Upper Egypt in the reign of Aurelian (270-275). In 274 Aurelian defeated Firmus, the leader of the allied rebels, and carried off a number of the Blemmyes to Rome, where they took part in his triumphal procession. The Blemmyes were, however, unconquered, and Probus (276-282) found it difficult to

[1] Strabo, xvii. 1. 2; Pliny, v. 8.

[2] "Blemmyis traduntur capita abesse ore et oculis pectori adfixis" (v. 8, 46).

[3] *Chronicon Pasch.*, p. 504-506.

turn them out of Upper Egypt, for the tribes of the Eastern and Western Deserts united against him; eventually he succeeded in gaining possession of Coptos, the most important city in Upper Egypt, for all the trade from the East passed through it.

During the early years of the reign of Diocletian (284-305) the inroads of the Blemmyes into Egypt became more and more frequent, and the Roman troops stationed at Syene and at the various posts in the Dodekaschoinos were unable to offer any effective resistance to the marauding bands on the river, and to stop those who invaded the Thebaïd from the desert was impossible. Diocletian was unprepared to send a large army into the Sûdân, and he therefore decided to withdraw his garrisons from Syene, Hiera-Sykaminos, &c., and to hand over the protection of the Dodekaschoinos to the Nobatae, a powerful tribe of nomads who lived in the Western Desert. The Nobatae appear to have come originally from Dâr Fûr and Kordôfân, and in Diocletian's time their settlements extended to the Oasis of Khârga; all the trade of the Southern Sûdân was in their hands, and their warlike and savage disposition made them suitable opponents of the Hamitic Blemmyes of the Eastern Desert. They were the descendants of the "Mentiu," or "Cattle-men," who were a terror to the Pharaohs, and the ferocity of their modern representatives, the "Baḳḳâra," or "Cattle-men," is too well known to need description. To the Nobatae Diocletian forthwith allotted lands round about Elephantine and on each side of the river, and he arranged to pay them annually a sum of money in return for their guardianship of Roman interests. At the same time he made an agreement with the Blemmyes, in which he undertook to give them yearly a certain payment in money provided that they ceased to raid Upper Egypt and the territory which belonged to the Romans.[1]

This done, Diocletian built a strong fortress on an island near Elephantine, and set up a temple and altars whereat the Romans and the Barbarians might adjust their differences in a friendly manner, and renew their oaths to each other in the presence of priests chosen by the various parties to the agreement. At Philae the Nobatae and the Blemmyes worshipped Isis, Osiris, and

[1] *τὲ καὶ Βλέμυσιν ἔταξε δίδοσθαι ἀνὰ πᾶν ἔτος ῥητόν τι χρυσίον ἐφ' ᾧ μηκέτι γῆν τὴν Ῥωμαίων λῄσονται* (Procopius, *De Bello Persico*, i. 19, p. 103).

ANAK DWELLINGS AT GEBEL MAMAN.

[From a photograph by Sir Reginald Wingate, K.C.B.

Priapus,[1] besides other gods. The Blemmyes were in the habit of sacrificing men to the sun. The arrangements made by Diocletian were the most natural under the circumstances, but he was the first ruler of Egypt who was astute enough to play off the tribes of the Western Desert against those of the Eastern Desert, and by means of two annual payments, which must have been after all comparatively small, obtain peace in Upper Egypt.

For a period of more than one hundred years Egypt ceased to be troubled by the Blemmyes, and it is tolerably certain that both they and the Nobatae kept their agreement with the Romans. However, towards the close of the reign of Theodosius II. (408-450) the Blemmyes for some reason or other either broke faith with the Romans, or overcame the Nobatae, and we find that they invaded certain territories which were regarded by the Romans as a part of Egypt. They actually took possession of the Oasis of Khârga, and defeated the Roman soldiers stationed there, and took numbers of the inhabitants captive. The captives they subsequently released and handed over to the governor of the Thebaïd, not, however, because they were afraid of the Romans, but because the Mazices, a Numidian tribe, were preparing to attack them.

In the reign of the Emperor Marcianus (450-457), Maximinus, the commander-in-chief of the Romans in Egypt, set out on an expedition to the south, and routed the Blemmyes and Nobatae with great slaughter, and then made them set free all the prisoners they had retained, and pay a huge fine, which was distributed among all those who had suffered injury or damage at their hands. Maximinus compelled them to give hostages for their future good behaviour, and to enter into an agreement to keep the peace for one hundred years. The sole stipulation which they appear to have made is a curious one. They asked permission to make annual pilgrimages to the temple of Isis at Philae, and to borrow the statue of Isis from time to time, in order that they might obtain the blessing of the protection of the goddess, and beg boons from her. From this it is clear that the worship of Isis of Philae was, even at this period, in a flourishing state. Maximinus

[1] The old Egyptian ithyphallic god Menu (?).

agreed to the stipulation, and so long as he lived there was peace between the Romans and the two great unruly tribes of the Sûdân. On his death, however, they came to an understanding with each other and once more invaded Egypt, and succeeded in taking the hostages whom they had given out of the hands of the Romans. The revolt was soon quelled by Florus, prefect of Alexandria, and once again the Blemmyes and Nobatae undertook to keep the agreement which they had originally made.

Towards the end of the reign of Justinian I. (527-565) the period of one hundred years, during which the Blemmyes and the Nobatae had agreed with Maximinus the general to keep the peace, expired, and it seems as if they must have begun at this time to make fresh trouble in Egypt, though there is no direct evidence in support of this supposition. Be this as it may, the wrath of Justinian fell upon them, and, partly for political reasons and partly as a result of his hatred of paganism, he determined to put a stop to the worship of Isis and of the other deities of her company at Philae, which had long been the home of religious fanaticism, and therefore a hotbed of conspiracy, unrest, and discontent. So long as the tribes of the deserts had an excuse for coming to Philae it was impossible to prevent them from gathering there annually in large numbers. The orders of Justinian in this matter were carried out by Narses, who went to Philae, and closed the great temple of Isis, and removed the statues of the gods and carried them away to Constantinople; he also confiscated the revenues of the sanctuary of the goddess, and threw her priests into prison.[1]

The deeds of Narses must have been approved of by large numbers of the Nubians, otherwise they could not have been performed, and there is little doubt that the conversion of the Nobatae to Christianity, which was brought about through the instrumentality of the Empress Theodora, about A.D. 540, prepared the way for the closing of the temple of Isis. Under Tiberius II. (578-582) the tribes of the Sûdân again made themselves troublesome, but their revolt was crushed by Aristomachus, the commander-in-chief of the Roman forces in Egypt, and we

[1] Procopius, *De Bello Persico*, i. 20

"ANAK" HOUSE AT GEBEL MAMAN ON THE OLD CARAVAN ROAD BETWEEN KASALA AND SAWAKIN.

[From a photograph by Sir Reginald Wingate, K.C.B.

hear nothing more of them for nearly a century. The Romans were fully occupied in keeping the Persians out of Egypt, and the nomads of the Eastern and Western Deserts were left to govern themselves in their own way.

APPENDIX TO CHAPTER XI.

AL-MAḲRÎZÎ'S DESCRIPTION OF THE BEJA.[1]

THE beginning of the country of Beja is from the city of Kharba, at the emerald mines in the desert of Ḳûṣ, about three[2] days' journey from that town. Jaheth mentions that there are no other emerald mines in the world, but in this spot. They are found in far extended and dark caverns, into which they enter with lights and cords, for fear of going astray, and with these they trace their way back. They dig for the emeralds with axes, and find them in the midst of stones, surrounded by a substance of less value, [i.e., mica], and inferior in colour and brilliancy. The extremities of Beja touch upon the confines of Habesh [Ethiopia]. The Beja live in the midst of the island, meaning the island of Egypt, as far as the shores of the salt sea, and towards the island of Sawâkin, and Nadha, and Dahlak. They are Bedouins, and fetch the herbs, wherever they grow, in leathern sacks. They reckon lineage from the female side. Each clan has a chief; they have no sovereign, and acknowledge no religion. With them the son by the daughter, or the son by the sister, succeeds to the property, to the exclusion of the true son, and they allege that the birth of the daughter, or sister's son, is more certain, because, at all events, whether it is the husband or some one else who is the father, he is always her son. They had formerly a chief, upon whom the minor chiefs depended, who lived at the village of Hejer, on the extremity of the island of Beja. They ride choice camels, of a reddish colour, the breed of which they rear, and the Arabian camel is likewise there met with in great numbers. Their cows are very handsome, and of various colours, with very large horns; others without any horns; their sheep are spotted, and full of milk. Their food is flesh and milk, with little cheese, though

[1] See Burckhardt, *Travels*, p. 503 ff.

[2] Al-Mas'ûdî says ten.

some of them eat it. Their bodies are full grown, their stomachs emaciated, their colour has a yellowish tinge. They are swift in running, by which they distinguish themselves from other people. Their camels are likewise swift and indefatigable, and patiently bear thirst; they outrun horses with them, and fight on their backs, and turn them round with ease. They perform journeys which appear incredible.

In battle the Beja pursue each other with their camels; when they throw the lance, and it adheres, the camel flies after it, and its master takes it again; but if the lance falls down, the camel lowers its hinder parts to permit the master to take the lance up from the ground. They are people of good faith; if any of them has defrauded his guest, the latter holds up a shirt on the end of his lance, and exclaims, "This is the tent-covering of such a one," meaning the guilty; the people then abuse the culpable until he satisfies the defrauded. They are very hospitable; if a guest arrives, they kill for him (a sheep); if there be more than three people, they slaughter a camel of the nearest herd, whether it belongs to them or to any one else; and if nothing else is at hand, they kill the camel upon which the guest arrived, and afterwards give him a better in return. Their arms are the lances called "Sebaye," with an iron point three *pics* in length, and a wooden shaft of four *pics*, for which reason they are called "Sebaye." The iron head is of the breadth of a sword. They very seldom deposit these lances, but keep them always in their hands. On the extremity of the wood is something like a handle, which prevents it from slipping through the hand. These lances are made by women, at a place where they have no intercourse with men, except with those who come to buy the lances. If any of these women bears a female child by one of these visitors, they permit it to live; but if a male, they kill it, saying that all men are a plague and a misfortune. Their shields are made of cow-skins full of hair; and others of their shields, called Aksomye,[1] are inverted in shape, and made of buffalo skin, as are likewise the Dahlakye, or else of the skin of a sea animal. Their bow is the Arabian bow, large and thick, made of the wood of Seder and Shohat; they use them with poisoned arrows: the poison is

[1] From the city Axum.

made of the root of the tree Falfa (or Galga), which is boiled over the fire until it dissolves into a glue. To try its efficacy, one of the people scratches his skin, and lets the blood flow; if the blood, upon being touched with the poison, is driven back, they know that the poison is strong, and they wipe the blood off, that it may not return into the body and kill the person. If the arrow hits a man, it kills him in an instant, even though the wound be not larger than the scratch made in cupping; but it has no effect except in wounds, and in blood, and it may be drunk without any harm.

The country is full of mines; the higher it is ascended the richer it is found to be in gold. There are mines of silver, copper, iron, lead, loadstone, marcasite, hamest, emeralds, and a very brittle stone, of which if a piece is rubbed with oil, it burns like a wick; other similar productions are found in their researches after gold; but the Beja work none of these mines except those of gold. In their valleys grow the tree Mokel [*dûm* palm ?], and the Ahlylej [myrobolan ?], and the Adkher, the Shyh [Artemisia?], Sena, Coloquintida, Ban [tamarisk?], and others. On the farthest confines of their country dates, and vines, and odoriferous plants, and others grow naturally. All sorts of wild animals are seen here, as lions, elephants, tigers, fahed, monkeys, weasels (?), civet cats, and a beautiful animal resembling the gazelle, with two horns of a golden colour; it holds out but a short time when it is hunted. Their birds are the parrot, the taghteit, the nouby, the pigeon called *narein*, the wood dove, the Abyssinian fowl, and others. Maribus omnibus in hâc regione testiculorum dexter abstrahitur: praecisa autem foeminarum labia pudendi, intensione primâ, ut medici dicunt, contrahuntur et sibi invicem radicitùs adhaerent; ante nuptias perforantur, cum rima ad mensuram inguinis virilis efficitur. Haec autem, quae jam rarior est, consuetodo, originem traxisse fertur ex antiquo pacis foedere, cum tyranno quodam inito, qui, ad gentem funditùs defendam, universis imperavit, ut masculorum liberorum testiculos, alterius autem sexûs mammas abscinderent: hi vero, diversâ ratione, maribus quidem mammas, foeminis pudenda exsecabant.

A race of Beja tear out their back teeth, alleging that they do not wish to resemble asses. Another of their races living on the extremity of their country is called Baza. Among them all the women are called by the same name, and so are the men. A Moslim merchant once travelled through their country, who, happening to be a handsome man, they called out to each other and said, "This is God descended from heaven;" and they kept looking at him from afar while he sat under a tree.[1] The serpents of this country are large and of many different species: it is related that a serpent was once lying in a pond, with its tail above water, and that a woman who came in search of water looked at it, and died in convulsions. Here lives a serpent without a head, not large, with both extremities (or sides) alike, and of a spotted colour. If a person walks upon its track, he dies; and if it is killed, and the person takes into his hand the stick that killed it, he himself is killed; one of these serpents was once killed by a stick, and the stick split in two. If any of these serpents, whether alive or dead, is looked at, the beholder will be hurt.

The Beja country is always in commotion, and the people are prone to mischief. During the Islâm, and before that time, they had oppressed the eastern banks of Upper Egypt, and had ruined many villages. The Pharaoh kings of Egypt made incursions against them, and at other times left them in peace, on account of their works at the gold mines; and the Greeks did the same when they took Egypt. Remarkable ruins of Greek origin are still to be seen at the mines, and their people were in possession of these mines when Egypt was conquered by the Moslems.

The interior Beja live in the desert between the country of Aloa and the salt sea, and extend to the limits of the country of Habesh. Their people rear cattle and are pastors; their way of living, their ships, and army, are like those of the Hadharebe, but the latter are a more courageous and more religious people, whilst those of the interior all remain infidels. They adore the devil, and follow the example of their priests: every clan has its priest, who pitches a tent made of feathers, in the shape of a dome, wherein he practises his adorations; when they consult him about their affairs, he strips naked, and enters the tent stepping backwards; he afterwards issues with the appearance of a mad

[1] Burckhardt says that when the Beja women saw him they uttered a shriek, and those who spoke Arabic exclaimed, "God preserve us from the devil!"

and delirious person, and exclaims, "The devil salutes you, and tells you to depart from this place, for that a hostile party (naming it) will fall upon you." If you ask advice about an expedition which you may be about to undertake against any particular country, he often answers, "March on, and you will be victorious, and will take booty to such an amount, and the camels you will take at such a place must be my property, as well as the female slave you will find in such a tent, and the sheep," &c. On the march, the priest loads his tent upon a camel destined for that sole purpose, and they believe that the camel rises up from the ground, and walks with great difficulty, and that it sweats profusely, although the tent is quite empty, and nothing is in it. Among the Hadharebe live some of those people who still retain this religion, and others who mix with it the Islam.

CHAPTER XII.

THE MUḤAMMADAN INVASION AND OCCUPATION OF THE SÛDÂN.

THE fortress of Babylon in Egypt fell into the hands of the Muḥammadans under ʻAmr ibn al-ʻÂṣî, general of Omar the Khalîfa, on the 9th of April, 641, and thus Egypt, and such portions of the Sûdân as were regarded as her possessions, at once became a province of the new Muḥammadan Empire. As soon as the fortress was taken ʻAmr at once set about occupying the principal divisions of Egypt, and sent troops into Alexandria, Damietta, and Tinnîs in Lower Egypt, and into the Fayyûm and other portions of Upper Egypt. About a year after the conquest of Egypt ʻAmr sent an expedition into Nubia[1] under one of his generals called ʻAbd-Allah bin Saʻd, whose force consisted of twenty thousand men.[2] Al-Masʻûdî tells us (chap. xxxiii.) that the Arabs attacked the Nubians, and discovered that they

[1] "In the history of Bahnase (Oxyrhinchus), and that of its valorous defence "against the Arab conquerors of Egypt, I find it stated, that a large army of "Bedjas and Noubas, headed by Maksouh, king of Bedja, and Ghalyk, king of "Nouba, came to the assistance of the Christian chief, Batlos, who was besieged "at Bahnase, by the officers of Amr Ibn el Aas. This black army is said to have "consisted of 50,000 men. They had with them 1,300 elephants, each bearing "upon its back a vaulted house made of leather, in which ten men took their "post in the battle. In the company of the Bedjas were a race of men of "gigantic stature, called El-Kowad, coming from beyond Souakin. They were "covered with tiger skins, and in their upper lips copper rings were fixed. The "Moslims defeated this army. There is a strange mixture of truth and romance "in this history, but the arrival of the Bedja army is so well authenticated by a "train of witnesses, that little doubt can remain of it having really taken place; "although the number both of men and elephants seems to be exaggerated. The "elephants of southern Nubia are, as far as I know, no longer used to ride "upon." (Burckhardt, *Travels*, p. 528.) The giants referred to above are clearly those who in modern times are known by the name of "Anaks."

[2] The authority for this statement is Al-Maḳrîzî. For the Arabic text, see Naʻum Bey Shucair, *History of the Sûdân*, vol. ii., p. 42.

were first-class archers, but he does not say where the fight took place. 'Abd-Allah stayed in Nubia for some time, and there is little doubt that he found his task not so easy as he had imagined; he was at length recalled by 'Amr, who, however, gave the Nubians no rest so long as he had power in Egypt. The Arabs appear to have entrenched themselves strongly at Aswân, which they made their frontier city, and they soon found that the Nubians were ever ready to cause them trouble, and to break out in revolt. When 'Abd-Allah returned to Fusṭâṭ (Cairo), the Nubians saw their opportunity, and, pouring northwards from the south, they invaded Egypt and laid waste the country far and wide.

For some years the Arabs watched these invasions in silence, but at length, in 652, 'Abd-Allah returned to the Sûdân and crushed the rebellion of the Blacks with merciless rigour. The capital of the new kingdom of the Blacks, who were now Christians, had been placed at Dongola (Old), a town situated on the east bank of the Nile, about 280 miles south of Wâdî Ḥalfa, by Silko, the king of the Blemmyes, about A.D. 450. To this town 'Abd-Allah sailed or marched, and, when he had battered down all its chief buildings, including the church, with stones which he hurled against them from slings, the natives cried out for peace. Their king Koleydozo[1] came out of the town with all "the signs of weakness, misery, and humbleness," and was graciously received by 'Abd-Allah, who granted him peace on the condition that he paid the annual tribute of slaves, which had already been agreed upon by 'Amr. Al-Maḳrîzî says that his *Bâḳṭ*,[2] or tribute, consisted of three hundred and sixty slaves, but Al-Mas'ûdî gives the number as three hundred and sixty-five, and says that besides these, there were forty slaves for the governor of Egypt, twenty for the governor of Aswân, five for the judge, and twelve for the inspectors, whose duty it was to see that the slaves were in a sound and healthy condition. The place fixed for the payment of the Baḳṭ was Al-Ḳaṣr (i.e., the Fortress), near the Island of Philae, on the western bank, six miles from Aswân. The king of Dongola having agreed to observe faithfully the stipulation which had been made by 'Amr, 'Abd-Allah made a treaty with him, the contents

[1] Burckhardt, *Travels*, p. 511.

[2] البقط.

of which, as given by Al-Makrîzî, who quotes Ibn-Selîm Al-Aswânî, are well worth recording here; it reads:—[1]

"In the Name of God, &c. This is a treaty granted by the "Emîr 'Abd-Allah ibn Sa'd ibn Abî-Sarh, to the chief of the "Nubians and to all the people of his dominions, a treaty binding "on great and small among them, from the frontier of Aswân to "the frontier of 'Alwa. 'Abd-Allah ibn Sa'd ordains security and "peace between them and the Muslims, their neighbours in Upper "Egypt, as well as all other Muslims and their tributaries. Ye "people of Nubia, ye shall dwell in safety under the safeguard of "God and His Apostle, Muḥammad the Prophet, whom God "bless and save! We will not attack you, nor wage war on you, "nor make incursions against you, so long as ye abide by the "terms settled between us and you. When ye enter our country, it "shall be but as travellers, not as settlers, and when we enter your "country it shall be as travellers, not settlers. Ye shall protect "those Muslims or their allies who shall come into your land and "travel there, until they quit it. Ye shall give up the slaves of "Muslims who seek refuge among you, and send them back to the "country of Islâm; and likewise the Muslim fugitive who is at "war with the Muslims, him ye shall expel from your country to "the realm of Islâm; ye shall not espouse his cause nor prevent "his capture. Ye shall put no obstacle in the way of a Muslim, "but render him aid till he quit your territory. Ye shall take care "of the mosque which the Muslims have built in the outskirt of "your city, and hinder none from praying there; ye shall clean it, "and light it, and honour it. Every year ye shall pay three "hundred and sixty head of slaves to the leader of the Muslims, of "the middle class of the slaves of your country, without bodily "defects, males and females, but no old men, nor old women, nor "young children. Ye shall deliver them to the governor of Aswân. "No Muslim shall be bound to repulse an enemy from you or "to attack him, or hinder him, from 'Alwa to Aswân. If ye "harbour a Muslim slave, or kill a Muslim or an ally, or attempt "to destroy the mosque which the Muslims have built in the out-"skirt of your city, or withhold any of the three hundred and "sixty head of slaves,—then this promised peace and security will "be withdrawn from you, and we shall revert to hostility, until "God decide between us, and He is the best of umpires. For our "performance of these conditions we pledge our word, in the name "of God, and our compact and faith, and belief in the name of "His Apostle Muḥammad, God bless and save him! And for "your performance of the same ye pledge yourselves by all that "ye hold most sacred in your religion; by the Messiah, and by "the Apostles, and by all whom ye revere in your creed and

[1] Stanley Lane Poole's translation (*Middle Ages*, p. 21); see also Burckhardt, *Travels*, p. 511.

"religion. And God is witness of these things between us and "you. Written by 'Amr ibn Shuraḥbîl in Ramaḍân in the year "31" (A.D. 652).

When the Nubians paid the Baḳṭ to 'Amr, they added forty slaves as a present for himself, but these he refused to accept, and returned them to Samkûs, the inspector of the Baḳṭ, who gave the Nubians wine and provisions for them. The additional forty slaves were always sent with the tribute, and in later times the Nubians received in exchange wheat, barley, wine, horses, and stuffs.[1] The Baḳṭ was paid regularly by the Nubians for a period of about six hundred years.

In the year 722,[2] under the rule of the Khalîfa 'Omar ibn 'Abd al-'Azîz, 'Obêd Allah ibn al-Ḥabbâb, the treasurer, carried out a general destruction of the sacred pictures of the Christians in Egypt. This resulted in a rising of the Copts in the Delta, which, though suppressed for a time, broke out again when the Coptic Patriarch was imprisoned. The Nubians were so enraged at the ill-treatment which their co-religionists received that their king Cyriacus marched into Egypt at the head of one hundred thousand men, and was only induced to return to his own country by the request of the Patriarch, who was hastily liberated.

Under the rule of the Beni 'Ommîa and the Beni 'Abbâs,[3] the Nubians sold several villages to the inhabitants of Aswân, and when Ma'mûn became Khalîfa (A.D. 813) their king appealed to him for protection against the men of Aswân. The matter was referred to the governor of Aswân, and the sale was confirmed.[4]

Under the rule of Ma'mûn the Beja, i.e., the tribes of the Eastern Desert, caused the Muslims a great deal of trouble, and at length, in 831, 'Abd-Allah ibn Jahân set out to do battle against them. This general defeated them several times, and finally made a treaty with their king Kanûn, who lived at Hejer. In this it was stipulated that the Beja should pay an annual tribute

[1] The exact amounts are given by Burckhardt, *Travels*, p. 512.

[2] Stanley Lane Poole, *Middle Ages*, p. 27.

[3] These tribes appear to have made their way into the Eastern Sûdân from Arabia in the eighth century, and to have settled on the Blue Nile and near the modern Sennaar.

[4] Burckhardt, *Travels*, p. 517.

of one hundred camels, or three hundred *dînârs*, that the country from Aswân to Dahlak and Nadha should be the property of the Khalîfa, who should be the overlord of the whole district. Further, the Beja were not to mention disrespectfully the name of Muḥammad, or his Kur'ân, or the religion of God, or to kill a Muslim, whether he were free man or slave, or to assist the enemies of the Muslims, or to rob a Muslim, wherever he might be; and if they did, they were to pay the blood fine ten-fold, and the value of the slave ten-fold, and the value of any Muslim tributary ten-fold. Muslim merchants and pilgrims were to be permitted to pass through the country in safety. Muslim runaways, or fugitives, and strayed cattle were to be given up, and in the latter case no fees were to be paid. The Beja were to be unarmed when travelling in Egypt. Muslims were to be allowed to trade in Beja land without molestation, their goods were not to be pilfered, and they were to pass through the land at will. No mosque of the Muslims was to be injured, and officers were to be allowed to enter Beja land to collect alms from the true believers. The Nubian king Kanûn ibn Azîz was to appoint an Agent in Upper Egypt to ensure the payment of the tribute as well as of fines. No Beja was to enter the Nuba country between Al-Ḳaṣr, near Philae, and Ḳubbân. This treaty was translated by Zakarya ibn Ṣâlah of Jidda and 'Abd-Allah ibn Isma'îl, and some of the inhabitants of Aswân were witnesses thereto.

About A.D. 833 the Nubians appear to have become somewhat lax in the payment of the Baḳṭ, and the Muslims of the frontier promptly stopped the supply of provisions which they had been accustomed to send to them. Zakarya ibn Bahnas, the king of the Nubians, urged by his son Fêrakî, then determined to cease to pay tribute, and if necessary to prepare to fight his overlord, the Khalîfa Mo'taṣim (833-842). Fêrakî set out for Baghdad in order to lay his father's case before the Khalîfa, and he was joined on his journey by the king of the Beja and his retinue. The Khalîfa received Fêrakî very kindly, and accepted his presents, giving him in return gifts which were double their value. He told Fêrakî to ask for any favour he wished, and the Nubian prince at once asked that certain Nubian prisoners might be set free; this the Khalîfa at once did. Fêrakî found great favour in his sight, and the Khalîfa made him a present of the house wherein he had alighted in Mesopotamia, and bought two houses for him in Cairo, one at Gîza, and one at Beni Wayl in Cairo. When Mo'taṣim inquired into the question of the Baḳṭ, he found that the gifts given by the Muslims to the Nubians exceeded in value their tribute; thereupon he refused to send them any more wine, and reduced the quantity of corn and of the stuffs which was to be given to them, and he decreed that the Baḳṭ was to be paid at intervals of three years. The Nubian king next demanded that the fortress of Al-Ḳaṣr should be removed from his territory to the frontier, and appealed for justice in the matter of certain lands which the inhabitants of Aswân had purchased from his slaves; in each case his suit was rejected by the Khalîfa, and the Baḳṭ was paid according to his decree.[1]

In 854 the Beja broke faith with the Muslims and declined to pay the tribute, which at that time consisted of four hundred slaves, male and female, a number of camels, two elephants, and two giraffes. They slew the Egyptian officers and miners who were working the emerald mines in the Eastern Desert, and then invaded Upper Egypt, and plundered the towns of Esna, or Asna, and Edfû, and drove out the inhabitants from these and many other cities. 'Ambasa, the Muslim governor of Egypt, wrote to his master Al-Mutawakkil at Baghdad, and asked for instructions. Notwithstanding the reports which had reached him of the savagery of the Beja and their country, Al-Mutawakkil determined to punish the rebels.

The Muslim troops were collected quickly at Kuft (Coptos), Esna, Erment, and Aswân on the Nile, and at Ḳusêr on the Red Sea, with large stores of weapons, horses, camels, &c. Seven ships were manned at Kulzum, and laden with stores, and they sailed for Sanga near 'Aydhâb,[2] the chief port on the African coast

[1] Ibn Selîm Al-Aswânî, quoted by Burckhardt, *Travels*, p. 514.

[2] 'Aydhâb was seventeen days' journey from Ḳûṣ on the Nile; it had no walls, and most of its houses were built of mats. It was formerly one of the first harbours in the world, because the ships of India and Yemen brought their merchandise there; it maintained its important position until

of the Red Sea. The commander, Muḥammad of Ḳumm, marched from Ḳûṣ, with 7,000 men, crossed the desert to the emerald mines, and even went near Dongola. 'Alî Bâbâ, king of the Sûdân, collected a large army, and prepared to meet him, but as his men were naked and armed only with short spears, they were at a great disadvantage. Their camels were, moreover, ill-trained and unmanageable. The Nubians skirmished from place to place, and had nearly worn out the Muslims, when the seven ships from Kulzum appeared off the coast. The Muslim general hung camel-bells round the necks of his horses, and when the Blacks came on to attack him, he suddenly charged them with the cry of "Allâhu Akbar," i.e., "God is the Great One." The clang of the bells on the horses' necks and the noise of the drums and the shoutings so terrified the camels, that they threw their riders and, turning tail, stampeded. 'Alî Bâbâ himself escaped, but his forces were defeated with great slaughter, and he sued for peace, and agreed to pay the arrears of the Baḳṭ, or tribute. Muḥammad of Ḳumm received him with honour, made him sit on his own carpet, gave him rich presents, and induced him to go to Fusṭâṭ, and later, in 855, to see the Khalîfa at Baghdâd.[1] 'Alî Bâbâ also undertook not to obstruct the work of the Muslims at the emerald mines.

A.D. 1420, when Aden took its place. It lay in a bare desert, and all provisions, and even water, were imported. Its inhabitants grew rich by the taxes which they levied on the merchants who thronged the place, and they took toll on every camel-load of goods; and they hired out to the pilgrims to Mekka the ships wherein they sailed to Jidda and back, thereby making much profit. Close to 'Aydhâb was a pearl fishery, and the divers, when not working, lived in the town. The people of 'Aydhâb lived like brutes, and were more like animals than men. The ships that carried the pilgrims were made without nails. They bound the planks with ropes made of cocoa-tree bark, and drove into them pegs made of palm-tree wood, and they poured over them butter, or oil made from a plant or taken from a large fish which devoured those who were drowned. The sails were of mats made from the produce of the Mokel tree. The men of 'Aydhâb overcrowded their ships, saying, "To us belongs the care of the ships, and to the pilgrims that of their own selves." The inhabitants of 'Aydhâb were Bejas, who were said to have no religion, and to be people of no understanding. Their males and females were constantly naked, some wearing rags round their loins, but many of them having no covering whatsoever.

[1] This narrative is told by Ibn Miskaweh, and is translated by Burckhardt, *Travels*, pp. 508-509, and by Poole, *Middle Ages*, pp. 41-42.

In 878 Abû 'Abd Ar-Raḥmân ibn 'Abd-Allah marched to the gold mines in the Eastern Desert, with 6,000 camels and a large number of men, and for a time he carried on work there, and obtained much gold. The local Arabs caused him much trouble, and he moved on to Shankir, to the south of Dongola; here he attacked the Nubians who were led by their king George, and defeated him.

In 956 the king of the Nubians attacked Aswân, and slew many of the Muslims there, and in the following year Muḥammad ibn 'Abd-Allah marched against him and defeated him. Muḥammad sent many Nubian prisoners to Cairo, where they were beheaded, and he captured Ibrîm (Primis), took its inhabitants captive, and returned to Cairo with 150 prisoners and many heads. A few years later the Nubians again invaded Egypt, and took possession of the country so far north as Akhmîm.

In 969 Gawhar, the governor of Egypt, sent a mission to George, king of Nubia, to receive the customary tribute and to invite him to embrace Islâm. George received the envoy Aḥmad ibn Solaim with great courtesy, and, presumably, paid the tribute, but he remained a Christian.

In 1005 the peace of Nubia was disturbed in a singular manner. A member of the royal 'Umayyad family,[1] who adopted the name of "Abû Raḳwa," i.e., "father of the leather bottle," from the leather water-skin which he carried after the manner of the Dervishes, took possession of Barka, defeated the troops of Ḥâkim, who had been sent against him, overran Egypt, and vanquished the Khalîfa's troops again at Gîza, where he encamped. He found it necessary to retreat to Nubia with his followers, where he was joined by the Nubians, but he was subsequently overcome, and his head and the heads of 30,000 of his followers were sent to Cairo, and thence in procession through all the towns of Syria on the backs of 100 camels, and then thrown into the Euphrates. Faḍl, the general who had brought about his defeat, was ill-rewarded for his services. He was unlucky enough to enter Ḥâkim's presence as he was cutting up the body of a beautiful little child whom he had just murdered. Faḍl was horrified, and, knowing that he had seen too much, went home,

[1] Abu Ṣâliḥ calls him Al-Walîd ibn Hishâm al-Khârijî.

made his will, and admitted the Khalîfa's headsman an hour later.[1]

In 1173 an expedition into Nubia was undertaken by the elder brother of Ṣalâḥ ad-Dîn (Saladin), who was called Shams ad-Dawlah Tûrân Shâh, and surnamed Fakhr ad-Dîn, first with the view of compelling the Nubians to pay tribute, and secondly to find out if it was a suitable country for the retreat of his brother Saladin in the event of his needing to fly from Egypt beyond the reach of his overlord Nûr ad-Dîn. Tûrân Shâh crossed into Nubia from Yemen, and, driving all the natives before him, he arrived at Ibrîm, or Primis, which was well supplied with provisions and arms. The Nubians made a stubborn defence, but were defeated, and their city was destroyed, and all its inhabitants, about 700,000 men, women, and children, were taken prisoners. In the city were found 700 pigs,[2] which the Muslims promptly killed. The Muslim conqueror ordered the cross on the church to be burned, and his followers pillaged the church, and the Muslim call to prayer was chanted from the top of its dome. The bishop of the district, who was in the city, was examined by torture, but he had no hidden treasure to reveal, and he was therefore made prisoner and thrown into the fortress on the hill, which was very strong. A large quantity of cotton was found in the city, and this Tûrân Shâh sent to Ḳûṣ in Upper Egypt and sold. Having left a company of horsemen in Ibrîm, with an abundant supply of food, arms, and ammunition, Tûrân Shâh departed.

Abû Ṣâliḥ tells us[3] that Saladin went with the Patriarch Anbâ Khâ'îl to beg for assistance from the Nubians when George was king of Nubia. George was filled with wrath when he heard of the treatment meted out to the Patriarch, and he collected 100,000 men and as many camels, and marched into Egypt, which he everywhere laid waste. At length he reached Cairo. Now this event, as Mr. Butler has already pointed out, took place in the reign of Marwân II., the last 'Umayyad Khalîfa (A.D. 750-

[1] Poole, *Middle Ages*, p. 129; Shucair, *History of the Sûdân*, ii., p. 50.

[2] Abû Ṣâliḥ, ed. Evetts and Butler, p. 267; Poole, *Middle Ages*, p. 197; Shucair, *op. cit.*, ii., p. 51.

[3] Ed. Evetts and Butler, p. 267.

754), and the Emîr of Egypt was not Saladin, but 'Abd al-Malik ibn Mûsâ ibn Nâṣir.

In 1174 Saladin's forces defeated the army of Kanz ad-Dawlah, the rebel governor of Aswân, who had marched against Cairo with an army of Blacks and Arabs. A battle took place near the village of Tûd, and the rebel's followers were routed with great slaughter. Kanz ad-Dawlah himself escaped, but he was killed soon afterwards.

For a period of about twenty years there appears to have been peace between the Nubians and Saladin, and at his death on March 4th, 1193, the port of Aswân became deserted, and the town fell into a state of decay.

In 1275 the Muslims annexed the Sûdân. This result was brought about by Dâwûd, the king of the Nubians, who refused to pay the Baḳṭ which had been fixed by 'Amr ibn al-'Âsî soon after the capture of Babylon of Egypt, and broke the terms of his treaty with the Muslims by seizing numbers of Arabs, and carrying them off as prisoners, both at Aswân and at 'Aydhâb, the chief port of the Beja on the Red Sea. Moreover, Dâwûd burned many water-wheels on the Nile, whereby much of the land went out of cultivation. The Egyptian governor of Ḳûṣ set out to do battle with him, but could not overtake him ; the governor, however, succeeded in seizing many Nubians, and the Lord of the Mountain,[1] and having taken these to Cairo, the Bahrite Mamlûk Khalîfa Rukn ad-Din Bêbars (1260-1277) ordered them all to be hewn in twain. Now it happened at this time that Shakanda, the son of the sister of Dâwûd, came to Cairo to ask assistance, and to plead against the injustice which he had suffered at his uncle's hands. Bêbars espoused the nephew's cause, and sent him, together with a large army under the command of two Amîrs, into Nubia to overthrow his uncle. The army consisted of horsemen, spearmen, bowmen, and men who were skilled in burning down the buildings of an enemy.

When the Muslim force arrived in Nubia it was met by Dâwûd's army, the spearmen of which were mounted on camels ; both sides fought bravely, but the Nubians were defeated, and fled. The Muslims advanced into Nubia by desert and by river, and

[1] I.e., the governor of the islands of Mîkâ'îl and of the province of Daw.

seized fortress after fortress, and slew many men, and took many prisoners. At length they reached the Island of Mîkâ'îl (Michael),[1] at the "head of the Cataracts," and drove back the Nubian boats, whereupon the Nubians fled to the islands in the Nile. Large numbers of cattle fell into the hands of the Muslims. Thereupon Ḳamr ad-Dawlah, the general of Dâwûd, swore allegiance to Shakanda, and, as the Amîr Fârḳânî gave him a safe-conduct, he went and brought back the people of Merîs to their towns, and all the fugitives. The other Amîr, Al-Afrâm, then besieged a tower on a small island in the river and took it. Here Dâwûd and his brother had taken refuge. Two hundred men were slain, Dâwûd's brother was taken prisoner, but Dâwûd himself escaped; he was pursued by the Muslim soldiers for three days, but they could not overtake him. His mother and sister, however, fell into the hands of the enemy. The Amîrs now established Shakanda as king of Nubia, and he agreed to pay annually three elephants, three giraffes, five panthers, one hundred camels of good stock, and four hundred cows. He promised to divide the revenue of his country into two parts, one of which was to be given to Bêbars or his successor, and the other to be devoted to the upkeep and guarding of the country.

The territory of the Cataracts, since it was near Aswân, was to belong to Bêbars; this territory was equal to one quarter of Nubia, and at that time produced cotton and dates. Besides all this, so long as the Nubians remained Christians, Shakanda undertook to pay annually one gold dînâr as poll tax, for every adult male of the population. He also swore a solemn oath to observe these conditions on behalf of himself, and his subjects also swore solemn oaths on behalf of themselves. The Amîrs then destroyed the churches of Nubia, and carried off everything of value which they found in them. They seized the persons of about twenty Nubian chiefs, and set free the Muslim prisoners from Aswân and 'Aydhâb. When Shakanda had taken the oath, he was set upon the throne and crowned king. He was compelled to give up to Bêbars all the property of Dâwûd, as well as all that of those who had been killed or taken captive, in addition to the Baḳṭ or tribute, which then consisted of four hundred head of

[1] Perhaps the Island of Sâî.

slaves and one giraffe; in return he was to receive one thousand *ardebs* of wheat, and his delegates three hundred.[1]

In 1287 Al-Manṣûr Ḳalâ'ûn sent an expedition into Nubia, which raided the country for a distance of fifteen days' journey south of Dongola. Before his generals returned to Cairo they established a garrison in that city, but so soon as they had retired the Nubians rose and drove out the garrison, and Ḳalâ'ûn was obliged to send a second army to Nubia to put down the revolt and to punish the rebels. The first expedition was undertaken as the result of a request made by Adûr, king of the Gates, who made complaints against Shemamûn, king of Nubia, and sent a gift of elephants and a giraffe to Ḳalâ'ûn. The king of Dongola then sent four hundred and twenty-six head of slaves, and two hundred cattle, which he caused to be taken to Ḳûṣ. When Shemamûn saw the Muslims approaching he fled, and a great number of his soldiers were slain. Jûrês, "the Lord of the Mountain," and one of the king's cousins were taken prisoners, and Shemamûn's nephew was appointed king; and the Muslims carried off large numbers of slaves, horses, camels, cattle, and stuffs. Shemamûn then appeared and drove out the Egyptian garrison, and his nephew went to Ḳalâ'ûn and told him what had happened. When the second expedition reached Aswân, the king of Nubia, i.e., Shemamûn's nephew, died, and a nephew of king Dâwûd was appointed in his stead. When the Muslim army entered Nubia, the soldiers massacred every one they found there, burned the water-wheels, and fed their horses on the crops.

When they reached Dongola they only found there one old man and one old woman, for Shemamûn and his followers had fled, and had taken refuge on an island which was fifteen days' journey from Dongola. When the Muslims arrived there, Shemamûn retired to "the Gates," a further distance of three days' journey. Here he was abandoned by his officers and by the bishop and the priests, who took away from him his crown and the silver cross which he wore. They returned to Dongola, and, having partaken of a meal in the Church of Jesus, they crowned as king the nephew of Dâwûd, who took the oath of allegiance, and undertook to

[1] See Burckhardt, *Travels*, pp. 514-516; Poole, *Middle Ages*, p. 271; and Shucair, *History of the Sûdân*, ii., p. 52.

pay the tribute. As soon as the Muslims returned to Egypt, Shemamûn reappeared, and all his soldiers flocked to his standard. Marching at their head, he attacked the palace at Dongola, made prisoner the new king, and so found himself master of the country once more. He then cut the throat of a bull, and having cut the hide into strips, he bound the body of his prisoner with them, tying him to a post. As the strips of hide dried, they shrank and cut into the ex-king's body, and caused his death. Shemamûn then slew Jûrês, "the Lord of the Mountain," and wrote and told Ḳalâ'ûn what he had done, and asked for his friendship, and promised to pay an increased tribute. His envoys took with them rich presents and many slaves, and as Ḳalâ'ûn took no steps to chastise Shemamûn we may assume that he condoned his behaviour.

In 1304 An-Nâṣir sent an expedition into Nubia to replace on the throne Amai, who had come to Cairo to implore his help; the leader of the Muslim troops was Sêf ad-Dîn Taktûba, governor of Ḳûṣ.

In 1311 Kerenbes, king of Nubia, went to Egypt after his brother's death, and took the appointed tribute with him. The following year Muḥammad ibn Ḳalâ'ûn sent 'Abd-Allah, the son of Sanbu, to Nubia, with an army under the command of 'Azz ad-Dîn Ibek, who was ordered to crown Sanbu king. Kerenbes and his brother Ibrahîm fled from Dongola, but they soon fell into the hands of the Muslims, and were sent to Cairo and cast into prison. Sanbu was crowned king, and the Amîr and his army returned to Cairo. Thereupon Kanz ad-Dawlah went to Dongola, slew the new king, and ascended the throne of Nubia. On this the Sulṭân took Ibrahîm out of prison and sent him to Nubia, promising him to set at liberty his brother Kerenbes so soon as he delivered Kanz ad-Dawlah bound into his hands. When Ibrahîm came to Dongola, Kanz ad-Dawlah submitted, and Ibrahîm arrested him, and would have sent him to Cairo only he (Ibrahîm) died three days later; the Nubians then unanimously elected Kanz ad-Dawlah to be their king.

In 1324 Kerenbes returned to Dongola with two Amîrs and a force of soldiers, and Kanz ad-Dawlah fled on their approach. Kerenbes was crowned king, but when the Muslims had departed,

Kanz ad-Dawlah attacked him, and once more defeated him, and once more ascended the throne of Nubia.

In 1365 the tribe of Kanz gained possession of Aswân and the desert of 'Aydhâb, and they robbed the caravans, and plundered travellers, until at length no merchant dared to travel in that region. A nephew of the king of Nubia revolted, and attacked Dongola at the head of an army of Arabs, and in the fierce battle which took place the king was slain and his followers were scattered. The loyal Nubians placed their late king's brother on the throne, and entrenched themselves in Daw. The rebel nephew, having made himself king, invited all the chiefs of the Arabs who had assisted him to a great feast, and on the appointed day they came to the rendez-vous. Whilst they were feasting all the houses round about were filled with wood and set on fire, and, as the guests rushed out in alarm from the building in which they were, they were cut down by the soldiers of the new king who were stationed at the door. In this way nineteen Amîrs and a large number of chiefs were slain. Not content with this, he fell upon the camp of the Arabs and massacred the greater part of them, and, having driven away the remainder, seized all their possessions. He then went to Daw, and, making peace with the last king's brother, joined with him in a petition to the Sulṭân that he would send them help to drive away the Arabs, and to regain possession of their kingdom. Their petition was granted, and a Muslim force was sent into Nubia. When its commander arrived there he learned that the king in the fortress of Daw was besieged by the Arabs. He passed on to Ibrîm, and soon after joined forces with the king of Nubia. Without waiting for the remainder of his army, he seized the Awlâd Kenz, and the Amîrs of the Akremî Arabs, and then marched on the west bank of the river to the Island of Mîkâ'îl, whilst the king of Nubia and his forces marched along the right bank. They attacked the island on both sides, and nearly all the Akremî were killed by arrows or by Greek fire. The Amîr Khalîl ibn Kûsûn returned to the Amîr Aktamûr with much spoil and many slaves.

With the consent of Aktamûr the king of Nubia took up his residence at Daw, for the town of Dongola was in ruins, and the nephew of the king was in Ibrîm; the former sent presents of slaves, horses, and dromedaries to the Sulṭân in Cairo, which arrived in due course and were accepted. On their way back the Muslim generals took with them the chiefs of the Awlâd Kenz and of the Akremî Arabs loaded with fetters. At Aswân they tarried seven days, and executed summary justice upon the slaves of the Awlâd Kenz against whom complaints were made.

In the same year the Sulṭân appointed Hosam, surnamed "Black blood," to be governor of Aswân, and sent to him the prisoners of the Awlâd Kenz who were in Cairo. When they reached Ḳûṣ, Hosam had them nailed to pieces of wood, and, having marched them in this state to Aswân, hewed them asunder there. Here he was compelled to fight the Awlâd Kenz, but was defeated, and most of his soldiers were wounded. The conquerors wreaked their vengeance on the people of Aswân, ravaged the country round about, burned and destroyed the houses, slew the men, and carried off the women.

In 1378 Kart, the governor of Aswân, sent to Cairo the heads of eleven chiefs, and two hundred men of the Awlâd Kenz in fetters; the heads were exhibited on the Bab Zuwêla. In the same year the governor arrested an official called Gôlam Allah, and seized a large number of swords which it was believed he intended to hand over to the Awlâd Kenz. At this time two members of that tribe were nailed to wood, and, having been led through the streets of Cairo and Fusṭâṭ in this state, were hewn asunder. In 1385 the Awlâd Kenz seized Aswân, and slew the greater number of its inhabitants. Husên, the son of Kart, was appointed governor. About three years later the Awlâd Kenz committed further outrages in Aswân and the neighbourhood. In 1395 a league of tribes marched against Aswân and pillaged the town and plundered the house of Husên, who had fled; the Muslims marched against them, but returned without having reduced the rebels. In 1397 Naṣr ad-Dîn, king of Nubia, fled to Cairo to beg assistance against his cousin. In 1403 Upper Egypt was in a state of desolation, and Aswân ceased to belong to the Sulṭân of Egypt. In 1412 the Ḥawâra tribe attacked and defeated the Awlâd Kenz, killed many men, carried off the women, and destroyed the walls of Aswân, leaving the town a mass of ruins. From this time until 1517, when Selîm reconquered Egypt, the Awlâd Kenz were masters of the Northern Sûdân, and the Khalîfa lost all authority over them.

From the facts derived from the works of Muhammadan historians given above, we see that the raids and expeditions of the Muslims into Nubia, which took place between 640 and 1400, with one or two exceptions, were confined to that portion of the country which lies between Aswân and Gebel Barkal, and that, speaking generally, no serious attempt was made by the Khalîfas to rule or occupy the Sûdân from Gebel Barkal to Kharṭûm. When we remember the conquests of the Arabs in Western Asia, Egypt, and other countries, it seems certain that the Khalîfas of Baghdâd and their viceroys in Egypt would have liked to obtain possession of the Nile Valley, and the adjoining countries, and we may be sure that they would have taken possession of the lands which produced slaves, and gold, and ivory if it had been at all practicable. The chief obstacle which stood in the way of their ambition was the Christian kingdom of Nubia, with its capital at Dongola, and there appears to be no doubt that the tide of the Muslim conquest from Egypt southwards was stayed by it for about seven hundred years. Christianity became the official religion of Nubia in the first half of the sixth century, and in spite of raids, persecutions, and the payment of heavy tribute, the dwellers on the Nile clung both to their own language and to the Christian religion, as they understood it, until the fourteenth century, when the Christian kingdom of 'Alwa on the Island of Meroe fell to pieces. The extraordinary people who occupied the banks of the Nile from Aswân to Dongola preserved also all the fundamental customs which had descended to them from Pagan times, and though they learned Arabic and talked it, their own language never fell into disuse.

The Christian Nubian kingdom, which extended from Aswân to the Blue Nile, came to an end through internal dissensions, and through the attacks made upon it by the peoples who lived on its eastern, western, and southern frontiers. Its fall was hastened by the rise to power of a number of Arab tribes, and of a powerful negro tribe called "Fûng." There is no doubt that Arabs in limited numbers had been crossing the Red Sea from the various provinces of Arabia and settling in the rich countries on the Blue Nile for centuries, even before the rise of Islâm. After the establishment of the Muḥammadan power it is quite certain that the immigration of the Arabs increased, and that their caravans travelled in all parts of the Sûdân where profitable business could be done. The progress of such immigrants, and also of the negro tribes to the south and east of Kharṭûm, was blocked by the Christian Nubian kingdom, and it was greatly to their interest to bring about its abolition.

During the fourteenth century the negro tribes between the Blue and White Niles began to obtain pre-eminence, and the descendants of the Muḥammadan settlers from Arabia to lose power, and a century later, on the downfall of the cities of Dongola and Soba, the capitals of the Christian Nubian kingdom in the north and south respectively, the negro tribes found themselves to be the greatest power in the country. Chief among these was the tribe of the Fûngs,[1] whose original home, according to some, was in the Shilluk country, and, according to others, in Dâr Fûr. Many origins have been suggested for them, but in the absence of definite knowledge probability is all that can be claimed for the most reasonable of them. But whatever their origin may have been, they fixed their capital at Sennaar, and their kingdom at the most flourishing period of its existence extended from the Third Cataract in the north to Fâzô'glî in the south, and from Sawâkin on the Red Sea on the east to the White Nile on the west. In 1493 the Fûngs were the dominant power in the Northern Sûdân, and in 1515 they founded their capital at Sennaar, with 'AMÂRA DUNḲAS as their king. Little is known of this king's personal exploits, but he must have been an astute ruler, for, observing how the power of the Turks was increasing, he strengthened his kingdom by making an alliance with 'Abd-Allah Gemâ'a, a tribal chief, and conquered the tribes on the Blue Nile between Fâzô'glî and Kharṭûm.

The founding of his kingdom at Sennaar followed as a matter of course. Twelve years after 'Amâra Dunḳas became king Selîm Beg, the Sulṭân of Turkey, defeated the Egyptian army outside Cairo (early in 1517), and four days later he entered Cairo in

[1] The Arabic opinions as to their origin are collected by Shucair in his *History of the Sûdân*, ii., pp. 71-73.

state as the lord of Egypt. He promptly sent a force to Sawâkin and Maṣaw'a, and entered Abyssinia, and 'Amâra Dunḳas feared that he would attack him. Thereupon he wrote and told Selîm that he could not comprehend why he had invaded his country, and that if he had done so for the sake of the religion of Islâm he must know that both he and his people were Arabs who had embraced Islâm, and who followed the religion of the Prophet of God, and that the greater number of his people were [descended from] Arabs of the desert.[1] With his letter he sent a series of genealogical tables which had been drawn up by an Imâm of Sennaar called As-Samarkandî, wherein it was shown that the Fûngs were descended from Arab tribes. When Selîm saw these tables he was struck with wonder at their contents and admitted the nobility of the Arabs of Sennaar. From this statement it is clear that the Fûngs embraced Islâm as a political measure; such tribes among them as were contented to lose their language, religion, and nationality became Muslims, and the rest left the country. The practical result of the diplomacy of 'Amâra Dunḳas was that Selîm took possession of Northern Nubia so far as the Third Cataract, and ruled it by means of *kashafa*,[2] or governors, whom he appointed over the larger towns, and the Fûng king ruled from the Third Cataract to Sennaar, presumably in peace. 'Amâra Dunḳas reigned from 1505 to 1534. He was succeeded by:—

1. 'Abd Al-Ḳâder,[3] his son, who reigned from 1534 to 1544.
2. Na'il, his brother, who reigned from 1544 to 1555.
3. 'Amâra ibn Sakâkîn, his brother, who reigned from 1555 to 1563. During his reign 'Abd-Allah Gemâ'a, shêkh of Ḳerrî, died, and left his district to his son 'Agîb Kâfût.
4. Dakîn ibn Na'il, surnamed Al-'Âdel, who reigned from 1563 to 1578.
5. Ṭabal, who reigned from 1578 to 1589.
6. Unsa I., who reigned from 1589 to 1599.
7. 'Abd Al-Ḳâder II., who reigned from 1599 to 1605.
8. 'Adlân ibn Aba, who reigned from 1605 to 1612.

[1] See Shucair, *op. cit.*, ii., p. 73.

[2] I.e., "governors," *kashafa* is the plural of *kâshif*.

[3] See Cailliaud, *Voyage*, tom. ii., p. 255.

During his reign 'Agîb, shêkh of Ḳerri, rebelled, and 'Adlân sent an army against him. A battle was fought at Kalmakûl, between 'Êlfûl and Kharṭûm, and 'Agîb was slain and his followers fled to Dongola. 'Adlân sent a free pardon to them by Idrîs ibn Muḥammad, and they returned with him to Sennaar, where 'Adlân treated them honourably, and made one of them, 'Agîl, governor of Ḳerrî. Shêkh Idrîs was born in 1507, and he died in 1650, aged 143 years.[1] An authority quoted by Na'ûm Shucair says that Islâm first entered Sennaar when Hârûn Ar-Rashîd was Khalîfa (A.D. 786-809).

9. Bâdî, or Sayyid Al-Ḳûm, who reigned from 1612 to 1615.

10. Rabâṭ, his son, who reigned from 1615 to 1643.

11. Bâdî abû Dhiḳn, who reigned from 1643 to 1678.

Bâdî made war on the Shilluks and captured many slaves. He then went further south to Gebel Taḳalî, and destroyed many villages on both banks of the White Nile, and carried large numbers of slaves back to Sennaar. Then he built villages wherein the members of each tribe could live by themselves, and to these he gave the names of the villages wherein they had lived in their own country, e.g., Taḳalî, Kadrô, Kank, Karkô, &c. He was a patron of learning, and fond of learned men, and he built a mosque in Sennaar with brass-framed windows; he also built a palace[2] which was surrounded by a wall, and which had nine doors. The Blacks whom he had captured on the White Nile became soldiers in his army.

12. Ansa II., his nephew, who reigned from 1678 to 1689.

In 1683 a severe famine broke out, and men were reduced to eating dogs; the country was swept by an epidemic of small-pox, and very many people died.

13. Bâdî Al-Aḥmar, i.e., Bâdî the Red, who reigned from 1689 to 1715.

In his reign some of the Fûng tribes rebelled, led by Shêkh Ardâb; Bâdî attacked them, and slew their leader and many of his men, and the rest fled to 'Aṭshân. In his reign lived Shêkh Ḥamed ibn At-Tarâbî, an Arab, whose tomb is at Sennaar.[3]

[1] Interesting accounts of his life are given by Shucair, *op. cit.*, ii., pp. 74-76.

[2] See Shucair, *op. cit.*, ii., pp. 78, 79.

[3] On the visit of Dr. Poncet to Sennaar, see Vol. I., pp. 1-17.

14. Ansa III., who reigned from 1715 to 1718.

He was the last descendant of 'Amâra Dunḳas to reign, and was deposed after a rebellion among the Fûng tribes in 1718.

15. Nûl, who reigned from 1718 to 1724.

16. Bâdî abû Shallûkh, who reigned from 1724 to 1762. In his reign 'Îyâsû I., 'Adyâm Sagad I., king of Abyssinia, invaded Sennaar because Bâdî had stopped certain presents which 'Îyâsû had sent to the king of France. A battle was fought on the Dinder river, and the Abyssinian army was defeated with great slaughter. 'Îyâsû I. was crowned 3rd Ḥamlê, 1682, and deposed 20th Magâbît, 1706; he was murdered in Ṭekemt (October) of the same year. In the reign of Bâdî M. le Noir du Roule was murdered at Sennaar (see Vol. I., pp. 11, 12).[1]

17. Nâṣer, who reigned from 1762 to 1769.

He was slain by Shêkh Muḥammad in the place to which he had been driven near Sennaar, and his brother was made king.

18. Isma'îl, who reigned from 1769 to 1778.

In the first year of his reign a severe famine broke out in the country, and in 1771 an extraordinary rise of the Nile took place.

19. 'Adlân II., who reigned from 1778 to 1789.[2]

He was the last of the Fûng dynasty of kings, and the powerful Hameg tribe usurped the throne. After his deposition anarchy prevailed throughout the country, and every man did what was right in his own eyes.

20. Awkal, who began to reign in 1789; he only reigned a few months, and having fled was succeeded by
21. Tabal II., who began to reign in 1789; he was killed by Nâṣer in Sennaar.
22. Bâdî V., who began to reign in 1789; he was killed by Nâṣer at Ad-Dâmer.
23. Ḥasab-raba, who began to reign in 1790; he died soon after his accession.
24. Nawwâr, who began to reign in 1790.
25. Bâdî ibn Ṭabal, who reigned from 1791 to 1821.

[1] See Shucair, *op. cit.*, ii., p. 80.
[2] For an account of his wars in Kordôfân see Shucair, *op. cit.*, ii., pp. 83-86.

26. Ranfi.

27. Bâdî ibn Ṭabal.

The most flourishing period in the history of the Fûng kingdom of Sennaar was in the reign of Bâdî Abû Shallûkh (1724-1762), when its fame reached Constantinople, and learned men from Egypt and Arabia flocked there and settled in and about the city of Sennaar.

During the rule of the Fûng kings there flourished in other parts of the Sûdân several dynasties of Shêkhs and semi-independent rulers, and among these may be mentioned :—

1. The 'Âbdallât Shêkhs, who were descended from 'Abd-Allah Gamâ'a, whose seat was at Ḳerrî, and whose territory extended from Ḥagar Al-'Asal, i.e., the "Honey Rock," to Sawba, or Sôba. They had authority over all the countries between Arbagî and the Third Cataract. In his *History of the Sûdân* Na'ûm Beg Shucair gives (ii., p. 99 ff.) the following list of them :—

1. 'Abd-Allah Gamâ'a, who was a contemporary of 'Amâra Abu Sakâkîn, the fourth king of the Fûng dynasty.
2. 'Agîb, who was surnamed "Al-Mângalûk."
3. 'Agîl.
4. Ḥamed Ash-Shemîk.
5. 'Uthmân, his son.
6. 'Abd-Allah II., ibn 'Agîl.
7. Mismâr ibn 'Abd-Allah.
8. Diyâb, or Arâdab wad 'Agîb.
9. Al-Amîn wad Mismâr.
10. 'Agîb ibn 'Abd-Allah.
11. 'Abd Allah III. wad 'Agîb.
12. 'Amr, brother of 'Agîb.
13. Muḥammad Al-Amîn ibn Mismâr.
14. Bâdî ibn Mismâr.
15. 'Abd-Allah IV. wad 'Agîb.
16. Nâṣer wad Al-Amîn.
17. Amîn II. ibn Nâser.
18. Nâṣer wad 'Agîb, who was a contemporary of Ismâ'îl Pâshâ.

KINGS OF FAZOGLI AND SHENDI

2. The seventeen kings of Fâzô'glî,[1] who reigned two hundred and fifteen years.

1. KALLAH	He reigned		50	years.
2. YAMNI	,,	,,	40	,,
3 IDRÎS, his son	,,	,,	30	,,
4. GÂBAR I.	,,	,,	15	,,
5. GÂBAR II., his son	,,	,,	2	,,
6. ZANKAR (?)	,,	,,	1	,,
7. RAWYÂ	,,	,,	2	,,
8. AMBADÎ, his son	,,	,,	4	,,
9. ATWARÔ	,,	,,	3	,,
10. ADARLÂ	,,	,,	15	,,
11. MAṬAR, his son	,,	,,	16	,,
12. FANKARÔ, his son	,,	,,	16	,,
13. ḲALBÂS,[2] his son	,,	,,	1	,,
14. ḲAMBÔ, his brother	,,	,,	2	,,
15. ḲAMBÂR	,,	,,	5	,,
16. AMÛSHAT,[3] his brother	,,	,,	1	,,
17. ḤASAN IBN ṬABAL	,,	,,	12	,,
			215	years.[4]

3. The sixteen kings of Shendî, who reigned two hundred and thirty-six years. Shendî was the capital of a district which was ruled by the Ga'alîn Arabs, and which practically represented the territory of the ancient Meroïtic kingdom. At an early period in the history of the Shendî kings their kingdom was divided into two parts, the part on the east bank of the Nile having as its chief town Shendî, and that on the west bank having as its chief town Matamma. The names of the kings of Shendî are:—

1. SA'ADAB DABÛS	He reigned		20	years
2. SULÊMÂN AL-'ADÂD	,,	,,	7	,,
3. IDRÎS I. IBN SULÊMÂN	,,	,,	35	,,
4. 'ABD AS-SALÂM	,,	,,	1	,,
5. FAḤAL IBN 'ABD AS-SALÂM	,,	,,	15	,,

[1] Given by Shucair (*op. cit.*, pl. ii., p. 102), on the authority of the last king.

[2] Slain by his brother.

[3] Slain by 'Adlân.

[4] See also Cailliaud, *Voyage*, tom. ii., p. 396.

6. IDRÎS II., his brother	He reigned	6	years.
7. DÎYÂB, his brother	,, ,,	12	,,
8. ḲANBALÂWÎ	,, ,,	3	,,
9. BISHÂRA	,, ,,	7	,,
10. SULÊMÂN IBN SALÂM	,, ,,	15	,,
11. SA'AD I., his brother	,, ,,	2	,,
12. IDRÎS III.	,, ,,	20	,,
13. SA'AD II., his son	,, ,,	40	,,
14. MASÂ'D, his son	,, ,,	13	,,
15. MUḤAMMAD AL-MAK	,, ,,	13	,,
16. NIMR, his son	,, ,,	17	,,
	Total	215	years.[1]

4. The twenty-six Sulṭâns of Dâr Fûr, who reigned for four hundred and thirty-one years :—

1. SULÊMÂN I.	who reigned from	1445 to 1476
2. 'AMR I.	,, ,,	1476 to 1492
3. 'ABD AR-RAḤMÂN I.	,, ,,	1492 to 1511
4. MAḤMUD	,, ,,	1511 to 1526
5. MUḤAMMAD ṢÛL	,, ,,	1526 to 1551
6. DALÎL	,, ,,	1551 to 1561
7. SHARAF	,, ,,	1561 to 1584
8. AḤMAD	,, ,,	1584 to 1593
9. IDRÎS	,, ,,	1593 to 1615
10. SÂLIḤ	,, ,,	1615 to 1622
11. MANṢÛR	,, ,,	1622 to 1639
12. SHÛSH	,, ,,	1639 to 1658
13. NÂSER	,, ,,	1658 to 1670
14. TÛM	,, ,,	1670 to 1683
15. KÛRÛ	,, ,,	1683 to 1695
16. SULÊMÂN II.	,, ,,	1695 to 1715
17. MÛSA, his son	,, ,,	1715 to 1726
18. AḤMAD BAKR	,, ,,	1726 to 1746
19. MUḤAMMAD DAWRA	,, ,,	1746 to 1757
20. 'AMR II., his son	,, ,,	1757 to 1764
21. ABU'L ḲÂSIM	,, ,,	1764 to 1768

[1] See Cailliaud, *Voyage*, tom. iii., p. 106.

22. TÊRÂB, his brother, who reigned from 1768 to 1787
23. ABD AR-RAḤMAN II. „ „ 1787 to 1801
24. MUḤAMMAD AL-FAḌL „ „ 1801 to 1839
25. MUḤAMMAD ḤASÎN „ „ 1839 to 1874
26. IBRAHÎM „ „ 1874 to 1875[1]

Of the history of Nubia from the First to the Third Cataract between the period of the downfall of the Arab power in Egypt and 1820 very little is known. It is said that about 1318 a number of the Jawâbir Arabs occupied the Nile Valley between the First and Second Cataracts; they seem to have been kinsmen of the Arabs of Nejd and 'Irâḳ (Mesopotamia). The district between the First Cataract and Sabû'a was, and is still, called the "country of the Kenûz." Between the Second Cataract and Gebel Dûsha, i.e., in Sukkôt, lived some of the Arabs who belonged to famous tribes, and in Mahass, i.e., between Gebel Dûsha and the Third Cataract, lived Arabs who declared they were descended from the tribe of Kurêsh. The latter founded a kingdom at Gebel Sâsî, near Dulgo, or Deligo. In 1520 the Arabs sent to Selîm and asked for help against the Jawâbir Arabs, and he despatched with the envoys a number of Bosnian troops, under the command of Ḥasan Ḳûshî, who drove the Jawâbir Arabs to Dongola, and only a few of them remained in Ḥalfa. The Bosnian soldiers built fortresses in Aswân, Ibrîm, and Sâî, and established themselves therein, and they drew a certain annual allowance from the treasury in Cairo.

After the death of Ḥasan the country was governed by "Kashafa" who were known by the name of "Al-Ghuzz." Soon after the Fûng kings became lords of Sennaar they wished to seize Northern Nubia, and sent an army to occupy the country. Ibn Janbalân, the chief of the Ghuzz, collected an army, and set out to fight the invaders. The two armies met near Ḥannek, and the Fûngs were defeated with great slaughter, and retreated, leaving their path strewn with their dead. It is said that their blood was collected in a pool by the victors, who built a "Ḳubba"

[1] For the details of their reigns see Shucair, *op. cit.*, ii., p. 113 ff.; for accounts of the kingdom of Fûr see the following chapter in the same work, p. 132 ff. The condition of the kingdom at the end of the XVIIIth century is fully described in Mr. Browne's *Travels*, of which mention has already been made (Vol. I., p. 23).

(Gubba) over it, and that this became the boundary mark between the territories of the Fûngs and the Bosnians. From this time until Ismâ'îl went to Sennaar in 1820 the Bosnians and their descendants appear to have been left severely alone by the Fûngs. Remains of many of their castles are still to be seen in Sukkôt and Mahass, both on the islands in the Nile, and on the river banks. They consist of a central fort surrounded by walls about fifteen cubits high and three cubits wide. Each wall had one tower on it about fifty cubits high, and was ascended by steps, or a ladder. Every tribe or clan had its castle, and in times of trouble the men made all their women and flocks go into the fortified part of it, and if attacked, they either went up on the towers and hurled stones at their enemies, or went out boldly and fought them with staves, and swords, and knives, and their women went out and took food to them, and encouraged them to do deeds of valour.

When Ismâ'îl passed through Nubia in 1820, the Kâshif Ḥasîn Ibn Sulêmân wished to prevent his advance, but was prevented from making the attempt by his brother Ḥasan. He then fled to Kordôfân with three hundred slaves, and slew Maḳdûm Musallim, and took his harîm and his treasury to the Sultân of Dâr Fûr, whose daughter he married. Meanwhile Ismâ'îl made Ḥasan chief of the country from Aswân to Ḥalfa, and gave him 293 acres of land and six purses of money, and the new Kâshif married as many Nubian women as he liked.

CHAPTER XIII.

THE RULE OF MUḤAMMAD 'ALÎ AND HIS DESCENDANTS IN THE SÛDÂN.

AFTER the capture of Cairo by Sulṭân Selîm in 1517 the military affairs of Egypt and of Nubia as far as the Third Cataract were managed by twenty-four Mamlûk Beys, whose actions were supposed to be controlled by a Pâshâ and a council of seven high officers of state. The principal military appointment was that of Governor of Cairo, or "Shêkh al-Balad," which at first was given to the ablest man among the twenty-four Beys. The country remained in a comparatively peaceful state until about 1700, when it was found that Bey after Bey throughout the land intrigued to obtain the governorship of Cairo, and that many murders took place as the result of their endeavours. By this time, too, the power of the Pâshâ of Egypt had become purely nominal, and the Beys, headed by the Shêkh al-Balad, were to all intents and purposes masters of the Turkish province of Egypt and Northern Nubia. In 1763 the famous 'Alî Bey became Shêkh al-Balad. In 1768 he rebelled against the Sulṭân of Turkey, and succeeded in persuading the Council of Seven to drive out the Pâshâ and to declare Egypt independent. In 1772 Muḥammad Abû Dhâhab, one of 'Alî Bey's generals, rebelled against him, and was declared Shêkh al-Balad; he was subsequently made Pâshâ of Egypt by the Sulṭân. After his death the supreme power was eventually shared by Ismâ'îl Bey and Murâd Bey, but in 1785 the Sulṭân despatched Ḥasan, his Lord High Admiral, to crush their authority and to make them pay the annual tribute. After a successful battle Ḥasan took Cairo, and chased Ismâ'îl and Murâd into Upper Egypt, where a fierce fight between the two forces took place. Ḥasan was, however, obliged to withdraw on account of the war which broke out between Turkey and Russia, and Ismâ'îl returned to Egypt and was made Shêkh al-Balad. He died in the year of the terrible plague, 1790.

In May, 1798, the French Expedition under General Bonaparte arrived in Egypt, and on July 5th Alexandria fell. Two years later Murâd Bey was made governor of a portion of Upper Egypt by Kléber, and in September of that year the French evacuated Egypt. Among those who had been sent by the Sulṭân to fight against the French was an Albanian called Muḥammad 'Alî, who was born at Cavalla in 1768. He married a daughter of the governor of his native town, and by her had three sons, Ibrahîm, Ṭusûn, and Ismâ'îl. At the age of thirty-three he was sent with his brother-in-law 'Alî Aghâ and three hundred men to attack the French, and after their departure from Egypt he was promoted to the command of one thousand men. Soon after the evacuation of Egypt by the French the country was filled with anarchy, caused by the struggle between the Mamlûks, who were known as Al-Ghuzz, the name of their chief tribe, and the Albanians, or "Arnauts," for the supreme power. Muḥammad Khusrûf, who had been made Pâshâ of Egypt after the departure of the French, attacked the Mamlûks with a force of 14,000 men, but he was defeated, and his guns and ammunition fell into the hands of the enemy.

For two years Cairo and the Delta were scenes of strife and turmoil, and this period was only brought to an end in May, 1805, by the people of Cairo electing Muḥammad 'Alî to be the Pâshâ of Egypt. A month or so later a *farmân* arrived from Constantinople appointing him governor of Egypt, but all the Mamlûk Beys, as well as the friends of Khurshîd Pâshâ, now became his foes. On August 18th the Beys with their followers forced their way into Cairo, and proceeded along the streets until they came to the main road called "Bên Al-Ḳaṣrên." Here they were suddenly fired upon, and when they turned to flee, they found all the side streets closed against them. Several cut their way through their foes, and escaped over the city walls, and many took refuge in the Mosque of Sulṭân Barḳûḳ. The latter surrendered, and some fifty of them were slain on the spot; the remainder were taken to the house of Muḥammad 'Alî, who ordered them to be fettered and kept in the courtyard until the next day. The following morning the heads of those who had been killed the day before were skinned, and the skins stuffed with straw before their eyes. The same night all but three of the remainder were tortured and put to death, and shortly after eighty-three heads were sent to the Sulṭân by Muḥammad 'Alí, with the boast that he had destroyed the Mamlûks.

On March 17th, 1807, about 5,000 British troops landed in Egypt with the view of bringing Muḥammad 'Alî to his senses, and proceeded to take Rosetta. They advanced into the town without opposition, but once inside a heavy fire was opened on them, and they only retreated with difficulty, having lost 185 men killed and 262 wounded. The heads of the slain were sent to Cairo, and stuck upon stakes on each side of the road which crossed the part of the city now covered by the Ezbekiya Gardens. A second attempt to take Rosetta was made, but it was followed by disaster, and the British lost in killed, wounded, and missing 900 men. The British prisoners were sent to Cairo, and were marched between the stakes whereon were displayed by hundreds the heads of their fellow-countrymen. In the September following, the British, finding that it was impossible to help the Mamlûk Beys, left Egypt. In 1811 Muḥammad 'Alî enticed 470 of the Mamlûks into the Citadel, and when they were inside, and ascending the sloping road which leads to the great gate, with the outer gate shut behind them, a murderous fire was opened upon them by the troops from the walls and the surrounding houses, and very few of them escaped. This was a signal for a general massacre of the Mamlûks throughout Egypt, and for two days the houses of the Beys were pillaged and destroyed, their women violated, and their friends and servants murdered.

The Mamlûks who managed to escape the general massacre fled first to Upper Egypt, and subsequently to Nubia. In 1819 Muḥammad 'Alî determined to conquer the Sûdân, first with the object of finding occupation for his troops, and secondly in order to get the gold which he was told existed there in fabulous quantities, and to collect a large number of slaves, of whom he intended to form a strong army. In 1820 he collected a force of about 5,000 Arabs and Turks, and in the summer of that year despatched them to Nubia under the command of his youngest son, Ismâ'îl. At Esna the Mamlûks offered some resistance, but this was speedily overcome, and Ismâ'îl advanced without much difficulty to Dongola, where, in a fierce fight, he utterly destroyed the power of the Mamlûks who had settled there, and were perpetrating terrible atrocities on the wretched Nubians. The Shaiḳîya tribe in the neighbourhood of the Island of Arḳo were foolish enough to attempt to stem the tide of invaders, and they paid dearly for their temerity.[1] Ismâ'îl reached Kharṭûm without mishap, and then proceeded to Sennaar, where he found the country torn with the dissension caused by 'Adlân and Ragab, both of whom had claimed the throne. Ragab had murdered 'Adlân, and had fled the country. Sennaar was taken without fighting, and, having been joined by his brother Ibrahîm, Ismâ'îl proceeded to Fâzô'glî, where he established the sovereignty of Egypt.

When Ibrahîm returned to Cairo, the natives rebelled, but Ismâ'îl quickly came back and put down the rebellion in the usual way. From Fâzô'glî he returned to Shendî, and, when there, accepted an invitation to a banquet to be given in his honour by Nimr, the Mek[2] of Shendî. When he and his followers had eaten, and were, most probably, drunk, Nimr, i.e., "The Panther," caused wood and scrub from the surrounding desert to be piled up round the house wherein the banquet was taking place, and set fire to, and Ismâ'îl and his followers were burned to death. This event took place in 1822, just after the founding of the city of Kharṭûm, which Muḥammad 'Alî intended to be the capital of the Sûdân.

While Ismâ'îl was taking possession of the kingdom of Sennaar, Muḥammad Bey, the Defterdâr, was sent to seize Kordôfân by Muḥammad 'Alî, and after a long struggle succeeded in his mission. When the news of the murder of Ismâ'îl reached him, he collected a large army and returned to Shendî to take

[1] Ismâ'îl had the ears of all the men and women he could find of the tribe cut off, and sent them to his father in Cairo! Cailliaud, *Voyage*, ii., pp. 58, 59. The Shaiḳîya fought two battles and were beaten both times.

[2] The word "Mek" is, it seems, a title, and is not to be confounded with *Melek*, "king." It is probably connected with the old Ethiopian root, መኰሐ "to be glorious," and in the life of Takla Maryâm we find a scribe called "Mekḥ Giyôrgîs," i.e., "Mekḥ George."

vengeance on Nimr and his town. He bombarded the town and destroyed the palace and most of the houses, then his soldiers entered and massacred every one they found. Nimr himself escaped, but his subjects suffered cruelly at the hands of the Turks and black men from Kordôfân, and the atrocities which were perpetrated are indescribable. Meanwhile the natives to the south again rebelled, and Muḥammad Bey had to return and fight several battles on the White and Blue Niles. At this time he captured the city of Al-Obêḍ (Al-Ubayyaḍ).

In 1825 OSMÂN Bey was appointed Governor of the Sûdân, and he made the recently founded city of Kharṭûm his headquarters. His rule lasted about one year, and was not very successful. He made Shêkh Shanbûl of Wad Medanî governor of the district from Ḥagar Al-'Asal to Gebel Fûng, but he was soon slain; Osmân Aghâ was appointed in his stead. At this time an epidemic of small-pox broke out in the country, and then came a famine, during which men ate dogs and donkeys. Osmân Bey died on April 22nd, 1826.

In 1826 MAḤḤU Bey of Berber ruled Kharṭûm for a few months. He was an honest and intelligent man with courteous manners, and he endeavoured to do good to the people. He built a government house in Kharṭûm, and to the south of the city is a large tree which is called after his name; he also dug a well at Berber. In the same year KHÛRSHÎD Pâshâ was appointed governor of the Sûdân. In 1828 he led an expedition against the Dinka tribes on the White Nile, and went to the mountains of Taḳalî and Fâshôda (Kodok). In 1830 he went south in boats and attacked the Shillûks, and slew large numbers of them, and returned to Kharṭûm with much spoil and many prisoners. In this year the Nile rose to an alarming height. In 1832 Khûrshîd marched against the Sabderât tribes and wasted their territory. In 1834 he built a mosque in Sennaar, and went to Kordôfân. In 1836 he went to Egypt viâ Dongola, and stayed in Cairo for a few months. On his return he was obliged to send an army under the command of Muḥammad Effendi to chastise the Abyssinians, who had come down from their mountains and killed many people and laid waste the country. Ragab, the son of Bashîr, their leader, was caught, and was brought to Khûrshîd at Ruṣêreṣ, where he was killed. In 1837 cholera broke out, and many of the notables died of the disease; when it reached Kharṭûm, Khûrshîd went to Shendî; in the same year a great star appeared which was visible at noon and shot forth sparks of fire! In 1838 the Abyssinians attacked Ḳallâbât, and did some damage.

In May, 1839, AHMAD Pâshâ was appointed Governor of the Sûdân; because of the size of his ears he was called "Abû Udân." On October 15th of this year Muḥammad Alî left Cairo to visit the Sûdân. He reached Kharṭûm on November 23rd, and stayed there twenty-two days. He set out for Fâzô'glî, and arrived there on January 18th, 1840, and returned to Cairo *viâ* Korosko on March 14th. A marvellous journey for a man seventy years of age! As the result of his personal inspection of the countries wherein he believed gold was to be found in large quantities, he determined to send expeditions into the Sûdân on a large scale for the purpose of bringing back gold and slaves in large numbers for his army. He interviewed the shêkhs and notables of Kharṭûm and Fâzô'glî, and no doubt came to an understanding with them as to what he required them to do. Under the rule of Aḥmad Pâshâ, the province of Tâka, or Kasala, was added to Muḥammad 'Alî's kingdom. Taking advantage of the enmity which existed between two of the Bega tribes, the Hadanduwa and the Ḥalânḳa, he succeeded in stirring up strife in the country, and then by an artifice managed to destroy a number of the people, and take possession of the villages and lands. He played one tribe off against the other, fought against all of them, and finally succeeded in reducing them to subjection. He then set over Tâka 'Amr Bey and Farḥât Bey in succession, and finally made Mûsa Ibrahîm, the nephew of Muḥammad Dîn, the Shêkh of the Hadanduwa, their governor. The taking of Tâka was as disgraceful as it was inexcusable, and it was carried out in a manner both cruel and shameful. The population of the district sent messengers to Aḥmad Pâshâ to announce their submission, but notwithstanding this, a company of four hundred "Arnauts," or Albanian mercenaries, were sent into the country to murder, plunder, burn, and destroy everything and everyone they could find, and they performed their mission thoroughly. Hundreds of unarmed men and women were slain at sight, and the wretched

VIEW OF THE VILLAGE OF KASSÂM, NEAR FÂZÔGLÎ, IN 1837.

[From Russegger, *Reisen*, Bl. 20.

VIEW OF THE BLUE NILE, NEAR FÂZÔGLÎ, IN 1837.

[From Russegger, *Reisen*, Bl. 16.

captives who were brought before Aḥmad were beheaded whilst he sat looking on in his tent. Forty-one of the shêkhs who had set out to come to Aḥmad with the soldiers had been shot on the way because they could not march fast enough.

Each captive "carried before him the stem of a tree as thick as "a man's arm, about five or six feet long, which terminated in a "fork, into which the neck was fixed. The prongs of the fork "were bound together by a cross-piece of wood, fastened with a

GEBEL KASALA, AS SEEN FROM THE NEW GOVERNMENT BUILDINGS.
[From Sir W. Garstin's *Report*, by permission of the Comptroller of H.M. Stationery Office.

"strap. Some of their hands, also, were tied fast to the handle "of the fork, and in this condition they remained day and night. "During the march, the soldier who is specially appointed to "overlook the prisoner, carries the end of the pole: in the night "most of them have their feet also pinioned together . . . ." "Then after all the conditions that were imposed had been "fulfilled, and the heavy contributions which had been required "from them under every variety of pretext had been also correctly "paid, the Pasha caused all the Sheikhs to assemble at once, as if "for a fresh conference, but forthwith had them all put in fetters, "together with 120 other people, and led away as prisoners. "The young and strong men were to be placed among the troops, "the women handed over to the soldiers as slaves; the Sheikhs "were reserved for punishment till a later day. Such was the "glorious history of the campaign against Taka as it was related "to me[1] by the European eye-witnesses." Under the rule of Aḥmad Pâshâ the Sûdân was divided into seven mudirîas, or administrative provinces, namely, Fâzô'gli, Sennaar, Kharṭûm,

VIEW OF AL-OBÊḌ IN 1837.

[From Russegger, *Reisen*, Bl. 16.

Kasala, Berber, Dongola, and Kordôfân, and a military commandant was set over each. Aḥmad Pâshâ died at Kharṭûm in October, 1844, and was buried there.

In 1844 AḤMAD Pâshâ Al-Maniklî was appointed Governor of the Sûdân, and his rule lasted for about two years.

In 1846 KHÂLID Pâshâ was appointed Governor of the Sûdân, and his rule lasted for about four years. In 1848 Ibrahîm Pâshâ, on account of Muḥammad 'Alî's failing health, was made Ruler of Egypt, but the disease from which he was suffering

[1] Lepsius, *Letters*, p. 200.

increased, and he died on November 10th of that year. He was succeeded by 'Abbâs Pâshâ, the grandson of Muḥammad 'Alî, on December 24th. On August 2nd, 1849, Muḥammad 'Alî died, heart-broken, it is said, because the British Government had cut down the number of his army to 18,000 men, and forbidden him to make use of his navy, which lay rotting in the harbour at Alexandria. He undoubtedly conferred great benefits on his country, and, in a fashion, was a patron of art and learning and a supporter of many reforms. He was greater as a warrior than as an administrator. He failed to see that the resources of Egypt were of an agricultural character, and encouraged industrial schemes which, had they been as successful as he wished, would have ruined his country. His character was a mixture of shrewdness, cunning, simplicity, cruelty, avarice, and generosity, and his love of wealth made him steal the revenues of tombs and religious institutions in Cairo, and take possession of nearly all the best land in Egypt. His policy in the Sûdân encouraged the slave trade to a degree hitherto unknown, and the cruelty and corruption of his officials there sowed the seeds of the rebellion which broke out thirty years later, and culminated in the rule of Muḥammad Aḥmad the Mahdî, and one of his Khalîfas, 'Abd-Allah.

In 1850 LAṬÎF Pâshâ was appointed Governor of the Sûdân.

In 1851 RUSTUM Pâshâ was appointed Governor of the Sûdân. He was stricken with an illness at Wad Medanî, and died in the following year, and was buried there.

In 1852 ISMÂ'îl Pâshâ was appointed Governor of the Sûdân. After making a tour in the Eastern Desert, he returned to Kharṭûm, and was recalled to Cairo.

In 1853 SELÎM Pâshâ was appointed Governor of the Sûdân.

In 1854 'ALÎ Pâshâ Sirrî was appointed Governor of the Sûdân, and in July of the same year 'Abbâs Pâshâ died, and was succeeded by Sa'îd Pâshâ, a son of Muḥammad 'Alî. About this time the Egyptian officials found it more and more difficult to collect the revenue, for the taxes were so heavy that the peasant farmers were ruined everywhere in paying them.

In 1855 'ALÎ Pâshâ Sharkas was appointed Governor of the

RIPON FALLS, VICTORIA NYANZA, THE SOURCE OF THE WHITE NILE.

[From Sir W. Garstin's *Report*, by permission of the Comptroller of H.M. Stationery Office

VICTORIA NYANZA AT THE RIPON FALLS.

[From Sir W. Garstin's *Report*, by permission of the Comptroller of H.M. Stationery Office.

Sûdân, and his rule lasted until 1858. During the visit of 'Abd Al-Ḥalîm Pâshâ cholera broke out, and very many people died of the disease. On January 16th, 1858, Sa'îd Pâshâ, the Khedive of Egypt, visited the Sûdân, and he was horrified at the state in which he found the country. He proclaimed the abolition of slavery, reduced the taxes on the water-wheels, made several sweeping reforms in the administration of the provinces, and established a camel-post between Kharṭûm and Cairo. He conceived the idea of connecting the Sûdân with Egypt by means of a railway, and Mougel Bey made a report on the subject. During the rule of 'Alî Pâshâ Sharkas Mr. John Petherick, H.B.M's Consul for the Sûdân, obtained permission to send a series of trading expeditions into the Sûdân. He left England in March, 1845, and was employed by Muḥammad 'Alî to search for coal, and subsequently investigated the mineral resources both of Egypt and the Sûdân. His expeditions to the country south of Kharṭûm took place in November, 1853, October, 1854, November, 1855, December, 1856, and February, 1858. He wrote an account of his travels, which was published in 1861,[1] and from this excellent work a very good idea of the state of the country may be gathered. He was accused of complicity in the slave trade, and his reputation suffered through many bitter attacks which were made on it. He appears to have been badly treated by the British Foreign Office, which abolished his consulate at Khartûm. In 1858 Mr. John Hanning Speke discovered that the Victoria Nyanza was the true source of the Nile.[2]

In April, 1860, in company with Captain J. A. Grant, he set out on another expedition to obtain further proof of the wonderful discovery he had made in 1858. Many of his statements were traversed by the late Sir Richard Burton (see *The Nile Basin*, 1864), but the priority and genuineness of Speke's discovery remain unquestioned.

In 1859 ARAKÎL Bey was appointed Governor of the Sûdân.

[1] *Egypt, the Soudan, and Central Africa*, W. Blackwood, Edinburgh, and London.

[2] Speke, *Journey of the Discovery of the Source of the Nile*, London, 1863; and *What Led to the Discovery of the Source of the Nile*, London, 1864.

THE SLAVE TRADE

In 1860 Ḥasan Bey Salâma was appointed Governor of the Sûdân.

In this year the Europeans who had traded with natives for ivory, gum, &c., realized that it was impossible for them to continue their business without aiding and abetting the slave trade, and, though they made a gallant stand against this shameful traffic, they saw that it was hopeless to resist successfully the results of the machinations of the corrupt Turkish officialdom at Kharṭûm and in Egypt. They therefore sold their trading concerns to Arabs, with the result that the state of the wretched black folk became worse than before, and in a year or two the slave trade increased to a frightful extent.

In March, 1861, Sir Samuel Baker set out to discover the sources of the Nile, with the hope of meeting Speke and Grant, who had been sent out by the British Government *viâ* Zanzibar with that object. He left Cairo in April, 1861, and, having explored all the country through which the Atbara flows, arrived in Kharṭûm on June 11th, 1862.

In July of this year Muḥammad Bey Râsikh was appointed Governor of the Sûdân. The state of Kharṭûm, the capital, at this time is described by Baker thus[1]:—

"A more miserable, filthy, and unhealthy spot can hardly "be imagined. . . . . . The town, chiefly composed "of huts of unburnt brick, extends over a flat hardly above "the level of the river at high water, and is occasionally "flooded. Although containing about 30,000 inhabitants and "densely crowded, there are neither drains nor cesspools; the "streets are redolent with inconceivable nuisances; should "animals die, they remain where they fall, to create pestilence "and disgust. Khartoum is the seat of government, the Soudan "provinces being under the control of a Governor-general, with "despotic power. In 1861 there were about 6,000 troops in the "town; a portion of these were Egyptians; other regiments were "composed of blacks from Kordofan, and from the White and "Blue Niles, with one regiment of Arnouts, and a battery of "artillery. These troops are the curse of the country: as in the "case of most Turkish and Egyptian officials, the receipt of pay "is most irregular, and accordingly the soldiers are under loose "discipline. Foraging and plunder is the business of the Egyptian "soldier, and the miserable natives must submit to insult and "ill treatment at the will of the brutes who pillage them."

[1] *Albert Nyanza*, New Edition, London, 1870, p. 8 ff.

On December 18th Baker left Kharṭûm for the south, and arrived at Gondokoro on February 2nd, 1863; here, on the 15th of the same month, arrived Speke and Grant. The former had walked the whole way from Zanzibar. They explained to Baker that they had been unable to follow the course of the Nile westward to the place where it entered the large lake called by the natives Luta N'zige,[1] which Speke believed to be a second source of the Nile, and Baker determined to proceed to this lake, and thus complete the splendid work which Speke and Grant had begun. Speke gave Baker minute directions as to the course he should follow, and on February 26th Speke and his companion sailed from Gondokoro for Kharṭûm in Baker's boats. On March 26th Baker set out on his march to the Luta N'zige. After innumerable delays caused by the idleness and obstruction of the natives, and by grievous sickness, starvation and fatigue, he arrived at the Luta N'zige on March 14th, 1864, and was the first European to look upon its waters. He says: "The glory "of our prize burst suddenly upon me! There, like a sea of "quicksilver, lay far beneath the grand expanse of water—a "boundless sea horizon on the south and south-west, glittering in "the noon-day sun; and on the west, at fifty or sixty miles' "distance, blue mountains rose from the bosom of the lake to a "height of about 7,000 feet above its level. . . . As an imperish- "able memorial of one loved and mourned by our gracious Queen, "and deplored by every Englishman, I called this great lake 'the "Albert N'yanza.' The Victoria and Albert Lakes are the two "sources of the Nile."[2]

In 1863 ISMA'ÎL, son of Ibrahîm Pâshâ, became Khedive of Egypt, and in the same year MÛSA Pâshâ Ḥamdî was appointed Governor of the Sûdân. "This man was a rather exaggerated "specimen of Turkish authorities in general, combining the worst "of Oriental failings with the brutality of a wild animal."[3] He is also described as "an unprincipled and cruel tyrant, who ruled "only by military power, and oppressed and plundered the "people";[4] and we are told that, in spite of the prohibition of

[1] I.e., the "dead locust Lake."

[2] *Albert Nyanza*, p. 308.

[3] Baker, *Albert Nyanza*, p. 8.

[4] Wells, *The Heroine of the White Nile*, p. 38.

the slave trade by the Porte, "this ruler, like all his predecessors, "did but little else, and thus amassed great wealth, and neglected "his duties as Governor."[1] Baker is an impartial witness, and it must be confessed that, judging from his description of the Sûdân at this time, the state of the country must have been appalling. The revenue was unequal to the expenditure, and fresh taxes were levied upon the inhabitants to an extent that paralyzed the entire country. Misgovernment, monopoly, extortion, and oppression were the accompaniments of the Turkish rule. The distance of Cairo from the Sûdân had an evil effect on the Egyptian official character. Every official plundered; the Governor extorted from all sides, and filled his pockets by obstructing every commercial movement with the view of obtaining bribes. Dishonesty and deceit characterized officials from the highest to the lowest, and each robbed in proportion to his grade. Soldiers collected the taxes and, of course, exacted more than was due. As a result, the natives produced just as much as they wanted and no more. The heaviest and most unjust tax of all was that on the water-wheels, on which the agricultural prosperity of the country depended. New settlers fled before the horde of tax-gatherers who alighted upon them, and thus whole tracts of country remained uncultivated. "The general aspect of the Soudan is that "of misery, nor is there a single feature of attraction to recom-"pense a European for the drawbacks of pestilential climate and "brutal associations. . . . Upon existing conditions the Soudan "is worthless, having neither natural capabilities nor political "importance; but there is, nevertheless, a reason that first "prompted its occupation by the Egyptians, and that is in force "to the present day. THE SOUDAN SUPPLIES SLAVES. Without "the White Nile trade Khartoum would almost cease to exist; "and that trade is kidnapping and murder. . . . The amount of "ivory brought down from the White Nile is a mere bagatelle as "an export, the annual value being about £40,000."[2]

Baker next goes on to explain how the ivory trade is worked. A penniless man borrowed £1,000 to make a slave-raiding expedition on the White Nile at 100 per cent. interest, agreeing to pay the lender in ivory at one half its market value. Having

[1] Wells, *op. cit.*, p. 38.

[2] *Albert Nyanza*, p. 11.

obtained the money, he hired vessels and from 100 to 300 Arabs and runaway villains, and bought rifles and large quantities of ammunition, and a few hundred pounds of glass beads. Each man was paid 45 piastres, or nine shillings, per month, for five months in advance, payment being made partly in cash and partly in stuffs for clothes, for which an exorbitant price was charged. The expedition set out in December, and when the leader came to the village of some negro chief, he stopped and made friends with him. He then agreed to help the chief to fight his enemies, and on a given night they went and bivouacked near the village where they lived. A little before daybreak, whilst the inhabitants were still sleeping, their huts were set on fire, and volleys of musketry poured in on them through the flaming thatch. The panic-stricken natives rushed out, and the men were shot down, and the women and children secured; the cattle were seized as the prize of victory. The women were fastened by the necks to forked poles, to which their hands were also tied, and the children were tied by their necks with a rope attached to the women, and were marched off to the victor's camp with the cattle. All the ivory found in the huts was seized, and the "trader's party" dug up the floors of the huts to find the iron hoes, and destroyed all the granaries. To obtain the iron or copper bracelets from the dead they cut off their hands. The "traders" then returned to the negro chief, who was delighted at the overthrow of his foe, especially when they gave him a present of cattle, and a captive girl of about fourteen.

The negro chief wanted cattle, and was prepared to exchange ivory for them, a tusk for a cow, a profitable business, for the cows cost nothing. One third of all the stolen animals belonged to "trader's" men. The slaves were next put up at auction among these men, who bought such as they required, the amount of their purchases being entered on their papers to be reckoned against their wages. Kidnapped women and children were sometimes ransomed for a certain number of tusks; if a woman attempted to escape she was flogged, or hanged, or shot. Frequently the "trader" picked a quarrel with his negro ally, whom he then murdered, his women and children becoming slaves. A raid of this kind produced usually ivory to the value of about £4,000, and the "trader's" own profit was represented by four or five hundred slaves, each of which was worth from five to six pounds—between £2,000 and £3,000. The slaves and ivory were then packed in boats and sent down the river under the charge of some of the "trader's" men, the rest of whom stayed in the country to obtain by plunder, massacre, and enslavement another cargo for the following season. The slaves were landed in parties at various places on the river, being received by agents, who transported them to Sennaar, and to Sawâkin and Maṣaw'a on the Red Sea, whence they were shipped to Arabia and Persia. When the "trader" returned to Kharṭûm he paid his original loan of £1,000 in ivory, and having a handsome profit, he was able to begin business as an independent merchant in ivory. In 1863 the Turkish officials pretended to discountenance the slave trade, yet the officers were paid in slaves! And every house was full of slaves, and nearly every European merchant was engaged in the slave trade. The slave raiders sailed their boats flying the English, French, Austrian, Turkish, and even the American flag. This picture is a gloomy one, but the witnesses to the appalling condition of misery in which the Sûdân was in 1863 are so numerous, and the agreement in their evidence is so universal, that there is absolutely no reason for doubting their testimony.

Soon after the accession of Ismâ'îl Pâshâ as Ruler of Egypt, in 1863, that energetic prince issued orders for the suppression of the slave trade, and there is no good reason for doubting the sincerity of his wish for the abolition of the trade in human beings. He held no foolish or sentimental ideas about the fitness of the Blacks to rule either their country or themselves, and he made no proposal to interfere with domestic slavery, an institution which has always been the fundamental principle of all native African society, for he well knew that, speaking generally, slaves were kindly treated by their owners, and that the disgusting brutality of the slave trade lay in the burning of the villages, the murders of the men, the kidnapping of the women and children, and in the driving of the slaves over hundreds of miles of burning desert, with the attendant deaths from sickness and starvation. What Ismâ'îl realized was that the leaders of the slave-raiding expeditions, both Arab and European, formed a serious menace to his authority in the Sûdân, and an effectual check to the extension of his territories. The European Powers urged him to destroy the slave trade, and he determined to do it, but as soon as he began to take the necessary steps his subjects in Egypt abused him for attacking the greatest of all the trading interests of the country, his officials declared he was not a true Muslim, and the English newspapers asserted that the suppression of the slave trade on the White Nile was merely a pretext for annexing the whole of the Nile Basin!

In 1865 JA'AFAR Ṣâdiḳ Pâshâ was appointed Governor of the Sûdân.

In 1866 JA'AFAR Mazhar Pâshâ was appointed Governor of the Sûdân.

Between 1863 and 1869 matters went from bad to worse, for every official in the Sûdân, realizing that the slave trade was threatened, made as much money as he could out of slaves while he had the opportunity. The actions of the Arab and European raiders justified Ismâ'îl's view that they were a serious menace to his authority, for some of them had secured from the Governors of the Sûdân leases of whole provinces, and they were *de facto* not only independent rulers in the territories leased by them, but enemies to any rule except that of lawlessness. Ismâ'îl's first great difficulty was to find men to carry out his wishes, for his officials in the Sûdân could not be trusted. Nearly every one of them had an interest in the ivory and slaves that had been collected, and were still waiting at stations up the White Nile. Many of the largest merchants at Kharṭûm employed exclusively bands of Arabs to raid slaves, and one of them had as many as 2,500 Arabs in his pay. These gangs were officered by deserters from the Egyptian army, were divided into companies, and were armed with muskets, &c. There were about 15,000 men thus employed in the Sûdân, and they raided about 50,000 slaves annually, and one "trader" called Aḳâd claimed the right of jurisdiction over 90,000 square miles of territory. Each "trader" established a series of stations, manned by about 300 of his men, throughout his district, and was thus able to occupy it effectively.[1]

[1] I owe these facts to Baker, *Ismailïa*, London, 1879, p. 1 ff.

SIR SAMUEL BAKER

Early in 1869 Ismâ'îl, who was now Khedive, selected Sir Samuel Baker to carry out the great work of reorganizing the Sûdân, and he issued a *farmân* wherein he authorized him to :—

1. Subdue the country south of Gondokoro.
2. Suppress the slave trade.
3. Introduce a system of regular commerce.
4. Open the Equatorial Lakes to navigation.
5. Establish a chain of military stations and commercial depôts, distant from each other a three days' march, throughout Central Africa, with Gondokoro as the base of operations.

Baker was to have the supreme command of the expedition for four years, beginning April 1st, 1869, and the power of life and death over every member of it. He was also given supreme and absolute authority over all the country south of Gondokoro included within the Nile Basin.

Baker left Suez on December 5th, 1869, and proceeded to Kharṭûm *viâ* Sawâkin, where he found that about half of the 30,000 people who formerly lived in the town had disappeared, that nearly all the Europeans had gone away, and that most of the population of the district had turned into brigands, and were hunting slaves on the White Nile. To his disgust, Baker discovered that Mazhar Pâshâ, the Governor of the Sûdân, had prepared for an expedition to Dâr Fûr eleven vessels and several companies of soldiers, and that he had given the chief command to one Kutchûk 'Alî, a notorious raider, who had made a large fortune out of slave-raiding and dealing! Thus the Khedive was doing his best to suppress the slave trade, and his Governor of the Sûdân was sparing no pains to support it. On February 8th, 1870, Baker left Kharṭûm with two steamers, thirty-one sailing vessels, and 800 soldiers. After steaming for 103 hours, he reached Fâshôda, now Kodok, and found it garrisoned by Egyptian soldiers under the command of 'Alî Bey, a Kurd, who told him that the Shilluk country was in good order, and that according to the Khedive's instructions he had exerted himself against the slave trade. This statement Baker doubted, and a few weeks later actually caught him in the act of kidnapping 155 slaves,[1] and he discovered that 'Alî levied a toll upon every slave whom the

[1] *Ismailïa*, p. 45.

traders' boat brought down the river, which he kept for himself. Baker insisted that the slaves should be set free, and this was done with great reluctance by the Governor of Fashôda, who explained that he had only been collecting the taxes! Finding it impossible to press to Gondokoro on account of the obstructing vegetation in the White Nile, Baker stopped at a favourable place, and founded the station of Tawfiḳîya. Whilst here, he stopped several boats laden with slaves and ivory; the former he liberated, and the latter he sent on to Kharṭûm, where it was confiscated. The complicity of the Sûdân officials was established beyond a doubt. In October Baker learned that the Egyptian Government had already leased to the "trader" Aḥmad Shêkh Aghâ[1] an area of 90,000 square miles of the territory which he was about to annex in the Nile Basin, for several thousand pounds sterling per annum, together with the monopoly of the ivory trade. Aḥmad paid £3,000 a year for his lease, and he foresaw that if the Government were established in his district, his raiding and trading would be at an end. The slave-hunters were actually the tenants of the Egyptian Government, and they naturally resented the purchase of ivory by the Government from countries already leased to traders. It was a difficult position for all concerned, for the Khedive, for his Governor of the Sûdân, for Baker, and for the trader. Baker himself was obliged to admit that Aḥmad had a grievance against the Government, and actually agreed with him that no ivory should be bought by any one else in the district leased to him until after the expiry of the contract on April 9th, 1872.

On April 15th, 1871, Baker arrived at Gondokoro, and on May 26th he officially annexed the country for the Egyptian Government. Twelve hundred men were paraded, with ten guns, and the Turkish flag having been run up, the officers saluted with drawn swords, the troops presented arms, and the artillery fired a royal salute. On May 14th, 1872, at Masindi, with the full approval of Kabba Réga, the former king, Baker took formal possession of the country of Unyoro in the name of the Khedive of Egypt. He next set to work to put the commerce of the country on a good footing, and purchased ivory for the Government with from

[1] For an acount of his agent, the infamous Abû Sa'ud, see *Ismailïa*, pp. 77, 138, 152.

1,500 to 2,000 per cent. profit. A few beads, three or four gaudy-coloured cotton handkerchiefs, a zinc mirror, and a fourpenny butcher's knife would purchase a tusk worth £20 or £30! And the natives found that such "luxuries as twopenny mirrors, four-"penny knives, handkerchiefs, earrings at a penny a pair, finger "signet rings at a shilling a dozen, could be obtained for such "comparatively useless lumber as elephants' tusks . . . . In "Unyoro each party to the bargain thought that he had the best "of it."[1] Baker built forts at Masindi, Fatiko, and Fuwêra, and administered justice in a rough-and-ready fashion with great success. All his troops were Muḥammadans, but the natives believed in nothing; even so the latter were "free from many vices that disgrace a civilized community." Early in 1873 Baker entered into friendly relations with M'tesa, king of Uganda, and thus the Egyptian dominions extended to within 2° of the Equator. On April 1st, 1873, Baker returned to Gondokoro, or Ismâ'îlîya, and his term of service to the Khedive expired. On his way down the river he learned that several cargoes of slaves had passed the Government station at Fashôda, and his informant, Wad Hôjoly, himself had 700 slaves, in three vessels, which he was taking down to a station a few days south of Kharṭûm. Moreover, the infamous Abû Sa'ûd had gone to Cairo to appeal to the Government, and to represent that Baker had ruined his trade.[2]

In 1873 David Livingstone, the celebrated explorer and missionary, died of dysentery on April 30th at Chitambo. His body was carried to the coast, and was buried in Westminster Abbey, April 18th, 1874. He was born at Blantyre, near Glasgow, March 19th, 1813. He discovered Lake Ngami in 1849; explored the Zambesi and Kuanza Basins to Loando in 1851-4; recrossed Africa and discovered the Victoria Falls in 1855; led an expedition up the Zambesi and Shirî Rivers, and discovered Lakes Shirwa and Nyassa in 1858-9; explored the Rovuma Valley in 1866, the Chambezi in 1867, and Lakes Tanganyika, Moero, and Bangweolo in 1867-8; was at Ujiji in 1869; navigated Tanganyika, was relieved by Stanley at Ujiji in 1871; parted from Stanley at Unyanyembe in 1872, and returned to Lake Bangweolo. His "Last Journals" were published in 1874.

[1] *Ismailïa*, p. 341.

[2] *Op. cit.*, p. 457.

In 1873 ISMÂ'ÎL Pâshâ Ayûb was appointed Governor of the Sûdân. He is famous for having initiated great reforms in the Sûdân, and he tried to stop the bribery and corruption which were rampant. He did excellent work in connection with clearing the Sudd, or blocks of vegetation, from the White Nile, and succeeded in re-opening the river to navigation in the following summer. On August 24th Baker reached Cairo, and had an audience of Ismâ'îl Pâshâ, to whom he explained the chart of the new territory which he had acquired for him. To Baker belongs the great credit of destroying the slave trade between Kharṭûm and Gondokoro, of opening up commerce on the Nile, and of carrying civilization to within 2° of the Equator. Had Ismâ'îl Pâshâ's servants in the Sûdân been faithful to their orders, the abominable traffic in human flesh would have been entirely wiped out from the Egyptian Sûdân.

Baker resigned his appointment in 1873, and was succeeded by Colonel C. G. GORDON, R.E., who left Cairo to take up his duties in the Sûdân early in the spring of 1874. His instructions were to carry on the work which Baker had begun, i.e., first, to crush the slave trade, which was then, in spite of all Baker's efforts, a thriving business; secondly, to establish law and order in the newly-acquired Egyptian provinces south of Gondokoro, and to develop trade on just lines. The Khedive's *farmân* made him "Governor of the Equatorial Provinces on the Nile," and his authority was to extend from Fâshôda (Kodok) to M'tesa's country to the south. The authority of the Governor of the Sûdân was not to extend south of Fâshôda. Gordon arrived at Gondokoro on April 15th, where he found Baker's garrison, and at once took steps to consolidate the Egyptian power in the country. He established a garrison of 160 soldiers at Bôr, north of Gondokoro, and sent a member of his staff, Colonel Long, on a mission to king M'tesa at Uganda. He next broke up several slave-traders' stations on the Bahr az-Zaraf, and established a station on the Sobat, which was so placed that he could control the traffic up and down the White Nile.

In the summer of 1874 Munzinger, the Consul of Britain and France, who lived at Naṣaw'a,[1] took the opportunity of the out-

[1] See Shucair, *History of the Sudân*, iii., p. 89.

SCENERY IN KORDOFAN.

[From a photograph by Lieutenant S. F. Newcombe, R.E.

break of a war between the Abyssinians and the Gallas to occupy Keren, the capital of the Abyssinian province of Bogos, with 1,500 men. And at the same time the district of Ailet, which lay between Ḥamâsîn and Maṣaw'a, was sold to the Egyptian Government by its treacherous governor. Thus the Egyptians became masters of Senhît. John, king of Abyssinia, sent an appeal by Colonel Kirkman to the European Powers against the proceeding, but naturally no action in the matter was taken by them.

When Gordon arrived at Gondokoro in April, 1874, he relieved the commandant, Raw'ûf Pâshâ, who proceeded to Kharṭûm. The king of Harar, Aḥmad, was dead, and had been succeeded by one Muḥammad, who was extremely unpopular with the people, for he had deposed their nominee to the throne, Sitra Amîr. The people of Harar sent to the Khedive of Egypt, and asked him to take over their province, and the task of occupying the same was given to Raw'ûf Pâshâ. He proceeded to Harar, with a sufficient force, and, having taken the country, hanged Muhammad without giving him an opportunity of defending himself.[1]

In the same year (1874) the Egyptians found it necessary to take possession of the kingdom of Dâr Fûr, for it had been clear for years past that it was impossible to put a stop to the slave trade so long as slave caravans could pass unhindered from the countries near the Equator to Egypt *viâ* Dâr Fûr and Kordôfân. Dâr Fûr appears to have been from time immemorial the centre of the slave trade, and from about the eighth century of our era to have been inhabited by a number of tribes, some of whom were partly of Arab descent, and by others whose origin is not clear. They were not, however, negroes. The kingdom of Dâr Fûr extended at one time to the Atbara, but the Fûng kings of Sennaar little by little filched the territory of the Dâr Fûrians until the White Nile became the boundary between the two nations. The Fûng kings were, about 1770, masters of Kordôfân, a province of Dâr Fûr, for a few years, but Dâr Fûr proper seems to have been always an independent state, and its line of Sulṭâns was unbroken for about four hundred years. In 1822 Kordôfân was conquered by the Defterdâr, Muḥammad 'Alî's son-in-law, who appropriated to himself the enormous spoil which he took, and treated the

[1] Shucair, *op. cit.*, p. 90. He says the country was taken October 11th, 1875.

natives with shameful cruelty, and mutilated hundreds of them.[1] In 1869 Ismâ'îl, Khedive of Egypt, decided that the time had come for him to give the natives some proof of his authority over Dâr Fûr, and he therefore despatched to the Baḥr al-Ghazâl an officer called Muḥammad al-Ballâli, with a force of 800 men, 400 of whom were Bâshbûzaḳ, or "Bashi Bazûks."

Among the great slave-dealers of Dâr Fûr at this time was Zubêr ibn Raḥama, who traced his descent back to Ghânim, a man of the tribe of 'Abbâs. When Zubêr understood for what purpose Al-Ballâlî had come, he collected an army and went against him, and, by a superior knowledge of the country and its methods of warfare, he caught him in an ambush, and burned his camp and completely destroyed his force. After this the fame of Zubêr increased in the Sûdân, and the tribes flocked to him, and for a few years he was the most powerful man in the country. In 1873 a dispute broke out between the Egyptian Government and the Sulṭân of Dâr Fûr, which assumed serious proportions in 1874, when the Sûdân authorities seized all the slaves in a caravan which had been despatched to Egypt. In retaliation the Sulṭân raided for slaves certain districts which had been leased to Zubêr, and stopped the supply of corn which he and his fellow slave-merchants had been in the habit of obtaining from Dâr Fûr. Zubêr, knowing his strength, determined to invade Dâr Fûr and bring the Sulṭân to reason, but when the Egyptian Government heard of this, Ismâ'îl decided to undertake the conquest of the country himself, and to employ Zubêr in the work. Zubêr was ordered to attack Dâr Fûr from the south, and Ismâ'îl Ya'kûb Pâshâ from the north. The Sultân of Dâr Fûr and two of his sons were killed in one of the battles which took place soon after, and the country became an Egyptian province. Zubêr was created a Pâshâ, but was not satisfied, for he wished to be made Governor of the territory which the Egyptians had gained chiefly by his skill and goodwill. He went to Cairo to urge his claims, but he was "detained" there[2]

[1] For an account of his acts, see Petherick, *Egypt, the Soudan and Central Africa*, p. 277 ff.

[2] Gleichen, *Anglo-Egyptian Sûdân*, p. 236.

until the end of 1898; he now lives at Geili on the Nile, about thirty miles north of Kharṭûm.[1]

Meanwhile Gordon had been working very hard, and had made the effect of his influence and personality felt all over the countries on the White Nile. On September 11th, about twenty-five shêkhs from the region of Gondokoro came and did homage to him, a striking example of the belief which the natives had at that time in him. He established a post on the Sobat, and stations at Nâṣer, Shâmbî, Makâraka, Bôr, Lâtûka, Lâdô, Reggâf, Dufilî (Ibrahimîya), Fatiko, and Fuwêra. His measures for the suppression of the slave trade were vigorous, and his officer, Yûsuf Bey, Governor of Fâshôda, intercepted a convoy of 1,600 slaves, and 190 head of cattle.[2] When Gordon left Cairo in March, 1874, he took with him the infamous slave-dealer Abû Sa'ud Al-'Aḳâd,[3] who had gone to Cairo to complain that Baker had ruined his business. When they arrived at Gondokoro Gordon gave him a position of trust, and set him over other slave-dealers, no doubt thinking that he would not do any mischief whilst he himself was near. He was, however, mistaken, for Sa'ud used his appointment to advance his interests in the slave-dealing business, and Gordon was obliged to discharge him promptly. How Gordon could ever have employed a man with such a past, which was well known to him, passes understanding, and suggests that he overrated his own powers of discernment. In 1874 Slatin Pâshâ visited the Sûdân. He reached Kharṭûm, *viâ* Aswân, Korosko, and Berber, in October, and then went on to the Nûba Mountains, and stayed some time at Delen, where there was an Austrian Mission. From here he explored the Naima and Kadero mountains. He returned to Austria in 1875.

In 1875 Gordon proposed to the Khedive to establish a station at Mombassa Bay, 250 miles north of Zanzibar,[4] but Ismâ'îl preferred the mouth of the Jûba River, and fitted out an expedition to go there, under the command of McKillop Pâshâ,

[1] A most interesting account of his life, dictated or written by himself, is given in Shucair's *History of the Sûdân*, iii., p. 60 ff.

[2] Gleichen, *op. cit.*, p. 234.

[3] See Shucair, *op. cit.* iii., p. 53, 128.

[4] Gleichen, *op. cit.*, p. 237.

and Colonels Ward and Long. This site being found unsuitable, McKillop occupied Port Durnford and the harbour of Kismayu. These places, however, belonged to the Sulṭân of Zanzibar, and as the expedition threatened to injure the trade of the merchants of Zanzibar, Great Britain intervened, and its further development was stopped. With great difficulty Gordon transported a steamer to the Lakes, and established stations on the west bank of the river; on the east bank the Bârî were hostile, and at Dufilî a party under Linant, one of Gordon's officers, was surprised and massacred. Whilst Gordon was in the south the Shilluk tribes rebelled against the cruelty and oppression of the Government, and but for Gessi's[1] presence there Fâshôda would have been lost to Egypt.

In 1875 a dispute broke out between the Abyssinians and Egyptians about the port of Zula and the district of Giuda, which Kirkman had occupied on behalf of King John of Abyssinia. In October Colonel Arendrup, on behalf of the Egyptians, sailed to Maṣaw'a, marched to Giuda and took possession of it; he then advanced to Adua, the Abyssinian capital. King John collected an army, attacked Arendrup and defeated him, killing 1,800 men and capturing 2,000 rifles; among the slain were 'Arâḳîl Bey, the agent of Munzinger, and Munzinger himself. The battle was fought on November 11th. Ismâ'îl promptly sent out another expedition, which arrived at Maṣaw'a on December 11th. It was under Râtib Pâshâ, and consisted of 15,000 men, and with them were Colonel Long and Prince Ḥasan Pâshâ. On March 7th, 1876, King John attacked the Egyptians at Ḳar'a, fifty-five miles from Maṣaw'a, and slew some 10,000 of them, and captured thousands of rifles, and twenty-five guns, and many prisoners.[2] The Egyptian army returned to Cairo in January, 1877. After the battle of Ḳar'a, Walda Mîkâêl laid waste the Ḥamâsin territory of Abyssinia; this act delayed the peace negotiations which were in progress, for King John knew that Walda Mîkâêl was supported by the Egyptians.

[1] Gessi was employed as interpreter to the British troops during the Crimean war, and joined General Gordon's staff in 1874; he died at Suez on April 30th, 1881.

[2] Gleichen, *op. cit.*, p. 238; Shucair, iii., p. 91.

In March, 1876, Gessi, by Gordon's order, circumnavigated the Victoria Nyanza, and found it was 140 miles long, and 50 miles wide; in July a steamer was put together, with heroic exertions, above Dufilî Falls, and a passage cleared to the Albert Lake. A treaty was made with M'tesa, King of Uganda, and Dr. Emin Effendi (Edward Schnitzer) was sent to him as Gordon's representative. In October Gordon left the Sûdân in disgust, for all his efforts to suppress the slave trade were nullified by the resistance of Ismâ'îl Yaḳûb Pâshâ, the Governor of the Sûdân, and his lying and corrupt officials.

In February, 1877, Gordon was persuaded to return to Egypt, and Ismâ'il made him Governor-General of the Sûdân and of the Equatorial and Red Sea Provinces, and gave him instructions to suppress the slave trade, to develop commerce, and to make peace with King John of Abyssinia. Gordon went to Maṣaw'a and made an arrangement with Walda Mîkâêl whereby his raids on Abyssinian territory came to an end, and he proceeded to Kharṭûm *viâ* Kasala and Ḳaḍâref. When he arrived there he found that a very serious rebellion had broken out in Dâr Fûr. It was led by Harûn, a kinsman of the late Sûlṭan of the province, and he was joined by all the neighbouring shêkhs and by every one who had a grievance against the Government and was interested in the slave trade. The number of men in open revolt amounted to many thousands, and Ḥasan Hilmî, the Governor of Dâr Fûr, was unable to maintain his authority. Gordon went to Dâr Fûr in June, and learned that the province of Baḥr-al-Ghazâl was also in revolt, and that Sulêmân, the son of Zubêr, had collected a large number of men and was ready to attack any force which the Government might send into the country. In July Harûn retreated before Gordon to Tûra,[1] and when a month later he went to Dâra, he found there Sulêmân and made him return to Shakka. Two months later Gordon went to Shakka, the chief centre of the slave trade, and sent Sulêmân to the Baḥr al-Ghazâl.

Thus, for the time, the slave trade was broken up. Meanwhile Walda Mîkâêl was giving trouble, and Gordon wished to seize him and send him to Cairo. At the end of 1877 Gordon visited the

[1] See Gleichen, *op. cit.*, p. 239; Shucair, *op. cit.*, iii., p. 93.

Red Sea provinces, and from Zêla went on to Harar. Here he found that the Governor, Raw'ûf Pâshâ, had ruled the people in a cruel fashion, and that he was a slave-dealer on a large scale; he therefore promptly dismissed him. In March, 1878, Walda Mîkâêl attacked Râs Baryôn, the commandant of the Abyssinian frontier, and defeated and killed him, and succeeded in obtaining possession of Gordon's letters to the Râs, wherein his views about Walda Mîkâêl were expressed. Osmân Pâshâ, one of Gordon's officers, supplied him with ammunition, and the Minister of War in Cairo wrote and congratulated Walda Mîkâêl on his victory! Nine months later Walda Mîkâêl made his submission to King John, which was accepted.

Notwithstanding that most of Gordon's time and attention was occupied in keeping the peace, such as it was, in the Sûdân, he managed to consider matters of commercial and practical utility. Among these was the scheme for uniting the Sûdân with Egypt by a railway. The scheme was an old one, which was proposed so far back as 1857 by Sa'îd Pâshâ, and the route was surveyed by Mougel Bey, the builder of the Barrage north of Cairo. In 1865 the country was examined by Messrs. Walker and Bray, but the railway was not begun. Subsequently Ismâ'îl ordered a line to be laid from Ḥalfa to the south, but after about fifty miles had been laid, at a cost of £450,000, the scheme was stopped. Gordon wished to make a line from Berber to the port of Sawâkin, which is the natural outlet for Sûdân produce, but the Khedive would not listen to the proposal. Meanwhile Gordon was doing splendid work in suppressing the slave trade, for in two months he seized fourteen caravans, and he settled a batch of 1,300 of Zubêr's old slave-soldiers in a district between Wadâi and Dâr Fûr.

The greatest event of the year 1878 was the campaign of Gessi against Sulêmân, the son of Zubêr, who revolted at the instigation of his father,[1] and seized the province of Baḥr al-Ghazâl. Gordon had long realized that it was hopeless to expect any support or help from Cairo, and he had good reason for believing that, in his inmost heart, Ismâ'îl's sympathies were with his own corrupt officials in the Sûdân, and that he regarded him

[1] See Gleichen, *op. cit.*, p. 241; Shucair, *op. cit.*, iii., pp. 96, 97 ff.

as an honest but visionary and troublesome reformer. Gordon knew too that with the success or failure of Zubêr's revolt the Egyptian Government in the Sûdân must fall or stand, but the corrupt clique in Cairo which toadied Ismâ'îl understood nothing of this, and cared for nothing except their gain and pleasure. Count Gleichen aptly points out that at this time Zubêr was in Cairo, being treated as an honoured guest, and that Nubar Pâshâ, who was well acquainted with Zubêr's successes as a slave-dealer, actually offered to send him to assist Gordon! The truth, of course, is that Ismâ'îl was constitutionally incapable of seeing eye to eye with the British in the matter of the slave trade, and his views about the rights of conquered or dependent people were fundamentally different from ours.

The rebellion headed by Sulêmân had for its object the seizing of the Sûdân, and he and his friends the slave-dealers had arranged to divide the country among themselves. Every tribe lent him its support, and sent men, for the Government of the country as administered by the Sûdân officials was most corrupt, oppressive, and abominable; its main object seemed to be to tax the native out of existence. Gessi left Kharṭûm in July, 1878, and on his way south to Shâmbî found the slave trade in full activity, the Government steamers and officials rendering to it every facility in their power. From Shâmbî he went to Rumbek, which he fortified, and stayed there till November. Here he learned that Sulêmân had surprised and massacred the troops at Dêm Idrîs, and that with his army of 6,000 men he was laying waste the country in all directions. Gessi's force consisted of 1,000 men and two guns. Gessi left Rumbek on November 17th, and arrived at Wâw, in the province of the Baḥr al-Ghazâl, on December 5th, and established a station there. From this place Sulêmân had carried off 10,000 women and children. Gessi then set out for Dêm Idrîs, and was attacked by Sulêmân on December 28th with 10,000 men; he was "repulsed with great loss after severe fighting." On January 12th, 28th, and 29th, 1879, Sulêmân again attacked Gessi, but he was defeated on each occasion. On March 11th Gessi set fire to Sulêmân's camp with rockets, and when its inmates rushed out Gessi's soldiers fell upon them; but pursuit was out of the question, for Gessi was short of ammunition. On

May 1st Gessi attacked Sulêmân's fort, which after three days' fighting he captured, with much spoil. Sulêmân himself escaped, and was pursued by Gessi, but without success. In July he set out again in pursuit of the rebel, and was fortunate enough to surprise him on the 15th, and to make him lay down his arms. Fearing that with the help of his friends Sulêmân might escape, Gessi shot him and ten other ringleaders,[1] and, with the help of the people, he hunted down the other dealers, and broke up their parties, and set the slaves free. Gessi's activity and boldness had enabled him to crush Sulêmân's revolt, and for a short period slave-trading ceased.

On June 25th, 1879, Ismâ'îl Pâshâ[2] was deposed, and was succeeded by his son, Tawfîḳ Pâshâ. In August Gordon arrived in Cairo to discuss Abyssinian affairs with the new Khedive, and the result was his mission to Abyssinia. He reached Maṣaw'a on September 6th, and Gura on the 16th, and arrived at Dabra Tâbôr, near Gondar, where the king of Abyssinia was staying, on October 27th. Here he was detained through the shilly-shallying of King John, but at length he was allowed to leave, and he started for Ḳallâbât, meaning to go on to Kharṭûm. Before he reached Ḳallâbât he was arrested by King John's orders and brought back through Abyssinia, and he arrived, after much privation, at Maṣaw'a on December 8th, and determined never to return to the Sûdân. During the second period of Gordon's rule in the Sûdân many administrative changes had been made. Several of the stations occupied by Baker had been given up, and the territory of Egypt in the Sûdân ceased at the Somerset Nile.

At the end of 1879 Raw'ûf Pâshâ was appointed Governor of the Sûdân. It will be remembered that he had been dismissed by Gordon from the governorship of Harar because he was trading in slaves and ill-treating the people of his province, yet this was the man whom the authorities at Cairo entrusted at this critical period with the rule of the Sûdân! Before six months had passed the slave-dealers were again active, and, favoured by the new Governor at Kharṭûm and his subordinates, raiding began

[1] For their names, see Shucair, *op. cit*, iii. p. 101.

[2] He was born in 1830 and died in 1895; he was the son of Ibrahîm Pâshâ and became Khedive in 1863, though the *farmân* was not issued until 1867.

again, and the export of slaves by the Dâr Fûr road to Egypt and the cross-country routes to Sawâkin and Maṣaw'a went on merrily. Gessi, of course, found his position under Raw'ûf intolerable, and therefore resigned his office in the Baḥr al-Ghazâl, and left Meshra ar-Reḳ for Kharṭûm on September 25th, 1880. His steamer, the *Sasia*, was towing boats with 400 men on board, and became blocked by the Sudd near Ghaba Ger Dekka. All efforts made failed to move the vegetable barrier, food ran short, fever killed one half of the men, and their dead bodies were eaten by the other half. On January 4th, 1881, Marno appeared in the *Burdên*, and brought food and help, and so saved Gessi's life. Gessi was succeeded in the governorship by Lupton Bey, the captain of a Red Sea merchant steamer. In 1882 the slave trade was flourishing in the Sûdân, and Sulêmân's friends were making up for lost time. Simultaneously the Sûdân was being "reorganized on paper" in Cairo, and the authorities were deciding that it was to be ruled by one governor, assisted by four subordinate governors, and decreeing that schools and courts of justice were to be established there, and making special arrangements for the suppression of the slave trade! Thus was dust thrown in the eyes of European powers.

In 1883 'Abd Al-Ḳâder Ḥilmy Pâshâ was appointed Governor of the Sûdân.

In 1883 'Ala Ad-Dîn Pâshâ was appointed Governor of the Sûdân.

In 1884 Gordon Pâshâ became Governor of the Sûdân for the second time.

In 1899 Lord Kitchener became Governor of the Sûdân, and he was succeeded in the same year (December 22nd) by Sir F. R. Wingate, K.C.B., Pâshâ.

CHAPTER XIV.

THE MAHDÎ IN THE SÛDÂN.

THE facts briefly stated in the preceding pages show clearly that in the sixty years which had elapsed since the occupation of the Sûdân by Muḥammad 'Alî in 1820, the country had been ruined by bad government, excesssive taxation, oppression, injustice, bribery, and, above all, by the infamous slave trade, which had been more or less aided and abetted by all the Rulers of Egypt. Thousands upon thousands of square miles of territory had gone out of cultivation, the water-wheels were broken in many places and had been left to rot, and about seven-eighths of the population had given up a settled life and become brigands, highway robbers, cattle-lifters, and slave-raiders. From the Equator northwards every man was dissatisfied with the Egyptian Government, and the desire for its abolition was boldly expressed on all hands. The natives in the towns had just tasted the blessings of Gordon's just and equitable government, and were becoming accustomed to his patient hearing of their petitions, and to the sight of the punishment which he meted out with unswerving justice to evil-doers, when he departed, and his place was taken by a notorious slave-dealer, whom the Khedive and his ministers set over their land. The slave-dealing tribes of Arab descent, hearing that the Government at Cairo talked of the suppression of their trade, were ready to revolt, and when they compared the number of the men available for the purpose with that of the Egyptian troops, they felt no doubt as to their success. Thus matters stood at the end of 1879 when Gordon left the Sûdân. All that was wanted to set the whole country in a blaze of rebellion was some one person, or an idea round which the elements of revolt could crystallize. Fate, or Fortune, supplied both a person and the idea; the person was Muḥammad Aḥmad, and the idea was one which, though thirteen hundred years old among Muslims, is ever new to the generation among which it reappears, viz., the regeneration of the Muḥammadan Dîn, or religion, by force of arms.

MUḤAMMAD AḤMAD,[1] now known as "the Mahdî," was born on the Island of Ḍarâr, in the neighbourhood of Dongola, about the year 1843; his father's name was 'Abd-Allah, and his mother's Zênab, and he claimed a descent from Arabs who had settled in Nubia from the Peninsula of Arabia. His pedigree is thus given by Shucair (iii., p. 114): Muhammad Al-Mahdi, the son of 'Abd-Allah, the son of Maḥal, the son of 'Abd Al-Walî, the son of 'Abd-Allah, the son of Muḥammad, the son of Ḥâgg Sharîf, the son of 'Alî, the son of Aḥmad, the son of 'Alî, the son of Ḥasab An-Nebî, the son of Ṣibr, the son of Nasr, the son of 'Abd Al-Karîm, the son of Ḥusên, the son of 'Aûn Allah, the son of Negen Ad-Dîn, the son of 'Uthmân, the son of Mûsa, the son of Abû Al-'Abbâs, the son of Yûnas, the son of 'Uthmân, the son of Ya'kûb, the son of 'Abd Al-Ḳâder, the son of Ḥasan the soldier, the son of 'Alwân, the son of 'Abd Al-Bâḳî, the son of Ṣakhra, the son of Ya'ḳûb, the son of Ḥasan As-Sabṭ, the son of Imâm 'Alî, the son of Abû Ṭâlib. His father was by trade a boat-builder, and when hard times came upon him he removed to Kharṭûm, and settled in Kararî, where he died and was buried, leaving a daughter called Nûr Ash-Shâm, and three sons, viz., Muḥammad, Muḥammad Aḥmad, and Ḥâmed. A fourth son, 'Abd-Allah, was posthumous. Ahmad's brothers worked at their father's trade, but Aḥmad devoted himself to books and learned the Ḳur'ân in the schools of Karari and Kharṭûm. He worked hard, and pleased his instructors, and went to Berber and studied under the famous Shêkh Muḥammad Al-Khêr.

From Berber he went to Kharṭûm and studied under Muḥammad Sharîf, an eminent professor of the Samânîya doctrine. He was modest, intelligent, and devout. At prayer-time he wept until the ground about him was moist, and all the time his shêkh

[1] The most complete account of the life and teaching of this man is given by Sir Reginald Wingate in his *Mahdiism* (second edition), and the best commentaries which the reader can have on both are Slatin Pasha's *Fire and Sword in the Sudan*, and Ohrwalder's *Ten Years' Captivity in the Mahdi's Camp*.

was instructing him he sat with bowed head.[1] He became a professor of religion in 1861, and in 1871 he and his brothers went to live on Abbâ Island, in the White Nile, near Kâwa. Here he led a life of fasting and prayer, and trained many disciples, and all the people regarded him as a most holy and learned man. His brothers made a good living by boat-building, for there was much timber on the island, and they supplied the wants of Aḥmad, which were few, for he lived in a cave hollowed out in the mud bank of the river.

One day his teacher, Muḥammad Sharîf, gave a feast to celebrate the circumcision of his sons, and he gave his guests an indulgence which permitted them to sing and dance. Aḥmad, hearing this, told his audience that no man could forgive sins, and singing, dancing, and music were contrary to God's commands. These words were reported to Muḥammad Sharîf, who promptly called upon his disciple to justify himself. Aḥmad humbly asked forgiveness, but his irate master abused him, and struck his name off the Samânîya order. Twice after this did Aḥmad ask for forgiveness, but his master repulsed him on each occasion with words of contumely and abuse. Aḥmad now applied to the Shêkh Al-Kurêshî, who lived at Masallamîya, to receive him into his order, and this shêkh agreed to do so. Just as Aḥmad was starting for Masallamîya, a message came from his former master telling him to appear before him, and he should receive a full pardon. Aḥmad declined to do this, saying that he was innocent of offence, and that he now sought no forgiveness from him. The dispute between Aḥmad and Muḥammad Sharîf created a stir, and people's sympathies were with the younger man. Numbers of men flocked to Abbâ Island to receive his blessing, and all the gifts given to him he distributed among the poor, thus gaining a great reputation for self-sacrifice and piety. He then travelled about among the religious folk in Kordôfân, and was everywhere received with open arms. He wrote a pamphlet wherein he called upon all true believers to help him to purify the religion of Islâm, which was becoming debased, and was being flouted by the Government officials; of this seditious work he gave copies to all his faithful admirers. Besides this, he preached the absolute

[1] Shucair, *op. cit.*, iii., p. 115.

equality of all men, and the community of all goods and possessions, and every man was to become a Muslim under penalty of death. A programme of this kind was certain to be popular, and Aḥmad knew well the character of the people to whom he preached. His social position was good, for he had married daughters of several of the chief Baḳḳâra (Baggara) shêkhs, and these connections gave him many friends.

Exactly when the idea came to him is not known, but in 1880 Ahmad seems to have made up his mind to personate the Mahdî, who according to Muslim tradition was to appear in the year of the Hijra 1300, i.e., A.D. 1882. Early in 1881 he had a serious quarrel with the Mudîr of Fâshôda as to the taxation of the district, and, knowing the feelings of the people, he openly defied him. In May, 1881, he took counsel with his co-religionists, and in August following, during the Ramaḍân fast, he boldly and publicly declared himself to be the Mahdî, whose advent was awaited, and he promised to purify the religion and to right all wrongs, and to abolish the Government with its iniquitous system of oppression and taxation. He would first take the Sûdân, then Egypt, and finally he would go and found a kingdom at Mekka which should last one thousand years. The Mahdî was at this time forty years of age, i.e., the same age as the Prophet when he declared his mission.

When Raw'ûf Pâshâ heard of the Mahdî's proclamation he sent Abu Sa'ûd, with 200 soldiers and one gun, to Abbâ Island to bring him to Kharṭûm. On their arrival, a member of the force called 'Alî Effendî shot a villager by mistake, whereupon the people rushed on the soldiers and massacred about 140 of them, and the rest with difficulty escaped to their boat. The Mahdî was now a rebel, and he was prudent enough to withdraw to the south of Kordôfân, beyond Gebel Taḳala to Gebel Ḳadîr; but he also took care to send out everywhere reports of his victory over the Government troops.[1]

On December 4th, 1881, Rashîd Bey, the Mudîr of Fâshôda, collected 400 soldiers and 1,000 Shilluks, and set out to attack the Mahdî at Gebel Ḳadîr; with him was the slave inspector Berghoff. He reached the Mahdî's position on the 9th at dawn, and his men

[1] See Slatin, *Fire and Sword*, p. 135; Shucair, *op. cit.*, iii., p. 130.

seeing wells rushed to drink; whilst thus scattered the Mahdî's men fell on them, and killed Rashîd and Berghoff and nearly all their followers. The news of the defeat spread far and wide in the Sûdân, and all the tribes in Dâr Fûr, Kordôfân, Sennaar, and in the Eastern Desert between Berber and the Red Sea were in revolt. Raw'ûf Pâshâ then collected a force of 4,000 men, which on March 18th, 1882, under the command of Nubar Pâshâ Yûsuf, set out for the Shilluk country. It reached Kâwa, stayed there for several weeks, and did nothing! Seeing that the troops were at Kâwa, Aḥmad Al-Makâshif, a relative of the Mahdî, besieged Sennaar with 1,000 of the Baḳḳâra; the siege was raised by Ṣâliḥ Bey after a fierce fight. The enemy retreated to Karkôg, and a few weeks later defeated a force sent against them at Masallamîya. Meanwhile Raw'ûf Pâshâ had been recalled and had gone to Cairo, and the government of Kharṭûm was carried on by Giegler Pâshâ, the head of the telegraph department, until the arrival of 'Abd Al-Ḳâder, the new governor, on May 11th, 1882. On the 3rd of May Giegler Pâshâ marched against the Baḳḳâra on the Blue Nile, and defeated them at Abû Ḥaraz, and on the 25th he gained another victory over them at Sennaar. He then returned to Kharṭûm. In June the Mahdî, whose followers had begun to invest Al-Obêḍ, surprised and routed Yûsuf Pâshâ, Governor of Fâshôda, near Gebel Ḳadîr, and took all his arms and ammunition, and a large quantity of stores. Soon afterwards the Mahdî captured Shatt on the White Nile, and put all the males to death; and on July 20th he destroyed a force of 1,000 Egyptians in Dâr Fûr.

In August the Mahdî found that he was master of three armies,[1] but his troops were defeated at Bâra, Al-Obêḍ was revictualled, and in a battle fought at Duwêm on the 28th he lost 4,500 men. Early in September the Mahdî led a force in person against Al-Obêḍ, and each of his three attacks on the 4th, 5th, and 6th respectively, was repulsed. His loss was about 10,000 killed, and his prestige suffered, for no force led by him in person had hitherto been defeated. About this time 'Alî Bey Satfi, with 3,000 troops, marched to the relief of Dâra, and engaged the enemy twice; the first time he was successful, and

[1] Gleichen, *op. cit.*, p. 244.

the second lost 1,130 men. In October the Mahdî besieged Al-Obêḍ and Dâra, and 'Abd Al-Ḳâder, the Governor of the Sûdân, telegraphed to Cairo for 10,000 men; in December Colonel Stewart was sent to Kharṭûm to make a report on the situation.

On January 5th, 1883, Bâra fell, and on the 17th Al-Obêḍ also, and 8,000 men, and rifles, arms and ammunition, five guns, and £100,000 in specie fell into the hands of the Mahdî, who took up his residence in the Government House at Al-Obêḍ. On February 29th 'Abd al-Ḳâder fought Aḥmad Al-Makâshif near Sennaar, and defeated him, and killed 2,000 of his men; on March 4th the rebel was attacked by Ṣâliḥ Aghâ, who defeated him and slew 547 of his men. 'Abd Al-Ḳâder was now superseded and 'Ala Ad-Dîn Pâshâ became Governor of the Sûdân. In response to 'Abd Al-Ḳâder's appeal for 10,000 men, Hicks Pâshâ was sent to Kharṭûm, *viâ* Sawâkin and Berber, with 10,000 untrained Egyptians, and he arrived on March 4th. Hicks left Kharṭûm on April 3rd for Kâwa, with about 5,000 men, and on the 29th he was attacked near Marâbia by Aḥmad Al-Makâshif, with 5,000 men; the rebel commander was defeated with great loss, and slain. On September 9th, Hicks left Kharṭûm with about 9,000 men, 5,500 camels, 500 horses, and 20 guns for Duwêm, which he reached on the 20th. He marched on Al-Obêḍ, *viâ* Khôr Abû Ḥabl, according to 'Ala Ad-Dîn's recommendation, and arrived at Shatt on the 24th. Meanwhile the Mahdî had collected some 40,000 men whom he had made to camp in the forest of Shekan. Hicks left Shatt on the 28th, and wandered on through a waterless country of which he knew nothing. His guides led him astray near Kasghil, and then ran away. He wandered about for three days and three nights, suffering greatly from the want of water, and then entered the forest wherein the Mahdî's men were.[1] Here, on November 5th, the enemy fell upon Hicks and his troops, and slaughtered men and animals mercilessly; only about 300 escaped death. Hicks and his Staff made a brilliant charge, and died fighting like men. The effect of this victory was to make the Mahdî master of all the Sûdân south of Kharṭûm, and

[1] For the supposed Itinerary of Hicks's Army, see Wingate, *Mahdiism*, p. 549.

he had now 21,000 rifles and 29 guns at his disposal, with ammunition, stores, specie, &c. And men all over the Sûdân believed that Muhammad Aḥmad was indeed the Mahdî, whose advent tradition had foretold.

Early in 1883[1] Slatin Pâshâ was ordered to nominate a local Sulṭân as King of Dâr Fûr, and to retire on Dongola *viâ* Kaja. It will be remembered that in 1882, after he had twice defeated Madibbo at Ingelêla near Dâra, he retired to Al-Fâsher to concentrate his forces. In 1883 he fought twenty-seven actions in his province, but little by little his men deserted him, and when the remainder heard of the annihilation of Hicks's army, Slatin found that the only course open to him was to surrender; this he did at Dâra in December, 1883.[2] He was then sent to Al-Obêḍ under the name of 'Abd Al-Ḳâder, and thence to Umm Durmân (Omdurman), where he remained a prisoner until his escape in 1895.

About the middle of 1883 Osmân Diḳna gathered together the Hadanduwa and the Bishârî and oṭher tribes of the Eastern Desert, and they revolted against the Government to such purpose that by December the Egyptian garrisons of Sinkât, Kasala, Ḳaḍâref, Ḳallâbât, &c., were in their hands. In October and November parties intended for Sinkât and Tokar were cut off, and on December 2nd about 700 men were annihilated near Tamanib. In the Baḥr al-Ghazâl, Jânḳî, Shêkh of the Dinkas, rebelled at Liffî on August 18th, 1882, on behalf of the Mahdî; towards the end of the year Lupton marched against him and defeated him with great slaughter at Telgona. Early in 1883 Jânḳî returned to Liffî and was again beaten; but in September he attacked Rufai 'Aghâ, an officer of Lupton's, at Dembo, and massacred him and all his men. The whole Dinka tribe then revolted, and Lupton had to retreat to Dêm Zubêr; after August 15th he was isolated.

After the annihilation of Hicks's army it was decided to abandon the Sûdân, for the simple reason that Egypt could neither produce an army, nor pay for one, which should be strong enough to crush the revolt in the Sûdân. The various Egyptian garrisons scattered throughout the country had, of course, to be withdrawn,

[1] Gleichen, *op. cit.*, p. 255. [2] See Shucair, *op. cit.*, iii., p. 187.

and the man chosen by the authorities to perform this work was General Gordon. He left London on January 18th, 1884, and reached Berber, *viâ* Korosko and Abû Ḥamed, on February 11th; he was accompanied by Colonel Stewart, who had been made his Deputy-Adjutant-General. At Berber he issued the decree authorizing the evacuation of the Sûdân, which it is said astonished the Mudîr, Husên Pâshâ Khalîfa, and practically sealed Gordon's own fate. On the 18th Gordon arrived at Kharṭûm, and the townsmen welcomed him. The enthusiasm was great at his assumption of power, at his remission of past and reduction of future taxes, and it lasted about nine days.[1] Soon after his arrival Gordon issued a proclamation to the people, in which he said:—

. . . . "I also give you the right to keep the slaves in your "service without any interference from the Government or any-"body else . . . ."

"Whereas my sincerest desire is to adopt a course of action "which shall lead to the public tranquillity, and being aware with "what regret you have regarded the severe and stringent measures "which have been taken by the Government for the suppression "of the traffic, and the seizure and punishment of all concerned "in the slave trade, as provided by the convention and by the "decrees, I therefore confer upon you these rights: that hence-"forth no one shall interfere with your property; that who-"ever has slaves in his service shall have full right to their "services and full control over them without any interference "whatsoever."[2]

When the first enthusiasm was over the people of Kharṭûm began to consider Gordon's position. He was Governor of the Sûdân, but he had no army, he forgave everybody, he freely remitted taxation, and he gave his support to the slave trade, which in years past he had done so much to crush. What did it all mean? Then men remembered that Cairo had been taken possession of by the British, who had determined to abandon the Sûdân, and they wondered when their country had been cast off by Egypt who was to rule it. Gordon announced that the Sûdân was now an independent kingdom, with himself as the Governor-

[1] Wingate, *Mahdiism*, p. 109. [2] *Ibid.*, Appendix to Book v., p. 551.

General, but no one in Kharṭûm regarded the man who had permitted Gessi to shoot Sulêmân, Zubêr's son, and had dismissed in disgrace Raw'ûf Pâshâ, the Governor of Harar, for slave-dealing, and had liberated thousands of slaves, as the permanent Governor of the country, the chief industry of which had, for thousands of years, consisted of slave-dealing and slave-raiding. Nor had the tribes between the White and Blue Niles and the Ga'alîn Arabs between Berber and Kharṭûm a different opinion, and they remembered that it was Gordon who issued the edict to eject the Gellabas from the southern districts, and that as a result of this drastic measure many of the people had not only lost fathers, brothers, and sons, but had been reduced to beggary. "Were they," Slatin pertinently asks, "likely to forgive Gordon this?"[1] Gordon's position was an impossible one, and the authorities had sent him to do a thing which was, for him, impossible. Neither the British nor the Egyptian Government realized how serious the situation was, and even Gordon himself appears to have underrated the strength and extent of the fanaticism which produced the rebellion, and to have overrated his ability to cope with it.

He appointed the Mahdî Sulṭân of Kordôfân by proclamation, and sent him some very fine clothes and a letter asking for the release of all prisoners. But the Mahdî was already *de facto* master of all the country south of Kharṭûm, and had tens of thousands of fanatical followers ready to fight for him to the death, whilst Gordon entered Kharṭûm with merely a small bodyguard.[2] The Mahdî knew well that Gordon could not take from him by force of arms what he had obtained, and when he wrote back to him he advised Gordon to surrender and save his life. This incident is both ludicrous and pathetic, and illustrates Gordon's attitude towards the rebellion.

In a very short time the natives made up their minds that Gordon was merely a stop-gap, and they began to consider who was to be their head after his departure. There was only one man whom the tribes admitted to be fit to hold his office, and that man was the notorious Zubêr; and it was for him that they clamoured. Gordon agreed with them, and asked the authorities

[1] *Fire and Sword*, p. 280. [2] *Ibid.*, p. 281.

to send Zubêr up to Kharṭûm to take over from him the rule in the Sûdân. The request was, however, refused on the ground that he had been a slave-dealer; therefore Zubêr was kept in Cairo. When the people in Kharṭûm learned the decision of the Government, they were much disappointed, and shêkh after shêkh began to demand that Kharṭûm should be handed over to him. Thereupon Gordon lined the forts with soldiers, and made ready for war. On March 16th he hazarded a fight, but his men "ran like hares and were massacred"; a week later the "Bashi-Bazouks" refused to obey orders, and were promptly disarmed. On March 10th the Mahdî called on Gordon to surrender, and sent him as a present a suit of Dervish apparel, which consisted of a coat, an overcoat, a turban, a cap, a girdle, and beads, and invited him to come out to him at once wearing this suit. Gordon called a council to consider this summons, and it decided to trust Gordon and resist; and Gordon accepted the trust. He was never allowed to leave Kharṭûm, and even on the most trifling boat journey he was always accompanied by vigilant townsmen,[2] whose *fetish* he had become.

Meanwhile Colonel Valentine Baker had set out in January to relieve Tôkar, with 3,700 men, but on February 4th at At-Teb he was attacked by 1,200 Arabs; his men literally ran away, and as they made no resistance 2,300 of them were slain. Baker and his officers escaped with difficulty, but 3,000 rifles and four Krupp guns fell into the hands of the enemy. Four days later Tawfîḳ and his men fought their way out of Sinkât, and they were all cut to pieces. General Graham was then sent to relieve Tôkar with a British force of 4,000 men; he defeated the rebels at At-Teb on January 29th, and again on March 13th at Tamâî. In April Ḳaḍâref surrendered to the forces of the Mahdî; on the 21st of the same month Karam-Allah,[3] the Amîr of Baḥr al-Ghazâl, forced Lupton Bey to surrender. Lupton was given a new name, 'Abd-Allah, and sent to Omdurmân, where he died on July 17th, 1888. On May 20th Berber was attacked, and, after some resistance,

[1] A translation of the document is given by Wingate, *Mahdiism*, p. 111 ff.; for the Arabic text, see Shucair, *op. cit.*, iii., p. 226.

[2] Wingate, *Mahdiism*, p. 116.

[3] He was executed at Al-Fâsher by 'Alî Dînâr in 1903; Gleichen, *op. cit.*, p. 259.

surrendered. On the 27th Karam-Allah called on Emin Bey at Lâdô to surrender, but he held on to his post, although his men were very greatly disaffected. Emboldened by his capture of Berber, Haddai marched into the Dongola province, where, however, he was defeated in July at Debba and Tani. On September 1st Mustafa Pâshâ Yâwar, the Mudîr of Dongola, with 400 men, attacked Haddai and Muḥammad Maḥmud, and their 3,000 men, and defeated them with great slaughter; both leaders were killed in the battle.

In the interval the British Government had decided to send out a Gordon Relief Expedition, and to Lord Wolseley was given the command of it; he arrived at Cairo on September 9th, and the expedition concentrated eventually at Korti in December.

Towards the end of August Gordon felt that the time had come to strike a blow at his enemies, who were hemming him in more closely each day, and on the 29th and 31st, his "fighting Pasha," Muḥammad 'Alî Pâshâ, set out for the Blue Nile with a large force. He defeated 'Abd al-Ḳâder at Gerêf, and Shêkh Al-'Obêḍ at Ḥalfâya, and gained two brilliant victories. On September 4th, however, the Shêkh Al-'Obêḍ fell upon his forces at Umm Dubbân at dawn, when they were tired and in disorder, for they had lost their way and had been wandering about all night, and Muḥammad 'Alî and 800 of his men were cut down, and 980 Remington rifles fell into the hands of the enemy.[1] This disaster took place about twelve miles to the east of the town of Al-'Êlafûn on the Blue Nile, a few miles above Soba, and was the more heart-rending because it happened after the brave "fighting Pasha" had gained a third victory at 'Êlafûn. After this defeat Gordon believed his position to be, humanly speaking, desperate, and he despatched the steamer "Abbâs" to Cairo[2] with Colonel Stewart, Herbin, Power, and a bodyguard of Greeks on board. The steamer left on September 10th, and was allowed to proceed safely so far as Habba in the Fourth Cataract, where she arrived on the 18th. Here the steersman ran her on a rock, and she sank, but Stewart and his companions managed to land. They entered a neighbouring village, and, having been invited into the

[1] Wingate, *Mahdiism*, p. 157; Shucair, *op. cit.*, iii., p. 251.

[2] See Shucair, iii., p. 258 ff.

house of Sulêmân wad Na'mân to drink coffee and to discuss the hire of camels, were murdered. The Arabs who murdered the party were collected by Faḳrî wad 'Uthmân, a blind man, and Sulêmân wad Ḳamr, the Shêkh of the Monasîr Arabs, assisted them. After the murder of Stewart and his party, another body of Arabs attacked the crew of the steamer, and only thirteen of them escaped.

On September 26th Gordon sent three steamers under the command of Nashî Pâshâ to meet the British Expedition, but this they did not do until January 21st, when they met the

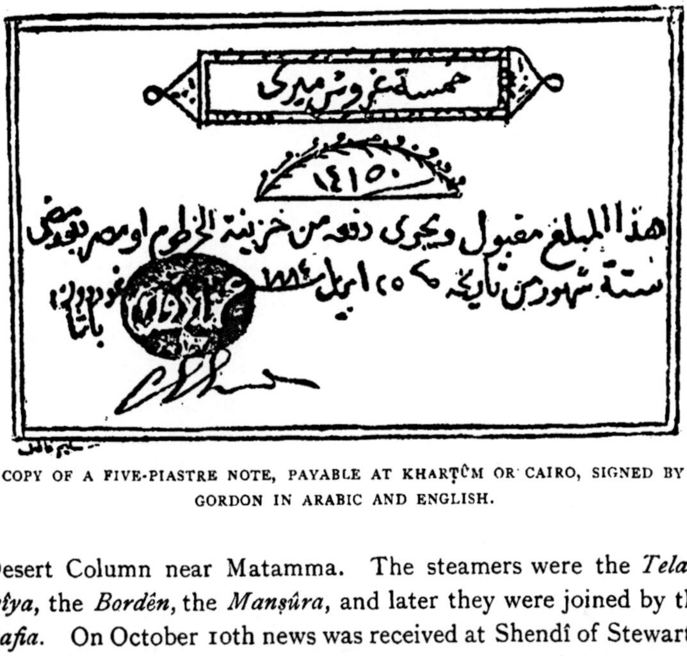

COPY OF A FIVE-PIASTRE NOTE, PAYABLE AT KHARṬÛM OR CAIRO, SIGNED BY GORDON IN ARABIC AND ENGLISH.

Desert Column near Matamma. The steamers were the *Telahwîya*, the *Bordên*, the *Manṣûra*, and later they were joined by the *Safia*. On October 10th news was received at Shendî of Stewart's death, and a steamer was sent to Kharṭûm to inform Gordon. The steamer returned to Shendî, and the attack on that town by Gordon's men went on for three months. Meanwhile nothing was heard of the British Expedition, and the hearts of men in Kharṭûm grew sick at the delay. After the disaster at 'Êlafûn the inhabitants "fell into despair and distress, and wept for their state," and Bûrdênî Bey [1] says that Gordon wept with them; it

[1] Quoted by Wingate, *Mahdiism*, p. 163 ff.

was "the first and last time I ever saw Gordon Pâshâ in tears." The day after the defeat the Mahdî sent 'Abd Ar-Raḥmân an-Nagûmî with 10,000 men to Kalâkala, and called upon every tribe to send men to besiege Kharṭûm. They did his bidding, and began to bombard the town from all sides. But Gordon had no fear, and one evening when his friend Bûrdênî suggested that he should have boxes of sand placed in the windows to stop the bullets, he was enraged, and at once had a lantern which would hold twenty-four candles brought to the room. He and his friend filled its sockets with candles, and lit them. Gordon then said, "When God was portioning out fear to all the people "in the world, at last it came to my turn, and there was no fear "left to give me; go, tell all the people in Kharṭûm that Gordon "fears nothing, for God has created him without fear." On November 12th a fierce fight between Gordon's men and the rebels took place, and the latter lost heavily. After the fight the rebels built forts between Omdurmân and Kharṭûm, and bombarded the latter town continuously.

On December 28th a River Column left Korti under General Earle, with orders to push on to Abû Ḥamed, and two days later a Desert Column left the same place to occupy Gakdûl Wells.

On January 5th, 1885, Faraḳ-Allah, the brave commandant of Omdurmân, was obliged to surrender, and all his men were taken prisoners. Thereupon the rebels began to cut off all supplies from Kharṭûm, and men began to starve. The crops on Tuti Island were sown and reaped under the fire of the guns from the fort! They produced 200 *ardebs* of corn (the *ardeb*=5½ bushels, or 300 pounds), and each *ardeb* Gordon bought for £12. When this corn and the biscuits were eaten, the town was carefully searched, but very little corn was found. A receipt was given to every man from whom corn was taken. Then men ate dogs, donkeys, skins of animals, palm fibre, and gum. The soldiers stood like logs of wood on the fortifications, and the corpses of civilians filled the streets. Then the cattle, 28 animals in all, were killed, and their flesh distributed among the soldiers.

On January 11th the Desert Column left Gakdûl Wells, 1800 strong, and on the 17th it engaged a force of 11,000 Dervishes at Abû Ṭleḥ ("Abû Klea"), which it defeated with great slaughter.

On the 19th it fought another battle at Abû Khrûg, and on that day Sir Herbert Stewart was mortally wounded.

On January 20th the rebels fired a salute of 101 guns, pretending that they had beaten the British, but Gordon was not deceived. On the 24th Sir C. Wilson left Gubat with two of Gordon's steamers which had arrived on the 21st at Matamma. Meanwhile in Kharṭûm the arrival of the British was expected, "but as day by day passed," says Bûrdênî Bey, "and we neither saw nor "heard anything of them, we began again to despair. Gordon "Pasha used to say every day, 'They must come to-morrow,' "but they never came." On the following Sunday, January 25th, Gordon observed that a great commotion was taking place at Kalâkala, and he felt sure that an attack on the town was imminent. He summoned his friends, and through Giryâgîs begged them to make a stand for the last time, for he had no doubt that in twenty-four hours the British would come. He was too much agitated to address his friends himself, and he felt that all the town was now believing that he had told them lies when he said the British were coming. Bûrdênî saw him after the meeting, and notes that the distress and anxiety of the last few months had turned his hair a "snowy white." If only a couple of English soldiers of the advancing force "could be paraded about "the lines of Kharṭûm," he used to say, "I should not fear the "enemy's attack." Gordon sat writing till midnight, and then lay down to sleep, but was awakened between 2 and 3 a.m. by the cries of the 50,000 Arabs, who had crept across the parapet[1] and over the filled-up ditch into the town.

For an hour he kept up a hot fire on them, but it was useless to stay the horde which thronged to the palace. He then left the roof and went to his room, and having changed his sleeping apparel for his white uniform, he stepped out at the head of the staircase. Here four men, Taha Shahîn, Ibrahîm Abû Shanab, Ḥamad Wad Aḥmad, and a certain Dongolâwî, rushed towards him as he stood in "a calm and dignified manner, his left hand "resting on the hilt of his sword." He asked, "Where is Muḥammad Aḥmad?" Shahîn attacked him at once with the words, "O cursed one, to-day is thy day" (i.e., thy time hath come),

[1] Ohrwalder, *Ten Years' Captivity*, p. 154.

and plunged his spear into his body. Gordon, it is said, made a gesture of scorn with his right hand, and turned his back, where he received another spear wound, which made him fall forward, and probably caused his death. The other three men rushed on him and hacked at him with their swords, and he must have died in a few seconds.[1] Gordon had a revolver in his hand, but he offered no resistance, and did not fire a shot.[2] His head was cut off at once[3] and sent to the Mahdî, and his body was dragged down the stairs into the garden, and stripped, and it lay there naked for some time; many Arabs came and plunged their spears into it. The head was taken over to Omdurmân and shown to Slatin Pâshâ[4] by Shatta, a black soldier; it was afterwards fixed between the branches of a tree and all who passed by cursed it, and threw stones at it. His body was finally thrown into a well[5]

[1] Bûrdênî Bey, quoted by Wingate, *Mahdiism*, p. 171.

[2] A wholly different version of Gordon's death is given by Neufeld in his *A Prisoner of the Khalifa.* It reads: "By the time Gordon had slipped into his "old serge, or dark tweed suit, and taken his sword and revolver, the advanced "Dervishes were already surrounding the Palace. Overcoming the guards, a "rush was made up the stairs, and Gordon was met leaving his room. A "small spear was thrown, which wounded him, but very slightly, on the left "shoulder. Almost before the Dervishes knew what was happening three of "them lay dead, and one wounded, at Gordon's feet; the remainder fled. "Quickly reloading his revolver, Gordon made for the head of the stairs, and "again drove the reassembling Dervishes off. Darting back to reload, he "received a stab in his left shoulder-blade from a Dervish concealed behind the "corridor door, and on reaching the steps the third time, he received a pistol "shot and spear-wound in his right breast, and then, great soldier as he was, "he rose almost above himself. With his life's blood pouring from his breast— "not his back, remember—he fought his way step by step, kicking from his "path the wounded and dead Dervishes; . . . and as he was passing through "the doorway leading into the courtyard another concealed Dervish almost "severed his leg with a single blow. Then Gordon fell."

[3] According to an authority quoted by Shucair (iii., p. 299) the actual murderer of Gordon was Muḥammad Nûbâwî Shêkh ibn Garar.

[4] *Fire and Sword*, p. 340.

[5] An eye-witness who visited the palace after the murder of Gordon says he saw his headless body, smeared with blood, lying at the foot of the stairs. He went upstairs, and passing three dead bodies entered Gordon's office, wherein he also took his meals, and saw on the table a plate with cooked eggs on it, a tin of preserved meat with a fork in it, a small spoon, and another plate with pieces of sugar on it. He next went into his bedroom and saw clothes hanging up over his bed, and looking-glasses, and his portmanteaus standing by the walls. (Shucair, *op. cit.*, iii., p. 299.)

at Kharṭûm. Gordon was murdered shortly before sunrise on Monday, January 26th, 1885.[1]

Thus died one of the greatest of Britain's sons, and it was a common saying among Muslims. "Had Gordon been one of us he "would have been a perfect man!" His bravery, generosity, and self-sacrifice won the admiration of his bitterest enemies.[2] We have it plainly stated by Sir Reginald Wingate,[3] the greatest living authority on Sûdân affairs, that the fall of Kharṭûm was not caused by treachery in the besieged, nor by the stratagems of the besiegers, but through starvation and long neglect. Only the cruel river filled the ditch which protected the town with mud, and then ebbed away. Over this swarmed the Mahdî's men, and nothing could stop them. Help was at hand, only one short hundred miles away—but hunger and despair decided the issue.[4]

For some time past Gordon has been the subject of much criticism;[5] some of it is friendly, but a great deal of it is of a decidedly

[1] He was born on January 28th, 1833, at Woolwich.

[2] Ohrwalder, *Ten Years' Captivity*, p. 169.

[3] *Mahdiism*, p. 156.

[4] *Ibid.*, p. 199.

[5] Compare the following from Sir Auckland Colvin's *The Making of Modern Egypt*, pp. 68 ff. On February 8th Gordon telegraphed that security in the Sûdân would be restored in a month (p. 69). On the 18th he proposed that Zubêr should be made Governor-General, and a K.C.M.G. (p. 72). Gordon reversed the order of his instructions, and instead of arranging for the evacuation of the Egyptian troops, urged that the Mahdî should be "smashed up" (p. 73). Gordon for the first time grasped the situation when he arrived at Kharṭûm. From that time he contended that evacuation was a mistake, and should be postponed until the Egyptian Government destroyed the authority which had superseded its own. He resolved to wreck that authority (p. 74). If the policy of evacuation were insisted on he would resign, and on March 25th he decided to remain (p. 75). The British Government and their Envoy over-estimated the influence which the latter could exercise in the changed conditions of the Sûdân. "Gordon Pasha, as the representative of Ismail Pasha, at the "zenith of that Khedive's power, and with slave-dealers only to contend against, "was one man; but he was another General Gordon altogether as the emissary "of Tewfik Pasha—Tewfik the protégé of Christian England, the prisoner only "yesterday of his own rebellious Egyptian Army—and with Muhammad Ahmed "El Mahdi as adversary. Gordon Pasha, in the days when he was Governor-"General, by his energy, his ubiquity, his matchless courage, his lofty single-"mindedness, his large generosity, and by the absolute authority with which he "was endowed, had been a name of terror to evildoers. But General Gordon, "shut up in Kharṭûm, authority wrenched from him, assistance from Egypt "unavailable to him, and with the Dervishes gathering around him, was not to

hostile character. What, however, is now plain is that when the authorities sent him to the Sûdân in 1884 they did not really understand the seriousness of the situation in that country. Affairs had developed so rapidly since Gordon left the Sûdân in 1879, and on lines so different from what he expected, that he himself probably failed to realize that he had undertaken to do what was impossible. Any one who has travelled in the Sûdân, and conversed with Europeans and natives who know what state the Sûdân was in at that time, cannot help hearing that, from an administrative point of of view, Gordon himself was impossible as a servant of the Government, and that he was often a thorn in the side of the authorities. It is said that his impulsive disposition, his generous emotions, his utter disregard for rules, orders, and precedents, his sometimes injudicious actions and fanaticism,

"be regarded as of great account" (p. 78). No one realized that the country had passed over to the Mahdi (p. 78.) But if the responsibility of misleading the British Government rests on Gordon, the Cabinet cannot escape censure for their selection of so unsuitable an envoy. Gordon, with all his splendid qualities, was the most unfit selection possible for a mission of which retreat was the leading feature ; for his task he was eminently and absolutely unsuited. His peculiarities were no secret. He was not made to obey. In his own Journal he writes, "I own to having been very insubordinate to Her Majesty's Government "and its officials. But it is my nature, and I cannot help it. I know if I were "chief I would never employ *myself*, for I am incorrigible." He thought he was directly guided by Providence, and his "impulsive and emotional nature "was beyond human control or comprehension. Years of solitary communing in "the African deserts, long days and nights of exhaustion and fatigue, fevers, "privation, wrestlings in prayer and spiritual strivings, had worked their "inevitable effect on the texture, both of mind and body" (p. 81).

Lord Fitzmaurice, in his *Life of Lord Granville*, London, 1905, says, "It is not disputed by the biographers of General Gordon that, once arrived at "Kharṭûm, he either forgot or deliberately put aside his instructions" (vol. ii., p. 385). Lord Granville wanted to recall Gordon (vol. ii., p. 401). Mr. Gladstone approved of Gordon's proposal to send Zubêr to the Sûdân, and at first Lord Granville did also (ii., p. 387). The four Ministers present at the meeting of the Cabinet which sent Gordon out were Lord Hartington, Lord Granville, Lord Northbrook, and Sir C. Dilke. Mr. Gladstone telegraphed his concurrence from Hawarden. Later he wrote : "Gordon remained in utter "defiance of the whole mind and spirit of our instructions. I do not see what "could have justified him, except (like Nelson at Trafalgar) a great success" (ii., p. 401). He also speaks of the "insufficient knowledge of our man, whom "we rather took on trust from the public impressions, and from newspaper "accounts, which were probably not untrue, but so far from the whole truth "that we were misled" (ii., p. 401).

caused his superior officers the gravest anxiety, and reduced them to despair.

At the same time it is generally agreed that the initial mistake, which resulted in his going to the Sûdân in 1884, was not made by him, and that had the advice of competent counsellors been taken he would not have been allowed to go there at all. But once sent, he should have been accompanied by a military escort sufficiently strong to show that he was supported by the Government, and that his orders would be, if necessary, enforced by arms. He was besieged in Kharṭûm on March 12th, 1884, and those who knew the extent of the rebellion felt and said that his case was hopeless: yet the Relief Expedition was not sanctioned till the following August. Sir Reginald Wingate says,[1] "There were no elements "of chance in the success of the expedition to relieve General "Gordon. It was sanctioned too late." And even when the expedition was ready to start it was, in direct opposition to the advice of the greatest authority on the subject, General Sir F. Stephenson, sent by the Nile instead of by the Sawâkin-Berber route. This involved sending the force a distance of 1,650 miles from its base at Cairo, by a river in which were innumerable obstacles in the shape of cataracts, rocks, and shoals. It had to proceed against the stream, thus making slow progress, and in boats every one of which would have to be specially constructed for the purpose.[2] All who were acquainted with the difficulties of the Nile route, and had had experience of past Egyptian expeditions into the Sûdân and possessed a competent knowledge of the country, strongly recommended the Sawâkin-Berber route, but to no purpose.

The Relief Expedition was at Matamma on January 21st, four days after the brilliant defeat of the combined forces of the Arabs under Mûsa wâd Helu at Abû Ṭlêḥ ("Abu Klea"), when four of Gordon's steamers arrived to obtain news, and to bring British soldiers to Kharṭûm. And Slatin Pâshâ asks, "Why did they "not send some Englishmen on board, no matter how few, and "despatch them instantly to Kharṭûm? If they could only have "been seen in the town, the garrison would have taken fresh "hope, and would have fought tooth and nail against the enemy;

[1] *Mahdiism*, p. 156. [2] Royle, *Egyptian Campaigns*, p. 313.

"whilst the inhabitants, who had lost all confidence in Gordon's "promises, would have joined most heartily in resisting the "Dervish attack, knowing that the relief expedition was now "certain to reach them."[1] Gordon had done his best to hold the town. He had made a paper currency,[2] and distributed honours and decorations almost daily, but what good were these now? No one believed his promises, and how could men faint from hunger, with only gum to chew, carry out his orders? The streets were filled with people who had died from starvation, even though Gordon had kept his men hungry by distributing hundreds of pounds' weight of biscuit and *dhurra* among the destitute poor. But if only *one* steamer[3] had arrived with news of a British victory[4] the inhabitants would have believed his words, and the town and the life of that fearless, brave, and gallant officer, who was courteous and generous to all, and careful for every one but himself, would have been saved. Father Ohrwalder's statement on this point is conclusive: "The unaccountable delay of the "English was the cause of the fall of Kharṭûm, the death of "Gordon, and the fate of the Sûdân. The Mahdî only made up his "mind to attack when he heard that they had delayed at Gubat. "He did not begin to cross over his troops till January 24th, and "it was not till Sunday night that the crossing was completed." After the defeat of his men at 'Êlafûn on September 4th Gordon saw that his position was indeed desperate, and from March 12th he had known that it was precarious. Still, for 311 days he stuck to his post and did his duty, in spite of want, hunger, neglect, and despair. The imagination fails to grasp how acute his mental sufferings were during the last five months of the siege, as he looked to the south daily from the palace roof and saw the enemy slowly but surely closing in on him, and to the north for the help which never came.

For six hours after the fall of Kharṭûm the town was given up

[1] *Fire and Sword*, p. 341.

[2] On November 12th Gordon had in the Treasury only £831, but his paper currency represented £42,000 more.

[3] See also the opinion of the fiki Medawî, quoted by Wingate, *Mahdiism*, p. 194.

[4] Ohrwalder says that if twenty red-coats had arrived Kharṭûm would have been saved (p. 167).

to pillage by the Arabs, and about 4,000[1] people were massacred; the bloodshed and cruelty which attended the massacre are said by Slatin[2] to be beyond description.

On January 28th, 1885, Sir Charles Wilson arrived with two steamers at Kharṭûm, and learned that the town had fallen and that Gordon had been murdered two and a quarter days previously. The news was generally known in England on February 5th, and the bitterness of a great national disappointment was felt to the fullest extent. All the gallantry and devotion of her officers and men had been unavailing; the costly Nile Expedition had proved a dismal failure; and Gordon had been allowed to perish. The main responsibility will always rest with the Government which so long delayed the despatch of the Relief Expedition, and then, as if to make its failure more certain, sent it by the wrong route.[3]

On February 13th the Desert Column, under Sir Redvers Buller, who had succeeded General Stewart, evacuated Gubat on the Nile, and retreated to Korti, which it reached early in March. The River Column succeeded in ascending the Fourth Cataract as far as Khulla, about 26 miles from Abû Ḥamed, and on its way fought, on March 10th, a decisive action, with brilliant results, at Kirbikan. General Earle was killed. At Salamât the Column destroyed house, water-wheels, palm-trees, and all property of Sulêmân wâd Ḳamr, and Faḳrî wâd 'Uthmân, who had arranged the murder of Colonel Stewart. On March 6th the Column arrived at Merawi.

Soon after the fall of Kharṭûm the British sent another Expedition to the Sûdân *viâ* Sawâkin under General Graham; Indian and Australian troops were enrolled in it. General Graham was ordered to crush Osmân Diḳna, to occupy the Eastern Sûdân, to build a railway to Berber, &c. The Expedition consisted of 13,000 men, and reached Sawâkin on March 12th. The season chosen for the Expedition was singularly unfortunate, as it

[1] Ohrwalder says (p. 162) that 10,000 people were killed, and that the streets were filled with headless corpses. The value of the sovereign sank to two-and-a-half dollars.

[2] *Fire and Sword*, p. 345; Ohrwalder, *Ten Years' Captivity*, p. 158.

[3] Royle, *Egyptian Campaigns*, p. 386.

coincided with the precise time of the year at which, twelve months before, the hot weather had compelled Graham to withdraw his army. The Expedition stayed at Sawâkin for two months, and fought actions at Tell Hashîm on March 20th, at Tûfrik on March 22nd, and at Tamâî on April 3rd. The railway was laid, 4 feet 8½ inches in single gauge, so far as Awtân, but work on it ceased on April 20th; the Expedition retired on May 17th.

In February the garrison of Ḳallâbât was relieved, in April the garrisons of Senhît and Amadib were relieved, Gîra was relieved in July, but on the 30th of the same month Kasala was starved into submission.

In March Sir Francis Grenfell became Sirdar of the Egyptian Army.

On June 22nd the Mahdî died, according to Slatin, of typhus fever, and according to Ohrwalder, of fatty degeneration of the heart. Before his death he nominated as his successor 'Abd-Allah At-Ta'âishî,[1] one of his four Khalîfas. Soon after the death of the Mahdî a revolt broke out in Dâr Fûr and Kordôfân, and Emin Pâshâ was obliged to withdraw from Lâdô and retreat to Wadelâî, whence he hoped to enter into relations with Kabarega, king of Unyoro. About this time the frontier of Egypt was fixed at Wâdî Ḥalfa, and the British force was withdrawn from Dongola on July 5th. Thus the Dervishes were free to raid the country so far north as the Second Cataract, and they took the opportunity of tearing up the railway and destroying the telegraph. Most of the daggers seen in the Sûdân in recent years are made from the rails and the fish-plates stolen at this time.

During the summer of 1885 the Khalîfa 'Abd-Allah matured the plan for the conquest of Egypt which the Mahdî had formulated. The plan was to send two columns to march along the river to Ḥalfa, and a third to cross the river from Abû Ḥamed to Korosko, thus cutting off from Egypt the frontier force at Ḥalfa. By the beginning of August the Amîr 'Abd al-Magîd was at Dongola with 4,000 men, and on the 24th the Amîr Wâd An-Nagûmî left Omdurmân with a large force for the north. In October

[1] See Shucair, *op. cit.*, iii., p. 392.

there was a Dervish force of 7,000 men at Hafîr, and another 3,000 at Abû Ḥamed. On November 17th about 8,000 Dervishes reached Dulgo, and a week later there were 7,000 at 'Amâra, a few miles from Ginnis and Kôsha. On December 29th Generals Stephenson and Grenfell, with 5,000 men, attacked the Dervishes at Kôsha and Ginnis and defeated them. 'Abd al-Magîd, eighteen chiefs, and 500 men were killed, and 300 wounded. This defeat was a serious check to the Khalîfa's advance.

On September 23rd of this year Osmân Diḳna was defeated by the Abyssinians and the Beni Amer, at Kufît, and 3,000 of his men were killed.

Early in 1886 Wâdî Ḥalfa was again made the frontier station of Egypt. In June the Dervishes arrived at 'Ukâsha, and tore up the railway between that place and Ambiḳôl Wells. In October 10,000 more left Berber, 1,500 of them having rifles, and this force had two or three steamers and a fleet of native boats; a month later their advanced guard of 2,000 men was at Abka, eight miles south of Wâdî Ḥalfa. In September Osmân Diḳna suffered defeat from the tribes on the Abyssinian frontier, and was obliged to run away.

In January, 1887, Mr. Charles Neufeld, a German merchant, joined a party of the men of the famous Kababîsh Shêkh Ṣâliḥ, intending to go to Kordôfân to open up a trade in gum and ostrich feathers. When the party arrived at the Oasis of Selîma, the Dervishes seized them, and the few who were not killed were taken to Dongola. There, with the exception of Neufeld, they were all beheaded, but he was sent on to Omdurmân, where he arrived on March 1st. On April 27th Colonel Chermside killed Nûr al-Kanzî and 200 Dervishes at Sarras. On May 17th, Shêkh Ṣâliḥ and a large number of his men were killed by the Khalîfa's men. He was the only man, it is said, of whom the Khalîfa stood in fear. In June the Abyssinians, under Râs Adal, advanced to Ḳallâbât, and defeated the Dervishes under Wad Arbâb, whom they killed. The Khalîfa sent reinforcements, whereupon the Râs threatened to invade the Sûdan. The Khalîfa then sent against him an army of 87,000 men under Abû Anga and Zâkî Tummâl, and a great battle was fought at Dabra Sin, thirty miles from Gondar, in August.[1] The Abyssinians were defeated, and the Dervishes entered Gŏndar and sacked it. In October the Dervishes again occupied Sarras, their force consisting of 2,500 men. In December a Dervish force led by Osmân wâd Adam (Ganu) fought an action against Zayid oḟ Dâr Fûr near Dâra, and repulsed him; in a second fight he routed him completely, and entered Al-Fasher. Zayid and his predecessor Yûsuf fled to the hills, but were killed soon after.

Early in 1888 the Dervish force retired to Gemai, and on June 4th the last detachment of British troops was withdrawn from Aswân, and the frontier was left entirely to the protection of the Egyptian army. On August 29th the Fort of Khôr Mûsa was captured by the Mahdî's men, and recaptured by the Egyptians. In this year a revolt broke out in Dâr Fûr. It was headed by a fanatic, an Anti-Mahdî, called Abû Gamêza ("Father of the Sycamore"), Shêkh of the Masalat tribe; he destroyed nearly one half of the Mahdî's force under Ganu at Kabkabîa in October, and large numbers of men deserted from the Mahdî in consequence. Throughout this year attacks were made on Sawâkin. On January 17th the Dervish camp at Handûb was attacked by friendlies, who captured it. The Dervishes, however, returned, and drove the friendlies into Sawâkin with considerable loss. Colonel (now Lord) Kitchener and Lieut. McMurdo were wounded. The object of the attack was to capture Osmân Diḳna. On March 4th the Egyptians made an unsuccessful sortie under Colonel Tapp. On September 17th about 500 Arabs attacked the Water Forts and began to fire on the town, and the besiegers pushed on their trenches to within 600 yards of the defences. General Grenfell arrived in November, and with a force of 2,000 Egyptians, 2,000 Sûdânî men, and 750 British troops, attacked Osmân Diḳna's force at Gamêza on December 20th. The defeat of Osmân Diḳna's followers was complete, for his trenches were rushed, and 500 out of his 1,500 men were killed. The attack ought to have been followed up, but no instructions to that effect were given, and the British troops were withdrawn.

On April 28th of this year Stanley and Emin met at Nsabe,

[1] On the prophet 'Îsî who appeared at this time, see Shucair, *op. cit.*, iii., p. 480.

and the Khalîfa, on learning of this, sent 4,000 troops to annihilate Emin. These arrived at Dufilî on October 15th, and their leader, 'Omar Ṣâliḥ, called on Emin to surrender. Emin's men preferred to resist, and for two months fighting went on between the two forces. On November 15th Reggâf was taken by the Dervishes, with large quantities of loot, several prisoners, despatches, flags, &c., which were sent on to the Khalîfa in Omdurmân. Some of these were sent on to General Grenfell at Sawâkin by means of Osmân Diḳna, and the worst fate was feared for Stanley and Emin. The advance of the Dervishes from Reggâf was prevented by Emin's men in December. In July the Abyssinian General Râs Adal attacked a Dervish force which, under Abû Anga, had invaded Abyssinian territory, and defeated it with great slaughter. The Râs made himself king of Gojam, and assumed the name of Takla Hâymânôt. At the end of the year the Khalîfa prepared to invade Egypt, and collected a large force under Wâd An-Nagûmî to carry out his plan.

On February 22nd, 1889, Abû Gamêza's army was destroyed at Al Fâsher by the Khalîfa's troops, and the Shêkh himself died the day following. Thus the Khalîfa's power became supreme once again in Dâr Fûr, and the invasion of Egypt was taken in hand seriously. In April the Amîr 'Abd al-Halîm arrived at Sarras with 1,000 men, and by May 5th about 1,500 more came. On June 22nd Wâd An-Nagûmî came, and joined his men to those of 'Abd al-Halîm, who had by this time crossed the river to Ma'tûḳa; the united force amounted to 4,000 men. In July Colonel Wodehouse engaged the force at Argîn, and killed 900 men and took 500 prisoners. Undismayed by this defeat and by the secession of 500 men, who returned to Ma'tûḳa and thence south, Wâd An-Nagûmî burnt his camp on August 4th and moved on northwards so far as Faras. Here he camped, but was shelled out by artillery fire, and on the 10th he camped on the hills two miles south of Balanga. On July 28th his force consisted of 3,300 fighting men, and 4,000 camp followers, and with these he moved on to the hills four miles south of Tushki, which he reached on August 1st. Here General Grenfell had concentrated his forces on the previous day. On August 3rd he discovered that Wâd An-Nagûmî was trying to avoid fighting, and that he wished to continue his journey northwards. General Grenfell therefore determined to make him fight, and, without waiting for the arrival of the squadron of the 20th Hussars, which was on its way, attacked him with Egyptian and Sûdânî troops, and stopped him at Tushki, twenty miles north of Abû Simbel. The Dervishes were defeated with great loss, for Wâd An Nagûmî and 1,200 of his men were killed, and 4,000 prisoners were taken. As the immediate result all the reinforcements which had been sent down the river to assist Wâd An-Nagûmî either retreated or deserted. General Grenfell shattered the Mahdiist vision of the conquest of Egypt, which was to be followed by that of the world, and struck a blow at the Khalîfa's power which it took years to recover.

In January, 1889, Abû 'Anga, the great Dervish leader, died. In February King John of Abyssinia determined to take vengeance on the Dervishes for the sacking of Gondar, and at the end of the month he marched against Matamma, the capital of Ḳallâbât, with an army of 87,000 men. He surrounded the town, which was held by Zâki Ṭummâl, with 60,000 men, and on March 9th completely defeated the Dervishes. At the end of the fight King John was accidentally shot, and, panic seizing the Abyssinians, they retreated. The Dervishes pursued them, and their retreat became a flight, and Zâki Ṭummâl killed many of them and captured King John's body.[1] Menelek II., King of Shoa, then seized the throne of Abyssinia, and now reigns as "king of kings of Ethiopia." In the latter part of this year Emin Pâshâ succeeded in reaching Zanzibar, and the Dervishes evacuated the Baḥr al-Ghazâl province, and Karam-Allah was withdrawn to Omdurmân.

On February 11th, 1890, Osmân Diḳna burned his camp at Handûb, and removed to Ṭôkar, which became his head-quarters. On October 7th he left Ṭôkar to attend a council to be held by the Khalîfa at Omdurmân. The crushing blow inflicted on the Dervishes at Tushki in August, 1888, had completely paralyzed the Khalîfa's organization. In the autumn of this year Sulêmân wâd Ḳamr, Stewart's murderer, was killed.

On January 27th, 1891, Colonel Holled-Smith attacked Osmân

[1] See Shucair, *op. cit.*, i.i., p. 486.

Diḳna's camp at Handûb and captured it. In February he advanced and took Trinkitat and At-Teb, and on the 19th, after a fight at Ṭôkar, he captured the village of Afafît, and slew 700 of Osmân Diḳna's followers. Osmân himself fled with about 300 men to Kasala, *viâ* Tamarîn. On the 22nd, General Grenfell visited Afafît, and congratulated the troops on their victory. The result of these operations was the re-opening of the Sawâkin-Berber road for trade. In this year several risings against the Khalîfa's rule took place in Dâr Fûr and Kordôfân, and Sulṭân 'Abbâs ruled in Gebel Marra. The Shilluks also rebelled, and Zâkî Ṭummâl was sent to reduce them. He made an alliance with the Nuers against the Shilluks, and they killed the Mek of the Shilluks. Soon after, however, the Nuers turned against the Dervishes and drove them out of the country south of Fâshôda. In December the Shilluks defeated their enemies at Fâshôda, and were then allowed to rest in peace for a short time. On Sunday, November 29th, Father Ohrwalder escaped from Omdurmân with some Sisters of the Austrian Mission, and a black girl called Adila; they reached Cairo on December 21st.

In 1892 Osmân Diḳna continued to raid the tribes near Sawâkin, and in the summer he attacked the post at Tamarîn, but was driven off by Major Hunter with a loss of 70 men. The Dervishes began again to give trouble on the frontier, and in December a fight took place in which Captain Pyne and twenty-six of his men were killed. During this year the Shilluks suffered a number of defeats at the hands of Zâkî Ṭummâl, who was, however recalled with his army, and he was obliged to evacuate Fâshôda. As the Italians were gaining power in Eritrea, he was sent to Ḳaḍâref and Ḳallâbât to arrest their advance. When he reported that this was impossible he was recalled to Omdurmân, and, having been invited into the house of Yâ'ḳûb (the Khalîfa's brother), was seized, disarmed, and made a prisoner. His house was searched, and 50,000 dollars and a large number of gold rings, &c., were found in it. The Ḳhalîfa had him walled up in a building in the shape of a coffin, and a little water was given him through a hole in the wall, but no food. He lingered for twenty-three days, without uttering a groan or complaint, and without begging: on the twenty-fourth day he died, and the Ḳhalîfa had him buried with his back towards Mekka, to destroy his hope of life in the world to come.[1] In this year the Ḳhalîfa, hearing that Europeans were advancing from Zanzibar on his southern provinces, withdrew his garrison, under 'Omar Ṣâliḥ, from Reggâf to Bôr, and in October he sent Abû Ḳirga to bring 'Omar Ṣâliḥ to Omdurmân; Abû Ḳirga, not wishing to go, fled to Fâshôda, and he was supposed to have deserted and joined the cause o Muzîl al-Muḥan, whose wish was to destroy the Khalîfa. The Khalîfa was afraid of the success of Muzîl al-Muḥan,[2] the "father of sandals," and sent a force of 4,000 men against him under Ibrahîm Khalîl, but this was unnecessary, for the fanatic's preachings were neglected.

In July, 1893, Osmân Azraḳ raided the village of Berîs, and the Egyptian Government established posts at the Oases of Khârga and Dakhla. In November the Dervishes raided Murât Wells, and killed Shêkh Ṣâliḥ. By the end of the year the movement started by Muzîl al-Muḥan had died out. In this year the Khalîfa became really alarmed at the growth of the Italian power in Eritrea, and he ordered a force to march eastwards from Kasala, the governor of which at that time was Musâ'id Ḳêdûm. A Dervish force of 12,000 men under Aḥmad 'Alî arrived at Kasala in November, and marched on to Aghûrdat, halfway to Maṣaw'a. Here it was overthrown by Colonel Arimondi, with only a force of 2,000 men and 42 officers, and on December 21st Aḥmad 'Ali was killed.

Abû Ḳirga, who had fled to Fâshôda in 1892, came to Reggâf in 1893, and sent a gift of ivory to the Khalîfa. When 'Omar Ṣâliḥ arrived in Omdurmân he reported that his former district was no longer in danger, and the Khalîfa sent 'Arabi wad Dafa' Allah to take command, and to take the garrison back from Bôr to Reggâf, and to put Abû Ḳirga in chains. When 'Arabi arrived, he wrote to Faḍl al-Mawla Bey, who was in command of some of Emin's men, and told him to bring Baert, the successor of Van Kerckhoven and leader of the Congolese Expedition, and his officers to him. Faḍl declined to do this, and Baert pushed on in order to establish posts on the Upper Nile in the interest of the Congo Free State.

[1] Slatin, *Fire and Sword*, p. 574.

[2] See the account of him given by Shucair, *op. cit.*, iii., p. 547.

His men under Faḍl met the Dervishes at Makaraki and Wandî; at the latter place a fight took place, and Faḍl was killed, together with about half of his men, in January, 1894.

In the summer of 1893 Abû Maryam, the successor of Osmân Ganu, the Dervish commandant of Shakka, attacked the Dinkas, but he was killed, his force nearly destroyed, and many fugitives from his army fled to Shakka. On January 2nd, 1894, Colonel

TWENTY-PIASTRE PIECES STRUCK BY THE KHALIFA A.H. 1311 (A.D. 1893).
No. 2, a specimen of the "Umla Gadîda," or "New money," contains 2 dirhams o. silver and 5 dirhams of copper.

Colvile arrived in Unyoro; he was appointed Chief Commissioner of Uganda in 1893, when the British Government took over the country. On February 4th Major "Roddy" Owen hoisted the British flag at Wadelâî. On July 17th Colonel Baratieri, with 2,510 men, marched from Aghûrdat, and surprised and took Kasala; he fortified the town, and the Italians held it for two and a half years. In this year the Khalîfa sent orders to Maḥmûd to re-occupy the Baḥr al-Ghazâl province, and he despatched 3,800 soldiers, under Hatîm Mûsa from Shakka towards the Belgian posts. The Belgians retired before him, and the Dervishes entered Faroge; Shêkh Ḥamed went over to the Dervishes. In this year Father Rossignoli, of the Austrian Mission, escaped from Omdurmân, and arrived in Cairo on October 20th.

On January 15th, 1895, Major Cunningham and Lieut. Vandeleur[1] planted the British flag at Wadelâî, in spite of the resistance caused by Kabarega, king of Unyoro.

In 1895 Osmân Diḳna raided the country round Ṭôkar. In the Baḥr al-Ghazâl, Hatîm Mûsa, finding that the Belgians had retired, retreated to Shakka, whereüpon, through want of food, most of his men deserted to Zemio; he then retreated to Kordôfân. Thus was the province free from Dervishes. In June Wâd Dafa' Allah retired from Reggâf to Shâmbî, frightened at the supposed advance of a European force, and the Khalîfa sent 4,000 men to help him; he then returned to Reggâf. On February 20th Slatin Pâshâ escaped from Omdurmân, and he arrived at Aswân on Saturday, March 16th.

On February 29th, 1896, an Italian army of about 37,000 men was defeated with great slaughter at Aduwa by the Abyssinians under Menelek II. They lost 7,000 killed, wounded and missing, and the Abyssinians captured 1,000 men and fifty-two guns. Their scattered forces were obliged to retreat towards Maṣaw'a, and were therefore unable to give assistance to their countrymen who were practically imprisoned by the Dervishes in the garrison of Kasala. Emboldened by the defeat of the Italians, the Dervishes attacked Sabderat on March 18th, and were repulsed; on April 2nd they attacked Mukram, and on April 3rd Tukruf, places close to Kasala, but they were beaten by the Italians under Colonel Stefani, and were compelled to retreat. On April 15-17 Colonel Lloyd from Sawâkin and Major Sidney from Ṭôkar, with a force of 1,000 men, and a party of friendly Arabs led by Shêkh 'Omar Tîta, killed about 100 of Osmân Diḳna's men, and wounded about 100 more, at Khôr Wintri. The rest of his force of about 600 men managed to escape to the hills, but his prestige

[1] This brave and distinguished officer, who was killed in action at the age of thirty-two, has found a sympathetic and truthful biographer in Colonel Maxse; see *Seymour Vandeleur*, London, 1906.

was destroyed, and there were no more fights in the neighbourhood of Sawâkin.

Early in March, 1896, partly with a view of assisting the Italians, and partly because it was felt that the time had come when a blow must be struck at the Khalîfa's power, the British Government determined to make an advance on Dongola. It was decided that the Expedition should consist of 9,000 Egyptian troops under the Sirdar, Sir Herbert Kitchener, who had succeeded Sir Francis Grenfell. On March 12th Colonel Hunter was ordered to advance to 'Ukâsha. On March 19th the

TRANSPORT OF SECTIONS OF LORD KITCHENER'S GUNBOATS BY RAILWAY.

Egyptian Government applied to the Commissioners of the Public Debt to advance £500,000 towards the expenses of the Expedition. Four out of the six Commissioners agreed, and the money was advanced. In the lawsuit which followed, the Mixed Tribunal in June ordered the Government to refund the money (already spent!) with interest, and this judgment was, on appeal on December 2nd, confirmed. The British Government, at the instance of Lord Cromer, lent the sum due, £515,600, which was paid into the Caisse on December 8th, and subsequently presented the amount to the Khedive's Government.

On April 2nd the Italians defeated a force of 5,000 Dervishes at Mount Mukram, and killed 800 of them. On May 24th the railway from Ḥalfa had reached Ambikôl Wells. On June 7th the Sirdar attacked the Dervish garrison at Ferket, with a River and a Desert Column, the two together consisting of about 9,000 men, and surprised it, and almost destroyed the entire force there. The Dervishes lost 1,000 killed, and 500 were made prisoners, and 'Osmân Azraḳ and forty chiefs were among the slain. The Sirdar sent on his troops to occupy Suwârda, which had until that time been the base for Dervish raids. Thus the Khalîfa's frontier army was destroyed. On June 17th Captain Mahon captured eleven boats laden with grain. On August 4th the railway was pushed on by Captain Girouard, R.E., to Kôsha, which on July 5th had been made the Sirdar's headquarters. On August 25th a rain-storm swept away part of the line at Sarras. Cholera appeared at Kôsha on July 15th, and carried off four British officers and two engineers who were putting together the gunboats. On September 18th the Sirdar's forces reached the Island of Tombos, and on the 19th the Dervishes under Wâd al-Bishâra were driven out of Hafîr by the gunboats and artillery. The Dervishes lost 200 men. New Dongola was occupied at 11 a.m. on the 23rd, and 900 prisoners were captured; these were converted into a black battalion and were added to the Sirdar's army. Debba, Korti, and Merawi, ten miles from the foot of the Fourth Cataract, were occupied a few days later. Merawi became the head-quarters of the Frontier Field Force, and the Sirdar returned to Cairo, leaving General Hunter in command of the province, which was placed under military law. The building of the railway was continued, and the rebuilding and re-inhabiting of New Dongola began at once. The Khalîfa, expecting the Sirdar to advance across the desert, began to fortify Omdurmân.

In 1897 the Sirdar continued his policy of advancing slowly, and making good every step taken by him towards the re-conquest of the Sûdân. The railway from Ḥalfa reached Kerma (201 miles) on May 4th, but long before this the Sirdar realized that its use, so far as the Expedition was concerned, was practically over. He therefore determined to build another line from Ḥalfa across the desert to Abû Ḥamed (231 miles); without such a line any advance on Berber and Omdurmân was practically impossible. The distance saved in cutting across the desert, instead of following the course of the Nile through the Second, Third, and Fourth Cataracts, is about 330 miles. The building of this line was sanctioned early in the year, and by May 4th about 15 miles of it had been actually laid. When the Ḥalfa-Kerma line was finished the whole of the railway battalion was set to work on the Ḥalfa-Abû Ḥamed line, and it advanced with marvellous rapidity under the direction of Captain Girouard, R E. The officer in charge of rail-head was Lieut. E. C. Midwinter, R.E., and the average rate of progress was 1½ miles per day. In June the Khalîfa decided to send a strong force under Maḥmûd to occupy the important strategic point Matamma, the capital of the Ga'alîn tribe, which lies on the west bank of the Nile a few miles south of Shendî. The Ga'alîn, an Arab tribe which is famed for the chastity of its women, wrote to the Khalîfa entreating him not to send an army there, and undertaking to defend their town against the "Turks." The Khalîfa was furious at this request, and ordered Maḥmûd to proceed to Matamma. The Ga'alîn sent shêkhs to Merawi to ask for help and rifles, saying they would resist Maḥmûd and throw in their lot with the Sirdar and the Egyptians. The Sirdar sent 6,000 rifles, and a large quantity of ammunition, but to send an army was, out of the question, for he could not feed it at Matamma, and the town itself was unequal to such a task. Besides, the possibility of treachery had to be taken into account. Before the rifles reached Matamma Màhmûd attacked the town, and though his first onset was repulsed, his second succeeded. Maḥmûd arrived at dawn on July 1st, and for three days the Ga'alîn kept him at bay, but when their ammunition was spent they had to surrender. The Dervishes entered the town and massacred about 2,000 men, besides women and children, and thousands died through the mutilation of their limbs which Maḥmûd had carried out on every male. The women were treated in an atrocious manner, and numbers of them drowned themselves in the Nile to escape dishonour; the old women were killed, and the girls were made prisoners. Practically the whole population of Matamma was destroyed. The few Ga'alîn who escaped made their way to Gakdûl Wells, and the Sirdar supplied them with rifles and ammunition, food, &c. The Shêkh 'Abd-Allah wâd Sa'ud was sent to Omdurmân, and the Khalîfa had him walled up in a hole in such a position that he could neither sit down nor stand upright, and then starved him to death. Maḥmûd's loss was 88 killed and 330 wounded.[1]

By the end of July the railway had reached mile 115 in the desert, and the Sirdar was obliged to consider the capture of Abû Ḥamed. On July 29th, General Hunter left Merawi and arrived at Abû Ḥamed on August 7th; a fierce fight took place, and 1,200 out of the 1,500 Dervishes who held it were either killed or taken prisoners. Major Sidney and Lieut. Fitz-Clarence were killed, and were buried a little to the south of the town. The quick march to Abû Ḥamed and the capture of the place are held to rank deservedly among the finest episodes of the campaign.

The fugitives from Abû Ḥamed made their way to the south and told their tale of woe as they went. As a result the Dervishes evacuated Berber, and a party of friendlies occupied it on September 7th; on the 13th General Hunter entered it with a number of troops. The Egyptian gunboats went on to Ad-Dâmar, a few miles south of the Atbara, and made it the advanced post of the army. A fort was built there, and the place was put in a state of defence. Meanwhile, Osmân Diḳna collected about 5,000 men at Adârama, a place on the Atbara river about ninety miles above Ad-Dâmar. On October 23rd General Hunter set out with a force to attack him, but when he arrived at Adârama he found that Osmân Diḳna had evacuated it two days previously, and that he was on his way to Abû Dalêḳ, a town in the desert between Omdurmân and Kasala. This was disappointing, but the result of Osmân's flight was excellent, for it rendered the Eastern Desert free from Dervishes, and the Berber-Sawâkin road was once more open for trade. On October 15th and 17th Commander Keppel bombarded Matamma, where Maḥmûd's force was, and he did the forts much damage. On October 31st the railway reached Abû Ḥamed, and it was decided to push it on to Berber. On November 1st General Hunter proceeded with the gunboats

[1] Shucair, *op. cit.*, iii., p. 597.

to the foot of the Sixth Cataract (Shablûka). On December 25th Kasala was taken over by the Egyptians, and the fort was occupied by Colonel Parsons.

In the Baḥr al-Ghazâl Chaltin's Column arrived at Beddên on the Nile on February 14th, and on the 17th he attacked 2,000 Dervishes and defeated them with great loss; before the close of the day he occupied Reggâf, and the Dervishes fled to the north.

On February 10th Maḥmûd, having been urged by the Khalîfa either to go forward and destroy the Egyptians or return to Omdurmân, began to move his army of 20,000 men across the river to Shendî, preparatory to marching on Berber. On March 2nd General Gatacre arrived with his force at Berber, then the head-quarters of Major Hunter, and on the 16th the Anglo-Egyptian force concentrated at Kenur, ten miles south of Berber. Meanwhile Maḥmûd had marched to Aliâb, about half way between Shendî and Berber, and on the 19th he left Aliâb, and set out across the desert for a place on the Atbara called Hûdî, where he intended to cross the river and advance on Berber. On the 20th the Sirdar with his force of 13,000 men encamped at Hûdî, and Maḥmûd crossed the river at Nakhîla, several miles higher up. The following day the Sirdar advanced to Râs al-Hûdî, thus setting his army between Maḥmûd and Berber. On the 25th the Sirdar sent a force to destroy Maḥmûd's garrison near Shendî, and to destroy that town. This was done, and much spoil was taken. On April 4th the Sirdar marched his whole force to Râs 'Adâr, nine miles from Hûdî and eleven miles from Nahkîla, and on the 5th General Hunter succeeded in making Maḥmûd show fight. On the 6th the Sirdar advanced to Umm Dabê'a, four miles from Khôr Abû 'Adâr, and on the 7th advanced to Mutrûs, one and a half miles from Maḥmûd. At 1 a.m. on the 8th the Sirdar's force set out for Maḥmûd's camp, and at 6.15 the guns opened fire, the bombardment continuing for an hour and a half. Soon after 8.15 the battle began, and lasted little more than half an hour.

Of Maḥmûd's force of about 14,000 men, 3,000 were killed or wounded, and 2,000 were taken prisoners; all his Amîrs were killed, and he himself was made captive. Osmân Diḳna escaped as usual. The rest of Maḥmûd's army fled to Adârama, and suffered many losses on the way, for hundreds of them died of thirst. The Anglo-Egyptian loss was 568 killed and wounded. On April 14th the Sirdar made his triumphal entry into Berber. The Sirdar ordered the Ga'alîn tribe to occupy Matamma, and thus the Nile Valley as far as the Sixth Cataract was in the hands of the Egyptian Government once more. During the winter no further advance was made by the Egyptian troops, for the Sirdar decided that the proper time to attack Omdurmân was at high Nile, i.e., about the end of August or the beginning of September.

In May, 1898, preparations for the advance on Omdurmân were taken in hand, and Fort Atbara was made the head-quarters of the Egyptian army in the Sûdân. Here the Sirdar's force of about 12,500 men began to concentrate in August, and by September 1st they reached a point about six miles north of Omdurmân. The gunboats steamed up to Tuti Island, and a howitzer battery was landed on the east bank, which soon opened fire on Omdurmân; its guns fired 50-pound shells of lyddite,[1] and after a few rounds the dome of the Mahdî's tomb was practically destroyed. Meanwhile the Khalîfa's army, which contained between 40,000 and 50,000 men, was moved out of Omdurmân, and it was reported that he intended to attack the Egyptians that very night. It is said that in a night attack lay the Dervishes' only chance of success, for they were only four miles away, and they could have crept up in the dark to the Sirdar's force, and it would have been impossible to fire on them with any effect until they were within 200 yards. The struggle would then have become a hand-to-hand fight, and the Egyptian losses would certainly have been very considerable, in any case very much greater than they actually were.

The Sirdar's answer to the report of the Dervish night attack was to send into the Khalîfa's camp men who pretended that they were deserters from the Sirdar, who was going to attack the Dervishes that night. No night attack therefore took place. At 5.30 a.m. on September 2nd the bombardment of Omdurmân was continued, and a few minutes later the advance of the enemy began. "It was a splendid sight. A huge amphitheatre, lit up by

[1] "On one occasion there were one hundred Dervishes praying in the court-"yard of the mosque; a lyddite shell burst in their midst, and only two came "out unwounded."—*Sudan Campaign*, p. 226.

"a blazing sun, in which a mass of fearless men, clad in gay-"coloured jibbahs, waving countless flags, and following reck-"less horsemen, were rushing forward with absolute confidence of "victory, and absolute contempt of death."[1] At 6.45 the artillery opened fire, and their shells burst in the Dervish ranks, but it did not stop their advance. Whilst one body of Dervishes attacked the southern face of the Sirdar's position, another rushed out from behind Gebel Surgham (Surkab) to attack the left flank. Presently the Guards opened fire, and next the Warwicks, the Highlanders, the Lincolns, and, later on, Maxwell's brigade. The Dervishes fell in heaps, but those behind pressed on until the foremost row were only 800 yards from the British force. Whilst the Khalîfa was attacking the British position, the Khalîfa's son, Shêkh Ad-Dîn, and 'Alî Wad Helu, with 10,000 men marched out on the Egyptian troops under Colonel Broadwood.

The Dervishes attacked with boldness, and Colonel Broadwood was so hard pressed that disaster must have followed had not the gunboat opened fire at close range, with deadly effect, and so saved the situation. These attacks on the position having failed, the 21st Lancers, about 320 in number, under Colonel Martin, were sent out to prevent the Dervishes from retreating to Omdurmân. Soon after they started they saw, as they thought, from 200 to 300 of the enemy concealed in a khôr, and they wheeled into line and charged. As they came near, the party of Dervishes was found to be about 3,000 strong, and these suddenly rose up and opened fire. The Lancers, however, rode on, charged through the mass of Dervishes, and fought their way out on the opposite side; then they dismounted, and opened fire on the enemy, and drove them out of the position. The Sirdar then ordered his force to evacuate the camp and to march on Omdurmân. About 9.30, when the leading brigades were close to the west side of Gebel Surgham, the third division of the great Dervish army, some 20,000 strong, led by the Khalîfa himself, rushed to the attack on the Sirdar's flank. The brunt of the attack was borne by the brigade of Colonel Macdonald, who, whilst carrying out the change of front ordered by the Sirdar, found himself about a mile distant from the rest of the army.

[1] *Sudan Campaign*, 1896 to 1899, by an Officer, p. 192.

The Dervishes, preceded by 300 or 400 mounted Baḳḳâra, attacked from the west, intending to break Macdonald's line, but never a man got within 300 yards of the fighting line. The Dervishes drove their banner-poles into the ground, and gathered round them, and died. But whilst Colonel Macdonald was still fighting, the Dervishes who were hidden behind the Kararî hills, to the north of Gebel Surgham, rushed out to deliver a second attack, thus threatening Macdonald both before and behind. The Dervishes were in two divisions, one led by Shêkh Ad-Dîn, and the other by 'Alî wad Helu, and they intended to envelop Macdonald. Seeing this, Macdonald coolly moved the men of his brigade into such a position that one portion of them faced north and the other west. When the Dervishes came up, they were received with a fire that no living thing could face and live, and at the same time Colonel Lewis's Brigade enfiladed the Khalîfa's ranks on the left. Colonel Wauchope's Brigade then came up, the fight ceased, and the Dervishes broke and fled. "The masterly "way in which Macdonald handled his force was the theme of "general admiration." The Dervish loss was 10,800 killed,[1] and 16,000 wounded; the Sirdar's entire loss was 48 killed, and 382 wounded. About 4,000 black troops surrendered, and some 1,222 of these were wounded; and three of Gordon's old steamers were captured.[2]

Soon after 3 o'clock the Sirdar entered Omdurmân, and was met by shêkhs bearing flags of truce, who said the people tendered their submission; this the Sirdar accepted, and the soldiers laid down their arms, whilst the people swarmed out of their houses and cheered the troops. The Khalîfa's house was shut and barred, and was shelled by the gunboats from the river. The Mahdî's tomb was then entered, and it was found to be much damaged by the fire from the gunboats and the howitzer battery; the top of the dome was knocked off, and there were several holes in it. The Khalîfa unfortunately escaped before the Sirdar entered Omdurmân, and made his way to the west, leaving

[1] Royle, *Egyptian Campaigns*, p. 571.

[2] See the fine accounts of the battle given by "An Officer," in *Sudan Campaign*, p. 191 ff., and by Colonel Maxse, in *Seymour Vandeleur*, and Royle, *Egyptian Campaigns*, p. 551.

untouched the dinner to which he had invited the Amîrs to come after his defeat of the Anglo-Egyptians!

As soon as steps had been taken to guard the town, the Sirdar went and set free the European prisoners, Charles Neufeld, Joseph Ragnotti, Sister Teresa Grigolini, and about thirty Greeks, and a large crowd of natives, many of whom had been

THE MAHDÎ'S TOMB AT OMDURMÂN BEFORE THE BOMBARDMENT OF THE TOWN BY LORD KITCHENER.

officials under the old Government; the total number of prisoners set free was 10,854. At 5 p.m. five Brigades reached the north end of Omdurmân, but it was nearly midnight before they had marched through the town and bivouacked. The cavalry pursued the fugitives until far into the night, but want of forage and stores then compelled them to return; the gunboats steamed 90 miles south of Kharṭûm, but could find no trace of the Khalîfa. When the arsenal was examined it was found to contain an enormous collection of weapons and stores of ammunition, including sixty cannon, Dervish spears, swords, banners, drums, rifles, and a lot of miscellaneous stuff picked up on the battle-field where Hicks was defeated. Two carriages, in one of which Gordon had driven, were also found,[1] and there were shirts of mail said to date from the time of the Crusaders.

At dawn on September 3rd the army marched out and bivouacked four miles south of Omdurmân, and parties were told off to bury the dead. Among these were numbers who pretended to be dead, but who jumped up when any one came near and either speared or shot the first soldier they met. Such shammers were promptly despatched, and incidents of the kind gave rise to the outrageous charge made in the *Contemporary Review* that the Sirdar ordered the Dervish wounded to be massacred, and that his soldiers wantonly killed wounded and unarmed Dervishes. The charge was as mischievous as it was untrue, as all who knew the Sirdar and the officers who were with him understood. British officers neither do such things, nor allow them to be done. It is notorious that the Sirdar might have had hundreds of unarmed men cut down as they rushed towards him when he rode through the town, and that he did all in his power to prevent unnecessary slaughter. At one time it was a question whether the Dervishes would spare his life, not whether he would spare theirs,[2] but as he rode coolly among them and promised them *amân*, i.e., "security," they laid down their arms, and no one touched them. We have it on the unimpeachable authority of Captain Adolf von Tiedemann, of the Royal Prussian General Staff, that he saw the Sirdar, wholly regardless of his personal safety, ride into narrow streets and courtyards, with uplifted hand, calling out *Amân*. The charge that Omdurmân was looted for three days was equally untrue. It was also said that the Sirdar did nothing to alleviate the sufferings of the wounded Dervishes, but as we know from the evidence of the *Daily News* correspondent, that 6,000 to 7,000 out of the 16,000

[1] For a picture of it, see *Sudan Campaign*, p. 222. In the other, Sa'îd Pâshâ had driven from Cairo to Kharṭûm.

[2] *Sudan Campaign*, p. 217.

MAJOR MARCHAND IN THE STEAM-LAUNCH THE "FAIDHERBE" TAKING POSSESSION OF FASHODA.

Dervishes wounded were treated in Hasan Effendi Zâkî's hospital, this statement is also seen to be without foundation.

One other important and most necessary thing[1] was done, at the request of, and with the approval of, many Muḥammadans. The Mahdî's tomb was destroyed, and his body taken from its grave, and burned in the furnace of one of the steamers, and the ashes thrown into the Nile. The head, it was said, was taken possession of by a British officer, but subsequently orders were issued to bury it, and a burial ceremony took place at Ḥalfa. Had the building been allowed to stand, and the body to remain in its grave the tomb would have become the centre of fanaticism and revolt, and the effect of the victory of law and order over lawlessness, barbarism, and savage despotism on the minds of the tribes for hundreds of miles round would have been ruined. The outcry raised against the act showed that there were even in 1898 some people in England who did not realize how completely the whole Sûdân had been held in the grip of Mahdiism, but the Muḥammadans understood their co-religionists, and knew that nothing short of the destruction of the Mahdî's body would bring lasting peace to the Sûdân, and prove that Muḥammad Aḥmad was, even in the eyes of Muḥammadans, an impostor. The ruins of the tomb proclaim to all passers-by the fate of one of the greatest of false teachers, and the lesson which they teach has sunk deeply into the minds of the natives.

On Sunday, September 4th, the Sirdar, with his staff and a large force, steamed over to Kharṭûm. The troops formed up into three sides of a square facing the ruined palace, on the staircase of which Gordon was murdered on January 26th, 1885; the Sirdar made a signal, and the British and Egyptian flags were run up flagstaffs erected on the palace, and the bands played "God save the Queen," and the Khedivial Hymn, whilst the gunboats saluted with twenty-one guns, and officers and men stood at attention. Three cheers were given for the Queen, and three for the Khedive, and the Guards' band played the "Dead March" in *Saul;* after a short service the Sûdânî band played Gordon's favourite hymn, "Abide with me."

On September 10th the Sirdar left for the south, and on his

[1] Royle, *Egyptian Campaigns*, p. 581.

arrival at Fâshôda on the 19th he found it occupied by Major Marchand; the British and Egyptian flags were hoisted,[1] and leaving a force there under Major Jackson, the Sirdar went on his way. A few days later the Egyptian flag was hoisted at Meshra ar-Reḳ. Major Hunter occupied Sennaar, Karkôj, and Ruṣêreṣ by October 1st, and Major Parsons defeated the Dervishes at Ḳaḍâref on September 22nd, and occupied the town. On December 26th Colonel Lewis defeated Aḥmad Faḍîl, cut up his force and killed about 500 Dervishes. On December 7th Colonel Collinson hoisted the British and Egyptian flags on the old fort at Ḳallâbât.

In January, 1899, Lord Cromer visited the Sûdân. In November, 1899, Colonel Sir Reginald Wingate[2] set out to attack the Khalîfa with a force of 3,700 men. On the 22nd he seized the camp of Aḥmad Faḍîl at Abû Adel, killed 400 of his men, and captured all the grain he was taking to the Khalîfa. On the 24th a fierce fight was fought at Umm Dabrêkât, and the Khalîfa and all his chief Amîrs, including 'Alî wad Helu and Aḥmad Faḍîl, were killed.[3] The Dervish loss was 600 killed, and 3,000 prisoners and 6,000 women and children were taken. It was this

[1] Major Marchand evacuated Fâshôda on December 11th.

[2] See Shucair, *op. cit.*, iii., p. 664.

[3] "As soon as Colonel Wingate's force had swept through the Dervish "position into the enemy's camp, the news at once spread that the Khalifa was "killed with most of his Emirs. Colonel Wingate immediately went to the "spot where the Khalifa was said to be lying. On the way a boy of 15 "caught hold of Major Watson's hand and said, 'The Khalifa is dead, I am his "son.' He took Major Watson to the place where his father lay. There was "the Khalifa lying in his forwah (sheepskin), his jibbeh riddled with bullets. "Lying over him were his two chief Emirs, Ali Wad Helu and Ahmed Fedil. "At each side of him were ten or a dozen of his chief Emirs, and in front of "him his faithful bodyguard, all dead. While Colonel Wingate was looking "at this terrible but noble spectacle of brave men dead, a small man was seen "to crawl out from under the slain. This was Yunis Deghemi, the former "Emir of Dongola. After a short time he began to speak, and at length "answered the questions put to him by Colonel Wingate. He said that when "the Dervishes failed to outflank the Egyptians and began to run before the "terrible fire the Khalifa called to his Emirs and said, 'I am not going away; I "shall die here; I call on you to stay by me and let us die together.' The Khalifa "took his forwah (sheepskin), sat down on it, and calmly awaited the end, "which was not long in coming. Later in the day, by order of Colonel "Wingate, the Khalifa and the Emirs who were killed were buried where they

FASHODA—MAJOR MARCHAND'S HOUSE AND SOME OF HIS GUNS.

[From a photograph by Miss Hilda Burrows.

fight which finally destroyed the power of Mahdiism in the Sûdân. The defeat of the Dervishes at Omdurmân restored that city to the Egyptians, but so long as the Khalîfa lived he was the visible personification of the Mahdî's movement, and many Muhammadans who saw him believed that he would one day be victorious. Only in the preceding August Khalîfa Sherîf[1] preached Mahdiism openly at Wad Madanî; but he was captured by Captain N. M Smyth, V.C., and tried by court-martial and shot. On August 26th the Atbara railway bridge was opened. On December 17th Colonel Mahon, D.S.O., occupied Al-Obêd.

On December 22nd Sir Reginald Wingate succeeded Lord Kitchener as Sirdar and Governor of the Sudân.

On January 18th, 1900, Captain F. Burges captured the notorious Osmân Diḳna in the Warriba Hills, to the south-west of Sawâkin ; he was first sent to Rosetta, but later to Damietta. Captain Burges was assisted by a Commandant of Police called Muḥammad Bey Aḥmad.[2] On March 4th 'Ali 'Abd Al-Karîm, the leader of a fanatical sect of Muḥammadans whose views were opposed to the Government, and several of his chief followers, were deported to Ḥalfa and placed under restraint.[3] The prompt action which Sir Reginald Wingate took in this matter is highly praiseworthy, for religious enthusiasts of the kind of 'Abd Al-Karîm should never be allowed to be at large. Their ultimate aim is always political power, and every one who preaches in the Sûdân equality and community of other people's possessions is always certain of a large following. The Mahdî adopted this method, with what success we have seen.

On November 29th Colonel Sparkes left Omdurmân with a force of nearly 400 men in steamers to occupy the Bahr al-Ghazâl province, and he arrived at Meshra ar-Reḳ on December 14th.

In December Lord Cromer visited the Sûdân a second

"fell by their own people with proper ceremonial. They lie in a beautiful spot, "near a large sheet of water surrounded by trees, and not so very far (some "forty miles) from Abba Island, the cradle of Mahdiism."—*Times*, December 9th, 1899.

[1] He lived at Shakâba, forty miles from Sennaar, and had with him Fâḍil and Bishra, two of the Mahdî's sons.

[2] Shucair, *op. cit.*, iii., p. 670.

[3] *Ibid.*, p. 671.

time, and on the 24th he delivered a speech of an important character.[1]

On January 1st, 1901, Colonel Sparkes made Tong his headquarters, and then made expeditions to Wâw, Fort Dessaix, Rumbek, Amadi, Kîrô and Shâmbî. Major W. Boulnois conducted a patrol to Dêm Zubêr, Telgôna, Fârôgê, and Chamamui, and returned to Tong on April 10th. In April the post which had been established at Kîrô was transferred to Mongalla, across the river, because Kîrô was claimed to be in Belgian territory. In June Colonel Sparkes visited Sulṭân Tambura of the Niam-Niams, and was well received, and he found the people to be of a "comparatively highly civilized order." In this month 'Alî Dînâr, who after the conquest of Omdurmân had been entrusted with the province of Dâr Fûr, began to pay tribute to the Government. In this year the Sûdân Government made two treaties as to the eastern frontier. The first was arranged by Colonel Collinson, Mudîr of Kasala, with Signor Martini, Governor-General of Eritrea, on February 28th, and the second by Colonel the Hon. M. G. Talbot, R.E., with Lieut. Colli at Kasala on April 16th. In April Major Gwynn, D.S.O., and Captain Smyth, V.C., surveyed the country about Fâmaka. The expedition, which left Nasser in January under Major Austin to explore the almost unknown, but rich gold-producing country to the south-east, nearly came to grief. It was arranged that the Abyssinians were to store supplies at Murle, on the north bank of Lake Rudolf, but when the party arrived they found that the Abyssinians had failed to keep their word. The party suffered greatly rom hunger and sickness, and thirty-nine of the fifty-three men died of starvation. During the year 1901 the Sûdân Government, notwithstanding its small staff of officials, and its limited means, explored its vast territories, organized and administered the country, established tribunals, and extended communications, and, in Count Gleichen's words, "settled down into an era of peace and growing prosperity."

In January, 1902, Captain A. M. Pirie occupied Dêm Zubêr and Chamamui; on the 10th of this month Lieut. Scott-Barbour was murdered by the Agar Dinkas, on the Naam River. Punitive

[1] An Arabic translation of the speech is given by Shucair, *op. cit.*, iii., pp. 677 ff.

THE BAḤR AL-GEBEL—KÎRÔ.

[From Sir W. Garstin's *Report*, by permission of the Comptroller of H.M. Stationery Office.

THE BAḤR AL-GEBEL—MONGALLA.

[From Sir W. Garstin's *Report*, by permission of the Comptroller of H.M. Stationery Office.

expeditions were quickly organized under Major Hunter and Captain L. Strack, who burned the Agar villages, and killed several of their men and carried off their cattle. The ringleader of the Agars, Myang Matyang, died of his wounds in July, and the Agars sued for peace. On May 15th a frontier treaty was signed at Adis Ababa by Menelek II., King of Abyssinia. In the spring or summer of this year the Shêkh As-Senussi died, having nominated his nephew, Aḥmad Ash-Sharîf, as his successor. His death put an end to the communications between the Senussi and 'Alî Dînar, Sulṭân of Dâr Fûr, which had been going on for three or four years. In July the Dervish Amîr 'Arabî Daf'a Allah surrendered to 'Alî Dînâr with 3,000 rifles.

In December, 1902, Lord Cromer visited the Sûdân a third time. On January 27th, 1903, Lord Cromer made a speech in the Grand Hotel, Kharṭûm.[1]

In March Colonel Sparkes marched from Kossinga to Ḥufrat An-naḥâs,[2] the famous copper mines in the south of Dâr Fûr. He found a number of shallow pits in a space about half a mile square. The place was deserted, for the former chief, Ibrahîm Murâd, went to Kafikingi when the Mahdî rose to power. In February Captain Armstrong was sent to open up relations with Yambio, the chief of the Niam-Niams. He was killed by an elephant on the 23rd, but the expedition was continued by Colour-Sergeant Boardman, R.M.A. On reaching the Niam-Niam country he was attacked by Mangi, the son of Yambio, and was obliged to retire. In August a Mahdî called Muḥammad Al-Amîn appeared and settled in Gebel Taḳalî, but he was captured by Colonel Mahon, C.B., D.S.O., and taken to Al-Obêḍ, where he was hanged on September 27th. In November work on the Atbara-Sawâkin Railway was begun. During the year 1903 good progress was made in the delimitation of the Abyssinian frontier by Colonel the Hon. M. G. Talbot, Major C. W. Gwynn, and Major C. E. Wilson, and a provisional agreement was made between the Sûdân and Congo Free State Governments about the territory between 5° and 5° 30′ north latitude. The capture of Aḥmad al-Ghazâlî on March 20th, and the death of the brigand

[1] An Arabic translation of it is given by Shucair, *op. cit.*, iii., p. 680 ff.

[2] For the route, see Gleichen, *op. cit.*, vol. ii., p. 103.

AN AGAR DINKA WOMAN AT SHAMBI.

[From a photograph by Miss Hilda Burrows.

Hakos on December 16th, brought peace to Wadai and the Abyssinian frontier respectively.

On January 27th, 1904, Captain P. Wood left Tong to visit Yambio, the Sulṭân of the Niam-Niams, with a view of establishing friendly relations with him. He was received with treachery and hostility, and found it necessary to destroy the village of Riketa, a son of Yambio. His losses on this occasion were Captain Haynes, who died of his wounds, two men killed, and eight wounded. Wood retired slowly to Mvolo (lat. 6° 6′ and 29° 58′) in order to keep in touch with the "Scientific Mission" of Lemaire, which had established itself in Anglo-Egyptian territory.

In May Sir Reginald Wingate visited Itang on the Baro River.

On May 23rd Ibrahîm wad Maḥmûd, the notorious slave-dealer of Gebel Gerok, was hanged at Wad Madanî. In spite of warnings given to him in 1903, he had continued his raids, and openly defied the Government, and eventually Colonel Gorringe, Governor of Sennaar, was sent with 800 men to capture him. Ibrahîm escaped from his village, but was caught and handed over to Major G. de H. Smith by Shêkh Aḥmad of Asôsa on March 3rd.

In August another religious enthusiast, called Adâm, who proclaimed himself to be the Mahdî, appeared near Senga on the Blue Nile. The Egyptian Ma'amûr of Senga, acting with most commendable promptitude, went out to capture him, and met him with his "twelve Apostles." Adâm refused to surrender, and in the fight which followed he and his "Apostles" were killed. The Ma'amûr was, unfortunately, killed also.

In September, Major O'Connell marched with a force of 340 rifles, and reduced to subjection the chiefs of Nûba, who had been in the habit of raiding the country south of Obêḍ.

During 1904 the efforts of the Sûdân Government towards the pacification of its country met with great success, and Count Gleichen tells us[1] that the desert west of Dongola, and the country of the Southern Atbâî and of the Gamîlâb tribe were visited, and certain districts mapped and surveyed. Posts too were established between the River Setît and Ḳallâbât, and the raids of the

[1] *Op. cit.*, p. 279.

Abyssinian brigands who infested the country were checked. The district about Gebel Tabi was explored, and garrisons established in the country of the northern Burun. As a result trade routes were opened up, to the great benefit of the natives. More effective control was established over the Shilluks near Fâshôda (Kôdôk), and more friendly relations between the Dinkas and the Nuers were entered into. In the Mongalla districts posts were established where necessary, and troops were quartered throughout the Nûba mountains. Sir Reginald Wingate visited Wâw in November, 1904.

As the attempt made in 1904 to establish peaceful negotiations between the Niam-Niams and the Egyptian Government had failed, Sir Reginald Wingate despatched a force against them under the late Major W. A. Boulnois, Governor of the Baḥr al-Ghazâl province. The eastern column of this force was under Captain A. Sutherland, and the western under Major Boulnois; the former was to attack Mangi, the son of Yambio, and the latter Yambio himself. On January 1st Captain Sutherland's force was concentrated at Mvolo, and on the 26th that of Major Boulnois left N'Doruma, 255 miles south of Wâw, and began to advance against Yambio. On the 30th Captain Sutherland came upon a post of Congo Free State troops at Iré (lat. 4° 55′, long. 29° 43′), which was a portion of Lemaire's "Scientific Mission"! It subsequently transpired that M. Lemaire had established five posts in Anglo-Egyptian territory, "in the interests of science." On February 25th Captain Sutherland's force joined that of Major Boulnois at Mangi's village. On January 30th Major Boulnois reached Zugumbia, and on the 6th he occupied the village of Yambio, who had fled into the bush. On the 8th the late Lieut. Fell located Yambio's position, and in the evening Major Carter captured him. Yambio received a mortal wound during the skirmish and died that night. His death relieved the country of a cruel chief, who had oppressed his people for years; the tribes came in soon after and tendered their submission to the Government. Major Boulnois died on his way back to Wâw, and Lieut J. L. Fell, late R.N., who cut the waterway through the great marshes of the Gûr River, died at Tambura of black-water fever. The other British officers who took part in this very successful expedition were Captain Sutherland, Major Carter, Major H. A. Bray, Captain H. Gordon, Captain A. J. Percival, D.S.O., Captain A. B. Bethell, R.A., who went alone on a mission to Tambura's country, notwithstanding the hostility of the Niam-Niams (Azande), Captain R. I. Rawson, and Captain S. K. Flint.[1]

[1] See the summary of their exploits in the *London Gazette* for Friday, May 18th, 1906, pp. 3443-3445.

PYRAMIDS OF MEROË.

CHAPTER XV.

CHRISTIANITY IN THE NORTHERN SUDAN.

OF the means by which Christianity was introduced into the Sûdân, who its introducers were, and when they took up their abode in the country, nothing is known with certainty. All the evidence which exists on the subject goes to show that Christianity did not make its way down the Blue Nile from Ethiopia into the Northern Sûdân, as some have thought and said, but that it entered Nubia from Egypt, as did the civilization of the ancient Egyptians, and that in the course of centuries it advanced to the southern end of the Island of Meroë, where the Christian kingdom of 'Alwâ flourished in the thirteenth and fourteenth centuries. The Christianizing of the Northern Sûdân was the result of the preaching of St. Mark in Alexandria, and the phase of Nubian Christianity known to us bears the marks and character of the form of Christian belief and teaching which were promulgated by the Jacobite (or Monophysite) Patriarchs of that city. According to a wide-spread tradition, emanating probably in the first instance from the Church of Alexandria, St. Mark preached in Alexandria about A.D. 69, and was the leader of the Christians and their Church there for some years. The traditions about the manner of his death vary; according to one he died a natural death, according to a second he was burned, and a third declares that his body was dragged over stones until it broke into pieces. Be this as it may, a considerable body of respectable tradition asserts that Christianity was preached in Egypt before the close of the first century, and it is certain that the new religion advanced southwards and spread quickly. The oldest authority for this view is Eusebius.[1]

In the third quarter of the second century, the number of

[1] *Hist. Eccles.*, ii. 16.

Christians in Egypt was large enough to necessitate the appointment of three bishops,[1] and in the reign of Severus (193-211) their number and influence were sufficient to bring upon them the wrath of the Romans, and a general persecution was the result.[2] In the second quarter of the third century the number of bishops was increased from three to twenty.[1] In the year 250 Decius issued his famous edict against the Christians, the object of which was to bring the people back to their ancient worship of the gods of Greece and Rome, and this could only be done by the stamping out of Christianity. The Roman officials everywhere were ordered to make the Christians renounce their faith, and those who apostatized were required to offer sacrifice and to burn incense to the gods. Each person who did this received a certificate from the magistrate setting forth that the Emperor's demands had been complied with. Large numbers, no doubt, sacrificed to the gods and renounced the Christian religion, but the "strong spirits" refused to do so, and these were hunted down without mercy. When caught, they were cast into prison, where many were done to death; in many respects the persecution of Decius resembled that inaugurated by Trajan (98-117).

With the death of Decius, who fell in battle against the Goths in Pannonia, the persecution stopped, but it was revived by Valerian (253-260). Many Christians in Egypt, of course, fled from their native towns whilst the persecutions of Decius and Valerian were in progress, and some have thought that the general adoption of the monastic life by the Egyptians dates from this period. This may be so, but it is impossible to assume that there were no Christians in Upper Egypt, especially in the Thebaïd at this time, and it is quite certain that some of these must have fled from the prison and tortures prepared for the Christians who refused to deny Christ. The most natural place for such to flee to would be the Nile Valley, south of Aswân, and if they did so, they must have carried Christianity with them. Apart from this, members of caravans trading between Egypt and the Sûdân would not fail to describe the events which were taking place in the former country, and the leading features of the new religion would be much discussed. Taking the probabilities

[1] Eutychius, *Annales*, i.

[2] Eusebius, *Hist. Eccles.*, vi. 1.

of the matter into consideration, it is impossible to think that individual Christianity was unknown in Nubia in the second and third centuries after Christ.[1] In the reign of Diocletian (284-305) a severe persecution of the Christians took place in Egypt, due partly to the hatred of the young men for military service, and partly to their refusal to take part in the worship of this Emperor. Those who fled to the south would be certain to find a refuge among the Blemmyes, who were at this time masters of Upper Egypt, and many, no doubt, retired from Egypt to Northern Nubia, where in the islands in the Nile and in the rocks of the hills they could lead the life of self-abnegation and religous contemplation, which was at the beginning of the fourth century becoming popular. Anthony the Great (born about 250) was in 311 a power in Egypt, and crowds of men were at that time obeying his teachings and emulating his example.

The persecution continued by Galerius (305-311) and Maximinus (305-313) only served to fill the hills and deserts with monks, and the Nitrian Valley in Lower Egypt under the rule of Ammon and the Thebaïd became filled with coenobites and anchorites. Indeed, if we may believe Bar-Hebraeus (*Hist. Dynast.*, text, p. 135), Christianity had penetrated not only all Egypt, but also the regions of the Sûdân and Nûba and Abyssinia[2] in the time of Constantine. It would be wrong to assume that conversion to Christianity had become general in Nubia and Abyssinia in the time of Constantine, but there is every reason to believe that there were in those countries numbers of Christians in the first half of the fourth century, although the Blemmyes, who were then the masters of the country between Aswân and Primis, were pagans and idolaters. The portion of the Nile Valley between the Second and Fourth Cataracts was far more suitable for the Christians to live in than the sterile region between Primis and Kôsha, a little above the head of the Second Cataract, and those who fled to this region probably followed the desert route to the west of the Nile. There are several large islands in the Nile

[1] Abû Ṣâliḥ (ed. Evetts, p. 265) says that the first Nubian who was converted from star-worship to Christianity was Baḥriyâ, the king's nephew; he built churches and monasteries in large numbers.

[2] وجميع اهل مصر من القبط وغيرهم وجمهور اصناف السودان من الحبشة والنوبة

above Kôsha, e.g., Sâî, Arnitti, Nilwatti, Wussi, Nilwa, Ertemri, Narnarti, and between the Third and Fourth Cataracts the number of them is considerable. In fact the remains of Christian buildings, churches, monasteries, &c., are found at comparatively frequent intervals all the way up between Hannek and Merawi, and many of these stand on sites which were occupied by the Christians so far back as the sixth century, when the Christian kingdom of Silko was founded, with its capital at Old Dongola.

But whether the Christians in Nubia during the fourth and fifth centuries were many or few, the people generally were pagans and idolaters. Olympiodorus,[1] who visited the country between 407 and 425, says that the Blemmyes, who occupied Nubia so far south as Primis, were heathen, and he makes no mention of Christians. The various tribes of the Blemmyes, i.e., the Bejas, who lived in the great Eastern Desert, were also pagans. Thus it is clear that the edict of Theodosius I. (378-395), decreeing that the whole of the Roman Empire should become Christian, had failed to abolish the worship of idols, which continued to flourish at Philae, Talmis (Kalâbsha), and other places in Nubia. The Blemmyes were, moreover, still pagans in the year 453; this fact is made known to us by Priscus,[2] the friend of Maximinus, who in the reign of Marcianus (450-457) went into Nubia on a punitive expedition against that people. The Nobatae had failed to fulfil[3] the agreement made with them by Diocletian to keep the Blemmyes in check, and the latter had invaded Upper Egypt and raided the country.

Maximinus, having severely punished the Blemmyes, made terms with them, and drew up an agreement with them which was to last one hundred years. They promised to pay for the damage they had done, to restore all the prisoners they had taken, and to give hostages; to the first and third of these clauses they had never before agreed. On their side, however, they stipulated that they should be allowed to visit the Island of Philae according

[1] Ed. Bekker, p. 62. [2] *Excerpt. legat.*, in Labbe, *Protrept.*, p. 40.

[3] See Revillout, *Mémoire sur les Blemmyes*, Paris, 1864; *Une Page de l'histoire de la Nubie*, in *Revue Égyptol.*, tom. iv., pp. 156 ff.; and *Second Mémoire sur les Blemmyes*, Paris, 1887.

to their ancient use and wont,[1] and that they should be allowed to borrow the statue of Isis, and to take it to a certain place in their own country, so that they might make petitions to the goddess in their own way. Here, then, we have a proof that the worship of Isis flourished at Philae and throughout the country of Northern Nubia more than fifty years after the famous Edict of Theodosius I. That a Roman general, with a great reputation for piety,[2] should agree to such a stipulation is strange, but it is more remarkable still that he should select Philae, the seat of the worship of idols, as the place wherein to sign the treaty, though we can readily understand that the Blemmyes would be more likely to regard the treaty as wholly sacred and binding if it were signed at the sanctuary of their great goddess. Thirty years later the condition of things was unchanged in Nubia, for Marinus of Flavia Neapolis in Palestine tells us in his life of Proclus,[3] that in his day Isis was still worshipped at Philae.

Of the progress of Christianity in the Sûdân during the first half of the sixth century we know nothing, but from the now famous Greek inscription which the Nubian king SILKO caused to be cut in the Egyptian temple at Talmis (Kalâbsha), it is clear that before the close of the century Christianity became the official religion of the country. This inscription was published for the first time by Gau from a copy made by him,[4] and its contents were discussed by Niebuhr;[5] another copy made by Cailliaud formed the subject of an exhaustive essay and of a translation by Letronne.[6] An excellent copy was also published by Lepsius,[7] and from this the uncial text given on p. 309 is taken; the transcription on p. 310 is that of Dittenberger.[8]

In this inscription Silko, who calls himself "*Βασιλίσκος* of the Nobadae and of all the Ethiopians," says that he came to Talmis

[1] Letronne has shown that this custom was at least 250 years old when Priscus wrote. *Histoire du Christianisme*, p. 68.

[2] This fact is well demonstrated by Revillout, *Blemmyes*, p. 45.

[3] Ed. Boissonade, Leipzig, 1814, p. 109, *Ἶσιν τὴν κατὰ τὰς Φίλας ἔτι τιμωμένην.*

[4] *Antiquités de la Nubie*, pl. 1, No. 1.

[5] *Inscriptiones Nubienses*, Rome, 1820.

[6] *Oeuvres Choisies*, tom. i., pp. 3 ff.

[7] *Denkmäler*, Abth. vi., Bl. 95.

[8] *Orientis Graeci Inscriptiones Selectae*, tom. i., p. 303.

and Taphis twice, that he fought against the Blemmyes, and that God gave him the victory once with three others, that once again he conquered [the Blemmyes], and that he made himself completely master of their cities, and established himself in them from the beginning with his troops. "I conquered them," he says, "and they made supplication to me: I made peace with them, "and they swore oaths to me by their idols [to observe it], and I "believed their oath, because they were good men." This done, he returned to the upper, i.e., the southern part of his own country. He continues, "Now that I have become *Βασιλίσκος*, not "only do I not follow after the other kings, but I march at their "head. Those who love to contend with me I do not permit to "dwell in peace in their own country, unless they entreat me for "forgiveness. For in the plains I am a lion, and in the hills I am "a bear (?)."[1]

"And I fought with the Blemmyes yet another time, from "Primis to Talmis. And I laid waste the countries of the peoples "above (i.e., south of) the Nobadae, because they would contend "against me. And as for the chiefs (*δεσπόται*) of the other "nations who would contend against me, I do not permit them to "take rest in the shade unless they bow their backs in homage "before me, and they cannot even take a drink in their own "houses. And as for those who offer resistance to me, I carry off "their women and their children."

The general meaning of this important inscription is quite clear. Silko warred against the Blemmyes and beat them on various occasions, and after his fifth fight he occupied their cities of Taphis (Tafa) and Talmis (Kalâbsha), which none of his predecessors had done; he also took their country so far south as Primis (Ibrîm). These victories he attributes to God. In his earliest campaigns the Blemmyes took the oath of allegiance to him, swearing to observe it by their idols. As a result of his victory he became *βασιλίσκος*,[2] i.e., chieftain, and he became greater than any of his predecessors. He raided the country of the tribes who resisted him, and he harassed the local Shêkhs (*δεσποται*) so mercilessly that they were always in the sun, and none of them found a chance to rest in the shade [of the trees

[1] More probably "oryx."

[2] Literally, "little king," or "kinglet."

of his native village], still less to take a drink of water in his own house. Such as resisted him suffered the loss of their wives and children. In the lower country he was a lion, and in the hills an oryx (?). Finally, we see that Silko was a Christian, and that his enemies were idolaters.

There is no need to discuss here the date of the inscription of Silko, for all that can be said on the subject, both for and against, has been said by Letronne. He was of opinion that it was written not earlier than the middle of the sixth century,[1] and was inclined to believe that it belonged to the period towards the end of that century. There is, however, one point which must be taken into consideration. Silko says that the Blemmyes took their oaths by their idols, and this suggests that the worship of Osiris and Isis at Philae was still flourishing. Now we know from Procopius[2] that Justinian (527-565) ordered Narses the Pers-armenian to go to Philae and put an end to the worship of Isis, and that this officer did so and closed the temple, and cast the priests into prison, and carried off the statues to Constantinople. This took place about 563, or, at all events, not many years before Justinian's death, but it is obvious that such a high-handed proceeding could not have been carried out by Narses unless the population generally concurred. Justinian may have felt that the custom of sacrificing human beings to the sun, which Procopius tells us was in force at Philae, and the worship of Priapus, were a disgrace to his empire, or, what is far more likely, he was anxious to seize the revenues of the temples of Isis and devote them to other purposes, but in either case there must have been in Nubia a large number of Christians who were prepared to further his views. Among such was Silko, who appears to have been urged to attack the Blemmyes about the time when the period of their treaty with the Romans for one hundred years expired. Silko crushed the Blemmyes and took their cities from Taphis to Primis, and then Justinian's envoy removed the statues of the gods from Philae, and closed the temple of Isis. The two events must have taken place about the same time, and it is difficult not to see in them the evidence of some special arrange-

[1] *Histoire du Christianisme*, p. 39.
[2] *De Bello Persico*, i., xix., pp. 59, 60.

ment made with Silko by Justinian or, according to some writers, by his Empress, Theodora.

The part which Theodora is said to have played in the conversion of the Nubians is described by Bar-Hebraeus[1] in his *Ecclesiastical History* thus:—About this time (i.e., between 540 and 548) there lived a priest called Julian, of the orthodox faith, i.e., Jacobite, who was at Constantinople in the service of the Pâpâ Theodosius of Alexandria. He was greatly concerned for the black people of the Nobades,[2] who lived on the southern border of the Thebaïd, and as they were heathen he wished to convert them. Julian told the Empress Theodora of his desire, and she begged Justinian to send him to Nubia. The Emperor, however, sent a certain bishop to Nubia, and with him went envoys and presents for the king of that country; not to be outdone, Theodora sent Julian also, and gave him a letter to the "Duke of the Thebaïd," wherein she said. "I and the Emperor "have determined to send [an envoy] unto the nation of the "Nobades, and behold I have sent Julian the priest on my own "behalf, and the Emperor hath sent other men, together with "objects of price. Do thou take good care that my [envoy] "entereth first, and let him make smooth the way for those [whom] "the Emperor hath sent." Now when the "Duke of the Thebaïd "had read the letter of the Empress, he did as she had commanded "him, and he detained the ambassadors of the Emperor until "Julian arrived, and he showed him the letter of the Empress. "And [Julian] taught and baptized the king and the nobles, and "he informed [them] concerning the schism which the Chalcedo-"nians had made, and how they had reviled the holy men, and "stablished a new faith besides that of Nicaea. And when the "ambassadors of the Emperor had arrived with the letters and "gifts, and said to the Nubians, 'Do not cleave unto those who "have been driven out and banned,' the king of the Nobades and "his nobles replied, 'We accept the honourable gifts of the "Emperor, and we will send [back] gifts twofold in return, but "we do not cleave to persecutors and calumniators. For behold, "we have already received holy baptism from this excellent man,

[1] Ed. Abbeloos and Lamy, tom. i., coll. 220 ff.

[2] ܥܡܐ ܐܘܟܡܐ ܕܢܘܒܕܝܣ

"and we cannot receive a second [baptism].' Thus were all the "people of Kushites converted to the orthodox faith, and they "became subjects of the throne of Alexandria. And Julian "remained there for a period of two years. And it is related "that from the third unto the tenth hour he stood and baptized "in caves full of water, naked, and with a girdle about him, and "the only part of his body which was out of the water was the "upper part thereof."[1] Whether this statement of Bar-Hebraeus gives the correct reason why the Nubians became Jacobites or not is comparatively unimportant, but it certainly supplies the connecting link between the wars of Silko and the removal of the statues of Osiris and Isis from Philae, and it suggests that some of the earliest of this king's campaigns against the Blemmyes took place before 550 The conclusion of the period of the treaty of one hundred years which had been made by Maximinus, and ratified by Florus, gave Justinian the opportunity he wanted, and he embraced it with the results already described.

According to John, Bishop of Ephesus, Julian took with him into Nubia the aged Bishop of the Thebaïd, and when he left Nubia to return to Constantinople he committed the newly Christianized people to his charge. The work of Julian was carried on by Longinus, who was appointed thereto by the Patriarch Theodosius on the day on which he died, and, in spite of all the opposition of his foes, Longinus succeeded in escaping from Constantinople, and he made his way, with two young men, into Nubia, where he built a church and established clergy, and taught the services and all the things which were ordered, according to the Christian faith. He stayed there about six years, and then, in obedience to certain letters which he had received from Alexandria, he proposed to leave the country; but the king and his nobles refused to allow him to depart, and it was only with difficulty that he did so. He then went to "Theodore, the aged Bishop of Pîlôn (Philae), "which is in the inner (i.e., southern) Thebaïd,"[2] and finally departed to Mareotis.

[1] The Syriac text will be found in Abbeloos and Lamy, i. coll. 229-234. Bar-Hebraeus drew his narrative from the work of John of Ephesus; see Cureton, *John of Ephesus*, Oxford, 1853, p. 223 ff.

[2] *John of Ephesus*, ed. Cureton, p. 228.

When once the statues of Isis and Osiris were removed from Philae Christianity spread rapidly in the country. Silko's successor, who was called EIRPANOME, or EIRPANOMOS,[1] was a devoted Christian, and either during or about the time of his reign the temples of Tâfa, Kalâbsha, Dakka[2] (Pselcis), Wâdî Sabû'a, 'Amâda, and Abû Simbel, were turned into Christian churches. Under the direction of the Bishop Theodore mentioned above, the pronaos of the temple of Isis at Philae was turned into a church, and two inscriptions at Philae published by Letronne[3] prove that he covered the walls with a coating of plaster to hide the figures of the Egyptian gods, and a third inscription, also at Philae, states that Theodore also built in the portion of the pronaos a sanctuary,[4] which was dedicated to Saint Stephen, under the diaconate of Posias. The transformation of the pronaos of the temple of Isis into a Christian church took place about 577, and about the same time the church at Dendûr, as M. Revillout has shown,[5] was built. Thus it is quite clear that by the end of the sixth century that portion of Nubia which lies between the First and Second Cataracts had been converted to Christianity.

The place chosen for the capital of the Christian kingdom of Nubia was Dongola, better known to-day as "Old Dongola," New Dongola being Al-Ûrdî; it is 351 miles from Ḥalfa by river, and stands on the east bank of the Nile. Dongola can easily be defended by a small force, and the choice of the site by the Nubian king who first settled there was a good one. The people who belonged to it probably lived on the west bank of the river, where there is a comparatively large area capable of cultivation. For nearly one hundred years after Silko founded his capital the Nubians were allowed to remain in peace, but soon after the conquest of Egypt by the Arabs in 640 they were attacked by the

[1] Revillout sees in this name a form of ERGAMENES: see *Blemmyes*, pp. 4, 6 ff.

[2] For the Greek inscriptions from Dakka and sites to the north, see Gau, *Monumenta Nub.*, plates xiii. and xiv.; Light, *Travels*, p. 270; Legh, *Narrative of a Journey*, London, 1820; Burckhardt, *Travels*, p. 106; Yorke and Leake, *Trans. Soc. Lit.*, vol. i. p. 225; Niebuhr, *Inscript. Nub.*, p. 10; Letronne, *Recueil*, p. 487; Letronne, *Recherches*, p. 370; Boeckh, *C.I.G.*; Lepsius, *Denkmäler*, Abth. xii., Bll. 13 and 14; Dittenberger, *Orientis Graeci*, tom. i., pp. 311 ff.; &c.

[3] *Hist. du Christianisme*, p. 80.

[4] κτισάμενος . . . τὸ ἱερὸν τοῦτο.

[5] *Blemmyes*, pp. 5 ff.

conquerors, who advanced to their capital, and, having captured it, laid upon the king the annual tribute known as the BAḲṬ. The facts concerning this are given elsewhere in this volume. In the various treaties which the Muslims made with the Nubians it is specially stipulated that the mosques shall not be injured, and that the Muḥammadans are to be allowed to trade and travel at will throughout the country, facts which seem to indicate that they considered it useless to attempt to convert the Christians to the religion of the Prophet. It is tolerably certain that the Nubians were kept in subjection by the Arabs, but at the same time they seem to have possessed, in the first half of the eighth century, considerable power. For, in 737, when the Copts were persecuted, and their Patriarch Khaîl was cast into prison, Cyriacus the king of Nubia marched into Egypt with 100,000 horsemen and 100,000 camels, and laid waste the country from Aswân to Cairo.[1] Cyriacus is said to have been the over-lord of thirteen kings, the chief of whom was Elkera, a Jacobite prince, and his dominions extended very far to the south, probably to the borders of Abyssinia.[2] When the governor of Cairo saw what had happened, he begged the Patriarch to ask Cyriacus to withdraw his troops, and the Nubian king did so.

About one hundred years later, Ibrahîm, the brother of the Khalîfa Al-Ma'mûn, sent a letter to Zacharias, king of Nubia, ordering him to pay the Baḳṭ, or tribute, which was fourteen years in arrears. The annual Baḳṭ consisted of about 400 men, therefore 5,600 men were due to the Egyptians from Zacharias. As Zacharias found it impossible to pay his debt, he sent his son George to Ibrahîm, who was then in Baghdâd, to say so, and to offer himself to the Khalîfa. Ibrahîm received him graciously, and granted all the petitions of Zacharias, and sent George back to Egypt with honour. George next went to see the Patriarch Anba Yûsâb (831-850 ?), and received his blessing, and then asked him to consecrate an altar so that he might take it back to the house of the amîr wherein he lodged. This was done, and the amîr ordered the wooden board to be struck on the roof of

[1] Poole, *Middle Ages*, p. 27; Abû Sâliḥ, ed. Evetts, p. 267.

[2] Letronne, *Histoire du Christianisme*, p. 36; Le Quien, *Oriens Christianus*, tom. ii., p. 662.

George's lodging, so that his friends might assemble at the house for prayers and hear the liturgy as in his own country. When George returned to Nubia his father founded a large church as a thank-offering to God for his son's safe return. This church was consecrated in 1020 by Anba George, Bishop of Natho, or Leontopolis.[1]

About the year 970, the Nubians, to a great extent, became an independent people, and they devoted their energies to the re-establishing of their power, and to the building of churches, monasteries, &c. In 1002 Raphael was king of Nubia, and he built at Dongola houses with domes of red bricks, similar to those which are found in Al-Irâḳ. The flourishing condition of the Nubian kingdom in the twelfth century is testified to by Abû Ṣâliḥ, the Armenian, who says of Dongola that it is a large city on the banks of the blessed Nile, and that it contains many churches and large houses and wide streets. Dongola had, in fact, taken the place of the old city of Napata, opposite to Gebel Barkal, and about this time had become the capital of the kingdom of Northern Nubia, which extended from the First to the Fourth Cataract. A few years ago, Mr. Carl Armbruster, of the Sûdân Civil Service, found three fragments of Greek inscriptions built into a wall at Dongola. With praiseworthy promptness he rescued them, and copies of the texts will be found in the *Journal of Theological Studies*, vol. iv., pp. 583 ff. Between the First and Second Cataracts there must have been many churches and monasteries, e.g., the "Monastery of Safanuf, king of Nubia,"[2] which was probably situated near Abû Simbel, and the Monastery of Ansûn at Tâfa, a few miles south of Philae, and the church of Saint Michael, which stood close to the frontier between Egypt and Nubia. On a large island about twelve miles south of Ḥalfa are the ruins of a Coptic church called Darbe.[3]

Abû Ṣâliḥ also mentions the Monastery of Michael and Cosmas, and the Monastery of Dêrâ, and says that the latter was near an ancient temple, between two great mountains, but their exact sites have not been identified. He speaks, too, of the city of Bansakâ as being large and handsome and containing many

[1] Abû Ṣâliḥ, ed. Evetts, p. 270. [2] *Ibid.*, p. 261.

[3] Crowfoot in Gleichen, *op. cit.*, i., p. 313.

churches, and the Monastery of Saint Sinuthius; as he says it was the abode of the "Lord of the Mountain" (see Vol. II., p. 193), and there was a gold mine near it, it certainly lay to the south of Wâdî Ḥalfa. On the west bank, near the Mountain of *Zîdân*, was the town which contained the Monastery of Abû Garâs, and which was the seat of a bishop. This town was probably near the Island of Sâî, where the pillars of a Coptic church, with crosses cut on them, may be seen to this day.

In the Oasis of Selîma, which lies fifty-five miles in the desert west of Saḳiat al-'Abd on the Nile, Mr. James Currie, Director of the Gordon College at Kharṭûm, saw the remains of "an old Christian convent, moderately well preserved, but the point of interest attaching to it is that it has apparently been built out of the

PLAN OF THE CHURCH IN THE CHRISTIAN MONASTERY IN THE WÂDÎ AL-GHAZÂL, NEAR ṢANAM ABÛ DÔM.

[From Lepsius, *Letters*, p. 219.

"ruins of something much older, to judge from the inscribed stones one notices."[1] From the neighbourhood of Sâî also came the sepulchral tablet of Iêsou, the Coptic Bishop, which was acquired for the Kharṭûm Museum by Mr. Crowfoot and myself in 1905. The numerous mines of gold and copper which existed between Dulgo and Kôya,[2] close to the Third Cataract, suggest that there were Coptic settlements near, and between Khandaḳ and Old Dongola Mr. Crowfoot has found remains of Christian, or older, sites at Firgi, Khalêwa,[3] Amentogo, Arab Hag, and a place a few miles to the east of Meganda.

[1] Quoted by Gleichen, *op. cit.*, i., p. 203; and see Crowfoot, *ibid.*, p. 313.
[2] Crowfoot in Gleichen, *op. cit.*, i., p. 313.
[3] Here Mr. Crowfoot found some Greek inscriptions.

At Bakhît Lepsius found the ruins of a church within a fortress which had "eighteen semicircular projecting towers of defence." The church was 63 feet long, and the whole nave rested on four columns and two pilasters. Close by are the ruins of the church of Magal, with monolithic granite columns 13½ feet high up to the capital, which is separated from the shaft, and is 1½ feet high, and 2 feet in diameter. It appears to have had five naves. At Gebel Deḳa are the ruins of a church which had three naves,[1]

CHRISTIAN MONASTERY IN THE WÂDÎ AL-GHAZÂL.

[From Lepsius, *Denkmäler*, Abth. I. Bl. 131.

and which stood inside a fortress with strong, massive walls. On Gimeti Island are traces of the ruins of a church.[2]

In the Wâdî al-Ghazâl are the ruins of a monastery with those of a church, built solidly of stone as high as the windows, and above them of burnt brick. The walls are plastered, and are painted on the inside. The vaulted apse is towards the east, and the entrances behind the western transept are towards the north and south. All the arches are round, and above the doors are Coptic crosses ✠. The building is 80 feet long and 40 feet wide, and stands in a great courtyard containing cells for the monks, built

[1] *Letters*, p. 231.

[2] Crowfoot in Gleichen, *op. cit.*, p. 315.

of stone, and a "cell" for the Abbot, which is 46 feet long. There are two churchyards, and in the eastern one Lepsius counted twenty tombstones, with inscriptions in Greek and Coptic.[1] This fact, taken with Mr. Armbruster's discovery[2] mentioned above, is important as showing that Greek was used throughout the kingdom of Dongola for ecclesiastical purposes, and it confirms the statement of Abû Ṣâliḥ, who says that the liturgy of the Nubians and their prayers are in Greek,[3] and that their land is under the jurisdiction of the see of St. Mark, the Evangelist, which consecrates [their bishops] for them. Thus, as Mr. A. J. Butler has pointed out, Christianity must have been introduced into Nubia before the translation of the Egyptian liturgy into Coptic. That this liturgy was originally in Greek is proved by the Greek sentences which are still preserved in the midst of the Coptic versions, and by the existence of the Greek liturgy of St. Mark, which is apparently the original of the Coptic St. Cyril.[4]

A few miles beyond Belal, at the foot of the Fourth Cataract on the south bank, are the remains of a Coptic church and fortified monastery.

The kingdom of Dongola was not, however, allowed to flourish in peace, and towards the middle of the twelfth century trouble broke out between the Nubians and the Sulṭân of Egypt about the country between the First and Second Cataracts. In the year 1173 Shams ad-Dawlah, an elder brother of Saladin, marched to Aswân, and, having collected boats, sailed up to Primis with a body of troops. Here he attacked the Nubians, and defeated them, and took their city, and made many prisoners. The Nubians were said to be 700,000 in number, and there were in the city 700 pigs, which the conquerors killed. In the city there was a large and beautiful church dedicated to the Virgin Mary, with a high dome, upon which stood a large cross. Shams ad-Dawlah had the cross burned, and the church pillaged, and the Muḥammadan call to prayer was chanted from its summit. A bishop who was in the city was

[1] For copies, see Lepsius, *Denkmäler*, Abth. xii., Bl. 22.

[2] The stone set up to commemorate Marcus is dated in the 528th year of Diocletian, i.e., A.D. 812.

[3] Ed. Evetts, p. 272.

[4] In Abû Ṣâliḥ, note i., p. 272.

tortured and then thrown into prison. Having left a number of men there to garrison the city, with supplies and stores of all kinds, Shams ad-Dawlah departed, carrying off with him a large quantity of cotton, which he sold at Ḳûṣ on his way down the river. Ibrîm had been captured by the Arabs before, in the reign of Muhammad ibn Ṭughg, the Ikhshîd (A.D. 935-946), by Muḥammad al-Khâzin.

Hitherto mention has been made only of the churches and monasteries of Northern Nubia, and we have now to consider those which existed in Southern Nubia, i.e., the country from the foot of the Fourth Cataract to the Blue Nile. The country on each side of the Fourth Cataract contains no ruins of any kind, but this is not to be wondered at when we remember that the routes to the upper country all crossed the desert to Berber or Shendî and did not run by the river. Ruins of Christian buildings are not found on the Island of Meroë, where, historical tradition tells us, a large and flourishing Christian kingdom existed at an early period, until we reach the south end of the Island, close to the Blue Nile. At a spot on the right bank of the Blue Nile, about twelve miles above Kharṭûm, stood the city of Sôba, or Suba, which was the capital of the great Christian kingdom of 'Alwa, or 'Aliya, the ÂLUT  of the hieroglyphic inscriptions. In late Christian times, i.e., about 1200, Nubia was divided into two great kingdoms, namely, the kingdom of Muḳurra, with its capital at Dongola, and the kingdom of 'Alwa, with its capital at Sôba. The district between Tâfa[1] and Philae was known as "Marîs," and its chief lived at Bagrash, which was probably near the modern Miḥarraḳah. The people of Marîs and those of Muḳurra were said to be descended from Himyar, and their ancestors to have come from Yaman, in Southern Arabia. The kingdom of 'Alwa included a portion of the land between the Blue and White Niles, and its capital probably consisted of two parts, one on each side of the Blue Nile.

Eastward of Sôba, according to Selîm al-Aswânî, is the river

[1] A tradition, quoted by Abû Ṣâliḥ and Selîm al-Aswânî, declares that Moses, before he became prophet, made an expedition into Nubia, and destroyed Tâfa, the people whereof worshipped stars and set up idols to them.

which dries up, and the bed of which is then inhabited.[1] The city is said to have contained handsome edifices and extensive dwellings, and churches full of gold, and gardens, and guest-houses wherein the Muslims live. The chief of 'Alwa was greater than the chief of Mukurra, and had a larger army, and his country was more extensive and fertile than that of Mukurra. He had great flocks of sheep and goats, and herds of cattle, fine horses, and cattle of a red colour. The religion of the chief and of his subjects was that of the Jacobite Christians, and their bishops were appointed by the Patriarch of Alexandria. Their [sacred] books were in the Greek tongue, and they were translated into the language of the country. Selîm adds, "The understanding of these people is inferior to that of the Nûbas." The rule of the chief was absolute and unquestioned. The tribes beyond 'Alwa worshipped the sun, moon, stars, fire, trees, and animals.

Abu Ṣâliḥ[2] says that the kingdom of 'Alwa was large, and consisted of vast provinces wherein were four hundred churches. The town stood between the Blue and White Niles, probably on the site of the modern city of Kharṭûm. Around it were monasteries, some at a distance from the rivers, and some on their banks. In the town was a large and spacious church, the largest of all the churches in the country, and it was called "Manbalî." There is no reason to doubt the existence of a large number of churches in 'Alwa, for many of them were in existence in the sixteenth century, and Alvarez tells us that he had talked to a certain "John of Syria," who declared that there were still in the country one hundred and fifty churches which contained crucifixes, and pictures of the Virgin Mary painted on the walls, and all old.[3] Each church stood within a fortress, as in Northern Nubia.

The ruins of Christian buildings which still exist on the Island of Meroë are very few, the most important being those which lie on the Blue Nile, about twelve miles from Kharṭûm; these are believed to be the remains of a part of the city of Sôba. Here at all events a Meroïtic temple stood in the early centuries of the Christian era, and on the portions of the pillars which still

[1] Burckhardt, *Travels*, p. 500.
[2] Ed. Evetts, p. 263.
[3] See Mr. A. J. Butler's note in Evetts, *op. cit.*, p. 264.

remain is cut the Coptic cross which proves that it was subsequently turned into a Christian church. This temple was built about the same time as the temples at Nagaa, judging by the colossal stone ram which was found there, and which is now in Kharṭûm; the ram is in the Palace garden, and a good picture of it is given by Count Gleichen in his *Handbook* (i., p. 228). The region where search should be made for Christian antiquities is along the Blue Nile. Mr. J. W. Crowfoot knows of the

RUINED CHURCH AT SIEDEVER, NEAR LAKE ṢÂNÂ, IN ABYSSINIA.

[From Sir William Garstin's *Report*, by permission of the Comptroller of H.M. Stationery Office.

existence of ancient remains at Anti (west bank), Rodis (east bank), Kasamba (west bank, three miles from Kâmlîn), Arbagi (west bank opposite to Rufa'a), Hassa Hissa (near Arbagi), and Sennaar, and some of these he has seen. These most likely mark the sites of Meroïtic towns, but among them will probably be found the remains of Christian buildings. Dr. Schweinfurth reports the existence of "some curious old Christian stone ruins and tombs," at Gebel Mamân, 201 miles from Sawâkin, on the "Ermenab" route to Kasala. Lastly, at Ḳaṭêna on the White

Nile were found some inscribed bricks and pottery of the Christian period; these are preserved in the Gordon College Museum.[1]

The most flourishing period of the Christian kingdoms of Muḳurra and 'Alwa was between 1100 and 1300, but at the beginning of the fourteenth century the power of the Muḥammadans was in the ascendant, whilst that of the Christians began to decline. Up to this time the Christian Church of Nubia had acted as a block to the advance of Muḥammadanism in the Sûdân, and for more than seven hundred years it had maintained its position in spite of all external persecutions and attacks. Towards the end of the thirteenth century the neighbourhood of Dongola became filled with Muslims, and a mosque was dedicated there to the worship of God in 1317. Subsequently the upper part of a church there was turned into a mosque,[2] but the exact date of this event is unknown. The immediate cause of the downfall of the Christian kingdom of Nubia was due to dissensions between the chiefs of 'Alwa and Muḳurra; and the Arab settlers in the north, and the negro tribes of the south, seized their opportunity, and wrested their dominions from them. In connection with this we must remember the loss of power and prestige which the Coptic Church in Egypt suffered about A.D. 1300, and this could not fail to have its effect in the Sûdân. From the time of Cyril, Patriarch of Alexandria (A.D. 1235), the Nubian Church was left practically to native guidance, with the result which we should naturally expect. In the second half of the fourteenth century there broke out in Egypt a fierce persecution of the Copts by the Muslims, due in a great measure to the insolence and arrogance of the Christians who were employed in every department of the government.[3] The Muslims burnt and destroyed Coptic churches everywhere, they beat and killed Copts in the open streets, and in the villages of Upper Egypt the Copts were so panic-stricken that they embraced Islâm, and pulled down their churches and built mosques in their places, and, whenever they could, married Muslim women. The same thing must have happened in Nubia, and the conversion of the upper part of the church at Dongola into a mosque probably dates from

---

[1] Crowfoot in Gleichen, i., p. 315.   [2] Crowfoot, *ibid.*
[3] See Renaudot, *Hist. Patriarcharum*, vol. i., p. 28; pp. 607-610.

this period. At all events, from about A.D. 1300 to the present day, the history of the Nubian Church is a blank page.[1]

A glimpse of the general condition of Nubia at the close of the fifteenth century is afforded us by Leo Africanus, or Ḥasan ibn Muḥammad, the Geographer,[2] and he says that the king of Nubia was engaged in continual wars with the people of Dâr Fûr and Kordôfân, who speak a language which no other people understand, and with the Bejas or Bishârîn tribes, who live upon the flesh of animals and milk; the latter took tribute from the king of Dongola and from the governor of Sawâkin. Nubia was divided into "fifteen kingdomes whereof agreeing much in rites and "customes, are subject unto fower princes onely." The principal town, Dongola, was "exceedingly populous," and contained 10,000 families, and its houses were built of a "kind of chalke," and covered with straw. Its people did a large trade in ivory, grain, sugar, sandal-wood, civet, and gold, of which there was "great "plentie" in the country, and in a kind of poison which was sold at one hundred ducats the ounce! The Nubians were governed by a woman, and they called their queen GANA. The spiritual condition of the Nubians he describes as most wretched and miserable, for having "lost the sinceritie and light of the Gospel, "they do embrace infinite corruptions of the Jewish and Muḥam-"madan religions." Whilst Alvarez was in Abyssinia the Nubians sent messengers to beg the "Prete" to appoint over them priests and persons to preach and administer the sacraments to them. These messengers said that the Nubians had often sent to Rome for a bishop, but as they received no assistance in this respect, they, little by little, lost all knowledge of the Christian religion, "and became infected with the impious and abominable "sects of the Iewes and Mahumetans." As the "Prete" was in sore need of clergy for his own churches he could not help the Nubians. Many of the churches in Nubia were destroyed by the Arabs, and the Portuguese travellers related that they saw pictures of saints painted on the walls.

[1] Nawâya Krestôs, king of Ethiopia (1342-1372), made war on Upper Egypt because the Governor of Cairo had thrown Abbâ Markôs, Patriarch of Alexandria, into prison, because he failed to pay the appointed tribute; the Patriarch was released, and he returned to his duties.

[2] Edited by Robert Brown, London, 1896, vol. iii., p. 836.

In the sixteenth century, about 1520, the Nubians were ruled by the Bosnians, who were sent into the Sûdân by Selîm after his conquest of Egypt, and about the same time the Arabs and Turks overran many parts of Ethiopia, and killed the Christians and destroyed their churches. The Portuguese missions to the Sûdân had for their object the conversion of the Abyssinians to the Roman faith, and nothing was done to help the Nubians, or to revive Christianity in their country.

APPENDIX TO CHAPTER XV.

THE INSCRIPTION OF SILKO, KING OF THE NOBADAE.[1]

TRANSLATION.

"I SILKO am Chieftain[2] of the Nobadae and of all the Ethiopians.

"I came to Talmis[3] and to Taphis.[4] Once, twice, I fought "with the Blemmyes, and GOD gave me the victory after the three. "I conquered them once and for all, and made myself master "of their cities, and for the first time I stablished myself therein, "together with my troops. I conquered them, and they made "supplication to me, and I made peace with them, and they "swore oaths to me by the images[5] of their gods, and I trusted "in their oaths that they were honourable men. Then I returned "into the upper part of my country.[6]

"When I had become Chieftain I did not follow behind other "kings, but [was] in the very front of them.[7]

"And as for those who strive with me for the mastery, I do "not permit them to live in their own country, unless they beg

[1] I am indebted to Dr. F. G. Kenyon for several valuable suggestions, which I believe make the meaning of some parts of this inscription clear for the first time.

[2] βασιλίσκος it is true = "regulus," but Silko was an independent king.

[3] Kalâbsha.

[4] The town near Wâdî Tâfa.

[5] I.e., images of Isis and Osiris at Philae.

[6] In the neighbourhood of Dongola.

[7] I.e., he was greater than any king known to him who had preceded him in Nubia.

"forgiveness from me. For in the Lower Country I am a lion, "and in the Upper Country I am an oryx (?).[1]

"I fought with the Blemmyes from Primis[2] to Talmis once. "And of the other Nobadae to the south I ravaged their lands, "since they contended with me. As for the chiefs of the other "nations who strive with me for the mastery, I do not permit "them to sit in the shade, but outside in the sun, and they cannot "even take a drink of water in their own houses.[3] As for those "who offer resistance to me, I carry off their wives and children."

THE INSCRIPTION OF SILKO AT KALÂBSHA.

(Lepsius, *Denkmäler*, Abth. VI. Bl. 95.)

1. ЄΓΩCΙΛΚΩΒΑCΙΛΙCΚΟCΝΟΥΒΑΔΩΝΚΑΙΟΛΩΝΤΩΝ
2. ΑΙΘΙΟΠΩΝΗΛΘΟΝЄΙCΤΑΛΜΙΝΚΑΙΤΑΦΙΝΑΠΑΞΔΥ
ΟЄΠΟ
3. ΛЄΜΗCΑΜЄΤΑΤΩΝΒΛЄΜΥΩΝΚΑΙΟΘЄΟCЄΔΩΚЄΝ
ΜΟΙΤΟ
4. ΝΙΚΗΜΑΜЄΤΑΤΩΝΤΡΙΩΝΑΠΑΞЄΝΙΚΗCΑΠΑΛΙΝΚΑ
ΙЄΚΡΑ
5. ΤΗCΑΤΑCΠΟΛЄΙCΑΥΤΩΝЄΚΑΘЄCΘΗΝΜЄΤΑΤΩΝ
6. ΟΧΛΩΝΜΟΥΤΟΜЄΝΠΡΩΤΟΝΑΠΑΞЄΝΙΚΗCΑΑΥΤ
ΩΝ
7. ΚΑΙΑΥΤΟΙΗΞΙΩCΑΝΜЄЄΠΟΙΗCΑЄΙΡΗΝΗΝΜЄΤΑΥ
ΤΩΝ
8. ΚΑΙΩΜΟCΑΝΜΟΙΤΑЄΙΔΩΛΑΑΥΤΩΝΚΑΙЄΠΙCΤЄΥC
ΑΤΟΝ
9. ΟΡΚΟΝΑΥΤΩΝΩČΚΑΛΟΙЄΙCΙΝΑΝΘΡΩΠΟΙΑΝΑΧΩΡ
ΗΘΗΝ
10. ЄΙCΤΑΑΝΩΜЄΡΗΜΟΥΟΤЄЄΓЄΓΟΝЄΜΗΝΒΑCΙΛΙCΚ
ΟC
11. ΟΥΚΑΠΗΛΘΟΝΟ̆ΛΩCΟΠΙCΩΤΩΝΑΛΛΩΝΒΑCΙΛЄ
ΩΝ

[1] ἄρξ can hardly mean a bear. He means, "I am as terrible as a lion to the men in the plains, and I am as strong and active as an oryx in the hills."

[2] I.e., Ibrîm.

[3] I.e., "I keep them flying from place to place in the desert, and they find no opportunity of visiting their villages, or of taking a drink in their houses."

12. ΑΛΛΑΑΚΜΗΝΕΜΠΡΟϹΘΕΝΑΥΤωΝ
13. ΟΙΓΑΡΦΙΛΟΝΙΚΟΥϹΙΝΜΕΤΕΜΟΥΟΥΚΑΦωΑΥΤΟΥϹ ΚΑΘΕΖΟΜΕ
14. ΝΟΙΕΙϹΧωΡΑΝΑΥΤωΝΕΙΜΗΚΑΤΗΞΙωϹΑΝΜΕΚΑΙΠ ΑΡΑΚΑΛΟΥϹΙΝ
15. ΕΓω ΓΑΡΕΙϹΚΑΤω ΜΕΡΗΛΕωΝΕΙΜΙΚΑΙΕΙϹΑΝωΜΕΡ ΗΑΡ (sic) Ξ̄ΕΙΜΙ
16. ΕΠΟΛΕΜΗϹΑΜΕΤΑΤωΝΒΛΕΜΥωΝΑΠΟΠΡΙΜʽΕωϹ ΤΕΛΗ (sic) ΛΕωϹ
17. ΕΝΑΠΑΞΚΑΙΟΙΑΛΛΟΙΝΟΥΒΑΔωΝΑΝωΤΕΡωΕΠΟΡ ΘΗϹΑΤΑϹ
18. ΧωΡΑϹΑΥΤωΝΕΠΕΙΔΗΕΦΙΛΟΝΙΚΗϹΟΥϹΙΝΜΕΤΕΜ ΟΥ
19. ΟΙΔΕϹΠΟΤ̄ΤωΝΑΛΛωΝΕΘΝωΝΟΙΦΙΛΟΝΕΙΚΟΥϹΙΝ ΜΕΤ̄ΕΜΟΥ
20. ΟΥΚΑΦωΑΥΤΟΥϹΚΑΘΕϹΘΗΝΑΙΕΙϹΤΗΝϹΚΙΑΝΕΙΜ ΗΫΠΟΗΛ̄ΙΟΥ
21. ΕΞωΚΑΙΟΥΚΕΠωΚΑΝΝΗΡΟΝΕϹωΕΙϹΤΗΝΟΙΚΙΑΝΑ ΥΤωΝΟΙΓΑΡ
22. ΑΝΤΙΔ(?)ΙΚΟΙΜΟΥΑΡΠΑΖωΤωΝΓΥΝΑΙΚωΝΚΑΙΤΑ ΠΑΙΔΙΑΑΥΤωΝ

TRANSCRIPT.

(Dittenberger, *Orientis Graeci Inscriptiones Selectae*, tom. i., p. 303.)

1. *Ἐγὼ Σιλκώ, Βασιλίσκος Νουβάδων καὶ ὅλων τῶν*
2. *Αἰθιόπων, ἦλθον εἰς Τάλμιν καὶ Τάφιν. ἅπαξ δύο ἐπο-*
3. *λέμησα μετὰ τῶν Βλεμύων, καὶ ὁ Θεὸς ἔδωκεν μοι τὸ*
4. *νίκημα. μετὰ τῶν τριῶν ἅπαξ ἐνίκησα πάλιν καὶ ἐκρά-*
5. *τησα τὰς πόλεις αὐτῶν. ἐκαθέσθην μετὰ τῶν*
6. *ὄχλων μου τὸ μὲν πρῶτον ἅπαξ, ἐνίκησα αὐτῶν*
7. *καὶ αὐτοὶ ἠξίωσάν με. ἐποίησα εἰρήνην μετ' αὐτῶν*
8. *καὶ ὤμοσάν μοι τὰ εἴδωλα αὐτῶν καὶ ἐπίστευσα τὸν*
9. *ὅρκον αὐτῶν, ὡς καλοί εἰσιν ἄνθρωποι. ἀναχωρήθην*
10. *εἰς τὰ ἄνω μέρη μου. ὅτε ἐγεγονέμην βασιλίσκος,*
11. *οὐκ ἀπῆλθον ὅλως ὀπίσω τῶν ἄλλων βασιλέων,*

12. ἀλλὰ ἀκμὴν ἔμπροσθεν αὐτῶν.
13. οἳ γὰρ φιλονικοῦσιν μετ' ἐμοῦ, οὐκ ἀφῶ αὐτοὺς καθεζόμ-
14. ενοι εἰς χώραν αὐτῶν, εἰ μὴ κατηξίωσάν με καὶ παρακαλοῦσιν.
15. ἐγὼ γὰρ εἰς κάτω μέρη λέων εἰμὶ, καὶ εἰς ἄνω μέρη ἄρξ εἰμι.
16. ἐπολέμησα μετὰ τῶν Βλεμύων ἀπὸ Πρίμ[εως] ἕως Τελ[μ]εως
17. ἓν ἅπαξ, καὶ οἱ ἄλλοι Νουβάδων ἀνωτέρω ἐπόρθησα τὰς
18. χώρας αὐτῶν, ἐπειδὴ ἐφιλονικήσουσιν μετ' ἐμου.
19. οἱ δεσπότ[αι] τῶν ἄλλων ἐθνῶν, οἵ φιλονεικοῦσιν μετ' ἐμοῦ,
20. οὐκ ἀφῶ αὐτοῦς καθεσθῆναι εἰς τῆν σκιάν, εἰ μὴ ὑπὸ ἡλίου
21. ἔξω, καὶ οὐκ ἔπωκαν νηρὸν ἔσω εἰς τὴν οἰκίαν αὐτῶν. οἱ γὰρ
22. ἀντίδικοὶ μου, ἁρπαζω τῶν γυναικῶν καὶ τὰ πωιδία αὐτῶν.

MODERN SÛDÂNÎ AMULET.

CHAPTER XVI.

CHRISTIANITY IN THE SÛDÂN—*continued.*

MODERN MISSIONARY ENTERPRISE.

THE first European in modern times who attempted to teach and preach Christianity in the Egyptian Sûdân was Father Knoblecher, who about the year 1848, a little before the Pope appointed a bishop over Kharṭûm, founded Roman Catholic mission stations on the White Nile. His first band of assistants were Fathers Beltrame, Dorvak, Morlang, Rylls, Ueberbacher, and Vinci, and eleven other devoted gentlemen, all of whom, save two, died of the fever of the country. The principal station was at a spot in lat. 5° 46′ N., about 916 miles south of Omdurmân, to which the natives gave the name of "Kanîsa," i.e., "Church," on account of the mission-church and buildings; these were situated on the east bank of the river, and the garden was on the west bank. By Europeans the place was known as "Heiligen Kreuz," or "Sainte Croix." Sir Samuel Baker visited this station[1] on January 24th, 1863, and found there about twenty grass huts, and another hut which served as a church. Herr Morlang told him that the mission was absolutely useless among such savages, who were utterly impracticable. He described the people as being far below the brutes, and lying and deceitful to a superlative degree. The fathers had decided to abandon the Mission, it being a total failure, and Herr Morlang had sold the whole village and station to Khurshîd Aghâ for 3,000 piastres, £30! Baker purchased a horse for 1,000 piastres, and called him "Priest." In the cemetery[2] of the station was the grave of Baron Harmer, a gallant Prussian gentleman who, whilst buffalo hunting, lost his life in saving that of a native. When Sir William Garstin[3] was on

[1] *Albert Nyanza*, p. 50.

[2] It is said that nearly sixty missionaries and lay-assistants were buried here. *Basin of the Upper Nile*, p. 94.

the White Nile he saw some of the lemon and orange trees of the mission garden still alive.

The next most important station was that of Gondokoro, 1,115 miles south of Kharṭûm, which Fathers Knoblecher and Vinci founded in 1848. Here the Austrians laboured for years, but without success of any kind. They built a church, with a bell for calling the natives to service, but the people would surround the church, and ring the bell all day and all night, and nothing could stop them. Baker visited the station in April, 1871, and saw lying there on the ground some sixty or eighty bushels of lemons which had fallen from the trees planted by the Christian Fathers. He tells us[1] that the Bâris, who were natives of the district, had pulled down the neat mission-house, and that they had pounded the bright red bricks of which the church was built into powder; this they mixed with grease and then used for smearing their naked bodies. "The missionary establishment itself was con-"verted into an external application for the skin; the house of "God was turned into 'pomade divine.' This was a result that "might have been expected by any person who had practical "experience of the Bâris." The Austrian Mission was, alas! a failure, and the White Nile stations were abandoned in 1864 or 1865. The brave and noble fathers did not understand either the country or the climate, and the imagination shudders at the sufferings of those who died of fever, and of their comrades who saw them die, and were powerless to alleviate their misery. The example of their lives, however, is not wasted.

The next pioneer of missionary enterprise was Alexandrine Petronella Francina TINNE, the daughter of Philip Frederic Tinne, and Henrietta, Baroness von Steengracht Capellen. She was born at the Hague in 1839, and her father died when she was five years old, leaving her the richest heiress in the Netherlands. She loved adventure, even when a child, and her first journey was to the North Cape. On her return she induced her mother to visit the East, and in due course Miss Tinne arrived at Cairo, where she adopted an oriental style of dress. She left Cairo at the end of the winter, but returned two years later, and, in the winter of 1859-60 she and her mother and an aunt sailed up the

[1] *Ismailïa*, pp. 107, 115.

Nile nearly as far as Gondokoro. In 1861 Miss Tinne made up her mind to visit Theodore, king of Abyssinia, with the view of extending Christianity in that country by her wealth and influence. About this time, it is said, King Theodore made an offer of marriage to Her Majesty Queen Victoria, and when he found that his letters were not answered he became furious, and his liking for Europeans turned to hate. Miss Tinne therefore abandoned her project, and decided to visit the White Nile once more. She left Cairo on January 9th, 1862, and in due course reached Korosko, where she hired one hundred camels to take her party across the desert to Abû Ḥamed.

When she arrived at Kharṭûm Mûsa Pâshâ was Governor-General, and she was horrified to learn that he was to all intents and purposes a slave-dealer. From Prince Halîm she obtained a steamboat,[1] and in May she began to ascend the White Nile; she was received with kindness by all except the slave-dealers, who feared and hated her, but who proposed to her to join them in their slave hunts! The fame of her wealth, and youth, and beauty was carried by the caravans to all parts of Africa, and the natives called her the daughter of the Sulṭân of Constantinople. The infamous slave-raider, Muḥammad Khêr, even offered to marry her, and make her Queen of the Sûdân! Miss Tinne succeeded on this journey in actually reaching Gondokoro, and she made her way into parts of the country, and explored a portion of the Sobat River never before visited by Europeans. At Gondokoro the hostility of the Bâris made it impossible for her to travel across the country westwards, and she therefore returned to Kharṭûm, where she found Dr. Steudner and Herr Theodor von Heuglin.

In the following year, 1863, Miss Tinne prepared a great expedition, and having taken Steudner and Heuglin into her service, and sent them on to Mashra ar-Reḳ to collect information, she set out from Kharṭûm, intending to travel through the country of the Niam-Niams, or Cannibals, towards the sources of the Nile. The expedition consisted of a steamer, two dahabîyas (house-boats), and two boats for baggage. The party

[1] The first steamboat that sailed on this part of the Nile was put together at Kharṭûm in 1846.

was composed of Miss Tinne and her mother, two European maids, and an Italian interpreter, and the boats carried two hundred soldiers and servants of different kinds, thirty mules and donkeys, four camels, a saddle horse, ammunition, and provisions for ten months. Among the stores were 3,000 pounds' weight of glass beads, and 12,000 ornamented shells! In due course the expedition reached a spot 600 miles south of Omdurmân, which from that time to the present day bears the name of "Maya bita Signora," or the "Lagoon of the Lady," because this backwater was first explored by Miss Tinne.[1] They then passed on to Mashra ar-Reḳ, where the expedition landed and prepared to march to the Kosanga and Gur Rivers and the country of the Niam-Niams.

As soon as Miss Tinne set out serious trouble began. The camels and some of the other animals died, and thus she lacked means of transport, and the slave-raiders in the district did all they could to obstruct. Heuglin and Steudner left the party to go and hire porters in the country to the west, but though they went as far as Wâw they failed to induce men to come back with them. Then both of them fell ill of fever, and Dr. Steudner died Heuglin then went into the Bongo country, where he obtained 150 blacks, and took them back to Mashra ar-Reḳ. Nothing daunted, Miss Tinne set out for the Gur River, which she and the other Europeans crossed in an indiarubber boat, but most of her baggage was ruined by water or lost. At length she reached the settlement of Biselli in the Bongo country, who apparently afforded her little help. There was a famine in the land, the animals died one after the other, and the supply of medicines was exhausted, and, to crown all her misfortunes, Miss Tinne's mother died of fever. Thereupon the expedition was abandoned, and Miss Tinne set out for Kharṭûm, but before this place was reached, her aunt, the two European maids, Contarini the interpreter, and a German gardener, to say nothing of natives, all died. Thus so far as the spreading of Christianity was concerned, or any useful effect on the slave-trade, this costly expedition was fruitless.

From a scientific point of view, however, this was not the case. Owing to Miss Tinne's generosity Heuglin was enabled to collect

[1] Junker's *Travels*, London, 1891, p. 38.

a vast amount of information about the birds, animals, and plants of the White Nile, which he published in *Reise in das Gebiet des Weissen Nil und seiner westlichen Zuflüsse*, 1862-1864. A large number of facts about the manners and customs of tribes whose very existence was until that time unknown, and the courses of the Gur, Kosanga, and Senna Rivers, were made out. Miss Tinne's expedition also was the first to discover the existence of a great lake, one of the sources of the Nile, which was further west than any known at that time. It is claimed by one of Miss Tinne's biographers that "the greatest result of this expedition "was, doubtless, the moral blow it struck at the internal slave-"trade," but it is difficult to see how this statement can be substantiated. Altogether Miss Tinne spent three years in the Sûdân.[1]

[1] On her return to Cairo, *viâ* Sawâkin and Suez, she began an action against the Governor-General of Kharṭûm for his complicity in the slave-trade. She next decided to settle in Egypt, and to build a castle on the Island of Rôḍa, but the Khedive prevented her from acquiring the necessary land, and she left the country with the intention of making a journey from Tripoli to Timbuctoo, across the desert. Eventually she prepared an expedition at Tripoli with the view of going to Bornu, then on to Lake Tchad, and returning *viâ* Wadâî, Dâr Fûr, and Kordôfân. She left Tripoli on January 28th, 1869, and reached Mûrzûk in Fezzan on March 1st, where she fell ill. On her recovery she made an arrangement with the Tuwârek chief to pass the summer in his country. One morning when she was journeying thither, as she was trying to stop a quarrel between some of her men, and addressing them with her right hand raised in the air, a Tuwârek struck at her hand with his sword and nearly separated it from the wrist. She staggered into her tent, where she was followed by other Tuwâreks, who killed her servants, and one of them struck her on the nape of her neck, intending to cut off her head. She fell on the ground, whereupon two of the natives rushed at her, stripped her almost naked, and then dragged her by her heels out into the sun, where they left her in order to go and join in the robbery of her chests, which were believed to be filled with gold. The Tuwâreks prevented any help being given to her, and they allowed no one to give her water, for which she asked very often, and she died in the course of the day, August 1st, 1869. The motive for the murder of this brave woman appears to have been robbery pure and simple. Accounts of her life will be found in Wells, *The Heroine of the White Nile*, New York, 1873 (?); Sir Harry Johnston, *The Nile Quest*, London, 1903, pp. 192 ff. (with portrait of Miss Tinne and details supplied by Mr. T. F. S. Tinne, her nephew); Heuglin, *Die Tinne'sche Expedition im Westlichen Nil-Quellgebiet*, 1863, 1864, Gotha, 1865; Nachtigal, *Relation de la Mort de Mlle. Alexina Tinne et voyage au Tibesti*, Paris, 1870.

From the facts given above it is clear that at this time the Sûdân offered a poor field for missionary enterprise, and in this connection the views on the subject expressed by Sir Samuel Baker in his *Ismailïa*[1] are of special importance:—

"If Africa is to be civilized, it must be effected by commerce, "which once established will open the way for missionary labour; "but all ideas of commerce, improvement, and the advancement "of the African race that philanthropy can suggest, must be "discarded until the traffic in slaves shall have ceased to exist. . . "Difficult and almost impossible is the task before the missionary. "The Austrian Mission has failed, and their stations have been "forsaken; their pious labour was hopeless, and the devoted "priests died upon the barren field. . . . The time has not yet "arrived for missionary enterprise in those countries; but at "the same time a sensible man might do good service by living "among the natives, and proving to their material minds that "persons do exist whose happiness consists in doing good to "others."

Baker then goes on to say what personal qualifications and outfit such a man ought to possess. He ought to be a good rifle shot and sportsman to secure the attention and admiration of the natives. He ought to be musical, and play the bagpipes, and be a skilful conjuror, and possess a magic lantern, magnetic battery, dissolving views, photographic apparatus, coloured pictures, &c. He ought to be a good surgeon and general practitioner, and be well supplied with drugs. He should set all psalms to lively tunes, and the natives would learn them at once. Devotional exercises should be chiefly musical. And if he had a never-failing supply of beads, copper rods, brass rings for arms, fingers, and ears, gaudy cotton handkerchiefs, red or blue blankets, zinc mirrors, red cotton shirts, &c., to give to his parishioners, and expected nothing in return, he would be considered a great man, whose opinion would carry considerable weight, provided that he only spoke of subjects which he thoroughly understood. A knowledge of agriculture, with a good stock of seeds of useful vegetables and cereals, iron hoes, carpenters' and blacksmiths' tools, and the power of instructing others in their use, together with

[1] Chapter xxvii., 2nd ed., London, 1879, p. 467.

a plentiful supply of very small axes, would be an immense recommendation to a lay missionary who should determine to devote some years of his life to the improvement of the natives.

These observations were written in 1873, after Sir Samuel Baker had finished his labours in the Sûdân, and they are clearly the result of a thorough experience and of first-hand knowledge of the country. In 1878 General Gordon, when Governor-General of the Sûdân, appealed to the Church Missionary Society to send a Mission to the Pagan tribes on the Upper Nile, and promised all possible help, but the Society was too much occupied in Uganda to respond, and in England no steps were taken to help the spread of Christianity in this portion of the Sûdân. In January, 1885, Gordon was murdered, and the Sûdân was closed to Europeans until the Sirdar, Lord Kitchener, captured Omdurmân in 1898.

A few months after the re-conquest of the Sûdân the American United Presbyterian Mission in Egypt began to consider what steps should be taken by its missionaries towards opening schools at Kharṭûm, and in generally making the Gospel known among the tribes which lived to the south of that city; and it was resolved, if possible, to establish a Sûdân branch of the Mission and stations in such places as were suitable for the purpose. The American Mission was prepared to an unusual degree for the proposed extension, for in its service were men who not only had a first-rate knowledge of the Arabic language, which is generally talked and understood in the Sûdân, but also great experience in dealing with natives, and these qualifications were backed by the prestige which accompanies successful work. The record of the Mission, which began its labours in 1854, was a good one, and, during the fifty years[1] which it had been in existence, the men who had directed its affairs had proved themselves over and over again to be not mere propagandists of the form of religion which they professed, but true helpers of education and progress and of the advance of civilization. Their schools all over Egypt were justly celebrated for the excellence of the teaching given in them, and the educational advantages which could be derived from them are

[1] See Dr. Andrew Watson's unostentatious account, *The American Mission in Egypt*, 1854-1896, Pittsburgh, 1898.

well illustrated by the large number of boys and young men in Government employ who owe their positions entirely to the education and training given to them in the schools of the American Mission. The Copts owe them a large debt of gratitude, for it was the American missionaries who showed them the advantage of an education given on Western lines in the English language, and taught them freedom of thought and methods of independence.

As a result of the decision of the American Mission, Dr. Watson, Dr. Kelly Giffen, and Mr. A. A. Cooper went to Kharṭûm on a mission of inspection, and on their return they recommended that work be undertaken in the Northern Sûdân, and in the Blue Nile region. In 1900 H. T. McLaughlin, M.D., and Dr. Kelly Giffen were ordered to proceed to the Sûdân to carry on missionary work. The Government, however, declined to allow them to work among the Muslims in the Sûdân, but at the same time pointed out that they might go and open as many stations as they pleased among the black tribes on the White Nile, to the south of Kharṭûm. Messrs. McLaughlin and Giffen went to Omdurmân, taking with them Mr. Gebera Hanna, whom they authorized to conduct meetings for the young men who had been trained in the Mission and were then in Government service. They then visited the White Nile, and returned to Egypt to report on the situation. In September, 1901, they returned to the Sûdân, taking their wives with them; and on March 2nd, 1902, they set out to establish a station on the Sobat River among the black Shilluks, or Shullas, about 560 miles south of Kharṭûm. On March 27th they arrived at a place called Dulêb Hill, which is situated on the north bank of the Sobat, and there they established an American Mission station.[1] On March 14th, 1903, Lord Cromer visited the station and found that it was "manifestly conducted on those sound, "practical, common-sense principles which, indeed, are strongly "characteristic of American Mission work in Egypt. No parade "is made of religion. In fact, the work of conversion, properly "so-called, can scarcely be said to have commenced." He found

[1] A very interesting account of their proceedings there has been written and published by Dr. Kelly Giffen, entitled *The Egyptian Sûdân*, and to this the reader is referred for details.

"numbers of Shillouks, men and women, working happily at the "brickkiln. Cotton of a good quality has been produced, and "the mission houses have been constructed by Shillouk labour. "The creation of establishments conducted on the principles "adopted by Mr. Giffen and Dr. McLaughlin cannot fail to "prove an unmixed benefit to the population amongst whom they "live."[1]

In 1902 Lord Cromer expressed surprise that none of the British Missionary Societies appeared to have devoted their attention to the Southern Sûdân, especially as its districts presented a far more promising field for missionary enterprise than the provinces whose populations are Muḥammadan. Also he saw no objection to the establishment of Christian schools at Kharṭûm, provided that parents were warned that instruction in the Christian religion is afforded, especially as there is a small number of Christians in the city.

In 1903 the American missionaries applied for the purchase of a considerable tract of land to teach the Shilluks agriculture.

In 1904 Lord Cromer and the Sirdar, Sir Reginald Wingate, were still of the opinion that "the time was still distant when "mission work could, with safety and advantage, be permitted "amongst the Moslem population of the Sûdân."

In answer to the request of Mr. McInnes, the Secretary of the Church Missionary Society in Egypt, who asked for an expression of opinion as to the prospects of missionary work in the Sûdân, Lord Cromer, on December 23rd, 1904, addressed a letter to the Church Missionary Society, in which he informed the Secretary that a large tract of country was, for the present, being reserved for them. The tract of country referred to is to the south of the Baḥr al-Ghazâl, and it extends south to about lat. 14° north;[2] to the north-east of it lies the sphere of the American Mission, and to the west and north of it is the Roman Catholic Mission sphere. Roughly speaking, it represents an area of about 25,000

[1] *Egypt*, No. 1 (1903), p. 89.

[2] It is bounded on the N. by the Baḥr al-Ghazâl; on the E. by a line drawn from the White Nile to Agiung-Twi, and the Abyssinian Frontier to lat. 5° N.; on the S. by the north border of the Congo Free State, the Lâdô Enclave, and Uganda; and on the W. by a line drawn from Mashra ar-Reḳ to N'darama.

SHILLUKS AT THE AMERICAN MISSION ON THE SOBAT RIVER.

[From a photograph by Miss Hilda Burrows.

square miles. In October, 1905, the Church Missionary Society in London sent out a party to found the "Gordon Memorial Soudan Mission," consisting of the Rev. F. B. Hadow, M.A., the Rev. A. Shaw, B A., the Rev. A. M. Thom, M.A., Mr. E. Lloyd, B.A., B.C., and Messrs. J. Comely and R. C. J. S. Wilmot, industrial agents. The party reached Kharṭûm on November 1st and Mongalla on January 8th, 1906. After exploring Mongalla and its neighbourhood, the party decided that it was not desirable to make that place the base of the Mission, and on the advice of Cameron Bey, the Mudîr, and Captain Logan, the Commandant, the mission boat was towed down the river to Bôr, about eighty-four miles to the north.[1]

It now remains to mention the work done by the Austrian Roman Catholic Mission in the Sûdân. As soon as possible after the taking of Omdurmân in 1898 the Austrian Mission reoccupied the site which had formerly been their headquarters at Kharṭûm before the rise of the Mahdî, and they found all their buildings and church in ruins; the boundaries of their garden could be made out, but when I saw it in December, 1899, ostriches were feeding in it! Monsignor Roveggio, the Bishop of Kharṭûm, with a small but devoted staff began to take up the broken threads of their work with energy. Soon afterwards the Austrian Fathers went to the south, and opened a station near Fâshôda, and it was visited in 1902 by Lord Cromer, who declared it to be well conducted[2] and to deserve the same amount of encouragement as that accorded to the American Mission. In 1903 Monsignor Gayer, the new Roman Catholic Bishop of Kharṭûm, visited the Baḥr al-Ghazâl and made arrangements for founding the mission station of Lûl, to the south of Fâshôda, about 477 miles from Omdurmân.[3] Lord Cromer suggested[4] that his operations should be confined to the west bank, as the Church Missionary Society was contemplating the foundation of a station at Mongalla. The station at Lûl was worked by five Fathers and three Sisters.

In 1904 the Austrian Missionaries established stations in the

[1] See the article in the *Church Miss. Intelligencer* for April, 1906, p. 262 ff.

[2] *Egypt*, No. 1 (1903), p. 90.

[3] See the view in Gleichen, *op. cit.*, i., p. 69.

[4] *Egypt*, No. 1 (1904), p. 95.

Tonga district and at Wâw, &c., and some of their number visited the Golo and Bongo tribes. Sir Reginald Wingate regards the work of the American and Roman Catholic Missions as that of civilizing agents, and says that the technical instruction which they are imparting to the Shilluks, Dinkas, and others, is very beneficial from a Government point of view.[1] Lord Cromer has stated clearly that "proselytism forms no part of "the programme of the British Government, either in countries "which form part of the dominions of the Crown, or in others "where British influence is in some degree predominant. . . . "Missionary enterprise is entirely in the hands of private "individuals, who receive no pecunairy aid from the Government. "The action of the latter is limited to securing perfect toleration "for all creeds, and to exercising such an amount of supervision "over missionary efforts as will ensure none but legitimate and "unobjectionable methods being adopted in order to convert "those who are not Christians to the Christian faith."[2]

Every one who knows the Sûdân and the exceedingly suspicious character of its people will readily understand the soundness of the policy and the wisdom of proclaiming it unequivocally. Slatin Pâshâ, whose unique experience of Sûdânî folk renders his opinion on the subject of the greatest value, says that missionary work among the pagan tribes is a civilizing one. The savages are taught by it the elements of common sense, good behaviour, and obedience to Government authority, rather than religion. He has never known any savage to be baptized, nor any to have been converted to Christianity, but, on the other hand, there is no doubt that the missionaries have had an improving effect on the character of the people amongst whom they have settled, and they have certainly gained their confidence.[3] It is therefore to be hoped that the Missionary Societies, whose servants are doing such good work in the Sûdân, will continue to support the "men on the spot" in all common-sense endeavours to promote the physical well-being of the natives, and the growth of trade, and that they will not allow themselves to be hurried by enthusiastic stay-at-home persons into attempts to obtain results, in the shape of "conversions," which for some time to come can

[1] *Egypt*, No. 1. (1905), p. 141. [2] *Ibid.*, p. 139. [3] *Ibid.* (1906), p. 125.

only be attended with loss to their cause, and which will do the native no permanent good, and cause the Government anxiety and trouble. The inhabitants of the "land of the whirring of wings, which is beyond the rivers of Kûsh," as Isaiah (xviii. 1) calls the territory wherein the Missions of the British, the Americans, and the Austrians are now labouring, have been pagans and idolaters, as we know of a certainty, for 6,000 years; and it seems only reasonable to suppose that many years must elapse before they will be able to make the results of the exalted truths of the Christian Religion manifest in their lives and works.

Finally, among the European institutions in the Sûdân which are working silently for the good of the people of that country, must be mentioned the school conducted by Father Ohrwalder in the heart of Omdurmân. The history of the trials and sufferings of this devout man are well known to every reader of Slatin Pâshâ's *Fire and Sword in the Sûdân*, and from Sir Reginald Wingate's translation of Father Ohrwalder's narrative which appeared under the title of *Ten Years' Captivity in the Mahdi's Camp*. After his escape from the Khalîfa's clutches, Father Ohrwalder laboured in Sawâkin, but as soon as possible he returned to Omdurmân, where he now directs a school with conspicuous success. He has cast in his lot with the natives of that town, and teaches the elements of civilization and practical religion to their children in his characteristic, whole-hearted manner. His continuous residence in the town gives to his work the consistency which is necessary for success, and the example of his life, his obedience to the Divine commands, and the thoroughness of his ministrations cannot fail to give to all the natives who are brought into contact with his personality some idea of the beauty of the religion of his Master, Christ, Whose loyal servant he undoubtedly is.

[1] ארץ צלצל כנפים. The allusion seems to be to the buzzing of the wings of the innumerable insects which live in the Southern Sûdân.

CHAPTER XVII.

THE GOLD MINES OF THE SÛDÂN

A GLANCE at the main facts of the history of the Sûdân for the last six thousand years will convince the reader that the principal inducements which made foreigners invade and occupy the country from the time of King Seneferu, B.C. 3700, to Muḥammad 'Alî, A.D. 1820, were the slaves which it produced, and the gold which lay hidden in its mountains and hills. The Egyptians welcomed the ivory, ebony, skins of animals, ostrich feathers, and spices, which the caravans brought northwards at intervals, but the objects which stirred their kings up to fight, and made them lead their troops over deserts and rocky cataracts for hundreds of miles, were not the love of conquest, and the desire to extend the blessings of the Egyptian civilization and religion to hordes of naked savages, but their greed for gold, and their need of the Sûdânî men to carry out their great works, to fight their battles, and to police their towns. The whole policy of the kings of Egypt towards the Sûdân was dictated and directed by their need of slaves and gold, and the example set by them was closely followed by Persians, Macedonians (Ptolemies), Romans, Arabs, and Turks.

In primitive times the Blacks traded with Egypt, and exchanged their gold, and ivory, and skins, for stone and porcelain beads and other ornaments, amulets, &c., and it is certain that numbers of the men who accompanied the caravans from the south would settle in Egypt. But the demand for Blacks was greater than the supply, and in the IVth Dynasty we find that Seneferu made a great raid into some part of the Sûdân and brought back a large number of prisoners, i.e., slaves. In the Vth and VIth Dynasties missions were sent into the Sûdân under Ba-neb-Ṭeṭ, Unȧ and Ḥer-khuf, and, besides the pygmies whom two of these generals

Reproduced from the painted casts of the relie

I.—A Nubian Village.

V.—Upper register: Tribute of the Nubians—rings of gold, vases of spice, bows, chains, ostrich feathers, fly-fla
Lower register: Tribute of the Nubians—panther skins, slaves, apes, ostrich, dogs, oxen, panthers, giraffe,

UBIA BY RAMESES II.

fs in the temple at Bêt al-Wâlî at Kalâbsha.

IV.—Prince Ȧmeni-ḥer-unemi-f.

II.—Rameses II. charging the Nubians.

III.—Prince Khā-em-Uast.

ers, ebony, the lion and other animals.
x, etc.

VI.—Rameses II., "Lord of the Two Lands (Egypt) of diadems," seated under a canopy and receiving the tribute of the Nubians. The king wears the double crown, and holds a club in his left hand.

obtained in the south, they brought into Egypt many other products of the Sûdân, including gold and slaves. It is quite clear that, more than three thousand years before Christ, a system of slave-raiding existed and flourished under the approval of the kings at Memphis, and that the chief base of the slave-raiders was at Aswân.

We have, unfortunately, no illustration of a slave-raid dating from this early time, but we are able to gain an excellent idea of the sçenes which took place from the reliefs which Rameses II. caused to be cut upon the walls of his little rock-temple at Bêt al-Walî in Nubia. These are represented on the accompanying plate, and are reproduced from the coloured cast made by Mr. Bonomi for Mr. Hay, which is now exhibited in the Fourth Egyptian Room of the British Museum. The left-hand top corner of the first section is mutilated, but what remains of the scene illustrates an attack made on a Sûdân village by the king and his followers. Here we see a woman squatting under a tree by a fire, and stirring the food which she is cooking in a pot; in the tree is an ape. Close by is the granary of the house, and the housewife stands among the trees, addressing three men, one of whom has come from the fight wounded, and is being led to his village by two friends. Near the woman are two children, naked, just as they are to this day. A little way off is a man running and shouting to unseen neighbours to come to him. Between two trees is a skin-clad man, holding a bow, who appears to have run away from the fight. Behind him is a fighting and struggling mass of black men, into whose midst the king, standing in his chariot, has charged. Rameses II. and his horses are drawn in colossal proportions, and he is about to shoot an arrow from his bow. The black men are being trampled under the feet of the horses, and several are already dead; the rest are powerless to resist, and their bows are useless. Behind the king are two chariots containing his sons, Åmen-ḥer-unami-f and Khā-em-Uast, and their drivers. There is no reason to assume that Rameses II. in person ever raided a village in the Sûdân, and chariots and horses, considering the nature of the ground, would not be of much use.

The end of the fight outside the village was always the same, for bows and arrows were of little use in fighting, at close quarters, men armed with metal-headed axes and hatchets, and handy short swords, daggers, and spears. Then came the day of reckoning, when the local shêkhs had to collect from the villagers the fine which had been laid upon them by the Egyptian officer, or his deputy, and *bakshîsh* had to be given in the shape of slaves, male and female, gold, &c., to the various servants of the Government, in order to get them out of the village. When the payment was a large one, the scene represented in the lower half of the relief was enacted. The king, or his chief officer, took up his position in some prominent place in or near the town, and the gifts, or tribute, were brought before him.

In the scene here given the tributaries are introduced by Prince Amen-ḥer-unami-f and by Àmen-em-Àpt, the son of Pa-ser, the Prince of Kash, or Nubia, and the latter is being invested with a garment by two Egyptians. On a stand between them rests a bar, with flowers above it, whereon are hung animals' skins and chains made of rings of gold. Immediately behind Àmen-em-Àpt are two stands, whereon are arranged large rings of gold, and leather bags, which were filled either with gold dust or precious stones. Next are seen heaps of red carnelian stones, bows, shields, chairs, large fans, ostrich eggs and feathers, logs of ebony, and the tusks of elephants, and then come men leading a lion, an oryx, and a bull, and the rear is brought up by a group of slaves. In the lower row the gifts are introduced by the Prince of Kash, and the Blacks bring skins, apes, a panther, a leopard, a giraffe, two bulls, with a negro's head between the horns, which terminate in hands stretched out in supplication, two hunting dogs, an ostrich, an oryx or ariel, and logs of ebony. The leader of the Blacks is dragged by an Egyptian into the presence of the king by means of the forked pole to which his neck is fastened, and to which his hands are tied. This instrument of torture was in use in the Sûdân during the last century, and each captive who was brought from Kasala to Shendî in 1843 was fastened to one

If we examine the scene represented on the next plate we shall find that the tribute sent to Thebes was, but for the omission of some of the wild animals, substantially the same as that paid to the Prince of Kash in Nubia. In the first register the chief of

THE PAYMENT OF TRIBUTE BY THE REPRESENTATIVES OF THE NUBIANS TO THE REPRESENTATIVE OF THE KING OF EGYPT AT THEBES.

[From Lepsius, *Denkmäler*, Abth. iii., Bl. 117.

the country of Mââm, with two feathers in his head-dress, is bowing with his head to the ground before the Egyptian governor, and by his side kneel the "Chiefs of Shesait," with their hands raised in adoration. They are followed by a Nubian lady dressed in Egyptian fashion, and by four Nubian chiefs. Immediately behind comes a chariot, shaded by an umbrella, and containing the queen of the country or tribe, which is drawn by cattle. She and the other Nubian notables wear the same kind of head-dress. By the side of the chariot walk two slaves, bearing offerings, and behind her are five slaves, wearing feathers in their caps; the first wears a linen tunic, and the four others leopard-skin tunics, with the tail of the animal attached. The rear is brought up by a negress, carrying a baby in a receptacle behind her shoulders, and leading a child, and by another woman, with a lighter skin, who is leading a child. The negress and her companions come from the country to the south of Kharṭûm. The offerings brought by this company consist of shields, chairs, head-rests, bedsteads, stools made of ebony and ivory, with cushions, bows, and gold. The gold was brought in two forms, viz., in rings and in dust.

In the second register the Blacks bring gold, , carnelian stones (*khenemet* 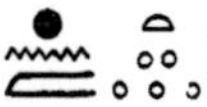), a giraffe, and oxen; and in the third they bring more gold and carnelians, large fans, skins, cattle, and balsam trees (?), or spice plants. Thus it is clear that the products of the Sûdân under the XVIIIth and XIXth Dynasties (B.C. 1600-1300) were practically what they are at the present time. Every object brought was a natural product of the country, and it is tolerably safe to assume that no manufacturing industry of any sort or kind was carried on in the Sûdân from one end to the other.

When the ancient Egyptians found that the ordinary caravans from the Sûdân did not bring a sufficient supply of gold and slaves, and that the tribes did not send the tribute of gold and slaves, which they were expected to pay, their kings sent at intervals expeditions into the country which reduced temporarily the people to obedience, and brought back to Egypt the booty which had been collected by the usual methods of burning villages and slaughtering men. From the Government point of view the results were unsatisfactory, for before the Egyptian soldiers had reached Aswân, the country behind them was in revolt, and a year or two later another expedition had to be despatched. Besides this, the bolder among the tribes on the frontier took to making raids in Upper Egypt, and it seems tolerably certain that from time immemorial the Nubians regarded the region between Aswân and Thebes as a portion of their own country. The first Egyptian kings who set to work seriously to convince the natives that the region in question belonged to Egypt were those of the XIth and XIIth Dynasties, about B.C. 2500. From Aswân they advanced step by step to Behen, or Wâdî Ḥalfa, and in the course of the following two hundred years they reduced to subjection the tribes on both banks of the river so far as the head of the Third Cataract. From the Mentiu, or "cattle-men," the ancestors of the "Baḳḳâra" of our own time, who lived on the west bank, they obtained the products of Dâr Fûr, and Kordôfân, and from the Ȧnti, or "Hillmen," the ancestors of the Blemmyes, Begas, and Bishâri tribes, who lived on the east bank, they obtained gold in considerable quantities.

When once the Pharaohs of the XIIth Dynasty had conquered these great tribes, they began to occupy sites on the banks of the Nile and to build fortifications on them close to the river. One of the earliest of these was near the modern village of Dâbûd, 13 miles south of Philae, and here the Romans built their station Parembole. Here was found a stele (now in Berlin) of Ȧmenemḥāt II., which leaves no doubt that the Egyptians occupied the site under the XIIth Dynasty. The next place chosen for a fort was near the modern village of Kalâbsha, between 35 and 40 miles south of Philae, and a third one was near the modern village of Dakka, about 30 miles further up the river. There was also a settlement near Korosko, 110 miles from Philae, and there is abundant proof that there were two or more at Wâdî Ḥalfa. It is probable that there were two or more stations on the river between Korosko and Wâdî Ḥalfa under the XIIth Dynasty, for it is unlikely that the garrison at the latter place would be left without the support of troops stationed nearer than Korosko. We may note that between Philae and Dakka, a distance of 63 miles, there were at least two stations, one near Dâbûd, and the other near Kalâbsha. From the nature of the Nile Valley between Philae and Dakka we see that there can never have been any large number of people living there, and this being so, the question naturally arises, "Why did the kings of the XIIth Dynasty build stations at Dâbûd and Kalâbsha?" There were two reasons: 1. They had to feed a garrison at Dakka, and later another at Ḥalfa, and places where the boats carrying the supplies could tie up for the night without being plundered were absolutely necessary. 2. The boats which carried food up the river would bring down Sûdân products, and strong, secure halting-places were as necessary when they came down the river as when they went up. These stations were, at first, probably of a purely military character, but so soon as they were securely established a small temple was built in each to the local god or gods. At these places the boats tied up for the night, and the guard turned out, and took steps to protect their loads until the time when their crews resumed their journey; and Government caravans travelling from south to north, or from north to south, could turn in and halt there for the night, or in times when the roads were unsafe.

Under the XIIth Dynasty Dakka was a station of great importance, and consisted of two portions, one on each side of the river. The reason of this is not far to seek. Just above the modern village of Ḳubbân is the entrance to a very old road which is used to this day, and which leads to the gold mines in the hilly region called "Wâdî al-'Ulâḳî" (or 'Ullâḳî). According to the Arab geographer Al-Idrîsî,[1] this region is situated in the country of the Begas, which is a large and sterile plain, without villages and without cultivation. The Wâdî, or Valley, itself has from time immemorial been inhabited by men who were occupied in the gold trade, and it has always been a sort of large village. Water was obtained from wells. The famous gold mines are situated in a plain, which is covered by vast masses of shifting sand. According to the same authority, the Arabs used to come by night, and each man would choose the place on which he intended to work. On the following day they came with camels and carried off a load of

[1] Ed. Dozy and de Goeje, Leyden, 1866, p. 31, text, p. 26.

sand to a well and washed it in wooden buckets, and when they had secured the gold from it, they poured quicksilver on it, and then melted the mixture.[1] From the Arabs the merchants bought the gold thus obtained and carried it into foreign countries. The natives of the place have no other occupation except this search for gold. The object of the Pharaohs of the XIIth Dynasty in invading Nubia is quite clear—they wished to possess themselves of the gold mines of 'Ulâkî, and having conquered the tribes who held them, they forced them to produce a regular supply, which was sent down the river under the protection of the soldiers stationed at the various points on the river already mentioned.

In the earliest times the natives of Wâdî 'Ulâkî contented themselves with washing gold out of the sand, but afterwards they found it necessary to dig into the veins of quartz which fill the rocks round about the valley, and then the labour of getting gold was very great. Now, deposits of quartz are found in many places in the Sûdân, and the richest veins are in the neighbourhood of the Second Cataract. As we should expect, the Egyptians became aware of this fact at a very early period, and the kings of the XIIth Dynasty took steps to occupy the country by establishing forts and garrisons, and to have the quartz crushed and the gold extracted under a Government monopoly. The first king to put this on a sure footing was Usertsen III., who built fortified outposts at Semna and Kumma, about forty miles south of Wâdî Ḥalfa, right in the heart of the district containing the richest quartz veins. The country round about could never have produced sufficient to feed the garrisons here and at the stations between this place and Aswân, and we may be sure that he provided for the safe transport of the grain, &c., coming up the river, and of the gold, slaves, &c., going down, by building numerous forts. The conquest of this part of Nubia was carried out at this time from a purely commercial point of view and for gain, and though the Pharaohs spoke of "enlarging the boundaries" of their kingdoms in their texts, their real object in invading the Sûdân was the getting of gold and slaves.

[1] Burckhardt (*Travels*, p. 15) thought the natives mistook micaceous sand for gold; but it is clear that his friends did not go far enough to reach the mines which undoubtedly exist there.

GOLD TRADE OF THE SUDAN

Under the kings of the XVIIIth Dynasty the whole of the quartz-producing districts near the Nile up to the Fourth Cataract passed into the hands of the Egyptians. Step by step, these kings advanced south, establishing stations and towns wherever they were needed, and, before the downfall of the dynasty, the viceroys of the Sûdân were absolute masters of all the trade routes, and of the river traffic, which they worked on behalf of the Pharaohs. Wherever there was a trade centre of importance a temple was built, and the size and grandeur of the building depended upon the amount of the offerings which the priesthood could extort from the worshippers who passed that way. In every station on the Nile under the XVIIIth Dynasty there was a small temple, which served not only as a place of worship, but as a storehouse for the valuable merchandise, which was placed directly under the care of the god to whom the building was dedicated. If we consider for a moment the position of the stations on the Nile in the quartz-bearing region between the head of the Second and that of the First Cataract, i.e., a distance of about 335 miles, we see that nearly all of them are on the west bank, i.e., that the garrisons had the river between them and the ferocious tribes of the Eastern Desert. And when all the stations whereat remains of temples and forts of the XIIth, XVIIIth, and XIXth Dynasties are enumerated, we see that between the limits mentioned above there were no less than twenty-one places where travellers by river or land would find Egyptian officials to help them. Beginning from the south, these stations were at Ṣulb, Dôsha, Saddênga and Suwârda, the Island of Sâî, 'Amâra, Semna, and Kumma, Gazîrat al-Malik, a site on the west bank of the Nile near Sarras, Ma'tûḳa, Wâdî Ḥalfa, Adda, Ibrîm and Derr, 'Amâda, Ṣabû'a, Miḥarraḳa, Korti, Dakka, Garf Ḥusên, Kalâbsha, Ḳartassi, and Dâbûd. It will be seen that whilst some stations were only ten miles from each other, others were as much as thirty.

It is probable that many other stations existed on the river between B.C. 1700 and 1300, but hitherto no remains of them have been found. Now, the quartz-bearing district referred to above was never famous for the production of slaves, for the simple reason that the strips of cultivable land on the river banks could not grow enough grain, &c., to support a considerable population, and we are therefore driven to conclude that the Pharaohs maintained this great chain of forts and temples on the Nile in connection with their gold monopoly. They did not put themselves to the trouble and expense of erecting such buildings for the sake of spreading abroad the blessing of the Egyptian civilization or religion in the Sûdân, but only because it enabled them to keep a firmer hold on their monopoly, and because it paid them handsomely to do so. Under the XVIIIth Dynasty the chain of forts and temples between Aswân and the foot of the Fourth Cataract, i.e., Napata or Merawi, was in a most effective state, and as Åmen-ḥetep II. made his way so far to the south as Wad Bâ Nagaa, it is pretty certain that the Pharaohs at that time were receiving gold from the country round about Sennaar and Fâzôglî.

Not content with drawing large quantities of gold from the Sûdân for their own use, the kings of Egypt, under the XVIIIth Dynasty, sent large quantities into Western Asia. Thus Kadashman-Bêl, king of Babylonia, begs Åmen-ḥetep III. to send him the gold about which he wrote, and says that if it comes within the season of harvest he will give him his daughter to wife.[1] Another king, Burraburiyash, asks Åmen-ḥetep IV. indignantly, "Why did you send me two manas of gold only?"[2] And he adds: "Send me much gold." Assur-Uballiṭ, a king of Assyria, writing to Amen-ḥetep IV., says, "In your land gold is "[as] dust. Gather it together . . . I am building a new house "and I would complete it, therefore send me the gold which I "require. When Assur-Nadin-Aḥi, my father, sent to Egypt, "twenty talents of gold were sent to him; and when the king of "Ḥanigalbat sent to your father, he sent back to him twenty "talents of gold also. And you should send me twenty talents of "gold."[3] Tushratta, king of Mitani, also writes[4] to Åmen-ḥetep III., saying, "You sent my father very much gold . . . let "my brother send me a very large quantity of gold, which cannot "be measured, and let him send more gold to me than he did to "my father. For in my brother's land gold is as common as

[1] Tell Al-'Amarna Tablet, Berlin, No. 3.
[2] *Ibid.*, London, No. 2.
[3] *Ibid.*, London, No. 9.
[4] *Ibid.*, No. 8.

"dust. And though gold is now very plentiful in my brother's "land, I pray that the gods may so ordain that it may become "ten times more plentiful even than it is now." Under the rule of the kings of the XIXth Dynasty it seems that the gold mines in the neighbourhood of the Second, Third, and Fourth Cataracts became unprofitable; at all events, we hear very little about them after the reign of Rameses II.

It is probable that Rameses I and his immediate successors found it impossible to maintain the forts and temples beyond Ḥalfa in an effective condition, and that they turned their attention to developing the mines in Wâdî 'Ulâḳî, a place which was much nearer Egypt, and the route to which gave far less trouble to defend. Moreover, the influence of Egypt over the Eastern Desert was greater than in former times, and the tribes which lived there brought their gold both to Ombos, the "gold city,"[1] the terminus on the Nile of one important desert route, and to Coptos, the termination of another. At this period of its history Egypt was able to absorb all the gold which could be brought into it, for the decoration of the funeral furniture, and ornaments of the dead, must have required as much of this metal as the jewellery and ornaments of the living.

The first king of the XIXth Dynasty who took steps to increase the import of gold into Egypt was Seti I., about B.C. 1370. According to an inscription published by Lepsius,[2] Seti I. was thinking about the countries from which the gold was brought, and the wish came into his mind to go and see the mines. He departed on his way up the river, and in due course set out on the desert road which leaves the Nile on the east bank near Edfû, and leads to the famous Emerald Mines of Gebel Zâbara near the Red Sea. As the king went along the road he thought about the lack of water on it, and wondered how the ordinary folk quenched their thirst. He quickly realized how they must suffer, and that unless some means for supplying water to travellers were found, caravans could not travel on that road, and it would be impossible

[1] In Egyptian NUBT, . The name is probably connected with *nub*, the word for gold.

[2] *Denkmäler*, iii. 40*b*.

to work the mines. Thereupon Seti resolved to dig a well, and with the help of his god he found a suitable place for digging one; he then collected workmen, who dug the well, and the water sprang up and filled it, and ran over the sides in such quantities that it seemed as if the two great sources of the Nile of the South and the Nile of the North had been tapped. After this the king established a station near the well, and built a temple. Rā was worshipped[1] in the sanctuary, Ptaḥ and Osiris in the hall, and Horus, Isis, and Seti were associated with the leading gods of the place. When this temple was finished and fittingly decorated, Seti came and worshipped in it. This temple lies on the old road to the Red Sea, at a distance of about forty miles from the Nile, and is known as the Temple of Radasîyah. This road was used in the reign of Åmen-ḥetep III., for Merimes, Prince of Kash, has left his name on the rock near the temple.

From another inscription[2] we learn that Seti I. dug a well on the old road leading from Ḳubbân on the Nile to the Wâdî 'Ulâḳî, at a place where several other kings had tried to find water, and that he, like them, was unsuccessful. These inscriptions show that Seti I. did his best to increase the import of gold by making communication easier between the Nile and the mines in the Eastern Desert. The activity of his son Rameses II. in this matter was not less than his own, for this king dug a well on the road which led to the mines in the Wâdî 'Ulâḳî, and he and his engineers were rewarded with the discovery of a splendid flow of water. From the time of Rameses II. onwards the kings of Egypt, whether Egyptian, Nubian, Persian, Macedonian, Roman, or Arabian, kept the mines working in the Wâdî 'Ulâḳî, and derived revenue from them. They protected the roads leading to them, and maintained stations on the Nile so far as Dakka for this purpose. It seems that the quartz reefs in the Nile Valley between Ḥalfa and the Third Cataract were worked out at a comparatively early period, i.e., during the XVIIIth or XIXth Dynasty, or at least that the working of them had become unprofitable.

Reference has been made above to the systematic attempt made

[1] See Chabas, *Inscriptions des Mines d'Or*, p. 6.

[2] See Prisse d'Avennes, *Monuments Egyptiens*, Paris, 1847, pl. xxi.

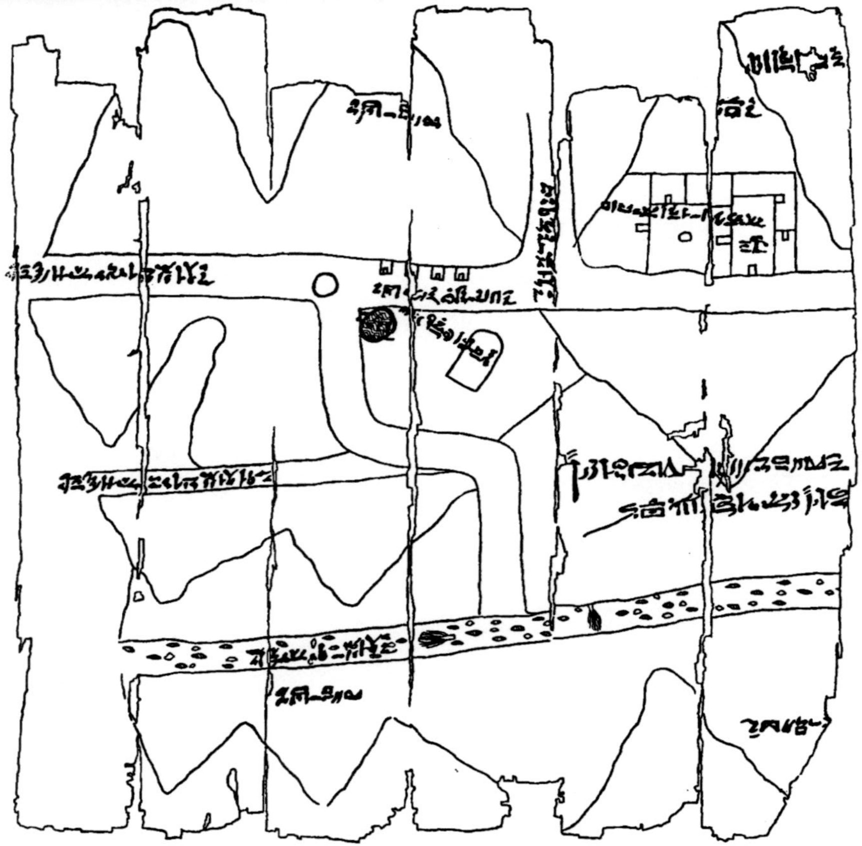

PLAN OF A GROUP OF GOLD MINES IN THE EASTERN SUDAN WHICH WERE WORKED IN THE REIGN OF SETI I., B.C. 1370.

[From a papyrus at Turin. Lepsius, *Auswahl*, Bl. xxii.

by Seti I. to develop the gold mines of the Eastern Desert, and a striking proof of this fact is afforded by the plan of certain gold mines on a papyrus which is preserved in the Museum of Turin.[1] The plan which is here reproduced shows us a portion of the gold-bearing country, with the mountains , on each side, and a valley with two roads and a cross path running between them. This is made certain by the legends 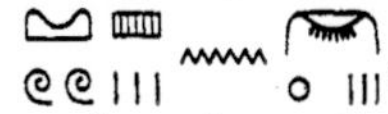, "mountains of gold," written four times on the plan. In the top right-hand corner, close to the road, is the "sanctuary of Amen; the holy mountain,"[2] wherein probably the gold was stored; and between the mountain on which it stands, and the next is a path leading to some locality, the name of which is not quite clear. Beyond the entrance to this path are four houses, which were set apart for the men who were overseers in the mines. Beyond these is a well, and the hieratic text further on says that the road leads to the sea. On the right-hand side of the winding path is another well or tank, filled with water, and round about it is a patch painted brown on the plan to represent the earth which is irrigated by the well. In the middle of the patch is a stele 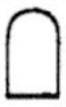, which is described as the "tablet of king Men-Maāt-Rā,"[3] i.e., of Seti I.; this seems to indicate that the well was dug by Seti I., who set up a stele to commemorate the fact. Further to the right are two lines of hieratic text, which were intended to form the title of the plan, for they read, "The mountains whereout they dig "the gold; they are depicted in red colour." The meaning of these lines was made out in 1852 by Dr. Birch, who had only Lepsius's reproduction of the plan in black and white to work from, and did not know that in the original the mountains were coloured red.[4] The road which leaves the middle of the winding path also "leads to the sea," and the lowest road of all is the main road

[1] First published by Lepsius, *Auswahl*, Bl. xxii., and later, in colours, by Chabas, *Les Mines d'Or*, Paris, 1862. See also Birch, *On a Historical Tablet of Rameses II.*, in *Archaeologia*, vol. xxxiv., pp. 357-391.

[2] 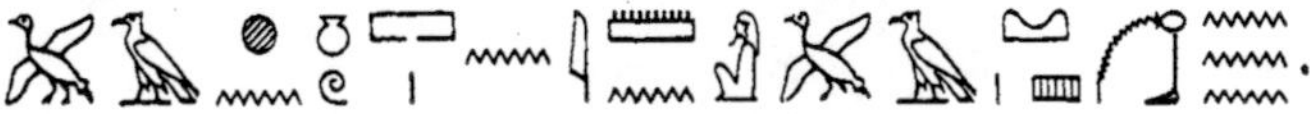

[3] 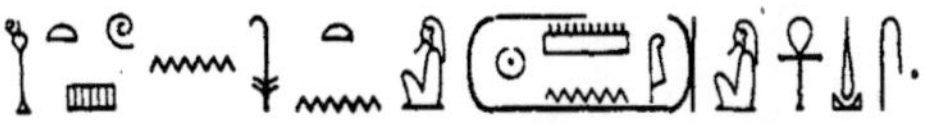

[4] A coloured plan was published by Chabas in 1862.

through the valley. On the original plan this last[1] is bestrewn with representations of coloured objects, which Birch and Chabas both believed to be sea-shells. There is, unfortunately, nothing on the plan which will help us to identify the site depicted, but there is little doubt that the gold mines were in the Eastern Desert between the Nile and the Red Sea, and they may well be some of those which were situated in the Wâdî 'Ulâḳî.

The Museum of Turin also contains the remains of a plan of the gold mines of the "mountain of Bekhani," , and the king's name mentioned in the fragmentary lines of text is Rameses II. The exact site of Bekhani is unknown, but it was probably situated in one of the valleys wherein quartz veins were found, to the south-east of the city of Coptos on the Nile. A facsimile of the fragments of this plan will be found at the end of Lieblein's "Deux Papyrus Hiératiques du Musée de Turin," Christiania, 1868.

The common Egyptian word for gold is *nub* , or , or , and the Egyptians distinguished between "gold of the mountain,"[2] and "gold of the river;"[3] the ore was called "gold on its mountain."[4] There was a difference too between mere "gold," , and "good gold," , and between "gold of the mountain," and "good gold of its mountain,"[5] there was also "gold of twice," and "gold of thrice,"[6] i.e., gold refined twice or thrice, or perhaps gold of one-third or two-thirds alloy; and there was a quality called "gold of the scale."[7] Another kind of

[1] It is called "The road of Thipamet," 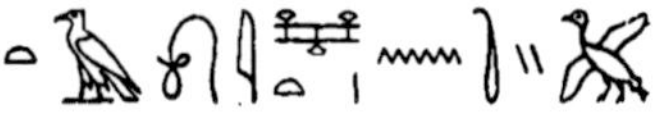

[2] 

[3] 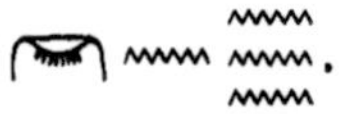

[4] 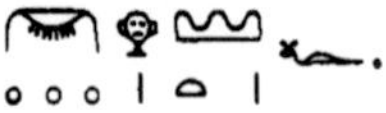

[5] 

[6] 

[7] 

gold was called *Katemet*, which has been compared with the Hebrew word for "fine gold," *kethem*, in Prov. xxv. 12, Job xxxi. 24, &c. A large quantity of gold came from Nubia, and this is called the "gold of Kash," and large quantities came from the Eastern Desert to the cities of Coptos, Edfû, and Ombos. Lastly, one kind of gold was called "white (or pale) gold," , and another "green gold," , as opposed to the kind which the Abyssinians call "red gold." From the monuments we see that gold was brought to Egypt in small nuggets and in dust, or melted into flat cakes, or bars (ingots), or bricks, or rings. The gold dust which came from the regions of Sennaar and Fâzôglî was tied up in bags (*ārfu*), and the metal in its other forms was often brought in boxes.[1] The principal gold weights were the *ṭeben*, , the *qet*, , = $\frac{1}{10}$th of a *ṭeben*, and the *peḳ*, , = $\frac{1}{128}$th of a *ṭeben*; Lepsius thought these weights = 90·959, 9·0959, and 0·7106 grammes respectively.

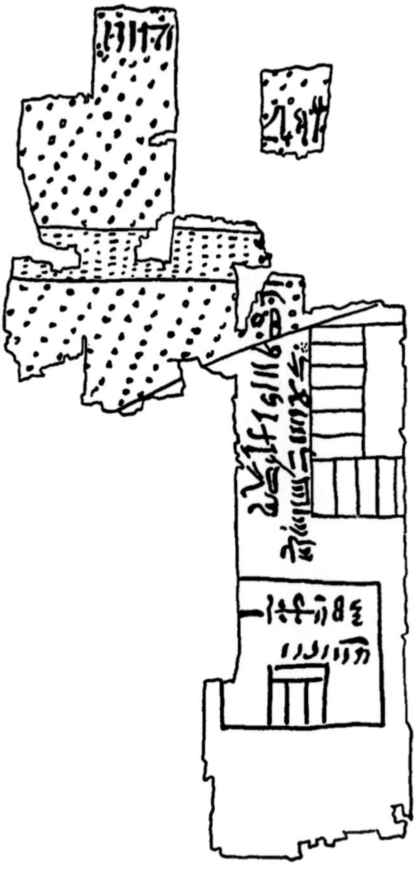

FRAGMENT OF A PLAN OF A GROUP OF GOLD MINES WHICH WERE WORKED IN THE REIGN OF RAMESES II. (B.C. 1330).

[From Lepsius, *Auswahl*, Pl. XXII.

The metal formed by the natural mixture of gold with silver was indicated by the sign ; this, because the sceptre

[1] See Lepsius, *Die Metalle*, p. 43.

has the value *tchām*.[1] Dr. Birch read the sign "*tchām*" and translated "pure gold"; [2] a better rendering is, however, "electrum."[3] This metal was brought into Egypt in bags, and also in the form of rings, and from the largeness of the quantities of it which are mentioned, it is clear that, as Lepsius says, it cannot have been gold of a very fine or pure quality. It was, however, a valuable substance, for it is mentioned in connection with gold, lapis-lazuli, and turquoise, and that it was a natural product is proved by the words "*tchām* of the mountains, and gold on its mountain" [4] (i.e., gold ore). The colour of *tchām* was much admired, and in the late period gold and silver were mixed together artificially, and the "electrum" of the classical writers was thus produced.

The mining methods of the ancient Egyptians were not very elaborate, and they appear to have been somewhat wasteful in character. The sites where the veins of quartz were thickest and most easily accessible were worked out first, but as soon as a vein ran deep, or a hard stone obstruction was met with, that section was abandoned. Where the veins were close to the surface the greatest trouble was taken to dig out every bit of quartz, as an examination of a mining site such as that near Semna on the Second Cataract will show. Here alternate layers of quartz and some hard stone are found, and the country for miles around is covered with flat pieces of dark stone which were broken in getting out the quartz. Whether the old mines would pay in the re-working is a matter which only mining experts can decide, but it is impossible not to think that with modern tools and modern methods much gold might be obtained from the quartz veins which have only been partly worked, and from others which were overlooked by the ancients. Muḥammad ʻAlî sent a party of men to make experiments with a view of reopening the mines in the Wâdî ʻUlâḳî, and the conclusion he arrived at was that the gold

[1] See Birch in Bunsen, *Egypt's Place*, vol. i., p. 574, No. 145; and vol. v., p. 519.

[2] Lepsius, *op. cit.*, p. 43.

[3] According to Pliny (xxxiii. 23) a mass of gold of which one-fifth was silver was called "electrum."

[4] 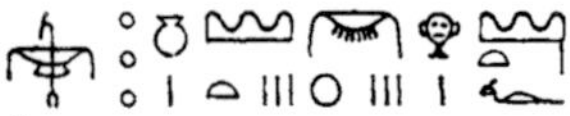, Lepsius, *op. cit.*, p. 46; Dümichen, *Hist. Insch.*, 31.

obtained by them only barely covered the expense of mining, and he therefore gave up the scheme. In this case the conclusion really depended on the honesty of his agents.

A great proportion of the gold and silver which entered Egypt annually between B.C. 1500 and 1200 must have come from the Eastern Desert, and for nearly 3,000 years gold must have formed the principal article of commerce borne by the caravans from the country now called the "Southern Atbai." We have, unfortunately, no information in the hieroglyphic inscriptions which enables us to calculate the exact amount or value of the gold and silver which were brought into Egypt annually, but that it was very great is evident from a statement made by Diodorus Siculus. In his first Book (chap. 48 ff.) this writer gives a description of the tomb of the king whom he calls "Osymandyas," who is really Rameses II.[1] After enumerating the reliefs which are to be seen on the various walls, he says that in one part is the figure of the king, painted in colours, who is engaged in offering to a god the gold and silver which he drew annually from the gold and silver mines of Egypt, and above it was an inscription stating the amount thereof. Diodorus, or Hekataeus, calculated what this sum amounted to in the money of his time, and says that it was equal to thirty-two millions of minas;[2] this sum in round figures is equal to about £80,000,000 sterling.[3] It is possible that a small proportion of the gold which was paid into the Egyptian treasury in the time of Rameses II. came from Northern Syria, but not very likely, seeing that this king's dominions stopped at the Nahr al-Kalb, or Dog River. The bulk of the gold and silver paid to Rameses II. came from the Eastern Desert and the districts near Sennaar and Beni Shanḳûl, and, though the estimate of its value given above may be excessive, it is quite clear from the figures quoted by Diodorus that the value of the precious metals which came into Egypt must have been very great indeed.

[1] Osymandyas = Usr-Maāt-Rā, , the first portion of the prenomen of Rameses II.

[2] ὑπογεγράφθαι δὲ καὶ τὸ πλῆθος, ὃ συγκεφαλαιούμενον εἰς ἀργυρίου λόγον εἶναι μνῶν τρισχιλίας καὶ διακοσίας μυριάδας. Ed. Didot, p. 41.

[3] The *mina* = 75 drachmae at 8*d*., or £2 10*s*. If the *mina* be calculated to be worth 100 drachmae, the total will be rather more than one-third higher.

About the working of the gold mines by the ancient Egyptians we obtain some valuable information from Agatharcides, who was born at Cnidus, probably at the beginning of the second century B.C. He wrote a work in five books on the Erythraean Sea about B.C. 120, and in the fifth he describes the manners and customs of the principal peoples who lived in the countries bordering on the Red Sea. From this Diodorus (iii. 12 ff.) transcribed the account of the working of the gold mines near the Red Sea, which may be summarized thus:—

To the south of Egypt, and on the borders of Arabia and Ethiopia, there is a place full of rich gold mines, whence with great expense, and toil, and difficulty, the gold is dug. The substance from which the metal is taken is a black stone seamed with white veins, and with shining patches. Those who are the overseers of the works at the mines employ a very large number of workmen, who are either condemned criminals, or prisoners of war, or men who, having been unjustly accused and cast into prison, have been banished to the mines, or men against whom the king had a spite. Frequently the last two classes are sent to the mines with all the members of their family, and their kindred, and these also are obliged to labour for the king's benefit. These wretched people work in fetters by day and by night, and chance of escape is impossible, for the guards and soldiers who are set over them keep strict watch, and as these speak only foreign tongues, it is impossible for them to be corrupted by the wretched miners either by bribes or entreaties.

The rock which contains the gold is very hard and solid, and they make it soft by lighting fires under it, after which they can break it with their hands. As soon as the stone is sufficiently softened, and is likely to break under the influence of a moderate effort, thousands of the wretched miners break it into pieces with the iron tools which are used in the working of stones. At their head is the skilled "ganger," who knows where to look for the veins of gold, and he shows the men where to dig. The most powerful among the wretched men who are condemned to work in the mines are told off to break the rock with iron picks, which they wield unskilfully, and with infinite labour. The galleries of the mines wherein this class of men work are not straight, but they follow the direction of the vein of quartz; and since in such crooked passages they have to work in the dark, they carry lamps attached to their foreheads. They change their position according to the nature of the rock and the position of the veins of metal, and dig down the rock above them in fragments. Thus they work incessantly under the eyes of a stern watcher, who meanwhile showers blows upon them.

As the fragments of quartz fall on the ground young children creep into the subterranean galleries, and collect them and carry them out to the entrances to the galleries. From these places men who are not more than thirty years of age take each a certain quantity of these fragments, and placing them in stone mortars they pound them with iron pestles until the ore is in pieces the size of a chick-pea (*ὄροβος*). The ore is then taken by women and old men and put in a row of mills, each of which is worked by two or three people, wherein the ore is ground as fine as powder. As the poor wretches who do this work are not allowed to pay any attention to the care of their bodies, and they wear no clothing, not even a rag to cover their nakedness, every one who looks upon their pitiable plight must be filled with commiseration for them. No respite is given to the sick, or the maimed, or the halt, and neither the weakness of old age, nor women's infirmities are accepted as a reason for rest or intermission of labour. All alike are forced to work, and any temporary relaxation of work is visited with an increased number of blows; finally many of them drop down dead through exhaustion. By reason of these sufferings, and being without hope in the future, these unfortunate beings await death with joy, for it is far preferable to life.

In the next stage the miners collect the ore which has been ground, and spread it out on sloping boards, over which they pour a stream of water, which carries away the earthy matters, leaving the gold lying on the boards. They repeat the washing process several times, and at length all the useless matter is eliminated, and the gold dust becomes pure and bright. Then other workmen take a measured quantity of the dust, and pour it into an earthenware vessel, and having added certain quantities of lead, salt, tin, and bran, they place on the vessel a cover which fits it tightly, and then set it in a furnace fire for five days and five nights continuously. At the end of this time they remove the vessel from the fire and set it aside to cool, and when they take off the cover they find nothing but pure gold inside it, for all the dross has disappeared. The gold, of course, weighs less than the powder which was put into the vessel to be smelted.

Thus it is clear that the processes of gold mining were difficult, and that the digging out of the ore involved great trouble. Finally Agatharcides tells us that the mines which he has been describing were discovered in very early times, and that they were worked by the most ancient kings.

CHAPTER XVIII.

THE MODERN SÛDÂN.

In the present and following chapters an attempt is made to describe briefly the principal facts connected with the country and people of the Sûdân as they exist in our time, so that the reader may be able to compare the modern conditions of the "Land of the Blacks" with the ancient records of its history. A description of this kind would naturally deal with the country itself and its provinces, first of all, but as the Nile and its tributaries form the most important features of the Sûdân, and the trade, and commerce of the country, and of every living thing in it, depend upon them for their existence, the first section of this chapter is devoted to the mighty river, which has for thousands of years formed one of the chief objects of veneration of the dwellers on its banks from the Central African Lakes to the sea.

I. The Nile.

The ancient Egyptians called the Nile-god Ḥep,[1] or Ḥāp,[2] and the earliest representations of him depict him in the form of a man, with female attributes; on his head he wears a cluster of lotus flowers, and he bears before him a table whereon are vases of water, flowers, &c. He dwelt in celestial regions, and poured out from his vases the life-giving waters, which appeared on earth from out of the two caverns, or Qerti, near the Island of Elephantine. The contents of one vase formed the Nile from Aswân northwards, and those of the other the Nile from Aswân southwards. That the Nile flowed into the sea was well known, but the Egyptians cannot have known, at all events with any certainty, where its sources were situated, though one would

1 

2 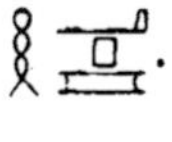

think that the caravan men from Dâr Fûr and Kordôfân would bring down from the natives of those countries accounts of the existence of great lakes in Central Africa. The famous hymn to the Nile, after enumerating the benefits which the god gives to gods and men, states that his "secret place cannot be explored, "and the place where he is is unknown";[1] elsewhere it is said that the Nile-god Ḥāp is One, that he created himself, and that his origin is unknown.[2] Whether the true sources of the Nile were known by the Egyptians, or guessed at by them, there is no evidence to show, but it is certain that the priests of Elephantine and Philae found it to their interest to declare that the sources of the Nile were at Philae, and according to the legend on the rock on the Island of Sâḥal in the First Cataract, it was to Elephantine that Tcheser, a king of the IIIrd Dynasty, sent when he wished to find out why the Nile had not risen for seven years to a proper height during the inundation.[3]

During the later period of Egyptian history Silsila was regarded as the frontier town between Egypt and Nubia, and an idea seems to have been prevalent that the home of the Nile-god was here; hence we find Rameses II. setting up an inscription on Gebel Silsila recording the establishment of two festivals in honour of the Nile-god. These were observed in June and August, and, as Dr. Stern pointed out, their modern Arab equivalents are the "Night of the Drop,"[4] which is observed on June 17th, and the "Cutting of the Dam," about the middle of August. The first of these festivals was celebrated in connection with the beginning of the rise of the Nile, and the Egyptians thought this was caused by the tears which Isis shed annually in heaven in commemoration of her first great lamentation over the dead body of her husband Osiris. Her tears were supposed to possess the power of increasing

[1] 

[2] , Stern, *Aeg. Zeit.*, 1873, p. 130.

[3] *Aeg. Zeitschrift*, 1873, p. 135.

[4] Lêlat al-Nuḳṭa. These festivals are well described by Lane, *Modern Egyptians*, vol. ii., p. 224 ff.

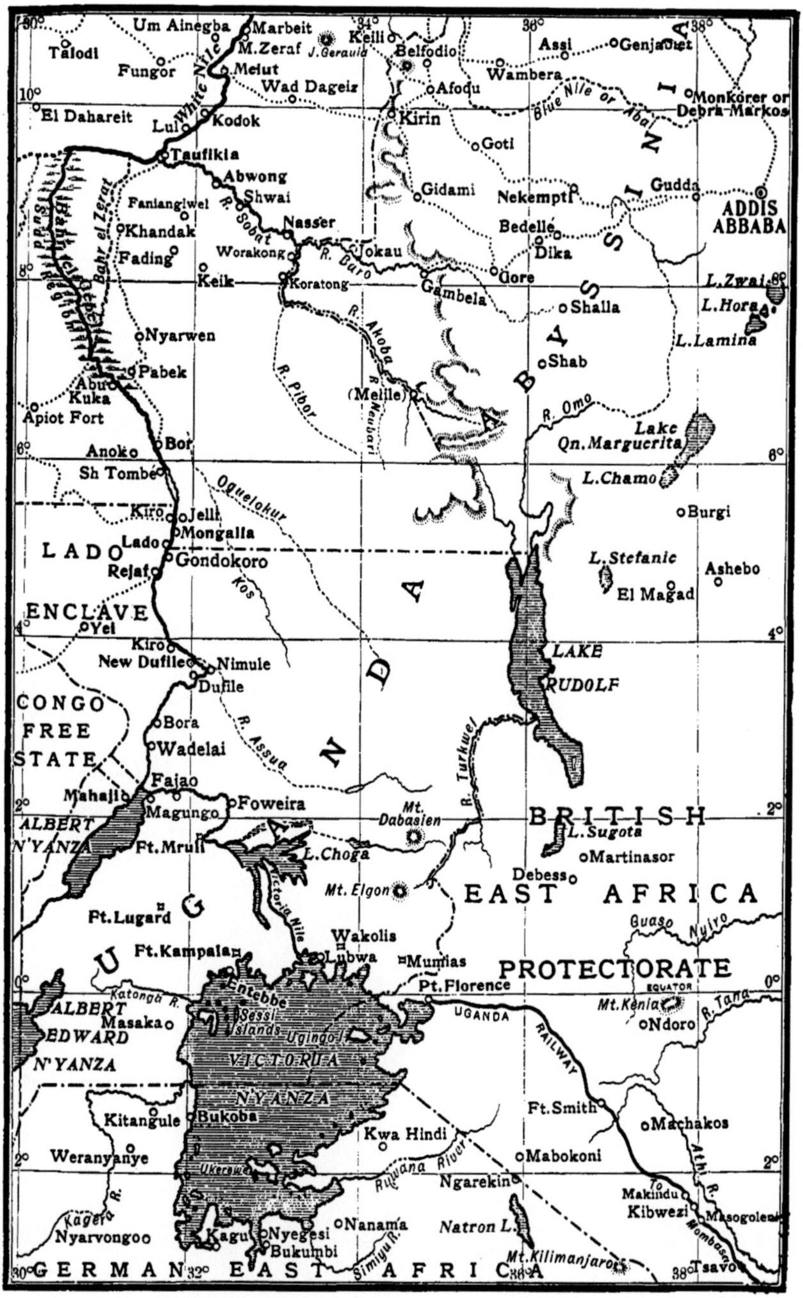

THE SOUTHERN SÛDÂN AND THE DISTRICT OF THE GREAT LAKES.

the waters of the river, and were the cause of the Nile-flood. According to another view the Nile and its flood proceeded from the body of Osiris, and Isis represented the land of Egypt which was made fertile thereby. The second festival was held when the Nile flood had reached its greatest height. In Egypt these festivals probably date from the time when the country became suitable for agricultural operations, but whether equivalents of these festivals existed in the Sûdân cannot be said, for nothing is known about the religious views of its people at this time. There is no evidence to show that the Egyptians knew the cause of the inundation, but some of the Sûdânî folk must have known that the flooding of the rivers in their country was due to heavy rainfall in the mountains.

About the origin of the name "Nile" there is diversity of opinion. According to some it is derived from the Greek *Νεῖλος*, but others say it comes from the Semitic word which occurs in Hebrew under the form *nakhal* נַחַל.

The mystery which has been diligently cultivated for centuries about the course of the Nile and its sources is more imaginary than real, and it is difficult not to think that if the ancients had really felt interested in the matter these things would have been described over and over again by ancient writers. Aristotle,[1] who wrote in the second half of the fourth century B.C., was well aware that floods were caused in Ethiopia and Arabia by summer rains which poured down in torrents, and he knew of the existence of the Pygmies, who fought with cranes, or, as Sir Harry Johnston suggests, with ostriches. Many of his statements are based on the authority of Hekataeus, who wrote on Egypt and visited the country B.C. 500. Eratosthenes (B.C. 276—196), the eminent geographer, who was appointed keeper of the Alexandrian Library by Ptolemy Euergetes, was well acquainted with the course of the Nile, and possessed a good deal of information about the country through which it flowed. He seems to have known of two great rivers, each of which flowed from a lake in Central

[1] Θεομὸν δὲ γίνεται ταχὺ τὸ συνιστάμενον ὕδωρ ἔν τε ταῖς χώραις καὶ ταῖς ὥραις ταῖς ἀλεειναῖς. Γίνεται δὲ καὶ περὶ τὴν Ἀραβίαν καὶ τὴν Αἰθιοπίαν τοῦ θέρους τὰ ὕδατα, καὶ οὐ τοῦ χειμῶνος, καὶ ταῦτα ῥαγδαῖα, καὶ τῆς αὐτῆς ἡμέρας πολλάκις, διὰ την αὐτὴν αἰτίαν. *Meteorologicorum*, I., viii. 19.

Africa, and the influence of the summer rains on one of them is described by him.[1] Aristocreon (Pliny, *Hist. Vat.*, v. 9), Caecilius Bion (Pliny, *Hist. Nat.*, xxviii. 57), Dalion (Pliny, *Hist. Nat.*, vi. 35), and Simonides are mentioned in such a way as to suggest that they were authorities on the geography of north-east Africa, and as the last named is said to have lived five years at Meroë he must have heard much about the country to the south and east of Kharṭûm.

Hipparchus, who flourished late in the second century before Christ, sketched the course of the Nile to the south, and made its sources to be three lakes.

Among the earliest travellers into the country south of Kharṭûm were the two centurions, who about A.D. 65 were sent by the Emperor Nero to report on the Sûdân. It is perfectly clear from the statements which they made to Seneca (see above, p. 172) that they reached the region of the Sadd, and if they could have forced their way through the obstruction, they would undoubtedly have reached the lakes. They were, of course, guided by local shêkhs who, by taking them up the White Nile, showed that they themselves understood the relation of the two great lakes to the Nile, and we may conclude that in the first century A.D. all the main facts about the course of the Nile and its lakes were known.

Ptolemy, the geographer, about A.D. 150 collected all the available information about the Nile from early travellers, and succeeded in forming a correct opinion as to the general course of the Nile. He made the Nile to flow out of three lakes, and placed its sources in the Mountains of the Moon, and if the identification of these mountains with the Ruwenzori range be correct, it is clear that Ptolemy was substantially right as to his facts. He made a mistake, however, in placing the sources of the Nile to the south of the Equator, but this may be due to the monastic copyists of his maps, and in such a matter no one would expect accuracy from them, especially as none of the early geographers, not even Ptolemy, had correct views about the extent and shape of Africa.

All the Muḥammadan geographers state that the springs of the

[1] Murray, *Historical Account of Discoveries and Travels in Africa*, London, 1818.

VIEW OF GONDOKORO IN 1905.

[From a photograph by Miss Hilda Burrows.

Nile are in the Mountains of the Moon; they are ten in number, and five flow into one lake, and five into another. From each lake two streams flow, and when all four have united the Nile is formed. The principal lake was called the "Lake of Likuri," Likuri being the name of a people who have been identified with the "Wakûri," who still live on Lake Victoria. These geographers knew of the existence of the mountains of snow, but they identified them with Gebel Kâf, which surrounded the world. The length of the Nile was stated to be 3,748 or 3,000 parassangs. Shams ad-Dîn,[1] who was born in the second half of the thirteenth century, says that the Nile springs flow from the Mountains of the Moon into two great lakes, which are four days' journey from each other, the eastern being called Kûkû, or Tamîm as-Sûdânî, and the western Damâdim, or Galgûr Hagamî. These lakes, he says, are in lat. 7° south, and from them flow four rivers which run from the Equator to lat. 7° north, into the great lake which is called in Arabic "Gami'a," i.e., the "gatherer together," and in the native language "Kûri" (or, Wakûri, the name of a tribe).

By the end of the seventeenth century a considerable amount of definite information about Lake Ṣânâ, and the Blue Nile and its course had been collected, chiefly through the observations of the Jesuits, Father Francisco Alvarez, Father Pedro Paez, and Father Jeronino Lobo, who visited Abyssinia in 1525, 1615, and 1622, and the sources of the Blue Nile in the Sakala Mountains of Gojam had actually been visited by Paez. The next European to see the sources of the Blue Nile was James Bruce of Kinnaird, who was in Abyssinia between 1770 and 1773. The investigation of the White Nile began in 1839, when Thibaut sailed up the river to within seven degrees of the Equator; two years later Werne, a German, reached Gondokoro, and about this time information about a great lake at a distance of several days' journey to the south began to filter down the river through the natives to Kharṭûm. In 1848 the missionaries Rebmann and Krapf actually saw the snow-covered "Mountains of the Moon," and they published accounts of Lakes Nyassa, Tanganyika, Baringo, and Victoria. These were the real pioneers of Nile discovery in the nineteenth century, and it was chiefly owing to the interest which

[1] Ed. Mehren, St. Petersburg, 1866, p. 88.

their narratives created, that scientific expeditions were despatched to identify the Mountains of the Moon and the great lakes which Ptolemy had plotted on his maps seventeen hundred years before, but which, in spite of the stories of the natives, modern geographers were too scientific to believe.

In 1857, guided by the published information of Rebmann and Krapf, Captain Richard Burton and Captain J. H. Speke discovered Tanganyika. Soon afterwards Burton fell ill, and then Speke travelled northwards by himself, and on August 3rd, 1858, discovered the Nyanza, to which he prefixed Her Majesty's name Victoria.[1] On March 16th, 1864, Sir Samuel Baker discovered the Luta Nzigi, i.e., Albert Nyanza, the most westerly of all the then known Nile lakes. In 1874 Lieut. Watson and Lieut. Chippendall, R.E., mapped the portion of the Nile called Baḥr al-Gebel, under the direction of General Gordon. In 1876 Gessi, by Gordon's orders, circumnavigated the Albert Nyanza, and he is said to have seen the Mountains of the Moon covered with snow. He also noticed that a large river flowed into the Albert Nyanza, but did not seem to think the discovery worth following up!

Between 1879 and 1898 the Sûdân was closed to every traveller from the north on account of the rebellion of the Mahdî, but very soon after the capture of Omdurmân, and the restoration of the authority of the Government in the Egyptian Sûdân, Sir William Garstin visited that country and made a rapid survey of the Nile Basin, and collected facts with the view of establishing a system of engineering works which would prove the salvation both of the Sûdân and of Egypt. In May, 1899, his report[2] was laid before both Houses of Parliament; it was the first statement about the capabilities of the river systems of the Egyptian Sûdân which had ever been made by a competent engineer. Never before had the region been viewed by the eye of a skilled irrigation expert, and never before had the relation which each river of the Nile system bore to the other, and the part each played in producing the River of Egypt, been accurately described. In the comparatively short examination of the White Nile which Sir William was able to make at this period he discovered that the only way by which

[1] On the feud between Burton and Speke, see Johnston, *Nile Quest*, pp. 128 ff.
[2] *Egypt*, No. 5 (1899).

the supply of water to Egypt by the White Nile could be increased was to make a channel through the vast swamp which exists between Shâmbî and Lake Nô, so that the waters which flow from the Victoria Nyanza might not be lost, and the water lost annually by evaporation, which he computed to be not less than 12,175,000,000 cubic metres, or 33,356,000 cubic metres per day, might be available for irrigation purposes.

In August, 1904, Sir William Garstin published his great *Report on the Basin of the Upper Nile,*[1] which embodied the results of five years' careful study of the Nile problem, and described the country through which the Nile and its tributaries flowed with great thoroughness. This work is intended primarily for irrigation engineers, but it is written in such an easy style that it possesses all the charm and fascination of a book of travels. Often the narrative breaks into picturesque description of the natural beauty of the country, and everywhere it reveals so great an appreciation of the marvellously beautiful scenery through which the great river flows, that the reader forgets he is perusing the matter-of-fact report of an irrigation engineer until he is reminded of the fact by tables of figures relating to volume, flow, discharge, &c., with which the work is provided. It is much to be regretted that such a valuable work as the *Report* was not printed on better paper and in a smaller size, so that it might range with the works of Cailliaud, Sir Samuel Baker, Petherick, Junker, Stanley, and other great Sûdân travellers. The last word on the Upper Nile Irrigation Scheme has, however, not yet been spoken, and when Sir William Garstin speaks it, we hope that it will appear not only in a convenient form, but in one which shall be worthy of the subject and of its master.

The true source of the Nile is Victoria Nyanza, or Lake Victoria,[2] which lies between the parallels of lat. 20′ north and 3° south, and the meridians of 31° 40′ and 35° E. of Greenwich. Its elevation is 1,129 metres above sea level at Mombasa. The deepest sounding yet obtained is 73 metres, but of the depth of the lake in the middle nothing is known. The lake is 400 kilometres long and 320 broad, and its area is 68,000 square kilo-

[1] *Egypt*, No. 2 (1904).

[2] The facts are derived from Sir William Garstin's *Report*, *Egypt*, No. 2 (1904).

metres ; its one outlet is the Victoria Nile. Its affluents on the north are the Sio, Nzoia, and Lukos ; on the east, the Nyando, Tuyayo, and Sundo ; on the west, Katonga, Ruizi, and the Kagera ; in German territory on the east are the Mara Dabash, Ruwana, and Mbalasati, and on the south the Mtuma, Suiuya, Moami, Wami, Lokungati, and the Ruiga. A current sets across the lake from the Kagera River to the Ripon Falls. The most important of all these is the Kagera, which is fed by the Nyavarongo, Akanyaru, and Ruvuvu, and if any one river can be said to have a special

ANKOLI DISTRICT, MOUNTAINS FORMING EASTERN BOUNDARY OF ALBERTINE RIFT VALLEY.

[From Sir W. Garstin's *Report*, by permission of the Comptroller of H.M. Stationery Office.

influence on the rise and fall of the waters of the lake, then the Kagera is the real source of the Nile. Sir William Garstin does not consider the Kagera to be the real source, but the lake itself. The catchment basin of the lake, including the lake itself, is 240,000 square kilometres. The terminus of the Uganda Railway on the lake is Kisuma, or Port Florence. There are several large islands in the lake, e.g., Buvuma, Loliu, Busoga, Bugala, and Ukerewe, and several groups of islands, e.g., those of Buvuma, Sessé, Kome, Damba, and Korne. The level of the water of the

THE KAGERA RIVER.

[From a photograph by Major Loughlin, King's African Rifles.

Reproduced from Sir William Garstin's "Report" by permission of the Comptroller of H.M. Stationery Office.

lake has been steadily falling for some years, and this fact is attributed to the steady shrinkage of the water surface which has been observed in other Central African lakes. The total amount of rain-water which enters the lake annually is computed at 138,750,000,000 cubic metres, and the amount which runs off into the Nile at 18,133,200,000 cubic metres. The amount lost by evaporation is 75,737,000,000 cubic metres. The mean daily discharge into the Nile is 49,680,000 cubic metres.

Other contributory sources of the Nile are Lake Albert Edward

LAKE ALBERT EDWARD. HEAD OF THE SEMLIKI RIVER.

[From Sir W. Garstin's *Report*, by permission of the Comptroller of H.M. Stationery Office.

and Lake Albert. Lake Albert Edward was discovered by Stanley in 1875, and lies between the parallels of lat. 0° 8′ and 0° 40′ south, and the meridians of 29° 32′ and 30° 6′ east. At the north-east corner it is connected by a long, narrow channel with the small lake called Ruisamba, or Dueru, though Lake Albert Edward is itself called Dueru by the Wanyoro. The area of the two lakes is 2,100 square kilometres; the larger is 70 kilometres long and 50 kilometres wide, and the smaller is 30 kilometres long and 16 or 17 wide. The catchment basin, including the lake itself, is in area 18,000 square kilometres, and the level of the lake is

965 metres above the sea. Both lakes lie in the western "Rift," which starts from the northern end of Lake Nyassa in lat. 10° 15′ south, and ends near Gondokoro.[1] The other Lakes in this rift are Tanganyika and Kivu. The only outlet of Lake Albert Edward is the Semliki River. In the Katwe Bay there are three islands, and in Lake Dueru two, viz., Chikalero and Naukavenga. The principal rivers which flow into Lake Dueru are the Makokia, Nuisamba, Lokoku, Sebu, Mbuku, Hima, Ruini or Nsongi, Dura, Yeria, Balariba, Msongi, Mpango, Igasha, Nakatera, Malluna,

VIEW ON THE SEMLIKI RIVER.

[From Sir W. Garstin's *Report*, by permission of the Comptroller of H.M. Stationery Office.

and Manobo; all these rise on the eastern face of the Ruenzori Mountains. The rivers which flow into Lake Albert Edward are the Rutshuru and Ruendu on the south; the Muwengu or Mtungi on the south-east, and the Nyamgasha or Nyamgashani, and the Dibirra on the north.

[1] The eastern "Rift" starts from the same place, follows the thirty-sixth meridian east of Greenwich, and either disappears at Lake Rudolph, lat. 4° north, or skirts the southern limits of the Abyssinian highlands, until it joins the similar depression now occupied by the Red Sea. In this "Rift" are Lakes Manjara, Natron, Naivasha, Al-Menteita, Nakuru, Hannington, Baringo, and Rudolph. See Garstin, *Report on the Upper Nile Basin*, p. 4; Gregory, *The Great Rift Valley*, London, 1896.

SEMLIKI RIVER

The connecting channel between Lake Albert Edward and Lake Albert is the Semliki[1] River. This river leaves the former lake in lat. 0° 8′ 30″ south, and following the line of the western "Rift" skirts the flanks of the Ruenzori, and after a course of 260 kilometres discharges its waters into the south end of Lake

UPPER FALL ON THE WAKKI RIVER, A TRIBUTARY OF LAKE ALBERT.

[From Sir W. Garstin's *Report*, by permission of the Comptroller of H.M. Stationery Office.

Albert in lat. 1° 9′ north. It runs through an almost impenetrable hedge of tropical vegetation; the rainfall below the snow peaks of Ruenzori is extremely heavy, and practically continues throughout the year, and the climate is often steamy to an extreme degree. Nothing is known of the river's course from where it enters the forest to its point of exit into Lake Albert, for

[1] Also called Issango, Kakoonda, and Kakibi.

Stanley rarely descended into the valley of the river. Between its head and its mouth the Semliki drops 285 metres.

Lake Albert,[1] into which the Semliki River flows, was discovered by Sir Samuel Baker in 1864. It lies within the parallels of lat. 1° 9′ and 2° 17′ north, and between the meridians of 30° 35′ and 31° 30′ east of Greenwich; its greatest length is 160 kilometres, and its greatest width 45 kilometres. It was circumnavigated by Gessi Pâshâ and Mason Bey. It receives from the Semliki River the overflow of Lake Albert Edward, and the entire drainage of the Ruenzori Mountains, and a great portion of that of the western hills. The catchment basin of the lake, including the valley of the Semliki River, has an area of 32,000 square kilometres, and the level of its waters is 680 metres above the sea. The principal rivers and streams which flow into it from the east are the Msisi, Ravasanja, Ngusi, Mponbi, Nyakabari, or Horo, with the Balbona, Jimangawu and Kagarandindu, the Wahamba, Lukajuka, Hoimi, Wakki, and the Waiga. All these rivers enter the lake in a series of cascades and waterfalls, and none of them is very long. The Victoria Nile enters Lake Albert in lat. 2° 17′ north. The northern end of the lake is a vast swamp of papyrus and ambatch several hundred square kilometres in extent.

The portion of the Nile between Lake Victoria at the Ripon Falls, and the point where it enters Lake Albert at Magungo, is 251 miles long, and is called the "Victoria Nile." Between its junction with Lake Albert and the eastern corner of Lake Nô in lat. 9° 29′ north, i.e., a distance of nearly 723 miles, the Nile is called the "Baḥr al-Gebel," or "Upper Nile." From the place where the waters of the Baḥr al-Gebel meet the waters of the Baḥr al-Ghazâl in Lake Nô, at the point called "Maḳren al-Buḥûr," to Kharṭûm, i.e., for a distance of about 600 miles, the Nile is called "Baḥr al-Abyaḍ," or "White Nile." The length of the Nile between the Ripon Falls and Kharṭûm is about 1,580 miles.

The rivers which flow into the Victoria Nile are: 1. The Kafu, which rises in the Unyoro country, and enters the Nile from the

[1] Called by the natives Muta N'zigi, or Luta N'zigi; this name means "dead locust."

west, near Mruli. 2. The Titi, near Mruli, from the north-west. 3. The Lenga, or Kubuli, on the east bank, opposite to Fuwêra. 4. The Dukhu, on the east bank, ten miles north of Fuwêra.

The rivers which flow into the Baḥr al-Gebel are: 1. The Tangi, on the east, at mile 15 from Lake Albert. 2. The Achwa, on the east, at mile 28; it rises in Mount Guruguru. 3. The Umi, on the east, at mile 40. 4. The Jokha, on the east,

JUNCTION OF THE ASUA RIVER WITH THE BAḤR AL-GEBEL.

[From Sir W. Garstin's *Report*, by permission of the Comptroller of H.M. Stationery Office.

at mile 85. 5. The Ayugi, on the east, opposite to Dufilî, at mile 130. 6. The Unyami, on the east, near the Ayugi. 7. The Asua, on the east, at mile 148; it is about 170 miles long. 8. The Atappi, on the north-east; it is a tributary of the Asua. 9. The Umi, on the east, at mile 173. 10. The Karpeto, on the east, at mile 183. 11. The Niumbi, on the east, at mile 195. 12. The Kiveh, on the east, at mile 199. 13. The Lugololo, on the east, at mile 216. 14. The Peki, on the east, at mile 220. 15. The Kît, or Baḥr Ramliya, on the east, at mile 234. 16. The Lakodero, on the east, at mile 245. Besides these, mention must be made of the large channel on the east of the Baḥr al-Gebel, which was discovered by Mr. E. S. Grogan[1] on his march from Bôr to the Baḥr az-Zarâfa, and called the "Gertrude Nile." Sir William Garstin investigated this channel in 1904, and found that the Gertrude Nile is no other than the river which the Dinkas call the "Atem." The course of this river is along the high land to the east of the Nile Valley; where

THE SOBAT RIVER.

[From Sir W. Garstin's *Report*, by permission of the Comptroller of H.M. Stationery Office.

it leaves the Baḥr al-Gebel is not known, but it enters it about mile 437 from Lake Albert. About 54 miles north of Bôr the Atem divides into two branches, that on the right being the Myding, or Mydang, and that on the left the Awai. A special map of the course of these rivers is given by Sir Willian Garstin in Appendix VI. of his *Report*.

Into the western end of Lake Nô (lat. 8° 29′ north) flows the Baḥr al-Ghazâl, or "Gazelle River," which receives the waters of all the streams that drain the watershed between the Congo and

[1] *From the Cape to Cairo*, London, 1900.

the Nile, i.e., in the area between lat. 5° and 8° north, and long. 24° and 30° east. The principal tributaries of the Baḥr al-Ghazâl river are the Rôhl, the Jân, and the Tonj, on the right, and the Baḥr al-'Arab, the Baḥr al-Ḥomr, and the Jûr on the left. Maṣhra ar-Reḳ, a place famous in the history of the

THE RIVER ABÂÎ, LOOKING UP-STREAM FROM THE BRIDGE OF AGAM DELDI.
[From Sir W. Garstin's *Report*, by permission of the Comptroller of H.M. Stationery Office.

slave-raiding expeditions in the Sûdân, was on "Kît Island," not far from the bifurcation (lat. 8° 44′ 50″ north) of the Baḥr al-Ghazâl, at mile 112 from Lake Nô.

The tributaries of the White Nile are the Baḥr az-Zarâfa, or "Giraffe River," and the Sobat, or Subat,[1] or the Baḥr al-Aṣfar,

[1] This is probably found in conjunction with *Asta*, "river," in the classical "Astasobas."

i.e., "Yellow River." The Baḥr az-Zarâfa enters the White Nile on the right or east bank, about 48 miles down-stream of Lake Nô, in lat. 9° 53′ 17″ north. The channel by which it is fed leaves the Baḥr al-Gebel 240 miles south of Lake Nô, and it receives on its way the waters from Khôr Too, Khôr Khos, and Khôr Kanieti, which come from the Latuka Hills. The course of the Baḥr az-Zarâfa was explored by Major Peake, R.A., and Captain Stanton in 1898, and by Mr. Grogan and Commandant Henri in 1900.

THE ABÂÎ, NEAR LAKE ṬÂNÂ.

[From Sir W. Garstin's *Report*, by permission of the Comptroller of H.M. Stationery Office.

The Sobat rises in the Abyssinian mountains, and for the first 260 miles of its course is known by the Abyssinians as the "Baro," by the Nuers as the "Kîr," and by the Anuaks as the "Upeno," and from its junction with the Pibor to the Nile it is called the Sobat or Baḥr al-Aṣfar. Its total length is about 460 miles. The tributaries of the Baro in its upper region are the Sako, right bank, Bonga, left bank; and the Khôr Gokau, or Garre, joins the Baro at Gokau and Machar. The Nigol, or Aluro, enters the Baro 17 miles below Itang, on the left bank.

The Pibor enters the Sobat 25 miles above Nasser, and 200 miles from its mouth. A tributary of the Pibor is the Agwei, also called Neubari, Ruzi II., and Adjonaro. The Akobo, or Juba River, enters the Pibor about 70 miles from its mouth. The Ajibir, or Ruzi I. River, enters the Akobo on the west bank about 80 miles from the south end of the Pibor. The Gelo enters the Pibor on the right bank, 26 miles above its junction with the Baro. The Mokwai, or Bela, enters the Pibor above

LAKE TSÂNÂ (ṢÂNÂ).

[From Sir W. Garstin's *Report*, by permission of the Comptroller of H.M. Stationery Office.

the Pibor-Sobat junction, and the Khôr Filus enters the Sobat on the left bank, about ten miles from its junction with the White Nile. The portion of the Sûdân through which these rivers flow has been explored in part by Major Gwynn, Major Austin, Mr. Wellby, Mr. O. Neumann, Signor Bottego, Captain H. H. Wilson, Mr. Macmillan, Colonel Artomonoff, Messrs. Faivre and Potter, Major A. Blewitt, Lieut. Comyn, and others. Excellent summaries of the results obtained by these travellers and officers will be found in Count Gleichen's *Handbook*, p. 131 ff.

The Sobat enters the Nile on the right bank, about 800 miles from Lake Albert, lat. 9° 22′ 8″ north, longitude 31° 31′ east. The water of the Sobat is at times of a "creamy white" colour, and at others a pale red, and it is probable that the White Nile derived its name from the milky colour given to its waters by those of the Sobat when in flood. The waters of the Nile are here of a greenish-grey colour, and Sir William Garstin notes that "for a long way down-stream a sharp line separates the two."

THE ABÂÎ, OR BLUE NILE, RAPIDS, NEAR THE FORD.

[From Sir W Garstin's *Report*, by permission of the Comptroller of H.M. Stationery Office.

The Sobat brings down an immense quantity of water, which probably equals that derived from the lakes, and the volume and velocity of this are sufficient to hold back the discharge of the White Nile. The country traversed by the Sobat is a rich alluvial plain covered with grass; large herds of cattle abound.

At Kharṭûm the White Nile is joined by the Blue Nile, or Abâî, on the east bank. The Blue Nile brings down an immense volume of rain-water from the Abyssinian mountains and forests

It begins to rise in June, reaches its maximum height in August, and falls rapidly in September. In flood time its waters are of a deep chocolate colour, but in the winter they are of a "beautiful limpid blue colour," and from this the river derives its name. The Blue Nile rises about 60 miles south of Lake Ṣânâ,[1] and flows northward into it at the south-west corner, and flows out again at the south-east corner of the lake.[2]

Lake Ṣânâ takes its name from "Ṣânâ," the largest of the

PORTUGUESE BRIDGE OVER THE RIVER ABÂÎ AT AGAM DELDI, ABOUT TWENTY-ONE MILES FROM LAKE ṢÂNÂ.

[From Sir W. Garstin's *Report*, by permission of the Comptroller of H.M. Stationery Office.

eleven islands which are in it. The other islands are Bergîdâ, Dabra Anṭônes, Dabra Maryâm, Dagâ, Deḳ, Galîlâ, Meṭrâkhâ, Meṣlê, Kebrân, and Rîmâ. Every island except Deḳ was inhabited by monks. The area of the lake is about 1,200 square miles; its greatest length is about 35 miles, and its breadth is about the same. It lies among the Abyssinian hills at an altitude of nearly 5,000 feet. After passing through a series of channels

[1] In Amharic Bâhr Ṣânâ ባሕር ፡ ጸና ፡ or ባሕር ፡ ጣና ፡

[2] See Mr. C. Dupuis's *Report upon Lake Tsana*, published in *Egypt*, No. 2 (1904).

it unites in a "fine broad stream about 200 metres wide." About 21 miles down-stream, at Agam Deldi, is the old Portuguese bridge, "a quaint, half ruinous old structure, very remarkable "as being still the only one spanning the Blue Nile in its whole "length."[1] The narrow gorge crossed by the bridge is a striking one, and the Falls of Tis Esat "are really exceedingly fine"; they are at the head of the gorge which is crossed by the bridge, and the river descends 150 feet in a single leap, into a profound abyss. Abyssinian writers say that the Abâî surrounds Gojâm in such a way that this country is always on its right bank, and that it rises in a place called *Sekût*,[2] to the west of Bagêmder and the Lake of Darâ (i.e., Lake Ṣânâ), and Bed. From this place it travels to Amḥârâ, then turns to the west, then passes Walaḳâ, and comes to the borders of Mûgâr and Shawâ (Shoa), and passing between Bîzâmâ and Gôngâ, it descends into the region of Shanḳelâ. Finally it enters the kingdom of Sĕnâr (Sennaar). After this it flows on and receives the waters of two great rivers, the Takazê,[3] which comes from Tegrê, and the Guangue,[4] which comes from Dembea, and then it runs to Dengûlâ (Dongola) and the country of Nôbâ (Nubia). The course of the Blue Nile from Lake Ṣânâ to the eastern frontier of the Sûdân is not well known, but it can hardly be less in length than 550 miles, and as Sir William Garstin puts the distance by river from Kharṭûm to Ruṣêreṣ at 426 miles, the total length of the Blue Nile must be about 1,000 miles.

From Lake Ṣânâ to Fâmaka, on the Abyssinian frontier, the river is called by its Abyssinian name, "'ABÂY,"[5] አባይ ፡ or "'ABÂWÎ," አባዊ ፡[6] but as soon as it enters the Sûdân its name becomes "Baḥr al-Azraḳ," i.e., the "Blue Nile." The Blue Nile must have borne the name of "'Abâî" in the time of Strabo, for he calls it "Astapos," which is a Graecized compound of *ast*, or *asta*, "water, river," and *'Abâi*, the name of the river.

[1] Arrangements are being made to build a bridge from Ḥalfâya to Kharṭûm, and I understand that work on the foundations has actually been begun.

[2] ሰኩት ፡ [3] ተከዜ ፡ [4] ጓንጕ ፡

[5] D'Abbadie transcribes *'Abbay*.

[6] The form 'Abâwî, አባዊ ፡ also occurs. See Pereira, *Chronica*, Lisbon, 1900, p. 634.

BLUE NILE, DINDER, RAHAD

The two tributaries of the Blue Nile are the Dinder and the Rahad. The Rahad rises in the Abyssinian mountains near Lake Ṣânâ, and enters the Blue Nile from the east close to Wad Madanî, 123 miles from Kharṭûm. The Dinder also rises in the Abyssinian mountains, and is about 250 miles long; it flows parallel with the Rahad for about 75 miles of its course, and enters the Nile from the east, about 40 miles above Wad Madanî, i.e., about 163 miles from Kharṭûm. The Dinder has been navigated in a steamer so far as Dabarkî, i.e., 120 miles from Kharṭûm, and Mr. Armbruster once steamed up the Rahad to Mashra Abîd, i.e., 420 miles from Kharṭûm.[1] The principal places on the Blue Nile are:—Sôba, or Sûba, 14 miles from Kharṭûm, 'Êlafûn, 18 miles, Kâmlîn, 61 miles, Rufâ'a, 94 miles, Masallamîa, 105 miles, Abû Ḥarâz, 117 miles, Wad Madanî, 123 miles, Sennaar, 213 miles, Runḳa and Sanga, 266 miles, Karkôj (Karkôg), 287 miles, Ruṣêreṣ, 382 miles, Fâmaka, 434 miles. Beyond these are Gebel Fâzô'glî, Gebel Ḳaba, Gebel Abû Ramla, and Gebâl Beni Shanḳûl.

Between Kharṭûm and the sea the great river, which is now called simply "Nile," receives but one tributary, viz., the Atbara, the "Astaboras" of classical, and the "Atbarâ"[2] of Abyssinian writers. According to Mr. Dupuis, the river Atbara is formed by the confluence of three large streams, the Goang, the Bulwena and the Gandwaha, a little to the south of Ḳallâbât, on the border of Abyssinia; other tributaries are the Salaam River,[3] which enters it on the east bank, about 100 miles north of Ḳallâbât, and the Setît River,[4] which also enters it on the east bank, a little to the north of Tomato. Its tributary, the Royan, joins it four miles east of Khôr Umbrega.[5] The upper portion of the Setît River is called by its old Abyssinian name, "Takazê."[6] A few miles north of Khashîm al-Girba is the well-known Fasher Ford, where the Ḳallâbât-Kasala road crosses the river. The character

[1] See Sir W. Garstin, *Egypt*, No. 2 (1904); Gleichen, *op. cit.*, i., p. 113 ff.

[2] I.e., አትባራ ፡ See Pereira, *Chronica de Susenyos*, text, p. 204, line 2.

[3] Also known as the Baḥr al-Ankareb.

[4] See Baker, *Nile Tributaries of Abyssinia*, London, 1867, pp. 136, 216, 468, 499; F. L. James, *Wild Tribes of the Sûdân*, London, 1863, p. 156 ff.

[5] Gleichen, *op. cit.*, p. 101.

[6] ተከዚ ፡

of the Atbara is torrential.[1] The rains begin in its upper basin in May, in June the "swelling of the springs" takes place, and this is followed by the arrival of dirty red water, and by the end of this month the flood water reaches the Nile, in years of heavy rain in the form of a high wave which literally drives the waters of the Nile over on to the western bank. The Atbara flood is at its highest in August. In September the river falls rapidly, in October it is fordable in many places, and by the end of November it is nearly dried up. The total annual discharge is estimated at 20,000,000,000 cubic metres. East of the Atbara is the Ḳâsh (Gash) River, which rises in the Abyssinian mountains, and flows north to Kasala, but a few miles to the north of this town it breaks up into channels, and disappears entirely. Further is the Baraka River, which rises in the Abyssinian mountains, and floods the country about Ṭôkar in the month of August. It should empty itself into the Red Sea, but it usually disappears in the desert before it reaches the coast.

Between Kharṭûm and Aswân there are on the Nile six great series of rapids, or "Cataracts,"[2] and five of them are in the Sûdân. The First Cataract lies between Aswân and Philae, and is about six and a quarter miles long. The Second Cataract is a little to the south of Ḥalfa, and its most difficult part is about fourteen miles long. The Third Cataract is at Ḥannek, but between Sarras and this place are the smaller cataracts of Semna, Ambiḳôl, Tangûr, 'Ukma, 'Ukâsha, Dâl, 'Amâra, and Khêbar. The Fourth Cataract is at Adramîya in the Shaikîya country, 250 miles from Ḥannek. The Fifth Cataract is at Wâdî Al-Ḥamâr. Between the Fourth and Fifth Cataracts are numerous small cataracts. The Sixth Cataract lies between Shendî and Kharṭûm about 194 miles south of Wâdî al-Ḥamâr, and is ten miles long. On the Blue Nile there is a series of cataracts which begins at Ruṣêreṣ, and extends southwards for some forty miles; and on the Baḥr al-Gebel, 140 miles north of Lake Albert, is the series of cataracts which is known as the Fôla, or Fûla, Rapids.[3]

[1] S. Baker, *Albert Nyanza*, pp. 3 ff.; Dupuis, special note, *Egypt*, No. 2 (1904), p. 226.

[2] Called by the Arabs "Shallâlât," or "Ganâdal."

[3] There are also the Yerbora Rapids, the Gougi Rapids, &c.

Here Sir William Garstin considers that a demonstration of the force and power of water is to be seen[1] which is not to be witnessed in any other cataract on the Nile. The Rapids begin in two or more falls with a drop of some sixteen or twenty feet, and a total width of nearly 200 feet. Below the falls the stream rushes down a very narrow gorge, with a heavy slope, enclosed between vertical walls of rock. This resembles a gigantic mill race, over 300 feet long. "The water tears through this channel in a glassy, "green sheet with an incredible velocity"; the width of the "gut"

THE BAḤR AL-GEBEL. FÔLA RAPIDS, LOOKING UP-STREAM.
[From Sir W. Garstin's *Report*, by permission of the Comptroller of H.M. Stationery Office.

is only about fifty feet, and in places it is less! At the foot of this race the river leaps into a cauldron about 160 feet long and forty feet wide, and fills it with a "boiling mass of white water, "lashed into foam. It is difficult, in words, to give even a faint "idea of this unique scene; . . . photographs do not satisfactorily "reproduce it. They cannot show the colouring of the picture, "or the wild beauty of the scene." On each side are vertical walls of rock from twenty to thirty feet high, polished black, and covered with masses of vegetation which resemble green velvet.

[1] *Egypt*, No. 2 (1904), p. 82.

"The inky blackness of the rocks and the variegated greens of "the foliage, contrast vividly with the seething mass of white "water, above which the spray is tossed high in the air in a "misty cloud. Above all a deep blue sky and a brilliantly clear "atmosphere add to the effect of an exceptionally lovely scene."

The INUNDATION, or Nile-Flood, is caused, as Aristotle said, by the rains which fall during the summer in the mountains of Abyssinia and the Sûdân, and which are brought down by the great tributaries of the river, the Baḥr al-Ghazâl, the Sobat, the Baḥr az-Zarâfa, the Blue Nile, and the Atbara or Atbarâ. The Sobat rises about the middle of April, the Baḥr az-Zarâfa about the middle of May, and the Baḥr al-Ghazâl begins to fill about the same time. Towards the end of the month the Blue Nile rises, and a little later the Atbara; the Nile-Flood is highest in August. The White Nile continues to rise, and does not fall till October, when it does so slowly. Between Tawfiḳîya and Kharṭûm the depth of the river varies from fifteen feet at low Nile to twenty-one feet in flood; and its width varies from one and a quarter to two miles. The "green water," which is seen at Cairo in June, appears at Duwêm a month earlier; its cause is said to be myriads of minute algae, which subsequently putrefy and stink. The dates of the arrival of the Flood at the various places down the river vary slightly each year. Sir William Garstin has calculated the river discharges as follows:—

1. The Victoria Nile. At the Ripon Falls, between 500 and 650 cubic metres per second.
2. The Baḥr al-Gebel. At Wadelâî, between 550 and 950 cubic metres per second. At Lâdô, between 600 and 700 cubic metres per second. The maxima are: 1,000 cubic metres per second in a low flood, and 2,000 cubic metres per second in a high one. By the time the river reaches Bôr half the water has been lost, and at the entrance to Lake Nô less than half enters the lake.
3. The Baḥr al-Ghazâl. At Lake Nô 20 to 30 cubic metres per second enter the lake during the summer.
4. The Baḥr az-Zarâfa. In flood this river contributed to the White Nile 80 to 160 cubic metres per second, but in summer only from 30 to 60.

5. The Sobat. In flood time 900 to 1,000 cubic metres per second.
6. The White Nile. At Kharṭûm the greatest discharge in flood time is about 1,700 cubic metres per second.
7. The Blue Nile. At Kharṭûm, in a good flood, between 10,000 and 12,000 cubic metres per second.
8. The Atbara. At least 3,000 cubic metres per second.

A series of calculations and measurements made in 1903 prove that the Nile north of the Atbara in flood time consists of very little more than the water which is contributed to it by the Blue

CATARACT AT SEMNA AND KUMMA.

Nile and the Atbara, in fact at this time the White Nile adds very little to these streams. During the spring and early summer, however, the water which reaches Egypt is supplied principally from Lakes Victoria and Albert, *viâ* the White Nile. It is calculated that about 1,150,000,000 cubic metres of water pass Berber in one day during an ordinary flood.

THE COURSE OF THE NILE IN THE SÛDÂN. By Article I. of the Treaty[1] between the Governments of Great Britain and Egypt, the Sûdân begins at the 22nd parallel of north latitude, and the course of the Nile from this point to Lake Victoria may be

[1] Signed, July 10th, 1899.

briefly described.[1] The mileage is that given by Count Gleichen, but it is understood that strict accuracy is not claimed for it.

The most northerly settlement in the Sûdân is on the Island of Faraṣ, twenty miles north of Ḥalfa, where there are remains of Egyptian, Roman, and Coptic buildings. At Ḥalfa, formerly a thriving town, are the head-quarters of the Ḥalfa province, and the terminus of the Sûdân Railway. Since the opening of the Atbara-Red Sea Railway, the greater number of the workshops have been removed to Atbara, and the decline of the town has begun, for numbers of Greeks have left it. Here was the terminus of the railway which ran to Kerma, but as the line did not pay, and the rails, which were practically new, were wanted elsewhere, the portion of it between Kôsha and Kerma has been taken up. On the west bank are the remains of a well-built Egyptian temple of the XVIIIth Dynasty.

From the Rock of Abû Ṣîr (seven miles from Ḥalfa) a fine view is obtained of the Second Cataract, the foot of which is close by. Here the district called Baṭn al-Ḥagar, i.e., the "Stone Belly," begins, and a more desolate, dreary country can hardly be imagined. It is about 120 miles long; on the east bank are nothing but sun-blackened rocks of savage aspect, and on the west bank is an interminable waste of yellow sand. In the bright sun, and under a blue sky, the blackened and polished rocks of the river present a picturesque contrast to the yellow sand on the west bank, and the patches of bright green vegetation on the islands in the stream lend a unique picturesqueness to the view. Near Ma'tûḳa (ten miles) are the remains of a temple of the XIIth Dynasty and those of an ancient Egyptian town. At Sarras (thirty-three miles) the railway turns off into the rocky country of the Eastern Desert. At Gazîrat al-Malik (forty miles) are the remains of an Egyptian temple of the XVIIIth Dynasty, which is built on the site of one erected by Usertsen III. of the XIIth Dynasty, and also those of a large fortress. At Semna and Kumma (43 miles), perched on the top of rocks 400 feet high, are remains of two Egyptian temples of the XVIIIth Dynasty.

[1] For full details, see Gleichen, *op. cit.*, i., pp. 23 ff.; Garstin, *Egypt*, No. 2 (1904); and Shucair, *op. cit.*, i., pp. 78 ff.

At Semna, on the west bank, are also the remains of a temple built by the Nubian king Taharqa (Tirhakah); the mountain beyond is Gebel Barga. The river here flows through a narrow channel, which has been eroded by its waters. The scenery is wild and grand. The Atiri, Ambiḳôl, Tangûr, and 'Ukma Rapids occur at miles 50, 57, 72 and 79 respectively. At 'Ukâsha (85 miles) is another rapid. Here the railway approaches the river.

At Dâl (98 miles) signs of cultivation begin; the cataract here renders navigation difficult. Near Gebel Firket (105 miles) the battle of Firket was fought on July 6th, 1896; near here is some cultivated land. The hills seen to the east are Gebel Idrîs and Gebel Ḥamra. Kôsha (113 miles) is the head-quarters of a district, and from here southwards much cultivated land is seen, and large numbers of palms. At Ginnis (115 miles) the battle was fought on December 30th, 1885. At 'Amâra (118 miles) are the remains of a temple of Rameses II. (west bank), and those of a Meroïtic temple (east bank). At Sâḳîyat al-'Abd (127 miles) a road starts for the Selîma Oasis, fifty-seven miles distant.

On the Island of Sâî, near 'Abri (130 miles), are the remains of two or three Egyptian temples, a Coptic church, and a Bosnian or Mamlûḳ fortress. Near Kuêka (135 miles), on the east bank, is Ḳubba Idrîs, the tomb of a famous shêkh and leader of the *Murghânî* doctrine. Suwârda (142 miles) stands among much cultivated land, and round about are some very fine trees. On the west bank are the remains of the temple of Queen Thi, B.C. 1450, commonly called the Temple of Saddênga; close by is Ḳubba Salîm. Near Ṣûlb (Gurgan Tau, 156 miles) are fine remains of a temple of Àmen-ḥetep III., husband of Queen Thi. Between Suwârda and Ṣûlb is Gebel Dôsha, the boundary between Sukkôt and Maḥass. At Tinnara are the remains of a Bosnian fort. At Dulgo (191 miles) are the remains of a temple of Seti I., B.C. 1370; here the railway rejoined the river. Passing the Kagbar, or Khêbar, Cataract (203 miles) Arduwân Island is reached at mile 212. Near Ḥannek (231 miles) is a series of rapids, and there are several small islands in the river. A little further on is Ḳubba Abû Faṭma (243 miles), and opposite is the Island of Tombos, with rock inscriptions of Thothmes I. On this Island is a fortress built by Muḥammad Wad Ṭunbul, king of Arḳô, and here are the tombs of his ancestors.

At Kerma (246 miles) was the terminus of the railway (201 miles from Ḥalfa). At Ḥafîr (248 miles) the Dervishes were defeated on September 20th, 1896. Between mile 252 and mile 272 is Arḳô Island, which is well cultivated and thickly populated. Two colossal Egyptian statues lie here, and in ancient times there must have been a large town on the island. From Dongola (280 miles), or Al-Ûrdî, to Merawi the Nile runs through a plain, and in many places the soil is rich and the cultivation abundant. A few miles to the south, at Kawa, on the east bank, are the remains of a small Egyptian temple, which was discovered and partly excavated by Col. the Hon. J. Colborne in 1885. Near Ḥannâg (291 miles) is the Fort of Wad Nimîr, king of Dongola. Near Aṣḥâba (296 miles) are the remains of some Muḥammadan (Bosnian ?) buildings. Near Sâti Bashîr (304 miles) is the island whereon the Mahdî is said to have been born. At Ḥandaḳ (320 miles) is a mosque, which has been built on the ruins of a Christian church, and the ruins of several churches existed here a few years ago.

About 21 miles from Ḥandaḳ is the well of Marḳûm, and three miles further on is the well of Aswânî; the people visit these springs in the summer, and bathe in their waters, and take hot sand baths there for an hour at a time. Those who suffer from stomach and other internal complaints derive great benefit from these baths. Dongola al-'Agûz, or "Old Dongola" (351 miles), is built on a hill on the east bank; here are ruins of a fort and of a Christian church, the upper part of which has been turned into a mosque. A town of considerable size existed here at one time, and it was the capital of the Dongola kingdom for about 600 years. The remains of a paved road leading to Merawi have recently been discovered. At Abû Ḳassi (356 miles) the course of the river changes to nearly east and west. On Tanḳâsi Island, near Dabba, are said to dwell some of the Fûng people who migrated thither from Sennaar.

Dabba (371 miles) was formerly a great trade centre, and here started roads for Omdurmân and Kordôfân. In the neighbourhood much petrified wood is found. Close by, at

Karad, are the remains of some buildings erected by the British in 1885. In the course of the next thirty miles several islands, fertile and well cultivated, are passed. At Abû Dôm Ḳashâbî the Nile bends and runs to the north-east. At Ambiḳôl (413 miles) cultivation becomes general. Kôrtî (416 miles) was the advanced base of the Gordon Relief Expedition in 1885; a road to Matamma *viâ* Gakdûl Wells starts here. Ḥannak (432 miles) was the capital of the Shâiḳîya Province. On an island between Ḥannek and Kôrtî was born 'Alî Mûrghânî, the son of Muḥammad 'Uthmân. Tanḳâsi (441 miles) is famous for its Tuesday weekly market, to which throng merchants from Dongola, Berber, and Kharṭûm. Close by are the ruins of Ḥôsh al-Ibyaḍ, an old Shâiḳîya town. Abû Dôm Ṣanam and Merawi (447 miles) are well cultivated and are most picturesquely situated. Merawi is the chief town of a province, and the abode of the Governor. The British camped here in 1885, and it was occupied by the Frontier Field Force in 1896. A road leads from here to Gakdûl Wells. Merawi can now be reached by train from Abû Ḥamed. The line was surveyed by Lieut. Newcombe, R.E., in 1904, and has its terminus at Karêma. On the right bank is Gebel Barkal, 302 feet high, and at its feet are the ruins of several temples; close by are several pyramids. On the left bank was situated the city of Napata, which as early as the XVIIIth Dynasty was the capital of the Northern kingdom of the Sûdân.

A few miles up-stream from Merawi is the foot of the Fourth Cataract, and from this place to Abû Ḥamed, 140 miles distant, the river is full of rapids which make navigation very difficult. After passing Nûrî, where there are several pyramids and remains of ancient temples, there are no antiquities on either bank. Excellent itineraries for the left and right banks, by Major Slade, R.A., and Col. the Hon. M. G. Talbot, R.E., respectively, are given by Count Gleichen in his *Handbook*, pp. 38-43.

Between Abû Ḥamed and the Atbara the country on both banks of the river is uninteresting; there is little cultivation, and even now the number of the inhabitants is not great As we advance south low ranges of sandstone hills appear, and villages and patches of cultivation become frequent on the western bank. At a little distance back from the east bank the whole country is a howling wilderness. Between Berber and the Atbara there is on the east bank a fairly broad strip of cultivation, but now that Berber is no longer the capital of the district it is probable that the general condition of the neighbourhood will become less flourishing than formerly. The railway runs on the east bank. After leaving Abû Ḥamed the river is full of rocks for a few miles, and navigation is difficult, but when these are passed the waterway is clear for about 50 miles. The Fifth Cataract is found near the Wâdî al-Ḥomâr, about 76 miles from Abû Ḥamed, and at low Nile is practically impassable.

The Atbara River enters the Nile on the east bank, 151 miles from Abû Ḥamed, and 200 miles from Kharṭûm. Between the Atbara and Shendî the country is uninteresting, and on each bank of the river the strip of cultivable ground is choked with thorn-growths and grass. Large patches of cultivation appear on the banks close to the river, but even now the natives find it hard to make a living. A large portion of the land went out of cultivation soon after Muḥammad 'Alî began to develop the slave trade, and during the rule of his successors the bulk of the population either fled and turned brigand, or remained on the land and were captured and sold for slaves. The ruin begun by him was completed by the Mahdî and the Khalîfa.

About 44 miles south of the Atbara, and 3½ from the Nile, on the east bank, is the site of an ancient Meroïtic city, which flourished between B.C. 300 and A.D. 200. Further to the east are the groups of pyramid-tombs under which its kings and queens and their families were buried. On or near the site of Shendî, 86 miles from the Atbara, another large Meroïtic city stood, but there is no evidence to show that it was the capital of the "Island of Meroë." A few miles to the south of Shendî, on the west bank, is Matamma, a town of the Ga'alîn Arabs, 2,000 of whom were slain by the Dervish leader Maḥmûd in 1897; it is the terminus of the road across the Bayûda Desert to Kôrtî and other places in the Dongola district. About 130 miles from the Atbara is the foot of the Sixth Cataract, commonly known as the Shablûka Cataract, which is about 10 miles long. Here the Nile flows through a channel about 500 feet wide, which it has made for itself in the granite rocks, and in flood time the current

A NATIVE HUT ON THE WHITE NILE.

[From a photograph by Miss Hilda Burrows.

is said to run at a rate of from seven to ten miles an hour. The river is studded with rocks and reefs nearly the whole way to Wad Ramla, and the water-way is frequently blocked by small islands; navigation here is very difficult. After Wad Ramla the cultivation increases, and every available acre on the islands all the way up to Kharṭûm is covered with crops. Four miles north of Kharṭûm, on the west bank, is the town of Omdurmân, and passing Tûtî Island the city of Kharṭûm, which is built in the angle formed by the junction of the White and Blue Niles, is reached. Kharṭûm is 480 miles from Merawi, 927 miles from Ḥalfa, and 1,730 miles from Cairo, by river; the distance from Kharṭûm to Cairo by railway and river is about 1,360 miles.

The river between Kharṭûm and Lake Nô is known as the "White Nile." After leaving Kharṭûm the river banks are flat, and the country is low and treeless.[1] The river is very shallow, and in some places is two miles wide, and the shelving banks make landing in boats impossible. Water-fowl and crocodiles are numerous, and in a strong wind the wide expanse of water is covered with comparatively high waves. Large crops are grown on the banks and islands as the river falls. Gebel Auli is passed on the east bank 28 miles from Kharṭûm, and Gebel Mandara on the west bank at mile 32. At Wad al-Karêl (34 miles) the river is three miles wide in flood time. At Al-Ḳatêna (55 miles) there was a settlement in the Christian period; fragments of pottery from this place are in the Museum at Kharṭûm. South of Ṣalahîya (59 miles) as far as Duwêm, i.e., for 66 miles, the banks are low; on the east the plain is covered with thick brush, and a dense growth of mimosa fringes the channel line. The scenery is "monotonous and uninteresting." The cultivation is chiefly on the islands and fore-shore, which the people water with *shadûfs;* the natives live in *tukls.* Near 'Amâra (109 miles) is the range called Gebel Arashkol; this mountain is volcanic, and its chief peak is Gebel 'Abd ad-Dâim. At Ad-Duwêm (125 miles), on the west bank, the river is divided by an island. The town contains 7,000 inhabitants, and is a large trading centre, with a good market. The transport service for Al-Obêḍ starts

[1] See Garstin, *Egypt*, No. 2 (1904), p. 106; Gleichen, *op. cit.*, i., pp. 52 ff.; Shucair, *op. cit.*, i., pp. 98 ff.

here, and the Kordôfân gum is brought here for shipment to Omdurmân. The Governor of the White Nile Province lives at Duwêm; the Government buildings, including a hospital, are "substantial." Here there is a Nile-gauge, and the river levels are recorded daily. A road to Sennaar starts here.

Five miles to the south is Ḥassanîya Island. Between Duwêm and Kawwa (146 miles) the river is about 750 yards wide, and in flood it is double this width; at low water it is 13 feet deep. Islands are numerous, and the mud flats are very wide. At Kawwa a British Inspector resides. It possesses a gum depôt, a small grain store, and a market; it is inhabited by the Ḥassanîya, the Ga'alîn, and the Danâḳla, who grow large crops on the mud-flats. The natives have much cattle, and thrive by boat-building, and the cutting of wood, which they supply to the steamers.

Abâ Island, usually written "Abba," is about 28 miles long; its northern end is near Shawal (163 miles). This island is long and narrow, and thickly wooded, and is higher at the southern than at the northern end. Here the Mahdî declared his mission, and here Sir William Garstin saw the ruins of his house in 1904. The country is open and high, with scattered bushes and mimosa. Kôz Abû Gûma (192 miles) is the head-quarters of a district of the same name. The telegraph line from Sennaar touches the White Nile here, and then proceeds southwards. The river is from 750 to 950 yards wide here. This place marks the limit of the "Sadd" vegetation on the north, and there are no swamps, properly so called. Here begins the country of the Negro, who takes the place of the Arab.[1]

At 'Abbâssîya Gadîda (200 miles) is a colony of old Sûdânî soldiers. At Abû Zêd (208 miles), for about 4 miles, the river spreads out to an immense width in a broad, shallow sheet. Upon its bed "fresh-water oysters" collect, and the broken shells form with the shingle a kind of "conglomerate" almost as hard as rock, which nothing but a specially adapted dredger could remove. In years of a very low river the water here is only 17 inches deep. The papyrus is first seen here, and hippopotami begin to be plentiful. At Danko Salîm (227 miles), by Masran Island, a reef of rocks "runs right across the river

[1] Garstin, *op. cit.*, p. 105.

"channel, and the only method of passing safely at low water is "to steer a course like the letter S." Masran Island is 27 miles long, and has Shilluk villages on it.

Gebelên (238 miles) is marked by a sort of amphitheatre of granite hills about a mile from the river on the east bank; the highest of the five peaks is about 330 feet high. The country on the right bank once belonged to the Dinkas, but it is now uninhabited, for the natives fled to the south to escape the slave-raiders.

For the next 60 miles the scenery is "dreary and monotonous. A fringe of thick forest marks the higher land. Between this

FÂSHÔDA (KÔDÔK).

[From Sir W. Garstin's *Report*, by permission of the Comptroller of H.M. Stationery Office.

the river winds through reedy islands bordered by the eternal belt of swamp" At Gebelên the *serût*[1] fly first makes its appearance; it is not poisonous, but is very troublesome. At Ḥellet ar-Renk (298 miles) the forest is very thick; a British Inspector lives here. Gebel Aḥmad Aghâ (353 miles) is named after Aḥmad Aghâ 'Antablî, a former governor of the district. This granite hill is about 340 feet high, is hog-backed in shape, and is about two miles east of the river. From this place to Kâkâ (391 miles), the country is almost uninhabited; in the river are several islands. At Old Kâkâ (404 miles) was a wooding

[1] On the effects of the bite of this pest, see Balfour, *Second Report of the Wellcome Research Laboratories*, p. 32. (Published by the Education Department, Kharṭûm, 1906.)

station. Between Kâkâ and Fâshôda a succession of grass islands is met with. On the west bank is a double line of Shilluk villages, the one on the edge of the swamp, and the other further inland. On the same side of the river are several "Khôrs." To land in this reach is impossible, for the marsh is very reedy and deep, and nothing but a hippopotamus can force its way through it.

At Fâshôda (Kodok, 459 miles) are the head-quarters of the province, with telegraph station, Government buildings, &c. Position 9° 53′ long., and 32° 1′ latitude. Major Marchand occupied it in June, 1898, and evacuated it in December of the same year. It was formerly an important trade centre. The station is on a small peninsula which juts out into the river, and on three of its sides is a deep swamp. It has an evil reputation for malarial fever. The climate is steamy and damp, and mosquitoes abound. In March the temperature ranges from 98° to 105° in the shade. At Lûl (477 miles) is the Austrian Mission station.

From this point onwards the scenery is very dreary. The west bank is lined with Shilluk villages, each of which is surrounded by groups of Dulêb palms (*Borassus Æthiopicus*). The *serût* fly drives the natives into the interior during the rainy season; there are no trees except palms to be seen, but hippopotami abound in the grass islands in the river. Tawfiḳîya (511 miles), on the east bank, is Sir Samuel Baker's old station, and stands on fairly high ground. The place is very unhealthy, and the white ants are a "serious nuisance."

The Sobat River joins the White Nile at mile 516; the country is flat and open. Near the junction, on the left bank of the Sobat, is the old fort, which was abandoned when Tawfiḳîya was occupied. On the north bank of the Sobat, seven miles from its mouth, is a station of the American Protestant Mission. Tonga Island begins at mile 521. The khôr which bounds it on the left is the so-called River Lolli, or Fanakama; according to Perthes's map its source is in Dâr Nûba, but Sir William Garstin doubts its being a river at all. It was partially explored by Marno in 1880 and by Col. Sparkes in 1899. For the next twenty-five miles the scenery is very monotonous, the banks are low, and beyond the swamps on each side of the river are vast grass plains. There is not a tree on the

TAWFIKIYA.

[From a photograph by Miss Hilda Burrows.

FLOATING SUDD ON THE WHITE NILE.

[From a photograph by Miss Hilda Burrows.

left bank, and the line of the horizon is only broken by the large ant-hills which dot the plain. The Baḥr az-Zarâfa enters the Nile at mile 547, at mile 600 is Maya Signora,[1] and there is nothing to be seen but swamps and a treeless plain. The water surface is covered with masses of floating "Sadd." Twelve miles further on Lake Nô is reached and the White Nile ends.

The next portion of the Nile, which extends from Lake Nô to Lake Albert, is called the "Baḥr al-Gebel," i.e., "Mountain River," or the "Upper Nile." The Upper Nile starts from the extreme eastern end of Lake Nô, and the region of the "Sadd" is here entered. "Sadd," a word derived from the Arabic word سد, meaning a "barrier" or "obstacle," is the name given to the barrier of floating weed which formerly blocked the navigation of the river between Shâmbî and Lake Nô, i.e., for a distance of about 250 miles.[2] The "Sadd" is formed chiefly of papyrus and the reed called *umm ṣûf*, i.e., "mother of wool;" the former grows to a height of from 17 to 20 feet, and the latter from 3 to 4 feet. These two, with the earth adhering to their roots, form the real obstruction. Other swimming plants assist, e.g., the Azolla, the Utricularia, the Otellia, and the Ambatch. Masses of these plants are broken from their places on the edges of the lagoons near the river by the wind during storms, and drift about, and in the rainy season when the swamps are full they find their way into the channel of the river. They are soon stopped by some bend in the river, and the channel is blocked. The masses of reed which follow are sucked by the current under the obstacle, and eventually "the whole becomes wedged into one solid block, "composed partly of earth, and partly of stalks and roots of "papyrus and reed, broken up by the extreme compression "into an inextricable tangle. So great is the pressure applied by "the water that the surface of the block is often forced several "metres above the water level." The thickness of the mass varies from 3 feet 6 inches to 23 feet!

All through the "Sadd" region the scenery is monotonous to a degree. Swamps and lagoons extend for miles on each side of

[1] The Signora was Miss Tinne; see above, p. 313.

[2] See Garstin, *Egypt*, No. 5 (1899); *Egypt*, No. 2 (1901); and *Egypt*, No. 2 (1904); and Gleichen, *op. cit.*, Appendix B., p. 299.

the river, and the marshes are covered with a dense growth of water-reeds, including the papyrus. Throughout this whole region, more especially between Bôr and Lake Nô, it is extremely rare to see any sign of human life.[1] Even the hippopotami appear to shun these swamps. There are no birds except a few night herons. Fish and crocodiles abound, and at sun-down the mosquitoes appear in millions. "The whole region has an aspect "of desolation beyond the power of words to describe. It must "be seen to be understood."[2] Well may Nero's centurions have reported unfavourably on the country as a place for Roman conquests!

At Ḥellet an-Nuer, or Aliab Dok, 139 miles from Lake Nô, on the west bank, is "Captain Gage's channel." It was discovered by Captain Gage, who followed its course for 40 miles, but was then stopped by the "Sadd." The Shâmbî station, or Ghaba Shâmbî (256 miles) is on the west bank of the Shâmbî Lagoon, about 1½ miles from the river, in lat. 7° 6′ 12″ north. It is a dreary-looking spot, but is nevertheless the chief Nile post of the Baḥr al-Ghazâl Province, and has a garrison of 25 men.[3] Near Abû Kûkâ (293 miles) the papyrus swamps cease, the western forest approaches the river, and the banks are dry. The village is invisible from the river.

At Kanîsa (304 miles), i.e., "the church," a station of the Austrian Mission was placed; it was abandoned in 1864 on account of the deadly effect of the climate on the Fathers. Here the forest is very thick. Between Kanîsa and Lake Powendael (344 miles) the country is desolate-looking and monotonous. This lake contains many small islands and is full of hippopotami.

Bôr (384 miles) is a collection of Dinka villages, which are well kept, neat, and clean. The huts are circular in shape, are plastered with mud, and have conical thatched roofs. Each has a small door, through which the inhabitants crawl. The people

[1] Garstin, *Egypt*, No. 2 (1904), p. 98.

[2] The positions of the nineteen Blocks into which Major Peake divided the "Sadd" in this region are shown in Sir W. Garstin's map (*Egypt*, No. 2 (1901), plates 2 and 3), and their distances from Lake Nô are given by Count Gleichen, *op. cit.*, p. 73.

[3] Gleichen, *op. cit.*, p. 75.

WOMAN GRINDING DHURRA AT KIRO IN THE LADO ENCLAVE.

[From a photograph by Miss Hilda Burrows.

seem to be comfortable and contented, and they have large herds of cattle. At Bôr the character of the marshes changes, and grasses take the place of papyrus and ambatch. The Dêm, or camp, of the Dervish leader Arabi Dafa'a Allah, is visible at mile 390. A few miles further south the scenery much resembles that of the Blue Nile; the forest is close to the river, the banks are high, and there is a profusion of creepers and undergrowth. About mile 410 the Bari *tukls* take the place of the Dinka

THE BAḤR AL-GEBEL—RIVER BANK AT BÔR.

[From Sir W. Garstin's *Report*, by permission of the Comptroller of H.M. Stationery Office.

huts, and the difference is at once visible. Further on the west bank is inhabited by the Aliab tribe, a cross between the Baris and Dinkas. Near the site of the Anglo-Egyptian station of Kirô (456 miles) the river scenery is fine, and "luxuriant tropical "vegetation abounds. Giant *Euphorbia* are a marked feature of "the forest. The whole of the banks and most of the trees are "covered with a velvety-looking mass of creepers. A bluff, three "to four metres high, projects into the stream. . . . The face of "this cliff is perforated by myriads of holes made by a very beauti- "ful and tiny species of bee-eater. These birds have rose-coloured "wings, with bronze-coloured bodies. They add much to the "beauty of a lovely scene."[1]

Kîrô (the Belgian station), 460 miles from Lake Nô, is the most northerly station of the "Lâdô Enclave;" it stands on the west bank in lat. 5° 12′ or 5° 13′ north. It is a picturesque-looking place, surrounded by forest, in which there are some fine trees. The bank, which is from 17 to 20 feet high, suffers from erosion, and pieces of it are frequently falling into the river. The huts are

THE BAḤR AL-GEBEL—LÂDÔ.

[From Sir W. Garstin's *Report*, by permission of the Comptroller of H.M. Stationery Office.

well laid out and neatly built. The cantonment is surrounded by a wooden stockade, in which Krupp guns are mounted. The commandant's house is a good one, and has a thatched roof and a deep verandah. On an island in the river vegetables and *paw-paw* trees are grown, otherwise there appears to be no cultivation. When Sir William Garstin visited Kîrô it possessed a small steamer, the *Van Kerckhoven*, called after the leader of the First Congo Expedition in 1889, and several steel sailing boats. The steamer was brought from the west coast in sections. The

[1] Garstin, *Egypt*, No. 2 (1904), p. 93.

WOMEN WASHING THEIR CLOTHES AT LADO.

[From a photograph by Miss Hilda Burrows.

garrison is recruited from the negro tribes round about. In two years the Belgians lost nine Europeans and 300 natives from fever. In 1905 some difficulty arose between Great Britain and the Congo Free State with respect to the territory on the Upper Nile. On May 8th, 1906, "an arrangement was signed by Sir Edward "Grey and Baron van Eetvelde, at Brussels, which stipulates that "the lease of 1894 of the Bahr-el-Ghazal shall be cancelled except "so far as regards the Lado *enclave*, which remains leased to King "Leopold during his reign under the present conditions. The

THE BAḤR AL-GEBEL. "EARTHQUAKE HILL." (GEBEL REGGÂF).

[From Sir W. Garstin's *Report*, by permission of the Comptroller of H.M. Stationery Office.

"arrangement further provides for the construction of a railway "from Lado to the Congo States frontier, the interest being "guaranteed by the Egyptian Treasury; the establishment of a "commercial port at the railway terminus; free navigation on the "Upper Nile for Congo and Belgian steamers; and free transit of "passengers and merchandise over the territories of the Egyptian "Sudan. Finally it is agreed that any differences as to the "delimitation of the frontier which may henceforth arise between "Great Britain and the Congo State shall be submitted to the "Hague Tribunal" (*Times*, May 9, 1906).

Mongalla (474 miles) is the most southerly post of the Sûdân Government on the Nile; it stands on the east bank, and is garrisoned by two companies. There is a Nile-gauge here. The forest has been cleared away, and huts for the men and houses for the officials have been built. Two miles further on is Shêkh Lâdô's house. The natives of this part of the country belong to the Bari tribe, but they are few in number. Lâdô (495 miles), on the west bank of the river, in lat. 5° 1′ 33″ north, was at one time the capital of the Equatorial Provinces of Egypt, and here Emin Pâshâ lived and governed. The houses are built of brick, and have conical thatched roofs; some of them rest on brick arches, which permit the air to pass beneath them. It is a desolate-looking spot, surrounded by a flat plain covered with bush. It is swampy in places. Food for the troops has to be brought from a long distance.

South of Lâdô the river winds its way between vast marshes, the banks are low, and the area of the country flooded is very great. Papyrus, reeds, and ambatch abound. There are numerous islands and channels in the river.

Gondokoro (504 miles) is the north frontier post of the Uganda Protectorate; it is on the east bank, and Gordon placed it in lat 4° 54′ 20″ north, and long. 31° 43′ 46″ east. The station stands on a high cliff from 18 to 20 feet above the water. Here were the church and houses of the Austrian Mission, but these have now disappeared, and the erosion caused by the river threatens to eat away the whole cliff. The huts for the garrison are built of bamboo and straw, and the house of the Collector and his staff is of brick, with a thatched roof. Here Sir Samuel Baker founded his town "Ismaïliya," with a garrison of 1,500 men; the remains of his lines are still to be seen, and a description of them is published by Count Gleichen in his *Handbook* (i., p. 81).

About eight miles above Gondokoro is Gebel Reggâf, i.e., "Earthquake Hill;" it stands on the west bank, not far from the river, and is about 350 feet high. This hill is a perfect cone, and its name suggests that it was a volcano.[1] To the north of the hill is the Belgian station of Reggâf, with its neat houses and

[1] The Arabic root رجف means "to quake," of the earth.

GONDOKORO. BY THE BANK IS A "DUG-OUT" CANOE.

From a photograph by Miss Hilda Burrows.

thatched roofs and verandahs.[1] There are no trees, and the country all round is open and bare of bush. Four miles up-stream the Kît River enters the Nile on the east bank; it rises in the Lumoga Mountains in lat. 3° 53′ north. About twenty-two miles from Gondokoro is Fort Berkeley, a collection of straw huts. Here the river is divided into three channels. Here is the north end of the Beddên Rapids. About mile 45 the Nile flows between two granite hills, each nearly 400 feet high. On the slopes of the western hill was the old fort of Kiri. Between

THE MURCHISON FALLS ON THE VICTORIA NILE.

[From Sir W. Garstin's *Report*, by permission of the Comptroller of H.M. Stationery Office. The original photograph is by G. Butcher, Esq.

miles 50 and 62 are the Gougi Rapids, and a little further on are the Yerbora Rapids. Near the northern end of these was Emin Pâshâ's fort Muggi. At mile 75 the Umi enters the Nile on the east bank; it is the boundary between the countries of Madi and Bari. Five miles on, on the west bank, is Emin's fort of Labori. At mile 95 the north end of Gebel Kurdu is seen on the west bank; this range is fully ten miles long, and some of its peaks are 350 feet high.

[1] Garstin, *Egypt*, No. 2 (1904), p. 90.

About mile 100 the Asua, or Assua, River joins the Nile on the east bank. The Asua rises in lat. 2° 20′ north, in the Suk Mountains, and is about 170 miles long. The scenery here is beautiful. Between this place and Nimuli are the Fola Rapids, which have been already described. On the left bank are the Kuku Mountains. At Nimuli (116 miles) is a garrison of two companies of Sûdânî soldiers, each under a British officer. The country is generally high and flat. The military station is about half a mile from the river, and behind it to the north-east are the Arju hills. Here the river runs between high banks, and in a series of rapids. About mile 121, on the west bank, is the Belgian station of Dufilî, lat. 3° 34′ 35″ north, and long. 32° 30′ east. Here is a collection of thatched houses within an enclosure. The armament consists of Krupp guns. Dufilî is a dreary spot, is very unhealthy, and black-water fever is said to be prevalent. At mile 193, and 40 miles from Lake Albert, is Wadelâî, which is situated on a rounded hill on the east bank. An English collector and a medical officer are stationed here, and their houses and the hospital are on the top of the hill. It is an unhealthy and fever-stricken place. From the hill fine views may be obtained, and to the south the Rubi Lake and the Albert Nyanza mountains are visible. On the east the country is of a "park-like character, "with grassy glades, alternating with open forest;" on the west is a bush-covered plain. The channel of the Nile is only about 450 feet wide here, and the river rushes along with a high velocity. Between Dufilî and Magungo the rivers Achwa and Tangi join the Nile on the east bank. About mile 233 Magungo is reached, and here the Baḥr al-Gebel, or Upper Nile, may for all practical purposes be said to begin. Magungo is about 747 miles from Lake Nô, and 1,359 miles from Kharṭûm.

Between Lake Albert and Lake Victoria the river is known as the "Victoria Nile," or the "Somerset River," and this section of it is about 255 miles long. The scenery for the first fifteen miles is in places very lovely. About mile 23 is the village of Fagao, where formerly caravans crossed the river by a ferry. A little above it are the Murchison Falls, and a mile or two on is the Island of Patosan. About mile 38 are the Karuma Falls, and at mile 68 is Fuwêra, which stands 1,060 metres

NATIVES IN AN AMBATCH CANOE NEAR GONDOKORO.

[From a photograph by Miss Hilda Burrows.

above the sea. This village is a large one; opposite to it the Lenga River enters the Nile. Near Mruli, mile 116, lat. 1° 39′ north, and on the right bank of the Kafu River, was Gordon's Fort. The Kafu rises in lat. 1° north, and is about seventy-five miles long; its tributaries are the Dubengi, the Lugogo, and the Maanja. At mile 124 Lake Choga is reached, and the river flows through it for more than fifty miles, on the west side. This lake is situated between lat. 1° and 2° north, and long. 32° 15′ and 33° 30′ east; it is joined at its south-east end by the Gogonio and Sensiwa Rivers. At mile 180 the Choga Lake is left. At mile 205 is Kakoji, and between this village and the Owen Falls at mile 243 there are falls and rapids all the way. About five miles further on are the Ripon Falls, over which the Nile flows out of Lake Victoria. As the Victoria Nile is about 250 miles long, and the Upper Nile is 747 miles long, and the White Nile 612 miles long, and the Nile between Kharṭûm and Cairo is about 1730 miles long, it is clear that the Ripon Falls are 3,339 miles from Cairo. If to this we add 130 miles for the length of one of the two great arms of the Nile from Cairo to the sea, the length of the Nile from the point where it leaves Lake Victoria to the sea is about 3,469 miles. Those who regard the Kagera River, which enters Lake Victoria at its southern end, as the true source of the Nile, add to these figures the length of Lake Victoria, 250 miles, and the length of the Kagera River, including that of one of its tributaries, the Akanyaru, which rises in lat. 2° 55′ south, and then say that the Nile is 4,000 miles long. Sir William Garstin, however, does not regard the Kagera as the source of the Nile, but Lake Victoria itself; we must therefore consider the length of the Nile to be not 4,000 miles, but about 3,469 miles.

Since the above paragraphs were written the Survey Department of Egypt has published a masterly treatise on the Nile, entitled *The Physiography of the River Nile and its Basin*, by Captain H. G. Lyons, R.E., the Director-General of the Survey Department. In this work the Nile Basin is discussed as a whole, and the general lines of its geology, climate, and hydrography, which together comprise its physiography, are treated scientifically for the first time. Throughout the volume are given many maps, plans, tables, &c., which illustrate and explain the letterpress of the various sections, and all the information given embraces the most recent results obtained by Captain Lyons and his staff, and by private investigators and travellers. Captain Lyons shows clearly how important it is that the Nile should be treated from the geographical as well as from the utilitarian point of view, and he is obviously correct in his conclusion that the study of the Nile geography is of the greatest value for all who are engaged in practical irrigation work. Want of space prevents our summarizing here many of the results given in this valuable supplement to Sir William Garstin's famous *Report*, but the following facts and figures are of general interest, and will be useful to many.

The area of the Nile Basin is about 2,900,000 square kilometres. The areas of Catchment Basins are:—

	SQUARE KILOS.	SQUARE MILES.
Lake Victoria	238,900	92,243
Lakes Albert and Albert Edward and Semliki River	54,100	20,889
Victoria Nile	75,600	29,190
Baḥr al-Gebel and Baḥr al-Zarâfa	190,700	73,632
Baḥr al-Ghazâl	552,100	213,175
Sobat River	244,900	94,560
White Nile	353,550	136,492
Blue Nile	331,500	127,998
Atbara	220,700	85,216
Nile	605,600	233,832
Nile	2,867,650	1,107,227

TABLE OF DISTANCES ON THE RIVER NILE.

PLACE.	DISTANCE.	FROM RIPON FALLS.
VICTORIA NILE—	MILES.	MILES.
Ripon Falls	—	—
Kakoji	40	40
Mruli	84	124
Foweira	47	170
Murchison Falls	48	218
Albert Lake	24	242

NILE DISTANCES

PLACE.	DISTANCE.	FROM RIPON FALLS
BAHR EL-JEBEL—	MILES.	MILES.
Bahr el-Jebel entrance	2	244
Wadelai	40	283
Nimule	94	378
Asua River	13	391
Fort Berkeley	78	469
Gondokoro	20	489
Lado	7	496
Mongalla	18	515
Bor	83	598
Kenisa	73	670
Ghaba Shambé	50	720
Hellet Nuer	112	833
WHITE NILE—		
Lake No	129	962
Taufikia	82	1,044
Dueim	391	1,435
Khartoum	124	1,560
NILE—		
Shendi	116	1,675
Atbara River	86	1,762
Berber	25	1,786
Abu Hamed	129	1,916
Merowe	149	2,065
Dongola	169	2,234
Wadi Halfa	277	2,510
Aswan	214	2,725
Luxor	136	2,861
Qena	40	2,901
Girga	77	2,978
Assiut	88	3,065
Cairo	247	3,312
Delta Barrage	14	3,326
Rosetta mouth	147	3,473

Total length of Nile . . . . . 3,473 miles.

II. The Country of the Egyptian Sûdân.

The Egyptian Sûdân is bounded on the north by the 22nd parallel of latitude, on the south by the Lâdô Enclave and by Uganda, which extends to the 5th parallel of north latitude, on the east by the Red Sea, Eritrea, and Abyssinia, and on the west by the French Congo and Wadai. The Lâdô Enclave is leased to H.M. Leopold II., King of the Belgians.[1] The area of the Egyptian Sûdân is generally estimated at 1,000,000 square miles. The population at the present time is said to be 2,000,000, but this estimate is a very general one. Before the Dervish rule, i.e., about 1880, Sir Reginald Wingate believes the population to have been about 8,525,000, but between that period and the year 1899 3,451,000 persons are said to have died of disease, and 3,203,000 to have been killed in external or internal war, and in 1903 he estimated the population to be 1,875,500 persons.[2] The Dervish policy was to wipe out the tribes which refused to swear allegiance to Mahdiism, and in this way whole districts were depopulated. Thus, prior to 1882, the district comprising the banks of the Rahad and Dinder Rivers contained upwards of 800 villages; in 1901 not a village remained there. Small-pox alone decimated the population, and wholesale butcheries like that of the Baṭṭahin, which Slatin Pâshâ describes, and like that of the Ga'alîn at Matamma, account for the disappearance of thousands of men.

The principal Rivers of the Sûdân have already been enumerated in the preceding section on the Niles. On these the very life of Egypt and the Sûdân depends, and the manner in which Nature provides the Valley of the Nile with water during the winter and summer is marvellous. The White Nile collects the waters of the Upper Nile, Baḥr al-Ghazâl, Baḥr az-Zarâfa, and the Sobat, and thus produces a regular supply the whole year round. The Blue Nile and the Atbara collect the waters which rush down from the Abyssinian mountains as the result of the summer rains, and pour them into the Nile in such quantities that the Nile Flood, or Inundation, is produced. They bring with them the scourings of forests and an enormous mass of mud, which has after several thousands of years formed the cultivable

[1] The text of the treaty is given by Count Gleichen, *Handbook*, ii., p. 286.

[2] *Egypt*, No. 1 (1904), p. 79.

land on the river banks between Kharṭûm and the Mediterranean Sea.

The Nubian Desert. On the east of the Nile the country between the river and the Red Sea so far south as the Atbara is practically a bare and stony desert. There are, however, many places in it where rain collects and permits the tribes to produce limited crops. From the Atbara south there is a good deal of cultivation, and many districts are very fertile. This is due to the water which falls as rain, and to the rivers which rise in the mountains which lie in Abyssinian territory, beyond the eastern frontier of the Anglo-Egyptian Sûdân. On the west of the Nile the Sûdân includes the southern part of the Libyan Desert and the Bayûda Desert. In places these deserts are seamed by ranges of low hills, which sometimes have peaks of considerable height, but the highest mountains in the Sûdân are those of Gebel Marra, which lie on the 13th parallel of north latitude, to the south-west of Al-Fâsher, in Dâr Fûr. Nearer to the White Nile are the Nûba Mountains, among which may be mentioned Gebel Abû Sinûn, Gebel Dêgo, Gebel Kôn, Gebel Abû Dôm, Gebel Têbûn, Gebel Kudr, Gebel Kadero, Gebel Taḳala, Gebel Gadîr, Gebel Gurûn, Gebel Morung, Gebel Werna, Gebel Tekem, &c. In the western desert are a few Oases, e.g., 1. the Oasis of Selîma, which lies on the Arba'în Road, about 78 miles south of the Oasis of Shabb, 55 miles west of Sâḳiet al-'Abd, and 120 miles south-west of Ḥalfa. It was visited by Mr. James Currie, Director of the Gordon College, in 1901, who examined the ancient remains there, and by Captain H. Hodgson in February, 1903, who estimated that there were 2,000 date trees there.[1] 2. The Oasis of Tundubî, 171 miles from Dongola.[2] 3. The Oasis of Lagia Kabîr, 166 miles from Dongola.[3] 4. The Oasis of Bîr Sulṭân, 283 miles from Dongola.[4] Here natron is found in a seam of from half an inch to two inches thick. Horns of the oryx and addax are found here in large numbers, and Captain Hodgson assumes that from time immemorial these were the tools which the natives employed in digging out the natron. 5. The

[1] Gleichen, *op. cit.*, vol. i., p. 203.
[2] *Ibid.*, vol. ii., p. 170.
[3] *Ibid.*, vol. ii., p. 168.
[4] *Ibid.*, p. 171.

Oasis of Tura. This oasis is, according to Count Gleichen, situated about 150 miles south of the Oasis of Lagia.

These and the other small oases have formed the chief factor in determining the routes of caravans across the desert, and it is tolerably safe to assume that travellers in all ages have journeyed by the same main routes because of the water and shade which the oases afforded. In a few places in the desert pools of water or WELLS exist; some of them have been formed in the first instance by Nature, and others by artificial means. The best known wells are those of Uḥmîr, Unḳât, Ṭarafâwî, and Nugîm, between

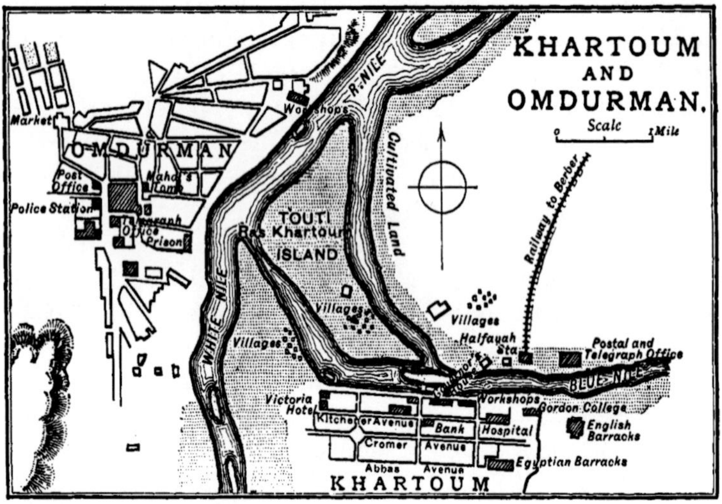

Aswân and Berber; the Wells of Murrât, between Abû Ḥamad and Korosko; the Wells of Handûb, Awtâw, Hambûk, Dassâbal, Harâtarî, Kûkrêb, Aryâb, and Albâk, between Sawâkin and Berber; the Wells of Maghâgha, Gakdûl, and Abû Tlêḥ, between Kôrtî and Matamma; the Seventy Wells in the Bayûda Desert, between Ambiḳôl and the Sixth Cataract; the Wells of Gabra, about 100 in number, between Dabba and Omdurmân; the Wells of Kagmar Ṣâfîya, Ẓabâ'î, Shuṭṭêr, and Mahtûl, between Obêḍ and Dabba; and the Wells of Umm Badr and 'Ain Ḥâmid, between Fâsher and Dongola.[1]

[1] See Shucair, *op. cit.*, i., pp. 22, 23; and Gleichen, *op. cit.*, Index *s.v.* "Wells."

PROVINCES OF THE SUDAN

For administrative purposes the Egyptian Sûdân is divided into EIGHT FIRST CLASS PROVINCES and FIVE SECOND CLASS; each Province has a chief town, and is divided into a number of Districts, as follows:—

FIRST CLASS PROVINCES.[1]

1. KHARṬÛM PROVINCE.[2] Its chief town is KHARṬÛM, and its Districts are Kharṭûm, Omdurmân, and Wad Ramla. The town of Kharṭûm was founded between the years 1820 and 1824 by the

THE PALACE AT KHARṬÛM.

[From a photograph by R. Türstig, Esq.

sons of Muḥammad 'Alî, and it stands on the angle of land between the junction of the White and Blue Niles, and nearly at the end of the left bank of the Blue Nile; it is 1,253 feet above the Mediterranean. The obvious meaning of the name, as I pointed out years ago, is the "trunk of an elephant," and the shape of the land near probably suggested the name "Kharṭûm" to the Arabs who first applied it to the town; but, on the other hand,

[1] For the old arrangement of provinces, see Shucair, *op. cit.*, i., pp. 69-72.

[2] For the boundaries of the provinces, see Gleichen, *op. cit.*, i., pp. 335 ff., and for the list of the tribes which inhabit them, see pages 273 ff., and 322 ff.

"Kharṭûm" may be the Arabic translation of an older name meaning the same thing, just as "Elephantine," the name which the Greeks gave to the island and town of Aswân, is a translation of its ancient Egyptian name "Ābu." If the name Kharṭûm means "elephant's trunk,"[1] the correct transliteration is "Khurṭûm" and not "Kharṭûm." The town of Kharṭûm which has sprung up under the rule of the British is built on the site of Muḥammad 'Alî's town, and this in its turn stood on the site of an older settlement; it is certain that a town existed here when the kingdom of Sôba flourished, and we may assume that one always stood here. Kharṭûm is the capital of the Egyptian Sûdân, and the seat of the Government. It is connected by a chain ferry with Ḥalfâya, or Kharṭûm North, and with Omdurmân by steamers which run at regular intervals. A little to the west of the railway terminus, on the opposite bank, is the Palace, built by Lord Kitchener on the site of the old Government Palace; to the south of its fine garden is a statue of General Gordon, and in the garden itself is a large stone Ram of Àmen which was brought from the ruins of Sôba, about 12 miles up the Blue Nile, on the east bank. Close by are the War Office and other Government buildings, the Post and Telegraph Office, the Office of Works, the British Barracks, and at the west end of the town are the Zoological Gardens. Eastwards are Slatin Pâshâ's house, the Sûdân Club, the Egyptian Officers' Mess, &c., and further up the river on the same bank is the Gordon College. A large mosque has been built in the south-western quarter of the town, the foundation stone of which was laid on September 17th, 1900. The Copts are building a church, and it is to be hoped that the British will soon build a church which for size and dignity shall be a worthy symbol of the Christian religion, and of the dominant power in the land.

The normal garrison consists of one battalion of British Infantry, three battalions of Infantry of the Egyptian Army, and forces of Cavalry and Artillery.[2] In rebuilding the town the British have been careful to provide for the construction of wide avenues, planted

[1] See Mas'ûdî, ed. B. de Meynard and P. de Courteille, tom. ii., p. 21, line 7. It is possible that the allusion is to the *tusks* of the elephant, for خرطوم also means the tushes of a boar or the long teeth of any animal.

[2] See Gleichen, *op. cit.*, i., pp. 3 and 49. It is understood that the garrison is to be increased.

A WOMAN DRAWING WATER AT OMDURMAN.

[From a photograph by Miss Hilda Burrows.

with trees, and all houses and other buildings have been erected on plans which have been approved by the authorities. The hottest months of the year are April, May, and June, and the cool and pleasant season begins about November 15th, and ends early in March. The population at the present time is nearly 10,000, but it is increasing rapidly, and in a few years will be very considerable.

The District of Omdurmân, more correctly "Umm Darmân," lies on the west bank of the Nile, about five miles from Kharṭûm. It takes its name from a little hamlet which stood just above the sandy bank of the river to the south end of the modern town of

THE MOSQUE AT KHARṬÛM.

[From a photograph by R. Türstig, Esq.

Omdurmân, and which was frequented by Arab merchants, who arranged their wares there before they crossed over to Kharṭûm. This hamlet existed for a considerable number of years, and is said by some to have been called "Omdurmân," i.e., "mother of *darmân*," because a thicket of *darmân* trees stood behind it;[1] if this be so, the trees must have been cut down by the inhabitants for firewood. Omdurmân was occupied by the Mahdî on January 5th, 1885, and he lived there with all his followers for a few months afterwards. After his death the Khalîfa 'Abd-Allah built a great Ḳubba over his tomb, and made Omdurmân the

[1] On the other hand "Umm Darmân" is a name given by the Arabs to the hedgehog.

capital, giving it the name "Bak'a al-Mahdî," i.e., the "Province of the Mahdî." Then he allowed his followers to build houses for themselves, and eventually Omdurmân became a town six miles long, and nearly three wide, and containing nearly 400,000 inhabitants. The Khalîfa then built a house of two storeys for himself close to the Mahdî's tomb, and also a large bazaar, wherein all kinds of Egyptian, Indian, and Yaman work could be brought. His so-called mosque, or "*hôsh*," was merely a large rectangular piece of land surrounded by a wall built of red, i.e., burnt, bricks; it was 460 yards long, and 350 yards wide, and had four doors. He set apart in the town a place which was called "Bêt al-Amâna," i.e., house of safe-keeping, or store-house, and he built the prison, of which such terrible stories are told in Slatin Pâshâ's *Fire and Sword*, and Ohrwalder's *Ten Years' Captivity*. The Khalîfa's sanitary arrangements were very primitive, and he allowed the people to fill the town with cess-pits, which Count Gleichen thinks were responsible for the disease of cerebro-spinal meningitis that was at one time so common in the town. The population is now about 46,000, and the garrison consists of two battalions of Infantry, and they have two Maxims.

2. SENNAAR PROVINCE. The chief town is Sanga, and its six Districts are Sennaar, Sanga, Abû Na'âma, Dinder (Abû Hashîm), Ruṣêreṣ, and Dâr Fûng. Sanga was founded by 'Abd-Allah wad al-Ḥasan about nineteen years ago. It stands on the left bank of the Blue Nile, and is about 266 miles from Kharṭûm. Sennaar was the capital of the Fûng dynasty of kings, who flourished from the beginning of the fifteenth to the beginning of the nineteenth century. Its position as a trade centre has been taken by Wad Madanî, which has a population of 14,000, and stands on the left bank of the Nile, 123 miles from Kharṭûm. Wad Madanî was founded by a religious teacher called Madanî, about A.D. 1800. The capital of the district of Dâr Fûng was formerly Gule, but it is now Keili, where the "Mek," or local chief, resides. Its inhabitants, the Ingassana, use boomerangs in hunting wild animals, and they have many curious and primitive customs. Their country is not well known.

3. KORDÔFÂN PROVINCE. The chief town of Kordôfân is Al-Obêḍ, and its eight Districts are Obêḍ, Bâra, Khûrshi (Umm

COTTON SPINNERS AT OMDURMAN.

[From a photograph by Miss Hilda Burrows.

Damm), Ṭayyâra, Nahûd, Tandik, Dilling, and Talôdî. This province lies between the White Nile and the eastern boundary of Dâr Fûr, and in its northern part the tribes which breed camels live. In the south are the Nûba hills, and "some of the views of the "hills looking over masses of forest are really beautiful" (Gleichen, i. 173). The elephant, giraffe, and antelope abound, the trees are filled with birds and monkeys, and snakes are said to be common. Dotted over the country are several mountains, or hills, and the province contains four principal lakes. The inhabitants obtain their water from rain, from the lakes and smaller pools of water, and from the famous *tabaldi* trees. These trees are naturally hollow, and vary in diameter from 10 to 25 feet, and the portion in which the water is stored—some are filled by the rain running into them along the branches, and others artificially—is often 20 feet high. The chief products of the province are gum, cattle, and ivory. When the British occupied the country in 1898 the whole region was found to have been laid waste by the Khalîfa, and of some of the most important towns it was difficult even to trace the ruins! "Everywhere the destruction was wanton and complete." The only inhabitants who defied the Mahdiists successfully were the Nûbas, who retreated to their hills, and were able to defend their villages with walls. The inhabitants are Nûbas and Arabs, and among the latter are the camel-breeders and the cattle-breeders, i.e., the Baḳḳâra, who are undoubtedly the descendants of the terrible "Menti" ("Cattle-men") of the Egyptian inscriptions. AL-OBÊḌ, or Al-Ubayyaḍ, the capital of the Province, is in lat. 13° 11′ north and long. 30° 14′ east, and Count Gleichen estimates that it contains about 10,000 people. It is 268 miles from Kharṭûm, to which town its gum is carried *viâ* Duwêm on the White Nile by a regular transport service. Al-Obêḍ was besieged by the Mahdi for six months, and fell on January 17th, 1883. NAHÛD, the chief town of a District of this name, lies 165 miles to the west of Al-Obêḍ, and is on the great trade route from Dâr Fûr, the eastern boundary of which forms the western boundary of Kordôfân.

DÂR FÛR is one of a line of ancient kingdoms running across Africa, which, according to Sir Reginald Wingate,[1] may be thus

[1] *Mahdiism*, p. 8.

enumerated: Senegambia, Bambara, Massina, Gando, Sokoto, Bornu, Bagirmi, Waddai, Dâr Fûr, Sennaar, and Abyssinia. A line of Sulṭâns reigned over Dâr Fûr from the early part of the fifteenth to the middle of the nineteenth century, several of them, apparently, being of Arab origin, and their territory extended so far to the east as the Atbara River. About 1740, however, the Fûng kings, whose capital was at Sennaar, occupied all the country between the Blue and White Niles, and defeated the people of Dâr Fûr in several engagements. Some 25 years later the Fûngs crossed the White Nile and seized the province of Kordôfân, but they only held it for a few years, and eventually they were driven back across the river. At the close of the eighteenth century Dâr Fûr was visited by Mr. W. G. Browne, one of whose objects was to travel southwards to discover the true source of the Nile, for he was convinced that the Blue Nile, whose source Bruce had discovered, was not the true Nile. Mr. Browne lived in Dâr Fûr for nearly three years (1792-1795), and his shrewd observations on the manners and customs of the people are singularly instructive and interesting.[1]

Soon after 1820 Dâr Fûr was conquered by Muḥammad Bey Defterdâr, the son-in-law of Muḥammad 'Alî, whose infamous cruelties have been described by Mr. Petherick. In 1874 Dâr Fûr itself was conquered by Zubêr Pâshâ on behalf of the Khedive of Egypt, and was annexed to Egypt. The limits of the present province are given by Gleichen (i. 184) as lat. 10° and 16° north, and long. 22° and 27° 30′ east, and its ruler is the Sulṭân 'Alî Dînâr, who pays an annual tribute to the Sûdân Government. The capital of Dâr Fûr is AL-FÂSHER, which took the place of Kôbî, or "Cobbe," as Mr. Browne writes the name, at the end of the seventeenth century. It is 388 miles from Obêḍ, and 650 miles from Kharṭûm. The province produces *dhurra*, millet, cotton, onions, simsim (sesame), cucumbers, pumpkins, &c., and the natives occupy themselves with the breeding of camels, horses, cattle, sheep, goats, &c. Salt is made at certain places, and the negroes of Gebel Marrado formerly worked iron on a small scale. The Arabs of Dâr Fûr, i.e., men of Arab descent, are Muḥammadans, and the Negroes are pagans.

[1] See *Travels in Africa*, 2nd Edition, London, 1806.

SHILLUKS ON THE WHITE NILE IN THEIR FAVOURITE ATTITUDE OF REST.

[From a photograph by Miss Hilda Burrows.

4. The Fâshôda Province, now known as Kôdôk, or the "Upper Nile Province." It extends from Gebelên in the north to parallel 5° north; on the west it is bounded by the eastern frontier of Kordôfân and the Baḥr al-Gebel, and on the east by the western and southern boundaries of Sennaar and the western border of Abyssinia down to the Uganda frontier. The principal town of the province is Kôdôk, and its four Districts are Renk, Kôdôk, Tawfîḳîya and Sôbât. Mongalla was formerly a District in this province, but on January 1st, 1906, it was formed into a separate province.

5. The Baḥr al-Ghazâl Province.[1] It is bounded on the north by Kordôfân and Dâr Fûr, on the south by the frontier of the Lâdô Enclave and a portion of the Congo-Nile water-shed, on the east by the Baḥr al-Gebel, and on the west by the French frontier. Its chief town is Wâw, and its three Districts are Wâw, Dêm Zubêr, and Awrambêk (Rumbek). The province in its lower portions is well watered, as may be seen from the large number of rivers which are in it.[2] The products are ivory, a species of fig, the *lulu* or "Sudan date," timber and honey, and iron is found everywhere in large quantities. Owing to the abundance of fuel in the Province the natives, i.e., the Gûrs and the Bongos, find no difficulty in smelting iron in small quantities, and it is they who have supplied the iron hoes which have been used in the country for untold generations. The principal inhabitants are Dinkas, Gûrs, Bongos, Golos, Ndoggos, and Kreich in the north, the Niam-Niams in the south, the Mittu, Wira, and Madi tribes in the east, and the Mandalla tribes in the west.[3]

6. The Kasala Province.[4] Its principal town is Kasala, and its three Districts are Kasala, Ḳaḍâref, and Ḳallâbât. The town

[1] For the history of the province since it declared in favour of the Mahdî in 1882, see Gleichen, *op. cit.*, i., p. 259 ff.

[2] I.e., the Adda, Akoli, Baḥr al-Arab, Baḥr al-Ghazâl, Baḥr al-Ḥomr, Biri, Bo, Boru, Bolako, Bongo, Buri, Chel, Duma, Gell, Ibba, Jur (Gûr) or Sueh, Kir, Leisi, Lau or Dok, Merridi, Naam, Mulmul, Ragaa, Rikki, Rodi, Shaliko, Siri, Sunni, Tong, and Wâw.

[3] Gleichen, *op. cit.*, i., p. 159.

[4] For the boundaries, see Gleichen, *op. cit.*, i., p. 336; and for the amended boundary, see the *Sudan Gazette*, No. 86, p. 415.

of Kasala is, with one exception,[1] the only permanent town in the Sûdân east of the Atbara. It stands on the right bank of the Ḳâsh (Gash) River, 1735 feet above the sea, and is 15 miles west of Sabderat on the Abyssinian frontier. Three miles to the east and south-east respectively are Gebel Mokran and Gebel Kasala, the highest parts of the latter being 2,600 feet above the town. The local shêkh is Sayyid 'Alî al-Mûrghânî, but his brother Sayyid Aḥmad acts for him. The total population of the town and district was estimated in 1904 at 46,000. As the rainfall is little, the people obtain most of their water from wells, which yield an abundant supply. Between June and October the country swarms with the *serûṭ* fly. The game found in the country between the Atbara and the Eritraean frontier is thus enumerated by Count Gleichen: Elephant, rhinoceros, buffalo, giraffe, roan-antelope, kudu, waterbuck, tora, hartebeeste, ibex, wild sheep (?), bushbuck, roebuck, Abyssinian duiker, oribi, dig-dig, and the following gazelles: Sommering's, Dorcas, Heuglin's, Isabella, and possibly Rufifrons; also hippopotamus, crocodile, turtle, wart-hog, pig, wild ass, lion, leopard, cheetah, serval; also various civet and wild cats, hares, wild dogs, baboons, and monkeys; ostrich, bustard, guinea-fowl, francolin, sand-grouse, geese, snipe, wild fowl, and quail.

Ḳaḍâref District has an area of about 11,000 square miles, and its inhabitants numbered 25,000 in 1904. It suffered greatly under the rule of the Dervishes, but was seized in 1898 by Colonel Parsons, who defeated its Dervish governor Aḥmad Faḍîl after a hard fight. The population of the town of Ḳaḍâref was in 1904 about 5,500. A British Inspector lives here for more than half the year, and the town is furnished with a detachment of Sûdânî troops from Kasala. Ḳallâbât District has an area of about 12,000 square miles, most of which is covered by forests. The town of Ḳallâbât is on the left bank of the River Abnaheir, a few miles from the Atbara. It was sacked by the Dervishes in 1886, and here in 1889, towards the close of a terrible battle, King John of Abyssinia was killed. His death was the means of turning the victory of the Abyssinians into a defeat, and the Dervishes con-

[1] I.e., Adârama on the Atbara, 78 miles above the junction of this river with the Nile. Capt. A. C. Parker reports a native tradition which says that the Ḳâsh has an exit in the Atbara near Adârama.

KHOR ARAB IN FLOOD.

[From a photograph by Lieutenant S. F. Newcombe, R.E.

tinued to be masters of the town until December, 1898, when Colonel Collinson hoisted the British and Egyptian flags. The inhabitants of the district and town are chiefly Takruris from Dâr Fûr, and in 1904 they numbered about 3,800.

7. The BERBER PROVINCE.[1] Its chief town is DÂMAR,[2] and its four Districts are Rubâṭâb, Berber Town, Berber District, and Shendî. The town of Berber[3] is a collection of mud huts, and stands on the east bank of the Nile, about 30 miles to the north of the Atbara; it formerly belonged to the kingdom of Sennaar, and its inhabitants submitted to Isma'îl Pâshâ, one of Muḥammad 'Alî's sons, without striking a blow. On May 26th, 1884, the town was captured by the Dervishes, who made it one of their strongholds, and its possession made them masters of the routes to Aswân, (245 miles), Sawâkin (242 niles), and Maṣaw'a (543 miles); it was evacuated by them after the fall of Abû Ḥamed, and occupied by Lord Kitchener on September 6th, 1897. It was formerly the capital of the Berber Province, and a very important place, in spite of the dust storms, which at times made life there well-nigh unbearable.[4] DÂMAR, the new capital of the Province, was a seat of learning in Burckhardt's days (*Travels*, p. 266), and was occupied by natives of Arab descent. Its governor was "Al-Faḳî al-Kabîr," i.e., the "Great Faḳî," or chief religious teacher of all the learned men there. He was reputed to possess supernatural power and knowledge, and was the final arbiter and judge in all disputes. On one occasion he caused the flesh of a lamb to bleat in the stomach of a man who had stolen it! There were several schools here in which young men from all parts of the Sûdân studied the Ḳur'ân and the Commentaries on it, and Muḥammadan Law, and theological philosophy; there was also a well-built mosque here. The great Faḳî lived in a small building, to which a chapel was attached. The natives traded with Dongola and Berber, and they made a kind of cotton stuff in the town, and mats of the *dûm* palm leaves. Burckhardt saw here ostrich eggs

[1] For its boundaries, see Gleichen, *op. cit.*, i. 335.

[2] The capital of the province was formerly Berber Town.

[3] Shucair, i., p. 88, reports a native tradition which derives the name of the town from "Barbara," a former queen!

[4] For a description of the manners and customs of the people of Berber, see the interesting section in Burckhardt, *Travels*, p. 215 ff.

and feathers, and wooden bowls used as ornaments on the walls of the houses, which had mats on the floor. A large trade is done in mats at Dâmar at the present time, and it is rapidly becoming an important trade centre.

The town of Shendî is said to have been at one time the largest in the Eastern Sûdân, and at present, though its population only numbers about 500, it bids fair to become a very important place. It is the residence of a British Inspector and of a Ma'amûr, or native Governor, and forms the head-quarters of four squadrons of Egyptian Cavalry, and of one field battery. There are large railway workshops here, and the railway station is a fine one. In the evening, when the north and south expresses are in, and the station is lit up by the electric light and crowded with natives of all kinds, it presents an animated and interesting scene, and one which many a traveller must be surprised to find in the Sûdân some 1,300 miles from Cairo. Little is known of the history of Shendî in the earliest times, but in or near the site of the modern town a large city must have stood at the time when the pyramids near As-Sûr and Bagrâwîya were built, between B.C. 500 and A.D. 200. The evidence derived from the reliefs in the chapels of these pyramids and from the sculptures on the columns of the temples at Nagaa shows that the Island of Meroë, or at all events that portion of it in which Shendî stands, was ruled by a succession of queens; each, according to Pliny, bore the title of "Candace."

The sculptures represent them as fine, large women, with bold features, and an extraordinary girth of body and development of hips. Whether or not these large-bodied queens were natives of the Island of Meroë cannot be said, but it seems as if they were, for Shendî and its neighbourhood have always enjoyed the reputation of producing beautiful women. Their large dimensions, however, were no doubt produced by artificial means, and to this day abnormally fat women are appreciated in many parts of Africa. Speke tells us that when he was in Karague he went to visit Wazezeru, the elder brother of king Rumanika, whom he found sitting side by side with his chief wife, with numerous wooden pots of milk in front of them. Of his wife he says: "I "was struck with no small surprise at the extraordinary dimen- "sions, yet pleasing beauty, of the immoderately fat fair one by "his side. She could not rise, and so large were her arms that, "between the joints, the flesh hung down like large loose-stuffed "puddings." On asking why his host had so many milk-pots there, Wazezeru pointed to his wife, and said, "This is all the "product of these pots: from early youth upward we keep those "pots to their mouths, as it is the fashion at court to have very "fat wives."[1] Speke also called on one of the sisters-in-law of Rumanika, and he found her "unable to stand except on all fours." He wished to obtain a good view of her, and to measure her, and he gives her dimensions thus: Round the arm, 1 ft. 11 in.; chest, 4 ft. 4 in.; thigh, 2 ft. 7 in.; calf, 1 ft. 8 in.; height, 5 ft. 8 in. "Meanwhile, the daughter, a lass of sixteen, sat stark-naked be- "fore us, sucking at a milk-pot, on which the father kept her at "work by holding a rod in his hand, for as fattening is the first "duty of fashionable life, it must be duly enforced by the rod if "necessary."[2] Dr. G. Schweinfurth gives a picture[3] of a Bongo woman of this class, and says that the thighs of some of the women of the tribe are "as large as a man's chest, and their measure- "ment across the hips can hardly fail to recall the picture in Cuvier's *Atlas* of the now famous 'Hottentot Venus.'" These he saw day after day, and he thinks they may well demand to be technically described as "Steatopyga."[4]

Some of these women wore long switch tails of bast, which contributed to their singular appearance.[5] Women of such form were known and appreciated among the ancient Egyptians, as may be seen from figures and models in the British Museum.[6] The portrait of the Queen of Punt, reproduced by Mariette,[7] also proves that the Egyptians knew of the existence of steatopygous women in other parts of Africa. Speke tells us that the specimens which he saw were produced by a superabundant diet of milk,

[1] Speke, *Journal of Discovery*, Dent's reprint, p. 172.

[2] *Ibid.*, p. 189.

[3] *Heart of Africa*, vol. ii., p. 121.

[4] The whole subject of Steatopygy is discussed, with illustrations, by Dr. H. Ploss in *Das Weib*, vol. i., pp. 202 ff.

[5] *Heart of Africa*, vol. i., p. 295.

[6] See the marble figure, No. 173; the ivory figure, No. 42 (Table-case L); dolls, Nos. 25, 26 and 33, in Case C; and No. 22906, in Case 192 (Third and Fourth Egyptian Rooms).

[7] *Deir al-Bahari*, plate 13, Leipzic, 1877.

and it is said in the Sûdân at the present time that women are fattened by feeding them on milk in which a certain herb is steeped. According to Bruce, who was in Shendî in October, 1772, the queen of the place, or "Sittina" as he calls her,[1] was a beautiful woman, and he describes her as being "scarcely forty, taller than "the middle size, with a very round, plump face, rather large "mouth, very red lips, and the finest eyes and teeth he had ever "seen. She wore a cap of solid gold on her head, hung round "with sequins, and about her neck were gold chains, solitaires, "and necklaces of the same metal. Her hair in ten or twelve "plaits hung down to her waist, and her shoulders and arms were "bare; her dress was a common white garment and a purple silk "stole, or scarf. She wore heavy bracelets and anklets of gold." It is only fair to say that Cailliaud made inquiries about this lady at Shendî, but could hear nothing of her, and it is clear from his narrative that he regarded as fictitious both the lady and Bruce's conversation with her![2] In connection with Shendî, mention must be made of the two brave women, Fâṭma, the mother of 'Uthmân al-Morghânî of Kasala, and her daughter Nefîsa, who resisted the Dervish Amîr of Shendî, Aḥmad Hamza, for months, and tried to keep the inhabitants loyal to the Government. (See Wingate, *Mahdiism*, p. 162.)

In 1814 Burckhardt passed a month in Shendî and collected a number of very important facts about the manners and customs of its inhabitants, its trade, &c.; these were published in his *Travels* (pp. 277-361), and from his narrative the following facts are derived. The town contains from 800 to 1,000 houses, some of which had courts 20 ft. square with high walls. The Mek, or Governor, was called Nimr, i.e., the "Tiger," who was akin to the Fûng tribes that lived near their capital, Sennaar; he was subject to the king of Sennaar, but up to a point his power was absolute. He imposed no tax on the merchants. Burckhardt described (pp. 224 and 280) the inhabitants as "people of frolic, "folly, and levity, avaricious, treacherous and malicious, ignorant "and base, and full of wickedness and lechery." They were shepherds, traders and husbandmen, who produced *dhurra*, millet,

[1] *Travels*, vol. vi., p. 448 (Edinburgh, 1813).
[2] The story is not doubted by Burckhardt.

wheat, water-melons and cucumbers. The cattle were very fine. Tigers, ariel, and ostriches were common in the neighbourhood. Crocodiles were numerous, and horses more numerous than at Berber. A market was held daily, and a large one once a week. Cows and camels were slaughtered daily for food, and milk, both fresh and sour, was brought in by the desert girls in the morning. Tobacco came from Sennaar and was freely indulged in, and snuff was much used. The chemists and druggists sold cloves, pepper, cardamoms, tamarinds,[1] sandal-wood, *ḥelba* (a tonic), *Libân* gum,

MODERN SÛDÂNÎ SILVER-WORK—CIGARETTE CASE.

gum arabic, *shishm* (for the eyes), antimony, *ḳerfa* bark (for fever), *tamar al-barr* (a digestive), &c. The trades were represented by sandal-makers, leather workers, blacksmiths, silversmiths, carpenters, and potters. Imported articles were the *senbil* perfume, the *maḥlab* condiment, soap, sugar, blue cambric, white cotton stuffs with red borders, blue-striped cloth, English calico, stuffs from Lyons and Florence, linen, sheepskins, beads of all kinds, coral, real and imitation, paper, pewter, copper, brassware, razors, files, thimbles, scissors, needles, nails, steels, sword-blades, tar, silver trinkets, bells, looking-glasses, &c. A caravan from

[1] From the Arabic *tamar Hindi*, i.e., the "Indian date."

Sennaar bringing dhurra, *dammûr* cloth, slaves, and gold arrived every six weeks. Gold came from Râs al-Fîl, four days' journey from Sennaar; at Sennaar it was worth 12 dollars an ounce, at Shendî 16, at Sawâkin 20, and at Jidda 22. The slaves were chiefly Nûbas. Other imports were ivory, rhinoceros horns, ebony, coffee, leather, leather water-flasks, shields made of giraffe and rhinoceros skin, honey, water-skins made of ox-hide, ostrich feathers, dates, and tobacco, and female slaves from Mahass.

Slaves were divided into three classes, those under ten years of age, those under fifteen, and those who were full grown. A boy of the second class was worth 15 or 16 dollars, and a girl from 20 to 25; a boy of the first class was worth 12 and a girl 15 dollars, and a full-grown man not more than 8 or 10 dollars. The Nûba slaves were considered to be the healthiest and to have the best disposition; of the western Negroes the Banda were most esteemed. As soon as a slave was purchased, he was circumcised and given a Muḥammadan name. Eunuchs were made at Zâwîyet ad-Dêr, near Asyûṭ in Upper Egypt, and this revolting trade was carried on chiefly by Coptic Christians, who were protected by the Government, to whom they paid an annual tax. The deaths resulting from the operation were rarely more than 2 per cent. A youth[1] who had been treated was worth 1,000 piastres at Asyût (about £10), and 250 were treated annually. Among the slave girls who arrived at Shendî and Asyût were several who, by reason of an operation[2] which had been performed upon them, probably by the merchants, were called in Arabic "*Mukhayyat*," i.e., "consutae." Girls in this state were worth

[1] "Puer, corpore depresso, a robustis quibusdam hominibus, super mensâ "continetur. Tunc emasculator, vinculis sericis sapone illitis, genitalia comprimit, et cum cultro tonsorio (dum puer pro dolore animo deficit) quam celerrime "rescindit. Ad hemorhagiam sistendam plagam pulvere et arenâ calidâ adurunt, "et post aliquot dies calido oleo inungunt. Dein vulnus cum emplastro aliquo, "quod inter Coptos arcanum est, per quadraginta spatium dierum donec "glutinetur curatur. Numquam de celotomia sub hoc coelo audivi." (Burckhardt, *Travels*, p. 330.)

[2] Browne (*Travels*, p. 347) says: "Mihi contigit nigram quandam puellam, "qui hanc operationem subierat, inspicere. Labia pudendi acu et filo con-"suta mihi plana detecte fuere, foramine angusto in meatum urinae relicto. "Apud Esne, Siout, et Cairo, tonsores sunt, qui obstructionem novaculâ "amovent, sed vulnus haud raro lethale evenit."

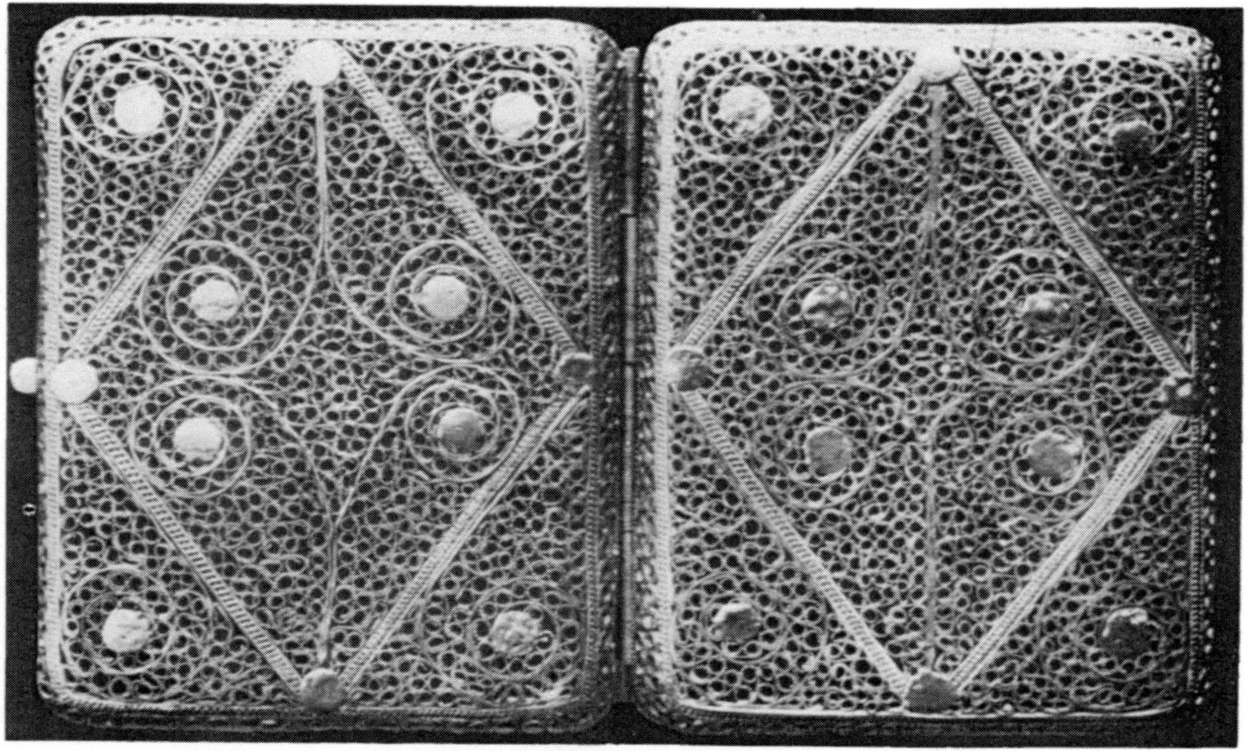

MODERN SUDANI SILVER WORK—CIGAR-CASE.

more than those who were not. The daughters of the 'Abâbda and Ja'afara Arabs, from Thebes to Sennaar, underwent excision, a fact which is also recorded by Strabo (καὶ τὰ θήλεα ἐκτέμνειν).[1] The treatment of slaves was kind, they were well-fed, not overworked, rarely flogged, and kindly spoken to; this was always the case in the town, but in the desert the disobedient slave often felt the whip. The male slave of indifferent character was tied to a long pole, one end of which was fastened to a camel's saddle, and in the other, which was forked, was placed the slave's neck, tied with a strong cord; his right hand also was fastened to the pole. Thus he marched the whole day behind the camel, and at night he was put in irons. Finally, Burckhardt says, "Slavery, in the "East, has little dreadful in it but the name; it is only by the "Turkish soldiers that slaves are ill-treated."

In 1822 Isma'îl Pâshâ, son of Muḥammad 'Alî, was treacherously burned to death, whilst he was eating his dinner, by Nimr of Shendî; in revenge Muḥammad the Defterdâr destroyed the town, and massacred nearly all its inhabitants.

8. The DONGOLA PROVINCE. Its chief town is MERAWI, and its six Districts are Arḳô, Khandaḳ, Dongola Al-Ûrdî, Dabba, Kôrtî, and Merawi. This Province lies to the west of Berber, and takes in the northern part of the great bend of the Nile. Merawi is a few miles below the foot of the Fourth Cataract, and is the residence of a Governor.

SECOND CLASS PROVINCES.

1. The GAZÎRA PROVINCE. Its chief town is WAD MADANÎ, and its six Districts are Wad Madanî, Abû Dulêḳ, Kâmlîn, Rufa'a, Masallamîya, and Manâgîl.

[1] On this Burckhardt remarks (p. 332): "Cicatrix, post excisionem clitoridis, "parietes ipsos vaginae, foramine parvo relicto, inter se glutinat. Cum tempus "nuptiarum adveniat, membranum, a quâ vagina clauditur, coram pluribus pro- "nubis inciditur, sponso ipso adjuvante. Interdum evenit ut operationem efficere "nequeant, sine ope mulieris aliquae expertae, quae, scalpello partes in vaginâ "profundius rescindit. Maritus crastinâ die cum uxore plerumque habitat; "undie illa Araborum sententia, 'Lêlat ad-dukhla mithl lêlat al-futûḥ,' i.e., post "diem aperturae, dies initus. Ex hoc consuetudine fit ut sponsus nunquam "decipiatur, et ex hoc fit ut in Aegypto Superiori innuptae repulsare lascivias "hominum parum student, dicentes, 'Tabûsnî walâ takharḳanî.' Sed quantum "eis sit invita haec continentia, post matrimonium demonstrant, libidini quam 'maxime indulgentes."

2. The WHITE NILE PROVINCE. Its chief town is DUWÊM, and its four Districts are Duwêm, Ḳaṭêna, Kawa, and Gadîd.

3. The RED SEA PROVINCE. Its chief town is "old" Sawâkin, and it has a District of the same name. The town of Sawâkin is built partly on an island, and partly on a portion of the mainland which is called Al-Ḳef;[1] these are joined by a road which is known as "Gordon's Gate and Causeway." The harbour is on the east side of the town. The place was originally colonized

SAWÂKIN—GENERAL VIEW.

[From a photograph by G. E. Mason, Esq.

by Arabs from Ḥaḍr al-Mût (which name has been corrupted into "Hadramout") in southern Arabia; some say they arrived there about A.D. 1800, and others say soon after the great spread of Islâm. For a description of the town about 100 years ago, see Burckhardt's *Travels*, p. 431; and for one of the modern town, see Gleichen, *Handbook*, pp. 94, 95. Now that the terminus of the Atbara-Red Sea Railway has been made at

[1] Burckhardt, *Travels*, p. 431.

MODERN SUDANI SILVER WORK.

Filigree work Matchbox. Amulet. Amulet Case.

Shêkh Mersa Barghût,[1] or "New Sawâkin," the importance of Sawâkin is certain to decline. This place is thirty-six miles north of Sawâkin, and is called after a certain Mersa, whose tomb stands on the northern point of the entrance to the harbour. Ṭôkar, the chief town of the Ṭôkar District, is situated at the mouth of the Khôr Baraka, fifty-six miles south of Sawâkin.

4. The MONGALLA PROVINCE. Its chief town is MONGALLA.

GORDON GATE, SAWÂKIN.

[From a photograph by G. E. Mason, Esq.

The boundaries of this Province are set out in the *Sudan Gazette*, January 1st, 1906, No. 86, p. 413.

5. The ḤALFA PROVINCE. Its chief town is ḤALFA, and its three Districts are Ḥalfa, Mahass (Dulgo), and Sukkôt (Kôsha). The province of Ḥalfa extends from Faraṣ Island (lat. 22° 10′ north) to Abû Fâṭma, near Kerma, and in 1904 its population was 30,800. The term Ḥalfa comprises Ḥalfa Town and the "Camp"; the former being nearly two miles to the north of the latter. Ḥalfa is the terminus of the Kharṭûm and Kôsha lines,

[1] More correctly *Burghûth*, برغوث; the word means "flea."

and contained large workshops, some of which have now been removed to Atbara Junction. Close by are the old fortifications, the barracks, the Sirdarîya, &c.

MINERALS IN THE SÛDÂN. For several thousands of years the Sûdân has been famous as a GOLD-producing country, and almost every ridge or vein of quartz shows signs of having been worked

SAWÂKIN BAZAAR

[From a photograph by Lieutenant P. Lord, R.E.

more or less some time or other. To this day, if a native finds a piece of quartz, he is not satisfied until he has broken it to see if there is any gold inside it. The richest gold-producing districts were formerly in the region which lies to the south and south-west of Lake Ṣânâ and Beni Shanḳûl. A considerable quantity of alluvial gold was found in the khôrs or beds of streams here.

Cailliaud says[1] that in his day the purest gold was found at Kamâmîl,[2] and that the less pure gold, which was of a yellowish-green colour, was mixed with silver. The market for gold from this neighbourhood was Sennaar, and hence it was called "Sennaar gold." A certain amount of gold was also found in Gebel Nûba, e.g., at Gebel Tîrâ and Gebel Shêbûn, to the west of Gebel Ḳadîr. Large quantities of gold must also have been found in the region

MAIN STREET, SAWÂKIN.

[From a photograph by G. E. Mason, Esq.

called "Atbâî," which lies between the 26th and 20th parallels of north latitude, and which is bounded on the west by the Nile from Kena to Halfa, and on the east by the Red Sea. The southern portion of this region belongs to the Sûdân, and is inhabited by the Bishârîn and Amarar tribes; there are no towns or villages in the whole district.

At one period of its history, gold-mining must have been carried on in this region on a large scale, for at Derahêb, about 208 miles

[1] *Voyage*, iii., p. 19.

[2] The pillar on which the names of the blessed in heaven will be cut is, according to Abyssinian writers, made of "red gold," i.e., pure gold.

from No. 6 Station on the Ḥalfa-Abû Ḥamed Railway, Colonel the Hon. M. G. Talbot, R.E., found[1] on the right bank of Wâdî Kamotît "a number of ruined stone houses arranged in streets, "and covering three or four acres. They are built in stone and "mud, but a few arches in lime are to be seen." Here also are a ruined castle of stone set in mud, with two or three pointed arches set in lime, and another building of nearly equal size in plan, and the ruins of a number of houses and shelters, on the left bank.

Here we have clearly the remains of a miner's colony, with the governor's house. A narrow-gauge railway has been constructed from No. 6 Station to Umm Nabâdî, and mining work is now being carried on there, it is said with great success. Another great centre for gold-mining was the Wâdî 'Ulâḳî, which is entered near Dakka, on the east bank of the Nile. COPPER is found at Ḥufrat an-Naḥâs, in the north-west of the Baḥr al-Ghazâl Province, and in the mountains near Sawâkin and in the Peninsula of Sinai; none of the mines have been properly worked yet. IRON is found in Dâr Fûr, Kordôfân, and Baḥr al-Ghazâl, and in some places the ore is so rich that it contains nearly 50 per cent. of the pure metal. Fuel is plentiful in these places, and the natives smelt the ore in small clay furnaces. A great deal of iron is found mixed with the sand in the river beds south of Sennaar. LEAD is obtained in small quantities from Gebel Kutum, to the west of Kôbî in Dâr Fûr. ANTIMONY comes from Gebel Marra. A deposit of LIGNITE has been found on the west bank of the river near Dongola, and a Company has decided to make trial borings on the east bank, and has sent out a diamond drill for the purpose. Lignite has also been found at Chelga in Abyssinia, and in the Peninsula of Sinai. NATRON occurs in large quantities at Bîr Naṭrûn on the Arba'în Road. SALT is found on the Atbara, at Sharshâr near Bâra, in the Oasis of Selîma, and in the Wâdî Ka'ab, to the west of Dongola. Of ALUM there is a large deposit in the Oasis of Shabb, i.e., the "Alum Oasis."

THE INHABITANTS OF THE SÛDÂN. The history of the various peoples and tribes who have inhabited the Nile Valley during the past ten thousand years is a subject of great difficulty, and general

[1] See the route described in Gleichen, *op. cit.*, ii., pp. 1-5. Gleichen (i. p. 87) gives the number of houses at 500.

agreement among ethnographers, even as regards its main facts, is not to be expected for some time to come. The traditions which the present inhabitants of the Sûdân possess concerning their ancestry cannot be accepted implicitly, and all their racial characteristics are not so clearly differentiated that hard-and-fast conclusions on all points can be arrived at. The oldest evidence on the subject, is, of course, that which is derived from the monuments, and tombs, and writings of the ancient Egyptians, and this is usefully supplemented by that found in the works of Greek, Roman, and Muḥammadan writers. The ancient Egyptian evidence proves that in the earliest times two kinds of people inhabited the Nile Valley between the Great Lakes and Middle Egypt, and that both these were included under the general name "Neḥesu," i.e., "Blacks." One of these peoples possessed the chief characteristics of the Negro, i.e., thick lips, wool for hair, &c., and the other, though black-skinned, lacked them. The Negro people lived probably in the region which stretched from the southern parts of the district now called Dâr Fûr and Kordôfân to the Equator, and formed the remote ancestors of the great belt of Black nations which stretched right across Africa from the modern Senegambia to Abyssinia.

The people who were brown or black-skinned, but not Negroes, lived in the regions to the north of the Negro country, and they must at one time have occupied parts of Egypt so far north as Asyût, if not farther. It goes without saying that from the earliest times these two black peoples must have mixed and intermarried, and it is probable that the nomadic instincts of both, which were in reality the result of their incessant quest for food, and trade, led them at regular intervals into each other's country. The physical conditions under which they lived cannot have been very different from what they were during the past century, and, during the historic period, and that immediately preceding it, there must have been frequent intercourse between the southern and northern portions of the Nile Valley. The Negroes were then, as now, pagans or heathen, that is to say, their magic, which was probably of a low kind, had not developed into religion, and there is no doubt that many of the features of the religion of the Egyptians whose writings are in hieroglyphics were derived from the Negro Magic of Central Africa. The description written under the Dynastic Period of King Unȧs, who slew, cut up, boiled, and ate his gods, who violated the dead bodies of his enemies in a shameful manner, who carried off men's wives whensoever the fancy took him, better suits that of a successful warrior and slave-raider in Central Africa than that of a king of Egypt, who was buried with all the religious pomp and ritual which were practised in Egypt under the Vth Dynasty. The black-skinned or brown non-Negro people had then, of course, many customs in common with the Negroes, but it is clear from the Pyramid texts that in the reign of Pepi I. they worshipped a god called Ṭeṭun, and that they had some kind of a religion. Down to the Roman Period the Egyptians worshipped the bull, Osiris himself being the "Bull of Ȧmentet," and, if we may believe the reports of the travellers [1] quoted by Professor Wiedemann,[2] the king of the crocodiles was, at the end of the eighteenth century, believed to live at Armant, eight miles south of Thebes, and a gigantic crocodile was held in veneration at Kharṭûm in the reign of Muḥammad 'Alî!

Many facts go to show the persistence of Negro influence on the beliefs, and manners and customs of the Dynastic Egyptians, and the most important thing of all in connection with this is the tradition which makes them to come from the land of Punt. It is unnecessary here to review all the theories which have been put forward by various scholars as to the position of this country, and we may accept without any misgiving the opinion of Professor Maspero and of Professor Naville, both of whom believe that it was situated in Africa, at a considerable distance to the south-east and south of Egypt. It could be approached by sailing down the Red Sea, and entering a certain port on the African coast, and it could also be reached by land, *viâ* the Sûdân and Southern Abyssinia. The products of the country as enumerated in the inscriptions of the great Queen Ḥātshepset suggest that Africa was their source, and that the particular

[1] Sieber, *Beschreibendes Verzeichniss*, Vienna, 1820, p. 59; Pückler, *Aus Mehemed Ali's Reich.* iii., p. 250.

[2] *Quelques Remarques sur le Culte des Animaux en Égypte*, Muséon, vi. 2, pp. 113-128.

region whence they came was in some part of the south-eastern Sûdân, or a neighbouring country.

There is no reason for assuming that the Egyptians knew of two countries of Punt, or that the Punt of the XVIIIth was different from that of the IVth Dynasty; we must therefore think that the "spice-land" of Punt was the home of one of the peoples who were the ancestors of the Dynastic Egyptians. The influence of their Punt ancestors shows itself in many ways, especially in the matter of their long, plaited beards, and the animals' tails which hung down behind from their girdles, and their head-dresses.[1] Some think that the men of Punt were Semites, but the evidence for this view seems unsatisfactory, and is, in many cases, insufficient. It is, of course, possible that a number of Semites entered Egypt by way of Punt, but, if this were so, we should have found traces of their Semitic speech in the early hieroglyphic inscriptions. All things considered, it seems tolerably certain that the men of Punt, who influenced the manners, customs, and beliefs of the people in the Nile Valley were of African origin; but how, or when, or why they acquired the superior qualities which enabled them to do this cannot at present be said.

The Egyptians under the XVIIIth Dynasty divided the world as known to them at that time into four parts, which were peopled by—1. RETH, or RET (older, Remt); 2. THEḤENNU; 3. ÅAMU; 4. NEḤESU. The first people, the Ret, i.e., "Men," were the Egyptians themselves. The Theḥennu were the Libyans, the Åamu were the people on the east of the Nile, and probably included the Nomads of Sinai and Southern Syria, and the Neḥesu were the Blacks. The Egyptians claimed to be of divine origin, their primitive home being the "divine land," or the "land of the spirits," i.e., Punt. The Theḥennu lived to the west of the Nile, and their territory stretched away to the south, so far probably as Kordôfân and Dâr Fûr; from the way in which their name is written it seems as if they were regarded by the Egyptians as "the foreigners who brought scent, spices, and gum."

[1] See the description of the curious green stone objects of the Archaïc Period published by Mr. F. Legge in the *Proceedings of the Society of Biblical Archaeology* for June, 1900.

The Ȧamu appear to have been looked upon as the "animal-men," i.e., hunters of wild animals and shepherds. From the above facts it is clear that the Egyptians were not scientific ethnographers, but their classification of the peoples of the world as known to them is useful, especially as it represents a very old tradition.

From the evidence of the Egyptian monuments we are justified in assuming that before the beginning of the Dynastic Period, the Nile Valley was inhabited by negroes, and by a brown or black-skinned people who are represented by the modern Nubians of Sukkôt and Mahass, and the Nûbas of Kordôfân, and that these mingled and intermarried with the desert inhabitants on the east and west banks of the Nile. Then came a time when the country north of the First Cataract was invaded by a people who entered Egypt from the East, and who brought with them a high order of civilization, the art of writing, superior methods of agriculture, and a certain knowledge of arts and crafts. These conquered the natives, and their rulers founded a kingdom in Egypt, and with the union of the power of the kings of the South and North Egyptian Dynastic history begins. These new kings of All Egypt, having established their kingdom, soon found it necessary to take steps to reduce to submission the dwellers in the Eastern and Western Deserts and the Blacks, and from the time of king Seneferu, B.C. 3700, to the reign of Rameses II., about B.C. 1330, the Egyptian texts are, at intervals, filled with accounts of slave-raids into the Sûdân, nearly all of which are of a more or less bloody character, and of conquests of Ta-Kenset, Uauat (Wawat), Kash (or Kesh), and Khent Ḥen-nefer, i.e., of the Nile Valley, from Aswân to the Baḥr al-Ghazâl. Among the peoples of this region were two who were regarded as especially brave, ferocious, and terrible, namely, the ȦNTI, or "Hill-men," who lived in the Eastern Desert, and the MENTI, or "Cattle-men," who lived in the Western Desert.

The Hill-men were fine, tall, strong men, mighty hunters and trained to the use of the bow and the boomerang, and their boldness and bravery, and rapidity of movement across their deserts, struck terror at all times into the Egyptians. To conquer them was impossible, for when pursued they retired to their mountain fastnesses, which were inaccessible; to follow them for any distance into the desert was out of the question on account of the absence of water. What the physical characteristics and appearance of the Cattle-men were we have no means of knowing. In Roman times we find the country of the Hill-men occupied by peoples to whom classical writers gave the names of Megabari, Blemmyes, and Ethiopians (i.e., not Abyssinians, but dwellers on the Island of Meroë), who are now generally admitted to belong to the Hamitic race. As their qualities and characteristics were identical with those of the Hill-men, it is only reasonable to think that they were the descendants of the Hill-men, and that the Hill-men themselves belonged to the Hamitic race. Whether the Hill-men were indigenous, or whether they entered the country from the north, their stock being replenished from time to time by new-comers, is not known. Of the Megabari, Blemmyes, and Ethiopians (i.e., Meroïtes), the last people were the most civilized, and the "Meroïtic" inscriptions, which have been found from the Blue Nile in the south to Philae in the north, are probably written in their language. The Blemmyes lived nearer to Egypt, the southern portion of which they frequently plundered, and their reputation for cruelty, robbery, and brigandage is too well known to need description. With the Blemmyes there is mentioned in the inscriptions of Adulis a group of tribes called "Bega"[1] and "Bugaeitai,"[2] and with them we may certainly identify the Baga, or Bejas, of Muḥammadan writers.[3] They were a fierce and warlike people, and possessed all the characteristics of the Blemmyes, and their ancestors, or predecessors, the Ȧnti, or Hill-men. For centuries they lived chiefly by plunder and brigandage, and they were generally at war with the sedentary tribes who lived on the Nile. The modern inhabitants of the land once held by the Blemmyes and Begas, or Bejas, are the tribes called 'Abâbdah, Bishârîn, Hadanduwa, Ḥâlanka, &c.

The peoples who lived in the deserts on the west of the Nile,

[1] Βεγά: see Dittenberger, *Orientis Graeci*, vol. i., p. 290.

[2] Βουγαειταί: *Ibid.*, p. 300.

[3] They have been identified by some with the inhabitants of the country of *Buka*, , mentioned in the hieroglyphic inscriptions.

among whom were the Menti, or "Cattle-men," were the descendants of the Theḥennu of the Egyptian inscriptions, and were known to classical writers as "Nubae," or Nubians, and "Nobadae," or "Nobatae." In Roman times the Nubians consisted of a league of the great tribes of the Western Desert,

DONGOLÂWÎ MERCHANT.

[From a photograph by R. Türstig, Esq.

and they were so powerful that Diocletian found it worth his while to subsidize them with an annual grant, and to employ them to keep the Blemmyes in check. In the second quarter of the sixth century a Nubian king called Silko embraced Christianity, and having defeated the Blemmyes in several battles, and occupied their towns of Kalâbsha, Dakka, and Ibrîm, he founded a

Christian kingdom in Nubia with Dongola as his capital. The northern part of this kingdom came to an end in the thirteenth century, and the southern portion of it about 100 years later.

The modern representatives of the Nubians, or perhaps more correctly the "vile people of Kash" mentioned in the Egyptian

SÛDÂNÎ WOMAN.

[From a photograph by R. Türstig, Esq.

inscriptions, are called "Barâbara," and their home is the Nile Valley between the First and Fourth Cataracts; the four principal divisions of this district are Ḥalfa, Sukkôt, Mahass, and Dongola. Akin to them are the Nûbas of Kordôfân,[1] whose language is cognate with that of the Barâbara of the northern Sûdân.

[1] Lepsius, *Nubische Grammatik*, Berlin, 1880, p. cxv.; see also Reinisch, *Die Nuba-Sprache*, Vienna, 1879.

The early investigators of the language of the Barâbara distinguished in it two dialects, namely, that of Dongola, and that of Kenûz, or the country from Philae southwards to Korosko. Lepsius proved the existence of a third dialect, that of Mahass and Sukkôt, and Reinisch distinguished a fourth, to which he gave the name "Fadîgî," which he regarded as the speech peculiar to Sukkôt. The dialects of Kenûz and Dongola are nearly the same, and the men of Kenûz and Dongola can understand each other without much difficulty; the Fadîgî and the Mahass dialects also are similar to each other. According to Count Gleichen, a man of Dongola cannot understand a man of Mahass, and he tells us that the Kenûz dialect is spoken from Shellâl to Korosko, the Fadîgî near Korosko and south, the Mahass dialect from Ḥalfa to Hannek, and the Dongola dialect from Kerma to Ambiḳôl.[1] Lepsius regarded the Barâbara as a purely African people, and thought that the difference which now exists between them and the Nûbas of Kordôfân was due to their intermarriage with Hamites and Semites, whereby some of their semi-negro characteristics have disappeared. Opinions differ as to the Barâbara. Mr. J. W. Crowfoot says, "They are an enterprising people, apt linguists, "and great travellers, very ready to take on a veneer of European "culture;" while Count Gleichen says, "The natives of Mahas and "Sukkôt lag behind, the fault being entirely their own; they are "of an extremely indolent nature, perpetually quarrelling among "themselves over questions as to ownership of land and date-"trees, and do little or nothing towards bettering themselves."[2] The Barâbara are Muḥammadans, and most of them speak Arabic.

Before referring to the Negro tribes of the Sûdân, mention may be made of the Arabs, who during the last 500 years have occupied large tracts of country, and made themselves masters of them. For several hundred years before the Arabs became Muḥammadans, numbers of them must have crossed the Red Sea and entered the country now called Eritraea and Abyssinia, and so made their way into the fertile country south of the Atbara, or even farther west, where they settled down and became more or less absorbed among the population. After the conquest of Nubia

[1] *Handbook*, i., p. 83. [2] *Ibid.*, pp. 84 and 318.

by the Muḥammadan Arabs about A.D. 650, we may assume that Arab immigration would increase, but it is unlikely that it attained to any large proportions until after the downfall of the southern half of the Nubian Christian kingdom, which had its capital at Sôba on the Blue Nile, about A.D. 1400 or somewhat later. After

SÛDÂNÎ YOUNG MAN.

[From a photograph by R. Türstig, Esq.

the conquest of Egypt by Selîm in 1517 a very considerable number of Arabs must have entered the Sûdân by way of Abyssinia and Egypt, and their influence and power in the country began then to grow steadily. Little by little they added to the territories on which they had settled, but so long as the Fûng Dynasty ruled at Sennaar, the progress of the Arab domination in the Sûdân generally was impeded, though the Fûng kings themselves had embraced Muḥammadanism. In the fourteenth century some knowledge of Muḥammadanism entered Dâr Fûr, and in its train came some of the manners and customs and the language of the Arabs. These were brought in by the Tungûr Arabs, who, leaving Tunis, travelled southwards, and occupied Bornu, Wadâi, and Dâr Fûr, where they settled at Gebel Marra. The natives of Dâr Fûr were Negroes, and their chief tribes were the Furâwa and the Dâgô, the latter being the dominant power in the land when the Tungûr Arabs under 'Alî and Aḥmad al-Makûr made their appearance. Aḥmad married a princess of Dâr Fûr, and, when her father the king died, he succeeded to the kingdom. Thereupon the Tungûr Arabs left Bornu and Wadâi in large numbers, and came to Gebel Marra, and practically crowded out the Dâgô tribe. When the Tungûr kings had reigned about 100 years, the last of them, Shan Durshîd, was dethroned by his half-brother Dâli, who became Sulṭân of Dâr Fûr. Dâli is famous as the author of the code of laws which was in force in 1874 when Zubêr conquered the country; he divided his kingdom into five provinces. Among his successors was Sulêmân, surnamed Solon, whose mother and wife were Arab women; under their influence Dâr Fûr became a Muḥammadan country. This took place at the end of the fifteenth century.

In the preceding paragraphs an attempt has been made to sketch the distribution of the inhabitants of the Sûdân in accordance with the broad historical facts which have come down to us, but some of these may be capable of a different interpretation when anthropologists and ethnographers have studied Sûdân ethnography in the country, and when the contents of such ancient graves as remain have been exhumed and examined by them. Up to the present, very few of the travellers in the Sûdân have possessed the technical knowledge and scientific training necessary to enable them to deal in a competent manner with the materials which surrounded them. Though men like Andersson, Alberti, Bastian, Burton, Browne, Burckhardt, Baines, Bowditch, Beurmann, Barth, Baker, Brehm, Clapperton, Cameron, Denham, Fleurist de Langle, Guilain, Güssfeldt, Heuglin, Hildebrandt, Klunzinger, Kaufmann, Krapf, Livingstone, Lenz, Lauder, New,

Nachtigal, Pechuël-Lösche, Pallme, Pruyssenare, Mungo Park, Rüppell, Russegger, Speke, Stanley, Thomas, Vogel, and others, have done splendid work in elucidating the manners and customs of the Black Tribes of North Africa, it cannot be said that any one of them was an anthropologist or ethnographer. Of those who have travelled and lived in the Sûdân, and investigated the

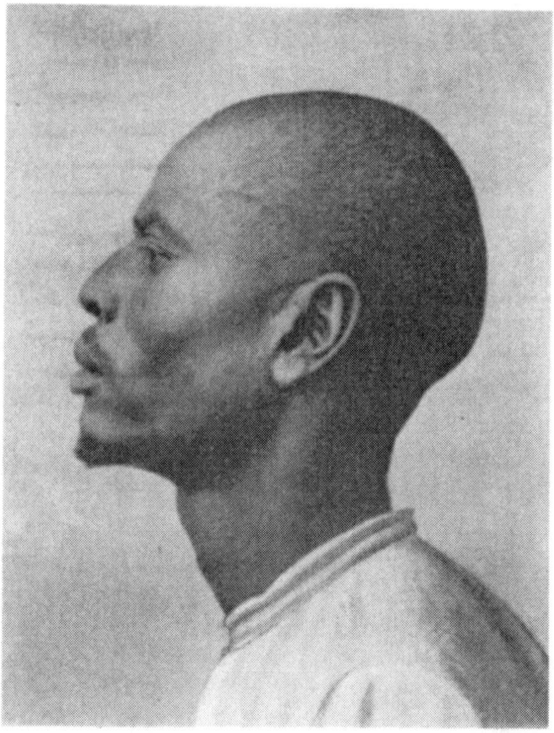

SÛDÂNÎ MAN.

[From a photograph by R. Türstig, Esq.

subject in a scientific manner, two names stand out prominently, i.e., those of Hartmann and Schweinfurth. The works of the former, *Die Völker Afrikas*, Leipzig, 1879; *Die Nilländer*, Leipzig, 1884; and other publications by him on the African peoples and their kinship and distribution, are most valuable contributions to the science of African anthropology, for they contain the results of a practical knowledge of the subject gained at first hand by residence in the Sûdân. Similarly Schweinfurth's *The Heart of Africa*, London, 1873 (translation by E. E. Frewer), forms a rich mine of facts collected by a trained mind during a period of three years' travel in the country. The researches made by Fritsch,[1] Falkenstein,[2] and others, also have a special value, and merit careful perusal. Among more recent works must be mentioned Prof. A. H. Keane's *Ethnology of the Egyptian Sudan*,[3] and *Die Heiden-Neger des Aegyptischen Sudan*, by Dr. Herman Frobenius, Berlin, 1893.[4] The last writer divided the peoples of the Sûdân into two great classes, i.e., Moslems and Heathen. The Moslems comprise four divisions:—1. Nubians, including the Barâbara, Bishârîn, Hadanduwa, &c. 2. The mixed Nûba tribes of Kordôfân. 3. The mixed Negro tribes of Dâr Fûr. 4. The Bakkâra Arabs. The Heathen of the Sûdân he divides into six series:—1. The Negroes who live in the swamp region, among whom he includes the Shulli (Lûri), the Shilluks (Jûr), the Anuaks, the Dinkas or Gangas, and the Bârî tribes, including the Shîr, Mûndar, Niâmbara, Fagelû, Kakuâk, Liggi, and Markhia. 2. The iron-working Negroes, i.e., the Bongo, the Mittu, Madi, Lubari, Kalikâ, Loggo, Brera, Abukaya (Oisila and Oigiga), Gogeri, Morû-Kodô, and Morû-Missa. 3. The Niam-Niams, or A-Sande, i.e., the "Great-eaters," and the Bomgîa. 4. The Mangbattu tribes. 5. The Lattuka. Strictly speaking, they live in Uganda territory. 6. The Batua, who also live beyond Egyptian territory. Under each series Dr. Frobenius adds a short description of the physical characteristics of each people or tribe, and describes succinctly their manners and customs, &c. In the map which accompanies his book, he shows by means of colours the distribution of the various series of peoples in the Sûdân in an effective manner.

A view wholly different from that usually held as to the manner in which the Nile Valley was peopled has been put forth by

[1] *Verhand. der Berl. Gesch. für Anthrop.* Sitz. v., February 17th, 1883, pp. 183-189.

[2] *Die Loango Expedition*, by P. G. J. Falkenstein and E. Pechuël-Loesche, Leipzig, 1879.

[3] *Journal of the Anthropological Institute*, November, 1884.

[4] The most recent commentator on Sûdân Ethnography is Mr. J. W. Crowfoot; see Gleichen, *op. cit.*, i., p. 317, *Ethnology of the Sudan.*

Sir Harry Johnston in his *Nile Quest*, London, 1903. According to him, the first men who entered Egypt and ascended the Nile came from the East—from India. They may have been so primitive, and ape-like, and of so undetermined a type, as not to belong definitely to any one of the three main species of humanity. They entered Egypt by the strip of land which (he assumes) joined

SÛDÂNÎ WOMAN.

[From a photograph by R. Türstig, Esq.

Arabia to Ethiopia. Many types of Asiatic animals came by this bridge, also man, possibly in the form of a low Negroid, represented to-day by the Congo Pygmies and the South African Bushmen. The region south of latitude 15° north was peopled by the Negro species, through southern Arabia. Egypt and Arabia were once a part of the domain of the Negroid Pygmies, but these were overwhelmed by the negrified Caucasians who came from Syria or Libya. About B.C. 7000, there were steatopygous men, showing Bushmen affinities, in Egypt, and they formed the servile class. Next came people similar to the Dravidians of India, or the Brahuis of Baluchistan, and after them an aquiline type of nearly pure Caucasian stock, probably from

A SÛDÂNÎ MAIDEN.

[From a photograph by R. Türstig, Esq.

Syria or Cyprus. The men of the northern half of the Nile Basin emigrated from the direction of Gallaland, or Somaliland, or Abyssinia, and their degenerate descendants exist in the Danâkil, Somali, and Galla of to-day. They became the main stock of the Egyptian population, and profoundly modified Negro Africa, their influence penetrating to Zululand on the south, and to the

Atlantic on the west. This Hamitic race was the mainstay of Ancient Egypt, and, assisted by the cognate Libyans, has been the main human agent in saving the Negro from slipping back into the life of the anthropoid ape. The Valley of the Lower Nile attracted many invasions from Europe and Asia, and from Libya, where the

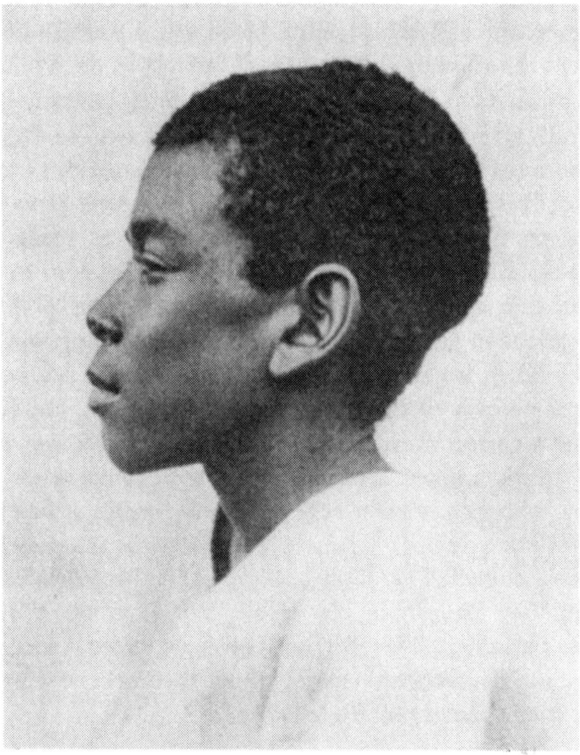

SÛDÂNÎ YOUTH OF NEGRO ORIGIN.

[From a photograph by R. Türstig, Esq.

dominant race was of Iberian stock. All the races, save the Hittites, were of Caucasian species. The Egyptians penetrated among the Negro tribes of the Central Sûdân and Equatoria; they had in their composition a certain proportion of Negro blood, besides the drop of it from their Hamitic ancestors, and they absorbed the earlier Negroid population of their country, and imported and intermarried with Negro slaves. But they were fully Caucasian in the vivid interest they took in nature, &c. After the early historical times relations between Egypt and the Upper Nile were severed. After the rise of Egyptian civilization B.C. 5000 the Egyptians easily impressed the Negroes of the south and the Libyans of the west by their power, and eventually taught them the art of working metals,'&c. In course of time the Negro race, through the Hamitic blood which was pouring into it, resisted the Egyptians, who lost all interest in the Sûdân.

If we understand this theory aright, it is fundamentally opposed to that of Hartmann, who maintained that the ancient Egyptians were descended from a purely African black-skinned race; and the labours of Maspero, Lefébure, and Wiedemann have proved from the religious ceremonies and social observances, as made known to us by the hieroglyphic texts, that a great deal is to be said in favour of this opinion. The proofs adduced from philological considerations in favour of this or that theory are not convincing, especially when we remember what inveterate tramps and wanderers the peoples of the Sûdân have always been, and it seems clear that a correct racial history of the Sûdânî folk can only be formulated by trained anthropologists and comparative ethnographers, who have a knowledge of Sûdânî peoples at first hand.

Lists of the principal tribes in the Sûdân at the present time have been compiled by Count Gleichen in his *Handbook*, and by Naum Bey Shucair in his Arabic *History of the Sûdân*, and both are valuable. The list here given is based upon that of Shucair, and the facts are collected from the works of Hartmann, Junker, Baker, Schweinfurth, and other travellers.

I. Negro and Negroid Tribes.

Agâr. A branch of the Dinkas. They live on the Rûl River in the Baḥr al-Ghazâl.

'Awra. In Dâr Fûr, their chief town being Galla between Kabkabîya and Kulkul.

Banḳû (Bongo). In the Baḥr al-Ghazâl. They smelt iron ore and work in iron. Their manners and customs are carefully described by Schweinfurth. They have no conception of immortality, and they do not believe in the transmigration of souls,

A WOMAN OF OMDURMAN.

[From a photograph by R. Tűrstig, Esq.

but they go in deadly fear of evil spirits, and their terror of witches and of their power passes understanding.[1]

BÂRÎ. A well-grown race who live near Bârî and Gondokoro. According to Baker (*Albert Nyanza*, p. 58) the negro type of thick lips and flat nose is wanting. Their features are good, but they

SÛDÂNÎ WOMAN WEARING THE RÂHAT, OR LEATHER GIRDLE.

[From a photograph by R. Türstig, Esq.

have woolly hair. They rub themselves with red ochre and tattoo their skins. They keep tufts of hair on the tops of their heads, wherein they stick feathers. They wear a neat lappet of beads or small iron rings in front, and a tail of fine strips of leather or cotton behind. Their huts have projecting roofs, and entrances about two feet high; they stand in enclosures formed by the

[1] *In the Heart of Africa*, vol. i., pp. 259-311.

euphorbia, on ground plastered with ashes, cow-dung, and sand. The dead are buried in these enclosures; a pole marks each grave, and on the top of it are fastened a few cocks' feathers. To the pole are tied skulls and horns of oxen. They used to poison their arrows with the juice of the root of a certain tree. Their bows were of bamboo, and their arrows, about three feet long, had detachable heads which fitted into sockets. Baker says the Bârî were held to be the worst tribe on the Baḥr al-Gebel. They wear no clothes, and are fond of singing, dancing, and strong drink.

Barḳad. Their chief place is Gebel Muskû, between Gebel Ḥarîz and Gebel Marra. They worship images in secret.

Barta. They live in Beni Shankûl, to the south of Fâmaka. They are akin to the Fûng tribes, and are nearly black in colour, and they have been said by some to possess "Caucasian" features. The men wear a girdle and a kind of tail, and the women go nearly naked. They are an industrious people, and they eat almost anything. They formerly paid £6,000 annually to the Egyptian Government. The Barta were discovered by Cailliaud.

Barti. Their chief place is Gebel Taḳâbû, three days to the north of Al-Fâsher; they speak Arabic as well as their own tongue.

Bîḳô. They live to the south of Dâra.

Budêyât. A nomad tribe to the west of the Natron Wells.

Burûn. A branch of the Hamags which lives in the mountains south of Khôr Dulêb.

Dâgô. They live in Gebel Dâgô, two days west of Dâra.

Dêwar. A branch of the Shilluks; they live to the west of the Dinkas.

Dinkas. They live to the east of the White Nile, near the Shilluks, between parallels 12° and 6° of north latitude. They are tall, comparatively slender men, with long heads, and wide noses, blunted at the tips; they have large mouths, with fleshy but not thick lips. The men despise all clothing and go naked; they live in grass-overed *tukls*, and sleep on beds of ashes of cow-dung. The women wear aprons before and behind, and sleep on mats. The men carry spears and clubs.

The Dinkas of the White Nile[1] migrated thither from the Baḥr al-Ghazâl.

FARÂTÎT. They live in the Baḥr al-Ghazâl, in the south-west of Dâr Fûr.

FÛR. Their chief place is Gebel Marra. They became Moslems in the fifteenth century, and kings of mixed origin reigned over them from 1444 to 1874.

GABLÂWÎYÛN. They live in Gebel Mûl, to the west of Dâr Fûr.

GABLÂYÛN. They live in Fâmaka, and are akin to the Fûng and Hamag tribes.

GÂNḲÎ. A tribe of the Baḥr al-Ghazâl, akin to the Dinkas.

GÛR (JÛR). Their country lies between those of the Dinkas and Banḳos; they are akin to the Shilluks, whose language they speak; they work in iron.

KÂGA AL-BADU. Their country lies to the north-east of Umm Shanḳa. They are expert hunters of the giraffe and the *darrak*.

ḲIMR. Their chief place is Abû 'Ushar, three days west of Kulkul.

KUBḲ. They live to the north-west of Gebel Marra.

ḲÛLÛ (Golos). They live in clean, well-built huts to the west of the Banḳu (Bongos). Their currency is iron hoes, forty of which purchase a wife.

ḲUMUZ. They live to the east of Fâmaka; their neighbours are the thievish Lâmḳasna.

LÂTÛKÂ. A cattle-breeding tribe to the east of the Baḥr al-Gebel. They live in bell-shaped *tukls*, and in each village is a high platform in three stages, on which are guards who keep watch day and night.

MÂDÎ. They live near the Bârî. They are a well-built people, and have long heads. Men and women cut their hair short; the men cover the right shoulders, but their left and their breasts are bare. They are good farmers, and live in neat *tukls*.

MAKÂRAK.[2] A branch of the Niam-Niams living in the Baḥr

[1] See Gleichen, *op. cit.*, i., p. 129; and especially Schweinfurth, *Heart of Africa*, vol. i., pp. 149-169.

[2] Junker says (*Travels in Africa*, p. 234) this name means "man-eaters."

al-Ghazâl. Their manners and customs have been described by Buchta, Hartmann, Junker, Marno and Schweinfurth.

MARÂRÎT. Their chief place is Galla, between Kabkabîya and Kulkul.

MASÂLÎT. Neighbours of the Ḳimr, *q.v.*

MÊDÛB. They live in Gebel Mêdûb, three days' journey from Taḳâbô, near the Arba'în Road.

MÛNA. Their chief place is Fâfâ. A number of them have become Moslems.

NIAM-NIAM, or NYAM-NYAM.[2] A famous people who live chiefly between parallels 4° and 6° of north latitude, and who were at one time computed to number 2,000,000. They call themselves A-SANDÎ, or A-ZANDÎ, which is the plural of a Dinka word meaning a "great eater;" because they were and still are eaters of human flesh, this word is said to mean "cannibals." Of Niam-Niam an Arabic plural has been formed, "Niamanjam"; the Mittu are said to call them "Makârak," the Bongos know them as "Man-yanya," the Dyurs as "O'Madyaka," and the Manbattu as "Babûngera." They are thought by some travellers to be akin to the Somali, or Galla, or Wahuma peoples; others make them akin to the Fan and the Manyema who live to the west of Lake Tanganyika. They are dark brown in colour, have well-built bodies of middle height, their heads are not long, their faces are broad, their noses are said by some to be of a Semitic type, but blunt at the tips and wide, they have thick lips, full cheeks, ears placed high, rounded chins, and small broad hands and feet. The hair is worn long by both men and women, and it falls over their shoulders, sometimes so far down as the middle of the body; they dress it in fantastic ways, and plait portions of it, and tie it in ornamental knots and bows. They tattoo various parts of their bodies, they wear long beards, and dress themselves in skins; necklaces made of beads of all kinds are much prized by them. They arm themselves with lances, shields, and daggers of curious shapes and forms. They live in groups of huts, but have neither towns nor villages. They are great hunters, and they keep dogs with pointed ears and tails curled up like those of pigs. They

[1] See Schweinfurth, *Heart of Africa*, vol. i., p. 416 ff.; vol. ii., p. 3 ff.

[2] Junker says this name means "man-eaters."

trap the elephant, and in former days collected large quantities of ivory. The men have many wives, and infidelity on the woman's part is punished often with death; to be the mother of many children reflects great credit on a woman, and causes her to be held in high honour. They love music of all kinds, singing and dancing, and they pass a great deal of time in playing the Mangala game on a long board, which stands on four legs, and has sixteen cavities, the pieces being twenty-four little stones or cowries. They cut off the hair as a sign of grief.

The bodies of the dead are decorated with feathers, &c., and are buried in a half-sitting position in hollows in the ground or in hollow trees. They sometimes make a chamber by the side of the grave in the ground, line it with boards, and build over it a *tukl*. The Niam-Niams are a very warlike people, and they make bold, steady, but cruel soldiers; they eat those who fall in battle, and many who die in the course of nature, and they revel in human fat, with which they smear their bodies. They also eat dogs, a custom which Schweinfurth believes to be allied to cannibalism. Their manners and customs have been well described by Junker, Schweinfurth, Buchta, and others, and all agree in saying that the Niam-Niams are the most intelligent people of the Baḥr al-Ghazâl Province. Their most recent visitor was Colonel Sparkes, and he says, "They are far superior to any other people I have met up here."[1] There is a striking similarity in their manners and customs to those of the early Egyptians, whose ancestors came from Punt, and it is not impossible that these and the primitive Niam-Niams may have come from the country of the Fan people, which may even have been Pun, or Punt.

NUWÊR, or NUWEHR. They live between the Sobat River and the Baḥr al-Ghazâl. Their men go naked, and rub their bodies with ashes of cow-dung, and stain their hair red and plaster it with ashes mixed with cows' urine. The married women wear a fringe of grass about their loins, and perforate their upper lip; in the hollow they wear an ornament of beads on an iron wire, which projects like a horn of a rhinoceros. The men wear coils of beads on their necks, heavy ivory bracelets and copper rings on their arms and wrists, and an iron spiked bracelet which they

[1] Gleichen, *op. cit.*, i. p. 161.

use for keeping their wives in order. They are tall and powerful, and carry lances and clubs, and live in large, well-built huts. They live by cultivating the ground, by hunting, and by fishing.

RUNAḲ. They live to the south-west of Dâgô.

SHÊRÎ. They live a little to the north of Gebel Lâdô, near the Bârî. The men are armed with lances, ebony clubs, bows always strung, and arrows; on their backs they carry a stool and a huge pipe. The women wear leather lappets, and tails made of strips of leather finely cut; they carry their children in skins slung from the shoulders.

SHILLUK. They live on the west bank of the White Nile, between Abû Island and Lake Nô; their capital was Fâshôda, and they are called by natives Shulla, or Ojallo. They are tall, but of slender proportions, and most of the men go naked; the women wear a certain amount of clothing. The men arm themselves with spears, shields, and clubs, and are said to be good soldiers, brave, independent, truculent, quarrelsome, obstinate, crafty, cunning, untrustworthy, &c.; Count Gleichen tells us that they are "the finest warriors in the Sûdân," and says that "their morals in relation to women are very good" (i., p. 193). According to Hartmann, they live in polygamy.[1] Their chief occupation is cattle-breeding, for nearly the whole of the Shilluk country is grass land; wives are obtained in exchange for cattle. Shilluk land is ruled by a Mek, and is divided into two provinces, Gerr and Loak, which are subdivided into 29 districts. An excellent account of the Shilluks is given by Count Gleichen in his *Handbook*, i., p. 193. It is based on the Reports made by Major Matthews, Father Banholzer, and the Rev. J. K. Giffen, and it contains much new and valuable information about this most interesting people, especially as regards their history and religion.[2]

SIMYÂR. A tribe akin to the Ḳimr and Masâlît, near whom they live.

SHULLA. A people of the same race as the Shilluks; they live at the head of the Baḥr al-Gebel, or Upper Nile.

TÂMA. A people who live near the Ḳimr.

ZAGHÂWA. They live four days' journey to the north of Al-Fâsher. A branch of the tribe, called Kamalt, lives near Dâra.

[1] *Die Nilländer*, p. 119. [2] See Schweinfurth, *Heart of Africa*, vol. i., p. 72 ff.

SHILLUKS AT FASHODA.

[From a photograph by Miss Hilda Burrows.

II. Nubians.

The Barâbara, or Nubians, who are to-day a mixture of Nûbas, Arabs, and Turks, may be divided into five groups:—I. The Danâḳala, whose kings ruled at Dafâr, old Dongola, Khandaḳ, and the Island of Arḳô, and who lived between the Third and Fourth Cataracts. II. The Maḥass, who live between the Third Cataract and Gebel Dûsha, and whose kings reigned at Gebel Sâsî. III. The Sukkôts, who live between Gebel Dûsha and the Second Cataract. IV. The Ḥalfas, who live between Ḥalfa and Sabû'a. V. The Kanûzî, who live between Sabû'a and the First Cataract. Many writers assume that the primitive Nûbas were akin to some of the Beja tribes, and have asserted that the ancient kingdoms of Meroë and Napata were founded by them, but facts in support of this view seem to be wanting.

III. Tribes of Hamitic Descent.

'Abâbdah. They live in the region of the 'Atbâî, from lat. 22° 30′ north to the Ḳena-Ḳuṣêr Road, and are divided into five groups:—I. 'Ashshânâb, whose seat is Aswân, and who live in the desert between Ḳena and Korosko (Kûruskû). II. Malîkâb, whose seat is at Darâw, and who live in the desert between that place and Berber. III. Fuḳarâ, whose seat is at Ramâdî near Edfû, and who live on both banks of the Nile between Ḳena and Korosko. IV. 'Ubûdîn and Shanâtîr, whose seat is Sayyâla, north of Korosko.

Bishârîn. There are three main divisions of this tribe. The first occupies the country on the Red Sea from Ḳuṣêr to the Atbara; the second lives on the Atbara; and the third in the Gazîra of the 'Atbâî. The Bishârîn claim to be descended from Arab ancestors, but this seems to be impossible. They divide themselves into the descendants of Umm 'Alî and Umm Nagî, the wives of 'Alî Ga'alan, a descendant of Bishar, the son of Kahl, and a descendant of Zubêr, whose wife was a sister of 'Abbâs, the uncle of the Prophet. The great 'Alîâb section of the Bishârîn are said to be the descendants of Umm Alî.

Beni 'Âmar. They live in the country between 'Aḳîḳ and Senhît, and likewise claim an Arab origin.

Ḥabâb. They live to the east of the Beni ʻÂmar.

Hadanduwa. They occupy the country between Khôr Baraka and the Atbara.

Ḥalânḳa. The seat of this people is Kasala.

Ummar'ar. Their territory lies between Berber and Sawâkin, and their chief place is Aryâb.

Sir Reginald Wingate speaks of a tribe of fine, tall men who live in the Eastern Desert, and who are generally known as "Anaks." They are probably the descendants of the tall, handsome men who are mentioned by classical writers in connection with their descriptions of the Island of Meroë, and of the Blemmyes.

IV. Tribes of Arab Descent.

ʻÂbdallâb. They live at Ḥalfâya. Their ancestor ʻAbd Allah assisted the Fûngs in founding their kingdom at Sennaar.

ʻAḳalyûn. Their district is between the Dinder and Blue Nile.

ʻAlâṭiyûn. On the Blue Nile between Ḥudêbât and Mashraʻ Tawla.

ʻArâkîyûn. In the neighbourhood of Abu Ḥarâz and Wad Madanî.

ʻArab al-Bashir. Their chief place was ʻUrêba.

Awlâd Ḥamîd. They live near the Habânîya.

Aḥâmada. They live near the Gimʻa.

Baḳḳâra Maḥâraba. Between Sennaar and Gebel Shaḳada.

Baḳḳâra al-Ḥawzâma. In the south of Kordôfân. Their chief place is Birka.

Barrîyât. Their chief place is Tûlû.

Baṭṭâḥîn. To the north of the Shukrîya tribe.

Beni Faḍl. In the neighbourhood of Al-Fâsher.

Beni Garrâr. In the east of Kordôfân, in the region of the ostriches and gazelles.

B eni Ḥasîn, or Awlâd Abû Rûf. In the country between Gebel Shaḳada and Khôr Dulêb. Their chief seats are Abû Ḥagâr and Marḳûm.

Beni Ḥasîn. In the neighbourhood of Masâlît.

Beni Helba. Their chief seat is Bulbul, west of Dâra.

ARAB TRIBES

BUDÊRÎYA. In Khûrshî and Ṭayyâra. They are said to be akin to the Ga'alîn.

DÂR ḤAMÎD. In the neighbourhood of the Kabâbîsh.

ḌBÂÎNA. Their chief places are Tûmât on the Atbara, and Gîra on the Setît, and Dûka.

DUGHÊM.

FÛNG. Descendants of this formerly very powerful collection of tribes are found at Renḳa, near Sennaar, Dabba, and Dongola. They were originally Negroes, but even in the time of Selim (1520) they pretended that they were descended from 'Abbâs, a near kinsman of the Prophet.

GA'ALÎN, or GA'ALÎYÛN. These tribes live in the country between Abû Ḥamed and Kharṭûm, and they are among the best and ablest of all the Arab tribes in the Sûdân.

GAM'ÎÂB. On the Nile between 'Aḳba Ḳurra and Shêkh Aṭ-Ṭayyib.

GAMÛ'ÎYA. On the White Nile from Omdurmân south.

GIM'A. Their chief place is Sharkîla.

GUWÂMA'A. Their chief place is Bara.

HABBÂNÎYA. Their chief place is Kâka in Dâr Fûr. Another tribe of the same name has its seat at Sharkîla.

ḤALÂWÎYÛN. In the neighbourhood of Masallamîa.

ḤAMADA. In the country between the Rahad and the Dinder, and their centres are Dabarkî and Dunkur.

HAMAG. A Moslemized Negro tribe. Their chief seat is Gebel Ḳalî, three days to the south of Karkôg.

ḤAMAR. At Abû Ḥarâz and Nahûd, in the district of the *tabaldî* or water trees.

ḤASÂNÎYA. In Gebel Gilif, in the Gakdûl Desert.

ḤAWÂWÎR. They are said to have come from Upper Egypt, and they live in the Desert of Gabra.

ḤAWÂTÎYA. To the west of Kabkabîa.

ḤUMR. In Uḍîa, between Birka and Shakâ.

ḤUMRÂN.

ḤUSSUNNÂT. Their chief place is Ḳaṭêna.

KABÂBÎSH. The greatest of all the tribes in Kordôfân. Before the revolt of the Mahdî they were said to number 250,000. Their chief centres are Âbâr, Ṣâfia, and 'Ên Ḥâmid.

KANÂNA. They live near Abâ Island on the White Nile.

KARÛBÂT. To the west of Kabkabîa.

KHAWÂBÎR. They trace their descent from the Beni Ummîa and the Beni 'Abbâs. They are great breeders of cattle and horses, and their chief centre is Wad'a.

KHAWÂLADA. Near 'Abûd in the Gazîra.

KHAWÂWÎR. They are neighbours of the Ḥasânîya and the Hawâwîr.

KHUZÂM.

KUWÂHLA. Near 'Abûd and Wad Madanî. Their nomads live on the west of the Dinder. Akin to them are the ḤASANÂT and the SHANÂBALA.

ḲUWÂHSAMA. They live to the north of Sennaar. Branches of this tribe are the 'ÂBDALLÂB, and the KAMATÎR, who live on the east of the Blue Nile between Runḳa and Ruṣêreṣ, and have their chief seat at Kharkôg.

LAḤAWÎYÛN. Nomads who live on the White Nile between Kawwa and Gebelên.

MA'ÂLÎYA. Their chief centre is Karkûd, to the north of Tuwêsha and Ḳôz al-Ma'âlîya.

MADANÎYÛN. Their chief centre is Wad Madanî, and they are called after their ancestor, Shêkh Madanî.

MAHÂRÎ.

MÂHARÎYA, who are said to be descended from Arabs from Yaman; their chief place is Dûr.

MASALLAMÎYA. They live on the Blue Nile.

MÎRAFÂB. They live to the south of the Rubâṭâb, and their chief seat is Berber. The four main divisions of the tribe are Ṣayyâm, Musṭafyâb, Labbayâb, and Raḥmâb.

MUNÂSÎR. On the banks of the Nile at the Fourth Cataract, and at Abû Ḥamed; their divisions are Wahâbâb, Kabbâna, Sulêmânîya, Kagûbâb, and Ḥabra.

MUSÊRÎYA. Kordôfân.

RAFÂ'ÎYÛN. Kâmlîn, on the Blue Nile.

RASHÂIDA, or Arabs from the Ḥijâz.

RUBÂṬÂB. They live to the south of the Munâṣîr. The three divisions of the tribe are Budêrîya, Farânîb, and Da'ifâb. They hold the views of Sûdânî folk who are "the companions of king

Adh-al-Kkr and the cap," and in their possession are the throne on which he sat, and the cap.

RUZÊḲÂT, a great tribe of Dâr Fûr, with its chief place at Shakâ.

SARÛRÂB. They live north of Omdurmân.

SHÂIḲÎYA, a tribe living in the country near the foot of the Fourth Cataract. Its main divisions are the 'Âdlânâb, Suwârâb, Ḥannîkâb, and 'Umârâb.

SHAMBATA. They live between Wad 'Abbâs and Sennaar.

SHUKRÎYA, a famous tribe which numbered 500,000 souls before the revolt of the Mahdî. Their chief centres are Rufâ'a on the Blue Nile, Al-Fâsher on the Atbara, Ḳaḍâref, Ḳala'a Arâng, Abû Dulêḳ, &c.

SULÊM. South of the Kanâna.

TA'ÂISHA. Their chief place is Mandawwa, near Kâka, whence came 'Abd Allah, the Khalîfa, in the region of the Farâtît.

TARGAM. Neighbour of the Masâlît.

TUMÂM. Their chief place is Birka.

'UṬÊFÂT. Their chief place is Ankâ.

'URÊḲÂT. Their chief place is Kutum.

YA'ḲÛBÂB. To the south of Sennaar.

ZABÂLLA'A. They inhabit the country between the Rahad and the Dinder. The only prophet they acknowledge is Abû Garîd, who was the founder of their sect, and whose tomb exists at Ḥellet Bunzuḳâ, between Karkôg and Ruṣêreṣ. Thus they say, "There is no god but God: Abû Garîd is the prophet of God." Their women are white in colour, and both men and women love pleasure, and the former fatten themselves, and are much addicted to perfumes.

ZAYYÂDÎYA. Their chief place is Mallîṭ. They trade in salt and natron, and derive their stock from Abû Zêd of Nejd.

The following are also given by Naum Bey Shucair (i. 63):—

AL-AGÂNIB. This name is given to those who have travelled into the Sûdân and other places.

AL-ḤAḌÛR. These are certain Egyptians who went from Cairo before the first "opening" of the Sûdân, and they live in Khandaḳ, Shendî, Masallamîya, and other places on the Nile, and occupy themselves with trade.

AL-AWLÂD AR-RÎF. This name is applied to the Egyptians, Turks, Europeans, and others, who went into the Sûdân after the first "opening."

AL-MAKÂDA, a term of abuse applied to the Abyssinians who are Christians.

AL-GABARTA, a name given to Abyssinians who are Moslems.

AT-TAKÂRANA, the people of Takrûr, to the south of Burnû; now known as Katkû.

AL-ḤALABAT, a name applied to tramps, showmen, jesters, and others who lead a careless and irregular life.

RELIGIONS. The dominant religion in the Sûdân is Muḥammadanism, and the Arabs have succeeded wonderfully in imposing the teaching of the Prophet on a large number of its inhabitants. Speaking generally, those who are not Moslems are pagans. The Arabs and the Negroes, or Negroid tribes, together destroyed the Christian kingdoms of Dongola and Sôba, and their teachings as regards polygamy and slave owning and holding have fitted in well with the natural manners and customs of the bulk of the Sûdânî folk. Islâm appeals to all their material characteristics and instincts, and it allows them a freedom of life which is condemned by Christianity, and promises them a heaven replete with sensual delights and happiness. On the other hand, it must be admitted that it has had a good effect upon the people of certain savage tribes, and the Arabs have certainly been the means of introducing the elements of civilization into places which otherwise would have been given up to the cult of devils and fetishes, and to nameless abominations of every kind. The great drawback to Islâm, apart from theological considerations, when viewed from a practical, European standpoint, is the unprogressive character of its teaching.

Though extraordinarily successful among many of the tribes of north-east Africa, and among several of the Negro peoples of the Sûdân, the teachers of Islâm have failed to eradicate many pagan beliefs, customs, and ceremonies, which appear to be among the fundamental peculiarities of their natures. Thus in Sennaar among the Moslem Fûngs phallic ceremonies were celebrated during the last century, and the Barta, like the ancient Egyptians, used the beetle as an amulet. The Hamags in Ruṣêreṣ and Fâzôglî at the season of harvest used to tie a dog to the leg of a couch (*anḳarêb*), and then every one present would strike or stab the poor creature until it was dead. The Barta also used to dance at the time of full moon round holy trees, and then make a great feast, during which the grossest debauchery reigned supreme. The Dâgô in Gebel Dâgô have a stone idol called Kanḳara, which they worship in secret. The Budêyât worship a special kind of tree. The Barḳad also worship images near Gebel Marra. The Dinkas have a dim belief in a good principle, the creator of things, which they call Deng-Dit. They also believe in the existence of the spirits of the dead, and they maintain a body of workers of magic called "Tît," who are supposed to repulse the evil spirits (Jok) who would attack them, and to make rain. The dead become the children of Deng-Dit. Mr. R. Türstig was witness of a ceremony performed in commemoration of a dead wife of Shêkh Bôr, during which a sheep was slain; on another occasion he saw a bull slaughtered, and the anointing of the bull and the bystanders with butter, and the dances of feather-bedecked women, all of which things were done for the benefit of a sick man.[1] The Dinkas appear to believe also in demoniacal possession. Sometimes when the "rain-maker" fails in his work, the bystanders fall upon him, beat him with their clubs, and then throw him into the river for the crocodiles to eat. Often the Tît are expert ventriloquists.

A number of important additional facts about the religious beliefs of the Dinkas have been collected by Major S. L. Cummins,[2] which may be thus summarized:—The Dinkas have a most elaborate list of gods and demi-gods. At the head of all is Deng-Dit, the "Rain-giver," with Abok, his wife; they have two sons, Kur-Kongs and Gurong-Dit, and a daughter, Ai-Yak. Their Devil is called L'wal Burrajok, and is the father of Abok, the wife of Deng-Dit. They account for their origin thus: Deng-Dit gave his wife a bowl of fat, and she and her children softened the fat over the fire, and began to mould from it men

[1] Quoted by Gleichen, *op. cit.*, i., p. 146.

[2] See Lord Cromer's *Report*, *Egypt*, No. 1 (1903), pp. 97 and 98.

and women in the image of the gods. Deng-Dit warned her against L'wal, or the Devil, who was his enemy, but Abok forgot, and with her children went to gather wood in the forest. There L'wal found the bowl, drank the greater part of the fat, and from the remainder proceeded to mould caricatures of men and women with distorted limbs, mouths, and eyes. Then, fearing the vengeance of Deng-Dit, he descended to earth by the path which then connected it with heaven. On discovering the result of her neglect, Abok hastened to her husband, who, greatly incensed, started in pursuit of L'wal. The latter, however, had persuaded the bird Atoi-toish to bite asunder with its bill the path from heaven to earth, and he thus escaped from the divine wrath. The Dinkas do not pray, but they offer sacrifices to their god, who, being rather of a malevolent than benevolent disposition, must be propitiated; the sky is to them the place of divinity, and the bowels of the earth the place of evil.

The Niam-Niams practise augury by means of wooden pegs dipped in water rolled on a flat stool, and by giving fetish-drink to hens; they call such ceremonies "borru." The Bârî believe in the existence of a kind of creator whom they call Mun, and also of evil spirits. The mother of their tribe was, they think, a serpent called Yukanye, and they keep tame serpents in their houses. The magicians, whom they call "Bunek," are held in great esteem, especially if they be successful rain-makers. In the country of the Blue Nile, in many places, the people worshipped the river, and made offerings to it. Witchcraft is common everywhere in the Moslem districts of north-east Africa, and at Sennaar the people used to believe that witches took the forms of hyaenas, and went about by night; at Fâmaka the black soldiers told Hartmann that they could cross the river by night in the form of hippopotami, and have intercourse with the women on the opposite bank of the Blue Nile. All over the same region a certain kind of python was held in great veneration by all the people, and in this respect the Sûdânî folk of to-day resemble the Abyssinians.

The Shilluks believe in a Great Creator, whom they call "Jo-uk," who is thought to be in a vague way connected with the events of their lives; they worship him and offer sacrifices to him in an indirect manner. In the beginning Jo-uk created a great white cow, which came up out of the Nile, and was called Deung Adok. The white cow gave birth to a son called Kola, who begat Umak Ra, or Omaro, who begat Makwa, or Wad Maul, who begat Ukwa, who became king. One day Ukwa saw two maidens, the lower parts of whose bodies were like those of a crocodile, come up out of the river, and after a time, during which they refused to have anything to do with him, he went up to them and laid hold of them. They screamed, and their father, who was part man and part crocodile, came up out of the river to see what was happening; he raised no objection to the proceedings, and Ukwa married the two maidens, who were called Nik-kieya and Ung-wad. Nik-kieya gave birth to two sons and three daughters, her eldest being Nyakang (or, Nik-kang or Nyakam), and Ung-wad to one son only, called Ju or Bworo. Meanwhile Ukwa married a third wife, whose eldest child, a son, was called Duwat. When Ukwa died Nyakang and Duwat quarrelled about the succession to the throne. In the end Duwat seems to have succeeded Ukwa, for Nyakang, and his sisters Ad-Dui, Ari Umker, and Bun Yung, his brother Umoi, and his half brother Ju, got wings and flew to the south of the Sobat River, which they found to be in the possession of the Arabs. These they drove out, and then founded a kingdom of their own. Nyakang, however, wished to people his country with men and women, and this he did by creating them from crocodiles, hippopotami, wild beasts, and cattle. So soon as the men and women appeared all their parents, the animals, were destroyed, so that the human race might never learn what its origin was.

The men and women who were made from the animals are called Shullî, or Shulla, i.e., common people, to distinguish them from Nyakang's descendants, who rule and perform all priestly functions to this day. Nik-kieya, the mother of Nyakang, is immortal. She usually appears in the form of a crocodile, and sometimes carries off a human being or an animal; this mark of her favour is much esteemed in a family. The great god Jo-uk is worshipped through Nyakang, and sacrifices offered to the latter are supposed to be received by Jo-uk, the father and source of all life, and of evil as well as of good. Jo-uk is omnipresent, and to him the dead go when they leave this world. In every village is a temple of Jo-uk, only it is called the "house of Nyakang," and sacrifices are made to the god once a year, at the beginning of the rainy season. An animal is slain with a holy spear, and the flesh is divided among the people, and cooked and eaten. The twenty-six kings who have reigned over the Shilluks from Nyakang are, according to Father Banholzer and the Rev. J. K. Giffen, as follows:—1. Dag (Dok). 2. Odage. 3. Kudit. 4. Dokodo (Dakkode). 5. Boj (Boiwj). 6. Tugo (Tuka). 7. Nya Dwai (Nya dwi). 8. Nya Ababdo. 9. Muko (Mu Kao). 10. Nya to (Nya ta). 11. Nyakong (Nik Kang). 12. Okun (Ukon). 13. Nya Gwatse

MEROÏTIC INSCRIPTIONS.

[From Lepsius, *Denkmäler*, Abth. VI. Bl. 2.

(Nkwaji). 14. Nyadok. 15. Akwot. 16. Ababdo. 17. Awin. 18. Akoj. 19. Nedok (Nyadok). 20. Kwad Keir (Kwat Ki). 21. Ajang (Ajung). 22. Gwin Kun (Kwoe Kon). 23. Yor Adodoit (Yur). 24. Akol. 25. Kur Wad Nedok. 26. Fadiet Wad Kwad Keir.[1]

LANGUAGES. The language most commonly used throughout the Egyptian Sûdân is ARABIC, the principal language of the Southern Semitic Group. A useful work which will serve as a guide to Sûdânî Arabic has recently been written by Captain

[1] These facts are taken from Giffen, *The Egyptian Sudan*, London, 1905; and from Father Banholzer's *Report*, summarized by Gleichen, *op. cit.*, i., p. 197 ff.

ALTAR WITH MEROITIC INSCRIPTION IN THE BRITISH MUSEUM (No. 892).

Amery, and published by the Government of the Sûdân.[1] Koelle's *Polyglotta Africana* may also be consulted. The NUBIAN language has, in a great measure, been reduced to writing by Lepsius, *Nubische Grammatik*, Berlin, 1880; and by Reinisch, *Die Nuba Sprache*, I. Grammatik und Texte; II. Wörterbuch (German-

ALTAR WITH MEROÏTIC INSCRIPTION IN THE BRITISH MUSEUM (NO. 901).

Nubian, and Nubian-German), Vienna, 1879, 8vo; and by Rüppell, *Reisen*, 1829. On the "Beja Languages," spoken in the Eastern Desert, see Almkvist, *Grammatik* (*Hadanduwa*), Upsala, 1880; Hartmann, *Die Bejah Zeit. Ethnog.*, 1882. The language of the

[1] *English-Arabic Vocabulary*, Cairo, 1905.

Barta has been discussed by Beltrame in *Il Sènnaar e la Sciangàllah*, Verona, 1879; Marno, *Reisen in Hoch Sennaar*, 1870-71; Salt, *Account of a Voyage to Abyssinia*, London, 1809; and several of the dialects in their district are also briefly treated of by Marno, Rüppell, and Munzinger. Valuable contributions to the study of the languages of the Niam-Niams, Shilluks, Nuwers, Dinḳas, Bârîs, Bongos, Golis, Gurs, &c., will be found in Schweinfurth, *Linguistische Ergebnisse* (*Zeit. für Ethnol.*), Berlin, 1873; *Heart of Africa*, London, 1873; Petherick, *Egypt, Sudan, and Central Africa*, London, 1853-58; Long, C. C., *Central Africa*, London, 1876; J. C. Mutterrutzner, *Die Dinka-Sprache in Central Afrika*, Brixen, 1866; *Thiermärchen*, *Z.D.M.G.*, Band xxi., 1867; *Die Sprache der Bari*, Text und Wörterbuch, Brixen, 1867; G. Beltrame, *Gram. e Vocab. della Lingua Denka*, Rome, 1882; *Il Fiume Bianco e i Denka*, Verona, 1881; Rueppell, *Reisen in Nubien, Kordofan*, &c., Frankfort, 1829; Brun-Rollet, *Excursion dans la Région Supérieure du Nil* (*Bulletin de la Soc. de Géographie*), iv., sér. ix., 1855; *Le Nil Blanc et le Soudan. Études sur l'Afrique Centrale*, Paris, 1855; F. Müller, *Die Sprache der Bari* (Grammar, Text, and Vocabulary), Vienna, 1864; *Die Musik-Sprache in Central-Afrika*, Vienna, 1886; R. W. Felkin and C. T. Wilson, *Uganda and the Egyptian Sudan*, London, 1882; Miani, *Viaggi celebri*, Milan, 1878; Antinori, *Il Marchese Orazio Antinori e la Spedizione Geografica Italiana nell' Affrica Equatoriale*, Perugia, 1883; Schuver, *Reisen im oberen Nilgebiet*, Gotha, 1883.

As regards the inscriptions written in hieroglyphics which are found at various places in the Sûdân, some are written in the language of ancient Egypt, and some in a language which has not hitherto been satisfactorily identified. The oldest of the former class were inscribed under the superintendence of Egyptian priests and officials who were well acquainted with the language, but the later inscriptions of this class are clearly copies made with more or less slavish fidelity from documents which the copyists did not understand. The latter class are written with pictorial characters similar to the ancient Egyptian hieroglyphics, and seem to be partly syllabic and partly alphabetic, and in what has been called a "demotic alphabetic writing." According to Lepsius (*Nubische Grammatik*, p. cxxi.), the language in which these inscriptions are written is that of the ancestors of the Begas, or Bejas, and the demotic alphabetic writing is one of the six kinds of writing which Eutychius, Patriarch of Alexandria, enumerates, and calls "Nûbî." Modern writers for convenience' sake have named it "Meroïtic." Dr. H. Brugsch made an attempt to decipher some of the Meroïtic inscriptions, and came to the conclusion that the language was akin to the speech of the Nûbas.[1] The most recent investigator of the question is Dr. H. Schaefer.[2]

[1] *Aegyptische Zeitschrift*, vol. xxv., 1887, pp. 1 ff., 75 ff.

[2] See *Die Aethiopische Königsinschrift des Berliner Museums*, Berlin, 1901; and see Erman, *Aegyptische Zeitschrift*, vol. xxxv., 1897, p. 152.

CHAPTER XIX.

THE BRITISH IN THE SÛDÂN.

Two days after the defeat of the forces of the Khalîfa and the capture of his town of Omdurmân on September 2nd, 1898, the Sirdar, Lord Kitchener, and his troops crossed over to Kharṭûm and hoisted the British and Egyptian flags on the flagstaffs which had been erected on the ruined Palace, wherein General Gordon was killed in January, 1885. This act, which proclaimed to all people that the rule of the Khalîfa was dead, and that the sovereignty of the Sûdân had passed into the hands of those who intended to make Kharṭum the capital of the country, was followed by a religious service of a most impressive and solemn character, in which representatives of every branch of the British and Egyptian Armies which had taken part in the campaign, returned thanks to Almighty God for the victory which He had given them. The manner in which the Anglo-Egyptian conquest was celebrated is unparalleled in the history of the Sudân for at least six thousand years. The victories of the ancient Egyptians and of the kings of Napata, the kings of Meroë, the Arabs, the Turks, Muḥammad 'Alî's son Isma'îl, and his son-in-law Muḥammad the Defterdâr, to say nothing of those of Muḥammad Aḥmad, the mystic and false Mahdî, and of his successor the Khalîfa 'Abd-Allah, were followed by murder and arson, and by the perpetration of atrocities of the most wanton and terrible character. Human blood was shed like water, property of all kinds was destroyed, and the energies of the conquerors were devoted to the burning of water-wheels, the destruction of crops, the raiding of cattle, and the abduction of girls and young women. When they had turned towns and districts into deserts they marched away.

The restoration of the Sûdân to Egypt was marked by none of these things, and the natives who were eye-witnesses of this fact perceived that a new power as well as a new kingdom had been born in the land. The awful, but still merciful slaughter, which that power had inflicted on the tyrannical and barbarous Baḳḳâra, or "Cattle-men," was proof positive that it was a very real one, and as the news travelled south along the banks of the rivers, in that swift and mysterious way with which all who know the East are familar, the natives everywhere rejoiced in their overthrow. With the capture of Omdurmân, however, Mahdiism was not destroyed, for according to Muḥammadan views the movement was still incarnate in the Khalîfa, and although he was in flight with a miserable remnant of his forces, the influence of his extraordinary personality was a factor in the situation which had to be reckoned with. More potent still was the fact that the body of the Mahdî himself still lay in his tomb, for so long as it remained intact the place where it rested would form a centre where religious and political fanatics, and renegades of every kind, could meet and conspire against the new Government. Orthodox Muḥammadans of all sects advised that it should be exhumed and destroyed, for they knew well the peculiar views which followers of the Mahdî would hold about his body and its resting-place, and every one competent to judge will approve of the steps which Lord Kitchener's officers took to bring about the destruction of both, and especially of the burning of the body. The fatalistic Moslems realised, when they saw this done, that its destruction had been written on the Tablet of Fate in heaven, and thus it became clear to them that the Mahdî was an impostor, and only one of the many false prophets who have risen among them. The shells fired by the gunboats had only partially wrecked the dome of the Mahdî's tomb, and Mahdiists believed that it was the power of their dead leader which prevented the guns from doing it further harm. To destroy this belief in the power of the Mahdî was the Sirdar's duty.

As soon as the Sirdar had sent down the river the British contingent, he began to look round on the towns of Omdurmân and Kharṭûm, and wherever he cast his eyes he found ruin and desolation. Omdurmân, the seat of the Mahdî's kingdom, was a filthy town some six miles long and in places nearly three miles wide, and was filled with hundreds of festering cess-pits which poisoned the whole place. Kharṭûm was in ruins, and it became clear that an entirely new town would have to be created. For hundreds of miles north and south the cultivable land was overgrown with ḥalfa grass and thorn bushes, the irrigation channels were choked, the water-wheels destroyed, the oxen that worked them had been slain and eaten, and for the past dozen years or more the palm trees had been neglected. The trade which had formerly been carried on along the main caravan routes had been well-nigh destroyed, the able-bodied male portion of the population had turned brigand, life and property were nowhere safe in the Sûdân, law and order had been abolished, and districts which had been formerly populous and thriving had become so many barren wildernesses. To this pass had the much vaunted rule of Muḥammad 'Alî and his descendants reduced the country, and the revolt of the Mahdî was the logical result of their rule and policy.

The hearts of men less stout than those of the Sirdar and his devoted band must have quailed when they saw the magnitude of the task which awaited them, but fear formed no part of their composition, and they set about the work of the reconstruction of the Sûdân kingdom with an energy which knew no limits. In solving the problems of war, as well as those of peace, which awaited them, they have signally displayed the courage, tact, commonsense and justice, which have earned for the British among the natives the name of "white men." The Sûdân has been ruled by the British for about eight years, and it will not be out of place to consider briefly what they have done in that country during this period, and the various works which they have undertaken in connection with its development.

The re-conquest of the Sûdân cost in all £E2,354,354.[1] Of this sum £E725,641 was spent on the Dongola campaign in 1896, the Wâdî-Ḥalfa-Kharṭûm railway cost £E300,000, and the balance, £E1,328,713, was absorbed by the subsequent military operations. And when we consider the magnitude of the results gained, it must be evident to all that better value for money was never obtained. From first to last the strictest, nay, the most absolutely

[1] Lord Cromer's most recent estimate is £E2,412,000, of which £E780,000 was paid by the British Government.

penurious economy was practised during the Expedition, there was no waste, and it may be added that there were no comforts, hardly even necessaries, either for officers or men, from the Sirdar himself to the private in a Black Battalion. The natives were surprised at the penurious administration of the Egyptian army, and in 1897 I heard many men wish for the return of the days of the Gordon Relief Expedition, during which money was poured out like water. When the Expedition was ended and Omdurmân captured, the same policy of economy was pursued, with what success is evident from the following facts. The revenue of the Sûdân was in 1898 £E35,000 and the expenditure £E235,000, and the deficit of £E200,000 was made good by the Egyptian Treasury. Since that time the revenue has increased steadily, and each year the sum which the Egyptian Treasury has been called on to furnish has been proportionately less; here are the figures as they appear in Lord Cromer's Reports:—

Year.	Expenditure. Civil and Military. £E.	Revenue. £E.	Deficit. £E.
1899	509,500	124,500	415,000
1900	598,000	140,000	417,179
1901	403,000	238,500	164,500
1902	517,000	270,000	247,000
1903	618,000	462,000	156,000
1904	629,000	576,000	53,000
1905	688,000	660,000	28,000 [1]

The revenue of the Sûdân is derived from taxes levied on land, houses, date trees, animals, boats, &c., from Customs dues, from royalties on ivory, &c., from tribute paid by the various nomad tribes, and from fees paid for game, liquor and fire-arms

[1] Count Gleichen gives the following (*Handbook*, p. 4):—

Year.	Revenue. £E.	Expenditure. £E.	Deficit. £E.
1899	126,596	511,693	385,097
1900	156,888	614,780	457,892
1901	242,309	629,969	387,660
1902	270,226	639,493	369 267
1903	462,605	810,019	347,414
1904	531,000	815,500	284,500

licences, from stamps of various kinds, from fees paid by litigants to the courts, from fees paid for the use of ferries, markets, slaughter-houses, &c.; and from the sale of lands which are the property of the Government. The land tax has varied from time to time, but, speaking generally, the tax on the best land is 60 piastres per *faddân* (=1·03808 acre), and on the least good 10 piastres. The incidence of this tax is carefully watched, and due allowance is made for the varying quality and position of the land in the different provinces. The land tax is generally paid in money, but sometimes, for various reasons, it is paid in kind, one-tenth (*'ushur*) of the crops being regarded as a fair equivalent. The house tax is practically one-twelfth of the annual rental value; it was fixed according to the ancient usage current in the province of Dongola. The date tax is 2 piastres on each tree, whether male or female. The tax on a camel is 20 piastres, on a horse 3, on a mule or donkey 3, on a sheep 1, on cattle 5 piastres per head, and on each goat half a piastre. Under the Dervish rule the tax on a camel was from 1,200 to 1,500 piastres, i.e., from £12 6*s*. to £15 7*s* 6*d*.; on cattle from 900 to 1,350 piastres per head; and on sheep and goats 100 piastres per head! The boat tax is two piastres per ardeb (i.e., 300 lbs.) on the carrying capacity of the craft. Game licences are of two kinds, A and B, the former costing £E25, and the latter £E5. A liquor licence costs £E50, and a licence to carry fire-arms from 25 to 50 piastres. Gum, ivory, ostrich feathers, and india-rubber paid a royalty of 20 per cent. *ad valorem* to the Government. In 1904 the royalty on ivory was reduced to 10 per cent., and as a result the value of the ivory exported rose from £E22,000 in 1903 to £E42,000 in 1905. When we know that the reduction of the duty has resulted in the wholesale slaughter of elephants, the Homr tribe killing no less than eighty-seven animals in one day, it is impossible not to regret the abolition of the Government monopoly. The old tax of from 300 to 500 piastres on every water-wheel has, most properly, been abolished. From Omdurmân northwards the Mahdî and the Khalîfa continued, substantially, the system of taxation which was in force before their rule, but in the southern provinces their will alone was law. Thus the province between the White and Blue Niles was made to deliver 100,000 ardebs of grain in Omdurmân, but as the collectors took care to provide for the private wants of themselves and their followers, it happened that nearly 300,000 ardebs were drawn from this one tract alone.[1] At the present time the taxes are collected honestly, and the natives have begun to realize that they do not have to pay them two or three times over; and each year, it is said, the tribes who own no land, but live by their flocks and herds, pay more readily the tribute which is laid upon them.

From the Statement of Accounts of the Sûdân Government for the year 1905, published by Colonel E. E. Bernard (*Sudan Gazette*, No. 95, 1906), we see that the revenue from the Provinces was £E216,579, and from the other Services £E448,832, i.e., £E665,411. The contribution by the Egyptian Government for civil expenditure was £E379,763, therefore the total revenue was £E1,045,174. The expenditure for the year was:—

Provinces	£E206,061
Departments	£E475,820
Total	£E631,881

The cost of maintenance of the Army in the Sûdân was £E186,757, and there was, therefore, a surplus of £E176,536.

The following extracts, which give the details of the receipts and show how the Revenue is obtained, and the receipts and expenditures of the Provinces, are of considerable interest:—

	£E.	£E.
1. Land Tax:—		
a. Taxed Land	48,970[2]	
b. Ushur (Tithe) . . .	30,453	79,423
2. Date Tax		15,595
3. Boat Tax		1,265
4. Animal Tax		19,381
5. House Tax		2,093
6. Road Tax		3,280
Carried forward . .		121,037

[1] Sir W. Garstin, *Egypt*, No. 5 (1899), p. 24.

[2] The *millims* are omitted.

	£E.	£E.
Brought forward . .		121,037
7. Royalties :—		
a. Gum	15,536	
b. Ivory	4,652	
c. Feathers	2,722	
d. India Rubber . . .	10	
e. Other Articles . . .	1,645	24,565
8. Tribute from Nomad Tribes . .		12,494
9. Woods and Forests . . .		16,714
10. By Sales :—		
a. Government Lands . .	2,619	
b. Salt	668	
c. Various	6,101	9,388
11. Customs Dues		96,648
12. Ferries		7,504
13. Stamped Paper		1,900
14. Licences :—		
a. Liquor	3,459	
b. Fire-arms	277	
c. Auctioneers and Pedlars .	1,197	
d. Game	1,527	
e. Prospecting	2,436	
f. Various	439	9,335
15. Slaughtering Dues . . .		4,183
16. Market Fees		7,216
17. Court Fees		5,575
18. Fines		4,966
19. Rent of Government Lands . .		4,512
20. Contribution to Pension Funds .		2,503
21. Mehkema Receipts . . .		2,701
22. Tax on Treasury Chest Remittances		425
23. Commission on Postal Money Orders		2,391
24. Sale of Postage Stamps . .		8,375
Carried forward . .		342,432

			£E.
	Brought forward . .		342,432
25.	Telegrams		17,571
26.	Transport :—		
	a. Steamers and Boats . .	104,643	
	b. Railways	172,249	276,892
27.	Various		27,095
28.	Refund by Egyptian Ministry .		1,397
		Total	665,387
	Contribution by Egyptian Government .		379,763
	Grand Total .		£E1,045,150

STATEMENT OF THE REVENUES AND EXPENDITURES OF PROVINCES AND DEPARTMENTS IN 1905.

	Receipts.		Expenditures.	
Provinces.	£E.	Mil.	£E.	Mil.
Baḥr al Ghazâl . .	7,058	084	22,850	198
Berber . . .	22,528	175	19,318	011
Blue Nile . . .	17,568	214	15,288	335
Dongola . . .	31,321	048	16,446	064
Ḥalfa	12,124	286	7,680	073
Kasala . . .	13,741	661	15,206	255
Kharṭûm . . .	16,370	842	16,243	225
Kordôfân . . .	37,501	877	23,005	936
Red Sea . . .	11,926	815	14,928	648
Sennaar . . .	17,655	989	25,846	840
White Nile . . .	10,980	401	16,039	377
Upper Nile . . .	17,801	315	13,208	441
	216,578	707	206,061	403
Departments.				
Civil Secretary . .	1,705	494	31,752	756
Legal	3,492	745	19,056	206
Education . . .	497	978	13,740	097
Agriculture and Lands	2,623	302	3,551	791
Game Preservation .	1,746	852	923	082
Carried forward .	226,645	078	275,085	335

	Receipts. £E.	Mil.	Expenditures. £E.	Mil.
Brought forward	226,645	078	275,085	335
Medical	1,002	417	14,085	869
General Central Services	13,248	584	27,365	741
Customs	97,989	063	6,359	670
Steamers and Boats	109,847	751	87,516	385
Posts and Telegraphs	30,532	230	30,442	638
Railways	174,962	466	126,225	623
Kharṭûm Town	9,785	710	15,674	532
Refund by Egyptian Ministry of War	1,397	884		
Contribution by Egyptian Government	379,763			
Governor-General's Office			7,131	711
Inspector-General's Office			2,416	948
Finance Department			17,602	377
Forestry ,,			14,567	126
Survey ,,			9,078	056
Cattle Plague Service			1,567	462
Public Works			46,761	516
Grand Total	1,045,174	183	681,880	989
Egyptian War Dept., for maintenance of Army in Sûdân			186,757	
Surplus 1905 passed to Reserve Fund			176,536	194
Grand Total			£1,045,174	183

The Reserve Fund of £E445,229 has been formed thus:—

I. Credit.	£E.
Surplus of 1902	20,454
Surplus of 1903	42,307
Carried forward	62,761

	£E.
Brought forward	62,761
Credit from Egypt in 1904	15,000
Surplus of 1904	140,932
Credit from Egypt in 1905	25,000
Surplus of 1905	176,536
Credit from Egypt for Public Works in 1906 . .	25,000
Total .	£E445,229

II. Debit.	Credit Opened. £E.	Balance Unexpended. £E.	Mil.
Partial cost of two Evaporators	20,454	1,929	149
Telegraph (Tawfîḳîya to Kîka)	14,650		
Steamers for Ferry . .	10,000	65	531
Pearl Fishery Service .	3,500	1,011	647
Roads and Communications .	17,750	7,345	844
Water Supply Works . .	20,250		
Tawfîḳîya Dockyard . .	800	61	670
Sanitation	2,500	1,486	189
Law Courts	4,000	2,751	
Cadastral Survey . . .	8,000	5,081	682
Apparatus for Gordon College	322	4	671
Public Works in 1905 . .	36,000	7,700	
Omdurmân Tramline . .	6,250	4,319	138
Wing to Gordon College . .	15,000	14,121	302
Expropriation of Land . .	14,606	14,119	532
Cattle Plague Service in 1905 .	9,000	5,651	266
Electric Lighting . . .	12,700	12,641	500
Engine for Stern Wheeler .	1,500	1,500	
Kharṭûm Roads in 1905 . .	1,000	264	340
Telephone Extensions . .	900	55	809
Telegraph (Tong to Mvolo) .	9,363	3,099	930
Relaying Kharṭûm Tramline .	600	167	343
Quarters at Ad-Dâmar . .	1,000	564	600
Carried forward . .	210,145	83,942	143

	Credit Opened. £E.	Balance Unexpended. £E.	Mil.
Brought forward . .	210,145	83,942	143
Special Grants to Provinces .	11,000	9,900	330
Telegraph (Rumbek to Bôr) .	21,235	20,609	547
Conversion of Ḥalfa Hotel into Offices	3,125	121	132
Contingencies	14,000	7,168	606
Various Services in 1906 . .	143,350	143,350	
Total	402,855	265,091	748
Unpledged Balance	42,374	42,374	
Grand Total . . .	£445,229	£307,465	748

One of the most urgent needs in connection with the development of the country is Easy means of Conveyance both for men and goods. The natives have from time immemorial used the river for this purpose as much as possible, but the mass of floating vegetation called sadd or sudd, which choked the river south of Lake Nô, and the Cataract of Shablûka and the cataracts between Abû Ḥamed and Ḥalfa, have always prevented the establishment of regular transport from the Sûdân to Egypt for merchandise in large quantities by river, at certain seasons of the year. As a result, the native merchants of Dâr Fûr and Kordôfân sent their goods and marched their slave-caravans by the "Arba'în [1] Road," through the Oases of the Western Desert to Asyût or Cairo, and, in order to shorten the journey by cutting off the bends and windings of the river, merchants who traded with the natives on the Blue Nile sent their wares from some town such as Ḳûṣ, or Darâw, or Korosko, through the Eastern Desert, *viâ* Abû Ḥamed and Berber. On the White Nile, i.e., the Nile between Kharṭûm and Lake Nô, the only obstacle to navigation is at the ford of Abû Zêd, where in years of very low Nile a *portage* is necessary. On the Upper Nile, now that the sudd has been removed, there is a clear water-way to Gondokoro. The Blue Nile is only navigable for steamers for

[1] I.e., the "Forty Road," because the journey along it from one end to the other occupied forty days.

six months of the year, and the Atbara is useless as a water-way the whole year through, but several of the rivers in the Baḥr al-Ghazâl Province have been ascended in steamers for very considerable distances from their mouths. When funds become available the Government will, no doubt, place steel boats and barges of shallow draught upon these rivers, and the development of trade will be greatly stimulated. A small steamer has been already placed on the Gûr River, with the view of opening up communication for trade purposes with the French Congo, but the Raffilî Falls at present obstruct the navigation to and from French territory, and nothing can be done until the rocks are blasted away. It is to be hoped that money may be forthcoming to extend and improve the Government Steamer Service in the Sûdân, and that Commander Bond, R.N., may be able to increase still further the benefits which his sound judgment, unostentatious work, and capable hands have bestowed upon the Sûdân.

After the rivers, the commonest and most natural means of communication are the Roads. Purely native roads in the Sûdân, as in Turkey in Asia, leave much to be desired. They are narrow, winding, and tortuous, and the natives would rather make their beasts travel double the distance than remove the obstacles in the way of their progress. During the last few years the authorities have taken the matter seriously in hand, and Lord Cromer reports that there are over 4,000 miles of good roads now in the Sûdân. The roads are tracks thirty feet wide, more or less straight, cleared of trees and stumps when they pass through forests or bush, defined by stones in the open country, and with ramps into and out of the *khôrs*. Along the 2,550 miles of road opened in 1905, some 121 wells were made, thirty-three of them by private enterprise. A road for wheeled traffic between the White and Blue Niles has been begun by Mr. Gorringe, who has already completed the section between Ruṣêreṣ and Gebel Agadî, a distance of twenty-four miles. He is now extending it to Renk, and when completed it will bring the southern districts of the Province of Sennaar into communication with a water-way open at all seasons of the year.

In connection with the roads of the Sûdân it is important to note the very thorough exploration of the country which has been made by the civil and military officials during the last few years. All the old native trade routes and caravan roads have been travelled over, the towns and villages, and the country between them, carefully described, the distances from place to place measured, and every point of interest, and every piece of information, which was thought likely to be of use to administrative officials and travellers, have been noted. Besides the old roads new country has been diligently explored, and new routes found out, and the probability and possibility of the development of trade along them have always been kept steadily in view. This most useful work has been unostentatiously performed by Capt. H. F. S. Amery, Capt. E. H. Armstrong, Mr. J. Baird, Capt. A. B. Bethel, R.A., C.-Sergeant Boardman, Major W. A. Boulnois, Major Bulkeley Johnson, Capt. V. Bunbury, Mr. Jennings Bramley, Capt. Bower, I.S.C., J. Butler Bey, Sorel Cameron Bey, Mr. E. Bonham-Carter, Capt. R. C. Carter, Colonel Collinson, Capt. T. Conolly, Mr. James Currie, Director of the Gordon College, Major de Rougemont, Capt. Dugmore, Lieut. H. L. H. Fell, R.N., Capt. C. E. Foster, Colonel Friend, Count Gleichen, Major C. W. Gwynn, D.S.O., R.E., Colonel Gorringe, Capt. H. R. Headlam, Colonel St. George Henry, Capt. H. Hodgson, Lieut. L. C. Jackson, R.E., Capt. Kenrick, Capt. C. Leigh, Capt. C. H. Leveson, Capt. C. H. Lewin, R.F.A., Mr. C. E. Lyall, Capt. H. D. W. Lloyd, Capt. H. G. Lyons, R.E., Colonel B. Mahon, C.B., D.S.O., Capt. McKerrell, Capt. E. G. Meyricke, R.E., Colonel Mitford, Capt. H. H. Morant, Mr. R. E. More, Capt. J. R. O'Connell, Capt. A. C. Parker, Capt. A. Percival, Capt. R. I. Rawson, Major Powell, R.E., Major H. V. Ravenscroft, Capt. C. Roberts, R.A., Capt. G. J. Ryan, Major G. de H. Smith, Colonel W. S. Sparkes, C.M.G., Capt. N. M. Smyth, V.C., Major E. A. Stanton, Governor of Kharṭûm, Lord Sudeley, Colonel the Hon. M. G. Talbot, R.E., Capt. A. A. C. Taylor, Lieut. A. M. Taggart, Capt. C. H. Townsend, Major Tudway, Major E. B. Wilkinson, Capt. H. H. Wilson, Capt. P. Wood, and others.

The "Routes" compiled by the above have been carefully edited, in some cases with additions, by Count Gleichen in the second volume of his *Handbook*, and many of them are to be obtained separately at the Sûdân Office in Cairo. A number of other "Routes" have been compiled by the editor himself and printed in the same volume, and this collection of "Itineraries" must always be regarded as one of the most important pieces of work done by British Officers in the Sûdân. All the useful facts collected by earlier travellers, such as Baker, Junker, and Schweinfurth, have been drawn upon, and there are many evidences that the information which has been collected by sportsmen and others in the Sûdân and Western Abyssinia during the last six years has been examined and sifted by Count Gleichen.

Side by side with the making of "Routes" the survey of the Sûdân has been carried on under the capable direction of Colonel the Hon. M. G. Talbot, R.E., and, as the result of the work of himself and of his assistants, the Sûdân Government has been able to publish a series of accurate maps of the country on a scale of about four miles to the inch. It is proposed to issue in all about 140 sheets, and of this number more than fifty have been already published; each sheet covers one degree of latitude,[1] and one and a half degrees of longitude. The country of the Sûdân was never so well known by any of its conquerors in the long course of its history, and the British are the first among them to survey it and to make maps of it.

From what has been said above it is clear that if the Sûdân is to be developed, other means of communication must be found besides the Nile and the roads, and for nearly thirty years before it was carried out the idea of connecting Kharṭûm with Cairo by railway was in the air.[2] The first section of the railway to Upper Egypt ended at Asyût, about 210 miles from Cairo, and from this town travellers to Kharṭûm usually went by river to Korosko, crossed the desert to Abû Ḥamed, and the rest of the journey they performed partly by camel and partly by boat. Many travellers preferred to take ship to Sawâkin, and then to cross the desert to Berber, and so on by camel or boat, or both, to Kharṭûm. A few hardy travellers with abundant means and leisure followed the course of the river the whole way from Cairo

[1] For the list of the sheets already published, see Gleichen, *op. cit.*, i., p. 349.

[2] The first to propose it was Sa'îd Pâshâ in 1860. Surveys were made by Mougel by Messrs. Walker and Bray in 1865, and by Mr. J. Fowler in 1871.

or Asyût to Kharṭûm, but it is obvious that the waste of time and money involved in such a journey prevented it from being generally adopted by merchants and officials. The administration of the Sûdân was carried on by means of the telegraph, of which there were several lines in the country. Thus there was the main line from Cairo to Kharṭûm, another from Kharṭûm to Kordôfân, a third from Kharṭûm to Fâzôglî, a fourth from Berber to Sawâkin, and smaller lines connected Kharṭûm and Berber with Maṣaw'a, Sawâkin, Kasala, Ḳallâbât, Ḳaḍâref, and many other places in the Eastern Sûdân.

In a fashion this arrangement worked fairly well, so far as the transmission of the orders of the Government were concerned, just as it does in Turkey in Asia at the present time, but a telegraph system cannot supply a Government with all the information it ought to possess, and the first to realize this to the fullest extent was Isma'îl Pâshâ. This Khedive determined to quicken the means of transport between Kharṭûm and Ḥalfa by building a railway on the east bank of the Nile, intending it to proceed through the Provinces of Sukkôt and Mahass to Dongola, thence to Merawi, and on to Kharṭûm *viâ* Berber and Shendî. A survey of the country was made, contracts were signed, and work began at Ḥalfa in 1877. In course of time the railway reached Sarras, 33 miles from Ḥalfa, and the road-bed was made for about 40 miles more ; the gauge was 3 ft. 6 in. The route chosen is, however, said by experts to have been a wrong one, and the object of the surveyors appears to have been to make the undertaking cost as much money as possible. The gradients are far too steep, and near the Ambiḳôl Wells and other places they are positively dangerous. The cost of the railway per mile was very high, and the Khedive decided, some say at the request of General Gordon, to stop the work. Even the section of the line which was laid was never properly worked, and many of the locomotives ordered for it were never put under steam. In 1887 I saw several of them still standing on the river bank, tied up in sheets of native calico, and scattered about in the mud, close to the water's edge, were numbers of the machines used in repairing locomotives; these were intended to be placed in the workshops which were never built. The decision to stop making the railway at Sarras was an unfortunate one; had the line been continued to Akasha ('Ukâsha) it would have been useful in bringing down dates from Sukkôt, and a reasonable tariff would have led to a development of trade.

The line from Ḥalfa to Sarras remained utterly useless until 1884, when the Royal Engineers of the Gordon Relief Expedition set it in order, and, having repaired the road-bed and continued it to 'Ukâsha, used it for military transport. When the British retired from the Sûdân in the spring of 1885, the Dervishes came north, tore up the rails for about 22 miles, and carried away as many of them, with bolts and fishplates, as they thought they required. Some of the sleepers they used for building huts for themselves, and others they burned to warm themselves at night, and to cook their food. In 1887 I saw a number of the "sleeper" huts made by the Dervishes and the remains of the charred wood, and to several places in the Cataract portions of the line, which the Dervishes could not take to pieces, had been dragged bodily from the road-bed, and thrown down the rocks near the water's edge. Curiously enough, the Dervishes did not interfere with the portion of the road-bed, 22 miles long, which Isma'îl's engineers made beyond Sarras. Between 1885 and 1896 the line from Ḥalfa to Sarras was just kept in working order and nothing more. The engines were old and in a dangerous condition, and there was no rolling stock worth mentioning. In 1896, when the Dongola Expedition was decided upon, the Royal Engineers once more took the railway in hand,[1] and the works which they carried out on it were of such a comprehensive character that they may be said practically to have rebuilt it. During the expedition the line was extended to Kerma, about 201 miles from Ḥalfa, and thus we see that the length of the extension added to the old Ḥalfa-Sarras line by the British was about 170 miles. The extension was of course hastily built, but it did splendid work, under the care and superintendence of a band of young Royal Engineer officers, among whom may be mentioned Lieutenants E. P. C. (now Sir Percy) Girouard, D.S.O., G. B. Macauley, A. G. Stevenson, H. L. Pritchard, H. A. Micklem, G. C. M. Hall, E. C. A. Newcombe, and R. B. D. Blakeney. For three or four years after the capture

[1] Lord Kitchener actually began to build a railway from Korosko to Abû Ḥamed, but he abandoned the scheme and made his line start from Ḥalfa.

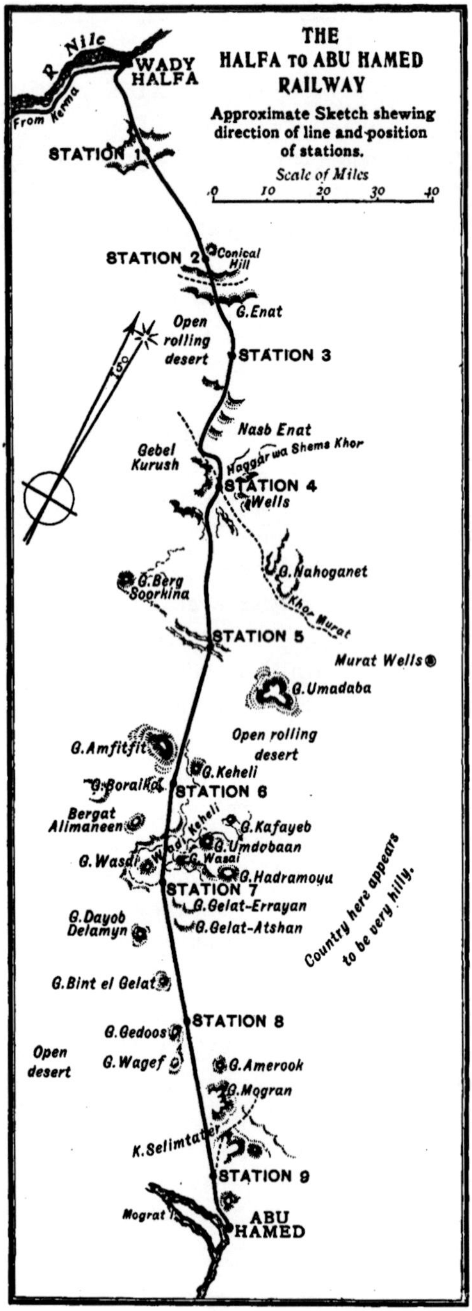

THE ḤALFA-ABÛ ḤAMED RAILWAY.
[From a plan by Sir E. Percy C. Girouard, K.C.M.G.

of Omdurmân the Kerma line was regularly worked, but unfortunately at a loss, and in 1902, whilst the working expenses amounted to £E23,500, the receipts from paying traffic were only £E3,526. The line was in a very bad condition, and as a large sum of money would have been required to repair it thoroughly, it was decided to close it. In 1903 the rails between Kerma and Kôsha were taken up and sent on to Atbara to be used in the construction of the Red Sea Railway, and the sleepers were stacked at Kôsha. At the present time the railways in the Sûdân are:—

1. The LINE FROM ḤALFA TO KÔSHA, about 108 miles long. The stations between the two termini are: Sarras 33 miles from Ḥalfa, Murrât 47 miles, Ambiḳôl Wells 64 miles, and 'Ukâsha 86 miles.

2. The LINE FROM ḤALFA TO KHARṬÛM, about 575 miles long.

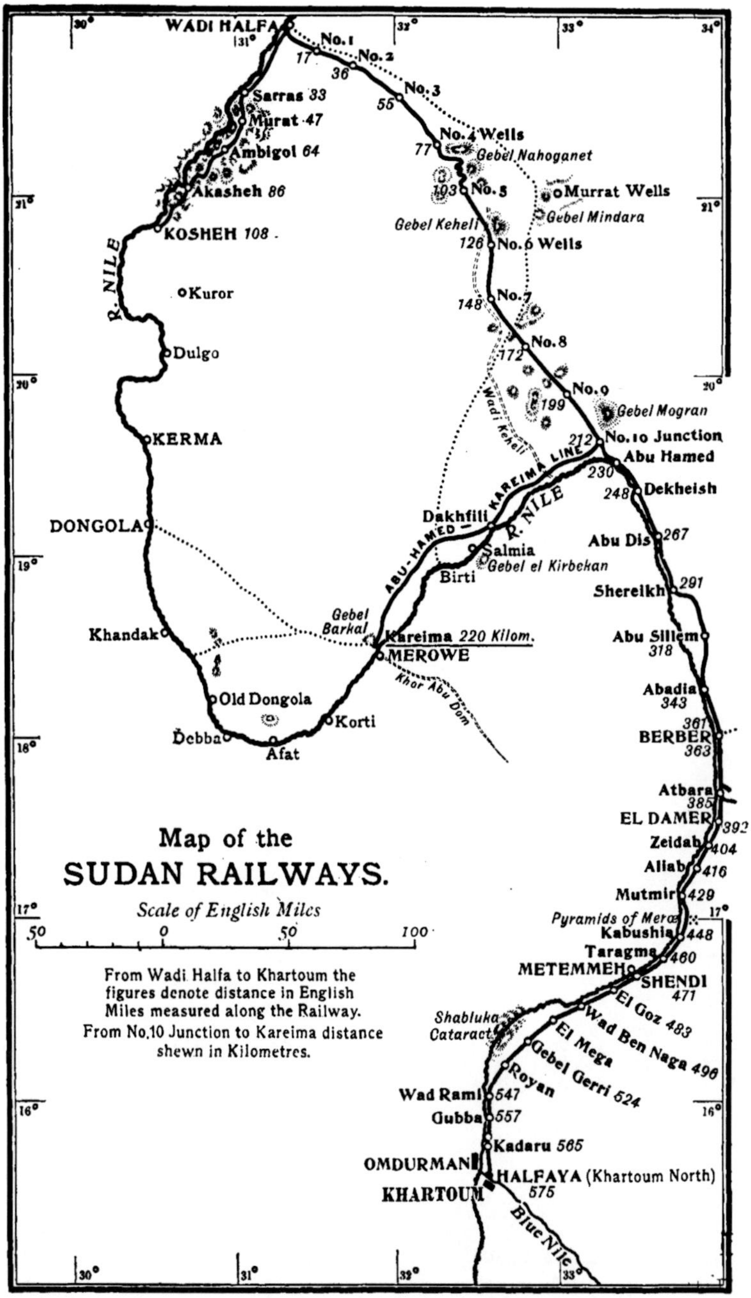

MAP SHOWING THE ROUTE OF THE ḤALFA-KÔSHA RAILWAY, AND THAT OF THE NEW RAILWAY FROM NO. 10 STATION TO KARÊMA IN THE DONGOLA PROVINCE.

[From a copy supplied by Capt. E. C. Midwinter, R.E.

The construction of this railway is one of the greatest of the works which have been done by the British in the Sûdân. When the advance to Dongola was effected in 1896, the idea was mooted that the Sirdar should proceed from Merawi to Matamma across the Bayûda Desert, and thence to Omdurmân, and for a time it seemed likely that the further advance of the Frontier Field Force

THE DRIVER OF THE "GEDAREF" AT NO. 4 STATION IN THE ABÛ ḤAMED DESERT.

would take place by this route. The Sirdar, however, thought otherwise, and he determined that his battalions should go forward by the Nile, and by the Nile only; in 1897 the places which he most wanted them to occupy were Abû Ḥamed, at the head of the Fourth Cataract, and Berber. The Frontier Field Force was already at Merawi, at the foot of this Cataract, about 140 miles from Abû Ḥamed, but the Sirdar was wondering the whole time if there was not some way whereby he could convey his supplies from Ḥalfa to Abû Ḥamed direct, a distance of about 230 miles, instead of sending them by rail to Kerma, 201 miles, by steamer from Kerma to Merawi, 246 miles more, and by camel to Abû Ḥamed another 140 miles, in all about 587 miles. At length he determined to make a railway from Ḥalfa to Abû Ḥamed, and this notwithstanding the objections raised by many engineers and

A DECORATED AMERICAN ENGINE ON THE ḤALFA ABU-ḤAMED RAILWAY.

others, who knew the desert very well, and who declared the thing to be an impossibility.

No map of the desert by any competent authority existed, and those who had crossed it from Korosko gave contradictory accounts as to details, but all agreed that there were no wells anywhere on the route of the proposed railway, and no water, and that it was so full of hills that no railway could be taken across it. The Sirdar was unmoved by any of these objections, for he *knew* the Abû Ḥamed desert better than any one else, and he was confident that his knowledge was correct. More likely than not he had ridden over every mile of it in years past, when he was quietly working out his plans for the reconquest of the Sûdân. His experience in the Gordon Relief Expedition taught him the difficulties which a General who succeeded in reaching Omdurmân would have to overcome before he got there, and that the greatest difficulty of all was the *country* and not the enemy. The exact route of the railway had, of course, to be planned by railway engineers, and a party was sent out to make the survey. When they returned they reported that about 100

A SHADY RESTING-PLACE.

miles from Ḥalfa the country rose to a height of from 1,200 to 1,500 feet, but that the ascent to the ridge and the descent from it were gradual, and that they had found a strip of "easy desert," which reached the whole way from Ḥalfa to Abû Ḥamed, along which the line might be laid. They had also noted two places in the desert, about 77 and 126 miles from Ḥalfa respectively, where they suggested that trial borings for water should be made; subsequently when wells were sunk there, water was found at the depth of 70 feet. The discovery at these places decided the route of the railway once and for all.

Without delay work was begun at Ḥalfa (the other terminus was actually in the possession of the Dervishes), and after May 4th, 1897, when the line to Kerma actually reached that place, the whole of the Kerma railway battalion was sent from the Nile to the Abû Ḥamed desert, and the line was pushed forward with astonishing speed and success.[1] It advanced at the rate of over a mile a day,

[1] The following description of the making of the line, by Mr. Knight, the able correspondent of the *Times* (September 11th, 1897), is excellent:—

". . . I walked to the end of the work and back. As this is a record "railway, and the methods employed are, I believe, in some respects unique, an "account of the order of the operations ought to be of interest. In the first "place, the banking of the section had been completed in the morning (for a "great part of the way no embankment was necessary, and the sleepers had "merely to be laid on the desert), so the 800 men who had been engaged on "this work were at the time of my arrival resting at the end of the formation, "to which the entire railway camp was to be moved in the evening. Still "further off, and out of sight, was the survey camp, under the command of "Lieutenant Pritchard, R.E., which I was unable to visit. On walking up the "line from the further end of the work I first met the 170 men who were "bringing up the sleepers from the train and laying them, and also 200 men, "divided into gangs of 10 each, who were carrying and placing in position the "heavy rails. No one shirked his work; on the left of the line hurried up the "sleeper carriers, each man with two or three of these on his shoulder; on the "right of the line worked the rail carriers, nine men to each rail, swinging along "with a fine stride. Backwards and forwards they went until they had emptied "the trucks of the mile and a half of material, which they did in a remarkably "short space of time. Immediately behind these I found a party of thirty men "and boys, the former bolting the fish-plates to the newly-laid rails, the latter— "the son of Hamuda, the Dervish general who fell at Firkeh, was among "them—holding the expansion pieces. Closely following these were 100 first "spikers, who spiked every other sleeper only; and a few rough straighteners, "whose work left the railway incomplete, but made it possible for the engine "and train to pass over. So just behind these came the train of material from "which the first-mentioned parties were unloading the rails and sleepers as fast "as they could handle them. Following the train and working on the portion of "line over which it had just passed came four fish-plate tighteners and sixty "final spikers, who spiked the alternate sleepers which had been left by the "first spikers working at the head of the train. Next came six rough "straighteners, whose work was preliminary to that of the next party of 100 "men who were employed in lifting and packing; then came 190 men boxing and "filling, and, lastly, a party of straighteners. It was a mile-long line of men "constructing a railway through all the stages of the work. Every advance of "the train, and of the successive working parties from section to section, meant "so many hundreds of yards more of completed railway thrust into the desert. "One realized this best when one sat on the train and felt it move on a little "way every few minutes. We timed our progress and found that we were, on

and in the month of October the telegraph brought us news at Merawi that on one day three miles of rail had been laid and spiked down. The record for the whole of that month was fifty miles. By May 4th about fifteen miles had been laid, and at the end of August the railway had reached mile 160, and on October 31st it entered Abû Ḥamed. The whole line, 231 miles long, was laid in six months, and the work was carried out during the hottest months of the year. The engineer officer whose name must ever stand out prominently in connection with this wonderful piece of work is Lieut. (now Sir Percy) Girouard, who had already displayed the powers of organization and resource which he possessed in the construction of the Kerma line, and he in turn was most ably supported by Lieutenants Macauley, Stevenson, Pritchard, Polwhele, Midwinter, and others. There was no opening ceremony, and there were no speeches and mutual congratulations; the locomotives alone did the "puffing." That trains should be running regularly into Abû Ḥamed in less than three months after it had been captured from the Dervishes seemed to be in the usual order of things! The distance saved by the railway between Ḥalfa and Abû Ḥamed is nearly 360 miles, and it enabled the Sirdar to dispense with a whole army of camels, and to obtain each supply of stores *three weeks* earlier than before.

From Abû Ḥamed the railway was continued to Atbara Fort without difficulty, a distance of 151 miles. After the capture of Omdurmân on September 2nd, 1898, a sum of £E300,000 was granted from the Special Reserve Fund to continue the railway from the Atbara to Ḥalfâya, opposite to Kharṭûm. The Atbara is crossed by a girder bridge 1,050 feet long, made by an American firm for £6,500; the substructure and the making and placing of the cylinders were carried out by an Italian contractor. At the northern end of the Atbara-Kharṭûm section a good deal

"the average, doing eighty yards in six minutes—a rapid rate for railway "construction, when it is borne in mind that they are here working with only "one shift of men. The absolutely finishing work on each section is done by a "party of 150 men who are employed on the final lifting, straightening, packing "and boxing. They follow on about three miles behind the main working "parties which I have described, thus allowing several heavy trains to pass "over the lines and settle it before these final adjustments and corrections are "made. . . ."

of cutting and banking had to be done, and towards the southern end the making of drainage cuttings and culverts cost much time and money. In spite of all this, the railway reached Ḥalfâya on December 31st, 1899, and the journey from its northern to its southern terminus could be made with comparative comfort in about thirty-six hours. At the present day the time occupied on the journey is only twenty-six or twenty-eight hours. The *train de luxe*, or, as the natives call it, *muftakhar*, i.e., the "proud," provides the traveller with every comfort, and supplies food and drink without difficulty. The sleeping berths are most comfortable, and the compartments are roomy; they are provided with electric light and fans, a flap-table, cane chairs, and wire-gauze and other shutters, which permit the occupant to admit as much or as little light as he pleases. Though the gauge is only 3 feet 6 inches, the width of the bodies of the coaches is nearly 9 feet. Every detail has been carefully thought out, and as the internal arrangements of the coaches represent the sum of the experience and needs of many desert travellers, the result is admirable. Each compartment contains two berths, but there is far more room in it for the occupants than in the ordinary Continental *train de luxe*, unless one of them overcrowds it with luggage. There are no baths on the train, but this causes no inconvenience, as the train stops long enough at Abû Ḥamed to allow travellers to enjoy the excellent baths which the authorities have established by the side of the station.

The stopping-places and stations on the Ḥalfa-Kharṭûm Railway, or the Sûdân Government Railway, are:—

	Miles from Ḥalfa.[1]	
No. 1.	17.	
No. 2.	36.	
No. 3.	55.	
No. 4.	77.	Here are wells on the east side of the line. Between Nos. 4 and 5 the country rises considerably, and in skirting Gebel Nahoganet the line makes a series of interesting curves.
No. 5.	103.	

[1] I am indebted to Capt. E. C. Midwinter, R.E., D.S.O., for these details.

Miles from Ḥalfa.		
No. 6.	126.	Here are wells on the east side of the line, a large triangle, and some workshops. On the east is the terminus of the short line which runs to the gold mines.
No. 7.	148.	
No. 8.	172.	
No. 9.	199.	Between Nos. 9 and 10, on the east, is Gebel Mugran.
No. 10.	212.	Here is the junction of the new line to Karêma.

	Miles From Ḥalfa.	
Abû Ḥamed	230.	
Mashra' ad-Dakhêsh	248.	The railway runs close to the river.
Abû Dîs	267.	
Sharêkh	291.	Here the line bends away into the desert.
Abû Sillem	318.	In the desert, some miles from the Nile.
Abidîya	343.	A village of some size.
Berber (North)	361.	Here the old caravan road to Sawâkin started.
Berber (South)	363.	
Atbara Junction	384.	Here the Sawâkin railway joins the Kharṭûm line.
Atbara	385.	
Ad-Dâmar	392.	The first station on the Island of Meroë.
Zêdâb	404.	
Alîâb	416.	
Mutmîr, or Mukhmîya	429.	
Umm 'Alî	437.	
Kabûshîa	448.	Nearest station for the Pyramids of Meroë.
Tarâgma	460.	
Shendî (Shindî)	471.	Here are several railway workshops.
Al-Ḳôz	483.	
Wâd Bâ Nagaa	496.	
Al-Mêga	511.	Here the railway leaves the river and cuts straight across the bend which contains the Shablûka Cataract.

	Miles from Ḥalfa.	
Gebel Gârî . .	524.	
Royan . .	538.	
Wâd Ramla .	547.	Here the railway approaches the river.
Ḳubba (Kubalab).	557.	
Kadaru . .	565.	
Ḥalfâya, or . . Kharṭûm North	575.	

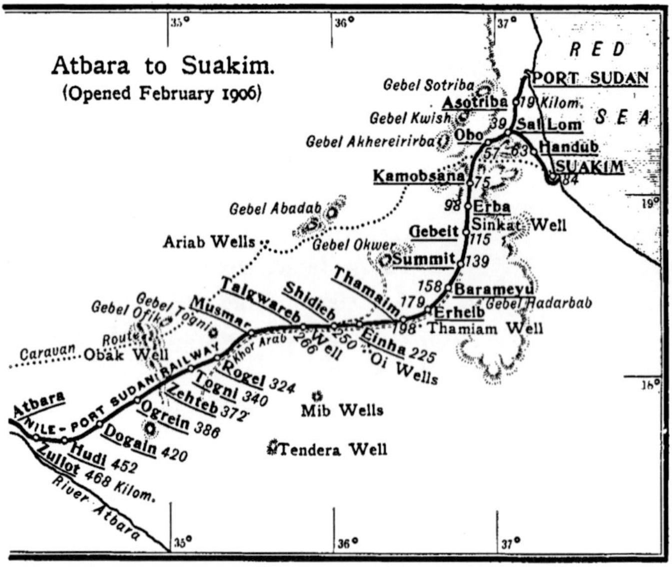

THE RAILWAY FROM ATBARA TO SAWÂKIN AND PORT SÛDÂN.

[From a copy supplied by Capt. E. C. Midwinter, R.E.

3. The LINE FROM THE NILE TO THE RED SEA. This railway leaves the Nile about one mile to the north of Atbara station, at a point called "Atbara Junction," or "Sawâkin Junction," and crosses the Eastern Desert to Sal-Lôm, where there is a junction. The line to the right runs south to Sawâkin, *viâ* Handûb, and that to the left runs north to Shêkh al-Barghûth, which is to be officially known henceforward as "Port Sûdân." The distance from Atbara to Sawâkin is 307 miles, and from the former place to Port Sûdân about the same. There are in all 331 miles of main

line, and 15 miles of sidings. The cost was about £E1,375,000, or about £E4,150 per mile. The steepest gradient is 1 in 100, and the sharpest curve 5 degrees. Work on the main line was begun in August, 1904, and the first through train from Atbara reached Sawâkin in safety on October 15th, 1905. The passengers were Messrs. Midwinter, Longfield, Sowerby, Lord, and Pelham, and the journey occupied 30 hours. Work was carried on simultaneously at each end of the line, but the Atbara section

RAILWAY SHOPS, SAWÂKIN.

[From a photograph by Capt. E. C. Midwinter, R.E., D.S.O.

advanced more quickly than that which started at Sawâkin, where there was much blasting to be done. Colonel Macauley, R.E., had the greatest difficulty in obtaining labour, and in the end recourse was had to the sturdy Egyptians. On several occasions there were bad "wash-outs" caused by rains in the mountains behind Sawâkin, whilst in the desert the men were often short of water. Colonel Macauley and Captain E. C. Midwinter had had much experience of such difficulties, and in the end they triumphed over them all.

The opening ceremony of the Nile and Red Sea Railway was performed by Lord Cromer, and took place on January 27th, 1906, at Port Sûdân. After a speech by Sir Reginald Wingate, Sirdar and Governor of the Sûdân, Colonel Macauley, R.E., Director of Sûdân Railways, made a statement of facts connected with the new railway, and tendered his thanks for assistance to Lieut. W. B. Drury, R..N, Capt. W. E. Longfield, R.E., Capt. M. E. Sowerby, R.E., Lieut. S. F. Newcombe, R.E., Lieut. P. C.

MATERIAL TRAIN LEAVING SAWÂKIN.

[From a photograph by G. E. Mason, Esq.

Lord, R.E., Hon. A. Pelham, Mr. R. W. Windham, Capt. E..C. Midwinter, D.S.O., R.E., Mr. C. Hodgson, Mr. G. B. Macpherson Grant, Mr. H. V. Hawkins, Maḥmûd Bey Khêr Allah, and five other native officers and gentlemen. Lord Cromer then made a speech worthy alike of the great occasion and the speaker. He pointed out that the railway had been made in fourteen months, that the distance from Berber to the sea was henceforward shortened by nearly 900 miles, that the railway would be the main artery of communication which would open out the Sûdân

THE SIRDAR INSPECTING THE CONSTRUCTION OF THE NILE—RED SEA RAILWAY.

[From a photograph by Lieutenant P. Lord, R.E.

to the world, that it would create a trade which, but for it, could never come into existence, that it was the first step in the execution of a series of works of great public utility which would be carried out by the British in the Sûdân, and he indicated what these works would be, and he stated that Port Sûdân and the Red Sea Railway would be open on equal terms to the trade of all the world. There would be no differential rates or duties to favour the trade of any one nation. After this speech Sir Rudolf von Slatin explained in Arabic to all the notables and local merchants

LAYING THE ATBARA-RED SEA RAILWAY.

[From a photograph by Lieutenant P. Lord, R.E.

the effect which the railway would have on their trade, and then in the name of His Majesty King Edward VII. and H.H. the Khedive, Lord Cromer declared the railway open. H.E. Muḥammad Pâshâ Chawarby then addressed the assembly in Arabic, and described to his auditors the great improvement which had taken place in the finances and conditions of Egypt under the influence of the British.

The opening of the Red Sea Railway is the most important of all the great works which Lord Cromer has effected by the help of Lord Kitchener, Sir Reginald Wingate, and their band of hard-working assistants in the Sûdân. For years past he has determined to have this railway made, for he says that without it the

Sûdân could never develop, and the country would remain shut in from the world, as it has been from time immemorial. The Ḥalfa-Kharṭûm Railway could never have done what this railway will do, and by no other means could the Sûdân have been given a seaport. Hitherto the Sûdân has never had an outlet for the energies of its people and the produce of its land, and for thousands of years before the coming of the British its tribes, having realized the impossibility of developing a large and profitable trade, have devoted themselves to inter-tribal fighting and wars. No one need wonder that the slave-raider turned the Sûdân into a happy hunting-ground, and that the only function which it seemed to perform in the scheme of the world was the production of slaves. Some years ago Lord Cromer delivered the *fellaḥîn* of Egypt from the oppression of a corrupt rule and placed them in the position of free men, and he has now done the same thing for the "Blacks" of the "Black Country." He it is who has brought the key and unlocked the Sûdân for the first time. This fact is patent to all, but it is only future generations who will be able to appreciate at its proper value the "first and preliminary step in the gradual execution of a large "scheme for the construction of works of public utility," which was announced to the world in such modest language on January 27th, 1906, at Port Sûdân. The stations on the Nile-Red Sea Railway are as follows:—[1]

PORT SÛDÂN	84 kilometres from Sawâkin.
Asotriba	19 kilometres from Port Sûdân.
Sal-Lôm Junction	39 ,, ,, ,, ,,
SAWÂKIN.	
Handûb	21 kilometres from Sawâkin.
Sal-Lôm Junction	45 ,, ,, ,,
Obo	57 kilometres from Port Sûdân.
Kamobsana	75 ,, ,, ,, ,,
Erba	98 ,, ,, ,, ,,
Gebêt	115 ,, ,, ,, ,,
"Summit"	139 ,, ,, ,, ,,
Barameyu	158 ,, ,, ,, ,,

[1] I owe this list to Capt. E. C. Midwinter, R.E., D.S.O.

THE NILE—RED SEA RAILWAY.

[From a photograph by Lieutenant P. Lord, R.E.

Erhêb	179	kilometres	from	Port	Sûdân.
Thamiam	198	,,	,,	,,	,,
Einha	225	,,	,,	,,	,,
Shidieb	250	,,	,,	,,	,,
Talgwareb	266	,,	,,	,,	,,
Musmar	299	,,	,,	,,	,,
Rogel	324	,,	,,	,,	,,
Togni	340	,,	,,	,,	,,
Zehteb	372	,,	,,	,,	,,
Ogrên	386	,,	,,	,,	,,
Dogain	420	,,	,,	,,	,,
Hûdî	452	,,	,,	,,	,,
Zullot	468	,,	,,	,,	,,
ATBARA JUNCTION	486	,,	,,	,,	,,

The fare from Atbara to Sawâkin is 307 piastres, first class.

4. THE LINE FROM ABÛ ḤAMED TO KARÊMA. This line runs in the desert on the right bank of the Fourth Cararact, and only approaches the Nile once *en route*, viz., at Dakhfilî; it is 138 miles long. It was surveyed and made under the direction of Capt. E. C. Midwinter, R.E., D.S.O., assisted by Mr. C. G. Hodgson, Locomotive Superintendent, Mr. G. B. Macpherson Grant, and Mr. H. V. Hawkins. It was opened by Sir Reginald Wingate on March 8th, 1906. By the opening of this line the Dongola Province is brought into direct communication with Ḥalfa, Kharṭûm, and the Red Sea, and it may be confidently predicted that its trade will receive a great stimulus thereby. It may be mentioned in passing that it will also enable the traveller to visit the ruins of the temples and the pyramid-tombs of the Nubian kings at Gebel Barkal and Nûrî, and, as steamers ply at regular intervals between Merawi and Kerma, he can proceed without difficulty to Dongola, and the islands of Arḳô and Tombos, where there are interesting remains of the Middle and New Empires.

Other lines contemplated are:—1. A branch from the Nile-Red Sea Railway to Kasala. 2. A line up the left bank of the Blue Nile. 3. A line to Al-Obêḍ to bring the gum of Kordôfân to Kharṭûm. Since the closing of the Ḥalfa-Kerma line the profits on the railway system of the Sûdân have increased considerably;

in 1905 the receipts were £E171,000, the working expenses £E118,000, and the profits £E52,000. The receipts from the railways in 1899 were £E31,000. One of the most important results of the opening of the Nile-Red Sea Railway is that coal is now cheaper in Kharṭûm than wood.

Since 1896, the year of the advance to Dongola, the TELEGRAPH system has been developed in a remarkable manner. The good work begun by that able officer, Lieut. Manifold, R.E., has been continued, and at the present time Kharṭûm is in direct communication with all the great towns of the Sûdân. About 3,925 miles of telegraph lines are open, and there are thirty-five telegraph offices in the Sûdân.[1] The principal lines are:—1. From Kharṭûm to Ḥalfa, both across the Abû Ḥamed Desert and along the river, *viâ* Dongola, Kerma, Kôsha, &c. 2. From Kharṭûm to Fâshôda and Tawfiḳîya. 3. From Berber to Port Sûdân and Sawâkin, and to Kasala, Ḳaḍâref, Ḳallâbât, and Wad Madanî. 4. From Kharṭûm to Sennaar and Ruṣêreṣ. 5. From Sennaar to Ḳôz Abû Gûma. 6. From Mashra' ar-Reḳ to Wâw and Tong.[2] 7. From Kharṭûm to Al-Obêḍ. The extension of the line from Tong to Rumbek is now being carried out. The receipts from telegrams in 1905 were £E29,000 and the working expenses were about £E30,000; in 1889 the receipts were £E3,500. In 1905 about 164,000 private telegrams were sent over the wires, while in 1901 the number was only 57,700.

In connection with the railways and telegraphs mention must be made of the Sûdân POSTAL SERVICE. This Service was established at Ḥalfa in 1897, and for the next year or two its chief customers were the officers and men of the Anglo-Egyptian Army. The natives, however, soon perceived the importance and value of a speedy and safe letter-post, and merchants and others hastened to make use of it. In the winter of 1901-2 the head-quarters of the service were removed to Kharṭûm, and the postal and telegraph services were united and placed under the direction of Captain Liddell, R.E. The head of the Khartûm Office is Mr. Williams, to whose experience and labours the Postal Department

[1] See the list in Gleichen, *op. cit.*, i., p. 219.

[2] This line was laid by Major Dale and Corporal Stead, R.E.

THE NILE—RED SEA RAILWAY NEAR GEBET.

[From a photograph by Lieutenant P. Lord, R.E.

in the Sûdân owes so much. The authorities have spared no pains, and it may be added no expense, in introducing for the benefit and convenience of customers most of the facilities which the public enjoy in Europe. The Parcel Service is excellent, money orders can be bought and cashed at about thirty offices in the Sûdân, and also on the stations of the Ḥalfa-Kerma Railway, which are visited at regular intervals by an official appointed for this purpose. During 1905 the value of the money orders which passed through the Sûdân Post Office was £E808,000. The convenience of the money-order system is greatly appreciated by the natives, both civil and military, for by means of it they send money to their friends and relatives in Egypt.

One of the most important works which have been carried out in connection with the means of communication in the Sûdân is the freeing of the Nile from the "Sadd," or "Sudd,"[1] with which in 1898 the river was blocked between the Sobat River and Shâmbî. In June, 1899, Sir William Garstin reported[2] that the Sudd was generally present in the Baḥr al-Gebel, the Baḥr az-Zarâfa, and the Baḥr al-Ghazâl, and their affluents, and that it even appeared at times on the White Nile between the Sobat River and Lake Nô. It has already been said that the Sudd is really the masses of *floating* vegetation, formed chiefly of papyrus, and the plant called *umm ṣûf* (i.e., "mother of wool"), that are driven by the winds into the channels of the rivers, which they block in a most effectual manner. There are three kinds of Sudd. The first contains plants the roots of which go down to the river bed, e.g., the papyrus, the common reed, and the feathery-headed grass. The second contains plants the roots of which are in the water and do not touch ground, e.g., the ambatch, the *umm ṣûf*, the wild bean, and a creeper with a purple flower. The third contains swimming plants only, e.g., the Pistia, Azolla, Utricularia, Aldrovandia, Ceratophyllum, Otellia, or "Ḳâḍi's Pudding," and the creeper Commellaria. Before Sir W. Garstin visited the Sudd region, and investigated the matter, it was thought that the Sudd seriously affected the

[1] See Lyons, *Physiography of the River Nile and its Basin*, Cairo, 1906, p. 132 ff.

[2] *Egypt*, No. 5 (1899), p. 15.

supply of water from the Nile in Egypt, but he has proved that it influences it to a very small degree. This is not to be wondered at seeing that it is the Sobat, the Blue Nile, and the Atbara which are the ruling factors in the production of the annual Nile flood. On the other hand, the Sudd when it blocked the Baḥr al-Gebel, or Upper Nile, seriously interfered with the navigation on the river, and it practically cut off all communication with the country south of Lake Nô. In some years the main channel of the White Nile was blocked by Sudd for a distance of 250 miles. Thus in 1863, 1864, and 1868 it was blocked; in 1870 Sir Samuel Baker found it blocked so far as Lake Nô. In 1872 both the Baḥr al-Gebel and the Baḥr az-Zarâfa were blocked. In 1874 Ayûb Pâshâ cleared the former river, but the channel was blocked again in 1878, and Emin Pâshâ could not ascend it. In 1879 and 1880 Marno cleared the river once more of Sudd. In 1880 Gessi Pâshâ was completely hemmed in by Sudd in the Baḥr al-Ghazâl, and he lost more than half his force by famine and fever. In 1881, 1884, 1895, and 1899 the Upper Nile was completely blocked by Sudd.

In 1899 the Egyptian Government determined to clear the river, and the work of carrying out their decision was entrusted to Colonel Peake, R.A. He left Omdurmân on December 16th, and by March 27th, 1900, his party had removed 14 blocks of Sudd in a length of about 83 miles of river. The total length of these blocks was about 8,666 yards, and the thickness of the Sudd varied from 5 ft. 6 in. to 20 ft. Colonel Peake worked with 5 gun-boats and 800 Dervish prisoners, guarded by 100 black soldiers, 5 English and several Egyptian officers, and some English non-commissioned officers. The method he employed was to cut the Sudd into rectangular blocks, which he hauled out of their places by steamers, and then allowed to float down the stream.[1] When Colonel Peake stopped work on March 27th only two more blocks remained to be removed, viz., No. 15 and No. 16. No. 15 was a reach of the river, about 23 miles long, blocked by Sudd the whole way. No. 16 was about 8 miles long, and really contained four blocks; it was removed in January, 1901, by Lieutenant Drury, R.N., assisted by one English sergeant of Marines. "Major Peake and all who "served with him may well be proud of the results of the season's

[1] Sir William Garstin, *Egypt*, No. 2 (1901), p. 39.

"work. He rendered a great service, both to Egypt and to the "Sûdân, by opening up this important river. The work was well "and thoroughly done."[1] "It is difficult to speak too highly of "the work done by Major Peake and his staff in 1900. Lieut. "Drury also deserves a word of special mention. The work was "very heavy. . . . The result has been an immense improvement "in the navigation of the river."[2]

In 1901 and 1902 Major Matthews cleared away about one half of block No. 15, but the rains stopped his work before it was finished. In January, 1904, Lieut. Drury, R.N., and Mr. Poole attacked the remaining portion of the block, but the former became so dangerously ill of malarial fever that he had to be taken back to Kharṭûm, just when success was in sight. Therefore steamers passing north and south had, in 1904, to follow the false channel through the shallow lakes. This, however, mattered little, for steamers plied at regular intervals between Kharṭûm and Gondokoro, the most northerly station of Uganda, and communication between these places was maintained throughout the year. Lieut. Drury's work was taken up by Engineer-Commander Bond, R.N., and Engineer-Lieutenant Scott-Hill, R.N. Between 1900 and 1904 a channel was cut through the Sudd on the Gûr River by Lieutenant Fell, R.N., the late Captain Saunders, and Colour-Sergeants Boardman and Sears.

Turning now to AGRICULTURE, we find that each year more and more land is being brought under cultivation, and that the natives are beginning to realize the blessing of peace in the country. In 1904 the area cultivated was equal to 529,239 acres, and in 1905 it had increased to 704,872 acres, i.e., a total increase of 175,633 acres. The principal crops raised were barley, cotton, dhurra, millet, maize, onions, lubia, beans, wheat, and simsim. There were 23,898 acres of cotton, and 22,000 of wheat. The planting of date trees is going on steadily, especially in the Dongola Province. The number of fruit-bearing trees there in 1885 was about 600,000, but in 1897 the returns furnished to Mr. Dawkins by the Maʻamûrs gave the numbers as 376,512. This decrease was due partly to the cutting down of the date trees by the Dervishes in the Ḥalfa District, and partly to the break-up of the date

[1] *Egypt*, No. 2 (1904), p. 120. [2] *Ibid.* (1901), No. 2, p. 39.

trade between Dongola and Ḥalfa caused by the Dervish revolt. Colonel Jackson, Mudîr of Dongola, reported in 1905 that the number of date trees in the province in that year was only 366,000, but that thousands more were being planted.

Intimately connected with the development of agriculture in the Sûdân are the great schemes for the IRRIGATION of the country which have been thought out by Sir William Garstin, who has examined the whole course of the Nile with the special purpose of finding out what can be done to regulate and improve the water supply of Egypt, and to extend irrigation both in that country and in the Sûdân. The result of his labours is to show that the destiny of Egypt is bound up with that of the Sûdân, and that the power which holds Egypt must also hold the Sûdân, for the simple reason that the very existence of Egypt is in the hands of those who have control over the waters of the Upper Niles and their great tributaries. Stated generally, the twofold problem which Sir William Garstin has to solve is how to obtain four thousand millions of cubic metres of water to enable the whole of the two millions of acres of cultivable land in Egypt, which are at present uncultivated, to be irrigated and made to produce crops. Next, what steps are to be, or can be, taken, whereby all the summer water in the Blue Nile will be used for the benefit of the Sûdân. It is understood that the waters of the White Nile must be reserved for Egypt and the river valley between Kharṭûm and Aswân. The only possible solution of the first part of the problem is to find some way of saving the waters of the Baḥr al-Gebel or Upper Nile, which are now wasted. This waste takes place as the river flows through the "Sudd" region, and is chiefly due to the evaporation which goes on over an expanse of marshes covering an area of about 35,000 square miles, and to the absorption of the water-plants which fill it.

The waste is so serious that at the point at which the river leaves the "Sudd" region it is from 50 to 80 per cent. less than when it entered it. No matter how high may be the water-level of Lake Albert, or how large the added volume brought in by the tributary streams which enter the river, the discharge of the Nile at the point where it issues from the "Sudd" area is practically constant at all seasons and under all conditions. Any works connected with the increasing of the present water supply, i.e., which shall enable the greater portion of the water entering the Baḥr al-Gebel from Lake Albert to reach the head of the White Nile near the junction of the Sobat, must be carried out between Bôr, about 100 miles from Gondokoro, and the junction of the Sobat, about 444 miles north of Bôr. To improve the channel of the Baḥr al-Gebel sufficiently to enable it to carry all the water required in the future is impossible, and the same may be said of the Baḥr az-Zarâfa, which is a much smaller river. Sir William Garstin therefore proposes to cut a channel between Bôr and the Sobat junction sufficiently large to take the entire future summer discharge of the Baḥr al-Gebel, or Upper Nile. This channel would practically be a huge canal, about 210 miles long, which would be provided with

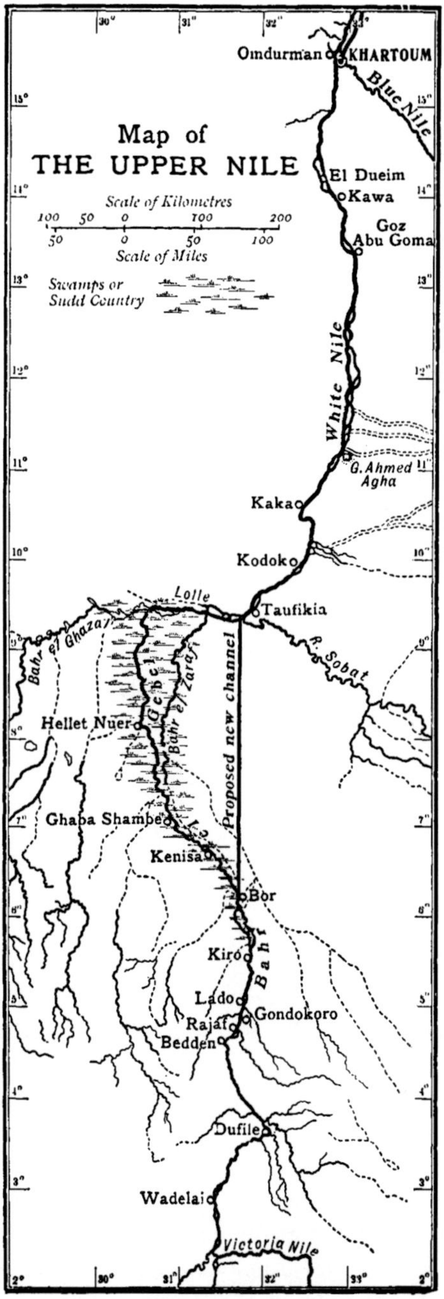

MAP SHOWING ROUTE OF SIR WILLIAM GARSTIN'S PROPOSED CANAL IN THE SÛDÂN.

[From Sir W. Garstin's *Report*, by permission of the Comptroller of H.M. Stationery Office.

a masonry regulator at each end. In the winter no water would be allowed to pass into the marshes, but in flood time the reverse would be the case, and only water sufficient for purposes of navigation would be allowed to enter the canal. The present long winding channel through the marshes would be replaced by a straight canal, very much shorter than the existing line. In this way a perfect control over the Upper Nile could at all seasons be obtained.

As regards the Blue Nile, Sir William Garstin proposes to construct one or more barrages or weirs on this river somewhere between the point where it issues from the hills and Kharṭûm. These works, which will raise the water-levels of the river, must be accompanied by large distributary canals on either bank. Other irrigation works contemplated in the Sûdân are in connection with the Ḳâsh, the Rahad, the Dinder, and the Atbara. The estimates of cost are:—

	£E.
Works on the Baḥr al-Gebel . .	5,500,000
Reservoir on Blue Nile . . .	2,000,000
Barrage on Blue Nile	1,000,000
Gazîra canal-system	2,000,000
Works on Ḳâsh River	500,000
Regulation of Lakes	2,000,000
	13,000,000

It is believed that when the whole of Sir William Garstin's scheme is completed, about 1,000,000 acres in the Sûdân will be brought under cultivation, and that the direct return, in the shape of land tax, at 50 piastres tariff per acre, will be £E500,000 a year. And Egypt will benefit by the extension of perennial irrigation from Aswân to the sea. In this way the Sûdân will prove to be, as Lord Cromer says, "a priceless possession to Egypt," and the life-giving waters, which are now wasted in the swamps of the "Sudd" area, will be brought to Egypt and will fill the heart of the farmer with joy, and put money in his pocket.

When the Anglo-Egyptian Army captured Omdurmân TRADE IN THE SÛDÂN was practically non-existent. The most important products of the country under Turkish and Egyptian rule were slaves and ivory; the market value of the former cannot be stated, but the export of the latter brought in from £E40,000 to £E60,000. As soon as possible after the Khalîfa's overthrow, Sir William Garstin visited the Sûdân and travelled through it, and in his opinion gum, ivory, and senna were the three articles most likely to be exported for some years to come. There was a demand for clothes, sugar, cheap hardware, and especially iron nails, tobacco, cheap cottons, and tea. He further reported that progress must be very slow, that the poverty and depopulation of the country were very great, that the people were an indolent race, the Arab scorning manual labour, and the Negro doing no work except under compulsion or under the goad of his personal necessities. South of Kharṭûm the natives needed to do very little work for a living, north of that place they had to work harder, for nature was less bountiful in her gifts. In spite of these facts, however, the authorities seized every opportunity of developing trade, and in 1904 the imports into the Sûdân, *viâ* Wâdî Ḥalfa, were valued at £E935,800, and the exports from the same place at £E303,502. The imports were: candles, cement, coffee, cotton stuffs, dates, drugs, flour, grain, iron and machinery, oil, petroleum, perfumery, provisions, rice, salt, soap, spirits, sugar, tallow, tea (100 tons!) timber, tobacco (158 tons), &c. The exports were: barley, butter, cotton, dates, *dhurra*, gum, ivory, ostrich feathers, palm trees, sinnamecca, sesame seed, skins, timber, lupines, wheat, &c. The imports, *viâ* Sawâkin, Sennaar, Kasala, Italian territory, and Lâdô, were valued at £E136,000, £E4,448, £E15,644, £E6,858, and £E2,000 respectively; and the exports at £E67,000, £E11,345, £E2,764 and £E4,753 (nothing from Lâdô) respectively. Thus the total imports were £1,100,750 in value, and the total exports £E389,364. The imports *viâ* Wâdî Ḥalfa in 1905 were valued at £E1,092,000, and the exports only £E251,000; for Sawâkin the figures are £E171,000 and £E58,000.

The above facts give abundant proof of the extraordinary success which has attended the efforts of the "small but very capable band of officials, ably directed by Sir Reginald Wingate," in the Sûdân. In connection with the trade of the country, attention must be called to the praiseworthy determination of the authorities to control the LIQUOR TRADE in the Sûdân. By an Ordinance promulgated in May, 1899, it was decreed that no one should trade in wine, spirits, &c., except under a licence, which costs £E50 a year. Every application for a drink licence is considered on its own merits, and with due regard to the size of the town, number of people in it, &c.

We may now briefly summarize what has been done for the people of the Sûdân themselves. One of the first things decided upon by Lord Cromer was the abolition of SLAVERY, but this was a matter of very great difficulty,[1] for slavery in all its forms has always been a fundamental institution among African peoples. In 1899 a Slavery Department was formed under the direction of Captain McMurdo, and in the same year Colonel (now Sir John) Maxwell, Governor of Omdurmân, reported that forty-seven persons had been condemned to various terms of penal servitude or imprisonment for dealing in or kidnapping slaves. In 1902 strenuous efforts were made to check slave-raiding on the Eastern Frontier, and the Sûdân Government began to deal with domestic slavery in a successful manner. In 1903 Sa'îd Ibrahîm, a powerful shêkh, was tried at Al-Obêḍ for slave-trading, and, in spite of his influence and popularity, was sentenced to five years' imprisonment. This action had a very decided effect upon the people, who clearly saw that the Government were in earnest in their efforts to put down the trade. Captain McMurdo, Mr. Gorringe, and Mr. Shakerley, all of the Slavery Department, worked with great success in the Abyssinian Frontier and in Kordôfân, and they entirely prevented large gangs of slaves from being smuggled down to the coast. In the same year great strides towards the abolition of domestic slavery were made in Egypt; according to Lord Cromer this was due to the fact that the Egyptians began to think that slave labour was more troublesome and more costly than free labour! This state of things had, of course, its reflex effect in the Sûdân.

In 1904 Colonel Gorringe succeeded in capturing the notorious slave-raider Ibrahîm wâd Maḥmûd, the terror of the Eastern Sûdân; the ruffian was hanged, his followers slain, and their

[1] See Lord Cromer's opinions in *Egypt*, No. 3 (1899), p. 31.

stronghold destroyed. The scene of Ibrahîm's operations was the country of the Burûn Negroes, and when Mr. Gorringe went through it after his namesake had captured the raider, he found that there were no children there, that the proportion of adults was seven men to one woman, and that there were no sheep, goats, poultry, or cattle in the villages. In this year the slave-trade received a very great check in the Sûdân, and sixteen persons suffered imprisonment for being concerned in it, with the result that people were beginning to dread the slavery laws.

In 1905 Colonel McMurdo found that the steady advance of civilization, improved means of communication, and the general opening up of the Sûdân were all tending to destroy the slave-trade. The British Inspectors were ever on the watch, and ever devising means which more and more convinced the raider that it was becoming too difficult and dangerous an undertaking to deal in, in fact that slave-raiding did not pay. Moreover, the natives themselves are beginning to realize that slavery is illegal and is punishable by law. Between January and September 1st, about sixty-seven slave-dealers were captured, tried, and convicted, and sixty-one of them received sentences of imprisonment varying from seven years to one. It must, of course, be some time yet before slave-raiding and domestic slavery can disappear from the Sûdân, but they will certainly come to an end when the country is opened up, and its wild parts are under effective control, and the people have work to do, and legitimate trading makes the slave-trade unprofitable. Meanwhile the British officials are doing a great and good work in a quiet and unostentatious manner, and their tactful and humane treatment of the natives will do more to bring about the result which we all desire than all the heroic measures and treaties which have ever been formulated. Isma'îl Pâshâ's decree, which ordered that slavery should cease in 1889, was not worth the paper it was written on, and in turn amused and irritated those who understood the question. General Gordon, the best of all judges, knew this quite well, and Colonel Stewart took the same view.[1]

As regards EDUCATION in the Sûdân, Lord Cromer states that in 1899 the only education obtainable was in the village schools,

[1] See *Egypt*, No. 11 (1883), p. 24.

with the exception of two Government schools, one at Ḥalfa and the other at Sawâkin. He decided to start two Government schools in each of the large towns, and to open a primary school at Omdurmân. The teaching was to be in the Arabic language, and to consist chiefly of reading, writing, arithmetic and Arabic. English was to be taught in the higher classes. In 1900 Mr. Bonham-Carter started an educational system which produced extremely good results, and reflected great credit on his foresight and energy;[1] in November of that year Mr. James Currie became Director of Education in the Sûdân, and Principal of the Gordon College. During that year it was decided to establish a certain number of *kuttabs*, or village schools, taught by trained Egyptian teachers, and a start was made at Kharṭûm, Omdurmân, Berber, Dongola, Wad Madanî, Ḥalfa, and Sawâkin.

Meanwhile the Gordon College was approaching completion, and when it was habitable Mr. Currie determined to place there: 1. A Sûdân Reference Library. 2. An Economic Museum. 3. A Meteorological Station and a small Observatory. 4. A small Analytical Laboratory. Without the College these schemes would have been impossible. In 1901 an efficient primary school was opened at Omdurmân; it was attended by 170 pupils, of whom 103 paid fees. A similar school was opened at Kharṭûm on October 1st, 1901; it was attended by 72 pupils, of whom 60 paid fees. In these and the village schools Mr. Currie decided to have the teaching done in the Arabic language, and both he and Lord Cromer were wholly opposed to the establishing of schools for the teaching of English, "for the sake of the supposed political "advantage which such teaching indirectly confers upon the "governing class." Only boys who are subsequently going into the Government service, or who are to follow commercial pursuits in which such a knowledge is necessary, should learn English, and the schools wherein it is taught should be good, and "it is nearly as important that at the present they should be few." They should also be fee-paying, though there might be a certain number of free scholars. The great need of the country was, and still is, a class of young men whose knowledge of reading, writing, and

[1] See *Egypt*, No. 1 (1901), p. 75.

arithmetic will enable them to occupy with advantage the subordinate places in the administration of the country. The lack of such retards the development of the country, and the "prevalent illiteracy" enables the petition-writer, the money-lender, and others, to victimize the people to a terrible degree.

In 1902 there were 215 pupils in the Omdurmân School, of whom 181 paid fees, and in the Kharṭûm School there were 115 pupils. In 1903 the number of pupils in the five educational establishments[1] in the Sûdân was about 600; they were of all nationalities, Blacks, Arabs, Egyptian Moslems, Copts, Greeks, &c. In 1904 Lord Cromer reported that "a very fair amount of progress" had been made by Mr. Currie in carrying out his plan formulated in November, 1901, viz.:—1. Creating a small artisan class. 2. Diffusing elementary education among the people. 3. Creating a native administrative class. At the same time, however, it was felt in that year that the time had come when the introduction of a new educational programme was inevitable, and Mr. Currie proposed to establish a good secondary school, and two higher primary schools, and "to provide increased accommodation at the Gordon College, so as to make that institution, even more than at present, the centre of the higher education of the country." To carry out this idea Lord Cromer provided £E15,000. At that time the three chief educational agencies at work at the Gordon College were: 1. A Training College for Schoolmasters and Judges in the Muḥammadan Courts, with 85 pupils. 2. A Primary School, attended by 150 boys. 3. Industrial Workshops, attended by about 70 boys. At the close of 1905 there were 1,533 boys under instruction at the various Government schools in the Sûdân. Of these, 392 were at the Gordon College, 229 at the higher elementary schools, 29 at the training colleges at Omdurmân and Sawâkin, and 723 at the elementary vernacular schools, which have now been established at 13 different centres.[2] The principle of levying an education rate was also sanctioned in that year, and it was decided to make a beginning in the Blue Nile Province and in Sennaar.

The educational system of the Sûdân now centres in the Gordon College at Kharṭûm, an institution which owes its existence to

[1] *Egypt*, No. 1 (1904), p. 94. [2] *Ibid.*, No. 1 (1906), p. 145.

the response of the British public to the appeal made to them at the end of 1898 by Lord Kitchener. The appeal brought in a sum of money sufficiently large to pay for the erection of the handsome building which now stands on the west bank of the Blue Nile, a little above Kharṭûm, and to provide an endowment fund of £100,000. Lord Kitchener's general idea was, "to give "the most practical, useful education possible to the boys for their "future in the Sûdân," and he intended Arabic to be the basis of education. These were his objects in appealing for means to establish the Gordon College, and when we come to consider the work which is now being done in the College itself, and in connection with it, it will be clear that its sphere of usefulness is far wider than that which was originally contemplated by Lord Kitchener. It is possible that during the first years of its existence the "Gordon School" would have been a better name for it than the "Gordon College," for it was originally intended to be a sort of "Higher Primary School," where education was to be given on the lines of the Aswân and Wâdî Ḥalfa Schools. The rapid development of the Sûdân, however, and the course of events in general throughout the country, especially during the last three or four years, have shown that, on the whole, the title of "Gordon College" is the best that can be given to the institution at the present time.

The handsome building is a very prominent object at Kharṭûm, especially when seen from Ḥalfâya, and reflects the greatest credit on the original designer, Fabricius Pâshâ, and on Colonel Friend, R.E., Director of Works, and others who carried out the work of construction. The opening ceremony was performed by Lord Kitchener on November 8th, 1902, in the presence of Sir Reginald Wingate, and a very large number of the military and civil officers of the Sûdân. During the ceremony, Mr. Currie, the Principal of the College, read a letter to Lord Cromer from Sir William Mather announcing his splendid gift of "the equipment "for a Department of Manual Training and Technical Instruction, "together with a Complete Apparatus for the establishment of "practical Workshops in the College." This equipment consisted of a steam boiler, steam engines, electric dynamos and motors, pumps and accessories for raising water from the Nile for the use of the College, machines and hand tools for wood and metal work, and sundry appliances for experimental illustration. Before the Gordon College was finished and opened, Mr. H. S. Wellcome, of the firm of Messrs. Burroughs and Wellcome, generously presented to the Institution an efficient analytical and bacteriological laboratory, equipped with all the necessary apparatus. An Economic Museum was also established there under the direction of Mr. Butler, of the Animals Preservation Department.

We may now refer to the work which has been done in the Gordon College in recent years, the facts here given being taken from Mr. Currie's *Report* recently issued. The Patron of the College is His Majesty King Edward VII.; the President, Lord Kitchener; the Hon. Treasurer, the Right Hon. Lord Hillingdon; and the Hon. Sec., Baldwin S. Harvey, Esq. The following are the Committee and Trustees: Lord Kitchener, Sir Reginald Wingate (*ex officio*), A. Falconer Wallace, Esq. (*ex officio*), Lord Cromer, Lord Rothschild, Lord Hillingdon, Lord Revelstoke, Sir Ernest Cassel, H. Colin Smith, Esq., Sir Henry Craik, Henry S. Wellcome, Esq., and Sir William Mather. The College now consists of three sections: a Primary School, a Training School for schoolmasters and judges in the Muḥammadan Courts, and the instructional Workshops. The Primary School is attended by 180 boys. The curriculum extends over four years, and is intended to fit a boy for some minor Government post. The Boarding House was in 1904 full, the number of boys being 25; it has been enlarged and now holds 50 boys. The boarding fee is £9 per annum. The Military School and the Training College are flourishing. The Workshops provide practical instruction in Carpentry, Fitting, Smiths' work, Moulders' work, Cotton-ginning, and a preliminary stage of mechanical Engineering, which includes the management and repair of Oil and Steam Engines, Pumping Machinery, and Turning.

It has been decided to devote a sum of £5,000 from Mr. Beauchamp's bequest to a considerable extension of the Workshops. Also the staff of the Higher School will contain a very efficient English element, and Mr. Drummond, of the School of Agriculture in Egypt, and Mr. Simpson, an Orientalist from Edinburgh, have already been appointed. The Workshops are under Mr. S. C.

Rhodes, and have produced already excellent results, and the Head Master of the Primary School and Training College is Aḥmad Effendî Hadayat. The Director of the Wellcome Laboratory is Dr. Andrew Balfour, who has published two most valuable Reports on his investigations into the Sûdân bacteriology. One important result of his labours is that Kharṭûm is now practically free from mosquitoes, and his discovery of the causes of certain diseases in Sûdân cattle must, in a very short time, greatly benefit the community. In this work the Government have been helped by Dr. Sheffield Neave, the Travelling Pathologist, whose appointment was made possible by Mr. Wellcome's generosity. Dr. Beam, the Chemist to the Laboratory, has carried out a series of analyses of the waters of Sûdân rivers, and has obtained important results.

Through the courtesy of Mr. James Currie I was enabled to go through a large portion of the Gordon College in February, 1905, and to see the arrangements which have been made by him and his staff for carrying out work there. I visited the Economic Museum and found the exhibits well displayed, and labelled in a clear and instructive manner. The collection is one of very considerable interest, and it is so arranged that a great deal of information may be gained about the products of the Sûdân in a comparatively short time. The Committee of the Museum have for their Secretary Mrs. Broun, an expert botanist and entomologist, possessing a special knowledge of Sûdân and Indian plants. In and about the Museum are many objects of interest, and among them visitors will note with interest the printing press and the lithographic stones from which General Gordon's proclamations were printed. Dr. Andrew Balfour explained to me the arrangement of the Laboratory, and also some of the experiments and processes wherefrom he was collecting important results. He proudly pointed out a number of bottled "specimens" connected with his researches into the effect of *marissa* (beer) drinking on the human stomach, and with "pigmentation" in the human skin. One remarkable specimen was a child in an embryonic state, the offspring of black parents, whose skin was quite white.

The arrangements seemed to be perfect, and that the utmost use was made of the appliances which Mr. Wellcome had given to the College was evident. When one looked round on the orderly rooms and the apparatus, it was almost impossible to realize that less than seven years ago the Dervishes were in possession of Kharṭûm, and that the town was a heap of ruins. Mr. J. W. Crowfoot, Inspector of Education, then showed me some of the class-rooms and their equipment, and the arrangements made for the well-being of the pupils, and all were excellent. No time has been lost in getting the educational machinery of the College into working order, but, on the other hand, there has been no undue haste. Mr. Currie has made good every step he has taken, and the goal which he has ever kept before him has been the education of the boys of the Sûdân on useful and practical lines. Some critics have complained that his system is too practical, but this is impossible. It would be a terrible thing for the country if the higher education of the people were to consist of "grammatical conundrums, and arid theological and metaphysical disputation," and it is quite certain that the course which he is following is in accordance with the wishes of Lord Kitchener, Lord Cromer, and Sir Reginald Wingate, who best know what are the true needs of the youth of the Sûdân.

The Gordon College is playing a most important part in the development of the country, and events have already justified Lord Kitchener's foresight in founding it. England unwittingly allowed Muḥammad 'Alî and his descendants to depopulate and ruin the Sûdân, and it has fallen to England's lot to repair the injury to it which they committed. Her soldiers, co-operating with the Egyptians, have crushed the Khalîfa and restored the country to the dominions of the Khedive, and some of the ablest of her sons are now shaping the future of the Black Country in the interests of peace and civilization, instead of those of the slave-raider. Philanthropists never gave money with a better object than the founding of the Gordon College, and it should afford great satisfaction both to them and to the originator of the scheme to note how wisely and judiciously, and with what regard to the true interests of the country their money is being spent.[1]

[1] For detailed information concerning the curriculum of the Gordon College, see the *Annual Report* (1904) *of the Education Department*, which may be obtained at As-Sûdân Printing Press, Kharṭûm.

The list of schools controlled or inspected by the Education Department, Kharṭûm, with the number and nationality of their pupils in 1905 and 1906, printed on the opposite page will interest all friends of Education in the Sûdân. I owe this list to the kindness of Mr. Currie, and much regret that want of space prevents the printing of all the information on the subject with which he has so generously provided me.

The establishment of a simple and humane system of criminal and civil JUSTICE, adapted to the requirements of the country, is due to the labours of Mr. Bonham-Carter, the Judicial Adviser to the Government of the Sûdân. The Sûdân Penal Code and the Sûdân Code of Criminal Procedure were enacted and applied for the first time in 1899, and both were drafted by Mr. W. E. Brunyate, of the Contentieux de l'État. The Sûdân Penal Code is an adaptation of the Indian Penal Code, and the Sûdân Code of Criminal Procedure of the Indian Code of Criminal Procedure. "All offences are ordinarily tried in the province in which they "have been committed, the smaller offences before a single "Magistrate, the graver crimes, after a preliminary inquiry by a "single Magistrate, before a Court of three Magistrates, called a "Mudir's Court, or Minor District Court, presided over by the "Mudir, or other high official. Except in unimportant cases, "there is a right of appeal from the judgment of a single "Magistrate to the Mudir. Judgments of Minor District Courts "and of Mudirs' Courts require confirmation, the former by the "Mudir, and the latter by the Governor-General. The Governor-"General possesses a general power of revision."[1]

In 1900 Mr. Bonham-Carter found that the "administration of justice reached a high level of excellence." Accused persons were tried with little delay, and criminal trials were characterized by fairness and patience, punishments being generally lenient. A good beginning was made in the administration of civil justice, and Courts for the administration of the Muḥammadan law were established in the principal towns of the Sûdân. Mr. Wasey Sterry was appointed to be Civil Judge at Kharṭûm. In 1900 all the Ḳâḍîs, or native administrators of Muhammadan law, were in receipt of a moderate monthly salary. A scale of fees was fixed,

[1] Mr. Bonham-Carter, in *Egypt*, No. 1 (1900), p. 53.

LIST OF SCHOOLS CONTROLLED OR INSPECTED BY THE EDUCATION DEPARTMENT, WITH NUMBER, NATIONALITY AND RELIGION OF THEIR PUPILS IN 1905-1906.

School	Province	Number of Pupils	Nationality			Religion			Nationalities of Natives			
			Natives	Egyptians	Miscellaneous	Moslems	Christians	Miscellaneous	Arabs	Blacks	Berberines	Mixed
Gordon College	Khartoum	103	103	—	—	103	—	—	97	—	1	5
" "	"	15	8	7	—	10	4	1	—	—	—	8
" "	"	182	116	65	1	159	20	3	27	41	5	43
" "	"	92	78	12	2	91	1	—	15	19	8	36
Khartoum	"	93	78	15	—	93	—	—	15	29	—	34
Omdurman	"	27	27	—	—	27	—	—	24	1	—	2
"	"	166	148	13	5	138	27	1	46	11	6	85
"	"	130	121	6	3	103	26	1	27	14	18	62
Halfa	Halfa	63	34	29	—	57	6	—	6	2	22	4
Suakin	Suakin	2	2	—	—	2	—	—	2	—	—	—
"	"	100	27	25	48	90	9	1	13	8	—	6
"	"	49	13	11	25	46	3	—	9	4	—	—
Berber	Berber	84	75	8	1	82	2	—	40	—	—	35
El Damir	"	34	32	2	—	34	—	—	16	—	—	16
Shendi	"	26	14	12	—	26	—	—	14	—	—	—
Metemma	"	21	21	—	—	21	—	—	21	—	—	—
Rufaa	Blue Nile	109	107	1	1	107	2	—	107	—	—	—
Wad Medani	" "	62	58	4	—	62	—	—	58	—	—	—
Kassala	Kassala	40	39	1	—	40	—	—	7	5	17	10
Gedarif	"	70	70	—	—	63	7	—	70	—	—	—
Dongola	Dongola	35	31	4	—	35	—	—	—	—	31	—
Geteina	White Nile	30	25	5	—	30	—	—	—	—	25	—
		1533	1227	220	86	1419	107	7	614	134	133	346

and these were handed over to the Government. These arrangements have had a very far-reaching effect in the country. In 1902 some 624 convictions for crime took place, and Mr. Bonham-Carter was satisfied that the system of criminal justice which had been introduced was suited to the requirements of the people. On the other hand, native ideas were found to be sometimes out of harmony with the law, especially in such matters as Slavery and the Game Laws. In the matter of the administration of Muḥammadan law, Mr. Bonham-Carter's efforts were ably seconded by the Grand Ḳâḍî, Muhammad Effendî Shakîr, and by Shêkh Muḥammad Hârûn, the Inspector of Muhammadan Law Courts. In 1904 the British civilian legal staff of the Sûdân consisted of a Legal Secretary to the Government (Mr. Bonham-Carter), a Chief Judge, three Judges, and an Advocate-General.

The systems of legal procedure both Criminal and Civil, and the manner in which they are administered by military and civil officials, have been fully discussed by Lord Cromer in his Reports,[1] and to these the reader is referred for information on the subject. Neither the systems nor the men who apply them may be perfect, but the practical result of their application by the said officials is that the natives are generally satisfied with the decisions of the Courts, and admit that they are just. Moreover, they obey them, and they know that the judgments of the Mudîrs and Magistrates, even when against them, are the result of honest investigation of their cases, and that bribery has played no part in forming them. In a country like the Sûdân, where there are so many groups of tribes, each with its own unwritten code of laws, and where large numbers of men prefer Muḥammadan to European Law, it must be many years before exact justice will be done in every case which is brought before the Courts, and before the last dissatisfied litigant will cease to exist. It may, however, be claimed, as the result of Mr. Bonham-Carter's efforts, that there was never a time in the history of the Sûdân when so little bribery in the Courts existed, and when the native was treated with such fairness, consideration, patience, and humanity as now. In many places the minds of the people are in such a backward state that "the principles underlying European systems of

[1] *Egypt*, No. 1 (1904), p. 88, and No. 1 (1905), p. 127 ff.

criminal jurisprudence lose their significance when applied to them." In support of this statement Mr. Bonham-Carter quotes the following cases:—

1. A native of southern Sennaar was tried for murder. He pleaded guilty, and said that he had killed his victim because he had cast the evil eye on his brother, thereby causing his death. The guilty man thought it was his duty to avenge his brother's death.

2. Taha Alî and Aḥmad Ḥamad were partners in a butcher's business. Taha Alî told his partner that ten and a half dollars belonging to the business had been stolen, but Ḥamad did not believe him, and accused him of theft. They agreed to go to a holy man (faḳîr) and try the matter. When the partners had stated their case, the faḳîr wrote certain formulae on a board, and then washed off the writing with water which he poured into a bowl. He then dipped a piece of bread into the water, and divided it between the two partners, who ate it. Soon afterwards Taha Alî was taken ill, and, returning to the faḳîr, told him that he had stolen the money; after this he became worse, and died a few hours later. The medical examination revealed no sign of poisoning.[1]

3. A Shilluk called Kwat wâd Awaibung was tried for murder. He pleaded guilty, and said: "Ajak wâd Deng, whom I murdered, owed me a sheep, but would not pay me. He said he would show me his work, and next day my son was eaten by a crocodile, which was, of course, the work of Ajak wâd Deng, and for that reason I killed him. We had had a feud for years, as I was a more successful hippopotamus-hunter than he was, and for that reason he was practising witchery over me and my family."[2] The majesty of the law was vindicated by a sentence of death passed on the prisoner, but it is good to know that on the Governor's recommendation it was reduced to a term of imprisonment and a fine.

In every department of the Government the officials are doing their utmost to promote the well-being of the people, and to protect the natural resources of the country. The Medical and Sanitary Department has, with very limited means, already worked wonders in freeing certain districts from the curse of the

[1] *Egypt*, No. 1 (1903), p. 77.

[2] *Ibid.*, No. 1 (1904) p. 89.

mosquito, and under the direction of Colonel Penton many districts have been rendered comparatively healthy. In the GOVERNMENT HOSPITALS 40,862 out-patients and 3,357 in-patients were treated in 1903, and since that year the numbers have increased; many natives willingly pay for treatment. The PRISONS Department, started by Captain Borton and now directed by Major Coutts, has worked with excellent results, and order is kept among the people by the Sûdân Police Force, which now numbers 1,820 men. The game and forests of the Sûdân are also objects of care. For the former a large tract of land has been set apart as a sanctuary, and wise Ordinances for regulating the shooting of rare animals and birds have been promulgated. Mr. Butler has established Zoological Gardens at Kharṭûm, but he is hampered by want of funds. Mr. Broun[1] has taken charge of the Woods and Forests, and the reckless cutting of trees which went on during the first few years after the restoration of the Sûdân will, it is hoped, be stopped. It would be a terrible thing if the Nile were to become like the Tigris between Baghdâd and Baṣra, where, away from the towns and villages, for hundreds of miles there is scarcely a tree to be seen. Before the advance of man both the forests and the wild animals must eventually disappear from certain portions of the country, but we may safely assume that their destruction will not now be reckless and wasteful.

Every attempt possible is being made to develop and utilize the natural resources of the country, and this work will be rendered easier as new means of communication are opened up. There seems to be no reason why COTTON should not be grown in considerable quantities in the Sûdân, especially when we read Mr. Nevile's Report on the subject. For this, however, a great deal more water will be required, and this cannot be supplied until some of Sir William Garstin's schemes have been carried out. There is no doubt that at the present time the agricultural development of the Sûdân is being sacrificed and retarded in the interests of Egypt. The Pearl Fisheries of the Red Sea may one day yield a good revenue, but to attain this result time is required.

[1] *Egypt* (1904), p. 91; (1905), p. 134.

From the brief summary of facts given above it is clear that the officials of the Sûdân Government have directed their attention chiefly to the present material interests of the Sûdân and its peoples, but they have done something also towards the encouragement of the study of the ancient history of the country and its languages. Sir Reginald Wingate has established a Museum of Antiquities in the Gordon College, and objects of interest are gradually coming into it. He arranged that excavations of the Pyramids of Meroë should be made in 1903, and two years later he made it possible for the work to be resumed, and for Mr. J. W. Crowfoot and myself to collect a number of antiquities from the country between the Second and Third Cataracts, which are now in the Museum at Kharṭûm. During this work the temple built at Semna by Tirhâḳâh in honour of Usertsen III., the first Egyptian conqueror of the Sûdân, was discovered and excavated, and a new and important set of facts was added to the ancient history of the country. Sir Reginald Wingate also decided to have the north wall from the chapel of one of the great Candace queens removed to Kharṭûm, and thus preserved one of the finest sculptures extant of the later Meroïtic Kingdom. Under his auspices, too, the clearing out of the temple at Ḥalfa, and other works at the same place were carried out by Mr. J. W. Crowfoot and Mr. P. Scott-Moncrieff, and it is to be hoped that he will see his way to excavate other sites, and to remove their antiquities to a place of safety in Kharṭûm. He has already caused some of the so-called "Anak" tombs to be excavated, and will, no doubt, as opportunity offers, continue the examination of other monuments of this class in the Eastern and Western Deserts. In all these works his efforts have been heartily seconded by Colonel E. E. Bernard, the Financial Secretary, who has cleverly managed to provide the necessary moneys. In connection with antiquities it may be noted in passing that in 1905 the Sûdân Government promulgated "The Antiquities Ordinance" (*Sudan Gazette*, p. 376 ff.), which provides for the better preservation of all antiquities that "were built, produced, or "made in the Sûdân or brought thereinto before the year 1783 o "the Gregorian Calendar."

Following the excellent example of the East India Company,

the Sûdân Government has decided to print works of linguistic importance written by its officers. *The Vocabulary of Sûdân Arabic,*[1] by Captain Amery, is a good and useful piece of work, and we hope it will be followed by a publication giving the texts of all the purely Sûdânî compositions which can be collected. Mr. Armbruster, Inspector of the Province of Kasala, has compiled an Amharic vocabulary of the Abyssinian language used in Kasala and its neighbourhood, and it should prove of considerable use to all the officials who are employed in administering the country near the Abyssinian frontier.[2] The excellent *Dictionary* of Isenberg (Amharic-English and English-Amharic) is unfortunately out of print, and very scarce, whilst the splendid *Vocabolario Amarico-Italiano* (Rome, 1901) of Guidi, and the *Dictionnaire de la Langue Amariññа* (Paris, 1881) of D'Abbadie, are very expensive works. The Sûdân Government deserves the hearty thanks of all who are interested in the languages of North-East Africa for undertaking the publication of such works, and considering the large number of able Oxford and Cambridge men who are now in its service, there is no reason why the Government should not, in years to come, produce works on the languages of the Sûdân which shall be as thorough and comprehensive as the famous Grammars of Lepsius and Almkvist on the Nubian and Hadanduwa Languages.

The Anglo-Egyptian Sûdân is ruled by a Governor-General assisted by a Secretary-General, an Inspector-General, a Legal Secretary, a Financial Secretary, an Agent-General stationed in Cairo, a series of Directors of Departments, a number of Governors of Provinces, called Mudîrs, who are in turn assisted by Inspectors and sub-Inspectors, and by native Ma'amûrs. The chief Departments are those of Surveys, Works, Education, Irrigation, Medicine and Sanitation, Woods and Forests, Agriculture and Lands, Railways, Steamers and Boats, Telegraphs and Posts, Customs, Game Preservation, Veterinary work, and Slavery Repression. The Sûdân comprises all the territories south of the 22nd parallel of north latitude which were in the possession of Egypt in 1882, and all which may be reconquered

[1] Kharṭûm and Cairo, 1905.

[2] This work is being printed at Cambridge, and will appear in 1907.

by the British and Egyptian Governments acting in concert. The British and Egyptian flags are used together throughout the Sûdân, both on land and water, except in the town of Sawâkin, where the Egyptian flag alone is used. In the Governor-General is vested the supreme military and civil command. He is appointed by Khedivial Decree, on the recommendation of His Britannic Majesty's Government, and can only be removed by Khedivial Decree, with the consent of His Britannic Majesty's Government. All Laws, Orders, and Regulations are made by Proclamations. The subjects of every Power trade in the Sûdân under equal terms. Egyptian goods entering the Sûdân pay no import duty, and the duties on goods from other countries do not exceed those on goods entering Egypt from abroad. Traffic in slaves in any form is absolutely prohibited, and the provisions of the Brussels Act of July 2nd, 1890, in respect of Fire-arms and Liquor are strictly enforced. Besides the above, the Anglo-Egyptian Convention of January 19th, 1899, which is the real CHARTER of the Sûdân, decreed that no Consuls, Vice-Consuls, or Consular-Agents should be accredited in respect of nor allowed to reside in the Sûdân, without the previous consent of His Britannic Majesty's Government. Without this last wise provision the progress of the Sûdân could not have been so great as it has been during the last eight years.

The present Governor-General, who is also Sirdar of the Egyptian Army, is Major-General Sir F. Reginald Wingate, K.C.B., K.C.M.G., D.S.O., &c. He is the first authority on all questions connected with the history and the origin of the idea of the Mahdî both among the mystic Persian Muḥammadans and the "traditionalists" of the West. His great knowledge of Arabic, and of the manners and customs, and of the phases of thought and religions of the Sûdânî tribes, has proved one of the main factors in the successes which have followed the Anglo-Egyptian Army in the Sûdân. His work, *Mahdiism, and the Egyptian Sûdân*, is an encyclopaedia of one of the most remarkable Moslem religious movements which ever took place, and will be for many years the leading guide to the student of the subject. Fate fittingly confided to his hands the destruction of the Khalîfa and of the Amîrs who clung to him, and it was meet that the historian of Mahdiism should be the instrument whereby the most baneful form of it which the world has ever seen should be finally crushed, and the claims of a mischievous impostor and rebel proved to be wholly vain.

Most intimately associated with Sir Reginald Wingate in the great work which he has carried out for many years is the present Inspector-General, Sir Rudolf von Slatin Pâshâ, K C.M.G., &c. The extraordinary experiences which this distinguished Austrian officer passed through during his long service and captivity in the Sûdân have given him an insight into the character of the Sûdânî peoples which is possessed by no other man. He is master of their languages and dialects, and he is able to look at things from their various standpoints, a faculty with which, to the same degree, few Europeans are endowed; while his patience and sympathy have caused him to be regarded as the friend of the native throughout the Sûdân. The Sûdân Government is fortunate indeed in possessing such an Inspector-General, and is to be congratulated on having placed him in a position where his unique knowledge can best be employed in the true interest of both the conquerors and the conquered.

To describe the work of all the Directors of Departments, and the results of the devoted labours of the past and present Mudîrs, which are all duly detailed in Lord Cromer's *Reports*, would occupy more space than can be spared in this work, but reference must be made to the quiet but ceaseless toil of one of the principal makers of modern Kharṭûm—Colonel E. A. Stanton, Governor of Kharṭûm since 1900. When he took over the duties of the Governorship from the capable hands of Colonel (now Sir) John Grenfell Maxwell, the town was, practically speaking, a heap of ruins, and the people, though suffering sorely from the effect of past oppression, were, as Colonel Maxwell reported,[1] just "beginning to appreciate the situation, and learning to under-"stand that the officials no longer prey upon them, but try to do "what is just and right, and to disentangle the truth from the "skein of lies that is generally put before you." With the help of Colonel Friend, Colonel Stanton set to work to make paths and roads, and then had them kept clean, and by degrees he has

[1] *Egypt*, No. 1 (1900), p. 58.

managed to make the natives appreciate the benefits of street sanitation. He has helped to plan and carry into execution many works of the greatest public utility, and by the establishment of steam trams in Kharṭûm and Omdurmân, and the construction of a road to the ferry, along the Blue Nile, he has conferred a great boon on all classes in Kharṭûm.

The town now contains many fine, broad roads and streets, with well defined pavements marked by kerb-stones, and the road along the river front is macadamized; in the matter of cleanliness Kharṭûm now compares favourably with many of the large towns in Egypt. Small wonder is it that it is now "practically "impossible to find a vacant house to let in either the second or "the third-class part of the town, and only one or two in the first-"class."[1] Few who visit Kharṭûm now can realize the filthy state and disorder of the town in 1899, and among those to whom credit is due for the decency and order which obtain there at the present time, Colonel Stanton's place is certainly not the least.

The Government of the Sûdân is, owing to the peculiarities and nature of its inhabitants, of a highly paternal character, but this under the circumstances cannot be avoided. Not only cannot the natives rule themselves, but they cannot take care of themselves, and in many particulars officials have to interfere promptly in their affairs to save them from the evil results of their own recklessness and ignorance. The peoples of the Sûdân have been oppressed for thousands of years, and the effects of this treatment are ingrained in them physically and mentally. It would be a great mistake to imagine that the innate characters of the various inhabitants of the Sûdân can be changed in one or two generations, and a greater mistake to think that any radical change has already been made. The natives who have Hamitic and Semitic blood in them will adapt themselves to their altered circumstances more quickly than the Negro or Negroid tribes, because some of their ancestors were descended from peoples who possessed civilizations of a comparatively high order, and the characteristics of these, latent in them, have not been obliterated wholly by the climatic and other conditions under which they live

[1] *Egypt*, No. 1 (1905), p. 147.

in Africa. The tribes of Hamitic and Semitic ancestry prefer fighting, highway robbery, and brigandage, to manual labour, just as, as we have already seen, their forefathers did thousands of years ago; and the Negroes, where free and independent, have never done more work than they were obliged to do in order to satisfy their personal needs or wishes. The best way to help both classes of natives to overcome their hereditary instincts is to open up their country, to develop trade, and to find for them occupation which will keep their minds from being influenced by fanatical teachers and religious impostors, and their hands from the works of rebellion.

All these things the British are doing with marvellous success at the present time. It is, however, important to remember that at intervals of years great waves of fanaticism have broken out among many Oriental peoples, and that at such times some of the strongest Governments have been swept away like chaff. Periods of religious unrest, or *malaise*, are certain to come again in the Sûdân as elsewhere, and it behoves the authorities to keep in readiness behind their moral influence material power sufficient to meet all the demands which may be made upon it. All will be well so long as the reins of government are in the hands of men who know and understand the native character, and who are able to make full allowance as they rule for the indolence, suspicion, ignorance, and fanaticism which characterize the people, especially in districts remote from towns. But a weak Governor-General, or injudicious taxation, or a great religious "revival" such as might take place as the result of the Pan-Islamic ideas now being promulgated in many parts of Turkey and Egypt, and above all the knowledge that the garrison at Kharṭûm was numerically weak, might tempt the tribes once again to fight for "liberty, equality, and a pure religion." Kharṭûm is 530 miles from the nearest sea-port, and the means of rapid communication consists of a single-line railway which passes for 300 miles through desert and hilly country, where it would be easy for the nomad tribes to tear up the line in dozens of places simultaneously. To the mere student of the history of the country who remembers that the "Hillmen," or Blemmyes, or Bejas in the Eastern Desert, and the "Cattle-men," or Nobadae of the Western Desert, successfully defied the power of Rome, the British force in the Sûdân at the present time seems insufficient, and there are several competent military experts who are of opinion that the garrison at Kharṭûm should be strengthened.

It has already been said that the Government of the Sûdân is of a highly paternal character, and we may now add that the "Father" of the country is Lord Cromer. A little more than three months after the capture of Omdurmân he visited Kharṭûm, so that he might see for himself the nakedness of the land, and the poverty and misery to which its scanty population had been reduced by forty-five years of Turkish "rule," and thirteen years of religious tyranny and cruelty, and might arrange with Lord Kitchener how the Sûdân was to be administered, and provide the necessary funds. He himself has told us that at that time the "prospect was certainly not encouraging." There was "scarcely a germ of civilization in the land, and a whole fiscal "and administrative system had to be created." Nothing daunted, however, he returned to Cairo and found money to carry on the government of the Sûdân, and despatched Sir William Garstin to the south to make an exhaustive report on the Nile Valley and Basin, the crops, the people, the animals, the Sudd, possible irrigation improvements, forestry, minerals, taxes, and trade. Sir William reported, as a result of a careful inspection, that there was reason to hope that the Sûdân Provinces would pay the expenses of their administration in course of time, but that the process of restoration would occupy many years. The country, he said, must have peace and quiet, just government, easy taxation, and simple sanitary measures which will tend to reduce mortality. He warned the Government, however, that the climate would levy a heavy toll in the shape of valuable lives, and his warning has been, alas, justified by events.[1] On July 10th, 1899, Lord

[1] From 1901 to 1904, both inclusive, nine British officers, two British non-commissioned officers, and thirty-two Egyptian or Sûdânî officers died of disease, mostly fever. During part of 1905 and part of 1906 there died, Major Boulnois, Lieut. Fell, Captain Sterling, Colour-Sergeant Boardman, Mr. Barron, Mr. Marsden, and six Egyptian and Sûdânî officers. From 1901 to 1905, both inclusive, ten British officers, one British non-commissioned officer, and twenty-three Egyptian and Sûdânî officers were invalided from ill-health. Further, it cannot be doubted that many civil and military officials, who have neither

Cromer and H.E. Boutros Ghali signed the famous constitutional treaty about the Anglo-Egyptian Sûdân, and from that day, humanly speaking, the salvation of the country was assured. Some two years later Lord Cromer again went to the Sûdân, and he was able to notice what had been the effect of the efforts made by the new Government to grapple with the formidable difficulties which they had to encounter, and he found that some progress had undoubtedly been made. The Khalîfa had been killed, Mahdiism had been crushed, and the inhabitants, having realized the falsity and worthlessness of the Khalîfa's rule, were beginning to give their attention to their business. In January, 1903, Lord Cromer again went to the Sûdân, and proceeded so far to the south as Gondokoro, examining the Government stations, and the American and Austrian Missions which had been established, and receiving deputations of natives, and hearing the experiences of the British officials on his way. On his return to Kharṭûm he and the Governor-General, Sir Reginald Wingate, were guests at the farewell dinner[1] which was given on January 27th to Bimbashi W. E. Bailey on his retirement from the Egyptian Army. After the Governor-General had described in eulogistic terms the valuable services of Captain Bailey, and expressed the regret which every one present felt at his departure, and announced the honours which H.H. the Khedive had been pleased to confer upon him, Lord Cromer made a memorable speech. He said that during his third journey through the Sûdân he had noticed a very great improvement, that trade was reviving as the

succumbed nor been invalided, have suffered severely in health from the praiseworthy zeal with which they have performed their work under conditions of special hardships. *Egypt*, No. 1 (1906), p. 119.

[1] The names of those present are :—Bimbashi Amery, Asser Bey, Captain Bailey, Colonel Bernard, Bond Bey, Borton Bey, Mr. H. Boyle, Colonel Briggs, Bray Bey, Dr. Wallis Budge, Mr. Butler, Bimb. Sorel Cameron, Mr. Bonham-Carter, Bimb. Charlton, Bimbashi Conolly, Lord Cromer, Mr. J. Currie, Al-Sâgh Dale, Bimb. Done, Drage Bey, Bimb. Flint, Count Gleichen, the Rev. L. Gwynne, Hall Bey, Mr. Drummond Hay, Henry Pâshâ, Sir W. Hill Bey, Howard Bey, Bimb. Hon. Cuthbert James, Bimb. Kennedy, Mr. Kershaw, Liddell Bey, Bimb. Maclean, Bimb. McArdagh, Bimb. McKay, Nason Pâshâ, Norbury Bey, Bimb. Owen, Bimb. Parker, Bimb. Parsons, Penton Bey, Phipps Bey, Mr. Poole, Ravenscroft Bey, Mr. Spring-Rice, Colonel Stanton, Bimb. Stockwell, Sutherland Bey, Sir F. R. Wingate, and Bimb. Young.

result of a return of confidence, and that there had been an advance along the whole line. The revenue was showing signs of elasticity, and the expenditure was under efficient control. Kharṭûm, from being a dust-heap, had become a handsome and well-organized town. The Schoolmaster, in the person of Mr. Currie, was abroad. A simple system of criminal and civil justice had been established by Mr. Bonham-Carter, the River Transport had been organized by Commander Bond, and a good medical service by Colonel Penton. The people had learned that the foreigners who visited their country were no longer slave-dealers, but the bitter opponents of slavery. But the Sûdân wanted more population, more railways, more irrigation, more British officials, more schoolmasters, and more public buildings. In fact, with the exception of sand, crocodiles, and hippopotami, there was not enough of anything in the Sûdân.

The Egyptian Government was paying £E350,000 a year for the Sûdân, and had agreed that the yearly increment of revenue in the Sûdân should be applied to Sûdân interests. They had handed over more than a half-a-million sterling to improve the railways, and could do no more. Lord Cromer then went on to speak of the need of a railway between the Nile and the Red Sea, and he promised his hearers that he would try to have it made; this has now been done. With reference to the governing agency in the Sûdân, he pointed out that the Egyptian is just as much a foreigner as the British official. The latter, it is true, was somewhat at a disadvantage, for he had to learn a difficult language; on the other hand, the British enjoyed the advantages derived from approved and inherited capacity to govern. The great need was a Sûdânî agency, and he thought that such might be created if high education were let alone for the time, and reading, writing, and arithmetic taught. He was not in favour of pushing instruction in English too hard. He wanted a railway to Kasala, another up the Blue Nile, a third to Al-Obêḍ, and a dam or two on the Blue Nile. The Sudd had been dealt with in a manner beyond all praise by Colonel Peake and Major Matthews, but he wanted dredgers to remove the mud from under the Sudd and elsewhere.

Turning to the question of the education of the British officials, he agreed that there might be some truth in the allegation that the British lagged behind other nations in the matter of education. On the other hand, the results of the British system of education were best seen in countries like the Sûdân. "A lad in whom "the sense of individual effort and personal responsibility has "been fostered at one of our public schools or military colleges "naturally becomes *capax imperii*, 'a strong character.' In the "free atmosphere in which his boyhood is passed he learns a "number of lessons which stand him in good stead in after-life as "one of an imperial race. He is no automaton, but acquires "unconsciously habits which fit him to shift and to think for "himself, to take responsibility, in a word to govern, and I may "add, to govern with justice and firmness." Men of this kind were to be found dotted all over the Sûdân, from Sawâkin to Al-Obêḍ, and from Ḥalfa to Gondokoro, and wherever they lived they were regarded by the natives as representatives of a just, humane, and righteous rule.

This speech was delivered in the large dining-hall of the Hotel at Kharṭûm, and all who were staying in the building were admitted to hear it. It was a remarkable speech in every way, and it helped those of the audience who were not members of the Sûdân Services to realize the bond which existed between His Majesty King Edward's great representative in Egypt and the Sûdân and every member of the British section of the governing agency of the country. It was wholly British in its simplicity, British in pure common-sense and modesty, and above all British in its tacit recognition of the right of the British to rule by virtue of their justice in dealing with conquered peoples, and their inherent ability to wield power the world over. Not a word was uttered which could indicate to the audience how Lord Cromer had himself toiled to bring about the results which he had seen; but praise, justly due, was unsparingly given to the band of Sûdân officials before him.

The manner of the speech was as interesting as the matter. It was delivered in simple, well-chosen words, and every sentence went home to its hearers. An earnest, hard-working man was addressing and encouraging earnest, hard-working men, and inciting them to work on fearlessly and undismayed. The wary British Lion was teaching his cubs how to rule and how to obey, and intimating to all whom it might concern that he would brook interference neither with himself nor with them—his family. Every official present felt that his own individual share in the great work of Sûdân development was known to Lord Cromer, and that full credit was given to him for it, and this knowledge has had far-reaching effects, and produced the splendid results which are annually described in Lord Cromer's reports.

From the time when this speech was made up to the present Lord Cromer has pushed on the schemes which he then indicated; the railway from the Nile to the Red Sea is an accomplished fact, and when the necessary surveys have been made we shall, no doubt, see other railways built, and Sir William Garstin's great irrigation works carried out. Lord Cromer has shown that Egypt and the Sûdân are one, and that the interests of the one country are locked up in those of the other; he has made the Egyptian a really free man, and slave-dealing and slave-raiding in the Sûdân are things of the past. All the world can see the marvellous changes which have been wrought by the determined and persistent efforts of the strong, far-sighted, broad-minded, and sagacious envoy of Great Britain in Cairo. And every true friend of civilization must rejoice that fate has placed the peoples of the Nile Valley in the hands of Lord Cromer, and of Sir F. Reginald Wingate, whose military achievements, linguistic acquirements, and personal qualities and sympathy, supremely fit him for his position of Governor-General of the Sûdân and Sirdar of the Egyptian Army. That they may continue to fill their high positions for many years to come, must be devoutly hoped by all who have the interests of the Sûdân at heart.

In conclusion, we may fittingly quote here the statement of the Inspector-General, Sir Rudolf von Slatin Pâshâ, on the general condition of the Sûdân at the present time. It represents the opinion of a very high authority, and of one who is not an Englishman, and it therefore possesses exceptional weight and importance. He writes:—"The justice of the Government is "recognized by every soul in the Soudan, by sedentary natives as "well as by the nomad Arabs, and I have never heard that even "the losing party suspected Government officials of having been "influenced by private reasons in giving a decision or sentence. "They have often appealed, but they have never complained of "injustice. Although there may still be sometimes a little dis- "satisfaction amongst the population, if an order is given which "does not fit in with their immediate views and inclinations, they "soon realize that such orders are issued in their interest and in "that of the public welfare. The people are daily gaining more "confidence in our good intentions, and are convinced that we "do our best to establish security in the country. The popula- "tion is becoming more active, and public wealth is increasing. "Whereas, in former days, a wealthy man was afraid to draw "upon himself the attention of the authorities and thus be "exposed to their despotic measures, now-a-days it is just the "contrary. Everyone wishes to be wealthy, or, at least, to be "considered as a man of means, because he knows that on account "of his wealth he may be consulted by the Government officials "on public questions, and be able to exercise some degree of "influence. The people give a great proof of their confidence in "the Government in sending their sons to Government schools. "Practically all the tribes of the Soudan are represented, and "there are so many applicants that we are forced to refuse a "certain number.

"If the Arab population gives proof of genuine progress in "civilization by better-built houses, bigger and cleaner huts, "and a large demand for furniture, which was unknown before, "so also the pagans inhabiting the southern part of the "Soudan prove their advance in their own way. Travelling "now on a steamer along the White Nile, one finds men and "women, who used only to wear beads and brass wire, in "possession of clothing, and they hesitate to meet you in their "former state of nudity. In former days, on seeing a steamer "stopping at the bank, they used to run away and flee into the "interior, fearing to be robbed or taken away as slaves. Now, "they meet the boats, greeting officials and travellers, and try "and sell their corn, chickens, &c., at as high prices as "possible. A great number of natives, especially of the Shilluk "and Dinka tribes, already know the value of money and goods,

" and the golden days when one could buy a bull or a sheep for " beads or copper wire worth a few pence have passed away. " This is, I think, a clear proof of the progress of civilization in " this part of the world.

" Public security prevails throughout the whole of the Soudan. " Considering the extent of the country, murder and highway " robbery are rare; there is comparatively little thieving, and " that nearly always amongst the natives, and not from the " white man. Our police is sound and good, and the Sheikhs " and Omdehs of villages and tribes, who are the pick of " the population, are responsible for safety and tranquillity in the " country. In consequence of this, there is no more slave-" raiding on a large scale, and Governors of provinces, who are " working hand-in-hand with the Slavery Department, state that " only isolated cases now occur.

" The conclusion at which I have personally arrived is that, by " treating the people with justice and making allowances for " their habits and customs, we have succeeded in gaining their " confidence, and that they have now ceased to be indifferent to " our efforts, and are willing to assist us to attain our object— " peace and prosperity in the Soudan." (*Egypt*, No. 1 [1906], pp. 119, 120.)

BIBLIOGRAPHY OF THE SUDAN

*** *Names compounded of "De," "Du," "De La," and "Des," will be found under D. Names compounded of "Von" will be found for the most part under the initial letter of the principal component.*

'ABD AL-LAṬÎF, THE PHYSICIAN.

Relation de l'Egypte par 'Abd al-Laṭîf . . . traduit et enrichi de notes historiques et critiques par SILVESTRE DE SACY. Paris, 1810.

ABÛ 'ABD ALLAH MUḤAMMAD IBN BAṬÛṬA.

Voyage dans le Soudan. Translated by DE SLANE. Paris, 1843.

ABUDACNUS, JOSEPHUS.

The True History of the Jacobites of Ægypt, Lybia, Nubia, &c., their Origin, Religion. . . . Translated by SIR E. SADLEIR. London, 1692. 4to.

The History of the Cophts, commonly called Jacobites, under the Domination of the Turk and Abyssinian Emperors. Translated from the Latin by SIR E. SADLEIR, Bart. London, 1693. 4to.

ABÛ-ṢÂLIḤ, AL-ARMANI.

The Churches and Monasteries of Egypt and some Neighbouring Countries. Edited and translated by B. T. A. EVETTS, *with Notes by* Mr. A. J. BUTLER. Oxford, 1895.

ABYSSINIA.

Abyssinia and the Soudan. Blackwood's Magazine, vol. CXXXVI., 1884.

L'Abyssinie et sa Grande Mission. Lyon, 1900.

The Ethiopic Didascalia, or the Ethiopic Version of the Apostolic Constitution received in the Church of Abyssinia. London, 1834.

Über der grossen Fluss in Südwest von Abessinien. Ausland, Jahrgang, 1841, Nr. 296.

ABYSSINIENNES.

Les Abyssiniennes et les femmes du Soudan Oriental d'après les relations de Bruce, Browne, Cailliaud, Gobat, D'Euny, Lejean, Baker, &c. Turin, 1876.

ADAMS, W. H. D.

Egypt, Past and Present . . . and Recent Events in the Soudan. London, 1885.

Recent Events in the Soudan. London, 1887.

AFEVORK, G. J.

Grammatica della Lingua Amarica. Metodo pratico per l'Insegnamento. Rome, 1905.

THE EGYPTIAN SUDAN

AFRICA.

A New Plaine and Exact Mapp of Africa, by R. WALTON. London, 1655.

Great Explorers of Africa; as told by its Explorers. 2 vols. London, 1894.

Protocol between Great Britain and Italy re Spheres of Influence in Eastern Africa. London, May, 1894.

Flora of Tropical Africa. 3 vols. H.M. Stationery Office, London.

AFRICAN ASSOCIATION.

Proceedings of the Association for Promoting the Discovery of Africa. London, 1790.

Rapport. Brussels, 1790.

Proceedings. London, 1798.

See also CUHN, E. W., *Geschichte der Untersuchung der Britt. Gesellschaft*, 1790.

AḤMAD IBN 'ABD AL-ḲÂDIR (S. AL. D.).

Histoire de la conquête de l'Abyssinie. Algiers, 1897. Ecole Supérieure des Lettres, Nos. 19, 20.

ALEXANDER, W.

Egyptian Monuments from Collections under Bonaparte. Engravings.

ALFORD, H. L. S., AND SWORD, W. D.

The Egyptian Soudan. Its Loss and Recovery. London, 1898.

ALMEIDA, M.

Historia General de Ethiopia. Coimbra, 1660.

ALMKVIST, H.

Die Bischari-Sprache (Tū-Beḍāwie) in Nordost Afrika beschreibend und vergleichend. Dargestellt von. . . . Upsala, 1881, 1885.

ALVAREZ, F.

Description de l'Ethiopie. Anvers, 1558.

Historia de las cosas d'Etiopia. Anvers, 1557; Saragose, 1561; Tolède, 1588.

Narrative of the Portuguese Embassy to Abyssinia, 1520—27. Hakluyt Society. London, 1881.

Verdadera Informcao da Preste Joaño das Indias, &c. Lisbon, 1540. Also in French, German, and Italian.

AMDA ṢĔYÒN, King of Ethiopia.

Histoires des guerres d'Amda Sĕyôn roi d'Ethiopie. 1894. Journal Asiatique, 1890.

Histoires des guerres d'Amda Sĕyôn. Paris, 1890.

AMÉLINEAU, E.

La Géographie de l'Egypte à l'Epoque Copte. Paris, 1893.

AMERY, H. F. S.

The Vocabulary of Sûdân Arabic. Khartûm and Cairo, 1905.

BIBLIOGRAPHY OF THE SUDAN

AMPERE, J. J. A.

Voyage en Egypte et en Nubie. Paris, 1882.

Voyage et Recherches en Egypte et en Nubie. Revue des Deux Mondes. Vols. XV.-XXIII., 1846-8.

ANDERSON, A. A.

A Romance of N' Shabé; or, Startling Events in South and Central Africa. London, 1891.

Twenty-five Years in a Waggon in the Gold Regions of Africa. 2 vols. London, 1887.

ANDRE, C.

Forschungreisen in Arabien und Ost-Afrika. Divers Voyages faits par Burton, Speke, Krapf, Rebmann-Erhart, etc. Leipzig, 1861.

ANSORAGE, W. J.

Under the African Sun. London, 1899.

ARAB WARFARE.

Souakim, 1885. London, 1885.

ARCHER, T.

The War in Egypt and the Soudan. 4 vols. London. 1885-7.

ARCHINARD, L.

Le Soudan français en 1889-90. Paris. 1891.

ARDAGH, SIR J.

Nilometers. Proc. Roy. Geog. Soc. 1889.

ARMBRUSTER, C.

Initia Amharica: Part I. Grammar; Part II. English-Amharic Vocabulary (with a phrase book); Part III. Amharic-English Vocabulary, (with a phrase book). Cambridge, 1907, etc. (In the Press.)

ASSENBUCH, L. VON.

Der Sudanaufstand und die Englische Politik. Unser Zeit. 1884, hf. 4, 5.

ATTERIDGE, A. H.

Towards Khartoum. The Story of the Soudan War of 1896. London, 1897.

ATKINS, SARAH.

See BELZONI, G.

AUSTIN, H. H.

Survey of the Sobat Region. Journ. Roy. Geogr. Soc. Vol. XVII., 495.

Among Swamps and Giants of Equatorial Africa. London, 1902.

AZEVEDO, L. DE.

Histoire de ce qui s'est passé en Ethiopie, Malabar, etc. Paris, 1620.

BAILLAUD, EMILE.

Sur les routes du Soudan. Toulouse, 1902.

BAINES, T.

Explorations in South-West Africa. London, 1864.

Voyages dans le Sud-Ouest de l'Afrique. Paris, 1868.

The Gold Regions of South-Eastern Africa. London, 1877.

BAKER, SIR B.

The River Nile. Min. Proc. Civil Eng. Vol. LX.

BAKER, SIR S. W.

Albert N'yanza and the great Basin of the Nile. 2 vols. 1866, 1872.

The Nile Tributaries of Abyssinia. London, 1867.

Ismaïlia: a Narrative of the Expedition to Central Africa. London, 1874, 1894.

Exploration du Haut Nil. Abrégé par H. VATTEMARE. Paris, 1880.

L'Afrique Equatoriale. Abrégé par H. VATTEMARE. Paris, 1880.

The Egyptian Question; being Letters to the "Times" and "Pall Mall Gazette." London, 1884.

BALDWIN, J. D.

Prehistoric Nations. London, 1869.

BALFOUR, DR. ANDREW.

First Report of the Wellcome Research Laboratories at the Gordon Memorial College, Khartûm. Khartûm, 1904. *Second Report.* Khartûm, 1906.

BALL, J.

Geology of the Aswan Cataract. Survey Dept., Cairo.

BALLIERE, H.

En Egypte: Journal d'un Touriste. Paris, 1867.

BARATIERI, O.

Les Anglais au Soudan et la question d'Abyssinie. Rev. des Deux Mondes. Paris, 1899.

BARATTI, G.

Travels of G. B. into the Remote Countries of the Abissins, or of Ethiopia Interior. London, 1670.

BARBIER DE MEYNARD, C., AND P. DE COURTEILLE.

Masoudi, Les Prairies d'Or. Arabic and French. 9 vols. Paris, 1861.

BARDONE, R.

L'Abissinie. Firenze, 1888.

BARESTE, E.

Monuments de la Haute Egypte et de la Nubie. L'Artiste, 1837.

BARGÈS, J. J. L., ABBÉ.

Le Sahara et le Soudan. Paris (no date).

BAROIS, J.

Les Irrigations en Egypte. Paris, 1904.

BARTH, H.

Travels and Discoveries in North and Central Africa in the years 1849-55. 5 vols. London, 1857.

Travels and Discoveries in North and Central Africa. London, 1890.

BIBLIOGRAPHY OF THE SUDAN

Bascià, G.

Sette Anni nel Sudan Egiziano. L'Esploratore, 1884.

Baschin, O.

Bibliotheca Geographica. Gesell. für Erdkund zu Berlin. Berlin (in progress).

Basset, R.

Les Apocryphes Ethiopiens. Paris, 1892 ff.

Histoire de la Conquête de l'Abyssinie. (XVIe Siècle.) Arabic and French. Paris, 1899 ff.

Notice sur le Magseph Assetat du P. Antonio Fernandes. Traduite du Portugais par R. B. Algiers, 1886.

Etudes sur l'Histoire d'Ethiopie. Paris, 1882.

Baude de Maurcelery, C.

L'Armée du Mahdi à vol d'oiseau. Paris, 1884.

Baumann, O.

In Deutsche Ostafrika während des Aufstandes. Wien, 1890.

Durch Massailand zur Nilquelle, 1891-3. Berlin, 1894.

Baumgarten, J.

Ostafrika, der Sudan und das Seengebiet. Land und Leute, etc. Gotha, 1890.

Beau de Rochas, A.

Oasis et Soudan. Paris, 1888.

Beccari, C.

Historia Aethiopiae. Rerum Aethiopicarum Scriptores Occidentales. Rome, 1905.

Bechet, E.

Cinq ans séjour au Soudan Français. Paris, 1889.

Beke, C. T.

Routes in Abyssinia. Proc. Roy. Geog. Soc. Vol. XIX. 1842.

An Enquiry into M. Antoine d'Abbadie's Journey to Kaffa in the Years 1843 *and* 1844 *to discover the Source of the Nile.* London, 1850.

The Languages and Dialects of Abyssinia and the Countries to the South with vocabularies of thirteen languages. Proc. Phil. Soc. Vol. II. 1845.

Travels and Researches. London, 1846.

The French and English in the Red Sea. London, 1862.

An Essay on the Sources of the Nile in the Mountains of the Moon. Edinburgh, 1848.

Bell, J. G.

Extract from a Journal of Travels in Abyssinia in the Years 1840-2. Miscellanea Aegyptiaca. Vol. I., pt. i., 1842.

Bellere, J.

Description historiale de l'Ethiopie. Anvers, 1598.

Beltrame, G.

Grammatica e Vocabolario della Lingua Denka. [*Spoken on the White Nile, north of the Equator.*] Roma, 1882.

BELZONI, G. B.
Narrative of the Operations and Recent Discoveries within the Pyramids, Temples, Tombs, and Excavations in Egypt and Nubia. London, 1820.
Voyages en Egypte et en Nubie, etc. 2 vols. Paris, 1821.
Fruits of the Enterprise exhibited in the Travels of Belzoni in Egypt and Nubia. By Sarah Atkins. London, 1821.

BELZONI, MRS.
An Account of the Women of Egypt, Nubia and Syria. Brussels, 1835.

BENNETT, E. N.
Downfall of the Dervishes. London, 1898.

BENT, J. THEODORE.
The Sacred City of the Ethiopians. London, 1893.
A Visit to the Northern Sudan. Journ. Roy. Geog. Soc., 1896.

BERKELEY, G. F.
The Campaign of Adowa and the Rise of Menelik. London, 1902.

BERKLEY, E.
The Pharaohs and their People. London, 1884.

BERLIOUX, E. F.
La Traite Orientale. Paris, 1870.

BERNATZ, J. M.
Scenes in Ethiopia, designed from Nature. London, 1852.

BERNON, L.
Recueil des Pièces curieuses apportées des Indes, d'Egypte, et d'Ethiopie. Paris, 1670.

BERRIDGE, F.
Abyssinia and its People. (*See* HOTTEN, J. C.) London, 1868.

BESANT, A.
The Story of the Soudan. The Atheistic Platform. London, 1884.

BETHUNE, G.
A Narrative of the Expedition to Dongola and Sennaar. Boston, 1823.

BETTON, C. S.
The Murchison Falls. Nature, June, 1902.

BEZOLD, DR. CARL.
Kebra Nagast, Die Herrlichkeit der Könige. Munich, 1905.
Das Arabisch-Aethiopische Testamentum Adami. Gieszen, 1906.

BIRCH, DR. S.
Sur l'origine des Egyptiens. Oriental Congress, 1873. Tom. II.
Inscription of Tahraka. Aeg. Zeit. 1880.
Copts. Encyclopædia Britannica.
Egyptian Inscription on the Rocks at Tangur. Proc. Soc. Bibl. Arch., Vol. VII., p. 121.
On a Historical Tablet of Ramesee II. Archæologia. Vol. XXXIV., pp. 357-391.

BIRCH, DR. S. (*continued*).

On some Monuments of the Reign of Tirhakah. Trans. Soc. Bibl. Arch., Vol. VII., p. 193.

On the Early Relations of Ethiopia under the Egyptian Monarchy. Proc. Roy. Soc. Literature, Jan. 1846.

BIRD, JAMES.

Observations on the Manners of the Inhabitants who occupy the Southern Coast of Arabia and Shores of the Red Sea. Journ. Royal Geographical Society. Vol. IV.

BISSING, F. W. VON.

Geschichte Aegyptens im Umriss von den ältesten Zeiten bis auf die Eroberung durch die Araber. Berlin, 1904.

BLANC, E.

Routes de l'Afrique sept. au Soudan. Bull. de la Société Géog. 1890.

BLANC, HENRY, M. D.

The Story of the Captives. Mr. Rassam's Mission to Abyssinia. London, 1868.

A Narrative of Captivity in Abyssinia. London, 1868.

BLANFORD, W. T.

Geology and Zoology of Abyssinia. London, 1870.

BLERZY, H.

L' Afrique Moderne. Histoire Physique, Races et Colonisation. Revue des Deux Mondes. Vol. LXXIII., 1868.

BLUNDELL, H. WELD.

A Journey through Abyssinia to the Nile. Journ. Roy. Asiatic Society. Vol. XV., 1900.

BODINI, C.

L' Abissinia degli Abissini. Torino, 1887.

BOEKEN, H. J.

Um und in Afrika. Köln, 1903.

BONCHAMPS, C. DE.

Une Mission vers le Nil Blanc. Bull. de la Soc. Géog., Paris, 1898.

BONFILS, F.

Albums photographiques, Egypte, Nubie, Palestine, &c. Paris, 1872.

Albums photographiques des Monuments et des Sites les plus célèbres de l'Orient. Paris, 1872.

BONNETAIN, P.

Dans la Brousse. Sensations du Soudan. Paris, 1895.

BONNETAIN, MME. P.

Une Française au Soudan. Paris, 1884.

BONOMI, J.

Egypt, Nubia, and Ethiopia. London, 1862.

BORCHARDT, L.

Nilhöhe und Nilstandmarken. Abh. d. Kgl. Preuss. Akkad. Wissenschaften. Berlin, 1905.

BORELLI, J.
Ethiopie méridionale. Paris, 1890.

BORELLI, OCTAVE BEY.
La Chute de Khartoum, 26 Janvier, 1885. Paris, 1893.

BOSSI, S.
Views in Egypt and Nubia. London, 1824-27, fol.

BOTELER, T.
Voyage of Discovery to Africa and Arabia. 1821-1826. 2 vols. London, 1835.

BOTTEGO, V.
Viaggi di Scoperta nel cuore dell' Africa. Roma, 1895.

BOURDARIE, P.
Fachoda, La Mission Marchand. Paris, 1899.

BOURDE, P.
La France au Soudan. Revue des Deux Mondes. Vols. XLII., XLIII. 1880-1.

BOURGUIGNON D'ANVILLE, J. B.
Dissertation sur les Sources du Nil. Mémoire de l'Académie des Inscriptions, 1759. Tome XXVI.

BOURKE, D. R. W. (See MAYO.)

BOURNE, H. R. F.
The Other Side of the Emin Pasha Relief Expedition. London, 1891.

BOWDICH, T. E.
An Essay on the Superstitions, Customs, and Arts common to the Ancient Egyptians, Abyssinians and Ashantees. Paris, 1821.
Travels in the Interior of Africa. London, 1820. (*See* MOLLIEN, G. T.)

BOYLE, ST. JOHN.
Travels of an Arab Merchant in the Soudan. Abridged from the French. London, 1854.

BRACKENBURY, H.
Narrative of the Advance of the River Column of the Nile Expeditionary Force. Edinburgh, 1885.

BRARD, PATER.
Der Victoria Nyansa. Petermann, Geog. Mitt. 1897.

BREASTED, J. H.
The Temples of Lower Nubia. Chicago, 1906.
A History of Egypt. 1906.
Ancient Records. 1906.

BREHM, A. E.
Reiseskizzen aus Nord-Ost Afrika .... Egypten, Nubien, Sennahr, Roseeres, und Kordofahn, 1847-1852. Jena, 1855.
Ergebnisse meiner Reise nach Habesch im Gefolge Seiner Hoheit des regierenden Herzogs von Sachsen-Koburg-Gotha Ernst II. Hamburg, 1863.

BRIDGMAN, H. L.

The New British Empire of the Sudan. National Geog. Mag., 1906.

BROCCHI, G. B.

Osservazioni fatte ne' Viaggi in Egitto, nella Siria e nella Nubia. 4 vols. Bassano, 1841-43.

BROCKENDEN, W.

Egypt and Nubia. 3 vols. London, 1846-9.

BROUN, A. F.

Report on the Woods and Forests of the Sudan. 1902.

Notes on Sadd Formation of the Upper Nile. Journ. Linn. Soc., July, 1905.

BROUSSAIS, E.

De Paris au Soudan. Marseille, Alger, Transsaharien. Algiers, 1891.

BROWN, R.

The Story of Africa and its Explorers. 4 vols. London, 1896.

BROWN, R. H.

The Fayûm and Lake Moeris. London, 1892.

BROWNE, C. E.

The Heroes of African Discovery and Adventure. London, 1883.

BROWNE, W. G.

Travels in Africa, Egypt, and Syria, 1792-8. London, 1806.

Nouveau Voyage dans la Haute et Basse Egypte, la Syrie, le Darfour. Paris, 1800.

BRUCE, J.

Travels to Discover the Source of the Nile in the Years 1768-73. 7 vols. London and Edinburgh, 1813.

An Interesting Narrative of the Travels of J. Bruce into Abyssinia to discover the Source of the Nile. Abridged, with notes and extracts from the Travels of Dr. Shaw, M. Savary, and the Memoirs of Baron de Tott. Boston, 1798.

Voyage aux Sources du Nil. 6 vols. Paris, 1790.

BRUCE, J., AND PETERSON, W.

Travels and Adventures in Abyssinia. Edinburgh, 1859.

BRÜCKNER, E.

Klimaschwankungen. Vienna, 1890.

BRUEL, G.

L'Occupation du bassin du Tchad. Moulins, 1902.

BRUGSCH, DR. H.

Die Geographie des alten Aegypten nach den altägyptischen Denkmälern. Leipzig, 1857.

Recueil de Monuments Egyptiens. Leipzig, 1862.

A History of Egypt under the Pharaohs. Translation by H. D. Seymour. London, 1879.

Entzifferung der Meroitischen Schriftdenkmäler. Zeitschrift für Aeg. Sprache, Bd. XXV. (1887), pp. 1-32, 75-97.

BRUGSCH, DR. R. (*continued*).

Das Aethiopische Goldgewicht. Zeitschrift für Aeg. Sprache, Bd. XXVIII. (1890), pp. 24-32.

Aethiopica. Zeitschrift für Aeg. Sprache, Bd. XXIX. (1891), pp. 25-31.

Vier bilingue Inschriften von Philä. Zeitschrift für Aeg. Sprache, Bd. XXVI. (1888), pp. 57-69.

Die Götter des Nomos Arabia. Zeit. Aeg. XIX., I.

Die Libysch-kaukasischen Völker-gruppen. Leipzig, 1885.

Die Negerstämme des Una-Inschrift. Zeit. Aeg., 1882.

Stele von Dongola. Zeit. Aeg., 1877.

Reise nach der grossen Oase El-Khargeh. Leipzig, 1878.

BRUN-ROLLET, N.

Le Nil Blanc et le Soudan. Paris, 1855.

BUCHTA, R.

Die Oberen Nil Länder; Volkstypen und Landschaften. Dargestellt in 160 *Photographien.* Berlin, 1881.

Der Sudan unter ägyptischer Herrschaft. Leipzig, 1888.

Der Aufstand im Sudan. Das Ausland, March, 1884.

BUDGE, E. A. WALLIS.

A History of Egypt. 8 vols. London, 1902.

Cook's Handbook to Egypt and the Sûdân. 2nd edition. London, 1906.

The Nile: Notes for Travellers. 10th edition. Cairo, 1906.

On the Orientation of the Pyramids in the Sûdân. 1899.

Gods of the Egyptians. London, 1904.

Life and Exploits of Alexander the Great. Ethiopic and English. London, 1896.

Contendings of the Apostles. Ethiopic and English. London, 1898, 1901.

Lives of Mabâ'-Ṣĕyōn and Gabra Krĕstôs. Ethiopic and English. London, 1899.

Miracles of the Virgin Mary. Ethiopic and English. London, 1900.

Life of Hannah. Ethiopic and English. London, 1900.

Magical Prayers. Ethiopic and English. London, 1900.

Life and Miracles of Takla Hâymânôt. Ethiopic and English. London, 1906.

BUNSEN, C. C. J.

Egypt's Place in Universal History. Translated by H. Cottrell, Esq., M.A. 5 vols. London, 1867.

BUONFANTI, M.

Le Sahara et le Soudan occidental. Relation de Voyages. Soc. R. Belge Géogr. Bulletin.

BURCKHARDT, J. L.

Travels in Nubia. London, 1819.

Reisen in Nubien und Arabien. Jena, 1820.

Arabic Proverbs; edited by Sir W. Ouseley. London, 1830 and 1875.

Arabische Sprüchwörter oder Sitten und Gebrauche der neueren Aegyptier. Weimar, 1834.

BURDO, AD.

Les Belges dans l'Afrique Centrale. Bruxelles, 1884.

BURETTE, H. A.

A Visit to King Theodore. By a Traveller lately returned from Gondar. London, 1868.

BURGES, J.

Notice sur le Soudan français. Paris, 1893.

BURLEIGH, W. B.

Desert Warfare, being a Chronicle of the Eastern Soudan Campaign. London, 1884.

Sirdar and Khalifa. London, 1898.

Reconquest of the Soudan. London, 1898.

Khartoum Campaign, 1898. London, 1899.

BURNEY, J.

A Chronological History of North-African Voyages and Discoveries. London, 1819.

BURROW, CAPT. G.

The Land of the Pigmies. London, 1898.

BURTON, J.

Plans, Drawings and Copies of Inscriptions of Temples, etc., from Kalabsha to Napata. Brit. Mus. Add. MSS. 25,649-51.

BURTON, SIR R. F.

First Footsteps in East Africa, or an Exploration of Harrar. London, 1856.

The Lake Regions of Central Africa. 2 vols. London, 1860.

BUTLER, A. J.

The Arab Conquest of Egypt. London, 1902.

BUTLER, COL. SIR W. F.

Campaign of the Cataracts, 1884-5. London, 1887.

Charles George Gordon. (*English Men of Action.*) London, 1889.

BUXTON, E. N.

Two African Trips. London, 1902.

CAILLIATTE, C.

Les Sources du Nil et les dernières explorations dans l'Afrique équatoriale. Paris, 8vo.

CAILLIAUD, FREDERIC.

Land of the Nile; or, Egypt Past and Present. London and Edinburgh, 1871.

Les Abyssiniennes et les Femmes du Soudan Oriental, d'après les relations de Cailliaud, etc. 1876.

Voyage à Méroé, etc. Années 1819-1822. Paris, 1826-1828.

Carte détaillée du Cours du Nil levée dans l'Expédition de 1819-22. Paris, 1824.

CAILLIAUD, FREDERIC (*continued*).

Voyage à l'Oasis de Thèbes. Paris, 1822-24.

Voyage à l'Oasis de Syouah. Paris, 1823.

CAILLIE, K., ET JOMARD, E.

Oeuvres complétées par les remarques et recherches géographiques sur le voyage de M. Caillie par M. Jomard. Paris, 1830.

CAIX DE SAINT AYMOUR, VICOMTE A. DE.

Relation de la France avec l'Abyssinie, 1634-1706. Paris, 1886.

Les intérêts français dans le Soudan Ethiopien. Paris, 1884.

CAMERON, CAPT. V. L.

The Soudan. Revue Coloniale Internationale. May, 1886.

The Future of the Soudan. National Review. Sept., 1885.

Our Duty in the Soudan. Contemporary Review. April, 1885.

CAMERON, D. A.

Egypt in the Nineteenth Century; or, Mehemet Ali and his Successors. London, 1898.

On the Tribes of the Eastern Soudan. Journ. Anthrop. Inst. Vol. XVI. 1887.

CAMPERIO, CAPT. M.

Setti anni nel Sudan Egiziano. (*Gessi, R.*) Rome, 1891.

CAPENNY, S. H. F.

The Khedivic Possessions in the Basin of the Upper Congo. Scot. Geog. Mag. Edin., 1899.

CARMOY, H.

Le Mahdi et les Associations religieuses Musulmanes. Revue Générale, May, 1884.

CASATI, G.

Ten Years in Equatoria. Translated by J. R. Clay. 2 vols. London, 1891.

CASTLEREAGH, VISCOUNT.

Journey to Damascus through Egypt, Nubia, Arabia Petræa, Palestine, and Syria. London, 1847.

CECCHI, A.

L'Abissins, etc. Da Zeila alle frontiere del Cafa. Soc. Geo. Ital. Roma, 1886.

L'Abissinia Settentrionale. Milano, 1887.

CHABAS, F. J.

Les Inscriptions des Mines d'Or. Paris, 1862, 1873.

CHAILLE-LONG, C.

Central Africa. Naked Truths of Naked People. London, 1876.

L'Afrique Centrale. Expéditions au Lac Victoria-Nyanza et au Makraka Niam Niam à l'Ouest du Nil Blanc. Paris, 1877.

CHAMPOLLION, J. F. (LE JEUNE).

Monuments de l'Egypte et de la Nubie. 4 vols. Paris, 1845.

Monuments de l'Egypte et de la Nubie. Continuées par Champollion-Figeac, E. de Rougé et G. Maspero. Paris, 1844-79.

CHARMES, G.

L'Egypte: Archéologie, Histoire, Littérature. Paris, 1891.

CHARTON, E.

Voyages anciens et modernes. 4 vols. Paris, 1853.

CHATELARD, E.

Projet de colonisation au Soudan. Paris, 1894.

CHAUVELOT, R.

Un Grand Politique: L'Empereur Menelik II. Paris, 1899.

CHAVANNE, J.

Die Sahara; oder von Oase zu Oase. Wien, 1879.

Die Mittlere Höhe Afrikas. Wien, 1881.

Afrika im Lichte unserer Tage. Leipzig, 1881.

Reisen und Forschungen im alten und neuen Kongostaate. Leipzig, 1887.

CHELU, A.

De l'Equateur à la Méditerranée: Le Nil, le Soudan, l'Egypte. Paris, 1891.

CHESNEL, E.

Les Anglais en Egypte; leurs défaites au Soudan. London, 1887.

CHOISY, A.

Chemin de fer transsaharien. Paris, 1895.

CHURCHILL, W. S.

The River War. London, 1899.

CLAPPERTON, H.

Journal of a Second Expedition into the Interior of Africa. London, 1829.

CLAPPERTON, H., AND DENHAM, D.

Narrative of Travels and Discoveries in Northern and Central Africa in 1822-1824. Boston, Mass. 1826. London, 1828.

CLARKE, J.

Specimens of Dialects: Short Vocabularies of Languages and Notes of Countries and Customs in Africa. Berwick-upon-Tweed, 1848.

CLARKE, SOMERS.

The Geography of Lower Nubia. Report Brit. Assoc. 1894.

COCHERIS, J.

Situation internationale de l'Egypte et du Soudan, juridique et politique. Paris, 1903.

COLBORNE, COL. HON. J.

With Hicks Pasha in the Soudan. London, 1884.

COLLIN, V.

La Question du Haut Nil au point de vue Belge. Anvers, 1899.

COLOMB, COL. E. VON.
Notice sur les Oases du Sahara et les Grandes Routes qui y conduisent. Nouv. Ann. des Voyages. 1860.

COLSTON, COL. R. E.
Reconnaissance from Berenice to Berber. Cairo, 1874.

COLVILLE, COL.
History of the Sudan Campaign, 1884-5. 2 vols. War Office, London, 1889.
The Land of the Nile Springs. London, 1895.

COLVIN, SIR A.
The Making of Modern Egypt. London, 1906.

COMBES, E.
Voyage en Egypte, en Nubie, dans le désert de Bayouda des Bischarys. Paris, 1846.

COMBES, E., et TAMISIER, M.
Voyages en Abyssinie. Paris, 1838.

COMBES, P.
L'Abyssinie en 1896. Paris, 1896.

CONDER, J.
A Popular Description of Egypt and Nubia. 2 vols. London, 1827.
The Modern Traveller. London, 1830.

CONGELMAN, W.
Chronique de Galâwdêwos (Claudius). Paris, 1895.

CONTI, ROSSINI.
Acta Marqorêwos. Paris, 1904.
Acta Yârêd et Panṭalewôn. Rome, 1904.
Al Rágali. Bulletino della Soc. Ital. di Esplorazioni. Milan, 1904.
Appunti ed Osservazione sui Re Zágue e Takla Haymanot. Rome, 1895.
Gli Atti di Abbâ Yonâs. Rome, 1903.
Beṣu'a Amlâk e il convento della Trinità. Rome, 1902.
Canti popolari Tigrai. Zeit. für Ass., Bd. XVII.
La Redazione Etiopica della Preghiera della Vergine fra i Parti. Rome, 1897.
Documenti per l'Archeologia Eritrea nella bassa valle del Barca. Rome, 1903.
Documenti per lo studio della lingua Tigrè. Florence, 1903.
L'Evangelo D'Oro di Dabra Libânos. Rome, 1901.
Il Gadla Filpos ed il Gadla Johannes. Rome, 1901.
I Loggo e la Legge dei Loggo Sarda. Florence, 1904.
Il "Nagara Gallá." Rome, 1904.
Note sugli Agau. I Appunti sulla lingua Khamta dell' Averghellé. Florence, 1905.
Rapport sur le Progrès des Etudes Ethiopiennes depuis, 1894-1897.
Ricerche e studii sull' Etiopia. Rome, 1900.
Storia di Lebna Dengel rè d'Etiopia. Rome, 1894.
Sulla Dinastia Zágué. Rome, 1897.
Tradizioni storiche dei Mensa. Rome, 1901.
Ricordi di un soggiorno in Eritrea. Asmara, 1903.

COOKE, LIEUT.-COL. A. C.

Routes in Abyssinia. Parliamentary Paper No. 3,964. Vol. XLIV., 1867-8. London, 1867.

COOPER, E. J.

Views in Egypt and Nubia. London, 1824-27.

COOPER, J.

The Lost Continent. London, 1875.

CORA, G.

Viaggi di G. Nachtigal nel Sahara e nel Sudan, 1869-74. "Cosmos," Torino, Vol. VIII., 1884.

COTTON. (See POWELL-COTTON.)

COULBEAUX.

Au pays de Menelik. Missions Catholiques, 1898.

CROMER, LORD.

Reports on Egypt and the Sûdân published annually, containing Facts about the Condition, Finance, Administration, etc., of both Countries. Published by the British Government in London. Translations in French and Arabic may be obtained in Cairo.

CUNY, DR. C.

Notice sur le Dar-Four et sur les Caravanes qui se rendent de ce pays en Egypte et vice versa. Bulletin de la Société de Géographie, 4 sér., Tom. VIII. Paris, 1854.

CURRIE, JAMES, DIRECTOR OF THE GORDON COLLEGE, ETC.

Reports on Education. Published at Kharṭûm.

Reports on the Gordon College.

CUST, R. NEEDHAM.

Notice of the Scholars who have contributed to the extension of our Knowledge of the Languages of Africa. Journ. Roy. Asiatic Society. N. S., 1882.

A Sketch of the Modern Languages of Africa. 2 vols. London, 1883.

CUZZI, G.

Fünfzehn Jahre Gefangener des falschen Propheten. Leipzig, 1900.

CZERNY, F.

Egipt i Mahdi w Sudani. Krakow, 1884.

D'ABBADIE, ANTOINE.

Dictionnaire de la Langue Amariñña. Paris, 1881.

D'ABBADIE, ARNAUD.

Catalogue raisonné des manuscrits Ethiopiens appartenant à A. d'Abbadie. Paris, 1859.

Douze ans dans la Haute Ethiopie (Abyssinie). Paris, 1868.

Géodésie d'une partie de la Haute Ethiopie, revue et rédigée par R. RADAU. Paris, 1860.

DAL VERME, L.

I Dervisci nel Sudan Egiziano. Roma, 1894.

Dandola, Emilio.
Viaggio in Egitto, nel Sudan, etc. Milano, 1854.

D'Arenberg, Prince, P.
Voyage au Soudan égyptien. Paris, 1904.

Darmesteter, J.
The Mahdi. London, 1885.

D'Athanasi, G.
Researches and Discoveries in Upper Egypt made under the Direction of Henry Salt, Esq. London, 1836.

D'Avezac-Macaya, Marie A. P.
Esquisse générale de l'Afrique. Paris, 1837, 1844.
Etudes de Géographie critique sur une partie de l'Afrique septentrionale. Paris, 1836.

De Bizemont, H. Vicomte.
Du Caire à Khartoum. Bull. de la Société Géog. Rochefort, 1883.
De Korosko à Khartoum, avec carte. Bulletin de la Société Géog. Paris, 1871.
Les grandes Entreprises Géographiques depuis 1870. Première partie: —Afrique. Paris.

Debono, A.
Fragment d'un Voyage au Saubat (affluent du Nil Blanc). Paris, 1861.

De Breves, Savary.
Voyages. Constantinople, Egypte, Afrique. Paris, 1630.

De Cadalvene, E., and De Breuvery, J.
L'Egypte et la Nubie. Paris, 1841.

De Champeaux, G.
A Travers les Oases Sahariennes. Paris, 1903.

Decken, Baron C. C. von der.
Reisen in Ost-Afrika in den Jahren 1859 *bis* 1865. 4 vols. Leipzig, 1869.

Deckert, Emil.
Der Aegyptische Sudan. Deutsche Revue, March, 1884.

Decle, L.
Three Years in Savage Africa. London, 1898.

De Constantin.
L'Archimandrite Païsi et l'Ataman Achinoff. Paris, 1891.

De Cosson, Major E. A.
The Cradle of the Blue Nile. London, 1877.

De Crozals, J.
Des races primitives de l'Afrique. Revue de Géog. Paris, 1881.
Le Commerce du Sel du Sahara au Soudan. Paris, 1896.

De Folleville, C.
Célèbres voyageurs des temps modernes. L'Afrique inconnue et les Sources du Nil. Limoges, 1884.

BIBLIOGRAPHY OF THE SUDAN

DEFREMERY, C., et SANGUINETTI, DR. B. R.

Voyages d'Ibn Batoutah. Arabic and French. 4 vols. Paris, 1874.

DE GASPARIN-BOISSIER.

Journal d'un Voyage—Vol. II., *L'Egypte et la Nubie.* Paris, 1850.

DE GOEJE, J.

Al-Idrisi. Leyden, 1866.

DE GUERVILLE, A. B.

New Egypt. London, 1905. Cheap edition issued in 1906.

DEHERAIN, H.

Le Soudan Egyptien sous Mehemet Ali. Paris, 1898.

Etudes sur l'Afrique—Soudan Oriental—Ethiopie—Afrique Equatoriale—Afrique du Sud. Paris, 1904.

DE LABORDE, LEON.

Voyage en Abyssinie, analyse critique, etc. Paris, 1838.

DELAFOSSE, M.

Essai sur le peuple et la langue Sara (bassin du Tchad). Paris, 1898.

DELAIRE.

Les Chemins de Fer du Soudan à travers le Sahara. Paris, 1877.

DE LANOYE, F.

Le Nil, son Bassin et ses Sources. Paris, 1870, 1873.

DE LA RENAUDIERE, F.

. . . *essais sur le progrès de la géogr. de l'intérieur de l'Afrique.* Paris, 1826.

DE LATURE, COUNT ESCAYRAC.

Le Désert et le Soudan. Paris, 1853.

Mémoire sur le Soudan, etc. Paris, 1855.

DE LAURIBAR, P.

Douze ans en Abyssinie. Paris, 1898.

DE LESSEPS.

Souvenirs d'un Voyage au Soudan. Nouvelle Revue, tome XXVI., 1884.

DE MALORTIE, BARON.

Egypt: Native Rulers and Foreign Interference. 2nd ed. London, 1883.

Crusaders' Armour in the Soudan. Interesting Discoveries in the Soudan. Aberdeen Journal, 1883. Tablet, 1883.

DEMANCHE, G.

Côte d'Ivoire et Soudan. Rev. Franç. de l'Etranger et des Colonies. Paris, 1895.

DE MARTONNE, E.

Dongola. Ann. de Géog. Paris, 1896.

La vie des peuples du Haut Nil. Annal. de Géog. Paris, 1896.

Hydrographie des Oberen Nil-beckens. Zeit. f. Erdk. Berlin, 1897.

DENHAM, D.

Travels and Discoveries in 1822-1824, *with a short Account of Clapperton's and Lander's Second Journey,* 1825-1827. London, 1831.

DENON, V.
Travels in Africa. 3 vols. London, 1803.

DERAMY, J.
Introduction du Christianisme en Abyssinie. Paris, 1895.

DE REICHENBERG, L'ORZA.
Souvenirs de Mission. Rouen, 1902.

DE RIVOYRE, L. D.
Aux Pays du Soudan. Paris, 1885.

DERMOTT, REV. J. V.
A Visit to the Island of Ukerewe. Proc. Roy. Geog. Soc., Vol. XIV., 1892.

DE ROUGÉ, E.
Chrestomathie Egyptienne. La Stèle du Roi Ethiopien Piankhi-Meriamen. Paris, 1876.

DESCOSTES, F.
Au Soudan, 1890-1891. Paris, 1893.

DE SLANE, M.
Histoire des Berbères et des Dynasties Musulmanes. 4 vols. (Arabic Text 2 vols.) Alger, 1855.

DES VERGERS, A.
Abyssinie: L'Univers; Histoire et Description de tous les Peuples. Paris, 1835.

DE THEVENOT, J.
Voyages de Thévenot en Europe, Asie et Afrique. 2 vols. Paris, 1664.

DE VLIEGER, REV. A.
Origin and Early History of the Coptic Church. Lausanne, 1900.

D'HERICOURT, C. ROCHET.
Voyage dans le pays d'Adel et le Royaume de Schoa. Paris, 1841.
Voyage sur la côte orientale de la Mer Rouge, etc. Paris, 1841.
Second voyage sur les deux rives de la Mer Rouge. Paris, 1846.

DILLMANN, C. F. A.
Chrestomathia Aethiopica. Leipzig, 1866.
Ueber die Regierung insb. die Kirchenordnung des Königs Zar'a-Jacob. Berlin, 1864.
Ueber die Anfänge des Axumitischen Reichs. Berlin Academy, 1879.
Grammatik der Aethiopischen Sprache. Leipzig, 1899.
Lexicon Linguae Ethiopicae. Leipzig, 1861, 1862.

DOMERGUE, A.
Sénégal et Soudan. Paris, 1895.

DOVE, C.
Kulturzonen von Nord Abessinien. Mitteilungen aus J. Perthes Geograp. Anstalt, Nr. 97, 1890.

DOVYAK (MISSIONÄR).
Physikalisch-geographische Beobachtungen am oberen Nil. Petermann, Geog. Mitt. 1859.

DOZY, R.
Al-Idrisi. Leyden, 1866.

DROUIN, E. A.
Les Listes Royales Ethiopiennes. Paris, 1882.

DROVETTI, B.
Voyage à l'Oasis de Dakel. Paris, 1821.

DU BOIS, AYME.
Mémoire sur la ville de Qoçeyr et ses environs et sur les peuples nomades. Description de l'Egypte. Tome XI. Paris, 1822.

DU CAMP, M.
Le Nil: Lettres sur l'Egypte et la Nubie. Paris, 1877.

DU CHAILLU, PAUL.
Adventures in the great Forests of Equatorial Africa. London, 1890.

DUJARRIC, G.
L'Etat Mahdiste du Soudan. Paris, 1901.

DÜMICHEN, J.
Die Oasen der Lybischen Wüste. Strassburg, 1877.
Der Aegyptische Felsentempel von Abu-Simbel und seine Bildwerke und Inschriften. Berlin, 1869.
Die Flotte einer Aegyptischen Königin. Leipzig, 1868.

DUNDAS (?).
Handbook of British East Africa. London, 1893.

DUNDAS, L. J. L.
Sport and Politics under an Eastern Sky. Edinburgh, 1902.

DUPOUY, E.
Les Chasses du Soudan. Paris, 1894.

DUPUIS, C. E.
A Report upon Lake Tsana and the Rivers of the Eastern Soudan. Cairo, 1904.

DUTTON, HENRY.
Narrative of a Journey through Abyssinia in 1862-1863. London, 1867.

DYE, A. H.
Le Bahr el Ghazal. Annal. de Géog. Paris, 1902.

DYE, W. MCE.
Moslem Egypt and Christian Abyssinia. New York, 1880.

EAST AFRICA.
Expedition in Ostafrika, 1861-62. Justus Perthes, Gotha, 1864.

EBERS, PROF. G.
Egypt, Descriptive, Historical, Picturesque. Translated by CLARA BELL. London, 1881.

EDEN, F.
The Nile without a Dragoman. London, 1871.

EDMONSTONE, SIR A.
A Journey to two of the Oases of Upper Egypt. London, 1882.

EDRÎSÎ (MUHAMMAD AL-IDRÎSÎ).
Description de l'Afrique et de l'Espagne. ED. DOZY and DE GOEJE. Leyden, 1866.

EGYPT, NUBIA, AND ABYSSINIA.
Society for the Diffusion of Useful Knowledge. London, 1868.

EGYPT AND THE SUDAN.
Annual Report of the Ministry of Public Works, 1892, etc.

EGYPTIAN QUESTION, THE.
Edinburgh Review, 1884, Vol. CLIX, p. 145 ff.

EHRENBERG, C. G., and HEMPRICH, W. F.
Reisen in Aegypten, Libyen, Nubien, und Dongola. Berlin, 1828.

ELLIOT, G. F. SCOTT.
Expedition to Ruwenzori. Journ. Roy. Geog. Soc., 1895.

ELTON, J. F., and COTTERILL, H. B.
Travels and Researches amongst the Lakes and Mountains of Eastern and Central Africa. London, 1879.

EMIN BEY.
Ueber Sudan und Aequatorialprovinz in Sommer. Das Ausland, 1882.

ENSOR, F. S.
Incidents of a Journey through Nubia. London, 1881.

ERMAN, A.
Die Aloa-Inschriften. Zeitschrift für Aeg. Sprache, Bd. XIX. (1881), p. 112 ff.
Zu den aethiopischen Hieroglyphen. Zeitschrift für Aeg. Sprache, 1897, p. 152.

ETHERINGTON, S.
Egypt, the Soudan, and Central Africa. Edinburgh, 1861.

ETHIOPIC LETTERS.
Ethiopic, Amharic, and Arabic Letters, written to HENRY SALT *by* RAS WALDÁ SELASE *and others.* British Museum Add. MSS. 19,343.

EURINGER, S.
Die Auffassung des Hohenliedes bei den Abessiniern: ein historisch-exegetischer Versuch. Leipzig, 1900.

EXCOFFON, A.
Plus loin que l'Oubanghi. Les Pères Blancs en Afrique. Paris, 1893.

FAIDHERBE, L. L. C.
Le Soudan Français. Lille, 1881-5.
Grammaire et vocabulaire de la langue Poul à l'usage de voyageurs dans le Soudan. Paris, 1882.

FALKENSTEIN, J.
Geschichte der wichtigsten Entdeckungsreisen. Dresden, 1828.

FALKENSTEIN, P. G. J., und PECHUËL-LOESCHE.
Die Loango Expedition. Leipzig, 1879.

FATMA, ZAÏDA.
L'Alkoran, 1861.

FELKIN, R. W.
Emin Pasha in Central Africa. London, 1888.
The Climate of the Egyptian Soudan. Journ. Balneology and Climatology, 1899.

FELKIN, R. W., and WILSON, C. T.
Uganda and the Egyptian Soudan. London, 1882.

FENZL, ED.
Bericht über die in Abyssinien gesammelten geographisch-statistischen Notizen. von Herrn Dr. Reitz auf seiner Reise von Chartum nach Gondar, etc. Wien, 1855.

FERLINI, G.
Cenno sugli Scavi operati nella Nubia e Catalogo degli Oggetti ritrovati. Bologna, 1837.
Relation historique des Fouilles opérées dans la Nubie. Rome, 1838.

FERNANDEZ CUESTA, N.
El Ejipto y la Nubia. Nuero Viajero Universal, Tom. I, 1859.

FIASCHI, T.
Da Cheren a Cassala: note di viaggio. Firenze, 1896.

FISCHER, G. H.
Am Ost Ufer des Victoria Nyanza. Petermann, Geog. Mitt. 1895.

FISHER, RUTH.
On the Borders of Pigmy Land. London, 1906.

FITZNER, R.
Der Kagera Nil. Ein Beitrag zur Physiographie Deutschen Ostafrika. Berlin, 1899.
Der Kagera Nil. Inaug. Diss. Halle, 1899.

FLAD, J. M.
Zwölf Jahre in Abessinien. Leipzig, 1887.

FLOYER, E. A.
Etude sur le Nord Atbai entre le Nil et la Mer Rouge. Cairo, 1893.
Abridged Notes on the Geology of the Northern Atbai. Journal Geological Society, 1892, Vol. XLVIII., p. 576 ff.
The Mines of the Northern Atbai. Journal Royal Asiatic Society, 1892, Vol. XXIV., p. 811 ff.

FORBES, ARCHIBALD.
Chinese Gordon. 12th edition. London, 1885.

FORNI, S.
Viaggio nell' Egitto e nell' Alta Nubia. 2 vols. Milano, 1859.

FOURNEL, J. H.
Etude sur la Conquête de l'Afrique par les Arabes. Duprat, Paris, 1857.
Les Berbères: Etudes sur la conquête de l'Afrique par les Arabes. Paris, 1875-1881.

FOURTAN, R.
Le Nil: son action géologique en Egypte. Bull. Inst. Eg., Cairo, 1894, 1895.

FOWLER, SIR J.
Report on the proposed Railway between Wadi Halfa and Shendy; and the Ship Incline at the First Cataract. Cairo, 1873.

FRITH, F.
Egypt, Nubia, and Ethiopia. London, 1862.

FRITZSCH, G.
Portraitcharaktere der altägyptischen Denkmäler. Verh. der Berl. Ges. für Anthrop. Sitz. V., 1883.
Die Eingeborenen Süd Afrikas Ethnographisch und anatomisch beschrieben. Leipzig, 1872.

FROBENIUS, H.
Die Heiden-Neger des ägyptischen Sudans. Berlin, 1893.
Die Erdgebäude im Sudan. Sammlung gemeinverständlicher wissenschaftlicher Vorträge, etc. Neue Folge. Heft 262, 1866.

FULLER, F. W.
Egypt and Hinterland to the Re-opening of the Soudan. London, 1903.

GAILLARDOT, C. H.
Sur les forêts pétrifiées et l'âge des grès en Nubie. Bull. de l'Institut Egyptien, 1873, No. 12.

GALLIENI, J. S.
Voyage au Soudan français. Paris, 1885.

GALLINA, F.
Apologhi ed Aneddoti volti in Lingua Tigriñña. Roma, 1902.

GAMBARDELLA, S.
L'Egitto e l'Etiopia. Napoli, 1890.

GARCON, A.
Guerre du Soudan. 1884.

GARSTIN, SIR WILLIAM.
Some Problems of the Upper Nile. Nineteenth Century and After, Vol. LVIII., 1905.
The Basin of the Upper Nile. 1904.
Report on the Sudan (Egypt No. 5). 1899.
Report as to Irrigation Projects on the Upper Nile, with 12 maps (Egypt No. 2). 1901.

GATELET, A. L. C.
Histoire de la Conquête du Soudan. Paris, 1901.

GAU, F. C.
Antiquités de la Nubie . . . commentées par B. G. NIEBUHR. *Inscriptions restituées et traduites par* M. LETRONNE. Paris, 1822.

GAYET, A. L.
Itinéraire illustré de la Haute Egypte. Les anciennes capitales des Bords du Nil. Paris (no date).

GEDDES, M.
Church History of Ethiopia. London, 1894.

GEDGE, E.
Notes on the Victoria Nyanza. Proc. Roy. Geog. Soc., Vol. XIV., 1892.

GENTIL, E.
La chûte de l'Empire de Rabah. Paris, 1902.

GESSI, F. PASHA.
Setti anni nel Sudan Egiziano. Milano, 1891.
Seven Years in the Sudan. London, 1892.

GIBBONS, MAJOR A. ST. HILL.
Africa from South to North. 2 vols. London and New York, 1904.
Nile and Zambesi Systems as Waterways. Geog. Journal, Vol. XVIII., p. 232 ff.

GIBSON, A.
Voyages and Travels. (Vol. II. deals with Africa.) London.

GIFFEN, T. KELLY.
The Egyptian Sudan. 1906. (Contains the history of the establishment of the American Mission on the Sobat.)

GILMOUR, T. L.
Abyssinia: the Ethiopian Railway and the Powers. London, 1906.

GLADSTONE, RIGHT HON. W. E.
Egypt and the Soudan. (Speech, February 12th, 1884.) London, 1884.

GLASER, E.
Die Abessinier in Arabien und Afrika. München, 1895.

GLEICHEN, COUNT A. E. W.
The Anglo-Egyptian Sudan. 2 vols. London, 1905.
Handbook of the Sudan. W.O.I.D. London, 1898.
Report on Nile and Country between Dongola, Suakin, Kassala, and Omdurman. W.O.I.D. London, 1898.
With the Camel Corps up the Nile. Nile Expedition, 1884-5. London, 1888.
With the Mission to Menelik. London, 1897.

GOBAT, S.
Journal of a Three Years' Residence in Abyssinia . . . with a Brief History of the Church of Abyssinia by PROFESSOR LEE. London, 1834.
Journal d'un séjour en Abyssinie pendant les Années 1830-1832. Paris, 1835.

GOETZEN, G. A. VON.
Durch Afrika von Ost nach West. Berlin, 1895.

GORDON, C. G.
Gordon and the Mahdi: Narrative of the War. London, 1885.
Journals at Khartoum. London, 1885.
Gordon's Last Journal. London, 1885.

GORDON, C. G. (*continued*).

The Soudan: 1882-1897. The Story of Gordon and the Great Betrayal. London, 1897.

Life of General Gordon. Edinburgh, 1900.

Parliamentary Papers:—

Correspondence respecting General Gordon's Mission to Egypt. 1884.

Further Instructions to General Gordon. 1884.

Text of General Gordon's Proclamation to the Inhabitants of the Sudan. 1884.

Relief of General Gordon. 1885.

GORDON, SIR H. W.

Events in the Life of C. G. Gordon. London, 1886.

GORDON, COL.

Voyage sur le Haut Nil. Bull. de la Soc. de Géog. Paris, Nr. 10, 1875.

GOSSELIN, P. F. J.

Géographie des Anciens. Paris, 1798-1813.

GOTTBERG, E.

Des Cataractes du Nil. Paris, 1867.

GRAHAM, MAJOR D. C.

Glimpses of Abyssinia. Letters, etc., edited by LADY ERSKINE. London, 1867.

GRANT, J.

Cassell's History of the War in the Soudan. London, 1885, etc.

GRANT, J. A.

Khartoum as I saw it in 1863. London, 1885.

A Walk across Africa; or Domestic Scenes from my Nile Journal. London, 1864.

Speke's and Grant's Travels in Africa. London, 1864.

GRANT, J. A.

Les Sources du Nil.

GRAY, W., and STAFF-SURGEON DOCHARD.

Travels in Western Africa. London, 1825.

GREGORY, J. W.

The Great Rift Valley. London, 1896.

GRIFFITH, MR. F. LL.

Tirhakah (in Petrie, *Tanis*, Vol. II., p. 29, plate 9, No. 163).

GROGAN, E. S., and SHARP, H.

From the Cape to Cairo. Revised ed. London, 1902.

GUESSFELDT, P.

Nil, Aegypten, Nubien, und Habesch nach astronom. Beobachtungen. Weimar, 1800.

GUETANT, L.

Marchand, Fachoda. La Mission Congo-Nil. Paris, 1899.

GUFFAREL, P.

Le Sénégal et le Soudan français. Paris, 1892.

GUIDI, IGNAZIO.

L'Abissinia Antica. Nuova Antologia, Giugno. Roma, 1896.

Due Notizie istoriche sull' Abissinia. Giornale della Società Asiatica Italiana, Vol. III., 1888.

La Storia di Hāyla Mikâ'ēl. Roma, 1902.

Le Liste dei Metropoliti di Abissinia. Roma, 1899.

Vita Za-Mikâ'ēl 'Aragâwī. Roma, 1896.

Sopra due degli Aeth. Lesestücke, etc. (Z. f. Ass. XI.).

Sulle conjugazione del verbo Amarico (Ibid. VIII.).

Documenti Amariññā. 1891.

Di due frammenti, etc. 1893.

Il Fetha Nagast. Roma, 1899.

Grammatica elementare della lingua Amariññā. Roma, 1890, 1891.

Il Marḥa Ewûr. 1896.

Proverbi, strofe e racconti abissini. Roma, 1894.

Qenē o Inni abissini. 1900.

Sulla reduplicazione delle consonanti Amariche. Milan, 1893.

Una squarcio della Storia ecclesiastica di Abissinia. (Bessarione, fasc. 49, 50.)

Lo Studio dell' Amarico in Europa. Paris, 1898.

Vocabolario Amarico-Italiano. Roma, 1901.

Annales Johannis I., Iyasu I. et Bakâffâ. 2 vols. Paris, 1905.

GUILLAUMET, E.

Le Soudan en 1894. Paris, 1895.

Tableaux soudanais. Paris, 1899.

GUILLEUX, C.

Journal de route de la Mission Saharienne (Mission Foureau-Lamy), Sahara, Soudan, Lac Tchad. Belfort, 1904.

GWYNN, C. W.

Surveys on the Proposed Sudan-Abyssinian Frontier. Journ. Roy. Geog. Society, Vol. XVIII., 1901.

HABERT, C.

Au Soudan; Excursion dans l'Ouest Africain. Paris, 1894.

HALEVY, J.

Travels in Abyssinia. Translated by J. PICCIOTTO. London, 1878.

HALIM, PRINCE, PASHA OF EGYPT.

Egypt and the Soudan. Nineteenth Century, May, 1885.

HALY, COL. R. H. O'GRADY.

The Nile above the Second Cataract. London, 1884.

HAMILTON, CHAS.

Oriental Zigzags; or Wanderings in Syria, Moab, Abyssinia, and Egypt. London, 1875.

HAMILTON, J.

Sinai, the Hedjaz, and Soudan . . . across the Aethiopian Desert from Sawakin to Chartum. London, 1857.

HARNIER, W. VON.

Reise am Nil von Assuan bis Chartum und Roseires. Petermanns Geog. Mitt., Gotha, 1861.

Reise am oberen Nil, etc. Darmstadt, 1866.

HARRIS, W. C.

The Highlands of Aethiopia. 3 vols. London, 1844.

HARTMANN, R.

Abessinien und die übrigen Gebiete der Ostküste Afrikas. Leipzig, 1883.

Der Nigritier. Ein Anthropologisch-Ethnologische Monographie. Berlin, 1876.

Die Nilländer. Leipzig, 1884.

Die Völker Afrikas. Leipzig, 1879.

Die Westliche Bayuda Steppe. Zeitschr. für All. Erdk. Berlin, 1865.

HASSAN IBN AHMAD, AL KHAIMI.

Zur Geschichte Abessiniens im 17 Jahrhundert. Berlin, 1898.

HASSAN, V.

Die Wahrheit über Emin Pasha. Berlin, 1893.

HASSE, J. G.

Praktisches Handbuch der Arabischen und Aethiopischen Sprache. Jena, 1793.

HASSENSTEIN, B.

Ostafrika zwischen Chartum und dem Rothen Meere bis Suakin und Massaua. Mitteilungen aus Justus Perthes. Gotha, 1861.

HAYES, J.

The Source of the Blue Nile. A Journey to Lake Tsana. London, 1905.

HEAWOOD, E.

The Egyptian Sudan and its History. Journ. of School Geog. Lancaster, Pa.

HEAWOOD, G.

Geography of Africa. London, 1903.

HEEREN, A. H. L.

Historical Researches into the Political Intercourse and Trade of the Carthaginians, Ethiopians, and Egyptians. Translated by D. A. TALBOYS. 2 vols. Oxford, 1832.

HENNEBERT, LT.-COL.

The English in Egypt. England and the Mahdi. Translated by B. PAUNCEFOTE. London, 1884.

HENNIKER, SIR F.

Notes During a Visit to Egypt, Nubia, the Oasis, Mount Sinai, and Jerusalem. London, 1823.

HENZE, H.

Der Nil, seine Hydrographie und seine wirthschaftliche Bedeutung. Angewandte Geog. Halle, 1903.

HERMANN, C. A.

Abessinia maa ja rahwas. Tartus, 1896.

HERTSLET, SIR E.

The Map of Africa by Treaty. London, 1896.

HEUGLIN, T. VON.

Reisen in Nord-Ost Afrika. Tagebuch einer Reise von Chartum nach Abessinien. Petermann, Geog. Mitt. Gotha, 1857.

Die Tinne'sche Expedition im Westlichen Nil-Quellgebiet. Gotha, 1865.

Reise nach Abessinien, den Gala Ländern, Ost Sudan, und Chartûm in den Jahren 1861 *und* 1862. Jena, 1868.

Reise in das Gebiet des Weissen Nil und seiner westlichen Zuflüsse, 1862-1864. Leipzig, 1869.

HEYLING, PETER.

Sonderbarer Lebenslauf und Reise nach Ethiopien. Halle, 1724.

HILL, G. B.

Colonel Gordon in Central Africa, 1874-79. London, 1897.

HILMY, PRINCE IBRAHIM.

Bibliography of Egypt and the Sudan. 2 vols. London, 1886.

HINDLIP, LORD.

British East Africa, Past, Present, and Future. London, 1905.

HODGSON, W. B.

Notes on Northern Africa, the Sahara, and Soudan in Relation to Ethnology Languages, etc. New York, 1844.

HOEHNEL, LUDWIG VON.

Ostäquatorial Afrika zwischen Pangani und dem neuentdeckten Rudolf See. Ergebnisse der Graf S. Telekischen Expedition. Gotha, 1887.

Zum Rudolf See und Stephanie See. Die Forschungsreise des Grafen S. Teleki in Ostäquatorial Afrika, 1881-1884. Wien, 1891.

Discovery of Lakes Rudolph and Stephanie by Count Teleki's Expedition. Translated by N. BELL. London, 1894.

HOLLAND, MAJOR T. J., and HOZIER, CAPT. H.

Record of the Expedition to Abyssinia: compiled by order of the Secretary of State for War. London, 1870.

HOLLOWELL, J. H.

Did the Gladstone Government Abandon Gordon? No. London, 1885.

HOLROYD, A. T.

Notes on a Journey to Kordofan in 1836-37. London, 1839.

HOLUB, E.

Eine Culturskizze des Marutse-Mambunda-Reiches in Süd-Central Afrika. Wien, 1879.

HOPE, C. W.

The Sadd of the Upper Nile. Annals of Botany, Sept., 1902.

HOPKINS, J. S.

A Winter's Journey up the Nile, 1876-77. Birmingham, 1878.

HORNER, J. S.

The Soudan and its Importance to Egypt. United Service Magazine, 1898.

HORNER, L.

Observations on Lepsius' Discovery of Sculptured Marks on Rocks in the Nile Valley in Nubia. Edinburgh, 1850.

HORNER, REV. G.

The Statutes of the Apostles, or Canones Ecclesiastici. Ethiopic, Arabic, and English. London, 1904.

HOSKINS, G. A.

Travels in Ethiopia. London, 1835.

Ethiopia versus Egypt, or Reply to a Critique on his Travels in Ethiopia. London, 1836.

HOTTEN, J. C., publisher of

Abyssinia and its People. London, 1868.

HUGHES, T.

Abyssinian Tributaries of the Nile. Macmillan's Magazine, Vol. XVII., p. 145.

HUGHES, T. P.

Notes on Muhammadanism. London, 1875.

Dictionary of Islam. London, 1896.

HUGHES, W.

Africa, the Red Sea, and the Valley of the Nile, including Egypt, Nubia, and Abyssinia. London, 1867.

HUTCHINSON, T. J.

Ten Years' Wanderings among the Ethiopians. London, 1861.

HUTTON, W.

A Voyage to Africa, etc. London, 1821.

IBN DUKMAK.

Part IV. of his Description of Egypt. (In Arabic.) Bûlâḳ Press, Cairo, A.H. 1309.

IDRISI, MUHAMMAD AL.

Géographie d'Edrisi. Traduite de l'Arabe en Français. . . . par P. AMÉDÉE JAUBERT. Paris, 1836-1840.

IRBY, C. L., and MANGLES, J.

Travels in Egypt and Nubia, Syria and Asia Minor, 1817 *and* 1818. London, 1823.

ISAACS, N.

Travels and Adventures in Eastern Africa. London, 1836.

ISAMBERT, A. J. and E.
Itinéraire Descriptif Historique et Archéologique de l'Orient. Paris, 1861 and 1878.

ISENBERG, C. W.
Grammar of the Amharic Language. London, 1842.
Dictionary of the Amharic Language. London.
Amharic Geography.
Universal History in Amharic.
Vocabulary of the Dankali Language.

ISENBERG, C. W., and KRAPF, L.
Journeys in Abyssinia. London, 1843.

ISMAIL PASHA.
Narrative of the Expedition to Dongola and Sennaar under the command of H. E. Ismail Pasha. London, 1822.

JACOBS, A.
Les Voyages d'Exploration en Afrique. L'Afrique australe et les nouvelles Routes du Soudan. Revue des Deux Mondes, Vol. X., 1857.

JAEGER, H.
Kamerun und Sudan. Berlin, 1892.

JAMES, F. L.
Wild Tribes of the Soudan. 2nd ed. London, 1884.
The Unknown Horn of Africa. An Exploration from Berbera to the Leopold River. 2nd ed. London, 1888.

JANKÓ, J.
Das Nil-Delta. Buda-Pesth, 1896.

JEPHSON, A. J. M.
Emin Pasha and the Rebellion at the Equator. London, 1890.

JEQUIER, G.
A propos d'une Stèle Ethiopienne. Recueil, XXVII., p. 170.

JESSEN, B. H.
South-Western Abyssinia. Journ. Roy. Geog. Soc. 1905.

JOHNSTON, C., M.R.C.S.
Travels in Southern Abyssinia in 1842, 1843. London, 1844.
Notices of Abyssinia. Syro-Egyptian Society, Original Papers, Vol. I., 1845.

JOHNSTON, SIR HARRY H.
The Nile Quest. A Record of the Explorations of the Nile and its Basin. London, 1906.
The Uganda Protectorate. London, 1902.

JOMARD, E. F.
Traversée du Désert de Nubie. Mém. Soc. Géog., Sér. III., Vol. VI., 1846, p. 186.
Voyage à la recherche des sources du Nil Blanc. Bull. Soc. Géog., Sér. IV., Vol. XII., 1856, p. 267; XIII., p. 71.

JOMARD, E. F. (*continued*).

Voyage de Dom Ignace Knoblecher. Ibid., 1852, p. 24.

Nouvelles d'Egypte et d'Ethiopie. Bull. Soc. Géog. Juillet, 1857.

Sur les rapports de l'Ethiopie avec l'Egypte. 8vo. Paris, 1822.

Sur la communication du Nil des Noirs ou Niger avec le Nil de l'Egypte. 8vo. Paris, 1825.

Remarques sur les découvertes géographiques faites dans l'Afrique Centrale, et le degré de Civilisation des Peuples qui l'habitent. Paris, 1827.

Premier voyage à la recherche des sources du Bahr-el-Abiad ou Nil-Blanc, sous le commandement de Selim Bimbachi. Paris, 1842.

Observations sur le voyage au Darfour suivies d'un vocabulaire Farnoui et des remarques sur le Nil-Blanc supérieur. Paris, 1845.

De la pente du Nil Blanc, etc. Bull. Soc. Géog. IX., 1848, p. 268.

Etudes Géographiques. Paris, 1839.

Itinéraire du voyage de Mohammed-Aly a Fansangoro. Mém. Soc. Géog., Sér. XI., Vol. XII., 1839, p. 253.

Notices sur la pente du Nil supérieur. 8vo. Paris.

JONES, SIR W.

Conversations with Abram, an Abyssinian, concerning the City of Gwender and the Sources of the Nile. Asiatick Researches. Calcutta, I. 1788.

JOUVEAUX, E.

Deux ans dans l'Afrique orientale. Tours, 1871.

JUDD, PROF. J. W.

A Report on the Deposits of the Nile Delta. Proc. Roy. Soc., Vol. LXI., 1886.

JUNKER, DR. W.

Travels in Africa, 1875-1878. *Translated by* A. H. KEANE. London, 1890.

Die Aegyptischen Aequatorial-Provinzen. Petermann, Mitt., Vol. XXVI.

KANDT, R.

Caput Nili. Berlin, 1905.

KATTE, A. VON.

Reise in Abessinien im Jahre 1836. Stuttgart, 1838.

KAUFMANN, A.

Das Gebiet des Weissen Flusses, und dessen Bewohner. Brixen, 1861.

KEANE, A. H.

North Africa. London, 1895.

Ethnology of the Egyptian Sudan. Journ. Anthropol. Inst., Nov. 1884.

Ethnology of the Egyptian Sudan. Encyclo. Brit., Vol. XVII., 1884.

KEAY, J. S.

Spoiling the Egyptians. A Tale of Shame. Told from the Blue-books. London, 1882.

KINGSTON, W. H. G.

Adventures in Africa by an African Trader. London, 1883.

Great African Travellers. London, 1885.

Travels of Mungo Park, Denham, and Clapperton. London, 1886.

KIRCHER, A.

Sources of the Nile. (See Bruce, "Voyage in Nubia," Vol. III.)

KIRKPATRICK, CAPT. R. T.

Lake Choga and Surrounding Country. Journ. Geog. Soc., 1899, Vol. XIII., p. 410.

KLOBB, LIEUT.-COL.

Dernier Carnet de Route au Soudan Français. Paris, 1905.

KLOEDEN, G. A. VON.

Das Stromsystem des Oberen Nil, etc. Berlin, 1859.

KLUNZINGER, C. B.

Bilder aus Ober Aegypten, der Wüste und dem Rothen Meere. Stuttgart, 1877.

Upper Egypt: its people and its products. London, 1878.

KNIGHT, E. F.

Letters from the Soudan. Reprinted from the "Times." London, 1897.

KNOBLECHER, I.

Reise auf dem Weissen Nil.

Voyage dans la région du Haut Nil.

KOETTLITZ, R.

A Journey through Somaliland and Southern Abyssinia . . . through the Sudan to Egypt. Journal Tyneside Geog. Soc., Vol. IV., 1901.

KOHN-ABREST, F.

L'Expédition anglaise et le Soulèvement du Soudan. La Tripolitaine, 1884.

KOLLMAN, P.

The Victoria Nyanza: the land, the races and their customs, etc. London, 1899.

KOTSCHY, THEO., and PEYRITSCH, JEAN

*Plantes Tinnéennes, publié aux frais d'*ALEXANDRINE TINNE *et* JOHN A. TINNE. Vienna, 1867.

KRALL, J.

Beiträge zur Geschichte der Blemyer und Nubier. Denkschriften Kais. Akad. der Wissen., 1898, zu Wien, Bd. XLVI.

Das Jahr der Eroberung Aegyptens durch Kambyses. Wiener Studien II., 1.

Grundriss der altorientalischen Geschichte. Wien, 1899 ff.

Ein neuer nubischer König. W. Z. M. XIV., p. 233.

KRAPF, J. L.

Grammatical Outline of the Galla Language.

Vocabulary of the Galla Language.

Travels, researches, etc. Journeys to Jaffa, Usambara, Ukambani, Shoa, Abyssinia and Khartoum. London, 1860.

KREMER, A. VON.

Aegypten Forschungen über Land und Volk während eines zehnjährigen Aufenthalts. Leipzig, 1863.

KROCHOW VON WICKERODE.

Reisen und Jagden in Nord-Ost-Afrika. 2 Bde. Berlin, 1867.

LAGRILLIERE BEAUCLERC, E.

Chambres de Commerce. Mission au Sénégal et au Soudan. Paris, 1898.

LAING, MAJOR A. G.

Travels in Africa. London, 1825.

LANDER, R.

Records of Capt. Clapperton's last Expedition to Africa. London, 1830.

LANIER, L.

L'Afrique. Choix de Lectures de Geographie. Paris, 1899.

LAPORTE, LAURENT.

Sailing on the Nile. Translated by V. VAUGHAN. Boston, 1872.

LATHAM, R. G.

Descriptive Ethnology. Vol. II. London, 1859.

LEACH, J.

Travels on the Nile. London, 1742.

LEAKE, W. M.

Journal of a voyage on the Bahr-Abiad, or White Nile. Journal Royal Geog. Society, Vol. II., 1832.

LE BEGUE, M. M. (COUNT DE GERMIENY).

De Saint Louis au Niger. Souvenirs de Campagne. Printed for private circulation. Paris.

LECERF, P. E.

Lettres du Soudan. Paris, 1895.

LEFEBURE, THEO.

Voyage en Abyssinie, 1839-1843. 6 vols. Paris, 1845-1854.

LEFEVRE, A.

Sur la Géologie de la Vallée du Nil jusqu'au Chardoun. Bulletin de la Société Géologique, Vol. X.

LEGH, T., M.P.

Travels in Egypt, Nubia, Holy Land, Mount Lebanon, and Cyprus, 1814. London, 1818.

Narrative of a journey in Egypt and the country beyond the Cataracts. London, 1816.

For Reviews of "*Travels*" see Monthly Review, Vol. LXXXIV.; Quarterly Review, Vol. XVI.; Edinburgh Review, Vol. XXVII.; Eclectic Review, Vol. XXV.

Reise durch Aegypten und in das Land oberhalb der Cataracten. Weimar, 1818.

LE JEAN, G.

Les Deux Nils. Paris, 1866.

Voyage en Abyssinie 1862 à 1864. *With Atlas.* Paris, 1872.

Empire d'Abyssinie et les Intérêts Français dans le Sud de la Mer Rouge. Revue des Deux Mondes. Paris, 1868.

Le Haut-Nil et le Soudan. Souvenirs de Voyage. Revue des Deux Mondes, Vol. XXXVII., 1862.

LELEWEL, J.

Géographie du Moyen Age. 5 Tom. Brussels, 1852-1857.

LEMAIRE, H.

En Abyssinie. A travers le Monde, Paris, New Series, 1899.

LE MASCRIER, J. B.

Description de l'Egypte. Paris, 1735.

LENZ, O.

Timbuktu. Reise durch Marokko, die Sahara und den Sudan. Leipzig, 1884.

Timbouctou. Voyage au Maroc et au Sudan. Paris, 1886.

LEPSIUS, C. R.

Auswahl der wichtigsten Urkunden des Aegyptischen Alterthums. Leipzig, 1842.

Denkmäler aus Aegypten und Aethiopien, 1842-1845. Berlin, 1849.

Explication des monuments de l'Ethiopie. Paris, 1885.

Discoveries in Egypt, Ethiopia, and the Peninsula of Sinai in the years 1842-45. London, 1852. 2nd ed. 1853.

Briefe aus Aegypten, Aethiopien und der Halbinsel des Sinai. Berlin, 1852.

Letters from Egypt, Ethiopia, and Sinai. Translated by J. B. HORNER. London, 1853.

Nubische Grammatik mit einer Einleitung über die Völker und Sprachen Afrikas. Berlin, 1880.

LE ROUX, H.

Menelik et nous. Paris, 1902.

LEROY-BEAULIEU, P. P.

Le Sahara, le Soudan, et les chemins de fer transsahariens. Paris, 1904.

LETRONNE, J. A.

Matériaux pour l'histoire du Christianisme en Egypte, en Nubie et en Abyssinie. Paris, 1832.

LE VAILLANT, F.

Voyage et Second Voyage dans l'intérieur de l'Afrique, 1780-85. Paris, 1780-96.

LEVI, G.

Osman Dekna chez lui. Le Caire, 1884.

LEYDEN, J.

A historical and philosophical sketch of the discoveries and settlements of Europeans in Northern and Western Africa. 1799.

Historical account of Discoveries and Travels in Africa. 2 vols. Edinburgh, 1817. Edited by H. Murray.

Histoire complète des voyages et découvertes en Afrique. 4 vols. 8vo. Paris, 1821.

LIDDELL, MAJOR J. R. E.

Journeys in the White Nile Region. Jour. Roy. Geog. Soc. 1904.

LIEBLEIN, J.

Handel und Schiffahrt auf dem Rothen Meere in alten Zeiten. Christiania, 1886.

Der Handel des Landes Pun. Zeitschrift für Aeg. Sprache. Bd. XXIV., 1886, pp. 7-15.

LIGHT, HENRY.

Travels in Nubia. London, 1818.

LINANT DE BELLEFONDS, E.

Journal of a voyage on the Bacher el Abiad or the White Nile. Journ. Roy. Geog. Soc., 1832.

L'Etbaye, pays habité par les Arabes Bicharieh. Paris, 1868.

LITTMANN, E.

Abyssinian Folk-Lore. Princeton University Bulletin, Vol. XIII., 1900.

Die Pronomina im Tigre. Zeit. für Ass. Bd. XII.

LIVINGSTONE, DR. D.

Missionary Travels and Researches. London, 1857.

A sketch Map of Livingstone's discoveries and Stanley's routes. New York and London, 1873.

LLOYD, A. B.

In Dwarf Land and Cannibal Land. London, 1899.

Uganda to Khartoum. London, 1906.

LOBO, J.

A Voyage to Abyssinia, by Father Jerome Lobo. Translated by DR. S. JOHNSON. London, 1735.

A Voyage to Abyssinia, with fifteen dissertations relating to Abyssinia. Translated by DR. S. JOHNSON. London, 1789.

A Short Relation of the River Nile. London, 1669.

Relations de l'empire des Abyssins, des sources du Nil, de la Licorne, etc. Paris, 1673.

Relation historique d'Abyssinie, Paris, 1728.

Reise nach Habessinien und zu den Quellen des Nils. 2 vols. Zurich, 1793.

Historia de Etiopia. Coimbra, 1659.

LOMBARDINI, E.

Essai sur l'Hydrographie du Nil. Milan, 1865.

LOPES DE LIMA, J. J.

Ensaios sobre a Statistica das Possessões Portuguezas na Africa occidental e oriental. Lisboa, 1844.

LUCAS, A.

The Blackened Rocks of the Nile Cataracts and of the Egyptian Desert. Cairo, 1905.

LUCAS, L.

On Natives of Suakin, and Bishareen Vocabulary. Journ. Anthropological Inst. VI., 1876.

LUDOLF, J.

Historia Æthiopica. Frankfurti ad M., 1681. Translation into English, London, 1684.

Appendix ad Historiam Æthiopicam. Frankfurti ad M., 1693.

Appendix Secunda ad Historiam Æthiopicam. Frankfurti ad M., 1694.

Commentarius ad suam Historiam Æthiopicam. Frankfurti ad M., 1694.

A new history of Ethiopia, made English by J. P. London, 1684.

Lexicon Æthiopico-Latinum. Frankfurti ad M., 1699.

LUGARD, SIR F. J. D.

British East Africa and Uganda. London, 1892.

The Rise of our East African Empire. 2 vols. Edinburgh, 1893.

The Story of the Uganda Protectorate. London, 1897.

Explorations in the country between Victoria Nyanza and Lake Albert Edward. Proc. Roy. Geog. Soc., Vol. XIV., 1892.

LUGARD, LADY.

A Tropical Dependency. London, 1905.

LUMBROSO, G.

L'Egitto dei Greci e dei Romani. Rome, 1895.

LYON, CAPT. G. F., R.N.

A Narrative of Travels in Northern Africa in the years 1818, 1819, 1820 . . . *Geographical Notices of the Soudan, etc.* London, 1821.

LYONS, CAPT. H. G.

On the variation in level of Lake Victoria Nyanza. Cairo, 1904.

The Rains of the Nile Basin, 1904. *Ditto,* 1905. Cairo, 1905-6.

The dimensions of the Nile and its Basin. Jour. Roy. Geog. Soc., 1905.

On the relation between variations of atmospheric pressure in North-East Africa and the Nile flood. Proc. Roy. Soc., Vol. A. LXXVI., 1905.

The Physiography of the River Nile and its Basin. London, 1906.

Notes on a portion of the Nubian Desert S.E. of Korosko. Quart. Jour. Geol. Soc., London, 1897.

MACDONALD, A.

Too Late for Gordon and Khartoum. London, 1887.

Why Gordon perished, or the causes which led to the Soudan disasters. London, 1896.

MACDONALD, J.

With Baker and Graham in the Eastern Soudan. Nineteenth Century, June, 1884.

MACDONALD, MAJOR.-GEN. J. R. L.

Journeys to the North of Uganda. Jour. Roy. Geog. Soc., 1899.

MACGUCKIN DE SLANE, BARON W.

Histoire des Berbéres. 1852.

MACKENZIE, W. C.

The Manurial value of Nile Mud. Jour. Khed. Agric. Soc. Cairo, 1899.

MACLAIRD and OLDFIELD.

Narrative of an Expedition into the interior of Africa, 1832-1834. London, 1837.

MACMASTER, M.

The Egyptian Soudan. London, 1885.

MACNEILL, M.

In pursuit of the Mad Mullah. London, 1902.

MAGE, A. E., and QUINTIN.

Voyage dans le Soudan occidental. Paris, 1868.

MAGYAR, L.

Voyages dans l'Afrique du Sud, 1849-57. Leipzig, 1859.

MAHLER, L.

Praktische Grammatik der amharischen (abessinischen) Sprache. 8vo. Wien, 1906.

MALTE-BRUN, V. A., et LEJEAN.

Nouvelles Annales des voyages par V. A. Malte-Brun et Lejean, Jan. 1862, *Nov.,* 1863, *Avril et Nov.,* 1865. Paris.

MANONCOURT, C. N. S.

Travels in Upper and Lower Egypt. Translated by H. HUNTER. London, 1799.

MANUEL, J.

Le Soudan ; ses Rapports avec le Commerce Européen. Bull. de la Société Geog., 1871.

Carte des Sources du Nil Blanc, et de ses Affluents. Paris, 1873.

MANZI, L.

Il commercio in Etiopia, ecc. Roma, 1886.

MARCHAND, J. B.

Vers le Nil Français. 1898.

MARIETTE BEY, AUG.

Description des fouilles exécutées en Egypte, en Nubie, et au Soudan, 1850-54. fol. Paris, 1863-67.

Deir el-Bahari. Text and plates. Leipzig, 1877.

MARKHAM, SIR C.

A history of the Abyssinian Expedition. London, 1869.

The Portuguese expeditions to Abyssinia in the fifteenth, sixteenth, and seventeenth centuries. Jour. Roy. Geog. Soc., Vol. XXXVIII.

MARNO, E.

Reisen im Gebiete des blauen und weissen Nil, in ägyptischen Sudan und den angrenzenden Negerländern in den Jahren 1869 *bis* 1873. Wien, 1874.

Reise in der ägyptischen Aequatorial-Provinz und in Kordofan in den Jahren 1874-1876. Wien, 1879.

MASPERO, G.

Dawn of Civilization. London, 1900.

Struggle of the Nations. London, 1900.

Passing of the Empires. London, 1900.

Histoire ancienne des peuples de l'Orient. Paris, 1904.

Essai sur la Stèle du Songe. Bibl. Egypt., Tom. III., p. 1. Paris, 1898.

Sur un décret d'Excommunication. Bibl. Egypt., Tom. III., p. 71. Paris, 1898.

Sur la Stèle de l'Intronisation. Bibl. Egypt., Tom. III., p. 135. Paris, 1898.

Stèle of King Horsiatew. Bibl. Egypt., Tom. III., p. 233. Paris, 1898.

Stèle of King Nastosenen. Bibl. Egypt., Tom. III., p. 239. Paris, 1898.

MASSAJA, G.

I miei trentacinque anni di missione nell' alta Etiopia. Roma, 1885.

In Abissinia e fra i Galla. Firenze, 1895.

MAUD, N. T.

Egypt and the Soudan in 1897-98. Jour. Soc. Arts, 1898.

MAUD, CAPT. P.

Exploration in the Southern Borderland of Abyssinia. Jour. Roy. Geog. Soc., 1904.

MAX-MULLER, W.

In ägyptischen Diensten. Leipzig, 1888.

Asien in Europa. Leipzig, 1893.

Aethiopien. Leipzig, 1904.

MAXSE, COLONEL F. I.

Seymour Vandeleur. London, 1905.

MAYO, EARL OF.

Sport in Abyssinia, or the Mareb and Tackazzee. London, 1876.

MEHEMET ALI, PASHA.

Premier Voyage à la recherche des Sources du Bahr-al-Abiad ou Nil-blanc, ordonné par Mohammed Aly. Paris, 1842.

MELLY, ANDRE D.

Lettres d'Egypte et de Nubie. Sept. 1850 *à Janvier* 1851. Privately printed. Londres, 1852.

MELLY, G.

Khartoum and the Blue and White Niles. 2 vols. London, 1851.

MERCIER, E.

La France dans le Sahara au Soudan. 3 tom. Paris, 1888.

MEYER, DR. E.

Geschichte des alten Aegyptens. Berlin, 1887.

MIANI, G.

Il Viaggio de G. Miani. Soc. Ital. Geog., Roma, 1875.

MICHEL, C.

Vers Fachoda à la rencontre de la mission Marchand à travers l'Ethiopie. Paris, 1901.

MITTERRUTZNER, J. C.

Die Dinka Sprache in Central Afrika. Brixen, 1866.

MOLLIEN, G. F.

Voyage dans l'intérieur de l'Afrique, aux sources du Sénégal et de la Gambia, fait en 1818. Paris, 1820.

MONDON-VIDAILHET, C.

La Langue Harari. Paris, 1902.
Manuel Pratique de la Langue Abyssine. Paris, 1891.
Grammaire de la Langue Abyssine-Amharique. Paris, 1898.
Chronique de Théodorus II. Paris, 1905.

MONNIER, M.

Mission Benger. Côte d'Ivoire et Soudan. Paris, 1894.

MONTEIL, C.

Soudan Français. Lille, 1903.

MOORE, F.

Travels in the Inland Parts of Africa. London, 1738.

MOORE, J. E. S.

Mountains of the Moon. London, 1901.

MOORE, J. H.

A new and complete collection of voyages and travels by Pocock, Norden, the Dutch Ambassador, and others. London, 1785 (?).

MORLAND, H.

Gleanings as to the present state of Abyssinia, and a short account of a visit to the hot springs of Ailaat. Trans. Bombay Geog. Soc., 1865.

MOURIEZ, P.

Histoire de Méhémet Ali (notes sur les mines d'or du Soudan et sur le voyage que fit Méhémet Ali, etc.). Paris, 1857.

MUHAMMAD IBN OMAR AT-TOUNSY.

Voyage au Darfour. Traduit de l'Arabe par PERRON. *Préface par* M. JOMARD. Paris, 1850.
Voyage au Ouadây. Paris, 1854.

MUELLER, FR.

Die Sprache der Bari (un des dialectes du Nil Blanc). Wien, 1864.

Ueber die Harari Sprache in Ostlichen Afrika. Kais. Akad. der Wissenschaften. Vol. XLIV. 1864.

Allgemeine Ethnographie. Wien, 1878.

MUENZENBERGER, E. F. A.

Abessinien und seine Bedeutung für unsere Zeit. Freiburg, 1892.

MUNZINGER, W.

Ost-Afrikanische Studien. Leipzig, 1864. Basel, 1883.

MURIEL, E. C.

Report on the Forests of the Soudan. 1901.

MURRAY, H.

Historical account of discoveries and travels in Africa, etc. Edinburgh, 1820.

MUSTAPHA MAGDALY.

Analyses quantitatives de l'eau du Nil, pendant dix mois de l'année. Mémoires de l'Institut Egyptien, Tom. I., 1862.

MYERS, A. B. R.

Life with the Hamram Arabs. . . . Sporting tour in the Soudan. London, 1876.

NACHTIGAL, DR. G.

Reise nach dem Bahr-el-Ghasal, etc. Petermann, Mitteilungen, 1873.

Sahărâ und Sûdân. Berlin, 1879-81.

Relation de la Mort de Mademoiselle Alexina Tinné. Bulletin de la Société Géographique, 1870.

Sur son voyage dans le Soudan. Bulletin de l'Institut Egyptien, No. 13, 1875.

NAVILLE, ED.

Deir el Bahari. Parts I.—V. London, 1895 ff.

NERAZZINI, C.

Itinerario in Etiopia. Roma, 1890.

NESTOR L'HOTE.

Lettres sur Egypte, Cossier, les Mines des Emeraudes.

NEUFELD, C.

A Prisoner of the Khalifa. London.

NEUMANN, O.

From the Somali Coast through Southern Ethiopia to the Sudan. Jour. Roy. Geog. Soc., 1902.

NEUMANN, R.

Nordafrika mit Ausschluss des Nilgebietes, nach Herodot. Leipzig, 1892.

NEW, C.

Life in East Africa. London, 1874.

NIEBUHR, B. G.

Inscriptiones Nubienses. Romae, 1820.

NORDEN, F. L.

Voyage d'Egypte et de Nubie. Copenhague, 1755.

Travels in Egypt and Nubia. 2 vols. London, 1757.

New Voyages and Travels. Vol. II. London, 1819.

The Antiquities, Natural History, Ruins, etc., of Egypt, Nubia, and Thebes . . . from drawings taken on the spot. London, 1792.

OGILBY, J.

Africa: being an accurate description of the regions of Egypt, Barbary, Libya . . . Ethiopia, and the Abyssines. London, 1670.

OHRWALDER, J.

Ten Years' Captivity in the Mahdi's Camp. From the original MS. by MAJOR F. R. WINGATE. London, 1892.

OLIVIER, A., VISCOUNT DE SANDERVAL.

Soudan français. Paris, 1893.

OLLONE, H. M. G.

De la Côte d'Ivoire au Soudan et à la Guinée. Paris, 1901.

OMBONI, T.

Viaggi nell' Africa Occidentale. Milano, 1845.

ORLEANS, PRINCE HENRY OF.

Une Visite à l'Empereur Ménélik. Paris, 1892, 1898.

OSIO, E.

La Spedizione inglese, 1867-1868. Roma, 1887.

OUDNEY, DR.

An outline of the discoveries in Central Africa made by Dr. Oudney, Major Denham, and Lieut. Clapperton. London, 1825.

OWEN, CAPT. W. F. W.

Narrative of voyages to explore the shores of Africa, Arabia, and Madagascar. 2 vols. London, 1833.

PAEZ, PEDRO.

Historia Aethiopiae. Vol. II. Romae, 1905.

PAIMBLANT DU ROUIL, A. F. M. J.

Explorateurs et Soldats. Marchand. Paris, 1899.

PALAT, B. E.

Campagne des Anglais au Soudan. Paris, 1884-1885.

PALLME, I.

Travels in Kordofan. Translated from the German. London, 1844.

PANCERI, DR. P.

Sur l'Infibulation chez les tribus du Soudan. Bulletin de l'Institut Egyptien, 1873, No. 12.

PARK, MUNGO.
Travels in Africa. London, 1816.

PARKE, T. H.
My Experiences in Equatorial Africa as Medical Officer of the Emin Pasha Relief Expedition. London, 1898.

PARKYNS, M.
Life in Abyssinia. London, 1853.

PARRY, MAJOR E.
Suakin, 1885. London, 1886.

PARRY, CAPT. F.
Narrative of an Expedition from Souakin to the Soudan. Jour. Roy. Geograph. Soc., London, 1874, pp. 152-163.

PARSON, C. S.
The Eastern Soudan. Proc. Roy. Artillery Inst., 1899.

PARTHEY, G. F.
Wanderungen durch das Nilthal. Berlin, 1834-1840.

PASSAGE, S.
Central Sudan. Berlin, 1895.

PAULITSCHKE, P.
Ethnographie Nordost Afrikas. Berlin, 1896.

PEACOCK, G.
The Guinea or Gold Coast of Africa, formerly a colony of the Axumites or Abyssinians. London, 1880.

PEARCE, N.
Life and adventures during a residence in Abyssinia from 1810-1819. London, 1831.

PEEL, HON. SYDNEY.
The Binding of the Nile and the New Sudan. London, 1904.

PENAZZI, L.
Sudan e Abissinia. Bologna, 1885.

PENEY, DR. A.
Mémoires sur l'Ethnographie du Soudan Egyptien. Revne d'Ethnographie, I., II., III.

PENSA, H.
L'Egypte et le Soudan Egyptien. Paris; 1895.

PEREIRA, F. M. E.
Chronica de Susenyos, rey de Ethiopia. Lisboa, 1892-1900.
Historia dos Martyres de Nagran. Lisboa, 1899.
O Elephante em Ethiopia. Lisboa, 1898.
Vida do Abba Samuel do Mosteiro do Kalamon. Lisboa, 1894.
Canção de Galadēwos rey de Ethiopia. Lisboa, 1898.
Historia de Minas. Lisboa, 1888.
Vida de Takla Haymanot. Lisboa, 1899.

PERROT, J. F. A.

Essai sur les Momies. Histoire Sacrée de l'Egypte et de la Nubie. Nîmes, 1844.

PERRUCHON, JULES.

Aperçu Grammatical de la Langue Amharique. Louvain, 1899.
Le Livre des Mystères du Ciel et de la Terre. Paris.
Histoire d'Eskender. Journ. Asiat., 1894.
Les Chroniques de Zar'a Yâᵉ qôb et de Ba'eda Mâryâm. Paris, 1893.
Notes pour l'Histoire d'Ethiopie. Revue Sémitique. Paris, 1893-1901.
Lālībalā, King of Ethiopia. Texte Ethiopien publié d'après un manuscrit du Musée Britannique. Paris, 1892.

PETERS, DR. CARL.

The Eldorado of the Ancients. London, 1902.
Das Deutsch Ostafrikanische Schutzgebiet. Leipzig, 1895.

PETHERICK, J.

Travels in Central Africa. 2 vols. London, 1869.
Egypt, the Soudan, and Central Africa . . . Sketches from sixteen years travel. Edin. and London, 1861.

PETRIE, W. M. F.

A History of Egypt from the Earliest Times to the XXXth Dynasty. London, 1894.

PEYRITSCH, JEAN, and KOTSCHY, THEO.

See Kotschy and Peyritsch (ante).

PFEIL, J. G.

Ost Afrika. Berlin, 1888.

PIAGGIA, C.

Dell' arrivo fra i Niam Niam e del soggiorno sul Lago Tzana in Abissinia. Lucca, 1877.

PIERRE, C. I., and MONTEIL, C.

L'Elevage au Soudan. Paris, 1905.

PIMBLETT, W. M.

Story of the Soudan War. London, 1885.

PINKERTON, J.

Voyages and Travels. 17 vols. London, 1808-14.

PLOWDEN, W. (edited by T. C. PLOWDEN).

Travels in Abyssinia and the Galla country, with an account of a mission to Ras Ali in 1848. London, 1868.

POCOCKE, R.

A Description of the East, etc. Vol. I. contains observations on Egypt. London, 1743.
Voyages dans l'Egypte, etc. 7 vols. Paris, 1772-73.
Beschreibung des Morgenlandes und einiger andern Länder, etc. Erlangen, 1771-73.

POMEL, A.
La Géologie du Soudan. Revue Géographique.

POMMEROL, JEAN.
Among the Women of the Sahara. Translated from the French by ARTHUR BELL. London, 1903.

PONCET, C. J.
A voyage to Aethiopia made in the years 1698-1700. London, 1709.
Nachrichten aus Aegypten, Nubien, Aethiopien oder Abyssinia. 1728.

PONCET, J.
Le Fleuve Blanc. Paris, 1863.

POOLE, STANLEY LANE.
A History of Egypt in the Middle Ages. London, 1901.

PORTAL, SIR G. H.
My Mission to Abyssinia, 1888. London, 1892.

POTAGOS, DR.
Dix années de voyages dans l'Asie Centrale et l'Afrique Equatoriale, 1867-77. Paris, 1885.

POUGEOIS, ABBE A.
L'Abyssinie, son histoire naturelle, politique et religieuse. Paris, 1868.

POWELL-COTTON, P. H. G.
A Sporting Trip through Abyssinia. London, 1902.

POWER, F.
Letters from Khartoum during the Siege. London, 1885.

PRAETORIUS, F.
Kebra Nagast. Fabula de Regina Sabaea apud Aethiopes. 1870.
Grammatik der Tigriña-Sprache. Halle, 1872.
Die Amharische Sprache. Halle, 1879.
Aethiopische Grammatik, etc. Porta Linguarum Orientalium, Pars VII., 1886.

PRAX, ...
Instruction pour le voyage de M. Prax dans le Soudan Septentrionale. Paris, 1847.

PRINGLE, MAJOR J. W., R.E.
With the Railway Survey to Victoria Nyanza. Jour. Roy. Geog. Soc. 1893.

PRISSE D'AVENNES, E.
Tribus Nomades de l'Egypte. Les Ababdeh. Revue Orientale, Paris, 1853, III. p. 337.

PROKESCH-OSTEN, A. VON (THE ELDER).
Das Land zwischen den kleinen und grossen Katarakten des Nil. Wien, 1831.

PROKESCH-OSTEN, A. VON (THE YOUNGER).
Nilfahrt bis zu den Zweiten Katarakten. Ein Führer durch Aegypten und Nubien. Leipzig, 1874.

PROMPT, M.

La Vallée du Nil. Bull. Inst. Eg. Cairo, 1891.
Réservoirs d'eau dans la Haute-Egypte. Bull. Inst. Eg. Cairo, 1892.
Soudan Nilotique. Bull. Inst. Eg. Cairo, 1893.
La Vallée du Nil. Réservoir des Girafes. Bull. Inst. Eg. Cairo, 1898.

PROUT, MAJOR H. G.

General Report on the Province of Kordofan. Cairo, 1877.

PRUDHOE, LORD.

Extracts from Private Memoranda kept by Lord Prudhoe on a journey from Cairo to Sennaar in 1829, *describing the Peninsula of Sennaar.* Journal Royal Geog. Society, Vol. V., 1835.

PRUYSSENAERE DE LA WOSTYNE, E.

Reisen und Forschungen in Gebiete des Weissen und Blauen Nil. Gotha, 1855.

PURDY, COL. E. S.

Psychometrical Observations taken at Fascher, Darfour, etc. Cairo, 1877.

PURVIS, J. B.

Handbook to British East Africa and Uganda. London, 1900.

QUATREMERE DE QUINCY, E.

Mémoires sur l'Egypte. 2 vols. Paris, 1811.

RAFFRAY, A.

Les Eglises Monolithes de la ville de Lalebela, Abyssinie. Paris, 1882.

RATZEL, PROF. F.

Die Naturvölker Afrikas. Völkerkunde, Bd. I. Leipzig (Bibliogr. Institut), 1885.

RAVENSTEIN, E. G.

The Climatology of Africa. British Assoc. Comm. Reports, 1883-1901.
Sir W. Garstin's Report on the Upper Nile. Egypt, No. 2, 1901. Geog. Journal, Vol. XVIII., p. 398 ff.

RAY, REV. J.

A collection of curious travels. London, 1738.

RECLUS, J. J. E.

Nouvelle Geographie universelle. Tome X. *L'Afrique septentrionale. Ire partie, Bassin du Nil: Soudan Egyptien, etc., etc.* Paris, 1884.

RECUEIL

de divers Voyages faits en Afrique et en L'Amerique, qui n'ont point esté encore publiez . . . avec des Traitez curieux touchant la Haute Ethyopie le débordement du Nil, la mer Rouge, etc. Paris, 1684. [*Par un témoin oculaire, qui a demeuré plusieurs années dans les principaux Royaumes de l'Empire des Abissins.*]

REED, J. H.

Fashoda and the Bahr-el-Ghazal. Manchester, 1899.

REINISCH, S. L.

Sprachen von Nord-Ost-Afrika. Die Nuba-Sprache: Nubisch-deutsches und Deutsch-nub. Wörterbuch. VII., 308, 240. Wien, 1879.

Die Barea-Sprache. Wien, 1874.

Die Bilin-Sprache, etc. Leipzig, 1883.

REPORT ON THE EGYPTIAN PROVINCES OF THE SOUDAN, RED SEA, AND EQUATOR.

War Office, London, 1884.

REULLE, M.

Au Soudan, 1893-1894. Reims, 1896.

REVILLOUT, E.

Mémoire sur les Blemmyes. Mém. preséntés à l'Acad. des Inscrip. et Belles Lettres. Sér. 1, Tom. XVII. Paris, 1874.

RIFAUD, J. J.

Voyage en Egypte, en Nubie et lieux circonvoisins depuis 1805 *jusqu'à* 1827. Paris, 1829.

Notice sur les travaux . . . en Italie, en Turquie, en Egypte, Nubie, etc. Paris, 1829.

Tableaux de l'Egypte, de la Nubie et des lieux circonvoisins . . . avec un vocabulaire des dialects vulgaires de la Haute Egypte. Paris, 1830.

Gemälde von Aegypten und Nubien und den umliegenden Gegenden. Wien, 1830.

RIMBAUD, J. A.

Lettres de J. A. Rimbaud. Egypte, Arabie, Ethiopie. Paris, 1899.

RITTER, C.

Die Erdkunde im Verhältniss zur Natur und zur Geschichte der Menschen, etc. Erster Theil, erstes Buch. *Afrika.* Berlin, 1822.

Ein Blick in das Nil Quell-land. Berlin, 1844.

RIZZETTO, R.

I commerci di Tripoli e quelli del Sudan. Roma, 1883.

ROBECCHI-BRECCHITTE, L.

Nell' Harrar. Milano, 1896.

ROBERTS, D.

Egypt and Nubia. Drawings by D. ROBERTS. *Historical descriptions by* W. BROCKEDEN. 3 vols. London, 1846. (Another edition, 5 vols., 1858.)

ROBERTS, EMMA.

Sketches and Tales in Egypt and Nubia. London, 1850.

ROBINSON, C. H.

Central Soudan. London, 1896.

ROCHAT, G.

Le Missioni evangeliche in Abissinia. Firenze, 1897.

RODWELL, J. M.

Ethiopic Liturgies and Hymns. Kitto's Journal of Sacred Literature. London, 1864-67.

ROHLFS, G.

Quer durch Afrika. Leipzig, 1874.

Land und Volk in Afrika. Leipzig, 1882.

Meine Mission nach Abessinien. Leipzig, 1883.

ROMAGNY, C. M.

Campagnes d'un siècle. Tunis, Soudan, etc. Paris, 1900.

ROMER, MRS.

A Pilgrimage to the Temples and Tombs of Egypt, Nubia, and Palestine. 2 vols. London, 1846.

ROSELLINI, IPPOLITO.

I Monumenti dell' Egitto e della Nubia. 3 vols. Pisa, 1834.

ROSIGNOLI, P.

I miei dodici-anni di prigionia in mezzo dei dervisci del Sudan. Mondovi, 1898.

ROSSI, E.

La Nubia e il Sudan. Constantinople, 1858.

ROWLEY, H.

Africa Unveiled. London, 1876.

Twenty Years in Central Africa. London, 1882.

ROYLE, C.

Egyptian Campaigns, 1882-1885. London, 1886.

RUEPPELL, DR. E.

Reisen in Nubien, Kordofan, und dem peträischen Arabien. Frankfurt am Main, 1829.

Aegypten politischer Zustand unter Mehemet Ali Pasha. Frankfurt am Main, 1838.

Zoologischer Atlas zu Reisen im nördlichen Afrika. Frankfurt, 1826.

RUNDALL, F. H.

The Highway of Egypt. London, 1882.

RUSSEGGER, J.

Beiträge zur Physiognomie, Geognosie, und Geographie des Afrikanische Toplandes. 1840.

Reisen in Europa, Asien und Afrika, 1835 *bis* 1841. (Vol. II. contains his travels in Egypt, Nubia, and the Eastern Sûdân.) Stuttgart, 1841.

RUSSEL, H.

The Ruin of the Soudan: cause, effect, and remedy. London, 1892.

RUSSEL, COUNT S.

Une Mission en Abyssinie. Paris, 1884.

RUSSELL, REV. M.

Nubia and Abyssinia. London, 1833.

SABRIJIAN, D.

Zwei Jahre in Abyssinien. 1886.

ST. JOHN, J. A.

Egypt and Mohammed Ali; or Travels in the Valley of the Nile. 2 vols. London, 1834.

Egypt and Nubia. London, 1845.

Oriental Album. Characters, costumes, and modes of life in the valley of the Nile. London, 1848.

Isis: an Egyptian Pilgrimage. London, 1853.

SALT, H.

A Voyage to Abyssinia and Travels into the interior of that Country. 37 *maps and plates.* London, 1809-1810.

Voyage en Abyssinie. Traduit de l'Anglais par P. F. HENRY. 2 vols. Paris, 1816.

SANDERVAL, O.

Soudan Français. Paris, 1893.

SANTALENA, A.

L'Insurrezione de Sudan. Treviso, 1881-1885.

SANTE STEFANO, G.

Viaggio in Etiopia. Cöln, 1860.

SAPETO, G.

Viaggio e missione cattolica fra i Mensa i Bogos e gli Habab. Roma, 1857.

Etiopia. Roma, 1890.

SARRAZIN, H.

Races humaines du Sudan Français. Chambery, 1901.

SARTORIUS, MRS. E.

Three Months in the Soudan. London, 1885.

SCHAEFER, H.

Urkunden der älteren Aethiopienkönige. I. Leipzig, 1905.

Zur Erklärung der "Traumstele." Zeit. für Aeg. Sprache, Bd. XXXV. (1897), p. 67.

Zur Inschrift des Taharka aus Tanis. Ibid. Bd. XXXVIII. (1900), p. 51 ff.

Die Aethiopische Königsinschrift des Louvre. Zeit. für Aeg. Sprache, Bd. XXXIII. (1895), pp. 101-114.

Eine Bronzefigur des Taharka. Ibid. pp. 114-116.

Nubische Ortsnamen bei den Klassikern. Ibid. p. 96 ff.

SCHAUENBERG, DR. E.

Reisen in Central Afrika. Lander, Clapperton, and Mungo Park. 1859.

SCHEFER, C. H. A., and CORDIER.

Recueil de Voyages, etc. Relation de l'Ambassade de D. Trevisan aupres du Soudan a Egypt, 1512. *Publié et annoté par* C. SCHEFER. Recueil de Voyages, 1884. No. 5. Paris.

SCHIAPARELLI, E.

Géographie de Nubie, etc. See Actes du X. Cong. des Orien. Sec. IV., 1894.

La Configurazione Geografica dell' alto Egitto. "Cosmos," Rome, Vol. XII., 1894-96.

SCHILLINGS, C. G.

With Flashlight and Rifle. Translated by T. WHYTE. 2 vols. London, 1906.

SCHINDLER, F.

Die Armee des Njegus Njegest Menelik II. Troppau, 1898.

SCHIRMER, H.

Le Sahara. Paris, 1893.

SCHLICHTER, H.

Ptolemy's Topography of Eastern Equatorial Africa. Proc. Roy. Geog. Soc., Sept., 1891.

SCHOENFELD, E. D.

Erythräa und der ägyptische Sudan. Berlin, 1904.

SCHUVER, J. M.

Reisen im Oberen-Nilgebiet. Petermann, Mitt. Ergänzungsheft 72. Gotha, 1883.

SCHWEINFURTH, G.

Beitrag zur Flora Aethiopiens. Berlin, 1867.

Im Herzen von Afrika. Reisen und Entdeckungen im Centralen Aequatorial Afrika 1868 *bis* 1871. 2 Tle. Leipzig, 1874.

In the Heart of Africa. Three Years' Travels and Adventures. 2 vols. London, 1873. 3rd ed., London, 1878.

De l'Avenir du Soudan Égyptien. L'Exploration, Tome 18, 1884.

SCHWEINITZ, H. VON.

Deutsch Ost-Afrika in Krieg und Frieden. Berlin.

SCHWEITZER, G.

Schnitzer, E. (*Emin Pasha.*) Berlin, 1898.

SCLATER, DR. P. L.

On the Mammals collected and observed by Capt. J. H. Speke during the East African Expedition. Proc. of the Zoolog. Soc. of London, 1864.

SCOTT-ELLIOTT, G. F.

A Naturalist in Mid-Africa. London, 1896.

SEANEANU, M.

*L'Abyssinie dans la seconde moitié du XVI*e *siècle.* Leipzig, 1892.

SEETZEN, U. J.

Dr. Seetzens linguistischer Nachlass. Wörter-Sammlungen aus Nordost Afrikanischer Sprachen. (See VATER, J. S.) Leipzig, 1816.

SENKOWSKI, J.

Reise durch Nubien und Nordäthiopien. Petersburger Zeitung, Vols. II., IV., VII. 1822.

SEPTANS, LIEUT.-COL. E.

Les Expéditions anglaises en Afrique. Paris, 1896.

SHARPE, S.

History of Egypt. 2 vols. London, 1877.

SHUCAIR, NAUM BEY, B.A.

The History and Geography of the Sudan. In 3 vols. Cairo, 1903. This work is in Arabic.

SIMON, G.

Voyage en Abyssinie et chez les Gallas Raïas. Paris, 1885.

Voyage en Abyssinie (l'Ethiopie). Paris, 1885.

SIMPSON, W.

Abyssinian Church Architecture. Sessional Paper, Royal Inst. Brit. Architects. London, June, 1869.

SIPP, C.

Central Soudan. Meissen, 1888.

SKINNER, R. P.

Abyssinia of to-day: an account of the First Mission sent by the American Government to the Court of the King of Kings. London, 1904.

SLATIN PASHA, SIR R. C.

Fire and Sword in the Soudan. London, 1896-1898.

Feuer und Schwert im Sudan, 1879-1895. Leipzig, 1896.

Nel Soudan Orientale, 1879-1895. "Cosmos," Rome, Vol. XII., 1894-96.

SMITH, A. C.

The Nile and its Banks: a Journal of Travels in Egypt and Nubia. 2 vols. London, 1868.

SMITH, A. D.

Through unknown African Countries. London, 1897.

An Expedition between Lake Rudolf and the Nile. Jour. Roy. Geog. Soc., 1900.

SMITH, F. H.

The Italian-Abyssinian Treaty. Un. Ser. Mag., New Ser., No. 14, 1897.

SMITH, H. F. H.

Pacification of the Sudan, etc. London, 1887.

Through Abyssinia. London, 1890.

SOLEILLET, P.

Obock le Choa le Kaffa. Une exploration commerciale en Ethiopie. Paris, 1886.

Voyages en Ethiopie. Rouen, 1886.

SOUTHWORTH, A. S.

Four Thousand Miles of African Travel. New York and London, 1875.

SPEEDY, MRS. C. M.

My Wanderings in the Soudan. 2 vols. London, 1884.

SPEKE, CAPT. J. H.

Journal of the Discovery of the Source of the Nile. London and Edinburgh, 1864.

What led to the Discovery of the Source of the Nile. London, 1864.

Les Sources du Nil. Paris, 1864.

Die Entdeckung der Nilquellen. 8vo. Leipzig, 1864.

Lake Victoria; a Narrative of Exploration. London, 1868.

STACQUEZ, DR.

L'Egypte, la basse Nubie, et le Sinai, 1862-1863. Liège, 1865.

STANDING, P. C.

The Mahdi of the French Soudan. Unit. Serv. Mag., London, 1900.

STANLEY, SIR H. M.

Through the Dark Continent. London, 1878.

In Darkest Africa. London, 1890.

Im dunkelsten Afrika. 2 Bde. Leipzig, 1890.

Magdala. The story of the Abyssinian Campaign of 1867-1868. London, 1896.

STECKER, A.

Reise von Tripolis nach der Oase Kufra. 1881.

STEEVENS, G. W.

With Kitchener to Khartoum. London, 1898.

STEGNER, F.

Die Nilzuflüsse in Abyssinien. 2 vols. Brunswick, 1867.

STEPHENS, J. L.

Notes of Travel in Egypt and Nubia. Revised and enlarged. London, 1876.

STERN, REV. H. A.

Wanderings among the Falashas in Abyssinia. London, 1862.

The Captive Missionary; being an Account of the Country and People of Abyssinia. London, 1868.

STEWART, COL.

Report on the Sudan. Egypt, 1883, No. 11. 1883.

STUART, H. W. V.

Egypt after the War. London, 1883.

STUHLMANN, DR. F.

Mit Emin Pasha ins Herz von Afrika. Berlin, 1894.

SUDAN, THE.

Report on the Egyptian Province of the Soudan. London, 1883.

The True Prophet in the Soudan. London, 1885.

Deux Campagnes au Soudan Français, 1886-1888. Paris, 1891.

Sudan Almanac. Cairo.

Sudan Gazette. Published monthly by authority of the Sudan Government. Cairo. First issue—March 7th, 1899.

SUDAN, THE (*continued*).

Sudan Campaign, by "An Officer." London, 1899.

Sudan Ordinances. See the List in Count Gleichen's *Handbook*, 2nd ed., Vol. I., p. 341, and in the *Sudan Gazette.*

SUDAN WAR.

Lives and Adventures of Heroes of the Soudan War. London, 1887.

SUDAN AND ABYSSINIA, THE.

A Visit to an Abyssinian Robber at home. Blackwood's Magazine, Oct., 1884, No. 828, pp. 481-497.

SWAYNE, H. G. C.

Seventeen Trips through Somaliland. London, 1903.

TABARIE, M.

C. G. Gordon le défenseur de Khartoum. Paris, 1886.

TAVERNA, E.

Le service du train dans la campagne des Anglais en Abyssinie. Paris, 1897.

TAYLOR, B.

Life and Landscape from Egypt to the Negro Kingdoms of the White Nile. London, 1854.

Eine Reise nach Central Afrika. Leipzig, 1855.

TEISSEIRE, R.

Marchand et la Question du Haut-Nil. Société de Géog. de Marseille, Nov. 1898.

TELLEZ, B.

The Travels of the Jesuits in Ethiopia. A New Collection of Voyages and Travels, Vol. VII. London, 1708-10.

TELLIER, L. H.

Etude Soudanaise. Paris, 1902.

TEYNARD, F.

Egypte et Nubie. Sites et monuments les plus intéressants pour l'étude de l'art et de l'histoire. 2 pts. Paris, 1858.

THEVENOT, JEAN.

Voyages de Thévenot en Europe, Asie, et Afrique, etc. Paris, 1664-1674.

THIERSCH, H. W. F.

Abyssinia. London, 1885.

THOMSON, JOSEPH.

In the Heart of Africa. From the Equator to the Pole. 1887.

To the Central African Lakes and back, 1878-1880. London, 1881.

Through Masailand. London, 1887.

THRUSTON, A. B.

African Incidents (Egypt and Unyoro). London, 1900.

TINNE, JOHN A.

Geographical Notes of an Expedition in Central Africa by three Dutch Ladies. Liverpool, 1864.

TRAILL, H. D.

From Cairo to the Sudan Frontier. London, 1896.

England, Egypt, and the Sudan. London, 1900.

TREATIES.

Treaties between the United Kingdom and Ethiopia, and between the United Kingdom, Italy, and Ethiopia, relative to the Frontiers between the Soudan, Ethiopia, and Eritrea. London, Treaty Series, No. 16, 1902.

TREMAUX, P.

Rapport sur le Voyage au Soudan Oriental. Paris, 1853.

Voyage en Ethiopie, au Soudan Oriental, et dans la Nigritie. Paris, 1862.

TREVISAN, D.

Le Voyage . . . auprès du Soudan d'Egypte. See Schefer, Recueil de Voyages, 1882.

TROTHA, T. W. VON.

Meine Bereisung von Deutsche Ostafrika. Berlin, 1897.

TUDELA, BENJAMIN (RABBI).

Reize in de jaren 1160-73 *door Europa, Azie, en Afrika.* (S. Keyser.) Leyden, 1846.

TURAIEV, B.

Monumenta Aethiopiae Hagiologica. St. Petersburg, 1902.

TWYFORD, A. W.

Notes relative to the proposed Expedition to discover the Sources of the White Nile. Proc. Roy. Geo. Soc., 1857.

UHLIG, C.

Expedition in Ostafrika. Petermann, Geo. Mitt., 1904.

ULE, OTTO.

Sahara und Sudan. Halle, 1861.

VALBERT, G.

Le Chemin de Fer du Soudan et les Trois Campagnes du Colonel Borquis-Desbordes. Revue des Deux Mondes, Vol. LIX., 1883.

VALENTIA, VISCOUNT.

Drafts and copies of papers relating to the History and Geography of India, Egypt, and Abyssinia. Collected by Viscount Valentia. (British Museum, Add. MSS. No. 19,348.)

Voyages and Travels to India, Ceylon, the Red Sea, and Abyssinia in 1802-6. 4 vols. London, 1809.

VANDELEUR, LIEUT. C. F. S.

Two Years' Travel in Uganda. Jour. Roy. Geog. Soc., 1897, Vol. IX., 369.

Campaigning on the Upper Nile and Niger. London, 1898.

VANDERHEYM, J. G.

Une expédition avec le Negous Menelik. Paris, 1897.

VAN DEVENTER, DR. L. W.

Les Anglais à la Découverte des Sources du Nil. De Gids, Sept., 1869.

VAN GHISTELE, J.

Voyage in landen . . . Arabien, Egypten, Ethiopien, Barbarien, etc. Gand, 1557.

VARTHEMA, L. [VERTOMANUS.]

Itinerario de L. di Varthema. Venetia, 1517.

The Travels of L. di Varthema, A.D. 1503-8. *Translated by* J. WINTER JONES. Hakluyt Soc., 1863.

Navigation and Voyages of L Vertomanus to the regions of Arabia, Egypt, Persia, Ethiopia, and East Indies. Translated by R. EDEN. Paris, 1577.

VAUCELLE, L.

Chronologie des Monuments antiques de la Nubie, etc. Paris, 1829.

VEITCH, SOPHIE F. F.

Views in Central Abyssinia. London, 1868.

VENTRE PASHA.

Hydrologie du Bassin du Nil. Bull. Soc. Geog. Khed., 1894.

Crues Modernes et Crues Anciennes du Nil. Zeit. f. Aegypt. Sprache, Bd. 34, 1896.

VERNER, CAPT. W.

Sketches in the Soudan. London, 1886.

VIGNE D'OCTON, P.

Terre de Mort—Soudan. Paris, 1892.

VIGNERAS, S.

Une Mission française en Abyssinie. Paris, 1897.

VIGNOLI, T.

Intelligenz im Thierreiche. Leipzig, 1879.

VILLOTEAU, G. A.

De l'Etat Actuel de l'Art Musical en Egypte. Paris, 1812.

VINGTRINIER, A.

Le Soudan Egyptien hier et aujourdhui. Revue du Monde Latin, Mars, 1884.

VIVAREZ, M.

Le Soudan Algérien. Paris, 1890.

VIVIAN, H.

Abyssinia. London, 1901.

VIVIEN DE ST. MARTIN, L.

Le Nord de l'Afrique dans l'Antiquité Grecque et Romaine. Paris, 1863.

Géog. génér. de l'Abyssinie. 1868.

VOGEL, DR. E.

Reise nach Central Afrika, 1853-4. Mitteilungen aus Justus Perthes Geographischer Anstalt, etc. Gotha, 1855.

VOLNEY, C.

Voyage en Syrie et en Egypte pendant les années 1783-1785. 2 Tom. Paris, 1787.

Travels through Syria and Egypt in the Years 1783-1785. 2 vols. London, 1787.

Recherches Nouvelles sur l'Histoire Ancienne. Paris, 1814.

VOSS, I.

Dissertation touchant l'origine du Nil et autres fleuves, etc. Paris, 1667.

VOSSION, L.

Khartoum et le Soudan d'Egypte. Paris, 1890.

VOYAGES AND TRAVELS.

A collection compiled from the library of the late Earl of Oxford. London, 1745.

Premier voyage à la recherche des Sources du Bahr-al-Abiad. Bull. Soc. Géog. Paris, 1840.

Relation de voyage sur le Fleuve Blanc, le Bahr-el-Chasal, le Sobatat . . . notice sur les trois variétés de la Tribu des Gniam-Gniam. Bulletin de l'Institut Egyptien, No. 6, 1862.

Extrait du Journal de voyage des Missionaires d'Alger aux Grands Lacs de l'Afrique équatoriale. Alger, 1879.

Le Jeune Voyageur en Egypte et en Nubie. Paris.

VUGLIANO, C.

Gli ultimi avvenimenti de Sudan. Frosinone, 1891.

WADDINGTON, REV. G., and HANBURY, REV. B.

Journal of a visit to some parts of Ethiopia. London, 1822.

WAGHORN, LIEUT. T., R.N.

Egypt as it is in 1837. London, 1837.

WAITE, P. C.

The Annual Rise and Fall of the Nile. Scot. Geog. Mag., 1904, Pt. II.

WAITZ, T.

Anthropologie der Naturvölker. Tom. 2. Leipzig, 1859-72.

WALDMEYER, TH.

Ten years in Abyssinia. London, 1886.

Ten years with King Theodorus in Abyssinia and sixteen in Syria. London, 1889.

WALKENAER, BARON C. A.

Recherches Géographiques sur l'Intérieur de l'Afrique Septentrionale. Paris, 1821.

Collection de relations de voyages par mer et par terre en différentes parties de l'Afrique, depuis 1400 *jusqu' à nos jours.* 21 vols. Paris, 1826-31.

WALKER, F. A.

Nine Hundred Miles up the Nile. London, 1884.

WALLER, H.

Livingstone: last journals in Central Africa. London, 1880.

WALLNER, F.

Hundert Tage auf dem Nil. Reisebilder aus Unter- und Ober-Aegypten und Nubien. Berlin, 1873.

WANSLEBEN, J. M.

A brief account of the rebellions and bloodshed occasioned by the anti-Christian practices of the Jesuits . . . in the Empire of Ethiopia. London, 1679.

WARD, J.

Our Sudan: its Pyramids and Progress. London, 1905.

WATKINS, O. S.

With Kitchener's Army: a Chaplain's experiences with the Nile Expedition. London, 1899.

WATSON, COL. SIR C. M.

Comparative vocabularies of the languages spoken at Suakin. London, 1868.
Notes to accompany a Traverse Survey of the White Nile from Khartoum to Rigaf. Jour. Roy. Geog. Soc., Vol. XLVI., 1877.

WATSON and CHIPPENDALL.

Survey of the White Nile. Cairo, 1874.

WEILL, R.

Recueil des Inscriptions Egyptiennes du Sinai. Paris, 1904.

WELLBY, M. S.

King Menelik's Dominions. London, 1900.
Twixt Sirdar and Menelik. London, 1901.

WEMMERS, J.

Lexicon Aethiopicum. Rome, 1638.

WERNE, F.

Expedition to discover the Sources of the White Nile, 1840-1841. 2 vols. London, 1849.

Feldzug von Sennaar nach Taka, Basa und Beni Amer, etc. Stuttgart, 1851.

African Wanderings: or, an Expedition from Sennaar to Taka, Base and Beni Amer. Translated by J. B. JOHNSTON. London, 1852.
Die Völker Ost Sudan.

WERNER, A.

Native Races of British Central Africa. London, 1906.

WERNER, C.

C. Werner's Nile Sketches, painted from nature during his travels through Egypt. London, 1871.

WHARTON, R.

Observations on Bruce's Travels. Newcastle-upon-Tyne, 1800.

WHITE, A. S.

The Development of Africa. London, 1892.

The Expansion of Egypt. London, 1899.

WIEDEMANN, A.

Aegyptische Geschichte von den ältesten Zeiten bis zum Tode Tutmes III. Gotha, 1884, 1888.

L'Ethiopie au Temps de Tibère. Le Muséon, Tome III., 1884, p. 117 ff. Louvain.

WILFORD, F.

On Egypt and other countries adjacent to the Cali river, or Nile of Ethiopia, from the ancient books of the Hindus. Asiatic Researches, Vol. III., 1807.

WILKINS, H. ST. CLAIR.

Reconnoitring in Abyssinia. London, 1870.

WILKINSON, SIR J. G.

Remarks on the country between Wady Halfeh and Gebel Berkel in Ethiopia. Journal Royal Geog. Society, Vol. XX., 1850.

WILLCOCKS, SIR W.

Perennial Irrigation. Cairo, 1894.

Egyptian Irrigation. London, 1899.

The Aswan Dam and after. London, 1901.

The Nile in 1904. London, 1904.

WILLIAMS, C.

How we lost Gordon. The Fortnightly Review, May, 1885.

WILLIAMS, DR. J.

Life in the Soudan. Adventures amongst the tribes, and travels in Egypt in 1881-1882. London, 1884.

WILLIAMS, REV. R. O.

North Africa, Physical, Historical, and Ethnological. University Quarterly, Vols. XXV.—XXX.

WILSON, REV. C. T., and FELKIN, R. W.

Uganda and the Egyptian Soudan. Stuttgart, 1883.

WILSON, SIR C. W.

What is to be done with the Soudan? The Asiatic Quarterly, April, 1886.

From Korti to Khartoum. London, 1886.

WILSON, CAPT. H. H.

A Trip up the Khor Filus and country on the left of the Sobat. Jour. Roy. Geog. Soc., 1902.

WILSON, R.

Voyages. 3 vols. London, 1806.

WINGATE, SIR F. R.

Mahdiism and the Egyptian Sudan. London, 1891.

The Sudan Past and Present. Minutes of Proceedings of the Royal Artillery Institution, Woolwich, 1892, Vol. XIX., p. 675 ff.

The Fate of the Sudan. Edinburgh Review, 1892, Vol. CLXXV., p. 232 ff.

The Rise and Wane of the Mahdi Religion in the Sudan. Proceedings of the Oriental Congress, 1892, p. 339 ff.

The Siege and Fall of Khartoum. United Service Magazine, 1892, p. 406 ff.

WINGATE, SIR F. R., and FATHER OHRWALDER.

Ten years' captivity in the Mahdi's Camp. London, 1892.

WINSTANLEY, W.

A visit to Abyssinia. London, 1881.

WOLFF, H., and BLACHERE, A.

Sahara et Soudan. Les Régiments de Dromadaires. Paris, 1884.

WOLVERTON, LORD.

Five months' Sport in Somaliland. London, 1894.

WOUVERMANS, H.

Les Sources du Nil. Bulletin de la Société Géog., Anvers, 1877.

WRIGHT, H. C. S.

Soudan '96. The Adventures of a War Artist. London, 1897.

WRIGHT, PROF. W.

Catalogue of the Ethiopic MSS. in the British Museum. London, 1877.

WYCHE, SIR P.

A Short Relation of the River Nile, of its Source and Current. London, 1673.

WYLDE, A. B.

'83 to '87 in the Sudan. London, 1888.

Modern Abyssinia. London, 1901.

WYNDHAM-QUIN, W. T.

The Soudan, its History, Geography, and Characteristics. A lecture. London, 1884.

YOUNG, T., M.D.

Observations on . . . some sepulchral inscriptions from Nubia. Archaeologia, Vol. XIX., 1819.

ZAIN-EL-ABIDIN.

Das Buch des Sudan. Aus d. Türk. übersetzt von G. ROSEN. Leipzig, 1847.

ZOEPPRITZ, C.

E. de Pruyssenaeres Reisen und Forschungen im Gebiete des Weissen und Blauen Nil. Petermanns Mitt. Erg., Gotha, 1877. No. 51.

Watson's und Chippendall's Aufnahme des Weissen Nil von Chartum bis Rigaf und Junker's Aufnahme des Sobat. Petermanns Mitteilungen, V.

ZOTENBERG, H.

Catalogue des MSS. de la Bibl. Nat. Fonds Ethiop. Paris, 1877.

ZURBUCHEN, J.

Reise nach Chartum, durch Kordofan und Darfur, 1879. Tagebuchblätter, Petermanns Mitt., Bd. 30. 1884.

ZWERG, A. W.

De Pygmaeis Aethiopiae populis dissertatio. Kiliae, 1727.

MAPS.

The best and most modern maps of the Sûdân are those of the ORDNANCE SURVEY, which are issued by the Director of Surveys of the Sûdân Government. Each map covers 1° of latitude, and 1½° of longitude. The scale is 4 miles to the inch. Price 1s. 6*d*. each. Published by the Intelligence Department, War Office.

INDEX

Àāḥ, Moon-god, i. 621, 624.
Aah-al-Kkr, ii. 439.
Àāḥmes I., i. 561; in the Sûdân, i. 562.
Àāḥmes, Queen, i. 623.
Àāḥmes-nefert-àri, i. 564.
Aala, i. 563.
Āamu, i. 505, 600; ii. 415, 416.
Āamu-ḥeru-shā, i. 517.
Āa-shāmu (?), i. 383.
Ab, i. 630.
Abâ Island, ii. 376, 434, 438.
Abâbda, ii. 407.
'Abâbdah, i. 496; ii. 417, 435.
'Abâbdah Arabs, i. 235.
Ababdo, ii. 444.
'Abâi, or Blue Nile, i. 19; ii. 362.
Abâi River, ii. 359.
Abala, ii. 160.
Âbâr, ii. 437.
Abaton, ii. 74.
'Abâwî, ii. 364.
'Abây, ii. 364.
Abbâ Island, ii. 242, 243.
'Abbâs Agha, i. 294.
'Abbâs Pâshâ, ii. 84, 218.
'Abbâs, steamer, ii. 250.
'Abbâs, Sultân, ii. 265.
'Abbâs, uncle of the Prophet ii. 435, 437.
'Abbâsîya Gadîda, ii. 376.
Abbeloos and Lamy, ii. 295.
'Abd- a Ḥalîm Pâshâ, ii. 220, 263.
'Abd al-Ḳâder, ii. 201.
'Abd al-Ḳâder II., ii. 201.
'Abd al-Ḳâder, Dervish, ii. 250.
'Abd al-Ḳâder Hilmy, ii. 239.
'Abd al-Ḳâder Pâshâ, ii. 244, 245.
'Abd al-Ḳâder (Slatin Pâshâ), ii. 246.
'Abd al-Ḳûrna, i. 573.
'Âbdallâb, ii. 436, 438.
'Abd Allah, ii. 436.
'Abd Allah, father of the Mahdî, ii. 241.
'Abd Allah At-Ta'âishî the Khalîfa, i. 213; ii. 260.
'Abd-Allah bin Sa'd, ii. 184, 185; Treaty of, ii. 186.
'Abd Allah Gemâ'a, ii. 200, 204.
'Abd Allah II. ibn 'Agîl, ii. 204.
'Abd Allah ibn Isma'îl, ii. 188.
'Abd Allah ibn Jahân, ii. 187.
'Abd Allah ibn Sanbu, ii. 196.
'Abd Allah III. Wâd 'Agîb, ii. 204.
'Abd Allah IV. Wâd 'Agîb, ii. 204.
'Abd-Allâh Wâd al-Ḥasan, ii. 396.
'Abd Allah Wâd Sa'ud, ii. 272.
'Âbdallât Shêkhs, ii. 204.
'Abd Al-Magîd, i. 96; ii. 260, 261.
'Abd al-Malik ibn Mûsa ibn Nâṣir, ii. 192.
'Abd ar-Raḥmân I. of Dâr Fûr, ii. 206.
'Abd ar-Raḥmân II., ii. 206.
'Abd ar-Raḥmân ibn 'Abd Allah, ii. 191.
'Abd as-Salâm, ii. 205.
Abeken, H., i. 62.
Abhat, country of, i. 518.
Àbhat, i. 605.
Àbhet, i. 612.
Abidîya, ii. 473.
Abka, ii. 261.
Abkûlgui, i. 44, 47.
Abnàheir, ii. 400.
Abok, ii. 441.
Abraham, i. 224, 464.
Abri, i. 444.
'Abri, ii. 371.
Àbskhent, ii. 95.
Ābu, i. 515, 519, 530, 533; ii. 394.
Abu Acmet, i. 313.
Abû Adel, ii. 280.
Abû Anga, ii. 261, 263, 264.
'Abûd, ii. 438.
Abû Dalêḳ, ii. 272.
Abû Dîs, ii. 473.
Abû Dôm Ḳashâbî, ii. 372.
Abû Dôm Ṣanam, ii. 373.
Abû Dulêḳ, i. 254; ii. 407, 439.
Abû Fâṭma, ii. 409.
Abû Gamêza, ii. 262, 263.
Abû Garâs, ii. 300.
Abû Garîd, ii. 430.
Abû Ḥ gâr, ii. 436.
Abû Ḥamed, i. 55, 59, 61, 62, 70, 76, 85, 100, 103, 104, 106, 113, 115, 184, 233, 253, 294, 470, 496, 497, 509, 549; ii. 93, 247, 252, 259, 261, 373, 458, 461, 467, 468.
——, baths at, ii. 472.

INDEX

Abû Ḥamed, capture by General Hunter, ii. 272.
——, capture of, i. 191.
——, desert, i. 244.
Abû Ḥamed-Karêma Railway, ii. 479.
Abû Ḥarâz, ii. 125, 126, 244, 365, 436, 437.
Abû Hashîm, ii. 396.
Abû Ḳassi, ii. 372.
Abukaya, ii. 424.
Abû Khrûg, ii. 253.
Abû Kirga, ii. 266.
Abû Klea, ii. 252, 257.
——, wells of, i. 110.
——, stern-wheeler, i. 99, 100, 102.
Abû Kûkâ, ii. 380
Abû Ḳûs, Abû Ḳussî, i. 107.
Abu'l Ḳâsim, ii 206.
Abûlay, i. 58.
Abû Maryâm, ii. 267.
Abû Na'âma, ii. 396.
Abû Nâga, i. 57.
Abuncis, ii. 168.
Abû Raḳwa, ii. 191.
Abû Ṣâliḥ, ii. 191, 192, 290, 298, 299, 302-4.
Abû Sa'ûd, ii. 228, 229.
Abû Sa'ûd Al-'Aḳâd, ii. 233.
Abû Sillem, ii. 473.
Abû Simbel, i. 39, 40, 53, 80, 81, 466, 507, 625, 636 ff., 640, 651; ii. 74, 75, 113, 264, 297.
——, temple of, i. 633.
Abû Ṣîr, Rock of, i. 53, 549; ii. 370.
Abû Ṭâlib, ii. 241.
Abû Ṭaliḥ, i. 99.
Abû Ṭlêḥ, ii. 252, 257, 392.
Abû Udân, ii 214.
Abû Ushar, ii. 431.
Abû Zêd, ii. 439, 458.
——, ford of, ii. 376.
Abydos, i. 54, 61, 251, 358, 386, 526, 538, 643, 652.
Abyssinia, i. 18, 20, 23, 31, 44, 47, 48, 105, 179, 507; ii. 105, 201, 203. 238, 254, 290, 298, 349, 368, 398.
Abyssinians, i. 5, 6, 7, 9, 10, 12, 21, 85, 216, 432; ii. 73, 213, 214, 231, 234, 261, 268.
—— eat raw meat, i. 18.
Acetuma, ii. 160.
Achwa, ii. 357, 386.
Acina, i. 543; ii. 162, 172.
Acridophagi, ii. 156.
Acug, ii. 160,
Adabuli, ii. 164.
Adam, i. 224, 464.
Adâm, religious impostor, ii. 285.
Adams, Mr., i. 248.
Adârama, i. 254; ii. 272, 273, 400.
Adarlâ, ii. 205.
Addà, i. 637; ii. 399.
Ad-Dâmar, i. 31, 250, 502; ii. 272, 473.
Addax, ii. 391.
Ad-Dîn, Shêkh, ii. 275, 276.
Ad-Dui, ii. 443.
Aden, ii. 190.
Adiabari, ii. 164.
Adila, ii. 265.
Adis Ababa, ii. 284.
Adjonaro, ii. 361.
'Adlân, ii. 212.
'Adlân II., ii. 203.
'Adlân ibn Aba, ii. 201.
'Âdlânâb, ii, 439.
Adramîya, ii. 364.
Adua (Aduwa), i. 85; ii. 234, 268.
Adulis, ii. 417.
Adûr, ii. 195.
Ægipa, ii. 164.
Ægipans, ii. 165, 175.
Aegis, i. 306.
Ælian, i. 522.
Ælius Gallus, ii. 167.
Æmilianus, M. J., ii. 175.
Aetheria, ii. 163.
Afafit, ii. 265.
Africa, i. 57, 76.
African Association, i. 29, 32, 33.
Africans, ii. 155.
Agam Deldi, ii. 359, 364.
——, Bridge of, ii. 363.
Agâr, ii. 428.
Agar Dinkas, ii. 282.
Agars, ii. 284.
Agatharcides, ii. 155, 340, 342.
Aggeh, i. 442.
Aghâ, i. 463.
Aghûrdat, ii. 266, 267.
'Agîb, ii. 202, 204.
'Agîb ibn 'Abd-Allah, ii. 204.
'Agîl, ii. 202, 204.
Agiung Twi, ii. 320.
Agole, ii. 160.
Agows, i. 20.
Agriculture, ii. 483.
——, at 'Amâra, i. 467.
Agriophagi, ii. 165.
Agrippa, M., ii. 165.
Agrospi, ii. 164.
Agwei, ii. 361.
Aḥâmada, ii. 436.
Āḥatiu-en-ḥeq, i. 565.
Ahlylej, ii. 181.
Aḥmad, ii. 206.
Aḥmad al-Ghazâlî, ii. 284.
Aḥmad 'Alî, ii. 266.
Aḥmad al-Makâshif, ii. 244, 245.
Aḥmad al-Makûr, ii. 422.
Aḥmad al-Maniklî, ii. 217.
Aḥmad Ash-Sharif, ii. 284.
Aḥmad Bakr, ii. 206.
Aḥmad Bey Khalîfa, i. 104.
Aḥmad Effendi Hadayat, ii. 494.
Aḥmad Faḍîl, ii. 280, 400.
Ahmad Ḥamad, ii. 499.
Aḥmad Hamza, ii. 404.
Aḥmad ibn Solaim, ii. 191.
Aḥmad, king of Harar, ii. 231.
Aḥmad of Derr, i. 442.
Aḥmad Pâshâ, ii. 214.
Aḥmad Shêkh, ii. 285.
Aḥmad Shêkh Aghâ, ii. 228.
Aḥmad Sîd al-Kôm, i. 10.
Ài, king, i. 625.
Aihetàb, i. 612.
Aikhentka, ii. 95.
Aina, well of, i. 641.
'Ain Ḥâmid, ii. 392.
Aithiops, ii. 163.

INDEX

Ai-Yak, ii. 441.
Ajak wâd Deng, ii. 499.
Ajang, ii. 444.
Ajibir, ii. 361.
Ajung, ii. 444.
Aḳâl, ii. 226.
Akaita, i. 632, 638.
'Aḳalyûn, ii. 436.
Akanyaru, ii. 352, 387.
Akaritha, i. 612
Akarkarḥent, ii. 95.
Akâsha, i. 86, 90, 92, 93, 94. 459.
'Aḳba Ḳurra, ii 437.
Aken, i. 543, 612.
Akhenthek, i. 612.
Akherkiu, i. 536.
Akhmîm, ii. 191.
'Aḳîḳ, ii. 435.
Akita, i. 549, 612, 643.
Akka, i. 525.
Akobo, ii. 361.
Akoj, ii. 444.
Akol, ii. 444.
Akoli, ii. 399.
Akremi Arabs, ii. 197, 198.
Aksha, i. 637, 638.
Aksomye, ii. 180.
Aktamûr, ii. 197.
Akwot, ii. 444.
'Ala Ad-Dîn Pâshâ, ii. 239.
Al-A'alâm, i. 551.
Alabastronpolis, i. 518.
Aladi, ii. 164.
Al-Afiâm, ii. 194.
Al-Âganib, ii. 439.
Al-Amîn Wâd Mismâr, ii. 204.
Alana, ii. 160.
'Alâṭiyûn, ii. 436.
Albâk, ii. 392.
Al-Ballâli, ii. 232.
Albanians, ii. 210.
Al-Barghûth, Shêkh, ii. 474.
Al-Baṣra, i. 471.
Alberti, ii. 422.
Albertine Rift Valley, ii. 352.
Albert N'yanza discovered, ii. 222.
Al-Debba, i. 107.
Aldrovandia, ii. 481.
Al-'Êlafûn, ii. 250.
Aleppo, i. 30, 604.
Alexander the Great, ii. 108.
Alexandria, i. 18, 62; ii. 157, 167, 168, 184, 210, 218.
——, Church of, ii. 288.
——, Library, ii. 347.
Al-Fâsher, ii. 246, 249, 262, 263, 391, 398, 430, 434, 436.
Al-Fûḳa'i, ii. 6.
Al-Gabarta, ii. 440.
Al-Ghuzz, ii. 207, 210.
Al-Ḥadûr, ii. 439.
Al-Ḥalabât, ii. 440.
Alî, Ḥaggi, i. 1.
'Alî of Tunis, ii. 422.
Aliâb, ii. 273, 473.
Aliab Dok, ii. 380.
Aliab tribe, ii. 381.
'Ali Abd Al-Karîm, ii. 281.
'Alî Aghâ, ii. 210.
'Alî Bâbâ, ii. 190,
'Alî Bey, ii. 209, 227.
'Alî Bey Satfi, ii. 244.
'Alí Dînâr, ii. 249, 282, 284, 398.
Al-Idrîsî, ii. 329.
'Alî Effendi, ii. 243.
'Alî Ga'alan, ii. 435.
'Alî Mûrghânî, ii. 373.
'Alî Pâshâ Sharkas, ii. 218.
Alî Pâshâ Sirri, ii. 218.
Al-'Irâḳ, ii. 209.
Alî Shalabi, i. 8.
Al-Islâm, i. 224.
'Alî Wâd Helu, ii. 275, 276, 280.
'Aliya, ii. 303.
Al-Ḳân, i. 532.
Al-Ḳaṣr, ii. 185, 188, 189.
Al-Ḳatêna, ii. 375.
Al-Ḳef, ii. 408.
Al-Kharṭûm, i. 42.
Al-Kirmân, i. 51.
Al-Ḳôz, ii. 473.
Al-Kurêshî, Shekh, ii. 242.
Al-Lâhûn, i. 551; ii. 7, 18.
Allan, Adriana, i. 18.
Al-Makhêrif, i. 114.
Al-Ma'mûn, ii. 298.
Al-Mângalûk, ii. 204.
Al-Maṣawwarât, i. 47.
Al-Mêga, ii. 473.
Almkvist, ii. 445, 502.
Al-Mutawakkil, ii. 189.
Aloa, ii. 182.
Al-Obêḍ, ii. 213, 217, 244, 245, 246, 281, 284, 375, 396, 479, 488, 509.
Al-Obêḍ, Shêkh, ii. 250.
Al-Ordi, i. 103; ii. 372.
Altakû, ii. 34, 35.
Altar at Wâd Bâ Nagaa, i. 287.
——, Meroïtic, i. 433.
Âlu-Âmen, Pyramid of, i. 382.
Al-Ubayyaḍ, ii. 213.
Alum, i. 217; ii. 412.
——, Oasis, ii. 412.
Al-Ûrdî, ii. 297.
Aluro, ii. 360.
Âlut, ii. 89, 303.
Alvarez, Father F., ii. 304, 307, 349.
'Alwa, i. 324; ii. 186, 199, 288, 303, 306.
Alwah, ii. 89, 98.
Al-Walîd ibn Hishâm al-Khâriji, ii. 191.
Amâda, i. 14, 458, 574, 598, 604, 629, 643, 651; ii. 297.
——, temple of Thothmes III. at, i. 599.
——, temple of Âmen-ḥetep II. at, i. 599.
Amadi, ii. 282.
Amadib, ii. 260.
Amai, ii. 196.
Amam, i. 2, 517, 518, 520, 521, 526.
Aman, i. 534, 536.
Amana, i. 524.
'Amâra, i. 60, 62, 444, 637, 651; ii. 110, 116, 119, 120, 122, 134, 170, 261, 371.
——, Cataract of, ii. 366.
——, excavations at, i. 468.
——, temple of, i. 467.

INDEX

'Amâra, on White Nile, ii. 375.
'Amâra Dunkas, ii. 200.
'Amâra ibn Sakâkîn, ii. 201.
Amasis, i. 426.
Amasis, a general of Psammetichus II., ii. 74.
Amasis I., i. 562.
Amasis II., i. 425; ii. 90, 91.
Amasis, son of Baba, the general i. 562, 563, 564, 565, 566, 567.
Amasis, son of Pen-nekheb, i. 563, 564, 565, 570.
Amathel, ii. 57.
Amather, i. 149.
Amazons, i. 23.
Ambadî, ii. 205.
'Ambasa, ii, 189.
Ambatch, ii. 173.
Ambikôl (Ambigôl), ii. 372.
——, Cataract of, ii. 366.
——, Road, i. 91.
——, Wells, i. 90, 91, 246, 438, 472; ii. 261, 270, 462, 464.
Āmemit, i. 370.
Åmen, i. 30, 67, 306, 368, 400, 561, 572, 584, 587, 599, 620, 622, 636, 637, 648; ii. 4, 5, 6, 7, 13, 15, 17, 19, 20, 21, 33, 41, 42, 49, 51, 52, 56, 58, 65, 76, 108, 112, 131, 135, 136.
——, College of, founded, i. 623.
——, double form of, ii. 3.
——, fame of, dwindles, i. 652.
——, festival of, ii. 15.
——, of Gebel Barkal, i. 143.
——, of Napata, i. 134, 137, 358; ii. 87, 95, 96, 143.
——, of Pa-Nebes, ii. 89.
——, of Pa-Qem, ii. 89.
——, of Tarukhet(?)-reset, ii. 79.
——, of Thebes, i. 358; ii. 143.
——, priests of, at Meroë, ii. 109; fly to Napata, i. 651, 652; memorial services of, i. 649; usurp royal powers, i. 645.
Amen, Ram of, i. 617, 618.
——, Ram sacred to, i. 597.
——, the Nubian, ii. 1.
——, two forms of, at Gebel Barkal, ii. 46.
Åmen-åbṭi, ii. 82, 83.
Åmen-Ār, Pyramid of, i. 357.
Åmen-Ārit (or, Ṭārit), i. 365; ii. 117.
——, Pyramid of, i. 357.
Åmen-Årq(ark)-neb, ii. 118.
——, Pyramid of, i. 425.
Åmenårṭās, ii. 28, 30, 33.
Åmen-åsru, i. 625.
——, lion usurped by, i. 618.
Åmen-em-åpt, prince of Kash, i. 630; ii. 326.
Åmen-em-ḥāt I., i. 553; ii. 19, 328.
——, in the Sûdân, i. 532, 534.
Åmen-em-ḥāt II., i. 539, 553.
——, in the Sûdân, i. 538.
Åmen-em-ḥāt III., in the Sûdân, i. 549, 554.
Amen-em-ḥāt IV., i. 552, 555, 573.
Åmen-ḥer-khepesh-f, i. 636.
Åmen-ḥer-unemi-f, ii. 325, 326.
Åmen-ḥetep I., i. 62?, 648, 649.
——, in the Sûdân, i. 564-567.
Åmen-ḥetep II., i. 463, 597, 598, 604, 616, 627; ii. 2, 124, 332.
——, brings seven dead kings to Egypt, i. 598.
——, temple of, at 'Amâda, i. 599.
—— ——, at Behen, i. 601.
——, travels of, i. 602.
Åmen-ḥetep III., i. 61, 67, 445, 448, 449, 454, 462, 480, 605ff, 630; ii. 45, 170, 334, 371.
Åmen-ḥetep IV., i. 607, 622; ii. 332.
Åmen-ḥetep, a priest, i. 604.
Åmen-ḥetep, high priest, i. 644.
Åmeni, i. 535, 536.
——, inscription of, i. 481.
——, stele of, i. 548.
Åmeni-em-ḥāt, i. 534, 553.
Åmeni of Menāt-Khufu, i. 534.
Åmen-ka-Ānkh, i. 362.
Åmen-khetashen, ii. 119.
——, pyramid of, i. 407.
Åmen-meri-Åsru, pyramid of, i. 419 ff.
Åmen-netek, pyramid of, i. 412.
Åmen-Rā. i. 137, 164, 427, 451, 587, 588, 591, 597, 605, 612, 618, 621, 624, 625, 626, 630, 633, 634, 635, 644, 651; ii. 8, 18, 33, 42, 45, 49, 57, 62, 63, 66, 70, 79, 106, 122.
——, temple of, at Semna, i. 482.
——, of Redesîya, i. 628, 629.
Åmen-Rā-khu-Åten, ii. 45.
Åmen-ruṭ-meri-Åmen, ii. 51.
Amen-Shipalta, Pyramid of, i. 373.
Åmen-Tahnamamip, ii. 119.
Åmenṭaket, i. 137.
Åmen-tarhaknen, ii. 66.
Åmen-tari (Rā-mer-ka), ii. 119.
Åmen-tarit, i. 412; ii. 120, 122, 127, 140, 142.
——, temple of, ii. 130 ff.
Åmen-Ṭārit = Candace, the foe of Petronius (?), ii. 169, 170.
Amen-taui-Kalbath, ii. 117.
Åmentet, i. 400; ii. 11.
——, Souls of, i. 385.
Amenti, i. 369.
Amentiu gods, i. 385.
Amentogo, ii. 300.
American Mission, i. 281.
Amery, Captain H. F. S., i. 41; ii. 444, 460, 502.
Amḥârâ, ii. 364.

INDEX

Amharic, i. 8, 432.
——, Vocabulary, ii. 502.
Åmḥet, ii. 22.
Amîn ibn Nâṣer, ii. 204.
Amiro, i. 381.
Ammon the Monk, ii. 290.
Ammonium, i. 56, 57; ii. 149.
Amnah, Tale of, i. 235ff.
Amodita, ii. 160.
Amoibichos, ii. 74.
Amon Ship(?)alak, i. 374.
'Amr, a shêkh, ii. 204.
'Amr Bey, ii. 214.
'Amr I. of Dâr Fûr, ii. 206.
'Amr II. of Dâr Fûr, ii. 206.
'Amr ibn al-'Âṣî, i. 184; ii. 185, 193.
Amr ibn Shuraḥbîl, ii. 187.
Amsu, i. 368, 386, 599, 625.
Amtel, i. 149.
Amtes, queen, i. 516.
Amu-kehek, i. 565.
Amulets, i. 105, 215 ff., 222; ii. 23, 205.
Amu-neb-hek, i. 565.
Ån, ii. 11.
Anaks, ii. 175, 184, 436,
——, tombs, ii. 501.
Anba George, ii. 299.
Anbâ Khâ'îl, ii. 192.
Anba Yûsâb, ii. 298.
Andatis, ii. 164.
Andersson, ii. 422.
Andetae, ii. 164.
Androgalis, ii. 160.
Andromeda, ii. 161.
Anerua . . . ru, ii. 80.
Angrab River, i. 251.
Anhai, Papyrus of, i. 370.
Ån-Ḥer, i. 604; ii. 45, 82.
Åni, Prince of Kash, i. 637.
Aniba, i. 643.
Animals, mythical, ii. 149.
Ankâ, ii. 439.
Ankarab River, i. 19,
Anḳarîb, i. 109, 205.
Ānkh-Ḥeru, ii. 24.
Ānkh-ka-Rā, ii. 84, 117, 119, 120.
Ānkh-nefer-åb-Rā, ii. 118.
Ānkh-s-en-pa-Åten, i. 624.
Ankoli, ii. 352.
Ån-Mut-f, i. 588.
An-Nagûmî, ii. 252.
An-Nâṣir, ii. 196.
Annu, ii. 22.
An-Nûr, i. 496.
Anokal, ii. 203.
Ånpu, i. 358, 421.
Ānqet, i. 599, 626.
Ansa II., ii. 202.
Ansa III., ii. 203.
Ansûn, ii. 299.
Ånt, ii. 26.
Åntefa, i. 530.
Anthony, a friar, i. 6.
Anthony the Great, ii. 290.
Anthropophagi, ii. 165.
Anti (Hill men), i. 532, 571, 588, 598, 631; ii. 174, 305, 328, 416.
——, figures, ii. 22.
Anti, on Blue Nile, ii. 305.
Ånti of Ta-Kenset, i. 562, 563, 564, 569, 604, 628, 629.
Antimony, ii. 412.
Antinori, ii. 446.
Antiquarium at Munich, i. 299, 382.
Antoninus, Itinerary of, i. 633.
Anuaks, ii. 360, 424.
Anubis, i. 160, 301, 362, 367, 370, 385, 386, 389, 391, 392, 400, 404, 418. 432.
Ånuqet, i. 548, 556, 625, 630, 633, 637.
Ape of Khonsu, i. 370, 381.
Ape of Thoth, i. 36.
Apes, i. 571; ii. 109.
Åpet, i. 643.
Aphek, ii. 38.
Aphrodisiacs, i. 221.
Aphroditopolis, ii. 9, 12, 25.
Apis, i. 400.
Apollo, ii. 164.
Apple, bitter, i. 3.
Åp-she, ii. 18.
Åpt, Festival of, ii. 14.
Åpthethua, i. 613.
Åpts, the, ii. 13, 17, 19.
——, temple of, at Gebel Barkal, ii. 79.
Åp-uat, i. 358.
Aqabet, i. 568.
Åqen, i. 543.
Āqleq, ii. 35, 41, 42.
Äqreq, mother of Tirhakah, ii. 35.
Årà, father of Ḥer-khuf, i. 520.
Araba, ii. 164.
'Arab al-Bashir, ii. 436.
Arabeta, ii. 160.
Arab-Hag, ii. 300.
Arabia, i. 217; ii. 154, 158, 164, 170, 199, 225, 340.
Arabia Felix, ii. 167.
Arabians, ii. 53.
Arabic, ii. 490.
——, *graffiti*, i. 365, 404.
——, language, i. 30, 33; ii. 444.
'Arabi Dafa' Allah, ii. 284, 381.
'Arabi wâd Dafa' Allah, ii. 226.
Arabs, i. 10, 33, 34, 36, 40, 42, 57, 82, 252, 259, 506, 507, 510; ii. 90, 167, 184, 199, 221, 324.
—— in the Sûdân, ii. 421.
—— of Singue, i. 44.
—— tribes, ii. 436.
Arafât, i. 32.
Arakîl Bey, ii. 220, 234.
'Arâkîyûn, ii. 436.
Aramasos, ii. 160.
Arambo, i. 35.
Aramus, ii. 160.
Arbâb, ii. 202.
Arbagi, i. 21; ii. 204. 305.
Arba'în Road, ii. 391, 432, 458.
Archers, ii. 16.
Archisarmi, ii. 164.
Arduwân, ii. 371.
Arek, i. 605.
Arendrup, Col., ii. 234.
Årersa, ii. 95.
Arerthet, i. 521.

INDEX

Argîn, i. 77, 81, 82, 83, 90; ii. 263.
Ar-ḥes-nefer, ii. 112.
Ariel, herd of, i. 325.
Arimondi, Col., ii. 266.
Aristocreon, ii. 162, 164, 348.
Aristomachus, ii, 178.
Aristotle, i. 522; ii. 347.
Ari-Umker, ii. 443.
Arju hills, ii. 386.
Årk-Åmen, i. 426.
Årkaret, ii. 79.
Årk-atalal (?) ii. 119, 120.
Ark-teten (?) ii. 143.
Arkenkherel, ii. 117.
——, Pyramid of, i. 367.
Arkiko, i. 18.
Arḳô, colossal statues of, i. 41, 557; ii. 372.
Arḳô, island of, i. 3, 35, 36, 51, 60, 62, 103, 556, 559, 651; ii. 212, 372, 407, 479.
Armant, ii. 414.
Armbruster, Mr. Carl, ii. 299, 365, 502.
Armlets from Meroë, i. 299 ff.
Armstrong, Capt., ii. 284, 460.
Arnaud, Mr., i. 322.
Arnauts, ii. 210, 214.
Arnitti Island, i. 444, 466; ii. 291.
Arq-Amen, ii. 109, 112, 113, 114, 115, 154.
Arrows, i. 286.
—— poisoned, ii. 180.
—— stone-tipped, ii. 107.
Årrpakha, i. 613.
Arsinoë, ii. 111.
Årsu, the Syrian, i. 640, 641.
Arta, ii. 69.
Artabatitae, ii. 165.
Artaghâsi, Island of, i. 102.
Artatama, i. 604.
Artemidorus, ii. 155, 158, 162.
Arthet, i. 517, 518, 520, 534.
Articula, Island of, ii. 162.
Artomonoff, Col., ii. 361.
Årua, ii. 81.
Åru-Åmen, ii. 118.
Aruḳa . . . th, ii. 80.
Aruruk (?), i. 612.
Åruthnait, ii. 82.
Aryâb, ii. 392, 436.
Asachae, ii. 164.
A-Sande, ii. 424.
A-Sandî, ii. 432.
Asara, ii. 164.
Ascalon, ii. 24.
Aᵉel, ii. 164.
Aṣḥâba, ii. 372.
'Ashshânâb, ii. 435.
Ashur, ii. 41.
Ashur-bani-pal, i. 487; ii. 40, 41, 46, 52.
——, Annals, ii. 50, 51.
——, and Tanuath-Amen, ii. 50.
Asia, i. 562; ii. 16.
Asiatics, i. 505, 531.
Askam, ii. 55.
Askân, i, 51.
Asmakh, ii. 54, 106.
Asna, ii. 189, 357.
Asôsa, ii. 285.
Aṣotriba, ii. 478.
Aspelta, ii. 58-65.
Asru, i. 421-424, 427.
Asru-meri-Åmen, ii. 118.
Åssâ, king, i. 515, 523, 524, 532.
As-Samarkandî, ii. 201.
As-Senussi, Shêkh, ii. 284.
Asses, i. 508, 543.
——, caravan of, i. 520.
Assessors, the Forty-two, i. 369, 384.
Aṣ-Ṣufra, ii. 152.
Aṣ-Ṣûr, i. 287; ii. 38.
Aṣ-Ṣûr, Pyramids of, i. 41, 49, 435; ii. 402.
Aṣ-Ṣûr, village of, i. 55.
Assur-nadin-aḥi, ii. 332.
Assur-Uballiṭ, ii. 332.
Assyria, ii. 30, 34, 35, 37, 40.
Assyrians, i. 652; ii. 34, 38, 40, 41.
Åst, mother of Thothmes III., i. 571.
Astaboras, i. 31, 55; ii. 157, 159, 365.
Astapos, ii. 364.
Astapus, ii. 153, 157, 159.
Astasobas, ii. 157, 359.
Åst-em-khebit, i. 648.
Åstersat, ii. 88.
Asua River, ii. 357, 386.
Asuru, i. 613.
Aswân, i. 3, 13, 21, 22, 23, 26, 27, 29, 31. 38, 53, 62, 64, 65, 68, 69, 78, 105, 463, 520, 530 639, 640; ii. 104, 105, 185, 187, 188, 191, 197, 198, 199, 207, 268, 289, 290, 328, 366, 394.
——, map of, i. 66.
——, tombs at, i 203.
——, views of, 67.
Aswânî, well of, ii. 372.
Aswân-Luxor Railway, i. 283.
Aswân-Shellal Railway, i. 574.
Asyût, i. 1, 8, 10, 23, 25, 508; ii. 9, 105, 406, 458, 461, 647.
Atab, Island of, i. 468.
Atappi, ii. 357.
Athâî, ii. 285, 411, 435.
Atbara, i 31, 55, 97, 114, 241, 250, 254, 264, 279, 281; ii. 83, 88, 221, 231, 272, 368, 373, 390, 391, 459, 464, 486.
——, Battle of, i. 178; ii. 253, 273, 274.
——, British cemetery at, i. 252.
—— Fort, i. 252, 256, 282; ii. 272.
—— Junction, ii, 473, 474, 479.
—— Railway Bridge, ii. 471.
—— ——, opened, ii, 280.
Atbara (Åtbarâ) River, i. 251, 252; ii. 365 ff., 374, 398.
——, discharge of, ii. 369.

INDEX

Atbara-Sawâkin Railway, ii. 284, 443, 474 ff.
Âtchakhar-Âmen, ii. 113, 114, 115.
Atef crown, i. 383, 400, 401.
Ateftkit, ii. 111.
Atem, ii. 358.
Âten, i. 622.
——, cult of, i. 623, 624.
Atharumaqu, i. 612.
Athlenersa, ii. 57.
Athribis, ii. 52, 53.
Atiri, ii. 371.
Atlantia, ii. 163.
Atlenersa, i. 139; ii. 27.
Atoi-toish, ii. 442.
'Aṭshân, ii. 202.
Attab, i. 444.
At-Tahra, i. 102.
At-Takârana, ii. 440.
Aṭ-Ṭayyib, Shêkh, ii. 437.
At-Teb, ii. 249, 265.
Atteva, ii. 161, 168.
Atwarô, ii. 205.
Āuapeth the rebel, i. 648, 649, 650; ii. 5, 8, 14, 21, 24.
Augustus, ii. 113, 161, 166, 167.
Âuḥa, i. 526, 527.
Aurelian, Emp., ii. 175.
Aurusha, ii. 612.
Auruspi, i. 164.
Austin, Maj., ii. 282, 361.
Autochthones, ii. 153.
Automoloi, ii. 54, 106.
Avaris, i. 561, 562.
Awai, ii. 358.
Awamba, i. 525.
Awâs al-Guarânî, i. 75.
Awin, ii. 444.
Awlâd Abû Rûf, ii. 436.
Awlâd ar-Rîf, ii. 440.
Awlâd Ḥamîd, ii. 436.
Awlâd Kenz, i. 197, 198.
'Awra, ii. 428.
Awrambek, ii. 399.
Awtân, ii. 260.
Awtâw, ii. 392.
Axum, i. 18; ii. 180.
'Aydhâb, ii 189, 193, 194, 197.
Ayrton, Mr. E. R. A., i. 640.
Ayûb Pâshâ, ii. 482.
Ayugi, ii. 357.
Azande, ii. 287.
A-Zandî, ii. 432.
Azolla, ii. 481.
'Azz ad-Dîn Ibek, ii. 196

BAAL, king of Tyre, ii. 38.
Baba, i. 563, 564, 566, 567.
Baboons, i. 28.
Babûngera, ii. 432.
Bâb Zuwêla, ii. 198.
Babylon, ii. 40.
Babylon of Egypt, ii. 184, 193.
Babylonians, ii. 74.
Bacata, ii. 160.
Bacchus, ii. 106.
Bâdî, ii. 202.
Bâdî V., ii. 203.
Bâdî abû Dhiḳn, ii. 202.
Bâdî abû Shallûkh, ii. 203.
Bâdî al-Aḥmar, ii. 202.
Bâdî ibn Mismâr, ii. 204.
Bâdî ibn Ṭabal, ii. 203, 204.
Baert, ii. 266.
Baga, ii. 417.
Bagémder, ii. 364.
Baghdad, ii. 189, 190, 199, 500.
Bagirmi, ii. 398.
Bagrash, ii. 303.
Bagrawîya, i. 62, 240, 287, 435.
——, Shêkh of, 268 ff.
Bagromeh, i. 55, 435.
Bahnase, ii. 184.
Baḥr al-Abyaḍ, i. 23; ii. 356.
Baḥr al-Anḳareb, ii. 365.
Baḥr al-'Arab, ii. 359, 399.
Baḥr al-Asfar (Sobat), ii. 359, 360.
Baḥr al-Azraḳ, ii. 364.
Baḥr al-Gebel, ii. 173, 350, 356, 366, 367, 379, 386, 481, 484, 485.
Baḥr al-Ghâzal, ii. 106, 232, 235, 264, 267, 273, 281, 320, 356, 380, 390, 459, 481.
Baḥr-al-Ghazâl, discharge of, ii. 368.
—— Province, ii. 236, 399.
Baḥr al-Ḥomr, ii. 359, 399.
Baḥr az-Zarâfa, ii. 230, 358, 360, 379, 390, 481, 485.
——, discharge of, ii. 368.
Baḥr bila-ma, i. 508.
Baḥriyâ, ii. 290.
Baḥr Ramliya, ii. 357.
Baḥr Ṣânâ, ii. 363.
Baḥr Yûsuf, i. 541.
Bai, i. 640.
Baibûkh, i. 227.
Bailey, Maj. W. E., ii. 508.
Baines, ii. 422.
Bairâm, i. 503.
Baird, Mr. J., ii. 460.
Baḳ'a al-Mahdî, ii. 396.
Bakennifi, ii. 14.
Bakenrenf, ii. 28.
Baker, Col. Valentine, ii. 249.
Baker, Sir Samuel, i. 76, 249, 251, 252, 258, 261, 522, 536; ii. 221, 223, 230, 238, 350, 351, 356, 365, 378, 384, 461.
——, appointed Governor of the Sûdân, ii, 227.
——, called a "steam engine," i. 270.
——, discovers Albert N'yanza, ii. 222.
——, on missionaries, ii. 317.
Baket, ii. 111.
Bakhit, ii. 301.
Baḳḳâra al-Ḥawzâma, ii. 436.
Baḳḳâra Maḥâraba, ii. 436.
Baḳḳâra, the, i. 85, 93, 172, 242, 276, 328, 564,: ii. 397.
Bakshîsh, i. 232.
Baḳṭ, or Tribute, ii. 185, 187, 188, 189, 190, 193, 194, 298.
Balance of the Two Lands, ii. 21.
Balance, the, i. 370, 381, 387.

INDEX

Balanga, ii. 263.
Balariba, ii. 354.
Balad Sûdân, i. 506.
Balbona, ii. 356.
Balessé, i. 524.
Balfour, Dr. A., i. 190; ii. 494.
Balii, ii. 165.
Ball, Mr. John, i. 474.
Balsam, i. 532.
——, trees, ii. 327.
Bambara, ii. 398.
Bamia, i. 217.
Bâ Nagaa (or Ban Nagaa), i. 57.
Banda slaves, ii. 406.
Ba-neb-Ṭet, ii. 324.
Bangles, i. 219.
——, gold, i. 305.
Banholzer, ii. 434, 444.
Banks, Sir Joseph, i. 29.
Banner, ii. 135, 136.
Bansaḳâ, ii. 299.
Baptism in Ethiopia, i. 514.
Bâra, ii. 244, 396, 412.
Barâbara, i. 13, 22, 26, 89, 91, 531; ii. 419, 435.
——, language of, ii. 420.
Baraka River, ii. 366.
Barakâwî dates, i. 471.
Barameyu, ii. 478.
Baratieri, Col., ii. 267.
Barce, ii. 104.
Barghût, ii. 409.
Bar-Hebraeus, 295.
——, quoted, ii. 290.
Bâri, ii. 314, 385, 429, 434, 442.
—— tribes, ii. 234, 313, 424.
—— tukls, ii. 381.
Barḳa, ii. 191.
Barḳad, ii. 430, 441.
Barkal, village, i. 206 ff., 216, 218, 222, 226.
Barḳûḳ, Sultân, ii. 210.
Barley, ii. 158.
Barnîk, i. 105.
Baro River, ii. 285, 360.
Barrage, ii. 236.
Barrenness, i. 36.
Barrîyât, ii. 436.
Barron, Mr., ii. 507.
Barrow, Sir John, i. 55.
Barta, ii. 430, 440, 441.
——, tribes of the, i. 44.
Barter, i. 3.
Barth, ii. 422.
Barti, ii. 430.
Bāru, the god, i. 628.
Baruat (Meroë), ii. 81, 82.
Baruḳa, ii. 81.
Bâshbûzaḳ, ii. 232.
Bashi-Bazouks, ii. 249.
Bashîr, ii. 213.
Basilis, ii. 162.
Basle, i. 29, 62.
Baṣra, ii. 500.
Bast, ii. 23; of Taret, Tert, Thert, ii. 79, 90, 96, 102.
Bastian, ii. 422.
Bata, i. 523.
Batâḥîn, ii. 436.
Baṭn al-Ḥagar, i. 31, 60 88; ii. 370.
Batta, ii. 160.
Battahîn, ii. 390.
Batua, ii. 424.
Batwa, i. 525.
Ba-ur-ṭeṭ, i. 515, 532.
Bayle, St. John, i. 24.
Bayûda Desert, i. 4, 58, 61, 509, 525; ii. 89, 182, 374, 467.
——, 70 wells of, ii. 392.
Bazungu, i. 525.
Beads, i. 217, 218.
——, The thousand, i. 226.
Beam, Dr., ii. 494.
Beauchamp Bequest, ii. 493.
Bêbars, ii. 193, 194.
Bed, ii. 364.
Beddên Rapids, ii. 385.
Bedjas, ii. 184.
Bedouins, ii. 179.
Bee, i. 306.
Beer, ii. 13.
Beetles, i. 222, 401; ii. 440.
Bega country, i. 630.
Bega, the, ii. 175, 328, 329, 417. (See Bejas.)
Bégaraviah, i. 287, 307.
Behen (Wâdî Halfa), i. 548, 553, 554, 563, 576, 599, 601, 605, 627, 637; ii. 75, 328.
Behent, ii. 111.
Behthalis, ii. 76.
Beḥutet, i. 482, 543; ii. 87.
Beja, ii. 187, 188, 189, 193, 291, 307.
——, described, ii. 179.
Bejas, ii. 417, 506.
Bekhani, ii. 336.
Bela, ii. 361.
Belak, i. 8.
Belal, i. 234; ii. 116, 302.
Belgians, ii. 268.
Bells, Gold, i. 305.
"Belly of Stones," ii. 93.
Beltrame, Father, ii. 312, 445, 446.
Belzoni, G., i. 40; ii. 313.
Bên al-Ḳaṣrên, ii. 210.
Beni 'Abbâs, ii. 187, 438.
Beni 'Âmar, ii. 435, 436.
Beni Amer, ii. 261.
Beni Faḍl, ii. 436.
Beni Garrâr, ii. 436.
Beni Hasan, i. 532, 534, 633; ii. 436.
Beni Helba, ii. 436.
Beni 'Ommîa, ii. 187.
Beni Shanḳûl, ii. 339, 410, 430.
Beni Ummîa, ii. 438.
Beni Wayl, ii. 189.
Bennu bird, i. 384.
Bent-anṭa, i. 636.
Berber, i. 31, 41, 49, 55, 61, 100, 104, 113, 114, 115, 184, 187, 209, 247-249, 254, 281, 294, 509; ii. 213, 217, 236, 241, 249, 271, 273, 373, 374, 458, 461, 462, 467.
——, entered by Sirdar, ii. 274.
——, evacuated by Dervishes, ii. 272.
Berber District, ii. 401.
—— Province, ii. 401.
—— Town, ii. 401.
Berber-Sawâkin road, ii. 272.

INDEX

Ber es-Soudan, i. 506.
Berghoff, ii. 243, 244.
Bergîdâ, ii. 363.
Beris, i. 23, 85 ; ii. 266.
Berkeley, Fort, ii. 385.
Berlin, i. 61, 149, 502, 547.
—— Museum, Ferlini's objects in, i. 299 ff.
Bernard, Col. E. G., ii. 453, 501.
Berressa, ii. 160.
Berti, ii. 90, 99.
Beruat, ii. 87.
Bêrût, i. 646 ; ii. 39.
Bes, the buffoon of the gods, i. 524.
Bes, the god, i. 57, 133; 134, 138; ii. 45, 69, 125, 151.
——, the dwarf god, i. 523.
Bêt al-Amâna, ii. 396.
Bêt al-Walî, ii. 325.
——, Temple of, i. 633.
Bethell, Capt. A. B., ii. 287, 460.
Bêth Nahrîn, i. 607.
Beurmann, ii. 422.
Bigga, Island of, i. 27, 72, 574, 598 ; ii. 74.
Bîbamû, i. 551.
Bîḳô, ii. 43.
Bintemôda dates, i. 471.
Bion, ii. 130, 164.
Bîr, i. 329.
Bîr al-Malḥ, i. 24.
Bîr at Maṣawwarât, i. 327.
Birch, Dr., i. 299, 533, 536, 538, 548, 605, 648 ; ii. 35, 335, 336, 338.
Bîr Daffer, i. 52, 53.
Birds, i. 234.
——, scaring, i. 267.
Birejik, i. 328.
Biremes, ii. 167.
Biri, ii. 399.
Birka, ii. 436, 437, 439.
Bîr Natrûn, ii. 412.
Birs, i. 315.
Bîr Sultân, ii. 391.
Biselli, ii. 315.
Bishar, ii. 435.
Bishâra, ii. 206.
Bishârîn Arabs, i. 70, 630 ; ii. 175, 328, 417.
——, three divisions of, ii. 435.
Bishra, ii. 281.
Bissing, F. W. von, i. 521.
Bitumen, stream of, ii. 160.
Bîzâmâ, ii. 364.
Blacks, i. 505, 512, 513, 539, 544, 548, 600, 631 ; ii. 413.
——, country of, i. 506.
——, decree against, i. 543.
——, described, ii. 154.
——, Land of, i. 2, 515 ; ii. 79.
Black Stone, i. 224.
Black Tribes, i. 515.
Blake, Mr., i. 109.
Blakeney, R. B. D., ii. 463.
Blemmyes, i. 28; ii. 158, 175, 176, 177, 178, 185, 290 ff., 309, 328, 417, 436, 506.
Blewitt, Major A., ii. 361.
Blood of bulls, ii. 91.
Blunt, Captain, i. 87.
Bo, ii. 399.
Boardman, Col.-Serg., ii. 284, 460, 483, 507.
Boat-building, ii. 376.
Boat of Amen, i. 646.
——, of Rā, i. 417 ; ii. 8.
——, of Tem, ii. 8.
——, of the Sun, i. 383, 425.
Boats, scarcity of, i. 439.
Bocchoris, ii. 28.
Boeckh, ii. 297.
Bogos, ii. 231.
Boggia, ii. 160.
Boiwj, ii. 444.
Boj, ii. 444.
Bolako, ii. 399.
Bomgia, ii. 424.
Bonaparte, Napoleon, ii. 210.
Bonarti, i. 2.
Bond, Engineer-Commander, ii. 459, 483, 509.
Bones of animals in tombs, i. 344.
Bonga, ii. 360.
Bongo, ii. 315, 322, 399, 424, 428.
—— woman, ii. 403.
Bonham-Carter, Mr. E., ii. 460, 490, 496.
Bonomi, Mr. J., i. 62 ; ii. 325.
Boomerangs, i. 520, 571.
Bôr, ii. 172, 230, 233, 266, 321, 358, 380, 485.
Bordein, the, Gordon's steamer, i. 255 ff.
Bornu, ii. 398, 422.
Boron, ii. 160.
Borru, ii. 442.
Bôr Skêkh, ii. 441.
Borton, Capt. N. T., i. 108, 109, 182 ; ii. 500.
Boru, ii. 399.
Bosnians, ii. 208, 308.
——, fortresses, ii. 207.
——, troops, ii. 207.
Bottego, Signor, ii. 361.
Boulnois, Major W., ii. 282, 286, 460, 507.
Bourriant, ii. 27.
Boutros Ghali, ii. 508.
Bowditch, ii. 422.
Bower, Captain, ii. 460.
Bows, i. 286 ; ii. 154, 159.
——, the fifteen, i. 531.
——, palm-stem, ii. 107.
Boyle, Mr. H., i. 264, 322.
Boys, Ethiopian, ii. 105.
Bracelet, i. 487.
Brahuls, ii. 426.
Bramley, Mr. Jennings, ii. 460.
Brass, ii. 153.
—— rings, ii. 154.
Bray, Maj. H. A., ii. 287.
Bread-stamps, i. 151.
Breeches of human hair, ii. 154.
Brehm, ii. 422.
Brendô (raw meat), ii. 73.
Brera, ii. 424.
Brevedent, C. F. Xaverius de, i. 1, 3, 6.
Briareus, i. 635.
Bricks, ii. 159.
Bridge, Portuguese, ii. 364.

INDEX

British Museum, i. 504.
——, Trustees of, i. 63, 113, 321, 323, 437, 502.
Broadwood, Col., i. 183; ii. 275.
Bronze bowl, i. 306.
—— boxes, i. 307.
—— pot, i. 345.
Brood mares, ii. 7.
Broun, ii. 500.
——, Mrs., ii. 494.
Brown, Maj. R. H., R. E., i. 551, 552.
Brown, Mr. R., ii. 307.
Browne, W. G., i. 26, 52, 506; ii. 207, 398.
——, Travels of, i. 23 ff.
Bruce, James, i. 5, 7, 8, 12, 23, 41; ii. 349, 404.
——, Travels of, i. 17 ff.
Brugsch, Dr. H., i. 486, 534, 541, 552, 568, 573, 648; ii. 84, 94, 447.
Brûndô (raw meat), ii. 73.
Brun-Rollet, ii. 446.
Brunyate, Mr. W. E., ii. 496.
Bubastis, i. 533, 556, 648, 652; ii. 2, 5, 14, 23, 29, 30.
Buchta, ii. 432, 433.
Budêrîya, ii. 437, 438.
Budêyât, ii. 430, 441.
Buffoon, i. 524.
Bugaeitai, ii. 417.
Bugala, ii. 352.
Buhen, i. 548.
Buiuuaua, i. 647, 648.
Bûlâḳ, i. 23, 150.
——, Museum of, i. 649.
Bulbul, ii. 436.
Bull, Bulls, i. 301, 384, 397; ii. 155.
——, three hundred fighting, ii. 108.
——, gold, ii. 101.
— —, wild, ii. 157.
—— of Amentet, ii. 414.
Buller, Sir Redvers, ii. 259.
Bullu Narti, i. 2.
Bulwena, ii. 365.
Buma, ii. 160.
Bunbury, Capt., i. 182; ii. 460.
Bunek, ii. 443.
Bun Yung, ii. 443.
Burckhardt, i. 34, 93, 105, 225, 437, 439, 463, 466, 476, 478, 494, 521, 634, 636; ii. 184, 185, 187, 189, 190, 195, 297, 304, 330, 401, 404.
——, travels of, i. 29 ff.
Burdên, i. 279; ii. 239, 251. See Bordein.
Bûrdênî Bey, ii. 251, 253, 254.
Burges, Capt. F., ii. 281.
Buri, ii. 399.
Burn Murdoch, Major, i. 93, 94.
Burnû, ii. 440.
Burraburiyash, ii. 322.
Burton, Sir R., i. 460; ii. 220, 350.
Burûn, ii. 286, 430.
——, Negroes, ii. 489.
Bus, ii. 173.
Bushmen, ii. 425.
Busiris, ii. 5, 14, 24.
Busoga, ii. 352.
Bussorah, i. 471.
Butler Bey, ii. 460.
Butler, Mr. A. J., ii. 192, 302, 304, 493, 500.
Buvuma, ii. 352.
Bwora, ii. 443.
Byssus, ii. 23, 24.

CADEUMA, ii. 160.
Caecilius Bion, ii. 348.
Caesars, i. 57.
Caesar, statues of, thrown down, ii. 168.
Cailliaud, i. 12, 23, 37, 56, 57, 59, 120, 122, 130, 131, 133, 134, 139, 153, 154, 155, 156, 159, 162, 163, 164, 169, 175, 201, 240, 267, 274, 275, 287, 328, 342, 348, 352, 353, 434, 441, 445, 453, 463, 466, 566; ii. 10, 124, 125, 147, 292, 351, 404, 411, 430.
Cailliaud, Travels of, i. 38.
Cairo, i. 5, 6, 8, 10, 22, 23, 25, 29, 30, 32, 36, 53, 54, 55, 64, 68, 92, 100, 250, 271, 272; ii. 191, 192, 196, 200, 209, 211, 458.
Calderari, Count, i. 98, 180, 181.
Callisthenes, Pseudo, ii. 108.
Cambusis, ii. 94, 161, 168.
Cambyses, ii. 84, 90, 91, 92, 105, 106, 153, 168.
——, attempts to conquer Sûdân, ii. 93.
——, store places of, ii. 94.
Camel Corps, i. 113, 115, 198.
Camels, i. 198.
—— bones, i. 344.
—— post, ii. 220.
—— transport, i. 470.
Cameron, Sorel Bey, ii. 321, 422, 460.
Canal in the First Cataract, i. 540.
Candace, i. 290, 357, 414; ii. 108, 117, 120, 131, 163, 168, 501.
——, attacks Premnis, ii. 169.
——, = Åmen-tāret (?), ii. 169.
Candace queens, ii. 402.
Candrogari, ii. 164.
Candy, P., i. 478.
Canimulgos, ii. 156.
Cannabis Indica, i. 221.
Cannibals, ii. 314, 432.
Cannon at Sâî, i. 463.
Cap, the, ii. 439.
Cape Guardafui, i. 571.
Capuchins, i. 5.
Carians, ii. 53.
Carnelians, i. 538; ii. 10, 327.
Carob trees, ii. 159.
Carriages in Omdurmân, ii. 278.
Carter, Captain, ii. 460.

INDEX

Carter, Major, ii. 286.
Carthage, ii. 89, 90.
Casmari, ii. 164.
Castle of Atab, i. 468, 469.
——, of Sâî, i. 595.
Castration, ii. 181.
Cat, i. 307.
——, Golden, ii. 160.
Catadupi, ii. 160.
Cataract, First, i. 13, 17, 18, 21, 39, 69, 505, 515.
——, Second, i. 13, 14, 15, 16, 29, 31, 39.
——, Third, i. 29, 53, 99.
——, Fourth, i. 50, 104, 114, 234.
——, Sixth, i. 4.
—— of Tangûr, i. 595.
Cataracts, head of, ii. 194.
——, Islands of, i. 496.
——, the Six, ii. 366.
—— on the Blue Nile, ii. 366.
Catholics flee from Sennaar, i. 5.
Cattle, i. 543.
—— breeding, ii. 398.
—— keepers, i. 564.
—— men, i. 588, 622; ii. 176, 416-418.
—— Sûdânî, i. 392.
Caucasians, ii. 426.
Cavalla, ii. 210.
Cecil, Lord Edward, i. 498.
Cedar trees, i. 646.
—— wood, i. 628.
Cemetery at Atbara, i. 252.
Censi, ii. 160.
Cepheus, ii. 161, 170.
Cepus, ii. 157.
Ceratophyllum, ii. 481.
Chabas, i. 541; ii. 334-336.
Chaltin's Column, ii. 273.
Chamamui, ii. 283.
Chambezi, ii. 229.
Champollion, i. 51, 60, 299, 534, 536, 576, 578, 601, 633, 637.
Charimortos, ii. 112.
Chel, ii. 399.
Chelga, ii. 412.
Chelonophagi, ii. 156.
Chermside, Col. Sir Herbert, i. 83; ii. 261.
Chickens, i. 332.
Chikalero, ii. 354.
Chippendall, Lieut., ii. 350.
Chitambo, ii. 229.
Choga, Lake, ii. 387.
Cholera, i. 91; ii. 214, 220, 270.
Christ, Dr. W., i. 307.
Christian church at Sâî, i. 60.
Christian VI., i. 13.
Christianity in the Northern Sûdân, ii. 288 ff.
Christians, Jacobite, ii. 304.
—— persecuted, ii. 289.
Church Missionary Society, ii. 318, 320.
Church of Jesus, ii. 195.
—— at Soba, i. 324.
Churches, 400 in 'Alwa, ii. 304.
—— in Nubia, i. 283.
—— destroyed, ii. 194.
—— ruined, i. 4.
Circumciser, i. 514.
Circumcision, i. 514; ii. 106, 156.
Cisori, ii. 165.
Cispii, ii. 165.
Civet cats, ii. 181.
Clarke, Mr. Somers, i. 82, 282, 283, 440.
Claudius, Emperor, ii. 170,
—— II., Emperor, ii. 175.
Cleopatris (Arsinoë), ii. 167.
Clubs, ii. 154.
——, iron-bound, ii. 157.
——, knotted, ii. 107.
——, leather-laced, ii. 89.
Cnidus, ii. 155, 340.
Coal, ii. 220, 480.
Cobbe, ii. 398.
Coffee, i. 105.
Coffins, earthen, ii. 154.
Cognac, i. 221.
Colborne, Col. the Hon. J., ii. 372.
Colchians, ii. 106.
Cold in Sûdân, i. 494.
Colli, Lieut., ii. 282.
Colligat, ii. 164.
Collinson, Col., ii. 280, 282 401, 460.
Colo-quintida, i. 3; ii. 181.
Colossi, the, i. 67.
Colvile, Col., ii. 267.
Colville, Commander, i. 102, 105.
Colvin, Sir Auckland, quoted, ii. 255.
Comeley, Mr. J., ii. 321.
Commellaria, ii. 481.
Comyn, Lieut., ii. 361.
Congo, i. 506; ii. 390.
—— Free State, ii. 266, 284, 286, 320.
——, French, ii. 459.
—— Pygmies, ii. 425.
Congolese Expedition, ii. 266.
Connaught, T.R.H. Duke and Duchess of, i. 272, 498.
Conolly, Capt. T., ii. 460.
Constantine, ii. 290.
Constantinople, i. 6, 17, 227; ii. 178, 204, 210, 294.
Consutae, ii. 406.
Contarini, ii. 315.
Contra-Pselcis, i. 634; ii. 111.
Contra-Syene, i. 520.
Contra-Talmis, ii. 111.
Contra-Taphis, ii. 111.
Cook, Messrs. Thos. and Son, i. 68.
Cooper, Mr. A. A., ii. 319.
Copper, i. 599, 642; ii. 2, 7, 412.
—— mines, ii. 158.
—— —— of Dâr Fûr, ii. 284.
—— ring, i. 305; ii 159.
Coptic Church at Soba, i. 43.
—— inscriptions, ii. 310.
—— in Sûdân, i. 464.
—— lamp, i. 487.
—— Saints, i. 50.
—— stele, i. 464.
Coptos, i. 535, 643; ii. 166, 189, 336, 337.

INDEX

Copts, i. 9, 283, 496; ii. 176, 306, 319, 394.
—— at Sâî, i. 462, 463, 464.
—— rising of, ii. 187.
Cornelius Gallus, ii. 166.
Coruscah, i. 318.
Cosmas, ii. 299.
Cosseir, i. 18.
Cotton, ii. 194.
—— at 'Amâra, i. 467.
—— stuffs, i. 105.
Couches, ii. 23.
Council of Seven, ii. 209.
Cows, i. 327.
Crandala, ii. 160.
Cranes, ii. 107, 347.
Crenellations, i. 517.
Critensi, ii. 164.
Crocodiles, i. 76.
——, god, i. 383.
——, hawk-headed, ii. 140.
——, worshipped at Khartûm, ii. 414.
Crocodilopolis, ii. 4, 12.
Crocotta, ii. 157.
Cromer, Earl of, i. 222, 264, 324; ii. 269, 280, 281, 284, 320, 321, 322, 450, 459, 470, 476, 477, 478, 486, 488, 490, 491, 495, 498, 507 ff.
——, and the Shilluks and Dinkas, i. 322, 323.
Crops, ii. 398, 483.
Cross, Coptic, i. 324, 463.
Crowfoot, Mr. J. W., i. 60, 329, 437 ff., 456, 457, 460, 487, 540, 547, 555, 583, 621, 637; ii. 147, 300, 305, 420, 495.
Crusaders, ii. 278.
Crusca (see Korosko),
Cucumber seeds, i. 221.
Cumi, ii. 164.
Cummins, Major S. G., ii. 441.
Cunningham, Major, ii. 268.
Cureton, Dr., ii. 296.
Currie, Mr. James, i. 438, 461; ii. 300, 391, 460, 490, 492, 509.
Curtius, L., i. 382.
Cush = Nubia, i. 535, 566.
Cutting of the Dam, ii. 344.
Cuvier, ii. 403.
Cynamolgi, ii. 165.
Cynocephali, ii. 157.
Cynocephalus, ii. 163.
Cynopolis, ii. 9, 25.
Cyprus, ii. 426.
Cyriacus, ii. 187, 298.
Cyrene, ii. 104.
Cyril, St., ii. 302, 306.
Cyste, ii. 160.

DABARKÎ, ii. 365, 437.
Dabba, i. 107; ii. 372, 392.
D'Abbadie, ii. 34, 502.
Dabeli, ii. 164, 165.
Dabra Anṭônes, ii. 363.
Dabra Maryam, ii. 363.
Dabra Sin, ii. 261.
Dabra Tâbôr, ii. 238.
Dabrôs, Island of, i. 82.
Dâbûd, ii. 111, 113, 114 328, 329.
Dafâr, ii. 435.
Dafûfa, i. 58, 59.
Dag, ii. 444.
Dagâ, ii. 363.
Daggers, i. 217.
Dâgô, ii. 430, 434, 441.
—— tribe, ii. 422.
Dahlak, ii. 179, 188.
Dahlakye, ii. 180.
Dahshûr, i. 515, 539.
Da'ifâb, ii. 438.
Dakarti, Island of, i. 52.
Dakhfilî, ii. 479.
Dâkhla, Oasis of, ii. 174, 266.
Dakîn ibn Na'il, ii. 201.
Dakka, i. 28, 74, 549, 555, 574, 629, 630, 631, 651; ii. 10, 75, 110-114, 168, 170, 297, 328, 329.
Dakkode, ii. 444.
Dâl, ii. 371.
——, Cataract of, ii. 366.
Dale, Major, ii. 480.
Dâli, ii. 422.
Dalion, ii. 162, 165, 348.
Dalîl, ii. 206.
Damâdim, ii. 349.
Damascus sword, i. 28.
Damba, ii. 352.
Dâmer, ii. 401.
Damerarchon, ii. 74.
Damietta, i. 8; ii. 184, 281.
Dammûr cloth, ii. 406.
Danâkala, ii. 435.
Danâkil, ii. 426.
Danaḳla, ii. 376.
Dancer of the god, i. 522.
Dancing, i. 195.
——, at Tushki, i. 78-80.
Dankêl, i. 287.
Dankelah, i. 55.
Danko Selîm, ii. 376.
D'Anville, i. 41.
Daphnae, ii. 54.
Dâra, i. 328; ii. 235, 245, 246, 262, 430.
——, Lake of, ii. 364.
Darâr, Island of, ii. 241.
Darâw, i. 31, 105, 509, 530; ii. 435, 458.
Darbe, ii. 299.
Darde, ii. 164.
Daressy, M. G., i. 531, 647.
Dâr Fertît, i. 53.
Dâr Fûng, ii. 396.
Dâr Fûngâra, i. 508.
Dâr Fûr, i. 23, 24, 25, 31, 52, 53, 105, 496, 506, 507, 509, 521, 562; ii. 83, 96, 105, 155, 171, 227, 239, 265, 282, 307, 391, 397, 458.
——, annexed by Egypt, ii. 231, 232.
——, revolt in, ii. 235, 260.
——, Sultans of, ii. 206, 207, 398.
Dâr Ḥamîd, ii. 437.
Darius the Great, ii. 104, 105.
Darkness, fear of, i. 220.
Dâr Mahass, i. 34, 35, 60, 441, 449, 450, 457, 549.
Dâr Mâra, i. 508.
Dâr Nûba, ii. 378.
Daron, ii. 164.
Darrak, ii. 431.

INDEX

Dâr Sukkôt, i. 60, 93, 438, 449, 450, 457, 464, 549.
Dassâbal, ii. 392.
Dates, i. 41.
—— at Merawi, i. 212.
—— of Dongola, i. 2.
—— tax, ii. 451.
—— trade, i. 96.
—— trees, ii. 483, 484.
——, Turkish, i. 472.
——, various kinds of, i. 471.
David, Col. E. F., i. 107, 109.
David, king of Israel, i. 195.
Davis, Mr. T. N., i. 607, 640.
Daw, ii. 193, 197.
Dawn, breath of, i. 186.
——, false, i. 100.
Dawûd, ii. 192, 194, 195.
Dbâîna, ii. 437.
Dead, disposal of, ii. 154, 159.
Debba, i. 107-109, 110, 113; ii. 250, 270.
Deche-Potasimto, ii. 74.
Decius, ii. 289.
De Horrack, ii. 55.
De Goeje, ii. 329.
Deḳ, ii. 363.
Delen, ii. 233.
Delligo (or Deligo), i. 35, 96, 437, 615; ii. 207.
Delta, i. 57, 362, 532, 533, 556, 645, 646, 647, 648; ii. 1, 2, 4, 29, 31, 35, 37, 38, 39, 40, 42, 49, 50, 187, 210.
De Maillet, i. 5, 6, 7, 8, 12.
Demba, Lake, i. 19.
Dembea, ii. 364.
Dembo, ii. 246.
Dêm Idris, ii. 237.
Demiourgos, i. 464.
De Morgan, Mr. J., i. 539, 604, 605.
Dêm Zubêr, ii. 246, 282, 399.
Dendûr, i. 27, 74; ii. 170, 297.
Deng Dit, ii. 441.
Dengûlâ, ii. 364.
Denham, ii. 422.
Denkmäler, the, i. 62, 277.
Denmark, i. 13.
Denna, ii. 160.
Denon, Vivant, i. 26, 27.
Dêrâ, 2, 299,
Derahêb, ii. 411.
Dêr al-Baharî, i. 298.
——, removal of royal mummies, &c., i. 649.
De Rougé, E., i. 627; ii. 4, 35, 46, 66.
De Rougé, J., ii. 66.
De Rougemont, Major, ii. 460.
Derr, i. 14, 15, 16, 17, 28, 29, 30, 31, 34, 440, 575, 651; ii. 107.
——, temple of, i. 634.
Dêr Sûllah, i. 53.
Dervishes, i. 84-86, 87, 89, 90, 93, 94, 95, 96, 97, 101, 102, 104, 106, 111, 113, 115, 179, 184, 187, 199, 209, 210, 211, 228, 254, 256, 261, 265, 274, 366.
——, at Nilwitti, i. 457.
Desert, Bayuda, ii. 391.
——, Gakdûl, ii. 437.
——, Libyan, ii. 391,
——, Nubian, ii. 391.
Desert Column, i. 110; ii. 252, 259.
Deserters, ii. 54, 106.
Dessaix, Fort, ii. 282.
Detrelis, ii. 160.
Deung Adok, ii. 443.
Devils, i. 268.
De Vogüé, i. 549.
Dêwar, ii. 430.
Dhurra, i. 3, 28, 40, 89, 212, 261, 262, 265, 439.
Dibirra, ii. 354.
Diḳna, i. 95.
Dilling, ii. 397.
Dillmann, Dr., i. 18.
Dimmi, ii. 50.
Dinder, ii. 203, 390, 396, 436, 437, 486.
Dinder River, ii. 365.
Dinkas, i. 322; ii. 246, 267, 286, 322, 358, 377, 399, 424, 428, 430, 441, 512.
——, origin of, ii. 441.
—— tribes, ii. 213
—— villages, ii. 280.
Diocletian, i. 28; ii. 176, 290, 291, 418.
Diodorus Siculus, i. 39, 538; ii. 28, 30, 54, 94, 109, 110, 112, 115, 153, 339.
——, quoted, ii. 58, 60, 340.
Dion Cassius, ii. 166, 167, 169.
Dionysos, i. 307.
—— masks, i. 294.
Direa, ii. 160.
Dittenberger, ii. 292, 297.
Dîyab of Shendî, ii. 206.
Dîyâb Wâd 'Agîb, ii. 204.
Dochi, ii. 164.
Dodekaschoinos, ii. 110, 114, 115, 176.
Dogain, ii. 479.
Dog-fish, ii. 155.
Dog king, ii. 164.
Dog River, ii. 339.
Dogs, ii. 156.
——, man-eating, ii. 108.
Dok, ii. 399, 444.
Dokodo, ii. 444.
Dollars, Khalîfa's, ii. 269.
——, Maria Theresa, i. 218.
Dongola, i. 10, 30, 34, 35, 41, 51, 62, 86, 90, 101, 102, 103, 104, 114, 125, 150, 198, 211, 509, 601; ii. 1, 291, 306, 364, 467, 480.
——, dialect of, ii. 420.
——, expedition, i. 93; ii. 463.
—— Fort, i. 106.
——, Kingdom of, i. 1.
——, New, i. 35, 103, 615; ii. 84, 372, 462.
——, Old, i. 35, 59, 61, 107, 615, 651; ii. 185, 190, 191, 195, 196, 197, 199,

200, 202, 207, 212, 213, 217, 241, 285, 297, 299, 302, 307, 372, 479.
Dongola, Old, described, i. 3, 4.
—— Province, ii. 407.
—— tale, i. 235 ff.
Dongola al-Ûrdî, i. 615.
Dongolâwîs, i. 216.
Donḳola al-'Agûz, i. 615.
Dôr, i. 646.
Doric columns, i. 633.
Dorvak, Father, ii. 312.
Dôsha, i. 38, 40.
——, temple of, i. 595.
Dove, i. 306.
Dozy, ii. 329.
Drage, Colonel W. H., i. 113, 181, 182, 203, 223.
Drake, Captain W. H., i. 331, 33?, 334, 337, 354.
Dravidians, ii. 426.
Dream, Stele of, ii. 51.
Dromedaries, ii. 198.
Drovetti, i. 40.
Drummond, Mr., ii. 493.
Drury, Lieut. W. B., ii. 476, 482.
Dubengi, ii. 387.
Dueru, ii. 353.
Dufilî, ii. 233, 234, 263, 357, 386.
—— Falls, ii. 235.
Dughêm, ii. 437.
Dugmore, Capt., ii. 460.
Dûka, ii. 437.
Dukhu, ii. 357.
Dulêb Hill, ii. 319.
—— palms, ii. 378.
Dulgo, i. 35, 96, 97, 437, 438, 439, 442, 615, 651; ii. 207, 261, 300, 371, 409.
Duma, ii. 399.
Dumana, ii. 160.
Dümichen, i. 533; ii. 338.
Dûm palm, i. 91; ii. 181.
Dunkur, ii. 437.
Dupuis, Mr. C., ii. 363, 365.
Dûr, ii. 438.
Dura, ii. 354.
Dust of Shêkh Idrîs, i. 469.
Duwat, ii. 443.
Duwêm, ii. 245, 368, 375, 376, 397, 408.
——, near Merawi, i. 234.
Dwarf, i. 138.
Dykes on the Nile, i. 555.
Dyroff, Dr. Karl, i. 382.
Dyurs, ii. 432.

Eagle, i. 306.
Earle, General, ii. 252.
Earthenware, i. 105;
—— jars, i. 345.
Ebers, i. 573.
Ebony, i. 526, 571; ii. 104, 105, 107, 520.
—— forests, ii. 165.
—— rods, ii. 108.
—— trees, i. 521; ii. 153, 159.
Edfû, i. 530; ii. 87, 189, 337, 435.
Edinburgh, i. 17.
Edos, ii. 160.
Education, ii. 489 ff.
Edwah, i. 551.
E. F. A., i. 478.
Eggs, i. 196, 332.
Egypt, i. 32, 47, 53, 61, 222, 280, 298, 337; ii. 34.
—— formed of mud, ii. 153.
——, tribute of, to Persia, ii. 104.
Egyptian civilization in the Sûdân, ii. 2.
Egyptians, i. 25, 33, 74, 83, 91; ii. 105, 106.
——, colony of, in Ethiopia, ii. 153.
Eight gods, the, ii. 17.
Einha, ii. 479.
Ekron, ii. 34.
'Êlafûn, ii. 250, 251, 258, 365.
Elamites, i. 648.
Electrum, ii. 338.
Elephant eaters, ii, 158.
—— grass, ii. 173.
—— hunts, i. 573; ii. 112.
Elephants, i. 105, 308, 525; ii. 108, 111, 155, 15?, 160.
Elephants, slaughter of, ii. 451.
——, the Sûdân, ii. 107.
—— tusks, i. 323
Elephantine, i. 13, 515, 517, 533, 539, 548, 553, 554, 556, 567, 588, 599, 606, 633, 637; ii. 49, 53, 54, 73, 74, 92, 105, 106, 167, 176, 394.
—— Island, i. 518, 574, 575; ii. 343.
Elephantomachi, ii. 156.
'Êlfûl, ii. 202.
Elias the Armenian, i. 12.
Elkera, ii. 298.
El-Kowad, ii. 184.
Ellesîya, i. 575.
Eltekeh, ii. 34.
Elysian Fields, i. 526, 644.
Embâba steamer, i. 258.
Emeralds, ii. 108, 181.
——, mines, ii. 179, 189, 190, 333
Emeus, ii. 160.
Emfras, i. 19.
Emin Pâshâ, ii. 235, 250, 260, 262, 263, 266, 384, 385, 482.
Emmàât, i. 643.
Enamel, blue and green, i. 301.
Endera, ii. 157.
Enenselsa, ii. 58, 62.
English in schools, ii. 490.
'Ên Ḥâmid, ii. 437.
Ephesus, ii. 296.
Epis, ii. 160.
Equator, i. 23, 508; ii. 240, 348.
Equatorial Provinces, ii. 235.
Equinox, ii. 153.
Eratosthenes, ii. 162, 347.
Erba, ii. 478.
Erbkam, G., i. 61, 125.
Ergamenes, ii. 109, 110, 112, 114, 154, 297.
Erhêb, ii. 479.
Eritrea, ii. 265, 266, 282, 390, 420.
Ermenab, ii. 305.

INDEX

Erment, ii. 189.
Erṭā-Ȧntef-Ṭeṭi, i. 537, 554.
Ertemri, ii. 291.
Eru, i. 449.
Esar, ii. 164.
Esarhaddon, ii. 37, 38, 39, 40.
—— appoints governors in Egypt, ii. 39.
Esest, i. 494.
Esna, i. 31, 530; ii. 189, 212.
Etbai (Atbai), ii. 339.
Ethiopia, i. 4, 22, 54, 56, 57, 61, 514, 558, 559; ii. 32, 54, 107, 153, 170, 264, 288, 308, 340.
—— described by Strabo, ii. 157.
——, forty-five kings of, ii. 163.
——, not Cûsh, i. 535.
Ethiopians, i. 21, 513; ii. 73, 105, 106, 107, 110, 153, 155, 158, 159, 292.
—— characters, i. 408.
—— described, ii. 158 ff.
——, Eastern, ii. 107.
——, Western, ii. 107.
Ethiopic, i. 8, 432.
Eumachus, ii. 109.
Eunuchs, ii. 406.
Euphorbia, ii. 381.
Euphrates, i. 328, 569, 570, 572, 598, 604; ii. 191.
Eusebius, quoted, ii. 289.
Eutychius, ii. 289, 447.
Eval, G. S., i. 478.
Evetts, Mr. B. T. A., ii. 192, 290, 298.
Evil eye, i. 214.
Evonymitae, ii. 162, 172.
Eye of Horus, i. 382.
—— of Rā, i. 307.
Eye-paint, i. 571.
Ezbekîya Gardens, ii. 211.

FABRICIUS Pasha, ii. 492.
Fâdassî, i. 44.
Fadiet Wâd Kwad Keir, ii. 444.
Fadîgî, ii. 420.
Fâdil, ii. 281.
Faḍl, ii. 191.
Faḍl al-Mawla Bey, ii. 266.
Fâfâ, ii. 432.
Fagao, ii. 386.
Fagelû, ii. 424.
Faḥal, ii. 205.
Faivre, M., ii. 361.
Fakhr ad-Dîn, ii. 192.
Faḳri wâd 'Uthmân, ii. 251, 259.
Falfa, ii. 180.
Falkenstein, ii. 424.
Fâmaka, ii. 282, 364, 365, 430, 431, 443.
Famine, ii. 202, 203, 213.
Fân, ii. 432.
Fanakama, ii. 378.
Fanḳarô, ii. 205.
Fans, ii. 327.
—— bearers, ii. 55.
Faraḳ-Allah, ii. 252.
Farânib, ii. 438.
Faras, i. 637; ii. 263.
——, island of, ii. 570.
Farâtît, ii. 431, 439.
Farêg, i. 98.
Farḥât Bey, ii. 214.
Farka, i. 93.
Fârḳânî, ii. 194.
Faroge, ii. 268, 282.
Fâsher, ii. 392.
—— Ford, ii. 365.
Fâshôda, ii. 213, 227, 228, 229, 230, 233, 243, 244, 265, 266, 280, 286, 321, 377, 378, 434.
—— Province, ii. 399.
Fatalism, i. 223.
Fatha, the, i. 224.
Fathers of Jerusalem, i. 5.
Fatiko, ii. 229, 233.
Fâṭma, ii. 404.
Fatme, i. 478.
Fayyûm, i. 551, 607; ii. 7, 18, 184.
Fâzôglî, i. 44, 47, 61; ii. 200, 212, 214, 217, 337, 332, 441, 462.
Fâzôglî, Kings of, ii. 205.
Feast in Abyssinia, i. 19.
Feathers, i. 525.
—— of vultures, i. 44.
Felkin, R. W., ii. 446.
Fell, Lieut. J. L., ii. 286, 460, 483, 507.
Fêrakî, ii. 188, 189.
Ferket, i. 34.
—— Battle of, i. 93, 94; ii. 270, 371.
—— Mountain, i. 94, 95, 96.
Ferlini, i. 277, 325, 339, 343, 373, 375, 382.
—— excavations by, at the Pyramids of Meroë, i. 285.
——, find by, i. 290, 291.
——, journey of, to Egypt, i. 294.
—— narrative of, in French, i. 313.
—— —— in Italian, i. 307.
Fertility of Sûdânî women, i. 36.
Festival of Ȧmen, ii. 15.
—— Apt, ii. 15.
—— New Year, ii. 15.
Fetish drink, ii. 442.
Fever, i. 32, 563.
Finger-nails, ii. 135.
Finger-rings from Meroë, i. 307.
Fire, ii. 163.
Firewood stations, i. 261-263.
Firgi, ii. 300.
Firmus, ii. 175.
First Cataract, Una's work at, i. 518.
Fish, ii. 155.
—— eaters, ii. 26, 92, 155.
—— traps, i. 112.
Fitz-Clarence, Lieut., i. 104; ii. 233, 272.
Fitzmaurice, Lord, quoted, ii. 256.
Flags, British and Egyptian, i. 322.
—— staffs for temples, i. 628.
Flavia Neapolis, ii. 292.
Fleurian, Father, i. 5.

INDEX

Fleuriot de Langle, ii. 422.
Flint, Capt. S. K., ii. 287.
Florence, i. 536.
Florus, ii. 179, 296.
Fola Rapids, ii. 174, 366, 367.
Fort of Sulu, i. 538.
Forts, Egyptian, in the Sûdân, i. 553, 651.
Forty Road, ii. 458.
Foster, Capt. C. E., ii. 460
Four Peoples, the, i. 534.
Four quarters of world, ii. 41, 79.
Fowler, Mr. J., ii. 461.
France, i. 5, 7.
Francis, St., i. 4.
Franciscans, i. 5, 6, 8.
Franke, *formatore*, i. 62.
Frankfort, Viscount, i. 83.
Franks, i. 13, 15.
Frederick William IV., i. 61.
Frey, J., i. 61.
Friend, Col., ii. 460, 492, 504.
Fritsch, ii. 424.
Frobenius, ii. 424.
Fruit trees cut down, i. 517.
Fukarâ, ii. 435.
Funeral at Barkal, i. 223, 224.
Fûng king, ii. 422.
—— Province of, i. 3.
—— tribe, ii. 199, 372, 430.
Fûngs, ii. 200, 208, 436, 437, 440.
—— defeated, ii. 207.
Fûr, ii. 431.
Fusṭaṭ, ii. 185, 190, 198.
Fuwêr, ii. 386.
Fuwêra, ii. 229, 233, 357.

GAALIN Arabs, i. 85, 216; ii. 205, 248, 271, 274, 375, 390, 437.
Ga'alîyûn, ii. 437.
Gâbar I., ii. 205.
—— II., ii. 205.
Gablawîyûn, ii. 431.
Gablâyûn, ii. 431.
Gabra, Desert of, ii. 437.
——, the Hundred Wells of, ii. 392.
Gabriel, i. 224.
Gadîd, ii. 408.
Gadsby, Mr., i. 548.
Gage, Captain, ii. 380.
Gaius Petronius, ii. 167.
Gakdûl, ii. 392.
—— Wells, i. 58, 110, 179; ii. 252, 272, 372.
Galerius, ii. 290.
Galga, ii. 181.
Galgûr Hagami, ii. 349.
Galîlâ, ii. 363.
Galla country, i. 61; ii. 428, 432.
Gallaland, ii. 426.
Gallas, ii. 160, 231.
Game, ii. 400.
Games of chance, i. 221.
Gamêza, ii. 262.
Gami'a, ii. 349.
Gamîâb, ii. 437.
Gamilâb tribe, ii. 285.
Gamu'îya, ii. 437.
Gana, Queen of Nubia, ii. 307.
Ganâdal, ii. 366.
Ganbreves, ii. 160.
Gando, ii. 398.
Gandwaha, ii. 365.
Gangas, ii. 424.
Gangrene, i. 223.
Gânḳî, ii. 431.
Ganu, ii. 262.
Garf Ḥussên (or Husên), i. 74, 633, 638, 651; ii. 75, 111.
Garodes, ii. 164.
Garre, ii. 360.
Garrisons in Egypt, ii. 54.
Garstin, Sir W., i. 525; ii. 172, 173, 174, 312, 352, 358, 362, 364, 365, 367, 368, 370, 375, 376, 378, 380, 382, 385, 387, 481, 482, 484, 486, 487, 507, 511.
——, reports of, on the Nile, ii. 350.
Gash River, ii. 366.
Gatacre, General, ii. 273.
Gate of Kalâbshah, i. 74.
Gates, the, ii. 195.
Gau, F. C., i. 54; ii. 292.
Gaugades, Island of, ii. 163.
Gawhar, ii. 191.
Gayer, Monsignor, ii. 321.
Gazelle bones, i. 346.
Gazelle Mountain, i. 125.
—— River, ii. 358.
Gazîra, i. 519.
—— Province, ii. 407.
Gazîrat al-Malik, i. 475, 540, 547, 563; ii. 370.
——, excavation of temple at, i. 488-493.
Gazzera, Signor C., i. 564.
Gebâl Beni Shanḳûl, ii. 365.
Gebel 'Abd al-Dâim, ii. 375.
Gebel Abû Dôm, ii. 391.
Gebel Abû Ramla, ii. 365.
Gebel Abû Sinûn, ii. 391.
Gebel Agadî, ii. 459.
Gebel Aḥmad Aghâ, ii. 377.
Gebel al-Ghazâl, i. 125.
Gebel An-Nagaa, i. 325, 326.
Gebel Arashkol, ii. 375.
Gebel Ardân, i. 47.
Gebel Auli, ii. 375.
Gebel Barga, ii. 371.
Gebel Barkal, i. 35, 36, 37, 51, 55, 59, 61, 62, 63, 64, 112, 114, 120, 122, 130 ff., 143, 144, 146, 149, 179, 201, 204, 205, 355, 427, 462, 502, 601, 617, 624, 651; ii. 23, 27, 33, 46, 51, 56, 57, 58, 66, 75, 89, 118, 199, 299, 373, 479.
——, granite lions from, i. i. 618-621.
——, historical stelae of, ii. 87.
—— pyramids, i. 41.
—— —— described, i. 152.
—— —— opened, i. 169 ff.
——, Temple of Amen Râ at, ii. 9, 10.
——, view of, i. 50.
Gebel Dâgô, ii. 430, 441.

Gebel Dêgo, ii. 391.
Gebel Deka, ii. 301.
Gebel Dôsha, i. 38, 52, 60, 449, 549, 553, 595, 596, 630; ii. 207, 371.
——, Egyptian remains at, ii. 451.
Gebel Fâzô'glî, ii. 365.
Gebel Firket, ii. 371.
Gebel Fûng, ii. 213.
Gebel Gârî, ii. 474.
Gebel Gerok, ii. 285.
Gebel Gurûn, ii. 391.
Gebel Gilîf, ii. 437.
Gebel Ḥamra, ii. 371.
Gebel Ḥarîz, ii. 430.
Gebel Idrîs, ii. 371.
Gebel Ḳaba, ii. 365.
Gebel Kadero, ii. 391.
Gebel Ḳadîr, ii. 243, 244, 391, 411.
Gebel Kâf, ii. 349.
Gebel Ḳalî, ii. 437.
Gebel Kasala, ii. 216, 400.
Gebel Kôn, ii. 391.
Gebel Kudr, ii. 391.
Gebel Kurdu, ii. 385.
Gebel Kutum, ii. 412.
Gebel Lâdô, ii. 434.
Gebel Mamân, ii. 305.
Gebel Mandara, ii. 375.
Gebel Marra, ii. 265, 391, 412, 422, 430, 441.
Gebel Marrado, ii. 398.
Gebel Mêdûb, ii. 432.
Gebel Mokram, ii. 400.
Gebel Morung, ii. 391.
Gebel Mûl, ii. 431.
Gebel Muskû, ii. 430.
Gebel-Nagaa, ii. 127.
Gebel Nahoganet, ii. 472.
Gebel Nûba, ii. 411.
Gebel Reggâf, ii. 384.
Gebel Sâsî, ii. 207.
Gebel Sesi, i. 442, 628.
Gebel Shaḳada, ii. 436.
Gebel Shebûn, ii. 411.
Gebel Surgham, ii. 275.
Gebel Surkab, ii. 275.
Gebel Tabi, ii. 286.
Gebel Taḳâbû, ii. 430.
Gebel Taḳala, ii. 243, 391.
Gebel Taḳalî, ii. 202, 284.
Gebel Tebûn, ii. 391.
Gebel Tekem, ii. 391.
Gebel Tîrâ, ii. 411.
Gabel Werna, ii. 391.
Gebel Zâbara, i. 630; ii. 333.
Gebelên, i. 531, 532.
Gebelên on the White Nile, ii. 377, 399, 438.
Gebêt, ii. 478.
Geese as sacrifices, ii. 22, 23.
Ge'ez, i. 432.
Geili, ii. 233.
Gell, ii. 399.
Gelo, ii. 361.
Gellâbs, i. 53.
Gellabas, ii. 248.
Gemai, ii. 262.
Gentil, i. 11.
George, king of Nubians, ii. 191, 192.
George, Saint, i. 50.
George, son of Zacharias, ii. 298.
Georgi, O., i. 62.
Gerêf, ii. 250.
Gerr, ii. 434.
Gerri, i. 4.
Gessi Pâshâ, ii. 234-239, 248, 259, 350, 356, 482.
Ghaba Ger Dekka, ii. 239, 259.
Ghâba Shâmbi, ii. 380.
Ghalyk, ii. 184.
Ghânim, ii. 232.
Ghûzêr 'Alî, i. 234.
Giegler Pâshâ, ii. 244.
Giffen, Dr. Kelly, ii. 319, 320, 434, 444.
Gilîf, i. 62.
—— desert of, i. 114, 115.
Gim'a, ii. 436, 437.
Gimeti Island, ii. 301.
Ginger, i. 105.
Ginnis, i. 89, 96; ii. 261, 371, 444.
Gîra, ii. 260, 437.
Giraffe River, ii. 358.
Giraffes, i. 514; ii. 189, 327.
Giraffes, as tribute, ii. 195.
Girgaui, i. 534.
Girouard, Sir Percy, i. 192; ii. 270, 271.
Gîsh, Abyssinia, i. 19, 20. 41.
Giuda, ii. 234.
Gîza, ii. 189, 191.
——, museum of, i. 547.
Gîzah, Pyramids of, i. 118.
Glaser, i. 18.
Glass, melted, ii. 154.
—— ware, i. 105.
Gleichen, Count, ii. 232, 233, 234, 236, 244, 246, 249, 282, 284, 285, 299, 300, 305, 306, 321, 365, 370, 380, 384, 386, 391, 392, 393, 394, 396, 397, 398, 399, 401, 408, 412, 420, 428, 431, 434, 441, 444, 451, 460. 461.
Gloploa, ii. 160.
Gnats, ii. 156, 157.
Goang, ii. 365.
Goats, i. 543.
—— flesh, i. 28.
God, the Ethiopian, ii. 159.
—— unity of, i. 224.
Gods of the Sûdân, mortal and immortal, ii. 154.
Gogeri, ii. 424.
Gogonio River, ii. 386.
Gojam, ii. 263, 349, 364.
Gokau, ii. 360.
Gôlam Allah, ii. 198.
Gold, i. 2, 533, 534, 541, 553, 631, 638; ii. 10, 23, 96, 167, 191, 214, 411.
—— caravans, i. 622.
—— dust, ii. 327, 337.
—— —— of Abkulgui, i. 44.
—— —— used as money, i. 44.
——, Egyptian word for, ii. 336.
——, export of, ii. 332.
——, green, i. 571.
——, how obtained, i. 538; ii. 155.

INDEX

Gold, 100 bars of, ii. 108.
—— mines, i. 534, 554, 630, 632, 642; ii. 113, 153, 158, 181, 182, 300.
—— ——, how worked, ii. 340.
—— —— in the Sûdân, ii. 324 ff.
—— rings, i. 306, 571; ii. 265, 327.
—— —— from Meroë, i. 301.
—— —— money, i. 44.
——, 700 talents paid to Darius per annum by Egypt, ii. 104.
——, smelting of the ore, ii. 340.
—— various kinds of, ii. 336.
—— white, green, and red, ii. 337.
Golden Cat, ii. 160.
—— House, ii. 154.
—— Temple, ii. 110.
—— Throne, ii. 110.
Golo, ii. 322.
Golos, ii. 399, 421.
Gondar, i. 12, 19, 20; ii. 238, 262, 264.
Gondokoro, i. 507; ii. 222, 226, 228, 229, 230, 231, 233, 349, 458, 483, 485, 508.
—— missionary station at, ii. 313.
—— ——, Austrian, ii. 384.
Gôngâ, ii. 364.
Gongi Rapids, ii. 366, 385.
Gordon, Capt. H., ii. 287.
Gordon, General C. G., i. 76, 95, 102, 259, 265, 270, 271, 322; ii. 230, 231, 233, 234, 235, 236, 237, 238, 239, 240, 247, 278, 279, 318, 350.
—— returns to Kharṭûm, ii. 247.
——, his proclamation, ii. 248.
—— prisoner in Kharṭûm, ii. 249.
Gordon, General C. G., his position desperate, ii. 250.
——, his paper money, ii. 251.
——, murder of, ii. 253 ff.
——, statue of, ii. 394.
—— steamers, i. 258; ii. 276.
Gordon College, ii. 300, 306, 490 ff.
Gordon's Gate at Sawâkin, ii. 408.
Gordon Memorial, Soudan Mission, ii. 321.
Gordon Relief Expedition, i. 83, 110, 231; ii. 250 ff., 257 ff.
Gordon, Mr., i. 17.
Gorringe, Col., ii. 285, 460.
Gorringe, Mr., ii. 459, 488, 489.
Gorthon, death of, i. 53.
Gospel, the, i. 57.
Goths, ii. 289.
Göttingen, i. 29.
Graffiti, i. 553.
Graham, General, his expedition to Sûdân, ii. 249, 259, 260.
Graham, James, i. 17.
Grain boats, ii. 270.
Grand Signior, i. 15.
Granite, i. 518.
—— quarries, i. 51, 531.
—— statues at Arkô, i. 35.
Grant, Capt. J. A., ii. 220, 221, 222.
Grant, Mr. G. B. Macpherson, ii. 476, 479.
Graucome, ii. 160.
Greeks, i. 242, 250, 291, 605; ii. 182.
—— bazaar at Atbara, i. 250.
—— fire, ii. 197.
—— inscriptions, ii. 302.
—— in the Sûdân, ii. 370.
—— merchants at Merawi, i. 184.
Green water, ii. 368.
Gregory, *Rift Valley*, ii. 354.
Grenfell, Lord (formerly Gen. Sir F.), i. 68, 76-78, 89, 95, 203; ii. 260, 261, 262, 263, 264, 265, 269.
Grey, Sir E. ii. 383.
Griffith, Col. G. B., i. 197.
Griffith, Mr. F. Ll., i. 531; ii. 35.
Griglioni, Sister, ii. 277.
Grogan, Mr. E. S., ii. 358.
Guangue, ii. 364.
Gubat, ii. 253, 258, 259.
Gubba Salîm, i. 606.
Guidi, ii. 502.
Guilain, ii. 422.
Gule, ii. 396.
Gulf of Arabia, i. 21.
Gum, ii. 221, 376.
Gundîla dates, i. 471.
Gûr, ii. 431.
—— River, ii. 286, 315, 459.
Gura, ii. 238.
Gurgan Tau, ii. 371.
Gurong-Dit, ii. 441.
Gûrs, ii. 399.
Guruguru, ii. 357.
Güssfeldt, ii. 422.
Gûwâma'a, ii. 437.
Gwin Kun, ii. 444.
Gwynn, Major C. W., ii. 282, 284, 361, 460.
Gwynne, Mr., i. 100.
Gymnetes, ii. 164.
Gystate, ii. 160.

Ḥa, land of, i. 539.
Ḥabâb, ii. 436.
Habânîya, ii. 436, 437.
Habba, ii. 250.
Habesh, ii. 179, 182.
Ḥabîr of caravans, i. 53.
Ḥabra, ii. 438.
Habûb, i. 192, 193.
Hachour, i. 435.
Hadanduwa, ii. 214, 246, 417, 436.
Haddai, ii. 250.
Hadharebe, ii. 182, 183.
Hadow, Mr. F. B, ii. 321.
Ḥaḍr al-Mût, ii. 408.
Hadramout, ii. 408.

INDEX

Hadrian, Emperor, ii. 174.
Hafîr, i. 101, 103, 105; ii 261, 270, 372.
Ḥagar al-Àsal, ii. 204, 213.
Ḥagg, or pilgrimage to Mekka, i. 32.
Ḥaggi, i. 32.
Ḥaggi Alî, i. 1, 6.
Ḥakim, ii. 191.
Hakos, ii. 285.
Ḥalânḳa, ii. 214, 417, 436.
Ḥalâwîyûn, ii. 437.
Ḥalfa, ii. 370, 496, 497, 503.
—— Province, ii. 409.
—— Railway, ii. 236.
—— -Abû Hamed Railway, i. 190, 191; ii. 271.
—— -Kerma Railway, i. 470, ii. 270.
—— -Khartûm Railway, ii. 464.
—— Kosha Railway, ii. 464.
Halfa grass, i. 260, 274.
Ḥalfâya, i. 4, 21, 41, 47; ii. 250, 394, 436, 471, 472, 474.
Halîm, Prince, ii. 314.
Hall, Lieut. G. C. M., i. 264; ii. 463.
Hall, Mr. H. R., ii. 112.
Hall of Osiris, i. 384, 396.
Ḥamada, ii. 437.
Hamadab, i. 59.
Ḥamad wâd Aḥmad, ii. 253.
Hamags, ii. 430, 437, 440.
Ḥamar, ii. 437.
Ḥamâ-în, ii. 231, 234.
Hambuk, ii. 392.
Ḥamed al-Shemîk, ii. 204.
Ḥamed ibn At-Tarâbî, ii. 202.
Hamest, ii. 181.
Hamilton, Rev. Dr., i. 29.
Hamites, ii. 420.
Hamitic race, ii. 427.
—— tribes, ii. 435.
Hammar Island, i. 107.
Hanbury, Rev. B., i. 34, 478.
Ḥandaḳ, ii. 372.
Hands cut off, i. 565.
Handûb, ii. 262, 264, 265, 392, 474, 478.
Ḥa-nebu, i. 629.
Ḥanigalbat, ii. 332.
Hanna, Mr. G., ii. 319.
Ḥannâk, ii. 372.
Hannek, i. 3, 52, 99; ii. 207, 291, 366, 371.
——, Cataract of, i. 559.
Ḥannikâb, ii. 439.
Ḥāp, ii. 11.
—— (Nile), ii. 343, 344.
Ḥāpi (Apis), i. 400.
Ḥāpi (Nile God), i. 66, 361, 383; ii. 49.
Harar, ii. 231, 236, 238, 248.
Harâtari, ii. 392.
Harmachis, i. 623, 637.
Harmer, Baron, ii. 312.
Harpocrates, i. 301, 417, 421, 557.
Harrow, i. 17.
Hartmann, ii. 423, 428, 434, 442, 445.
Ḥarua, ii. 30.
Harûn, ii. 235.
Hârûn ar-Rashîd, ii. 202.
Harvest, ii. 441.
Ḥasab-Raba, ii. 203.
Ḥasan, ii. 208.
Ḥasan the admiral, ii. 209.
Ḥasan, Aghâ of Derr, i. 28, 34.
Ḥasan Bey Salâma, ii. 221.
Hasan Effendi Zâki, ii. 279.
Ḥasan Hilmi, ii. 235.
Ḥasan ibn Muḥammad, ii. 307.
Ḥasan ibn Tabal, ii. 205
Ḥasan Kûshi, ii. 207.
Ḥasan Pâshâ, Prince, ii. 234.
Ḥasanât, ii. 438.
Ḥassanîya Island, ii. 376.
—— tribe, ii. 375, 437.
Ḥashîsh, i. 221, 222.
Ḥasîn ibn Sulêmân, ii. 208.
Hassa Hissa, ii. 305.
Hathor, i. 301, 307, 327, 576, 592, 599, 625, 636, 637, 643; ii. 45, 125.
Hathor capitals, i. 161, 454.
—— pillars, i. 637.
——, tree of, i. 384.
Hatim Mûsa, ii. 268.
Ḥātshepset, i. 571, 573, 598, 623: ii. 414.
Hawâra, i. 552; ii. 198.
Ḥawâtîya, ii. 437.
Hawâwîr, ii. 437.
Hawk, stone, i. 391, 621.
Hawk-headed crocodile, ii. 140.
Hawk-nome, i. 362.
Hawkins, Mr. H. V., ii. 476, 479.
Hay, Mr., ii. 325.
Haynes, Capt., ii. 285.
Headlam, Captain H. R., ii. 460.
Heat, great, i. 290.
—— at Gebel Barkal, i. 51.
—— in the Sûdân, ii. 157.
Heart, weighing of, i. 381, 387.
Hebdomecontacometae, ii. 160.
Hebrews, i. 195, 535.
Hebsi, ii. 80.
Heeren, Prof., i. 56, 57.
Ḥeḥ, land of, i. 538, 541, 543, 544, 553.
Heiligen Kreuz, ii. 312.
Hejer, ii. 179, 187.
Hekataeus, ii. 339, 347.
Helâwa, i. 2.
Heleii, ii. 157.
Heliopolis, i. 621, 622, 624; ii. 8, 22.
Heliostats, i. 334.
Ḥellet an-Nuer, ii. 380.
Ḥëllet ar-Renk, ii. 377.
Ḥellet Bunzûka, ii. 439.
Hemp, Indian, i. 221.
Ḥen-Nefer, i. 562.
Ḥennu, i. 532.
Henry, Col. St. George, i. 282; ii. 460.
Ḥep (Nile), ii. 343.
Herakleopolis, ii. 4, 5, 7, 12, 14, 17.
—— Princes of, i. 529, 530.

Herbagi, i. 21.
Herbin, Mr. ii. 250.
Hercules, i. 307; ii. 154, 159.
Ḥer-Ḥeru, first priest king, i. 645, 646, 647; ii. 2.
Ḥeripeṭmai, ii. 21.
Ḥeriu-shā, i. 533, 553, 568.
Ḥer-khu, i. 2, 515, 526, 533; ii. 324.
——, inscription of, i. 520.
—— meets Una, i. 520.
Hermitages, ruined, i. 4.
Hermopolis, i. 137; ii. 5, 6, 7, 12, 14.
—— Parva, ii. 5, 14.
Herodotus, i. 39; ii. 28, 29, 34, 53, 54, 55, 91, 93, 104, 105, 106, 107, 110, 153.
—— and Lake Moeris, i. 551, 552.
Heroopolis, ii. 166.
Ḥeru, ii. 41.
Ḥeru-em-ḥeb, a priest, i. 625; ii. 41.
Ḥeru-em-khut, i. 623.
Ḥeru-ḳer-taui, ii. 27.
Ḥeru-khent-Khatthi, ii. 23.
Ḥeru-khuti, i. 605, 626, 644.
Ḥeru-nekht, ii. 56.
Ḥeru-nest-aṭebui (?), i. 485.
Ḥeru-Rā-kha-kau, Fort, i. 548.
Ḥeru-sa-atef, ii. 75, 87.
—— reign, ii. 75-82.
Ḥeru-seḥ[er]-taui, ii. 27.
Ḥesert, ii. 49.
Hesperiae, ii. 165.
Hesperu Ceras, ii. 165.
Ḥet-Benben, i. 625.
Ḥet-Bennu, ii. 12, 15.
Ḥet-khā-em-Maat, name of temple of Ṣulb, i. 612.
Ḥet-ka-Ptaḥ, ii. 21.
Ḥet-Khent, ii. 111.
Hetley, F., i. 478.
Ḥet-menen-khā-em-Maāt, i. 612.
Ḥet-nub, i. 518.
Ḥet-urt, ii. 12.

Heuglin, Herr T. von, ii. 314, 316.
Hezekiah, ii. 33, 34, 35.
Hicks Pâshâ, Gen., ii. 278.
——, his defeat and death, ii. 245.
Hiera-Sykaminos, ii. 111, 162, 172, 176.
Hijâz, i. 32; ii. 238.
Hildebrandt, ii. 422.
Hill-men, i. 568, 588, 598, 604, 622, 631; ii. 174, 416, 417.
Hima, ii. 354.
Himantopodes, ii. 175.
Himyar, ii. 303.
Hipparchus, ii. 348.
Hipponon, ii. 6, 12.
Hippopotamus, i. 41, 105; ii. 376.
—— goddess, i. 383.
Hirth, Mr. G., i. 382.
Hittites, ii. 427.
Hobbs, Captain, i. 255.
Hodgson, Mr. C. G., i. 437, 497, 503; ii. 476, 479.
Hodgson, Capt. H., ii. 391, 460.
Hoes, iron, ii. 399.
Hoimi, ii. 356.
Holroyd, i. 478.
Holy Mountain, i. 137; ii. 45, 46, 57, 61.
Homer, i. 522.
Ḥomr tribe, ii. 451.
Honey, i. 221, 230, 525; ii. 80, 90.
Honey Rock, ii. 204.
Hora, ii. 160.
Hornemann, i. 52.
Horo, ii. 356.
Horse, ii. 7, 17, 23.
——'s bones, i. 344.
——s of Dongola, i. 105.
—— in Egypt, the, i 565.
——s' scalps worn, ii. 105.
Horton, Mr. W. H., i. 437, 497.
Horus, i. 306, 362, 370, 386, 389, 391, 392, 398, 418, 421, 526, 547, 568, 625,

629, 633; ii. 16, 17, 82, 135.
Horus and Set set up the ladder, i. 527.
——, eyes of, i. 301, 305.
——, Four Children of, i. 361.
—— of Behen, i. 576, 584, 599.
—— of Behutet, i. 482.
—— of Edfu, i. 543.
—— of Kenset, i. 595.
—— of Māām, i. 575, 576.
—— of Ram of Amen, i. 597.
—— of Sekhem, ii. 24.
—— -Rā, i. 384.
—— -Set, ii. 33.
Hosam, ii. 198.
Hôsh al-Ibyaḍ, ii. 373.
Hoskins, G. A., i. 103, 105, 117, 118, 120, 122, 130, 133, 134, 139, 149, 150, 151, 152, 153, 154, 156, 162, 163, 164, 169, 201, 235, 240, 267, 274, 276, 328, 342, 348, 352, 353, 428, 435, 440, 453, 454, 463, 466, 496, 557, 558, 559; ii. 10, 147, 148.
——, Travels of, i. 55 ff.
Hospitals, ii. 500.
—— in Omdurmân, ii. 279.
Houri, i. 226.
House of a Thousand Years, ii. 80.
—— of the Eight Gods, ii. 17.
House tax, ii. 451.
Ḥuā, land of, i. 553, 554.
Ḥudêbât, ii. 436.
Hûdî, ii. 273, 479.
Ḥufrat An-Naḥâs, ii. 284, 412.
Human sacrifices, ii. 177.
Ḥumr, ii. 437.
Ḥumrân, ii. 437.
Hunter, Major (afterwards General) Sir A., i. 86, 89, 104, 113, 192; ii. 265, 269, 270, 273, 280.
Ḥurbasa, ii. 24.

Husên Pâshâ Khalîfa, ii. 198, 247.
Ḥussunnât, ii. 437.
Huu, i. 536.
Hyalus, ii. 159.
Hyksos Kings, i. 559, 561, 562, 599.
Hylophagi, ii. 156.
Hypaton, ii. 160.

IBBA, ii. 399.
Iberians, ii. 427.
Ibis-nome, i. 362.
Ibn Jaubalân, ii. 207.
Ibn Miskaweh, ii. 190.
Ibn Selîm al-Aswânî, ii. 186, 189.
Ibrahîm, ii. 298.
Ibrahîm of Dâr Fûr, ii. 207.
Ibrahîm, brother of Kerenbes, ii. 196.
Ibrahîm Pâshâ made ruler of Egypt, ii. 217.
Ibrahîm, son of Muḥammed Ali, ii. 210, 212.
Ibrahîm Abû Shanab, ii. 253.
Ibrahîm ibn 'Abd-Allâh, a name of Burckhardt, i. 30.
Ibrahîm Khalîl, ii. 266.
Ibrahîm Murâd, ii. 284.
Ibrahîm wâd Maḥmûd, ii. 285, 488, 489.
Ibrahimiya (Dufili), ii. 233.
Ibrîm, i. 22, 26, 28, 29, 31, 463, 599, 643; ii. 168, 174, 191, 192, 197, 207, 293, 303.
Ice at Aswân, i. 71.
Ichthyophagi, the, ii. 106, 15.
Idrîs, Shêkh, i. 444, 456, 458, 471.
—— ——, Ḳubba of, i. 458 ff.
Idrîs ibn Muḥammad, ii. 202.
Idrîs of Dâr Fûr, ii. 206.
Idrîs, son of Yamni, ii. 205.
Idrîs I., ibn Sûlêmân, ii. 205.
Idris II., ii. 206.
—— III., ii. 206.
I-em-ḥetep, i. 400.
Iêsou, Abbâ, i. 464, 465; ii. 300.
Igasha, ii. 354.
Ikhshîd, the, ii. 303.
Image of Amen-ḥetep III., i. 623, 624.
Images, worship of, ii. 430, 441.
Imâm Âlî, ii. 241.
Incense, ii. 90, 521.
—— trees, i. 521.
India, i. 21, 34; ii. 170, 189.
Indians, Calantian, ii. 105.
India-rubber, ii. 451.
Ingassana, ii. 396.
Ingelêla, ii. 246.
Innocent XII., i. 5.
Inundation, the, ii. 153, 157.
——, heights of, i. 550.
——, how caused, ii. 368.
Ionians, ii. 53.
Ipoto, i. 524.
Ipsodorae, ii. 164.
'Irâḳ, ii. 207.
Iré, ii. 286.
Iron, ii. 412.
—— fetters of a slave, i. 366.
—— mines, ii. 153, 158, 181.
—— money, i. 105.
—— working, ii. 398.
Irrigation Dept., i. 71.
—— schemes, ii. 484.
Îsa, the Robber, i. 495, 496, 606.
Isaac, i. 464.
Isenberg, ii. 502.
Isis, i. 72, 160, 306, 365, 383, 385, 395-398, 421, 432, 591, 633; ii. 112, 118, 122, 134, 136, 154, 159, 176.
—— and the Nile, ii. 344.
—— goddesses in Nubia, ii. 82.
Isis, of Philae, ii. 177, 292, 294.
—— Selqet, i. 394.
——, temple of, at Philae, i. 13.
—— —— closed, ii. 178.
Islâm, i. 82; ii. 182, 186, 191, 200, 201, 408, 440.
—— enters Sennaar, ii. 202.
Island of Bigga, i. 598.
—— Sâî, i. 595, 601, 606.
—— Senmut, i. 598.
Islands of the Blessed, i. 524.
Ismâ'îl, ii. 203.
Ismâ'îl Bey, ii. 209.
Isma'îl Pâshâ, i. 35, 69, 87, 90, 105, 258, 271; ii. 204, 218, 235, 462.
—— becomes Khedive of Egypt, ii. 222.
——, deposition of, ii. 238.
—— and the slave trade, ii. 225, 226, 237.
Isma'îl Pâshâ Ayûb, ii. 230
Ismâ'îl, son of Muḥammad 'Alî, ii. 208, 210, 212.
—— burnt to death, ii. 407.
Ismâ'îl Ya'kûb Pâshâ, ii. 232, 235.
Ismaïlia, steamer, i. 258.
Ismâ'îlîya (Gondokoro), ii. 229, 384.
Issango, ii. 355.
Isveli, ii. 165.
Italians, i. 242; ii. 267, 269, 270.
—— in Eritrea, ii. 265, 266.
—— defeated, i. 85, 86, 268.
Itang, ii. 285, 360.
Ituri River, i. 524, 525.
Iuaâ, i. 607.
Ivory, i. 521, 525, 526, 554, 571; ii. 10, 104, 221, 223, 399, 451.
—— trade, ii. 228.
—— —— working of, described, ii. 224.
'Îyâsu I. invades Sennaar, ii. 203.
Îyâsûs, king of Abyssinia, i. 10, 11, 12.

INDEX

JA'AFAR Mazhar Pâshâ, ii. 226.
Ja'afar Ṣâdiḳ, ii. 226.
Ja'afara Arabs, ii. 407.
Jaalîn, i. 85.
Jackals, i. 269, 344.
Jackson, Colonel, ii. 280, 484.
Jackson, Lieut. L. C., ii. 460.
Jacob, i. 464.
Jacobites in Nubia, ii. 296.
Jaheth, ii. 179.
James, Mr. F. L., ii. 365.
Jân, ii. 359.
Jânḳî, ii. 246.
Jawâbîr Arabs, ii. 207.
Jeddah, i. 18.
Jerusalem, ii. 34, 37.
——, Fathers of, i. 5.
Jesuits, i. 1, 7, 12.
—— expelled, i. 5.
Jews, ii. 167.
Jidda, i. 18, 31; ii. 188, 190, 406.
Jimangawu, ii. 356.
John, king of Abyssinia, ii. 231, 234, 235, 236, 238, 264, 400.
John of Ephesus, ii. 296.
John of Syria, ii. 304.
Johnson, Major Bulkeley, ii. 460.
Johnston, Sir H., ii. 316, 347, 350, 425.
Jokha, ii. 357.
Jomard, i. 24.
Jones, Sir W., i. 19.
Joseph = Brevedent, i. 6.
Josephus, ii. 94.
Josiah, ii. 73.
Jo-uk, ii. 443.
Ju, ii. 443.
Juba, ii. 160.
—— River, ii. 233, 361.
Judah, ii. 33, 73.
Judgment Scene, i. 369, 381, 384.
Julian, a priest, ii. 295, 296.
Junker, ii. 351, 428, 461.
Jupiter, ii. 106, 154.
Jupiter Ammon (or Hammon), i. 56; ii. 91, 93, 163.
—— Sarapis, ii. 136, 141.
Jûr (Gûr), ii. 359.
Jûrês, ii. 195, 196.
Justice, ii. 496.
Justinian, Emperor, ii. 178, 294.

KA-ÂAT, ii. 117.
Ka'aba, i. 224.
Kaau, i. 517.
Kabâbîsh, ii. 437.
Kabarega (Kabba Réga), ii. 228, 260, 268.
Kabbana, ii. 438.
Kabenât, Island of, i. 50.
Kabkabîa, ii. 262, 432, 437.
Kabôdi, i. 98.
Kabûshîyâ, i. 41, 56, 331, 334, 497, 503; ii. 473.
Ḳaḍâref, ii. 235, 246, 249, 265, 280, 399, 400, 439, 462.
Kadaru, ii. 474.
Kadashman Bêl, ii. 332.
Kaddin, i. 98.
Kadero, ii. 233.
Kadesh, i. 598; ii. 38.
Ḳâḍî's Pudding, ii. 481.
Kadro, ii. 202.
Kafikingi, ii. 284.
Kafu, ii. 356, 387.
Kâga al-Badu, ii. 431.
Kagarandindu, ii. 356.
Kagbar Cataract, ii. 371.
Kagera, ii. 352, 387.
Kagmar, ii. 392.
Kagûbâb, ii. 438.
Kaheni, ii. 22.
Ka-ḥeseb, ii. 11, 14.
Kahl, ii. 435.
Ḳaja, ii. 246.
Kâḳâ, ii. 377, 378, 437, 439.
——, Old, ii. 377.
Kakibi, ii. 355.
Kaknak, ii. 424.
Kakogi, ii. 387.
Kakoonda, ii. 355.
Ḳala'a Arâng, ii. 439.
Kalâbsha, i. 13, 73, 87, 574, 599, 629, 638, 651; ii. 111, 170, 291, 292, 297, 328, 329.
Kalâkala, ii. 252, 253.
Ḳal'at an-Nagîl, i. 129.
Ḳal'at Ma'atûka, i. 549.
Ḳalâ'ûn, ii. 195, 196.
Ḳalbâs, ii. 205.
Kali, i. 604.
Kalikâ, ii. 424.
Kalka, i. 426; ii. 118.
Ḳallâbât, ii. 214, 238, 246, 260, 261, 265, 280, 285, 365, 399, 400, 462.
Kallaḥ, ii. 205.
Kalmakûl, ii. 202.
Kaltela, ii. 118.
—— Pyramid of, i. 426 ff.
Kamalt, ii. 434.
Kamâmîl, i. 44; ii. 411.
Kamatîr, ii. 438.
Ḳambâr, ii. 205.
Kambasuṭen, ii. 94.
Kambô, ii. 205.
Kâmlîn, ii. 305, 365, 407, 438.
Kamobsana, ii. 478.
Ḳamr ad-Dawlah, ii. 194.
Kamâna, ii. 438, 439.
Ḳanbalâwî, ii. 206.
Kandake, i. 357.
Ka-nefert, i. 421.
Ka-nekht-khā-em-Nept, ii. 75.
Kanîsa, Mission of, ii. 312, 380.
Kanîsa ul - Faḳîr Maṣawwarât, i. 47.
Kank, ii. 202.
Kanḳara, ii. 441.
Kantat, i. 109.
Kanûn ibn Azîz, ii. 187, 188.
Kanûzî, the, ii. 435.
Kanz, tribe of, ii. 197.
Kanz ad-Dawlah, ii. 193, 196, 197.
Ka-qem, ii. 22, 23.
Ḳar'a, ii. 234.

INDEX

Karabîn, i. 44.
Karubât, ii. 438.
Karad, ii. 373.
Karague, ii. 402.
Karam-Allah, ii. 249, 250, 264.
Karari, ii. 241.
—— hills, ii. 276.
Kararîsh tribe, i. 496.
Kar Bêl-matâti, ii. 53.
Karei, i. 607.
Karêma, ii. 473.
—— -Abû Hamed Railway, ii. 373.
Karert, ii. 82.
Kari, i. 604, 632.
Karka, ii. 118.
Karkĕmîsh, ii. 74.
Karko, ii. 202.
Karkôg, ii. 244, 280, 365, 437.
Karkûd, ii. 438.
Karnak, i. 54, 67; ii. 13, 30, 33, 38, 41, 42.
Karpeto, ii. 357.
Kart, ii. 198.
Ḳartassî, i. 651.
Karṭept, ii. 94, 95.
Kartera, ii. 118.
Karuma Falls, ii. 386.
Karuthet, ii. 82.
Kas, i. 536.
Kasala, i. 31, 86, 214, 217, 246, 305, 339, 502; ii. 235, 260, 265-268, 273, 282, 366, 400, 404, 436, 462, 479, 487, 502, 509.
—— Province, ii. 399.
Kasamba, ii. 305.
Ḳasâu, ii. 81.
Kash (Cûsh), i. 535, 536 ff., 573, 592, 595, 622, 626, 628, 629, 631, 637, 642; ii. 39, 62, 66, 72, 326, 334, 400, 416, 486.
—— = Southern Sûdân, i. 536.
——, gold of, ii. 337.
—— prince of, i. 554.
—— River, ii. 366.
Kashafa, the, ii. 201, 207.
Kashgil, ii. 245.
Kashta, ii. 27, 28.
Ḳaṣr Towago, i. 60.
Kassâm, ii. 215.
Kassingar, i. 114, 191, 232.
Ḳaṭêna, ii. 305, 408, 437.
Katha . . . ., i. 612.
Katimar, ii. 117.
Katkû, ii. 440.
Katonga, ii. 352.
Katwe Bay, ii. 354.
Kaufmann, ii. 422.
Kâwa, ii. 242, 244, 245, 372, 408.
Kawwa, ii. 376, 438.
Keane, A. H., ii. 424.
Kebkebîya, ii. 428, 438.
Kebiân, ii. 363.
Kedesh, i. 609.
Kefa, i. 612.
Kefîyah, i. 214.
Kefla 'Abâi, i. 20.
Keili, ii. 396.
Kelham, Sergeant-Major, i. 108, 109, 240.
Ḳena, i. 18, 471, 642.
Ḳenbetu, i. 572.
Kenensat, ii. 2, 3.
Kenreth, i. 418; ii. 117.
Kenrethreqnen-m, ii. 117.
—— ——, Pyramid of, i. 417 ff.
Kenrick, Capt., ii. 460.
Kenset, i. 562, 564, 593, 595, 598, 604, 628; ii. 45.
Kensetiu, i. 563.
Kentakit, ii. 117.
Kentha - Ḥebit, ii. 117, 169.
——, Pyramid of, i. 357.
Kentkit, ii. 169.
Kenufi, i. 383, 384.
Kenur, ii. 273.
Kenûz, ii. 207.
—— dialect, ii. 420.
Kenyon, Dr. F. G., i. 175; ii. 308.
Keppel, ii. 272.
Keren, ii. 231.
Kerenbes, ii. 196.
Kerkis, ii. 74.
Kerma, i. 87, 97, 98, 99, 100, 101, 106, 188, 443, 470, 472; ii. 93, 270, 370, 372, 409, 463, 468, 470, 479.
Kermân, i. 559.
Ḳerri, ii. 262, 204.
Kesh (Cûsh), i. 564, 605, 628, 633.
Ḳetshi, i. 612.
Key of the Sûdân, i. 249.
Khā-em-Uast, ii. 325.
Khaîl, Patriarch, ii. 298.
Khalêwa, ii. 300.
Khâlid Pâshâ, ii. 217.
Khalîfa 'Abd Allah, i. 64, 77, 90, 96, 97, 106, 177, 209, 606.
——, his plans for conquest of Egypt, ii. 260.
—— begins to invade Egypt, ii. 263.
——, escape of, ii. 277.
——, defeat of, ii. 280.
Khalîfa Sherif, ii. 281.
Khalîl ibn Kûsûn, ii. 197.
Khamsîn (Khamâsîn, Khamsûn), i. 51.
Khanak, i. 97.
Khandaḳ, i. 615, 651; ii. 300, 407, 439.
Khā-nefer, a pyramid, i. 518.
Kharba, ii. 179.
Khârga, Oasis of, i. 9, 10, 23, 85, 508; ii. 93, 176, 177, 266.
Kharṭûm, i. 21, 38, 47, 54, 61, 62, 78, 95, 102, 209, 264, 285, 321, 324, 480, 485, 488, 500, 502, 503, 506, 508, 519, 547, 567, 597, 621; ii. 89, 199, 212, 217, 375, 450, 462.
—— besieged and bombarded, ii. 252 ff.
——, city of, ii. 394.
—— described by Baker, ii. 221.
—— founded, ii. 212.
——, governors of, i. 271.
——, meaning of name, ii. 393.

Kharṭûm, Museum at, i. 436, 477, 502.
——, North, ii. 474.
——, schools in, ii. 318.
—— taken by the Mahdî, ii. 254.
—— occupied by Lord Kitchener, ii. 279.
—— Province, ii. 393.
Khas, i. 604.
Khashîm al-Girba, ii. 365.
Khati I., i. 529.
—— II., i. 529.
Khawâbîr, ii. 438.
Khawâlada, ii. 438.
Khawâwîr, ii. 438.
Khêbar, Cataract of, ii. 366, 371.
Khebit, ii. 66.
Khemennu, i. 626 ; ii. 14.
Khemer, i. 536.
Khemthithet, ii. 111.
Khennutiu, i. 569.
Khen-Setcher, i. 517.
Khensu, i. 134, 135, 306, 526, 527 ; ii. 52, 66, 70.
Khensu-Arṭâs, ii. 69.
Khensu - em - Uast - Nefer-ḥetep, ii. 45.
Khent, or Image, i. 623.
Khent = Sûdân, i. 562.
Khent-ḥen-nefer, i. 561, 566, 567, 568; 632 ; ii. 416.
Khent-Khatthi, ii. 23.
Khent-khat-ur, i. 538.
Khent-Nefer, ii. 24.
Khent-ruhi, ii. 69.
Kheper-ka-Rā, ii. 118, 119.
Kher-Āḥa, ii. 8, 22, 24.
Kheta, i. 605, 631, 636, 637 ; ii. 38.
——, Prince of, i. 627.
Khnem-ab-Rā, i. 425 ; ii 118.
Khnemu, i. 384, 421, 467, 531, 556, 571, 584, 587, 592, 594, 599, 601, 603, 605, 612. 626, 630, 633 ; ii. 3, 74, 112, 122, 135, 150.
—— temple at Elephantine, i. 574.
Khnemu-Rā, ii. 49.
Khneph, i. 384.
Khnoubis, i. 384.
Khnoumis, i. 384.
Khnouphis, i. 384.
Khonsu, i. 370, 418.
Khôr Abû 'Adâr, ii. 273.
Khôr Abû Ḥabl, ii. 245.
Khôr Baraka, ii. 409, 436.
Khôr Dulêb, ii. 430, 436.
Khôr Filus, ii. 361.
Khôr Gokau, ii. 360.
Khôr Kanieti, ii. 360.
Khôr Khos, ii. 360.
Khôr Mûsa, i. 84 ; ii. 262.
Khôr Too, ii. 360.
Khôr Umbrega, ii. 365.
Khôr Wintri, ii. 268.
Khu-en-Åten, i. 622.
Khuit, ii. 23.
Khu-ka-Rā, i. 139 ; ii. 57.
Khulla, ii. 259.
Khûrshi, ii. 396, 437.
Khurshîd Aghâ, ii. 312.
Khurshîd Pâshâ, i. 285 ; ii. 210, 213, 214.
Khu-taui-Rā, king, i. 485, 486, 487.
——, statue of, at Kharṭûm, i. 555.
Khut-en-Åten, i, 623.
Khuzâm, ii. 438.
Kilgû, i. 44.
Kilma dates, i. 471.
Kipkip, ii. 50.
Ḳimr, ii. 431, 432, 434.
Kings, how chosen, ii. 153, 155, 159.
——, mutilation of, ii. 150.
Kinnaird, i. 17.
Kir, ii. 362, 399.
Kirbikân, ii. 259
Kiri, ii. 385.
Kirkman, Col. Sir J., ii. 231, 234.
Kirô, ii. 282, 284, 381, 382.
Kirsh, ii. 75.
——, temple of, i. 633.
Kismayu, ii. 234.
Kisuma, ii. 352.
Kît, ii. 357, 385.
Kît-Island, ii. 359.
Kitchener, Lord, i. 34, 63, 68, 88, 89, 105, 321 ; ii. 239, 262, 318, 448, 477, 492, 495, 507.
Kitchener, Col. F. W., i. 233.
Kiveh, ii. 357.
Kivu, ii. 354.
Kléber, ii. 210.
Klunzinger, ii. 422.
Knoblecher, Father, ii. 312, 313.
Knot of Hercules, i. 307.
Knowles, General, i. 85.
Kôbi, i. 53, 508 ; ii. 398.
Kôdôk, ii. 213, 227, 228, 230, 286, 377, 378, 399.
Koelle, ii. 445.
Kôka, i. 52.
Koke, i. 35.
Kola, ii 443.
Koleydozo, ii. 185.
Kome, ii. 352.
Konegoi, ii. 156.
Konosso, Island of, i. 531, 556, 604 ; ii. 74.
Kordôfân, i. 24, 31, 61, 105, 179, 285, 295, 506, 521 ; ii. 96, 105, 155, 171, 175, 208, 213, 217, 231, 242, 248, 265, 458, 462.
—— Province, ii. 396.
——, revolt in, ii. 260.
Korne, ii. 352.
Koroscoff, i. 14.
Korosko, i. 14, 31, 55, 61, 62, 81, 87, 294, 295, 496, 531, 534, 536, 548, 553, 574 ; ii. 93, 105, 214, 247, 314, 328, 420, 458, 461, 468.
——, mosque of, i. 75, 76.
——, views of, i. 74.
—— -'Abû-Hamed Railway, ii. 463.
Korti, i. 4, 35, 110, 111, 509 ; ii. 75, 259, 270, 372.
Kosanga, ii. 315.
—— River, ii. 315.

INDEX

Kôsha, i. 95, 96, 97, 438, 442, 443, 468, 469, 470 ff.; ii. 89, 116, 261, 270, 290, 370, 371, 409, 464.
Koskam, i. 20, 21.
Kossinga, ii. 284.
Kotschy, i. 24.
Koye, i. 34; ii. 300.
Kôz Abû Gûma, ii. 376, 480.
Ḳôz al-Ma'âlîya, ii. 438.
Ḳôz-Ragab, i. 31.
Krall, Dr., i. 648.
Krapf, ii. 349, 350.
Kreich, ii. 399.
Kuanza, ii. 229.
Kubalab, ii. 474.
Ḳubba, ii. 474.
Ḳubba, near Ḥannek, ii. 207.
Ḳubba Abû Faṭmâ, i. 559; ii. 371.
Ḳubba Idrîs, i. 444, 445, 459 ff.; ii. 371.
Ḳubba Salîm, i. 455, 456, 606, 621; ii. 371.
Kubbân, i. 74, 534, 574, 629, 631, 632, 633, 634, 638, 651; ii. 111, 188, 329, 334.
Kûbî, ii. 412.
Kubḳ, ii. 431.
Kubuli, ii. 357.
Kudit, ii. 444.
Kuêka, ii. 371.
Kufit, ii. 261.
Ḳuft, ii. 189.
Kûkreb, ii. 392.
Kûkû, ii. 349.
—— Mountains, ii. 386.
Kulkul, ii. 428, 431, 432.
Kulzum, ii. 189, 190.
Ḳumm, ii. 190.
Kummah (or Kumma), i. 40, 61, 476, 480, 481 487, 540, 541, 552, 563, 571; ii. 116, 330, 370.
——, Fort of, i. 549.
——, graffiti at, i. 479.
——, Nile registers at, i. 550.
Kummah (or Kumma) temple of Thothmes III. at, i. 592.
—— village and temple of, i. 479.
Ḳumuz, ii. 431.
Ḳur'ân, i. 33, 214, 217, 224, 226, 230, 234, 457; ii. 188, 241.
Kurar, i. 444.
Kurbag, i. 210.
Kurêsh, ii. 207.
Kur-Kongs, ii. 441.
Kûrkûr, Oasis of, i. 521.
Ḳûrna, i. 600.
Kurru, i. 170; ii. 116.
——, pyramids of, i. 125.
Ḳûrta, i. 574, 651; ii. 111.
Kûrû, ii. 205.
Ḳuruâr-ḥi (?), ii. 46.
Kurumut, ii. 69.
Ḳuruses, i. 612.
Kuru-tanen-Âmen, ii. 66, 69.
Kur Wâd Nedok, ii. 444.
Kûṣ, i. 298; ii. 179, 189, 190, 192, 193, 195, 196, 198, 303, 458.
Ḳuṣêr, i. 18, 642; ii. 189.
Kush, ii. 41, 323.
Kushites, ii. 296.
Kutchûk 'Alî, ii. 227.
Kuttabs, ii. 490.
Kutum, ii. 439.
Kuwâhla, ii. 438.
Ḳuwâhsama, ii. 438.
Kuwêkka, i. 458.
Kuyunjik, i. 487; ii. 30.
Kwad Keir, ii. 444.
Kwat Ki, ii. 444.
Kwat wâd Awaibung, ii. 499.
Kwoe Kon, ii. 444.

LABBAYÂB, ii. 438.
Labori, ii. 385.
Labyrinth, i. 551, 552.
Ladder, i. 527.
Lâdô, ii. 233, 250, 260, 368, 384, 487.
Lâdô Enclave, ii. 320, 382, 390, 399.
—— Shêkh, ii. 384.
Lafargue, i. 478.
Lagîa, i. 24.
Lagia Kabîr, ii. 391.
Laḥawîyûn, ii. 438.
Lake Albert, i. 525; ii. 222, 235, 350, 353, 484, 485.
—— described, ii. 356.
Lake Albert Edward, i. 525; ii. 353.
Lake Al-Menteita, ii. 354.
Lake Bangweolo, ii. 229.
Lake Baringo, ii. 349, 354.
Lake Damâdim, ii. 349.
Lake Dueru, ii. 354.
Lake Hannington, ii. 354.
Lake Kûkû, ii. 349.
Lake of Likuri, ii. 349.
Lake Manjara, ii. 354.
Lake Moeris, i. 550, 551; ii. 104.
—— ——, existence of, disproved, i. 552.
Lake Moero, ii. 229.
Lake Naivasha, ii. 354.
Lake Nakuru, ii. 354.
Lake Natron, ii. 354.
Lake Ngami, ii. 229.
Lake Nô, ii. 351, 356, 358, 368, 375, 379, 458, 481, 482.
Lake Nyassa, ii. 229, 349, 354.
Lake Rudolf, ii. 282, 354.
Lake Ṣânâ, ii. 349, 363 ff.
Lake Shirwa, ii. 229.
Lake Tanganyika, ii. 229, 349.
Lake Victoria, ii. 222, 350, 351.
Lakodero, ii. 358.
Lāmersekni, ii. 5, 12.
Lâmḳasna, ii. 431.
Lamp, dedication of, ii. 101.
Lampreys, ii. 155.
Lances, i. 3.
Land of the Blacks, i. 506, 515, 600; ii. 340.
—— of Men, i. 505.
—— of the Spirits, i. 138, 523.

INDEX

Land tax, ii. 451.
Lane, Mr. E., i. 226; ii. 344.
Languages, ii. 444.
Lapis lazuli, ii. 17, 23.
Laṭîf Pâshâ, ii. 218.
Lâtûka (place), ii. 233.
—— Hills, ii. 360.
Lâtûkâ (tribe), ii. 431.
Lattuka, ii. 424.
Lau, ii. 399.
Lauder, ii. 422.
Lausanne, i. 29.
Laws of Egypt and Ethiopia, ii. 153.
Lea, ii. 160.
Leach, Colonel, i. 68.
Lead, ii. 181, 412.
Leake, ii. 297.
Lebanon, i. 628.
Lefébure, ii. 428.
Legge, M. F., i. 513; ii. 415.
Legh, Thomas, i. 34; ii. 297.
—— meets Burckhardt, i. 31.
——, travels of, i. 26.
Leigh, Capt. C., ii. 460.
Leigh, I. W., i. 478.
Leipzig, i. 29, 62.
Leisi, ii. 399.
Lêlat al-Nuḳṭa, ii. 344.
Lemaîre, ii. 285, 286.
Lenga, ii. 357, 387.
Le Noir du Roule, ii. 203.
Lenz, ii. 422.
Leo Africanus, ii. 307.
Leontopolis, ii. 299.
Leopards, ii. 108, 156.
—— skins, ii. 107.
Leopold II., ii. 390.
Lepsius, Dr., i. 80, 115, 118, 125, 129, 134, 139, 149, 150, 153, 154, 163, 169, 201, 240, 277, 295, 296, 297, 299, 339, 342, 348, 352, 353, 356, 404, 407, 466, 467, 500, 502, 534, 541, 547, 550, 552, 557, 558, 573, 602, 605, 617; ii. 10, 57, 84, 147, 292, 335, 337, 419, 445, 502.
——, travels of, i. 61 ff.
Le Quien, ii. 298.
Letorzec, P. C., i. 37, 41, 52, 368, 478.
——, travels of, i. 38.
Letronne, ii. 292 ff., 297.
Leuce-Come, ii. 167.
Leupitorga, ii. 160.
Leveson, Capt. C. H., ii. 460.
Lewin, Capt. C. H., ii. 460.
Lewin, Captain H. F. F., i. 331, 332, 333, 334, 335, 337, 341, 354.
Lewis, Colonel, i. 89, 183 196; ii. 276, 280.
Libân, i. 521.
Libya, ii. 104, 158.
——, Higher, ii. 155.
Libyans, i. 505, 531, 577, 631, 633, 638, 641; ii 13, 53, 74, 415.
Licences, game, ii. 451.
——, liquor, ii. 451.
Liddell, Capt., ii. 480.
Lieblein, ii. 336.
Life, symbols of, i. 305, 306.
Liffi, ii. 246.
Liggi, ii. 424.
Light, ii. 297.
Lignite, ii. 412.
Likuri, ii. 349.
Limir-Patesi-Ashur, ii. 53.
Linant, an officer, ii. 234.
Linant de Bellefonds, i. 24, 47, 551, 552; ii. 66, 87.
Linen, i. 3, 105.
Linthuma, ii. 160.
Lions, i. 58; ii. 157, 159.
—— at Nagaa, i. 325.
—— banner, ii. 136.
——, gold, i. 305.
——, granite, i. 618, 619.
——, 100 slain by Amenhetep III., i. 622.
—— -serpent, ii. 137.
—— skins, ii. 107.
Lippi, M., i. 9, 11.
Liquor traffic, i. 250.
Livingstone, Dr., ii. 229.
Lloyd, Col., ii. 268.
Lloyd, Mr. E., ii. 321.
Lloyd, Capt. H. D. W., ii. 460.
Loadstone, ii. 181.
Loak, ii. 434.
Loando, ii. 229.
Lobo, Father Jeronimo, ii. 349.
Lobsters, ii. 155.
Lockyer, Sir Norman, i. 276.
Locusts, salted, ii. 156, 165.
Logan, Capt., ii. 321.
Loggo, ii. 424.
Loin cloths, i. 260.
Lokuku, ii. 354.
Lokungati, ii. 352.
Loliu, ii. 352.
Lolli River, ii. 378.
Long, Colonel C., i. 177, 231; ii. 230, 234, 446.
Longfield, Capt. W. E., ii. 475, 476.
Longinus, ii. 296.
Longompori, ii. 165.
Lord, Lieut. Percy, R.E., i. 324, 325, 326, 327, 330, 331; ii. 475, 476.
Lord of the Mountain, ii. 193, 300.
Lot, i. 16.
Lotus, ii. 154.
Lotus, gunboat, i. 96.
Louis XIV., i. 4, 8, 12; ii. 2.
Louvre, ii. 2.
Lubari, ii. 424.
Lucan, i. 19.
Lugogo, ii. 387.
Lugololo, ii. 357.
Lukajuka, ii. 356.
Lukos, ii. 352.
Lûl, ii. 378.
—— Mission station, ii. 321.
Lulu, the, ii. 399.
Lumoga Mountains, ii. 385.
Lupton Bey, ii. 239, 246, 249, 424.

Lusehan, ii. 39.
Luta N'zige, ii. 222, 350.
Lüttge, Dr., i. 534.
Luxor, i. 30, 54, 67, 647; ii. 13, 30.
L'wal Burrajok, ii. 441.
Lyall, Mr. C. E., ii. 460.
Lyddite, ii. 274.
Lyme, i. 26.
Lyons, Capt. H. G., i. 86, 536 ff., 553, 579, 584, 601; ii. 166, 387, 388, 460.

MAĀ-AMEN, i. 644.
Maā-kheru, i. 422.
Ma'âlîya, ii. 438.
Mäām, i. 575, 576, 599; ii. 327.
Maāmam, i. 28.
Maanjá, ii. 387.
Maāt, i. 358, 370, 396, 397, 400; ii. 111.
Maāti, Hall of, i. 369.
Ma'atûka, i. 563, 651.
Macadagale, ii. 160.
Macauley, Col. G. B., ii. 463, 474, 475.
MacDonald, General i. 87; ii. 275, 276.
Macé, i. 11.
Macedonians, ii. 324.
Machar, ii. 360.
Machell, Lieut., i. 85.
McInnes, ii. 320.
Mackay, Lieut., i. 193.
Mackenzie, Mr. C. C. F., i. 503.
McKerrell, Capt., ii. 460.
McKillop Pâshâ, ii. 233, 234.
McLaughlin, Dr. H. T., ii. 319, 320.
Macmillan, ii. 361.
McMurdo, Col., ii. 262, 482, 488.
Macrobii, ii. 164.
Madani, Shêkh, ii. 438.
Madanîyûn, ii. 438.
Madi, ii. 385, 424, 431.
—— tribe, ii. 399.
Madibbo, ii. 246.
Madina, i. 551.
Madînat al-Fayyûm, i. 551.
Madînat Habu, ii. 30, 42.
Madwa, i. 24.
Magassa, ii. 160.
Maghâgha, ii. 392.
Magic, ii. 441.
——, white, i. 219.
Magungo, ii. 356, 386.
Mahârî, ii. 438.
Mâharîya, ii. 438.
Mahass, ii. 207, 208, 371, 409, 462.
Mahdî, Muhammad 'Aḥmad, the, i. 77, 90, 97, 105, 208, 228, 229, 270, 458, 606.
——, his pedigree, ii. 241.
——, his life and revolt, ii. 240 ff.
——, his programme, ii. 243.
——, his successes, ii. 244, 245.
——, master of the Sûdân, ii. 246.
—— appointed Sulṭân by Gordon, ii. 248.
—— sends Gordon Dervish apparel, ii. 249.
——, death of, ii. 260.
——, his body destroyed, ii. 279, 449.
——, his tomb, ii. 277, 396.
—— —— destroyed, ii. 274.
Mahdiism, i. 76; ii. 279, 504, 508.
—— crushed by Wingate, ii. 281.
——, history of, by Sir F. Wingate, ii, 241.
Mahdiists, i. 86.
Maḥḥu Bey, ii. 213.
Maḥmûd, the Dervish General, i. 253, 254, 264, 278; ii. 206, 267, 273, 374.
—— at Matamma, ii. 271.
Maḥmûd, uncle of Mahdî, i. 77.
Maḥmûd Bey Khêr Allah, ii. 476.
Mahon, Col., C. B., i. 101, 183; ii. 270, 281, 284, 460.
Mahtûl, ii. 392.
Mai, i. 612.
Maidens, Ethiopian, ii. 108.
Mai-khentka, ii. 95.
Mail, shirts of, ii. 278.
Mâithariâa, i. 612.
Makârak, ii. 431, 432.
Makâraka, ii. 233.
Makaraki, ii. 267.
Maḳdûm, ii. 208.
Makhi-taui, ii. 21.
Makokia, ii. 354.
Maḳren al-Buḥûr, ii. 356.
Maḳrîzi, ii. 184, 185, 186.
——, his account of the Beja, ii. 179.
Maksouh, ii. 184.
Makwa, ii. 443.
Malîkâb, ii. 435.
Malli, ii. 160.
Mallît, ii. 439.
Mallos, ii. 160.
Malluna, ii 354.
Malta, i. 30.
Mama, ii. 160.
Mambli, ii. 160.
Mamlûks, i. 22, 26, 27, 29, 30; ii. 210.
—— Beys, ii. 209.
——, massacre of, ii. 210.
Mamuda, ii. 160.
Ma'mûn, Khalîfa, ii. 187.
Manâgîl, ii. 407.
Manbalî, ii. 304.
Manbattu, ii. 432.
Mandalla, ii. 399.
Mandawwa, ii. 439.
Mandulis, i. 599.
Manetho, i. 539; ii. 27.
Manfalût, i. 1.
Mangbattu, ii. 424.
Mangi, ii. 284, 286.
Manifold, Lieut. M. G. E., i. 241; ii. 480.
Manobo, ii. 354.
Manṣûr, ii. 206.
Manṣûra, i. 222, 251.

Mansura, steamer, i. 258.
Manyanya, ii. 432.
Manyema, ii. 432.
Maqu, i. 612.
Marâbia, ii. 245.
Mara Dabash, ii. 352.
Maraga, ii. 116.
Maragga, i. 35.
Marârît, ii. 432.
Mārāuat, ii. 111.
Marcasite, ii. 181.
Marchand, Major, ii. 280, 378.
Marcianus, Emp., ii. 177, 291.
Mardîn, i. 328.
Marea, ii. 53, 54.
Māreiui, i. 638.
Mareotis, ii. 296.
Margaret, H.R.H., the Princess, i. 272.
Mariette, i. 62, 149, 150, 340, 626; ii. 4, 38, 46, 58, 63, 403.
Marigerri, ii. 164.
Marinus, ii. 292.
Marîs, ii. 303.
Marissa, ii. 158.
Mark, Saint, ii. 288, 302.
Markhia, ii. 424.
Markûm, ii. 436.
——, Well of, ii. 372.
Marno Bey, i. 259; ii. 239, 378, 446, 482.
Marsden, ii. 507.
Martin, Colonel, ii. 275.
Martini, Signor, ii. 282.
Martyrs, Era of, i. 464. 465.
Mārubiua-Åmen, ii. 66.
Mary the Virgin, ii. 302.
Masâ'd, ii. 206.
Masadâglia Bey, i. 76.
Masalat tribe, ii. 262.
Masâlit, ii. 432, 434, 436, 439.
Masallamîya, i. 285; ii. 242 244, 365, 407, 438, 439.
Maṣawa, i. 12, 18, 31; ii. 201, 225, 230, 231, 234, 235, 238, 239, 266, 268, 401, 462.
Maṣawwarât, i. 240.
—— described by Cailliaud, i. 47, 48, 49.
—— al-Kirbikân, i. 57.
—— an-Nagaa, i. 57, 326, 355, 407.
—— aṣ-Ṣufra, i. 56, 57, 326, 327, 329, 355; ii. 116, 146 ff.
Mascoa, ii. 160.
Mashakit, i. 637.
Mashat, ii. 101.
Mashra Abîd, ii. 365.
—— ad-Dakhêsh, ii. 473.
—— Tawla, ii. 436.
Mashu, i. 2.
Māshuasha, ii. 14.
—— chiefs, i. 647; ii. 24.
—— depart to Sûdân, ii 55.
Masindi, ii. 228, 229.
Masindomacam, ii. 160.
Masks of Dionysos, i. 307.
Mason Bey, ii. 366.
Maspero, Prof., i. 340, 514, 523. 547, 549. 551, 626, 649; ii. 46, 52, 63, 73, 414.
Masran Island, ii. 377.
Massina, ii. 398.
Mas'ûdî, al, i. 179, 224, 507; ii. 184, 185, 394.
Matamma, i. 58, 61, 113, 179, 187, 188; ii. 205, 251, 253, 257, 274, 372, 374, 390, 467.
—— bombarded, ii. 272.
—— destroyed by Mahmûd, ii. 271.
—— of Kallâbât, ii 264.
Maṭar, ii. 205.
Matarîya, ii. 22.
Matchai, i. 631.
Mātchaiu, i. 533. 553.
Mātet Boat, ii. 22.
Māthaka . . . . ., i. 612.
Māthaun, i. 612.
Mâthen, i. 604.
Māt . . . . ḥenen, ii. 58.
——, Stele of, ii. 66 ff.
Mather, Sir W., ii. 492.
Matthews, Major, ii. 434, 483, 509.
Ma'tûḳa, ii. 263, 370.
Māturu, i. 612.
Maud, Mr., of *The Graphic*, i. 100, 109, 189; ii. 214, 215, 216.
Maumarum, ii. 160.
Mauritania, ii. 165.
Maximinus, ii. 177, 178, 290, 291, 296.
Maxse, Colonel F. I., i. 233; ii. 268.
Maxwell, Sir J. G., i. 86, 87, 241, 498; ii. 275, 488, 504.
Maya bita Signora, ii. 315, 379.
Mazices, ii. 177.
Mbalasati, ii. 352.
Mbuku, ii. 354.
Meat, eaten raw, i. 81.
——, eaters of raw, ii. 69, 70.
Mecindita, ii. 160.
Medawi, ii. 258.
Medes, ii. 74.
Medical Dept., ii. 499.
Medicines, i. 105, 218, 219.
——, native, i. 220.
Medimni, ii. 164.
Medîna (Madîna), i. 32.
Mediterranean Sea, i. 601; ii. 9, 24.
——, Islands of, i. 623.
Medoë, ii. 164.
Mêdûb, ii. 432.
Mêdûm, ii. 4, 7.
——, Pyramid of, i. 118, 515.
Megabarei (or -bari), ii. 157, 158, 164, 417.
Megada, ii. 160.
Meganda, ii. 300.
Mega-nei, ii. 160.
Megasthenes, ii. 41.
Megatichos, Mount, ii. 160.
Megiddo, i. 572; ii. 73.
Mehat, ii. 82.
Meḥit, ii. 111.
Mehren, ii. 349.

Meḥtet-en-usekh, i. 648.
Meḥti-em-sa-f., i. 524.
Mek, the title, ii. 212.
Mekh Gîyôrgîs (George), ii. 212.
Mekhenteqnent, ii. 95, 96.
Mekhetsa (or -sai), ii. 81.
Mekhsherkherthet, ii. 95.
Mekhu, tomb of, i. 519.
Mekka, i. 30, 31, 33, 224; ii. 266.
Melly, B., i. 478.
Melons, i. 458.
Memnon, ii. 161, 170.
Memnones, ii. 164.
Memphis, i. 56, 120, 144, 515, 518, 519, 523, 529, 532, 533, 557, 632, 643; ii. 4, 7, 11, 19, 28, 30, 33, 38-40, 49, 52, 90, 91, 104, 325.
——, capture of, ii. 8.
Men, i.e., Egyptians, i. 505.
Menȧ, i. 512; ii. 2.
Menȧt, i. 426.
Menāt-Khufu, i. 534.
Mendes, i. 635; ii. 5, 14, 24.
Menelek II., ii. 264, 268, 284.
Menes, i. 512.
Menḥi-khent-Seḥetch, ii. 19.
Men-Nefer, ii. 20, 21.
Mennu-khā-em-Maāt, i. 620.
Menthu, i. 531, 584, 591, 644; ii. 24.
Menthu-em-ḥāt, ii. 41, 42.
Menthu-ḥetep I., i. 530, 531.
—— II., i. 531.
—— III., i. 531, 532, 537.
Menthu-ḥeteps, i. 553.
Menthu-ḥetep, an official, i. 539.
Menthu-Rā, i. 556.
Menti (Cattle-men), ii. 397, 416.
Menti of Asia, i 629.
Menti-nu-Satet, i. 612.
Mentiu, ii. 176, 328.
Mentiu of Asia, i. 562.
Mentu, i. 588.
Menu, the god, i. 195, 368, 386, 396, 531, 556, 559, 625, 627; ii. 45, 122, 177.
Merawi, i. 36, 38, 51, 58, 59, 64, 98, 104, 108, 109, 111 ff, 177 ff, 466; ii. 56, 259, 270, 271, 291, 372, 373, 407, 462, 467, 651.
——, antiquities of, i. 114 ff.
Mercenaries, Greek, ii. 53-55.
Mer-en-Ptaḥ I., i. 638, 639.
Mer-en-Rā, king, i. 519, 520, 524.
Merimes, ii. 334.
Meri-Rā Pepi I., 516.
Meris, ii. 194.
Merkanesh, ii. 24.
Merkanshu, ii. 8, 21.
Mer-ka-Rā, ii. 58.
Meroë, Island of, i. 18, 41, 55, 58, 59, 62, 120, 149, 159, 240, 241, 321, 467, 483, 497, 500, 564, 622; ii. 81, 82, 83, 93, 95, 104, 105, 106, 111, 116, 117, 153, 157, 160, 162, 165, 172, 175, 199, 288, 303, 348, 374, 435, 473.
—— ——, shape of, ii. 158.
——, city of, Ferlini's excavations at, i. 287.
——, Pyramids of, ii. 473.
—— —— described, i. 357 ff.
—— ——, excavation of, i. 341 ff.
—— queens of, i. 300, 402, 414, 415.
—— army of, ii. 163.
Meroë, mother of Cambyses, ii. 153.
Meroïtes, ii. 417.
Meroïtic inscriptions, i. 429 433.
—— kingdom, ii. 115.
—— sculptures, i. 500.
—— writing, ii. 446.
Merridi, ii. 399.
Mersa, ii. 409,
——Barghût, Shêkh, ii. 409.
Mersekér, i. 591.
Mer-Tem, city, ii. 12, 18.
Merthet, ii. 82.
Merti, ii. 22.
Mes, Prince of Kash, i. 639.
Mesaches, ii. 164.
Meshra ar-Rek (Mashra' ar-Rik), i. 259; ii. 239, 280, 281, 314, 315, 320, 359, 480.
Meskher, i. 520.
Meslê, ii. 363.
Mesopotamia, i. 87, 112, 217, 227, 280, 449, 607, 609; ii. 189, 207.
Messiah, the, ii. 186.
Mest, city of, ii. 8, 24.
Mestha, i. 361.
Mesuth Rā, ii. 91.
Metamma, i. 110.
Metammeh, stern-wheeler, i. 102.
Metcha, i. 517, 518, 534.
Metet, ii. 80.
Methu, i. 520.
Metrâkhâ, ii. 363.
Meyricke, Capt. E. G., ii. 460.
Miani, ii. 446.
Mice, ii. 34.
Michael, St., ii. 299.
Micklem, Lieut. H. A., i. 97; ii. 463.
Midas, ii. 91.
Midwinter, i. 264, 279, 280, 437, 497, 503; ii. 271, 472, 475, 476, 479.
Miḥarraḳa, ii. 111, 303.
Mîkâ'îl, Island of, ii. 193, 194, 197.
Millet, ii. 158.
Milukhkhi, ii. 34, 37.
Mimaut, Monsieur, i. 287.
Minerals, ii. 410.
Mines, i. 458, 621.
Mîraîâb, ii. 438.
Mismâr ibn 'Abd Allah, ii. 204.
Mission, American, in Sûdân, ii. 318, 378.
——, Austrian, ii. 265, 268, 317, 321.
——, British (C.M.S.), ii. 320, 321
Missionary enterprise in the Sûdân, ii. 317 ff.

Missions founded on the White Nile, ii. 312.
——, Portuguese, ii. 308.
Mitani, i. 604 ; ii. 332.
Miter, the, i. 22.
Mitford, Colonel, ii. 460.
Mittu, ii. 399, 424, 434.
Moami, ii. 352.
Modunda, ii. 164.
Moggore, ii. 160.
Mograkeh, i. 95.
Mokeltree, ii. 181.
Mokwai, ii. 361.
Moltke, Von, i. 110.
Molum, ii. 160.
Mombasa, ii. 351.
—— Bay, ii. 233.
Monasîr Arabs, ii. 251.
Money, i. 218.
—— iron, i. 105.
Mongalla, ii. 282, 283, 286, 321, 384, 399.
—— Province, ii. 409.
Monkeys, i. 571.
Monophysite belief, ii. 288.
Montmorency, Hon. R. H. de, i. 83.
Moon, Mountains of, ii. 172, 348, 349, 350.
Moon-god Ȧāḥ, i. 621, 624.
Morant, Capt. H. H., ii. 460.
More, Mr. R. E., ii. 460.
Morgan, Mr., i. 334.
Morghâni, Shêkh, i. 459.
Morlang, Father, ii. 312.
Morocco, i. 76.
Morrada, i. 17.
Morû-Kodô, ii. 424.
Morû-Missa, ii. 424.
Moses in Nubia, ii. 303.
Moshi, i. 10, 23, 36.
Moslems, ii. 182.
Môṣul, i. 227, 228.
Mo'taṣim, ii. 188,
Mothitae, ii. 164.
Mougel Bey, ii. 220, 236, 461.
Mount Arafât, i. 32.
Mount Barkal, i. 130.
Mount Pisgah, i. 525.
Mpango, ii. 354.
Mponbi, ii. 356.
Mruli, ii. 357, 387.
Msisi, ii. 356.
Msongi, ii. 354.
M'tesa, ii. 229, 230, 235.
Mtuma, ii. 352.
Mtungi, ii. 354.
Mûgâr, ii. 364.
Muggi, ii. 385.
Mughess, i. 23.
Mughrât Wells, i. 91.
Mugrum, i. 55.
Muḥammad, Captain, i. 444.
Muḥammad the Defterdar, ii. 212, 231, 407.
Muḥammad, king of Harar, ii. 231.
Muḥammad the Prophet, i. 131, 221, 460 ; ii. 186, 188, 203.
Muḥammad of Ḳumm, ii. 190.
Muḥammad Abû Dhâhab, ii. 209.
Muḥammad Al-Amîn, a Mahdî, ii. 204, 284.
Muḥammad al-Ballâli, ii. 232.
Muḥammad al-Faḍl, i. 52 ; ii. 207.
Mûḥammad Alî, i. 31, 33, 34, 35, 41, 285, 554, 574 ; ii. 84, 96, 240, 323, 338, 374, 393, 414.
——, life of, ii. 210.
——, his rule in Sûdân, ii. 209 ff.
—— visits Sûdân, ii. 214.
——, death of, ii. 218.
Muḥammad 'Ali Pâshâ, ii. 250, 251.
Muḥammad al-Khâzin, ii. 303.
Muḥammad al-Khêr, ii. 241.
Muḥammad al-Mak, ii. 206.
Muḥammad Bey, ii. 213.
Muḥammad Bey Aḥmad, ii. 281.
Muḥammad Bey Râsîkh, ii. 221.
Muḥammad Dawra, ii. 206.
Muḥammad Dîn, ii. 214.
Muḥammad Effendi, ii. 213.
Muḥammad Effendî Shakîr, ii. 498.
Muḥammad Hârûn, ii. 498.
Muḥammad Ḥasîn, ii. 207.
Muḥammad ibn 'Abd Allah, ii. 191.
Muḥammad ibn Ḳalâ'ûn, ii. 196.
Muḥammad ibn 'Omar, i. 24, 25.
Muḥammad ibn Tughg, ii. 303.
Muḥammad Ibrahîm al-Amîn, i. 265 ff.
Muḥammad Khêr, ii. 314.
Muḥammad Khusrûf, ii. 210.
Muḥammad Maḥmud, ii. 250.
Muḥammad Nûbâwî Shêkh, ibn Garar, murderer of Gordon, ii. 254.
Muḥammad Pâshâ Chawarby, ii. 477.
Muḥammad Sharîf, ii. 241.
——, his quarrel with the Mahdî, ii. 242.
Muḥammad Ṣûl, ii. 206.
Muḥammad 'Uthmân, ii. 373.
Muḥammad Wâd Ibrahîm, Shêkh of Barkal, i. 201 ff.
Muḥammad Wâd Tunbul, ii. 372.
Muḥammadans, i. 25, 32, 33, 75.
—— law, i. 33.
Mûtl, i. 43.
Mukhmîya, ii. 473.
Muko (Mu Kao), ii. 444.
Mukram, ii. 268, 270.
Muḳurra, ii. 303, 304, 306.
Müller, D. H., i. 18.
Müller, F., ii. 446.
Müller, Mr. M., ii. 63.
Müller, Mr. W., i. 541.
Mulmul, ii. 399.
Mulukhîya, i. 217.
Mummies, robbery of, i. 646
Mûn, ii. 442.

Mûnâ, ii. 432.
Munâṣîr, ii. 438.
Mungo Park, ii. 423.
Munich Royal Museum, Ferlini's objects in, i. 299.
Munkar, i. 224, 225.
Munzinger, ii. 230, 446.
Murâd Bey, ii. 209, 210.
Mûr'anîya doctrine, ii. 371.
Murât (Murrât), Wells of, i. 193; ii, 266, 392, 464.
Murchison Falls, ii. 386.
Murle, ii. 282.
Murtek, ii. 118.
——, Pyramid of, i. 382 ff.
Mûsa Ibrahîm, ii. 214.
Musâ'id Ḳêdûm, ii. 266.
Mûsa of Dâr Fûr, ii. 206.
Mûsa Pâshâ, ii. 314.
Mûsa Pâshâ Ḥamdî, ii. 222.
Mûsa Shêkh, i. 531.
Mûsa wâd Helu, ii. 257.
Musallim the Maḳdûm, ii. 208.
Museum, British, i. 447.
——, Khartûm, i. 436, 494.
Musêrîya, ii. 438.
Musk-maidens, i. 226.
Muslims, ii. 186, 241.
Musmar, ii. 479.
Mustafa Pâshâ Yâwar, ii. 250.
Musṭafyâb, ii. 438.
Mustapha, i. 237.
Mut the goddess, i. 160, 301, 362, 397, 626; ii. 4, 38, 43, 45, 52, 56, 58, 65, 66, 70, 117, 132, 134.
—— of Nubia, i. 134, 137.
Muta N'zigi, ii. 356.
Mut-khā-neferu, ii. 30.
Mutmîr, i. 331; ii. 473.
Mut-nefert, i. 570.
Mutrus, ii. 273.
Mutterrutzner, ii. 446.
Muwengu, ii. 354.
Muzil al-Muḥan, ii. 266.
Mvolo, ii. 285, 286.
Myang Matyang, ii. 284.
Myding, ii. 358.
Myrrh, i. 532, 571; ii. 90.
Myrson, ii. 160.

NAAM, ii. 282, 399.
Nabataeans, ii. 167.
Nabû-shezib-anni, ii. 53.
Nachtigal, ii. 316.
Nadha, ii. 179, 188.
Nagaa, i. 47, 48, 58, 138, 240, 286, 324, 325, 330, 467; ii. 119, 122, 131, 139, 152, 305.
——, buildings at, i. 327.
——, temples of, ii. 143 ff.
Nag' Ḥamâdî, i. 64, 65.
Nagîl Castle, i. 129.
Nahoganet, ii. 472.
Nahr al-Kalb River, ii. 39, 339.
Nahûd, ii. 397, 437.
Na'il, ii. 201.
Naima, ii. 233.
Nakatera, ii. 354.
Nakhêla, i. 253.
Nakhîla, ii. 273.
Nakîr, i. 224, 225.
Napata, i. 28, 36, 59, 64, 234, 290, 306, 427, 600, 601, 615, 620, 637, 651; ii. 1, 2, 3, 6, 9, 10, 27, 28, 35, 39, 45, 46, 49, 52, 53, 54, 73, 82, 93, 104, 116, 117, 154, 161, 163, 168, 172, 299, 332, 373, 435.
——, endowment of gods of, ii. 83.
Napoleon, i. 26, 38, 54.
Napoleon, Prince, ii. 66.
Napt, ii. 111.
Narekîheb, i. 610.
Narnarti, ii. 291.
Narses, ii. 178, 294.
Narukiheb, i. 612.
Nâṣer, ii. 203, 233.
Nâṣer of Dâr Fûr, ii. 206.
Nâṣer Wâd 'Agîb, ii. 204.
Naṣḥi Pâshâ, ii. 251.
Nason, Col. F. J., i. 324.
Naṣr ad-Dîn, ii. 198.
Nasser, ii. 282, 361.
Nastaâbusaknen, ii. 66.
Nâstasenen, ii. 75, 110.
——, reign of, ii. 84-103.
——, translation of Stele of, ii. 97 ff.
Natho, ii. 299.
Natron, ii. 391, 412.
—— Wells, ii. 430.
Naukavenga, ii. 354.
Naumburg, i. 61.
Navectabe, ii. 164.
Navi, ii. 164.
Naville, Prof., i. 512, 513, 549, 553, 560; ii. 111, 414.
Nawâyâ Krestôs, ii. 307.
Nawwâr, ii. 203.
Nazareth, i. 495.
N'darama, ii. 320.
Ndoggos, ii. 399.
N'Doruma, ii. 286.
Neave, Dr. S., ii. 494.
Neb-Maāt-Rā, name of Āmen-ḥetep III. as god, i. 612.
Nebt-Tatet, i. 636.
Nebuchadnezzar II., ii. 74.
Necho, ii. 73.
Necklaces, i. 306.
—— from Meroë, i. 301-303.
Nedok, ii. 4 4.
Needles, i. 105.
Nefer-āb-Rā, i. 427.
Nefer-ānkh-āb-Rā, i. 422.
Nefer-ḥetep, king, i. 556.
Nefer-khā, ii. 58.
Nefert-āri, i. 639, 637, wife of Rameses II.
Nefer Tem, i. 362, 386, 421; ii. 45.
Neferus, ii. 12.
Nefîsa, ii. 404.
Negroes, i. 216, 449, 506, 560; ii. 413, 424.
—— kings, i. 407.
—— tribes, ii. 200.
—— —— in the Sûdān, ii 428.
Negroid Pygmies, ii. 425.
Nehanat, ii. 82.

INDEX

Neharina, i. 607.
Nehárq, ii. 117.
Nehāu, ii. 111.
Neherin, i. 604, 609, 612.
Nehernu, ii. 38.
Neḥesu, i. 505, 512, 539; ii. 413, 415.
Neḥi, prince of Kash, i. 573, 576, 591, 595.
Neḥsi, i. 560.
Neḥsi-Rā, i. 559.
Neith, i. 531; ii. 14, 25.
——, temple of, ii. 91.
Nejd, ii. 207, 439.
Nekau, prince of Saïs, ii. 39, 40, 41, 52.
Nekau (Necho), ii. 73.
Nekhebet, i. 575, 588, 599.
Nekht-Ḥeru-na-shennu, ii. 24.
Nemareth the rebel, i. 648; ii. 4, 5, 7, 9, 12, 14, 16, 17, 26.
Nemkhi, ii. 69.
Nephthys, i. 160, 383, 387, 396, 397, 404, 421.
Nepita, i. 600.
Nept, i. 600, 615.
Nero, ii. 161, 162, 380.
—— sends centurions up the Nile, ii. 348.
—— sends soldiers into the Sûdân, ii. 170 ff.
Nes-Ànḥer, ii. 69.
Nes-ba-Ṭeṭ, i. 646.
Nes-Mut, ii. 69.
Nesnaqeti (or-ḳeti), ii. 14, 24.
Nesthentmeḥ, ii. 16.
Net, i. 531.
Netch-ka-Àmen, ii. 56.
Netch-neteru, ii. 75.
Netek-Àmen, ii. 118, 119, 122, 125, 126, 134, 141, 142, 170.
—— pyramid of, i. 412.
Neter, town of, ii. 4, 11.
Neter-ḥet-Sebek, ii. 12.
Neter-taui, i. 642.
Neubari, ii. 361.
Neufeld, Mr. C., ii. 261.
—— released, ii. 277.
Neufeld on Gordon's murder, ii. 254.
Neumann, Mr. O., ii. 361.
Nevile, Mr., i. 325, 326, 330; ii. 500.
New, ii. 422.
Newcombe, E. C. A., ii. 463.
Newcombe, Lieut. S. F., R.E., i. 330; ii. 373, 476.
New Year Festival, ii. 15.
Ngaiyu, i. 524.
Ngusi, ii. 356.
Nî, i. 572, 598.
Niamanjam, ii. 432.
Niâmbara, ii. 424.
Niam Niams, ii. 282, 284, 285, 286, 287, 314, 315, 399, 442.
Niebuhr, i. 18, 22; ii. 292, 297.
Night of the Drop, ii. 344.
Nigol, ii. 360.
Nigroae, ii. 165.
Nik-kang, ii. 443.
Nik-kieya, ii. 443.
Nile, i. 8, 9, 19, 386, 440, 507, 601, 633; ii. 40, 154, 161.
—— Basin, ii. 350.
—— ——, area of, ii. 388.
——, Blue, i. 19, 21, 42, 61, 62, 151, 324, 521; ii. 1, 362.
—— ——, discharge of, ii. 369.
—— ——, works on, ii. 486.
——, course of, in the Sûdân, ii. 369 ff.
—— distances, ii. 388.
—— flood, ii. 345.
—— ——, how caused, ii. 368.
—— gauge, ii. 376, 384.
—— —— at Halfa, i. 86.
——, Gertrude, ii. 358.
—— god, i. 66, 383; ii. 143.
—— ——, two festivals of, ii. 344.
—— goddess, i. 421.
——, history of, ii. 343.
Nile, hymn to, ii. 344.
——, islands in, ii. 291.
—— Lakes, ii. 348.
——, length of, ii. 389.
——, North and South, i. 395.
——, origin of name, ii. 344.
—— registers, i. 550.
——, supposed sources of, ii. 153, 344.
——, true source of, ii. 220.
——, Upper, ii. 356.
—— —— described, ii. 379 ff.
—— ——, discharge of, ii. 368
——, Victoria, ii. 356, 386.
—— ——, discharge of, ii. 368.
——, views of Diodorus on, ii. 153.
——, White, i. 23, 42, 58, 324, 521, 562; ii. 356.
—— —— described, ii. 375.
—— ——, discharge of, ii. 369.
——, worship of, ii. 442.
Nili Paludes, ii. 172.
Nilwa, ii. 291.
Nilwatti, Nilwitti, Island of, i. 444, 456, 457; ii. 291.
Nimr, ii. 213
Nimr, Mek, ii. 404, 407.
Nimr of Shendi, ii. 206, 212.
Nimuli, ii. 386.
Nine Nations (or Tribes) of the Bow, the, i. 81, 598, 626.
Nineveh, i. 227; ii. 30, 38, 39, 40, 41, 50, 52, 74.
Nisacaethae, ii. 165.
Nisan, ii. 38.
Nisyti, ii. 165.
Nit, ii. 25.
Nitrian Valley, ii. 290.
Niumbi, ii. 357.
Nkwaji, ii. 444.
Noa, ii. 160.
Nôbâ, ii. 364.
Nobadae (Nobatae), ii. 176-178, 291, 292 ff., 295 ff., 308 ff., 418, 506.

Nomades, ii. 156, 160.
Nome standards, i. 362.
Norden, Capt., i. 22, 29.
----, Travels of, i. 13 ff.
Noubas, ii. 184.
Nsabe, ii. 262.
Nsongi, ii. 354.
Nûba, ii. 285.
—— Mountains, ii. 233, 286, 391.
Nubae, ii. 158, 418.
Nubar Pâshâ, ii. 237.
Nubar Pâshâ Yûsuf, ii. 244.
Nûbas, i. 61; ii. 304, 397, 404, 416.
Nubei, ii. 164.
Nûbî language, ii 447.
Nubia, i. 13, 21, 22, 24, 26, 30, 32, 34, 39, 52, 53, 60, 61, 75, 82, 121, 122, 144, 152, 176, 463, 505, 532, 534, 537, 562, 563, 565, 570, 573, 597, 598, 604-606, 621-625, 627-629, 633, 636, 638, 640, 642, 643; ii. 1, 3, 28, 30, 39, 45, 50, 54, 58, 73, 91, 109, 153, 289, 326.
——, four princes of, ii. 307.
——, 15 kingdoms of, ii. 307.
——, names of, i. 535, 539.
Nubian Desert, i. 30, 31.
—— Language, ii. 445.
Nubians, i. 81, 84, 93, 531, 538, 541, 562, 563, 568, 605, 625, 626; ii. 2, 3, 5, 6, 53, 74, 92, 104, 115, 166-169, 185, 187, 416, 418, 435.
—— described, ii. 92, 93.
——, Jacobite, ii. 152.
Nubt, ii. 24.
Nuers, ii. 265, 280, 360.
Nugîm, ii. 392.
Nuisamba, ii. 354.
Nûl, ii. 203.
Nulwa, i. 453.
Numidians, ii. 109.
Nups, ii. 160.
Nûr ad-Dîn, ii. 192.
Nûr al-Kanzî, i. 83; ii. 261.
Nûr Ash-Shâm, ii. 241.
Nûri, i. 114, 234; ii. 116, 373, 479.
——, pyramids of, i. 41, 59, 115 ff., 153, 169, 274.
Nut, ii. 18.
Nuwêr, ii. 433.
Nuzûl, i. 182.
Nya Ababdo, ii. 444.
Nyadok, ii. 444.
Nya Dwai, ii. 444.
Nya Gwatse, ii. 444.
Nyakaibari, ii. 356.
Nyakang (Kong), ii. 443, 444.
Nyamgasha, ii. 354.
Nyamgashani, ii. 354.
Nyando, ii. 352.
Nyato, ii. 444.
Nyavarongs, ii. 352.
Nzoia, ii. 352.

OASES, i. 508, 458.
Oasis, god of, i. 513.
Oasis of Dâkhla, ii. 174.
—— Jupiter Ammon, ii. 91, 93.
—— Kharga, i. 51; ii. 93, 174.
—— Minor, ii. 174.
Obêḍ, ii. 285.
'Obêd Allah ibn al-Ḥabbâb, ii. 187.
Obelisk-House, i. 625.
Obo, ii. 478.
Obodas, ii. 167.
O'Connell, Maj. (formerly Capt.), ii. 285, 460.
Odaenathus, ii. 175.
Odage, ii. 444.
Œcalices, ii. 165.
Ogrên, ii. 479.
Ohrwalder, Father, ii. 241, 253, 255, 258-260, 265, 323, 396.
Oigiga, ii. 424.
Oils, i. 105; ii. 158.
Oisila, ii. 424.
Ojallo, ii. 434.
'Okâsha, Shêkh, i. 93.
Okmah, i. 92, 93.
Okun, ii. 444.
Old Cairo, ii. 22.
Oldfield, Capt., i. 98, 99, 282.
Olympiodorus, ii. 291.
O'Madyaka, ii. 432.
'Omar ibn 'Abd al-'Azîz, ii. 187.
'Omar Ṣâliḥ, ii. 266.
'Omar Tita, ii. 268.
Omaro, ii. 443.
Ombos, ii. 333, 337.
Omdurmân, i. 41, 110, 173, 178, 201, 202, 209, 240, 241, 264, 271, 272; ii. 246, 254, 375, 449, 463.
——, Battle of, ii. 274-276.
—— surrenders, ii. 252.
——, town of, ii. 395 ff.
Ophthalmia, i. 32.
Opium, i. 221, 222.
Oppert, Dr., i. 648.
Orambis, ii. 160.
Orsum, ii. 160.
Oryx, ii. 391.
Osiris, i. 67, 160, 169, 195, 383, 397, 400, 421, 432, 524, 540, 547, 643; ii. 33, 106, 112, 117, 122, 134, 176, 414.
——, cult of, at Napata, i. 167.
—— gods in Nubia, ii. 82.
——, Hall of, i. 396.
——, House of, i. 369.
——, Judgment of, i. 358.
—— Khenti Amenti, i. 362, 369.
——, Lord of Ṭaṭṭu, i. 362.
—— and the Nile, ii. 344.
—— of Philae, ii. 294.
—— pillars, i. 633, 634, 635, 636.
—— at Semna, i. 477.
——, statue of, from Gazîrat al-Malik, i. 493.
—— —— at Semna, i. 60.
Osmân Aghâ, ii. 213.
Osmân Azraḳ, i. 94, 95; ii. 266, 270.

INDEX

Osman Bey, i. 296, 339, 340; ii. 213.
Osmân Diḳna, i. 95, 253; ii. 246, 261, 262, 263, 264, 265, 268, 269, 272, 273, 281.
Osmân Ganu, ii. 267.
Osmân Pâshâ, ii. 236.
Osmân wâd Adam, ii. 262.
Osorkon I., i. 648.
Osorkon III., ii. 28.
Osorkon the rebel, ii. 23.
Ostrich feathers, ii. 10, 451.
Osymandyas, ii. 339.
Otellia, ii. 481.
Other World, the, i. 369, 370, 384, 385, 407, 523, 524; ii. 17.
——, four divisions of, i. 505.
Owen Falls, ii. 387.
Owen, Major "Roddy," i. 91; ii. 267.
Oxen, white, ii. 8, 22.
Ox-gall, i. 19.
Oxyrhynchus, ii. 4, 6, 12, 15, 184.

PA-ÅSÅR-NEB-ṬEṬ, ii. 14.
Pa-Ba-neb-Ṭeṭ, ii. 14.
Pa-Bas, ii. 24.
Pa-Bast, ii. 14.
Paez, Father Pedro, ii. 349.
Page, Mr., i. 99.
Paget, J., i. 478.
Pagsarca, ii. 160.
Pa-Ḥāp, ii. 24.
Pa-Ḥebi, ii. 24.
Paḳerer, ii. 24.
Pakhoni, i. 464.
Paḳrer, ii. 39, 40, 41, 49.
Palermo Stele, i. 514.
Palestine, i. 449, 505, 627; ii. 35, 37, 38, 292.
Paley, i. 57.
Paliurus plant, ii. 156.
Pallme, i. 24; ii. 423.
Palm branches, i. 398.
—— shoots, i. 438.
—— trees, i. 1, 3, 260.
Palugges, ii. 164.
Pa-Matchet, ii. 12, 15.
Pamphagi, ii. 165.
Pan, ii. 154, 159.
Pa-Nebes, ii. 79, 82, 83, 89, 111.
Pa-neb-ṭep-aḥet, ii. 12.
P-ānkh-åluru, ii. 75, 88.
Pānkhi, i. 144 ff.
Pannonia, ii. 289.
Panthers, ii. 108, 159.
—— skins, i. 385, 571; ii. 108.
Pa-nub, ii. 11.
Paoletti, i. 478.
Pa-Pek, ii. 6, 14.
Paper currency, ii. 258.
Pa-Ptaḥ, i. 633.
Papyrus, ii. 173, 376, 380.
Pa-Qem, Pa-Qemt, ii. 82, 89.
Pa-Qem-Åten, ii. 90, 96, 102.
Pa-Rā, i. 635.
Paradise, i. 224, 226.
Pa Rā-sekhem-kheper, ii. 11, 18.
Pa-rehu, i. 571.
Parei, i. 301.
Parembole, ii. 111, 113-115, 328.
Parenta, ii. 160.
Parker, Capt. A. C., ii. 400, 460.
Parrots, ii. 108, 181.
Parsons, Col., ii. 273, 280, 400.
Paschal, a friar, i. 6.
Pa-Sekhet-neb-Rehesaui, ii. 24.
Pa-Sekhet-nebt-Saut, ii. 24.
Pa-Sept, ii. 24, 39, 40, 41, 49.
Pa-ser, ii. 326.
Pasunka, i. 612.
Paṭā-Åstet, ii. 23.
Paṭa-nub, ii. 69.
Pa Teḥuti-åp-reḥeḥ (or reḥeḥui), ii. 14, 24.
Pathenf, ii. 24.
Patiga, ii. 160.
Patis, ii. 160.
Patosan, Island, ii, 386.
Patricia, H. R. H. the Princess, i. 272.
Pa-ur, Prince of Kash, i. 625, 637, 643.
Payne Knight, Mr., i. 100.
Peake, Colonel (formerly Major), R.A., ii. 380, 509.
—— and the Sudd, ii. 482.
Pearls, ii. 108.
—— fisheries, ii. 190, 500.
Pebbles on graves, i. 225.
Pebekhen-nebiu, ii. 21.
Pechuël-Lösche, ii. 423.
Pectoral offered to Ṭeṭun, i, 589.
Pedjoul, i. 91.
Pedley, Captain O., i. 64, 67, 68, 72, 98, 240.
Pef-tchāā-Bast, ii. 4, 7, 17.
Peḥqennes, ii. 111.
Peki, ii. 357.
Pelekos, ii. 74.
Pelham, the Hon. A., ii. 476.
Pelham, Hon. H. G. G., i. 437, 497.
Pelkha, ii. 87.
Pellegrini, Signor A., i. 514.
Pelly, Miss, i. 498.
Pelusium, ii. 34, 90.
Pelusium Daphnae, ii. 53.
Pemau, ii. 24.
Peni . . . . ., ii. 21.
Penn, Messrs., i. 258.
Pen-nekheb, i. 564, 565.
Pennut, i. 643.
Pentaurt, ii. 24.
Penth-bekhent, ii. 24.
Penton, Col., ii. 500, 509.
Pepi I., 121, 195, 516, 519, 524, 526; ii. 414.
——, death of, i. 517.
Pepi II., i. 522, 523, 526, 529.
Pepi-nekht, i. 517.
Percival, Captain A. J., ii. 287, 460.
Pereirà, F. M. E., ii. 364, 365.
Perfumes, i. 307.
Perorsi, ii. 165.
Perron, Dr., i. 25.

INDEX

Persea tree, i. 384, 398; ii. 159.
Persia, ii. 225.
Persian Gulf, i. 471.
Persians, ii. 95, 104, 105, 178, 324.
Perui, i. 421; ii. 117.
Perusii, ii. 165.
Peṭā-Ȧmen, a priest, ii. 69.
Petā-Ȧmen-neb-nest-taui, ii. 25.
Peṭā-Ȧst, ii. 8, 24.
Peṭā-Ȧsteta, ii. 21.
Peṭā-Ḥeru-sma-taui, ii. 24.
Peṭā-Khensu, ii. 52.
Peten-Ḥert, ii. 111.
Petherick, Mr. J., ii. 220, 232, 351, 398, 446.
Petronius, Prefect, i. 28; ii. 161, 167, 168.
Phaliges, ii. 164.
Phallic ceremonies, ii. 440.
Phanes, ii. 90.
Pharaohs, i. 65, 98, 299, 622, 626; ii. 17, 176.
Pharbaetites, ii. 24.
Philae, Island of, i. 13, 26, 27, 30, 31, 38, 67, 72; ii. 74, 105, 110, 111, 113, 166, 167, 176, 185, 188, 291, 292, 294.
——, worship of Isis at, ii. 177, 178.
Philostratus, i. 522.
Phoenicians, ii. 92.
Phrygia, ii. 91.
Phthouris (Phturis), i. 60; ii. 161, 168.
Piānkhi, i. 59, 120, 144 ff., 169, 201.
Piānkhi, husband of Ȧmenȧrṭās, ii. 30.
Piānkhi-meri-Ȧmen, i. 600; ii. 2-26, 27, 42, 45, 46, 53, 56.
Piānkhi Senefer-Rā, ii. 56.
Pibor River, ii. 361.
Pide, ii. 160.
Pidibotae, ii. 160.
Pierret, ii. 2.
Pigmentation, ii. 494.
Pigs, ii. 192, 302.
Pîlôn, ii. 296.
Pindicitora, ii. 160.
Pinnis, ii. 160.
Pipes (tobacco), i. 105.
Pirie, Capt. A. M., ii. 282.
Pistia, ii. 481.
Pithecussae, ii. 109.
Pithom, Stele of, ii. 111.
Pittara, ii. 162, 172.
Plague, i. 563.
Plenariae, ii. 160.
Pleyte, Dr., ii. 33.
Pliny, i. 59, 543; ii. 94, 153, 160, 169, 170, 171, 172, 175, 338, 348.
Ploss, Dr., ii. 403.
Plunkett, Colonel, i. 69.
Pococke, Dr., i. 13.
——, Travels of, i. 22.
Poison, traffic in, i. 525.
Poll tax, ii. 194.
Pomades, i. 105.
Poncet, i. 6, 7, 12, 23; ii. 202.
——, Travels of, i. 1.
Poppies, i. 221.
Poole, Stanley Lane, ii. 186, 187, 192, 195, 298, 483.
Portais, Father, i. 22.
Port Durnford, ii. 234.
Port Florence, ii. 352.
Port Sûdân, ii. 474, 476, 478.
Posias, ii. 297.
Postal Service, ii. 480.
Potter, Mr., ii. 361.
Pottery, Christian, ii. 375.
Powell, Major, ii. 460.
Powendael, Lake, ii. 380.
Power, Mr., ii. 250.
Premnis, i. 28; ii. 168, 169, 174.
Priapus, i. 635; ii. 176.
Price, Mr. H. E., i. 275.
"Priest," the horse, ii. 312.
Primis, i. 22, 26, 28, 575, 599, 643; ii. 161, 191, 290, 291, 293, 294, 302.
Prince of Kash, establishment of, i. 566.
Priscus, ii. 291.
Prisse d'Avennes, ii. 42, 334.
Prisons, ii. 500.
Pritchard, H. L., ii. 463.
Proaprimis, ii. 160.
Probus, Emp., ii. 175.
Proclus, ii. 292.
Procopius, ii. 176, 179, 294.
Prosda, ii. 160.
Prudhoe, Lord, i. 617, 624; ii. 118.
——, Travels of, i. 54.
Prussia, i. 61.
Pruyssenare, ii. 423.
Psammetichus, ii. 158.
Psammetichus I., i. 53; ii. 58, 106, 164.
Psammetichus II., i. 427; ii. 74.
Psammetichus III., i. 91; ii. 90.
Psammetichus, son of Nekau, ii. 52.
Psammetichus, son of Theokles, ii. 74.
Psebo, ii. 159.
Pselcis, i. 74, 634; ii. 111, 114, 161, 167.
Ptaḥ, i. 625, 632, 634, 636, 644; ii. 7, 8, 19, 21, 33, 42, 49, 82.
Ptaḥ of the South Wall, ii 21.
Ptaḥ-Seker-Ȧsȧr, i. 358.
Ptoenphae, ii. 164.
Ptolemaïs Epithêras, ii. 111.
Ptolemies, i. 57, 169, 510; ii. 324.
Ptolemy I., ii 109.
Ptolemy II., i. 154; ii. 109, 111, 115, 157.
Ptolemy III., ii. 112.
Ptolemy IV., ii. 112, 115, 118.
Ptolemy V., ii. 115.
Ptolemy the Geographer, ii. 110, 172, 348.
Ptolemy Lathyrus, ii. 163.
Puarma, ii. 5, 12, 25.
Pückler, ii. 414.
Punt, i. 138, 512, 513, 515, 523, 532, 538, 554, 571, 572, 573, 599, 612, 626, 628, 642; ii. 414, 415, 433.

INDEX

Punt, chiefs of, i. 626.
——, Queen of, ii. 403.
Pygmies, i. 138, 515, 516 ii. 158, 163, 324, 347.
—— described, i. 525.
Pygmy, the dancing, i. 522 ff.
Pyne, Captain, ii. 265.
Pyramids of Aṣ-Ṣûr, i. 274.
—— —— described, i. 323.
—— Bagrâwîya, i. 323.
—— Gebel Barkal, i. 240.
—— —— described, i. 152 ff.
—— —— opened, i. 169.
—— of Kurru, i. 240.
—— of Meroë, ii. 131.
—— ——, groups of, i. 273 ff.
—— ——, No. 11 of, excavated, i. 498 ff.
—— ——, Southern group described, i. 416 ff.
—— of Tanḳâsî, i. 240.
—— of Zûma, i. 240.
Python, worship of, ii. 442.

QANTUR, i. 125.
Qaruqamisha, i. 613.
Qeb, i. 418, 421.
Qebḥsennuf, i. 361.
Qebti, i. 643.
Qehaq, i. 642.
Qelhetat, ii. 46.
Qem-baiu-set, ii. 94.
Qem-ur, ii. 23.
Qepqepa, ii. 50.
Qerti, ii. 343.
Qetshi, i. 609.
Qetu folk, i. 569.
Quarries, i. 458.
—— of Ḥet-nub, i. 518.
—— at Meroë, i. 355.
—— at Nagaa, i. 326.
—— at Tombos, i. 559.
Quartz, i. 541.
Queen, the fat, i. 467.
Quicksilver, ii. 330.
Qurui, i. 612.

RÂ, i. 385. 421, 625; ii. 3, 8, 14, 22, 62, 82, 91, 135.
Rā-Āpepi, i. 561.
Rabât, ii. 202.
Rab-saki (Rabshakeh), ii. 40.
Radasîyah, Temple of, ii. 334.
Rafâ'îyûn, ii. 438.
Raffilî Falls, ii. 459.
Ragaa, ii. 399.
Ragab, ii. 212, 213.
Ragnotti, Joseph, ii. 277.
Rahad. ii. 390, 437, 486.
—— River, ii. 365.
Rā-Harmachis, i. 80, 421, 635, 636; ii. 18.
Rahât, the, i. 213, 236.
Râ-Ḥerukhuti, i. 574, 635; ii. 45.
Raḥmâḥ, ii. 438.
Railway, Abû Hamed to Karêma, 479.
——, Aswân to Shellâl, i. 69.
——, Atbara to Red Sea, ii. 476.
——, Ḥalfa to Kerma, ii. 463, 476.
——, —— to Kharṭûm, ii. 464.
Railway survey, ii. 462.
Rain at Aswân, i. 71.
—— makers, ii. 441.
—— water, ii. 163, 165.
Raisins, i. 221.
Ram of Åmen, i. 616, 617; ii. 3.
Rams' heads, i. 306.
Rā-Maat-neb, pyramid of, i. 403.
Ramaḍan, i. 31.
Ramâdî, ii. 435.
Rā-ma-uā-neferu, i. 637.
Rā-mer-ka, ii. 119.
Rameses, ii. 344.
Rameses I., 633, 648.
—— in the Sûdân, ii. 333.
Rameses II., i. 57, 81, 462. 646, 648; ii. 10, 74, 325, 336. 339, 371.
——, his 111 sons and 67 daughters, i. 634.
—— in the Sûdân, i. 630 ff.
—— reswathed, i. 649.
Rameses II., temple of, at 'Amâra, i. 468.
——, ——, at Arnitti, i. 466.
Rameses III., i. 641, 645, 648.
Rameses IV., i. 643.
Rameses V., i. 643.
Rameses VI., i. 643.
Rameses VII., i. 644.
Rameses VIII., i. 644.
Rameses IX., i. 644, 645.
Rameses X., i. 645, 648.
Rameses XI., i. 645.
Rameses XII., i. 645.
Rā-nefer, ii. 23.
Rā-Neḥsi, i. 559.
Ranfi, ii. 204.
Raphael, ii. 299.
Raphia, ii. 38.
Râs Adal, ii. 261, 263.
Râs 'Adâr, ii. 273.
Râs al-Fîl, ii. 406.
Râs al-Hûdî, ii. 273.
Râs al-Kharṭûm, i. 42.
Râs Baryôn, ii. 236.
Rashâida, ii. 438.
Rashîd Bey, ii. 243. 244.
Râs Muḥammad, i. 32.
Râtib Pâshâ, ii. 234.
Ravasanja, ii. 356.
Ravenscroft, Major H. V., ii. 460.
Rawlinson, Sir H., i. 227.
Rawson, Captain R. I., ii. 287, 460.
Raw'ûf Pâshâ, ii. 231, 236, 238, 239, 243, 248.
Rawyâ, ii. 205.
Rebaru, ii. 95.
Reb-Khenṭent, ii. 95.
Rebman, ii. 349, 350.
Redesîyah, i. 630, 631.
——, temple of, i. 628.
Red Sea, i. 18, 48, 54, 217, 505, 513, 516, 554, 571. 630, 638, 642, 643; ii. 95, 112, 155, 158, 163. 165, 189, 190, 199, 225, 233, 500.
—— Canal, ii. 74.
—— Province, ii. 408.
—— Railway, ii. 464.
Reeds, bundles of, i. 14.

Reggâf, ii. 233, 263, 266, 268, 273, 384.
Reḥent, ii. 18.
Rehrehsa, ii. 80, 81.
Reinisch, ii. 419, 445.
Rejaf, ii. 173.
Religions, ii. 440 ff.
Renaudot, ii. 306.
Renk, ii. 399, 437, 459.
Renni, ii. 160.
Ren-seneb, i. 556.
Reservoir, ii. 128, 148.
Rest Camp at Aswân, i. 68, 71.
Retennu, i. 599.
Reth, ii. 415.
Reuter's Correspondent, i. 100.
Revillout, ii. 291, 292, 297.
Rhadata, ii. 160.
Rhinoceros, ii. 108, 157.
Rhizophagi, ii. 156, 157.
Rhodes, Mr. S. C., ii. 493.
Riketa, ii. 285.
Rikki, ii. 399.
Rîmâ, ii. 363.
Rimak, ii. 434.
Rings, ii. 135.
——, gold, i. 305, 306.
——, silver, i. 305, 306.
Ripon Falls, ii. 219, 352, 356, 368, 387.
River Column, ii. 252, 259.
River discharges, ii. 368.
—— worship, i. 20.
Roads, ii. 459.
Roberts, Capt. C., ii. 460.
Rodi, ii. 399.
Rodis, ii. 305.
Rogel, ii. 479.
Rôhl, ii. 359.
Romans, i. 510; ii. 120, 167, 324.
—— in the Sûdân, ii. 166 ff.
—— rule in Nubia, i. 28.
Rome, ii. 166, 175, 506.
Rosellini, i. 299, 536, 537.
Rosetta, ii. 211, 281.
Rossignoli, Father, ii. 268.
Rothschild, Hon. C., i. 150.
Roule, M. le Noir du, Travels of, i. 4.
Routes, ii. 460.
Roveggio, Monsignor, ii. 321.
Rovuma Valley, ii. 229.
Royalties, ii. 451.
Royân, ii. 365, 474.
—— River, i. 251.
Royle, Mr. C., i. 85, 254; ii. 259.
—— quoted, ii. 257, 273, 276.
Rubâṭâb, ii. 401, 438.
Rubi, Lake, ii. 386.
Ruendu, ii. 354.
Ruenzori, ii. 354, 355.
Rufa'a, ii. 305, 365, 407, 439.
Rufai 'Aghâ, ii. 246.
Ruiga, ii. 352.
Ruini, ii. 354.
Ruisamba, ii. 353.
Ruizi, ii. 352.
Rûl River, ii. 428.
Rumâ-Âmen, ii. 66.
Rumanika, ii. 402, 403.
Rumbek, ii. 237, 282, 399, 480.
Rundle, Gen. Sir Leslie, i. 83, 89, 113, 177, 180, 183, 187, 198, 199, 200, 223, 230.
Runka, ii. 365, 438.
Rüppell, i. 24; ii. 445.
Ruṣêres, i. 61; ii. 213, 280, 364, 365, 366, 396, 438, 441, 459.
Russegger, J., i. 24.
——, Travels of, i. 61.
Rustum Pâshâ, ii. 218.
Rutshuru, ii. 354.
Ruvuvu, ii. 352.
Ruwana, ii. 352.
Ruzêḳat, ii. 439.
Ruzi I. River, ii. 361.
—— II. River, ii. 361.
Ryan, Capt. G. J., ii. 460.
Rylls, Father, ii. 312.

SA'AD I., ii. 206.
Sa'ad II., ii. 206.
Sa'adab Dabûs, ii. 205.
Sab, ii. 69.
Sâba Bey, i. 85.
Sabaco, i. 558.
Sabderat, ii. 268, 400.
Sabderât tribes, ii. 213.
Sabnâ, i. 517.
Sab'ûa, ii. 207.
Sacrifices, bloodless, i. 624.
——, human, ii. 294.
Sadd, ii. 348, 376, 379, 481.
——, regions of, ii. 172.
Saddên, temple of, i. 453.
Saddênga, i. 62, 453, 614, 651.
——, temple of, i. 606; ii. 371.
Sadler, Colonel Hayes, i. 579.
Saea, ii. 160.
Safanuf, ii. 299.
Safia steamer, ii. 251.
Ṣâfîya (Sâfia), ii. 392, 437.
Sâḥal, Island of, i. 540, 548, 556, 640; ii. 344.
Sa Hathor, i. 538, 539, 553.
Sâî, Island of, i. 31, 34, 38, 40, 52, 60, 62, 439, 444, 457, 458, 462 ff, 466, 595, 601, 606, 651; ii. 194, 207, 291, 300, 371.
——, Castle of, i. 461, 462.
Sa'îd Ibrahîm, ii. 488.
Sa'îd Pâshâ, i. 149; ii. 218, 236, 461.
—— visits Sûdân, ii. 220.
Sainte Croix, ii. 312.
St. Martin, i. 18.
Saîs, ii. 11, 14, 19, 28, 39, 40, 52, 53, 91.
Sâḳiat (Sâḳîyat, Sâḳiet) al-Abd, i. 444; ii. 300, 371, 391.
Sakkala (Sakala) i. 20.
—— Mountains, ii. 349.
Ṣaḳḳâra, i. 518.
Sako, ii. 360.
Saksakṭit, ii. 95.
Salaam River, i. 251; ii. 365.
Ṣalâḥ ad-Dîn (Saladin), ii. 192, 193, 302.
Ṣalahîya, ii. 375.
Sale, quoted, i. 224.
Sallier Papyrus, i. 561.

INDEX

Sâliḥ Aghâ, ii. 245.
Ṣâliḥ Bey, ii. 244.
Ṣâliḥ, Shêkh, ii. 261, 266.
Sâliḥ, Sultan, ii. 206.
Salîm, Ḳubba, i. 455, 456.
Sal-Lôm, ii. 474.
—— Junction, ii. 478.
Salt, Mr. Henry, i. 40; ii. 446.
Salt, i. 217, 494; ii. 398, 412.
——, rock, i. 105; ii. 159.
——, well, i. 24.
Samânirku, i. 612.
Samânîya doctrine, ii. 241.
—— order, ii. 242.
Sàmensā. ii. 81.
Sa-mer-Åmen, ii. 75.
Samkûs, ii. 187.
Samos, ii. 169.
Samuda Bros., i. 258.
Ṣânâ, Lake, ii. 349, 361 ff., 410.
——, Island of, ii. 363.
Ṣanam Abû Dôm, i. 114, 122, 177, 186, 188, 210, 214, 232; ii. 300.
Sanbu, ii. 196.
Sandstorm, i. 51.
Sanduma, ii. 160.
Sanga, ii. 189, 365, 396.
Sansa, ii. 160.
Sapakhi, ii. 69.
Sapalul, i. 627.
Sape, ii. 164.
Sa Ptaḥ Mer-en-Ptaḥ, i. 640
Sarcophagus, i. 518.
Sargon, i. 227, 228; ii. 30.
Sarras, i. 54, 83, 84, 85, 88, 89, 90, 437, 438, 440, 472, 495, 496, 497; ii. 261, 262, 366, 370, 462, 463, 464.
Sarurâb, ii. 439.
Sasia steamer, i. 258, 259; ii. 239.
Satans, i. 227, 229.
Satet, i. 531, 556, 588, 599, 625, 630, 633.
Sath barge, i. 518.
Sati, i. 548, 575; ii. 16, 112.

Sâti Bashîr, ii. 372.
Satiu, i. 533.
Satu, i. 592.
Sa·yrs, i. 28; ii. 165, 175.
Saunders, Capt., ii. 483.
Saut (Asyût), i. 647.
Sawâkin, i. 10, 31, 97, 111, 179, 184, 222, 225, 227, 236, 239, 249, 262, 281, 305, 323; ii. 200, 201, 263, 268, 281, 401, 461, 462, 478.
—— described, ii. 408.
—— Junction, ii. 474.
——, New, ii. 409.
—— -Berber Railway, ii. 260.
—— —— road, ii. 265.
—— —— route, ii. 257.
Sawba, ii. 204.
Sayâla, Sayyala, i. 27; ii. 435.
Ṣayyâm, ii. 438.
Sayyid Aḥmad, ii. 400.
Sayyid ʿAlî al-Morghânî, ii. 400.
Sayyid al-Ḳûm, ii. 202.
Scales, i. 643.
Scammi, ii. 160.
Scarabs, i. 305.
Scents, i. 105, 218.
Schaefer, Dr., ii. 58, 84, 85, 94, 96, 447.
Schiaparelli, i. 515.
Schlieffen, Graf Wilhelm von ii. 84.
Schools, ii. 490, 497.
—— at Nilwitti, i. 456.
—— near Dulgo, i. 443.
—— of Ḳubba Idris, i. 460.
Schutzer, Dr. E., ii. 235.
Schuver, ii. 446.
Schweinfurth, ii. 305, 403, 423, 424, 430-436, 446, 461.
Scorpions, ii. 38, 156.
Scotland, i. 17.
Scott-Barbour, Lieut., ii. 282.
Scott-Hill, Lieut. E., ii. 483.
Scott-Moncrieff, Mr. P. D., i. 329, 583.
Scudamore, Mr., i. 100.

Sea-calves, ii. 155.
—— -turtles, ii. 156.
Seänkhka-Rā, i. 532.
Sears, Colour-Sergeant, ii. 483.
Seb, i. 526.
Sebaye, ii. 180.
Sebek, i. 383, 625, 626.
Sebek-em-ḥeb, i. 583.
Sebek-ḥetep I. 555.
Sebek-ḥetep III., i. 558, 559.
Sebek-ḥetep IV., i. 556.
Sebennytus, ii. 24.
Sebosus, ii. 162.
Sebu, ii. 354.
Secande, ii. 164.
Secundum, ii. 164.
Seeds, i. 105.
Seetzen, i. 24.
Sêf ad-Dîn Taktûba, ii. 196.
Segasmala, ii. 160.
Seh[er]-taui, ii. 57.
Seḥetep-taui-f, ii. 56.
Sehreset, ii. 82.
Sekaruḳat, ii. 82.
Seker, i. 358; ii. 7, 8, 19.
Seker-Åsar, i. 400.
Seker-neb-sehetch, ii. 18.
Sekheper-en-Rā, i. 139; ii. 57.
Sekhet, i. 301, 421; ii. 122.
Sekhet-Åaru, i. 369, 526, 644.
Sekhet-am, i. 612.
Sekhet-en-Åm, i. 629.
Sekhmakh, ii. 87, 88.
Sektet Boat, ii. 22.
Sekût, ii. 364.
Selîm, ii. 198.
Selîm Pâshâ, Governor of Sûdân, ii. 218.
Selîm, Sultân, i. 463, 495; ii. 200, 201, 207, 209, 308, 421.
Selîm al-Aswânî, ii. 303, 304.
Selîma, Oasis of, i. 2, 10, 23, 25, 96, 508, 509, 521; ii. 261, 300, 371, 391, 412.
—— described, i. 51, 52.

Selîma, princess, i. 24, 52.
Sem priest, i. 477.
Semberritae (Sembritae), ii. 54, 106, 158, 164.
Sembobitis, ii. 164.
Semerkha, i. 512.
Semiramis, ii. 108.
Semliki River, i. 525; ii. 354, 355.
Semna (Semnah), i. 40, 53, 60, 61, 62, 283, 440, 472, 475, 481, 497, 502, 538, 540, 553, 563, 571, 637, 643, 651; ii. 42, 116, 330, 370, 501.
——, Cataract of, i. 479; ii. 366.
——, Fort of, i. 549.
——, Nile register at, i. 550.
——, Temple of Thothmes III. at, i. 476, 478, 580 ff., 584 ff.
Semneh, stern-wheeler, i. 72.
Semti, i. 195.
Semti folk, i 569.
Sha'abân, i. 220.
Shaât, i. 536, 592, 629.
Shabaka, ii. 28, 29, 30, 33, 36.
Shabataka, ii. 31, 32, 33, 35.
Shabb, Oasis of, i. 2, 23; ii. 391.
Shablûka, Cataract, i. 4; ii. 273, 374, 458, 473.
Shadûf, ii. 375.
Shahâda, i. 224.
Shahîn Effendi, i. 183.
Shahîn, Taha, ii. 253.
Shaikaru, ii. 81.
Shaiḳîya Arabs, i. 35, 36, 211, 212; ii. 212, 439.
Shâi-qa-em-Ånnu, ii. 22.
Shairetana, i. 642.
Shakâ, Shakka, ii. 235, 267, 268, 437, 439.
Shakaba, ii. 281.
Shakanda, ii. 193, 194.
Shakerley, ii. 488.
Shaliko, ii. 399.
Shalklal, ii. 119, 120.
Shallâlât, ii. 366.
Shamash-shum-ukin, ii. 40.
Shambata, ii. 439.
Shâmbî, ii. 233, 237, 268, 282, 351, 379, 380, 481.
Shams ad-Dawlah, ii. 192, 302, 303.
Shams ad-Dîn, ii. 349.
Shanâbala, ii. 438.
Shanâtîr, ii. 435.
Shanbûl, Shêkh, ii. 213.
Shan Durshîd, ii. 422.
Shanḳelâ, ii. 364.
Shankir, ii. 191.
Shankpîtah (?), ii. 121.
——, temple of, ii. 144.
Sharaf, ii. 206.
Sharêkh, ii. 473.
Sharkîla, ii. 437.
Sharkrar, ii. 119, 120.
Sharruludari, ii. 24, 40, 41, 52.
Sharshâr, ii. 412.
Shârûhen, i. 562.
Shashanq I. = Shishak, i. 648, 652.
Shashanq the rebel, ii. 5, 14.
Shasu, the, i. 627, 641.
Shāt, i. 612.
—— stone, i. 601.
Shataui, i. 625, 637.
Shatt, ii. 244, 245.
Shatta, ii. 254.
Shaw, Rev. A., ii. 321.
Shawâ, ii. 364.
Shawal, ii. 376.
Sheeps' tails, ii. 154.
Shêkh al-Balad, ii. 209.
Shellabi, Shêkh, i. 496, 497.
Shellâl, i. 69, 70, 71, 81, 240, 502.
Shemamûn, ii. 195, 196.
Shemik, i. 536.
Shendî, i. 21, 31, 41, 47, 56, 58, 62, 331, 334, 337, 497; ii. 116, 212, 271, 273, 366, 374, 401, 462, 473.
—— described, ii. 402, 405.
—— destroyed, ii. 273.
——, kings of, ii. 205.
Shentch wood, i. 519.
Shep-en-Åpt, ii. 28, 33.
Sheps, i. 626.
Sherîf Pâshâ, i. 258.
Shesait, ii. 327.
Shibba, i. 129, 196, 216, 231.
Shidieb, ii. 479.
Shields, crane-skin, ii. 107.
——, ox-hide, ii. 154, 157.
Shilluks, i. 54, 322; ii. 202, 213, 243, 265, 286, 319, 322, 424, 434, 512.
——, religion of, ii. 442.
—— villages, ii. 378.
Shiri River, ii. 229.
Shîr Mûndar, ii. 424.
Shoa, ii. 264, 364.
Shoes, i. 105.
Shu, ii. 19.
Shucair, ii. 370, 392, 393, 401, 428, 439.
——, quoted, ii. 192, 195, 200, 201, 202, 203, 204, 205, 237, 231, 233, 234, 236, 238, 241, 242, 243, 246, 249, 250, 254, 260, 262, 264, 266, 272, 280, 281, 284.
Shukrîya, ii. 436, 439.
Shullas, ii. 319.
Shullî (or Shulla), ii. 424, 434, 443.
Shurwa dates, i. 471.
Shûsh, ii. 206.
Shutter, ii. 392.
Sib', Sib'e, ii. 30.
Ṣidkai, ii. 34.
Sidney, Major, i. 104, 234; ii. 268, 272.
Sieber, ii. 414.
Silk, i. 105.
Silko, ii. 185, 291, 418.
——, Inscription of, ii. 292, 308 ff.
Silsila, i. 625; ii. 344.
Silver, i. 599; ii. 23.
—— mines, ii. 153, 181.
—— rings, i. 305.
—— —— from Meroë, i. 301.
—— useless, i. 3.
Simbarri, ii. 164.

INDEX

Simoes, ii. 156.
Simonides, ii. 162, 348.
Simpson, Mr., ii. 493.
Simyar, ii. 434.
Sinai, Peninsula of, i. 32, 412, 415, 505, 512, 515, 529, 538, 621, 642.
Sinat, ii. 164.
Singar, i. 609.
Singue, i. 44, 47.
Sinjirli, ii. 39.
Sinkât, ii. 246, 249.
Sinuthius, ii. 300.
Sio, ii. 352.
Sirbitum, ii. 165.
Sirdar (Lord Kitchener), i. 68, 72, 177.
Siri, il. 399.
Sirius, ii. 157.
Sistrum, i. 137; ii. 7, 17.
Sitra Amîr, ii. 231.
Sittina, ii. 404.
Skins, i. 217, 520, 554.
—— for crossing Nile, i. 42.
Slade, Maj., R.E., ii. 373.
Slatin Pâshâ, i. 94, 113, 178, 179, 183, 188, 200, 201, 202, 217, 230, 231; ii. 233, 241, 243, 246, 248, 254, 257, 259, 260, 323, 390, 394, 477, 504, 511.
——, escape of, from Omdurmân, ii. 268.
—— on Mission work, ii. 322.
Slavery, ii. 488.
——, abolition of, proclaimed, ii. 220.
——, Burckhardt's opinion of, ii. 407.
Slaves, i. 2, 554; ii. 104, 406.
—— caravans, i. 622.
—— labour, i. 533, 621.
—— market at Dongola, i. 105.
—— raiding, earliest instance of, i. 522.
——, runaway, i. 198.
—— trade, i. 25; ii. 218.
—— ——, how worked, ii. 223-225.
Slave trade increases, ii. 221.
Slings, ii. 16.
Sma-Beḥuṭet, ii. 24.
Small-pox, ii. 202, 213, 390.
Sma-taui, ii. 91.
Smelt, Rev. Charles, i. 28, 31.
Smendes, i. 646, 647.
Smerdis, ii. 91.
Smith, Col. Sir C. Holled, i. 576, 577, 584; ii. 264.
Smith, Mr. G., ii. 51.
Smith, Major G. de H., ii. 285, 460.
Smyth, Capt. N. M., ii. 281, 282, 460.
So, i. 29, 30.
Soap, i. 218.
Sôba, i. 42, 43, 62, 324; ii. 89, 116, 151, 200, 204, 250, 303, 365, 394.
——, the ram of, ii. 305.
Sobat River, ii. 230, 233, 314, 358, 359, 360, 368, 378, 390, 433, 481, 485.
——, discharge of, ii. 369.
——, Mission station on, ii. 319.
Sokoto, ii. 398.
Soleb (Ṣolib, Ṣulb), i. 34, 144.
——, temple of, i. 608-615.
Solon, ii. 422.
Solstice, summer, ii. 153.
Somaliland, ii. 426.
Somerset Nile, ii. 238, 386.
Songs, Berberi, i. 80.
Souls of Rameses II., i. 632.
Sowerby, Capt. M. E., ii. 476.
Sparkes, Col. W. S., ii. 281, 282, 284, 378, 433, 460.
Spears, horn-tipped, ii. 107.
Speke, Capt. J. H., ii. 220, 221, 222, 350.
—— quoted, ii. 402-403.
Spells, i. 222.
Spermatophagi (or Spermophagi), ii. 156, 157.
Sphingium, ii. 162.
Sphinx, i. 623.
Sphinx, sand cleared from, i. 605.
—— at Sôba, i. 42.
Sphinxes, ii. 108, 157.
—— at Meroë, i. 287.
Spices, i. 105.
—— plants, ii. 327.
Spiders, ii. 156.
Spintum, ii. 160.
Spirits, belief in, i. 220.
——, evil, i. 268.
——, land of, i. 523.
—— in pyramids, i. 267.
Spong, Surgeon-Capt. C. S., i. 194.
Stadasis, ii. 161, 168.
Stambûl, i. 216.
Stanley, Sir H., i. 220, 524; ii. 229, 262, 351, 353, 356.
Stanton, Col. E. A., i. 42, 324; ii. 460, 504, 505.
Star appears in the Sûdân, ii. 214.
Statet, i. 386.
Statues of Tombos, i. 559.
Stead, Corporal, ii. 480.
Steamers on Nile, i. 258; ii. 459.
Steatopygy, i. 48; ii. 403.
Stefani, Antoine, i. 285, 286, 287, 288, 291, 293, 295, 314, 316, 317, 318, 320, 343.
Steindorff, ii. 46, 51.
Stele of the Coronation, ii. 58, 60 ff.
—— of Dongola, ii. 84.
—— of the Excommunication, ii. 70.
—— of Piānkhi, ii. 4.
—— of Pithom, ii. 111.
Stenning, Mr., i. 331.
Stephen, St., ii. 297.
Stephenson, General Sir Frederick, i. 95; ii. 257, 261.
Step-pyramid, i. 357.
Sterling, Capt., ii. 507.
Stern, Dr., ii. 344.
Sterry, Mr. W., ii. 496.
Steudner, ii. 314, 315.
Stevani, Col., ii. 268.

Stevenson, Lieut. A. G., i. 241 ; ii. 463.
Stewart, Col., ii. 245, 247, 250.
——, murder of, i. 85 ; ii. 251.
Stewart, Sir Herbert, i. 110.
——, death of, ii. 253.
"Stone Belly," i. 31 ; ii. 370.
Strabo, i. 39, 55 ; ii. 41, 54, 93, 106, 153, 157, 166, 167, 175.
Strack, Capt. L., ii. 283.
Strates, i. 20.
Struthophagi, ii. 156, 158.
Sûdân abandoned by Egypt, ii. 246.
——, absence of ancient remains in, i. 511.
—— annexed by Arabs, ii. 193.
——, area of, ii. 390.
——, boundaries of, ii. 390.
——, British in, ii. 448.
—— budget, ii. 453.
—— caravan, i. 23.
——, deserts of, ii. 391.
——, desolation in, i. 452.
—— destroyed by Muḥammad 'Alî's policy, ii. 240.
——, Egyptian influence in, i. 513.
——, extent of, i. 506.
——, inhabitants of, ii. 412.
——, irrigation of, ii. 351.
——, Kitchener's advance in, ii. 269.
—— languages, ii. 444.
——, meaning of, i. 506.
—— Military Railway, i. 65.
——, minerals of, ii. 410.
——, the modern, ii. 340.
—— Oases, ii. 391.
——, population of, ii. 390.
—— Provinces—revenues of, ii. 455.
—— religions, ii. 440 ff.
—— revenue, ii. 451.
——, seven Provinces of, under Aḥmad Pâshâ, ii. 217.
Sûdân, thirteen Provinces of, ii. 393 ff.
——, travellers in, i. 1 ff.
——, tribute of, ii. 326.
"Sudan Campaign," i. 85, 102.
Sudd, i. 239, 259 ; ii. 230, 481.
——, regions of, ii. 172, 173.
Sudeley, Lord, ii. 460.
Sueh, ii. 399.
Sueki, i. 442.
Suez, i. 32, 470 ; ii. 227.
—— Canal, i. 71.
Sugar, i. 105, 217, 494.
Sûḥna, i. 216.
Suicide, ii. 154.
Suinya, ii. 352.
Suk Mountains, ii. 386.
Sukkôt, i. 31, 40, 459, 461, 471 ; ii. 207, 208, 371, 409, 462.
—— dates, i. 455.
——, temple of, i. 453.
Ṣulb, i. 34, 35, 37, 38, 40, 41, 52, 53, 55, 60, 62, 144, 149, 439, 443, 471, 497, 502, 596, 620, 621, 624, 651 ; ii. 45, 371.
——, hawk standard of, i. 621.
——, temple of, 608-615.
—— ——, excavations at, i. 445 ff., 449, 450, 451.
Sulêm, ii. 439.
Sulêmân (Solon), ii. 422.
Sulêmân I., ii. 206.
Sulêmân II., ii. 206.
Sulêmân, son of Zubêr, i. 259 ; ii. 235, 236 ff., 248.
Sulêmân Al-'Adâd, ii. 205.
Sulêmân ibn Salâm, ii. 206.
Sulêmân Wâd Ḳamr, i. 85 ; ii. 251, 259.
—— killed, ii. 264.
Sulêmân Wâd Na'mân, ii. 251.
Sulêmânîya, ii. 438.
Sulphur well, i. 92.
Sulu-n-Diffe, i. 537, 538.
Summara, ii. 164.
"Summit," ii. 478.
Sun, men sacrificed to, ii. 177.
——, oaths sworn by, i. 54.
——, an object of fear, ii. 154.
Sun-god, ii. 136.
Sundo, ii. 352.
Sunni, ii. 399.
Sunnu, i. 530.
Sunt, ii. 81.
Ṣûr, ii. 116.
Susa, ii. 91.
Sutekh, i. 561.
Suten-ḥenen, ii. 12, 14, 17, 18.
Suten-ḥet, ii. 12.
Sutherland, Capt. A., ii. 286.
Suwârâb, ii. 439.
Suwârda, i. 95, 444, 449, 451, 452, 453, 454, 651 ; ii. 270, 371.
Swabey, Capt., i. 251, 254, 282, 283.
Swêni, i. 24, 53.
Sydop, ii. 160.
Syene, i. 509, 512, 519, 530 ; ii. 160, 161, 162, 165, 166, 167, 168, 176.
Syenitae, ii. 160.
Syllaeus, ii. 167.
Syrbotae, 8 cubits high, ii. 164.
Syria, i. 6, 18, 30, 32, 505, 565, 570, 572, 598, 599, 604, 605, 622, 623, 625, 627, 628, 640-642 ; ii. 35 37-40, 70, 161, 170, 191.
——, North, i. 449.
Syrians, i. 571, 577, 607, 646 ; ii. 53.
Syrtes, ii. 165.

TAA-EN-ÀMEN-SETEP-EN-NETERU, ii. 113.
Ta'âisha, ii. 439.
Ta-an, ii. 24.
Ṭabal, ii. 201.
Tabal II., ii. 203.
Tabaldi trees, ii. 397, 437.
Table of the Sun, ii. 92.
Tablet, the Preserved, i. 220.

INDEX

Tacaze (or Takazê) River, i. 549; ii. 157, 364.
Tachompsos, ii. 105, 111, 160.
Tadu, Island of, ii. 163.
Tâfa, ii. 111, 293, 297, 299, 303.
Tafnekhth, ii. 4-26, 28.
Taggart, Lieut., ii. 460.
Taha 'Alî, ii. 499.
Taharq, i. 482, 483; ii. 35.
Taharqa, ii. 36, 37, 38, 42-46, 51, 52, 56, 116, 170.
——, his temple to Usertsen III., ii. 43.
——, temple of, ii. 371.
Tâha Shahîn, ii. 253.
Ta-ḥeḥet, ii. 75, 88.
Tails worn by women, ii. 403.
Taiutchait, ii. 12.
Tâka = Kasala, i. 31, 339; ii. 214, 217.
Taḳâbô, ii. 432.
Taḳalî, ii. 202, 213.
Takarta, ii. 69.
Ṭākehet-'Amen, ii. 36, 43, 45.
Ta-Kenset, i. 121, 134, 485, 486, 527, 575, 593, 600, 612, 619, 630; ii. 56, 69, 416.
Ta-Kenset of the Blacks, i. 539.
Takla Hâymânôt, ii. 263.
Takla Hâymânót II., i. 19.
Takla Maryâm, ii. 212.
Takrûr, ii. 440.
Takrûris, ii. 401.
Talbot, Col. the Hon. M. G., i. 50, 119, 120, 130, 133, 154, 155, 180; ii. 282, 284, 373, 412, 460, 461.
Talgwareb, ii. 479.
Talmis, i. 73; ii. 111, 170, 291, 292, 293.
Tâlôdî, ii. 397.
Tama, ii. 162, 172, 434.
Tamaai, stern-wheeler, i. 102.
Tamâî, ii. 260.
Tamakhith, ii. 95.
Tamanib, ii. 246.
Tamarin, ii. 265.
Tamarinds, i. 105.
Tambura, ii. 286, 287.
Tambura, Sultân, ii. 282.
Tamîm as-Sûdânî, ii. 349.
Tammuz, ii. 38.
Tandamanie, ii. 51.
Tandik, ii. 397.
Ta-Neḥesu, i. 505, 506.
Tanen-Àmen, ii. 69.
Tanenbuta, ii. 69.
Ta-neter, i. 599; ii. 26.
Tanganyika, ii. 350, 354.
Tangi, ii. 357, 386.
Tangûr, i. 596; ii. 371.
——, Cataract of, i. 606; ii. 366.
Tani, ii. 250.
Tanis, i. 533, 556, 560, 646, 647, 652; ii. 35, 36, 40, 41.
——, kings of, i. 647, 648.
Tanḳâsî, i. 122, 170, 187, 198, 214, 216, 218; ii. 116, 373.
—— fair, i. 399.
—— Island, ii. 372.
——, pyramids of, i. 125.
Tanpu, i. 612.
Tantarene, ii. 160.
Tanuath-Amen, ii. 42, 46, 53, 56.
——, his name, ii. 51, 52.
——, stele of, ii. 47 ff.
Taphis, ii. 111, 293, 294.
Tapp, Col., ii. 262.
Taqnat, ii. 81.
Taqtetet, ii. 95.
Ṭarabîl, name of pyramids in the Sûdân, i. 41, 228, 264, 267.
Tarafâwî, ii. 392.
Tarâgma, ii. 473.
Tarbushes, i. 105.
Ta-Resu, i. 610, 612, 629.
Taret, ii. 79.
Targam, ii. 439.
Tarreqet, ii. 95.
Tartan, ii. 40.
Tarukhet (?)-reset, ii. 79.
Tarumen, ii. 95.
Taruṭi-peḥt, ii. 94.
Tasheṭ-khensu, i. 648.
Ṭaṭ, i. 418.
Ta-tchennian, i. 612.
Ta-tchesert, i. 386.
Tatehen, ii. 6, 15.
Tathem, i. 517.
Tattu, i 362, 386.
Tau-āa-qen, i. 561, 562.
Ta-Uatchet, ii. 111.
Tauḥibit, ii. 21.
Ta-urt, i. 160, 383, 400, 421, 626.
Taurus, ii. 165.
Tawfîḳ Pâshâ, ii. 238.
Tawfîḳîya, i. 82 ff.; ii. 368, 399.
—— founded, ii. 228.
Taxes, i. 530; ii. 451.
—— levied by priests of Àmen, i. 644.
Tayf, i. 31, 33.
Taylor, Capt. A. A. C., ii. 460.
Ṭayyâra, ii. 397, 437.
Tcha-ab, statue of, i. 488.
Tcham, land of, i. 517.
Tchart, ii. 94, 95.
Tcharukha, i. 607.
Tcheser, king, i. 512; ii. 344.
Tchestcheset, ii. 174.
Tcheṭ-Àmen-àf-ānkh, ii. 14.
Tcheṭ-Amen-àuf-ānkh, ii. 24.
Tcheṭ-khiau, ii. 24.
Tchu-ā, i. 514.
Tea in the Sudan, i. 455.
Teck, Prince Francis of, i. 182.
Tefaba, i. 529.
Tegrê, ii. 364.
Telahwîya, ii. 251.
Telegraphs, ii. 462, 480.
Telgona, ii. 246, 282.
Tell al-'Amarna, i. 622, 623.
Tell Hashîm, ii. 260.
Telmes (Termes), i. 599.
Tem, (Temu), i. 385, 526, 621, 624; ii. 4, 8, 11, 21, 22, 45.
Tem-Kheperà, ii. 22.

Temple of the Gold Bull, ii. 101.
—— of Sukkot, i. 60.
Temple-forts in the Sûdân, ii. 331.
Temples turned into churches, ii. 297.
Templeman, Dr., i. 13.
Tenedhbai, i. 287.
Ṭenḳ, pygmy, i. 522 ff.
Tenupsis, ii. 164.
Têrâb, ii. 207.
Teres, i. 520.
Tergedus, ii. 162, 163, 172.
Tert, ii. 90.
Tessata, ii. 160.
Tetȧ, king, i. 516.
——, pyramid of, i. 514.
Tetȧān, i. 563.
Ṭet-Ānkh-Ȧmen-taa-en-Rā, ii. 112.
Ṭeṭun, i. 121, 477, 485, 486, 556, 527, 575, 584, 587, 588 ff., 593, 604; ii. 3, 41-45, 412.
Ṭeṭun-khenti-nefert, ii. 61.
Thakhisa, i. 598, 599.
Thamiam, ii. 479.
Tharebenika, i. 610.
Thȧresina, i. 610.
Tharubnika, i. 612.
Tharusmȧ, i. 612.
Tharutharu, i. 612.
Thatice, ii. 160.
Thebaïd, ii. 167, 174-176, 177, 295, 296.
——, Christians in, ii. 289.
Thebans, i. 561; ii. 115.
Thebes, i. 48, 57, 67, 159, 298, 427, 531, 561, 568, 600, 606, 625, 643, 644, 648, 651, 652; ii. 1, 2, 4, 6, 9, 13, 14, 26, 27, 28, 30, 40, 41, 42, 45, 46, 52, 53, 93, 166.
——, kings of, i. 647.
—— plundered by Assyrians, ii. 50.
——, Princes of, i. 529, 530, 532, 561.
Theḥennu, i. 505, 612, 628, 633; ii. 13, 415.
Thekansh, ii. 12.
Themeḥ, i. 2, 520.
Themistocles, ii. 91.
Thena, ii. 160.
Thenteremu, ii. 24.
Thent-sepeḥ, i. 648.
Thent-taā, i. 563.
Theodora, Empress, ii. 178, 295 ff.
Theodore, king of Abyssinia, ii. 314.
Theodore of Philae, ii. 296, 297.
Theodosius I., ii. 291, 292.
Theodosius, Pâpâ, ii. 295.
Theodotus, ii. 175.
Theokles, ii. 74.
Theon Ochema, ii. 165.
Thert, ii. 96.
Thesma-nefer-ru, ii. 76.
Thet-taui. ii. 7, 11, 19.
Thi, Queen, i. 454, 607, 608, 612, 614, 622; ii. 371.
Thi, wife of Ȧi, i. 625.
Thibaut, ii. 349.
Thiersch, H., i. 382.
Thipamet, ii. 336.
Thita, i. 612.
Thom, Rev. A. M., ii. 321.
Thompson, Sir E. Maunde, i. 175, 323, 437.
Thoth, i. 36, 137, 160, 370, 392, 396, 397, 418, 421, 426, 576, 591, 594, 626, 637, 644; ii. 7, 17, 45, 112, 113, 122.
—— the "twice great," i. 370.
——, month of, ii. 6, 11.
Thothmes I., i. 61, 540, 548, 567, 594, 595, 596; ii. 371.
—— in the Sûdân, i. 568-570.
Thothmes II., i. 61, 480, 537, 583, 593, 595.
—— in the Sûdân, i. 570.
Thothmes III., i. 53, 60, 61, 449, 463, 477, 480, 481, 483, 484, 487, 537, 549, 613, 625, 627, 628, 630; ii. 42.
Thothmes III. and Usertsen III. at Dôsha, i. 596.
—— embracing Usertsen III., i. 587.
—— in the Sûdân, i. 571 ff.
—— kills 120 elephants, i. 573.
Thothmes IV., i. 536, 538, 623.
—— in the Sûdân, i. 604, 606.
Thread, i. 105.
Throne of gold, ii. 89, 90.
Thuaa, i. 607.
Tiberius, ii. 113.
Tiberius II., Emp., ii. 178.
Tiedemann, Capt. A. von, ii. 278.
Tiger grass, ii. 173.
Tigris, i. 112; ii. 500.
Timosthenes, ii. 162.
Tinara, i. 31, 439; ii. 371.
Tinne, Miss A. P. F., ii. 313 ff., 379.
Tinnis, ii. 184.
Tirhâḳâh, i. 51, 59, 122, 169, 487; ii. 35, 501.
——, temple of, i. 132 ff.
——, ——, excavated, i. 482-490.
Tirikanlat (?), Tirikanletau (?), Pyramid of, i. 408 ff.; ii. 119.
Tis Esat, Falls of, ii. 364.
Titi, ii. 357.
Titus, ii. 174.
Tobacco, i. 34.
Tôf (raft), i. 479.
Togni, ii. 479.
Tôkar, ii. 246, 249, 264, 265, 268, 366, 409.
Tolles, ii. 164.
Tomato, ii 365.
Tombos, Island of, i. 51, 62, 99, 559, 568, 570; ii. 270, 371, 479, 568, 570, 651.
——, quarries of, i. 60.
Tomo, Giorgio, i. 368.
Tom-tom, i. 79.
Tong, ii. 282, 285, 399, 480.
Tonga, ii. 322.

Tonj, ii. 359.
Tonobari, ii. 164.
Tor, i. 18, 32.
Tortoises, i. 508.
Toski, i. 76, 77, 78, 90.
Townshend, Col., i. 183, 196; ii. 460.
Trade, ii. 486.
Trajan, Emp., ii. 174, 289.
Travellers in Sudan, i. 1 ff.
Tree of Hathor, i. 384.
Tree worship, ii. 441.
Triad, Osirian, i. 500.
Triakontaschoinoi, ii. 166.
Trinkitat, ii. 265.
Triremes, ii. 74, 167.
Troglodytae, i. 562, 569; ii. 155, 156, 158, 163.
Tu-ā, i. 514.
Ṭu-ȧb, i. 630; ii. 61, 70.
Ṭuamutef, i. 361.
Ṭuat, i. 369, 385, 505; ii. 17, 18.
Tûd, ii. 193.
Tudmur, i. 216.
Tudway, Major, i. 183; ii. 460.
Tûfrik, ii. 260.
Tugo, Tuka, ii. 444.
Tukl, tukul, i. 113, 178, 206; ii. 375.
Tukruf, ii. 268.
Tûlû, ii. 436.
Tûm, ii. 206.
Tumâm, ii. 439.
Tûmât, ii. 437.
Tunbul, ii. 372.
Ṭunbus, i. 559.
Tundubi, Oasis of, ii. 391.
Tungur Ārabs, ii. 422.
Tunis, i. 24, 25; ii. 422.
Tunkul, i. 103, 104.
Tûra, ii. 235.
Tura, Oasis of, ii. 392.
Ṭura, quarries of, i. 516.
Tûrân Shâh, ii. 192.
Turdannu, ii. 30, 40.
Turks, i. 25, 26, 40, 42, 109, 510; ii. 324.
Turquoises, i. 538; ii. 23.
Türstig, R., ii. 441.
Turusu, i. 612.
Tushki, i. 76, 77, 78; ii. 263, 264.
Tushratta, ii. 332.
Tusks of elephants, ii. 107, 108.
Tusûn, ii. 210.
Ṭut-ȧb (Gebel Barkal), ii. 45.
Tut-ānkh-Åmen, i. 624, 625.
Tuti Island, ii. 252, 274, 375.
Tutzis, i. 633; ii, 111.
Tuwêsha, ii. 438.
Tuyayo, ii. 352.
Typhon, i. 133; ii. 125.
Typhonium, i. 132, 133; ii. 125.
Tyre, ii. 38, 39.

UAFTH-TĀT-SEMT-SEMT-NEBT, ii. 75.
Uahmāni-Åmen, ii. 69.
Uasarken, ii. 14, 22.
Uaseb (?), ii. 15.
Uast, ii. 13.
Uatchet, i. 575, 588.
Uatch-ka-Rā, ii. 57.
Uau, i. 536.
Uauaiu, i. 533, 553.
Uauat, i. 517, 518, 519, 521, 534, 572, 573, 643; ii. 416.
—— = Northern Sûdân, i. 536.
'Ubûdîn, ii. 435.
Udamos, ii. 74.
Uḍîa, ii. 437.
Ueberbacher, Father, ii. 312.
Uganda, ii. 229, 230, 235, 267, 318, 390, 424.
—— Protectorate, ii. 384.
—— Railway, ii. 352.
Uḥat, i. 521.
Uḥmîr, ii. 392.
Ujiji, ii. 229.
'Ukâsha, i. 86; ii. 261, 269, 371, 463, 464.
——, Cataract of, ii. 366.
'Ukma (Ukmah), i. 92; ii. 371.
——, Cataract of, ii. 366.
Ukon, ii. 444.
Ukwa, ii. 443.
Ul-Makâda, ii. 440.
Umak Ra, ii. 443.
'Umârâb, ii. 439.
'Umayyad, ii. 191.
Umi, ii. 357, 385.
Umla Gadîda, ii. 267.
Umm 'Alî, ii. 435, 473.
Ummar'ar, ii. 436.
Umm Badr, ii. 392.
Umm Dabê'a, ii. 273.
Umm Dabrêkât, ii. 280.
Umm Damm, ii. 397.
Umm Darmân, ii. 395.
Umm Dubbân, ii. 250.
Umm Durmân, ii. 246.
Umm Nabâdî, ii. 412.
—— —— mine, ii. 247.
Umm Nagî, ii. 435.
Umm Shanḳa, ii. 431.
Umoi, ii. 443.
Um-Soof (or Sûf), ii. 173, 379, 481.
Un, city, ii. 14, 15, 16.
——, nome, ii. 12, 17.
Unȧ, ii. 324.
——, career of, i. 516.
——, journeys of, i. 516 ff.
—— meets Ḥer-khuf, i. 520.
Unȧs, king, ii. 414.
Unguents, i. 307.
Ung-wad, ii. 443.
Unḳât, ii. 392.
Unmatur, i. 55.
Un-nefer, an official, ii. 69.
Unsa I., ii. 201.
Unu-Åmen, i. 646.
Unyami, ii. 357.
Unyanyembe, ii. 229.
Unyoro, ii. 228, 229, 260, 267, 268, 356.
Upeno, ii. 360.
Urbim, ii. 160.
Urdamanie, ii. 51.
'Urêba, ii. 436.
'Ureḳât, ii. 439.
Usekht boat, i. 518.
Usertsen I., i. 412, 413, 534-538, 553, 576, 601, 627.
—— builds dykes, i. 555.
—— in the Sûdân, i. 548.

Usertsen II., i. 637.
—— in the Sûdân, i. 539.
Usertsen III., i. 38, 60, 121, 195, 449, 462, 476, 477, 483, 484, 491, 492, 493, 496, 510, 553, 564, 571, 575, 585, 587, 588 ff., 601, 604, 625; ii. 42, 45, 116, 330, 501.
—— and Thothmes III. at Dôsha, i. 596.
——, decree of, i. 542.
— — in the Sûdân, i. 539. 549, 533.
——, stele of, i. 541, 544 ff.
Usibalci, ii. 165.
Usr-âb, ii. 58.
Usr-Maāt-Rā, ii. 2.
Utcha-Ḥeru-Resenet, ii. 91.
Utchat, i. 307.
'Uṭêfât, ii. 439.
'Uthmân, ii. 204.
'Uthmân al-Morghânî, ii. 404.
Utricularià, ii. 481.
Uu-en-Rā-nefert, ii. 14.

VALERIAN, ii. 289.
Valerius Largus, ii. 167.
Vandeleur, Seymour, ii. 268.
Van Eetvelde, ii. 383.
Van Kerckhoven, ii. 266.
Van Kerckhoven, steamer, ii. 382.
Ventriloquists, ii. 441.
Venus, Hottentot, ii. 403.
Vermilion, ii. 107.
Verseau the Jesuit, i. 5, 6.
Verus, Emp., ii. 174.
Vespasian, Emp., ii. 174.
Victoria Nile, ii. 356.
Victoria Nyanza, ii. 220, 351, 352.
Villiers, Mr. Fred, i. 100, 189, 190.
Vinci, Father, ii. 312.
Vines, i. 517; ii. 82.
Vod Benaga, i. 313.
Vogel, ii. 423.
Vulcan, ii. 163.
Vulture, i. 306.

WAD'A, ii. 438.
Wâd 'Abbâs, ii. 439.
Wâd Agîb, i. 21.
Wadâi, i. 25; ii. 236, 285, 390, 398, 422.
Wâd al-Bishâra, i. 101, 102, 103; ii. 270.
Wâd al-Karêl, ii. 375.
Wâd an-Nagûmî, i. 76-78, 90; ii. 260, 263, 264.
Wâd Arbâb, ii. 261.
Wâd Bâ Nagaa, i. 47, 286, 287, 324, 325, 330, 331, 412, 502, 602, 622; ii. 116, 118, 119, 120, 122, 124, 126, 134, 152, 170, 332, 473.
Wâd Dafa' Allah, ii. 268.
Waddington, G., i. 34, 478.
Wadelâî, ii. 260, 267, 268, 368, 386.
Wâd Habashî, i. 251.
Wâd Hôjoly, ii. 229.
Wâdî Abû Dôm, i. 114.
Wâdî al-'Alâḳi, i. 534.
Wâdî al-Awâiteb, i. 57.
Wâdî al-Banât, i. 49.
Wâdî al-Ghazâl, Church of, ii. 300, 301.
Wâdî al-Ḥagar, i. 60.
Wâdî al-Ḥamâr (or Ḥomâr), ii. 366.
Wâdî al-Khawânib, i. 534.
Wâdî al-Kirbikân, i. 325; ii. 124.
Wâdî Aṣ-Ṣufra, i. 324, 327; ii. 146, 147.
Wâdî Awateb, i. 325.
Wâdî Ghazâl, i. 234.
Wadî Ḥalfah (Halfa), i. 31, 34, 38, 39, 40, 53, 61, 62, 70, 77, 82-87, 436, 437, 449, 536, 538, 553, 573, 599, 601, 638, 651; ii. 75, 83, 105, 110, 113.
——, frontier of Egypt, ii. 260.
——, temples at, i. 576 ff.
—— Railway, ii. 462.
Wâdî Hammâmât, i. 643; ii. 30.
Wâdî Ka'ab, ii. 412.
Wâdî Ma'atûḳa, i. 549.
Wâdî Nagaa, i. 509.
Wâdî Sabu'a, i. 14, 74, 634, 638, 651; ii. 297.
Wâdî Ṭâfa, ii. 308.
Wâdî Ṭarâbîl, plan of, i. 359.
Wâdî 'Ulâḳî (al-'Ullâkî), i. 549, 555, 574, 630, 638, 642; ii. 10, 104, 110, 113, 329, 330, 333, 336, 338, 412.
Wâd Madani, ii. 213, 218, 281, 285, 365, 407, 436.
——, town, ii. 396.
Wâd Maul, ii. 443.
Wâd Nimîr, ii. 372.
Wâd Ramla, ii. 375, 393, 474.
Wahâbâb, ii. 438.
Wahamba, ii. 356.
Wahuma, ii. 432.
Waiga, ii. 356.
Wakki River, ii. 355, 356.
Wakûri, ii. 349.
Walaḳâ, ii. 364.
Walda Mîkâêl, ii. 234-236.
Walker & Bray, Messrs., ii. 236, 461.
Wambutti, i. 525.
Wami, ii. 352.
Wandî, ii. 267.
Wansleben, i. 22.
Wanyoro, ii. 353.
War boat, i. 518.
—— correspondents, i. 100.
—— song, i. 79.
Ward, Colonel, ii. 234.
Warriba Hills, ii. 281.
Water Forts, ii. 262.
—— tank at No. 6 Station, i. 245.
—— trees, ii. 397.
—— wheels, i. 3, 104; ii. 193, 195, 220.
Watson, Dr. Andrew, ii. 318, 319.
Watson, Lieut., ii. 350.
Wauchope, Col., ii. 276.
Wâw, ii. 237, 282, 286, 315, 322, 399, 480.
Wazezeru, ii. 402, 403.

INDEX

Weapons, i. 105.
Weather, i. 334.
Weidenbach, E., i. 61.
Weidenbach, M., i. 61.
Weill, R., i. 515.
Well at Nagaa, i. 326.
—— at No. 6 Station, i. 246.
—— of Rameses II., i. 632.
—— of Seti I., i. 630; ii. 333.
—— of the Sun, ii. 8.
Wellby, Mr., ii. 361.
Wellcome, Mr. H., i. 221, 223; ii. 493.
Wells, ii. 459.
——, list of, ii. 392.
——, the Seventy, ii. 392.
Werne, ii. 349.
Whip, the, i. 210.
Whiston, Surgeon-Captain, i. 194.
White Ḳubba, i. 234.
White Nile Province, ii. 408.
White Wall, ii. 11, 19.
Wiedemann, Prof. A., i. 486, 515, 523; ii. 4, 55, 74, 414.
Wiggett, J. S., i. 478.
Wilbour, Mr., i. 539.
Wild, Mr. J., i. 62.
Wilkinson, Major E. B., ii. 460.
Wilkinson, Sir J. G., i. 574.
Wilmot, Mr. R. C. J. S., ii. 321.
Wilson, C. T., ii. 446.
Wilson, Capt. H. H., ii. 361, 460.
Wilson, Maj. C. E., ii. 284.
Wilson, Sir C., ii. 253, 259.
Windham, Mr. R. W., ii. 476.
Wine, i. 221; ii. 156.
—— of Rhodes, i. 174.
Wingate, Sir F. R., i. 96, 113, 178, 183, 188, 189, 201, 204, 205, 231, 321-323, 326, 339, 340, 348, 375, 436, 437, 464, 480, 498, 500, 501, 502, 577, 579, 583; ii. 239, 247, 249, 250, 251, 255, 257, 258, 281, 285, 286, 320, 322, 323, 390, 397, 404, 436, 477, 479, 487, 495, 501, 503, 511.
Wingate, Sir F. R., defeats and kills Khalîfa, ii. 280.
Winged Disk, i. 543.
Wira, ii. 399.
Witchcraft, ii. 442.
Wodehouse, Colonel, i. 77, 81, 84; ii 263.
Wolf, fire-breathing, i. 268.
Wollen, Lieut. W. R. G., i. 264.
Wolseley, Lord, i. 83, 110; ii. 250.
Women rulers of Meroë, i. 48.
——, steatopygous, ii. 402.
—— warriors, ii. 154.
Wood, Capt. P., ii. 285, 460.
Woods and Forests, ii. 500.
Wussi Island, i. 444; ii. 291.

XÊT, ii. 27.

YÂ'KÛB, Khalîfa's brother, ii. 265.
Ya'ḳûbâb, ii. 439.
Yaman, ii. 303, 438.
Yambio, ii. 284, 285, 286.
Yamni, ii. 205.
Yârâ, i. 44.
Yellow River, ii. 360.
"Yellow Maria," i. 87, 88, 91.
Yembo, i. 32.
Yemen, ii. 189, 192.
Yerbora Rapids, ii. 366, 385.
Yeria, ii. 354.
Yor Adodoit, ii. 444.
Yorke, ii. 297.
Young, Dr., i. 299.
Yukanye, ii. 443.
Yûsuf, ii. 262.
Yûsuf Bey, ii. 233.
Yûsuf Pâshâ, ii. 244.

ẒABÂ'Î, ii. 392.
Zabâlla'a, ii. 439.
Zafr, gunboat, i. 106.
Zaghâwä, ii. 435.
Zakarya ibn Bahnas, ii. 188.
Zakarya ibn Ṣâlah, ii. 188.
Zâkî Tummâl, ii. 261, 264, 265.
Zanḳar, ii. 205.
Zanzibar, ii. 222, 229, 233, 234, 264, 265.
Zâwîyat al-Karâdsa, i. 551.
Zawyet ad-Dêr, ii. 406.
Zayid, ii. 262.
Zayyâdîya, ii. 439.
Zêdâb, ii. 473.
Zehteb, ii. 479.
Zela, ii. 236.
Zemio, ii. 268.
Zênab, ii. 241.
Zenobia, Queen, ii. 175.
Zêt, ii. 27.
Zîdân, ii. 300.
Zmanes, ii. 160.
Zoton, ii. 160.
Zubêr, ii. 236, 237, 248, 249, 422.
Zubêr, brother-in-law of Abbâs, ii. 435.
Zubêr ibn Raḥama, ii. 232.
Zubêr Pâshâ, ii. 398.
Zugumbia, ii. 286.
Zula, ii. 234.
Zullot, ii. 479.
Zûma, i. 170; ii. 116.
——, Pyramids of, i. 129.

Printed by Gilbert & Rivington Ltd., St. John's House, Clerkenwell, E.C.

Lightning Source UK Ltd.
Milton Keynes UK
UKOW051127211211

184179UK00001B/38/P

9 781616 404550